GLOBAL PERSPECTIVES ON ADR

# GLOBAL PERSPECTIVES ON ADR

*Edited by*

Carlos Esplugues
Silvia Barona

intersentia
Cambridge – Antwerp – Portland

Intersentia Publishing Ltd.
Trinity House | Cambridge Business Park | Cowley Road
Cambridge | CB4 0WZ | United Kingdom
Tel.: +44 1223 393 753 | Email: mail@intersentia.co.uk

*Distribution for the UK:*
NBN International
Airport Business Centre, 10 Thornbury Road
Plymouth, PL6 7 PP
United Kingdom
Tel.: +44 1752 202 301 | Fax: +44 1752 202 331
Email: orders@nbninternational.com

*Distribution for the USA and Canada:*
International Specialized Book Services
920 NE 58th Ave. Suite 300
Portland, OR 97213
USA
Tel.: +1 800 944 6190 (toll free)
Email: info@isbs.com

*Distribution for Austria:*
Neuer Wissenschaftlicher Verlag
Argentinierstraße 42/6
1040 Wien
Austria
Tel.: +43 1 535 61 03 24
Email: office@nwv.at

*Distribution for other countries:*
Intersentia Publishing nv
Groenstraat 31
2640 Mortsel
Belgium
Tel.: +32 3 680 15 50
Email: mail@intersentia.be

Global Perspectives on ADR
Carlos Esplugues and Silvia Barona (eds.)



ISBN 978-1-78068-139-9
D/2014/7849/10
NUR 820

British Library Cataloguing in Publication Data. A catalogue record for this book is available from the British Library.

# PREFACE

Modern societies are increasingly complex. This complexity tends to be accompanied by a continuous escalation in litigiousness. The more developed a society is, the more disputes tend to exist. Moreover, these tend to be increasingly heterogeneous and complicated. This situation has a direct effect both on the State's system of justice and on the implementation of the principle of access to justice for citizens. Figures show the growing inability of the State, the single holder of the monopoly of justice in recent times, to cope with this situation. The State tries to tackle this soaring reality by way of different tools. Thus many national regulations on civil procedure have undertaken reforms in the last years, in an attempt to make it quicker and more tailored to the needs of the parties. Additionally, huge amounts of money have been invested in the strengthening of the State's system of justice.

Unfortunately all these measures taken so far by many State legislators seem to have not been fully successful. The judiciary seems increasingly incapable of giving a valid response to the continuously growing number of disputes lodged before them, disputes of different nature and difficulty which deserve a quick, sound, affordable and, in many cases, specialised response. Already overworked courts face a huge workload and this fact directly affects access to justice for citizens; delayed justice implies in too many cases absence of justice.

This circumstance creates an increasing feeling of failure as regards the ability of the State to preserve and ensure the fundamental right of access to justice to citizens. The enormous budgetary effort made by many States as regards the judiciary has been insufficient in providing citizens with a valid and certain response to their legal problems. In addition to that, this situation does not only exist in Western countries; it tends to repeat itself in many other parts of the world. And the true problem is that, far from stopping, it will most probably continue to grow in the future thus putting the whole State's system of justice under increasing pressure, precisely at a time when many countries are facing budgetary constraints.

Citizens have long tried to surmount this situation in different ways. In some cases, they have adopted a purely passive attitude. In certain cases it seems more sound and inexpensive to leave the dispute unresolved than to refer it to State courts that in too many cases will render a late, unspecialised and not always certain response. In other situations, citizens have tended to explore the possibility of referring their disputes to non-judicial means of dispute resolution:

the so-called alternative dispute resolution devices. Arbitration, mediation, conciliation or negotiation are all embodied within this movement. Each one of them enjoys a different level of acceptance and implementation.

Certainly, problems undergone by the judiciary in many countries have entailed a correlative increasing resort to ADR devices as a way to ensure access to justice to citizens, at least in certain areas of law. Nevertheless, the use of ADR has been different in the several geographical areas of the world and has also varied regarding the specific ADR device referred to and the kind of disputes involved. Arbitration has so far been the most commonly used tool, although nowadays mediation is also gaining popularity.

ADR devices allow citizens to find responses to their need of justice. Many of these devices are not new insofar as they have long existed in national legislation, although the problems generated by complex modern society have granted them a certain image of novelty. In any case, the response provided by ADR devices is subject to some criticism of a different kind. From a justice standpoint, ADR may be regarded with some caution insofar as it is a private response which entails costs for citizens and that gives rise to a response not controlled by the State. From a systemic standpoint, the response provided has tended to be too limited in terms of the number of cases dealt with and of the sectors affected by it. Moreover its expansion has entailed a reproduction of some of the most criticised vices of the judiciary: growing costs, lack of speediness or absence of certainty in the response provided. In fact, within the ADR movement these problems favour mediation rather than arbitration.

The State has long enjoyed the monopoly on justice, but this time seems to be coming to an end. The State as the single provider of justice services for citizens seems to be under growing scrutiny. Despite all the moves undergone and the huge budgetary effort made by the State, it seems incapable of ensuring access to justice to citizens in this complex modern society in which we live. Mistrust of the judiciary has favoured growing resort to ADR devices for citizens but, at the same time, these devices seem not to form a global and real alternative to State courts insofar as they enjoy a limited use and provide a reduced response to a huge problem.

Complex societies and complex problems require complex solutions. And assuring full access to justice for citizens seems to demand an elaborated and sophisticated response too. It is time to offer citizens flexible and easily tailored solutions for them far away from doctrinal responses. That implies that State courts and ADR devices should no longer be viewed as real and separate alternatives lacking any contact with each other.

ADR can no longer be approached as a global alternative to State courts with the aim of leaving courts aside. State courts and non-judicial methods of dispute resolution should not be considered as two juxtaposed and independent realities which run parallel each other with no contact whatsoever. Sophisticated and collaborative responses are needed for citizens to have their duty to receive speedy, affordable and certain redress ensured. That implies a reshaping of the notion of full access to justice for citizens which should be based on the understanding of State courts and ADR as two different realities that actually interact when necessary to ensure citizens gain redress.

This new approach to access to justice means that it is for the parties to decide freely whether they refer their dispute to State courts or to ADR or to any of the mixed devices that increasingly exist in practice. This option must be chosen by them freely and taking into account their situation and legal expectations. It should not be directed or favoured by the State in any case and should not be based on budgetary concerns. We are not dealing with a budgetary question, namely whether the State should spend more or less on the judiciary and whether resort to ADR devices by citizens may result in some saving by the State. Acceptance by the State of the role played by the ADR movement should not come accompanied by a correlative weakening or impoverishment of the judiciary. The situation is different; we are simply offering citizens a multi-gear solution for having their disputes resolved and it is for them to decide how to approach and tackle them.

The new understanding of access to justice supposes that this basic fundamental right should no longer be understood as access solely to State courts of justice. On the contrary it should signify access to any of the existing available instruments for the parties to have their dispute resolved. The time of fully alternative responses is gone and a new era of proposals' plurality is arriving. The traditional concept of access to justice now implies a reference to a certain number of possibilities for the parties to obtain redress to their disputes. This opens up a new horizon for them that is much more easily adapted to their needs. But in order for this to be operative, citizens must be well aware of the existence of this alternative and, relatedly, of what ADR means, implies and supposes for them.

This book is based on this new understanding of access to justice and it looks to the future. Accordingly it approaches the reality of ADR in some of the most relevant countries of the growing Asian-Pacific economic area, the area in which the game of the future will be played. These countries tend to share the same problems of a growing number of disputes in a framework of overworked State courts and enormous amounts of money spent on the judiciary by national governments as in Western countries. But because they have different legal and historical backgrounds the response provided by them distinguishes one from another.

The book is written by leading academics and practitioners and it makes reference to both the existing legal basis for ADR in each of these jurisdictions and the way these rules are implemented. It offers an exhaustive analysis of the existing situation in these nations and tries to trace some common trends for the future development of ADR in this area of the world. Insofar as ADR has historically been a reality very much linked to common law countries and because some of the major Asia-Pacific States still belong to the British Commonwealth, a necessary reference to two European common law countries, Britain and Ireland, is also included. Despite the historical link between these two countries, their origin, culture and legal responses vary and allow the reader to compare them with the development that is currently happening far away, in the Asia-Pacific area.

This publication marks the way ahead. We hope that it will become a useful tool for practitioners and academics. The future of ADR and, by way of its potential interaction with State courts, of the understanding of what access to justice really means and implies for citizens, needs to ensure that all those involved in justice – judges, parties or legal practitioners – have a clear understanding of the existence of ADR as a complementary way to solve disputes, of its significance, consequences, advantages and also of those difficulties that its use may entail. With this book we want to contribute to this goal.

This book is direct result of the Research Project DER2010–17126 sponsored by the Ministry of Education of Spain on 'La experiencia del arbitraje y la mediación en los sistemas anglosajones y asiáticos y su incorporación en el nuevo modelo de justicia española del siglo XXI', to which many of the authors belong.

We would like to finish this preface by thanking Ms María Aranzazu Gandía Sellés, PhD student and assistant at the Department of International Law of the University of Valencia for her constant and valuable help and support in editing the present book.

Carlos Esplugues and Silvia Barona
Valencia, 22 January 2013

# CONTENTS

# TABLE OF CASES

## AUSTRALIA

- *Ezekiel-Hart v. Law Society (ACT)* [2012] ACTSC 135
- *Idoport Pty Ltd v. National Australia Bank* [2001] NSWSC 427
- *Mabo v. State of Queensland (No 2)* (1992) 175 CLR 1
- *Newcastle City Council v. Paul Wieland* [2009] NSWCA 113
- *Tapoohi v. Lewenberg (No 2)* [2003] VSC 410

## CANADA

- *Moore v. Bertuzzi*, 2012 ONSC 597
- *Noble China Inc v. Lei* (1998) 42 OR (3d) 69; 42 BLR (2d) 262
- *Rains v. Molea*, 2012 ONSC 4906
- *The United Mexican States v. Cargill Inc.*, 2011 ONCA 622

## EUROPEAN COURT OF JUSTICE

- ECJ Judgment of 17.11.1998, in case C-391/95, *Van Uden Maritime / Kommanditgesellschaft in Firma Deco-Line and others* (*ECR* 1998 p. I-7091)
- ECJ Judgment of 26.10.2006, in case C-168/05, *Mostaza Claro* (*ECR* 2006 p. I-10421)
- ECJ Judgment of 06.10.2009, in case C-40/08, *Asturcom Telecomunicaciones* (*ECR* 2009 p. I-9575)
- ECJ judgment of 10.02.2009, in case C-185/07, *Allianz (formerly Riunione Adriatica di Sicurtà)* (*ECR* 2009 p. I-663)

## ENGLAND AND WALES

- *AES Ust-Kamenogorsk Hydropower Plant LLP v. Ust-Kamenogorsk Hydropower Plant JSC* [2013] UKSC 35
- *African Fertilizers and Chemicals NIG Ltd (Nigeria) v. BD Shipsnavo GmbH & Co Reederei KG* [2011] EWHC 2452 (Comm)
- *Aird v. Prime Meridian Ltd* [2006] EWCA Civ 1866
- *Allianz SpA etc v. West Tankers* (C-185/07) [2009] 1 AC 1138; [2009] 1 All ER (Comm) 435; [2009] 1 Lloyd's Rep 413; [2009] 1 CLC 96; [2009] ILPr 20

- *Associated Electric and Gas Insurance Services Ltd v. European Reinsurance Co of Zurich* [2003] UKPC 11
- *Barnetson v. Framlington Group Ltd* [2007] EWCA Civ 502; [2007] 1 WLR 2443
- *Bea Hotels NV v. Bellway LLC* [2007] EWHC 1363 (Comm).
- *Bevan Ashford (a firm) v. Geoff Yeandle (Contractors) Ltd (in liquidation)* [1998] All ER (D) 138
- *Bradford & Bingley plc v. Rashid* [2006] UKHL 37; [2006] 1 WLR 2066
- *Bremer Vulcan v. South India Shipping Corporation Limited* [1981] AC 909, HL
- *Brown v. Rice* [2007] EWHC 625 (Ch)
- *C v. D* [2007] EWCA Civ 1282; [2008] 1 Lloyd's Rep 239
- *Cable & Wireless v. IBM United Kingdom Ltd* [2002] 2 All ER (Comm) 1041
- *Canonway Consultants Ltd v Kenworth Engineering Ltd* [1997] ADRLJ 95
- *Carleton v. Strutt & Parker* [2008] EWHC 424
- *Clyde & Co v. Bates van Winkelhof* [2011] EWHC 668 (QB)
- *Cumbria Waste Management Ltd v. Baines Wilson* [2008] EWHC 786 (QB)
- *Dallah Real Estate & Tourism Holding Co v. Pakistan* [2010] UKSC 46; [2010] 3 WLR 1472
- *Downing v. Al Tameer Establishment* [2002] EWCA Civ 721
- *Dunnett v. Railtrack plc* [2002] 1 WLR 2434, CA
- *Emmott v. Michael Wilson & Partners Ltd* [2008] EWCA Civ 184
- *English Churches Housing Group v. Shine* [2004] EWCA Civ 434
- *Farm Assist Limited (in liquidation) v. The Secretary of State for the Environment, Food and Rural Affairs (No 2)* [2009] EWHC 1102 (TCC); [2009] BLR 399; 125 Con LR 154
- *Fiona Trust and Holding Corporation v. Privalov* [2007] UKHL 40; [2007] 4 All ER 951; [2007] EWCA Civ 20
- *Fulham FC (1987) Ltd v. Richards* [2010] EWHC 3111 (Ch); [2011] 2 All ER 112
- *Guangzhou Dockyards Co Ltd v. ENE Aegiali I* [2010] EWHC 2826
- *Halpern v. Halpern (No 2)* [2007] EWCA Civ 291
- *Halsey v. Milton Keynes General NHS Trust* [2004] EWCA Civ 576; [2004] 1 WLR 3002; [2004] 4 All ER 920
- *Itochu Corporation v. Johann M.K. Blumenthal GMBH & Co KG & Anr* [2012] EWCA Civ 996
- *Jivraj v. Hashwani* [2011] UKSC 40; [2011] 1 WLR 1872
- *JSC BTA Bank v. Ablyazov* [2011] EWHC 587 (Comm)
- *Lesotho Highlands Development Authority v. Impreglio SpS* [2006] 1 AC 22, HL
- *Lombard North Central plc and another v. GATX Corporation* [2012] EWHC 1067 (Comm)
- *Martin Dawes v. Treasure & Son Ltd* [2010] EWHC 3218

- *Mary Harvey v. Motor Insurers' Bureau* (QBD (Merc) (Manchester), Claim No: 0MA40077, 21.12.2011, unreported)
- *McMillan Williams v. Range* [2004] EWCA Civ 294; [2004] 1 WLR 1858
- *Michael Wilson & Partners v. Sinclair* [2012] EWHC 2560
- *Midgulf International Ltd v. Groupe Chimiche Tunisien* [2010] EWCA Civ 66; [2010] 1 CLC 113
- *Mobil Cerro Negro Ltd v. Petroleos De Venezuela SA* [2008] EWHC 532 (Comm)
- *Oceanbulk Shipping and Trading SA v. TMT Asia Ltd* [2010] UKSC 44; [2010] 3 WLR 1424 (reversing [2010] EWCA Civ 79; [2010] 1 WLR 1803)
- *P4 Ltd v. Unite Integrated Solutions plc* [2006] EWHC 2924 (TCC)
- *Petrochemical Industries Co. (KSC) v. Dow Chemical Co.* [2012] EWHC 2739 (Comm)
- *Pioneer Shipping v. BTP Tioxide Ltd ('The Nema')* [1982] AC 724
- *Reed Executive plc v. Reed Business Information Ltd* [2004] EWCA Civ 887; [2004] 1 WLR 3026
- *Shashoua v. Sharma* [2009] EWHC 957
- *Shell Egypt West Manzala GmbH v. Dana Gas Egypt Ltd* [2009] EWHC 2097 (Comm)
- *Shipping Ltd of India v. TTMI Ltd of England ('The Amer Energy')* [2009] 1 Lloyd's Rep 293
- *Smith v. Weiss* [2002] All ER (D) 356
- *Sulamerica CIA Nacional de Seguros SA v. Enesa Engenharia SA* [2012] EWCA Civ 638
- *Svenska Petroleum Exploration AB v. Government of the Republic of Lithuania (No 2)* [2006] EWCA Civ 1529; [2007] QB 886
- *Swain Mason and others v. Mills & Reeve (a firm)* [2012] EWCA Civ 498
- *Turner v. Grovit* (2001) [2001] UKHL 65; [2002] 1 WLR 107
- *Unilever plc v. The Proctor & Gamble Co.* [2000] 1 WLR 2436, CA
- *Venture Investment v. Hall* [2005] EWHC 1227 (Ch)
- *Virani Ltd v. Manuel Revert y Cia SA* [2003] EWCA Civ 1651; [2004] 2 Lloyd's Rep 14
- *West Tankers Inc v. Allianz SpA and another* [2012] EWHC 854 (Comm)
- *West Tankers Inc v. Allianz SpA v. Generali Assicurazione Generali SpA* [2012] EWCA Civ 27
- *Westacre Investments Inc v. Jugoimport-SDRP Holding Company Ltd* [1999] APPLR 05/12
- *Wuhan Ocean Economic & Technical Cooperation Co. Ltd and another v. Schiffharts-Gesselschaft 'Hansa Murcia' MBH & Co. KG* [2012] EWHC 3104
- *Yukos Capital SARL v. OJSC Rosneft Oil Company (No 2)* [2012] EWCA Civ 855; [2012] WLR (D) 186

## FRANCE

- *Aïta v. Ojjeh* (Cour d'appel de Paris, 18.2.1986, 1 Chambre Supple. (1986) *Revue de l'Arbitrage* 583)
- *Bleustein v. Société True North et Société FCB International* (Trib. de Commerce de Paris, Ord. réf, 08.10.2002, (2003) *Revue de l'Arbitrage* 189)
- *Gouvernement du Pakistan v. Société Dallah Real Estate & Tourism Holding Co.* (Cour d'appel de Paris, Pôle 1 – Ch. 1, n° 09/28533, 17.02.2011, (2011) *Revue de l'Arbitrage* 286)
- *S.A.J. & P. Avaxv. Société Tecnimon* (Cour d'appel de Reims, cour de renvoi, 02.11.2011, n° 10/02888, (2012) *ASA Bulletin* 189)
- *Société Hilmarton v. Société OTV* (Cour de Cassation, 1st Chambre Civil, 23.03.1994, (1994) *Revue de l'Arbitrage* 327)
- *Société PT Putrabali Adyamulia v. Société Rena Holding et Société Mnogutia Est Epices* (Cour de Cassation, 1 Chambre, 29.06.2007, (2007) *Revue de l'Arbitrage* 507)

## HONG KONG

- *A v. R* [2009] 3 HKLRD 389
- *Democratic Republic of Congo v. FG Hemisphere Assocs. LLC* [2011] 4 HKC 151
- *FG Hemisphere Associates LLC v. Democratic Republic of Congo* [2010] 2 HKC 487, CA
- *Gao Haiyan and another v. Keeneye Holdings Ltd and another (No 2)* [2012] 1 HKC 491
- *Gao Haiyan and Xie Heping v. Keeneye Holdings Ltd* [2011] 3 HKC 157
- *Golden Eagle International (Group) Ltd v. GR Investment Holdings Ltd* [2010] 3 HKLRD 273
- *Hak Tung Alfred Tang v. Bloomberg LP* [2010] HKEC 1227
- *Ng Fung Hong Ltd v. ABC* [1998] 1 HKC 213
- *Pacific China Holdings Ltd v. Grand Pacific Holdings Ltd* (2012) HKEC 645; (2011) HKLRD 611

## ICSID[1]

- *Abaclat and others v. Argentine Republic (*ICSID Case no. ARB/07/5, formerly *Giovanna a Beccara and others v. Argentine Republic*)
- *Barnmore Demolition and Civil Engineering Ltd, Alandale Logistics Ltd, et al., and Bayindir Insaat Turizm Ticaret Ve Sanayi AS v. Islamic Republic of Pakistan* (ICSID Case no. ARB/03/29)

1 Available at: https://icsid.worldbank.org/ICSID/FrontServlet.

- *Occidental Petroleum Corporation and Occidental Exploration and Production Company v. Republic of Ecuador* (ICSID Case no. ARB/06/11)
- *Salini Costruttori SpA and Italstrade SpA v. Kingdom of Morocco* (ICSID Case no. ARB/00/4)
- *SGS Société Générale de Surveillance SA v. Islamic Republic of Pakistan* (ICSID Case no. ARB/01/13)
- *World Duty Free Company Limited v. Republic of Kenya* (ICSID Case No. ARB/00/7)

## INDIA

- *Abdul Kadir v. Madhav Oak*, AIR 1962 SC 406
- *Aboobakar Latif v. Reception Committee*, AIR 1937 Bom 410
- *Ace Pipeline Contracts Pvt Ltd v. Bharat Petroleum Corporation Ltd* (2007) 5 SCC 304
- *Afcons Infrastructure Ltd v. Cherian Varkey Construction Co. (P) Ltd* (2010) 8 SCC 24
- *Alcove Industries Ltd v. Oriental Structural Engineers* (2008) 1 ArbLR 393 (Del), 423
- *Apparel Export Promotion Council v. Prabhati Patni* (2005) 3 ArbLR 518 (Del), 530
- *Arvind Construction Co Pvt Ltd v. Kalinga Mining Corpn* (2007) 6 SCC 798
- *Aurohill Global Commodities Ltd v. MSTC Ltd* (2007) 7 SCC 120
- *B.P. Moideen Sevamandir v. A.M. Kutty Hassan* (2009) 2 SCC 198
- *Babubhai Tansukhlal v. Madhavji Govindji & Co.*, AIR 1931 Bom 343
- *Bharat Aluminium v. Kaiser Aluminium Technical Services* (Civil Appeal No. 7019 of 2005) (2012) 9 SCC 552
- *Bharat M. Nagori v. Satish Ashok Sabnis* (2003) 6 BomCR 257
- *Bharat Rasiklal Ashra v. Gautam Rasiklal Ashra* (2012) 2 SCC 144
- *Bharat Sanchar Nigam Ltd v. Motorola India Pvt Ltd* (2009) 2 SCC 337
- *Bhatia International v. Bulk Trading SA* (2002) 4 SCC 105
- *Bihar State Mineral Development Corpn v. Encon Builders (I) (P) Ltd* (2003) 7 SCC 418
- *Booz Allen & Hamilton v. SBI Home Finance Ltd* (2011) 5 SCC 532
- *BSES Ltd v. Fenner India Ltd* (2006) 2 SCC 728
- *CDC Financial Services (Mauritius) Ltd v. BPL Communications Ltd* (2003) 12 SCC 140
- *Centrotrade Minerals & Metals Inc. v. Hindustan Copper Ltd* (2006) 11 SCC 245
- *Chandrabhan Bilotia v. Ganpatrai & Sons*, AIR 1944 Cal. 127
- *Chetandas Daga v. Radhakissen Ramchandra*, AIR 1927 Bom 553
- *Chief Signal v. Hytronics Enterprises* (2006) 2 ArbLR 343 (AP)

- *ITI Ltd v. Siemens Public Communications Network Ltd* (2002) 5 SCC 510
- *Ivory Properties & Hotels Pvt Ltd v. Nusli Wadia* (2011) 2 BomCR 559
- *Jagdish Chander v. Ramesh Chander* (2007) 5 SCC 719
- *Jagmohan Singh Gujral v. Satish Ashok Sabnis* (2004) 1 BomCR 307
- *Jain Studios v. Shin Satellite Public Co. Ltd* (2006) 5 SCC 501
- *J.B. Engineers Pvt Ltd v. Union of India* (2011) 5 SCC 758
- *J.G. Engineers (P) Ltd v. Union of India* (2011) 5 SCC 758
- *J.S. Ocean Liner LLC v. MV Golden Progress* (2007) 2 BomCR 1
- *Keshav Singh Dwarkadas Kapadia v. Indian Engineering Co.*, AIR 1969 Bom 227
- *Keshav Singh Dwarkadas Kapadia v. Indian Engineering Co.* (1971) 2 SCC 706
- *K.K. Modi v. K.N. Modi* (1998) 3 SCC 573
- *K.N. Govindan Kutty Menon v. C.D. Shaji* (2012) 2 SCC 51
- *Konkan Railway Corpn Ltd v. Rani Construction Pvt Ltd* (2002) 2 SCC 388
- *Kumaon Mandal Vikas Nigam Ltd v. Girja Shankar Pant* (2001) 1 SCC 182
- *Ladli Construction Co. (P) Ltd v. Punjab Police Housing Corpn Ltd* (2012) 4 SCC 609
- *Magna Leasing & Finance Ltd v. Potluri Madhavilata* (2009) 10 SCC 103
- *Maharashtra State Electricity Board v. Datar Switchgear Ltd* (2003) 2 BomCR 81
- *Maintech Engineers v. Jogindra Steel Tubes Ltd* (1993) 51 DLT 463
- *Marketing Federation India Ltd v. Gains Trading Ltd* (2007) 5 SCC 692
- *McDermott International Inc. v. Burn Standard Co. Ltd* (2006) 11 SCC 181
- *M.D., Army Welfare Housing v. Sumangal Services Pvt Ltd* (2004) 9 SCC 619
- *Momentous.ca Corpn v. Canadian American Association of Professional Baseball Ltd* (2012) SCC 9
- *Moradabad Development Authority v. VR Construction & Engineering Co.* (2007) Supp ArbLR 80
- *Morgan Securities and Credit (Private) Ltd v. Modi Rubber Ltd* (2006) 12 SCC 642
- *M.R. Engineers & Contractors (P) Ltd v. Som Datt Builders Ltd* (2009) 7 SCC 696
- *M.R. Power Projects v. State of Arunachal Pradesh* (2009) 4 GauLR 154
- *Mukesh H. Mehta v. Harendra H. Mehta* (1995) 5 CompLJ 517 (Bom)
- *N. Srinivasa v. Kuttukaran Machine Tools Ltd* (2009) 5 SCC 182
- *N. Radhakrishnan v. Maestro Engineers* (2010) 1 SCC 72
- *Nandos Indage v. Nando's Resources BV* (2009) 4 BomCR 139
- *Narayan Prasad Lohia v. Nikunj Kumar Lohia* (2002) 3 SCC 572
- *National Ability SA v. Tinna Oil and Chemicals Ltd* (2008) 3 ArbLR 37 (Del)
- *National Agricultural Coop. Marketing Federation India Ltd v. Gains Trading Ltd* (2007) 5 SCC 692

- *National Highways Authority of India v. Afcons Infrastructure Ltd* (2008) 3 ArbLR 56
- *National Insurance Co. Ltd v. Boghara Polyfab (P) Ltd* (2009) 1 SCC 267
- *Natraj Studios (P) Ltd v. Navrang Studios* (1981) 1 SCC 523
- *Nirma Ltd v. Lurgi Lentjes Energietechnik GmbH* (2002) 5 SCC 520
- *Northern Railway Administration, Ministry of Railways v. Patel Engineering Co. Ltd* (2008) 10 SCC 240
- *Novartis Vaccines and Diagnostics Inc. v. Aventis Pharma*, judgment of 03.10.2007 in Arbitration Petition No. 302 of 2007, Bombay High Court (unreported)
- *NTPC v. Singer Company* (1992) 3 SCC 551
- *Numaligarh Refinery Ltd v. Daelim Industrial Co. Ltd* (2007) 8 SCC 466
- *Olympus Superstructures Pvt Ltd v. Meena Vijay Khetan* (1999) 5 SCC 651
- *OPBK Construction Pvt Ltd v. Punjab Small Industries* (2008) 3 Arb LR 189 (P&H)
- *Oriental Instruance Co. Ltd v. Unitech Ltd* (2008) 1 Arb LR 187 (Del)
- *P. Anand Gajapathi Raju v. PVG Raju* (2000) 4 SCC 539
- *Pandey & Co. Builders Pvt Ltd v. State of Bihar* (2007) 1 SCC 467
- *Paramita Constructions Pvt Ltd v. UE Development India Pvt Ltd* (2008) 3 ArbLR 522
- *Percept D'Mark (India) Pvt Ltd v. Zaheer Khan* (2006) 4 SCC 227
- *Phulchand Exports Ltd v O.O.O. Patriot* (2011) 10 SCC 300
- *Powertech World Wide Ltd v. Delvin International General Trading LLC* (2012) 1 SCC 361
- *P.R. Shah Share & Stock Brokers v. BHH Securities* (2012) 1 SCC 594
- *Prima Buildwell (Pvt) Ltd v. Lost City Developments LLC* (2011) 3 ArbLR 350
- *Prima Developers v. Lords Co-operative Group Housing Society Ltd* (2009) 2 ArbLR 387
- *P.T. Thomas v. Thomas Job* (2005) 6 SCC 478
- *R.M. Investments & Trading Co. P. Ltd v. Boeing Co.* (1994) 4 SCC 541
- *R.S. Avatar Singh and Co. v. Indian Tourism Development Corpn Ltd*, AIR 2003 Del 249
- *R.S. Jiwani v. Ircon International Ltd* (2010) 1 BomCR 529 (FB)
- *Rambaksh Lachmandas v. Bombay Cotton Co.*, AIR 1931 Bom 81
- *Ramesh Kumar v. Furu Ram* (2011) 8 SCC 613
- *Rashtriya Ispat Nigam Ltd v. Verma Transport Co.* (2006) 7 SCC 275
- *Renusagar Power Co. Ltd v. General Electric Co.* (1984) 4 SCC 679
- *Rickers Verwaltung GmbH v. Indian Oil Corpn Ltd* (1999) 1 SCC 1
- *Rukmanibai Gupta v. Collector, Jabalpur* (1980) 4 SCC 556
- *Salem Advocates Bar Association v. Union of India* (2003) 1 SCC 49
- *Sakuma Exports Ltd v. Louis Dreyfus Commodities* (2012) 1 BomCR 547
- *SBP & Co. v. Patel Engineering Ltd* (2005) 8 SCC 618

- *Seidel v. TELUS Communications Inc.* (2011) SCC 15 (CanLII)
- *Shin-Etsu Chemical Co. Ltd v. Aksh Optifiber Ltd* (2005) 7 SCC 234
- *Shree Ram Mills Ltd v. Utility Premises (P) Ltd* (2007) 4 SCC 599
- *Shreejee Traco (I) Pvt Ltd v. Paperline International Inc.* (2003) 9 SCC 79
- *Shri Lal Mahal Ltd v. Progetto Grano SpA* (Supreme Court, 3 July 2013 in Civil Appeal No. 5085/2013)
- *Smita Conductors Ltd v. Euro Alloys Ltd* (2001) 7 SCC 728
- *S.N. Prasad v. Monnet Finance Ltd* (2011) 1 SCC 320
- *State of Goa v. Praveen Enterprises* (2011) 3 ArbLR 209
- *State of Maharashtra v. Hindustan Construction Co. Ltd* (2010) 4 SCC 518
- *State of Punjab v. Jalour Singh* (2008) 2 SCC 660
- *Sukanya Holdings (Pvt) Ltd v. Jayesh H. Pandya* (2003) 5 SCC 531
- *Sumitomo Heavy Industries Ltd v. ONGC Ltd* (1998) 1 SCC 305
- *Sundaram Finance Ltd v. M.K. Kurian*, AIR 2006 Mad 218 (DB)
- *Sundaram Finance Ltd v. NEPC India Ltd* (1999) 2 SCC 479
- *Tata Industries Ltd v. Grasim Industries Ltd* (2011) 3 Bom CR 326
- *Travancore Devaswom Board v. Panchamy Pack (P) Ltd* (2004) 13 SCC 510
- *Union of India v. Master Construction* (2011) 12 SCC 349
- *Union of India v. Popular Construction Co.* (2001) 8 SCC 470
- *Union of India v. Singh Builders Syndicate* (2009) 4 SCC 523
- *United India Insurance Co. Ltd v. Ajay Sinha* (2008) 7 SCC 454
- *Venture Global Engg. v. Satayam Computer Services Ltd* (2008) 4 SCC 190
- *Videocon Industries Ltd v. Union of India* (2011) 6 SCC 161
- *Vijaya Bank v. Maker Development Services Pvt Ltd* (2001) 3 BomCR 652
- *Visa International Ltd v. Continental Resources (USA) Ltd* (2009) 2 SCC 55
- *Vishal Exports Overseas Ltd v. Ind Agro Synergy Ltd* (2007) 3 ArbLR 502 (MP)
- *Voltas Ltd v. Rolta India Ltd* (2011) 113 BomLR 393
- *Wellington Associates Ltd v. Kirit Mehta* (2000) 4 SCC 272
- *Yashwitha Constructions (P) Ltd v. Simplex Concrete Piles India Ltd* (2008) 4 Andh LT 266
- *Yenepoya Minerals & Granites P Ltd v. Maharashtra Apex Corpn Ltd* (2004) 2 ArbLR 47 (Kar)
- *Yograj Infrastructure Ltd v. Ssang Yong Engg & Construction Co. Ltd* (2011) 9 SCC 735
- *Z.I. Pompey Industrie v. ECU-Line NV* (2003) SCC 27

## IRELAND

- *Barnmore Demolition and Civil Engineering Ltd v. Alandale Logistics Ltd, et al.* [2010] No 5910P

## JAPAN

- *Hayakawa v. Aoki*, Japanese Supreme Court, Judgment of 5 March 1958, Minshu vol. 12, no. 3, p. 381
- *Kokusan Kinzoku Kogyo Co. Ltd v. Gurd Life Co.*, Japanese Supreme Court, Judgment of 15 July 1975, Minshu vol. 29, no. 6, p. 1061
- *Nihon Kyoikusha v. Feld*, Japanese Supreme Court, Judgment of 4 September 1997, Minshu vol. 51, no. 8, p. 3657
- *Ohara v. Kawanishi*, Osaka High Court, Judgment of 20 February 1974, Hanreijiho no. 746, p. 42
- *Osaka Nyuseihin Co. Ltd v. Nagano Kanzume Kogyo Co. Ltd*, Japanese Supreme Court, Judgment of 14 June 1958, Minshu vol. 12, no. 9, p. 1492
- *Sumitomo Fudosan Systemconstruction Co. Ltd v. Kato*, Tokyo High Court, Judgment of 9 October 1990, Kin'yu shojihanrei no. 863 p. 42.

## KOREA

- *HIWOOD Inc. v. HIWOOD Inc.* [Judgment of the Korean Supreme Court of 18.10.2012 (Case No. 2010da10300)]
- *Hun-Keun Yoo, Receiver of Eastern Sea Pulp Corp. (Reorganization Company) (Currently Moorim P & P Co. Ltd) v. Majestic Woochips Inc.* [Judgment of the Korean Supreme Court of 26.02.2003 (Case No. 2001da77840)]
- Judgment of the Korean Supreme Court of 09.12.1986 (Case No. 86do51147)
- Judgment of the Korean Supreme Court of 05.12.1995 (Case No. 95da21868)
- Judgment of the Korean Supreme Court of 23.06.2000 (Case No. 98da55192)
- Judgment of the Korean Supreme Court of 23.07.2000 (Case No. 98da55192)
- Judgment of the Korean Supreme Court of 26.02.2003 (Case No. 2001da77840)
- Judgment of the Korean Supreme Court of 25.06.2004 (Case No. 2003da5634)
- Judgment of the Korean Supreme Court of 14.10.2004 (Case No. 2003da70249, 70256)
- *KOICA v. Hi-Net Trade Co. Ltd* [Judgment of the Seoul High Court of 12.09.2007 (Case No. 2006na107687]
- *KOICA v. Hi-Net Trade Co. Ltd* [Judgment of the Korean Supreme Court of 24.06.2010 (Case No. 2007da73918)]
- *Korea Heavy Industry and Construction Corp. v. Gold Star Cable & System Corp.* [Judgment of the Korean Supreme Court of 14.04.1992 (Case No. 91da17146)]
- *Kyphon SARL v. Taeyeon Medical Co., Ltd.* [Judgment of the Korean Supreme Court of 15.03.2012 (Case No. 2010da63133)]
- *LG Electronics Inc. v. Daewoo Electronics Corp.* [Judgment of the Korean Supreme Court of 19.01.2012 (Case No. 2010da95390) (en banc)]

- Ruling of the Korean Supreme Court of 14.06.2007 (Case No. 2006ma910)
- *Taeyeon Medical Co., Ltd v. Medtronic, Inc* [Judgment of the Korean Seoul High Court of 08.07.2010 (Case No. 2009na22763)]

NEW ZEALAND

- *Methanex Motunui Ltd & Methanex Waitara Valley Ltd v. Joseph Spellman* [2004] 1 NZLR 95 (NZCA)

PAKISTAN

- *HUBCO v. WAPDA* (2000) 16 *Arbitration International* 469
- *SGS v. Federation of Pakistan*, SCMR 1694

PHILIPPINES

- *ABS-CBN Broadcasting Corpn v. World Interactive Network Systems (WINS) Japan Co. Ltd* [G.R. No. 169332, 11.02.2008]
- *Allen v. Province of Tayabas* [G.R. No. 12283, 25.07.1918]
- *Benguet Corpn v. Department of Environment and Natural Resources et al.* [G.R. No. 163101, 13.02.2008]
- *Chan Linte v. Law Union and Rock Insurance Co. Ltd* [G.R. No. 16398, 14.12.1921]
- *Chang et al. v. Royal Exchange Assurance Corporation of London* [G.R. No. L-3567, 20.08.1907]
- *China Chang Jiang Energy Corporation (Philippines) v. Rosal Infrastructure Builders* [G.R. No. 125706, 30.09.1996]
- *Chung Fu Industries (Philippines) Inc. et al. v. Court of Appeals et al.* [G.R. No. 96283, 25.02.1992]
- *Cordoba v. Conde* [*G.R. No. 1125*, 24.08.1903]
- *Eastboard Navigation Ltd v. Juan Ysmael and Co. Inc.* [G.R. No. L-9090, 10.09.1957]
- *Fort Bonifacio Development Corpn v. Domingo* [G.R. No. 180765, 27.02.2009]
- *Gammon Philippines, Inc. v. Metro Rail Transit Development Corpn* [G.R. No. 144792, 31.01.2006]
- *Korea Technologies Co. Ltd v. Hon. Alberto A. Lerma et al.* [G.R. No. 143581, 07.01.2008]
- *Philrock, Inc. v. CIAC* [412 Phil. 236, 2001]
- *Prudential Guarantee and Assurance Inc. v. Anscor Land Inc.* [G.R. No. 177240, 08.09.2010]

- *Puentebella et al. v. Negros Coal Co. Ltd et al.* [G.R. Nos. 26216 & 26217, 06.03.1927]
- *Wahl et al. v. Donaldson, Sims & Co.* [G.R. No 1085, 16.05.1903]

## SINGAPORE

- *AAY v. AAZ* [2011] 1 SLR 1093
- *ALC v. ALF* [2010] SGHC 231
- *AZT v. AZV* [2012] SGHC 116
- *Doshion Ltd v. Sembawang Engineers and Constructors Pte Ltd* [2011] SGHC 46
- *Equinox Offshore Accommodation Ltd v. Richshore Marine Supplies Pte Ltd* [2010] SGHC 122
- *Giant Light Metal Technology (Kunshan) Co. Ltd v. Aksa Far East Pte Ltd* [2012] SGHCR 2
- *Government of the Republic of the Philippines v. Philippine International Air Terminals Co. Inc.* [2007] 1 SLR 278
- *Ho Wing On Christopher and others v. ECRC Land Pte Ltd (in liquidation)* [2006] SGCA 25
- *Hyundai Engineering v. Sembawang Kimtrans* [2001] 1 SLR 739
- *John Holland v. Toyo Engineering Corpn (Japan)* [2001] 2 SLR 262
- *Kempinski Hotels SA v. PT Prima International Development* [2011] SGHC 171
- *Larsen Oil and Gas Pte Ltd v. Petroprod Ltd* [2011] SGCA 21
- *Lock Han Chng Jonathan v. Goh Jessiline* [2008] 2 SLR(R) 455
- *Ng Chin Siau v. How Kim Chuan* [2007] 2 SLR(R) 789
- *Pioneer Shipping v. BTP Tioxide Ltd ('The Nema')* [1982] AC 724
- *Quarella SpA v. Scelta Marble Australia Pty Ltd* [2012] SGHC 166
- *Tjong Very Sumito v. Antig Investments* [2009] 4 SLR(R) 732; [2009] SGCA 41

## SWEDEN

- *Jilkén v. Ericsson*, Case no. T 2448-06, 19.11.2007 (NJA 2007)
- *Korsnäs AB v. AB Fortum Värme*, Case no. T 10321-06 (NJA 2010)
- *Profilgruppen v. KPMG*, Case no. T 1085-11 (www.arbitration.sccinstitute.com/files/102/1023796/T%201085-11_eng.pdf#search="KPMG")

## SWITZERLAND

- *A v. B, C, D* (Federal Supreme Court judgment of 21.03.2011, Case no. 4A_574/2010)

- *A v. Fédération Internationale de Football Association (FIFA)* (Federal Supreme Court judgment of 9.1.2009, Case no. 4A_460/2008 len/)
- *AG v. Y* (Federal Supreme Court judgment of 6.8.2012, Case no. 4A_119/2012)
- *Union des Associations Européennes de Football (UEFA) v. Association Z* (Federal Supreme Court judgment of 22.12.2008, Case no. 4A_392/2008/ech)
- *X v UCI, CONI & FCI* (Federal Supreme Court judgment of 18.6.2012, Case no. 4A_488/2011)
- *X v. Y* (Federal Supreme Court judgment of 20.2.2009, Case no. 4A_600/2008)
- *X. Lda, Administradora de Insolvencia v. Y* (Federal Supreme Court judgment of 15.10.2012, Case no. 4A_50/2012)

## USA

- *Aerojet-General Corp. v. Am. Arbitration Ass'n*, 478 F.2d 248 (9th Cir. 1973)
- *Alexander v. Gardner-Denver Co.*, 415 U.S. 36 (1974)
- *Allied-Bruce Terminix Cos. v. Dobson*, 513 U.S. 265 (1994)
- *ANR Coal v. Cogentrix of N. Caro., Inc.*, 172 F.3d 493 (4th Cir. 1999)
- *Armendariz v. Found Health PsychCare Sers., Inc.*, 6 P.3d 669 (Cal. 2000)
- *Asoma Corp. v. M/F Faros D.C.N.Y. 2001* [2001 WL 1588929, vacated C.A.2d, 2002, 53 Fed. Appx. 581]
- *AT&T Techs., Inc. v. Commc'ns Workers of Am.*, 475 U.S. 643 (1986)
- *AT&T Mobility LLC v. Concepcion*, 131 S.Ct. 1740 (2011)
- *Availl, Inc. v. Ryder Systems, Inc.*, 110 F.3d 892 (2d Cir. 1997)
- *Banc One Acceptance Corp. v. Hill*, 367 F.3d 426 (5th Cir. 2004)
- *Bechtel do Brasil Construções Ltda v. UEG Araucária Ltda*, 638 F.3d 150
- *Blue Cross Blue Shield of Mass., Inc. v. BCS Ins. Co.*, 671 F.3d 635 (7th Cir. 2011)
- *Booth v. Mary Carter Paint Co.*, 202 So2d 8 (Fla Dist Ct App 1967)
- *Botello v. COI Telecom, LLC*, 2010 U.S. Dist. LEXIS 138572 (W.D. Tex. Dec. 30, 2010)
- *Bowen v. Amoco Pipeline Co.*, 254 F.3d 925 (10th Cir. 2001)
- *BP Exploration Libya Ltd v. ExxonMobil Libya Ltd*, 11–20547, 2012 WL 3065317 (5th Cir. 30.07.2012)
- *Buckeye Check Cashing, Inc. v. Cardegna*, 546 U.S. 440 (2006)
- *Burton v. Bush*, 614 F.2d 389 (4th Cir. 1980)
- *Cabinetree of Wisconsin, Inc. v. Kraftmaid Cabinetry, Inc.*, 50 F.3d 388 (7th Cir. 1995)
- *Chen-Oster v. Goldman, Sachs & Co*, 785 F. Supp. 2d 394 (S.D.N.Y. 2011)
- *Citibank, NA v. Stok & Assocs., PA*, 387 F. App'x 921 (11th Cir. 2010)
- *Cole v. Burns Int'l Security Servs.*, 105 F.3d 1465 (D.C. Cir. 1997)
- *Commonwealth Coatings Corp. v. Continental Cas. Co.*, 393 U.S. 145 (1968)

- *Compania Panemena Maritima v. J.E. Hurley Lumber Co.*, 244 F.2d 286 (2d Cir. 1957)
- *Cone Mem'l Hospital v. Mercury Constr. Corp.*, 460 U.S. 1 (1983)
- *Consorcio Ecuatoriano de Telecomunicaciones SA v. JAS Forwarding (USA), Inc.*, 685 F.3d 987 (11th Cir. 2012)
- *Contec Corp. v. Remote Solution Co.*, 398 F.3d 205 (2d Cir. 2005)
- *Cox v. Ocean View Hotel Corp.*, 533 F.3d 1114 (9th Cir. 2008)
- *Dean Witter Reynolds, Inc. v. Byrd*, 470 U.S. 213 (1985)
- *Doctor's Associates, Inc. v. Casarotto*, 517 U.S. 681 (1996)
- *EEOC v. Waffle House, Inc.*, 534 U.S. 279 (2002)
- *Emilio v. Sprint Spectrum, L.P.*, 315 F. App'x 322, 324 (2d Cir. 2009)
- *Erie R.R. Co. v. Thompkins*, 304 U.S. 64, 78 (1938)
- *Fantastic Sams Franchise Corporation, v. FSRO Association Ltd., et al.*, 683 F.3d 18 (1st Cir. 2012)
- *Fidelity Fed. Bank, FSB v. Durga Ma Corp.*, 386 F.3d 1306 (9th Cir. 2004)
- *Figueiredo Ferraz e Engenharia de Projecto Ltda v. Republic of Peru*, 2001 WL 6188497 (2d Cir. 14.12.2011)
- *First Options of Chicago, Inc. v. Kaplan*, 514 U.S. 938, 115 S.Ct. 1920 (1995)
- *Gilmer v. Interstate/Johnson Lane Corp.*, 500 U.S. 20 (1991)
- *Gonzalez v. West Suburban Imp., Inc.*, 411 F. Supp. 2d 970 (N.D. III 2006)
- *Gov't of United Kingdom v. Boeing Co.*, 998 F.2d 68 (2d Cir. 1993)
- *Green Tree Fin. Corp v. Bazzle*, 539 U.S. 444 (2003)
- *Green Tree Fin. Corp.-Alabama v. Randolph*, 531 U.S. 79 (2000)
- *Gulf Guar. Life Ins. Co. v. Conn. Gen. Life Ins. Co*, 304 F.3d 476 (5th Cir. 2002)
- *Gulf Petro Trading Co. v. Nigerian Nat'l Petroleum Corp.*, 512 F.3d 742 (5th Cir. 2008)
- *Halide Group, Inc. v. Hyosung Corp.*, F. Supp. 2d 1, 2010 WL 4456928 (E.D. Pa., 2010) (No. CIV. A. 10-02392)
- *Hall Street Associates LLC v. Mattel Inc.*, 552 US 576 (2008) (Sup Ct)
- *Hay Group, Inc. v. EBS Acquisition Corp.*, 360 F.3d 404 (3d Cir. 2004)
- *Haynsworth v. The Corporation*, 121 F.3d 956 (5th Cir. 1997)
- *Hoeft v. MVL Group*, 343 F.3d 57 (2003) (2d Cir) US
- *Howsam v. Dean Witter Reynolds, Inc.*, 537 U.S. 79 (2002)
- *In re California Title Ins. Antitrust Litig.*, 2011 U.S. Dist. LEXIS 71621 (N.D. Cal. 27.06.2011)
- *In re Kinoshita & Co.*, 287 F.2d 951 (2d Cir. 1961)
- *In Vilches v. Travelers Co.*, 413 Fed. Appx. 487 (3d Cir. 09.02.2011)
- *Intercarbon Bermuda, Ltd v. Callex Trading & Transport Corp.*, 146 F.R.D. 64 (S.D.N.Y 1993)
- *Intergen NV v. Grina*, 344 F.3d 134 (1st Cir. 2003)
- *International Electric Corp. v. Bridas Sociedad Anonima Petrolera Industrial y Commercial*, 745 F. Supp 172 (S.D.N.Y. 1990)

- *Iran Aircraft Indus. v. Avco Corp.*, 980 F.2d 141 (2d Cir. 1992)
- *Island Territory of Curacao v. Solitron Devices, Inc.*, 356 F.Supp. 1 (S.D.N.Y.), aff'd, 489 F.2d 1313 (2d Cir. 1973)
- *Itoman (USA), Inc. v. Daewoo Corp.*, 68 N.Y.2d 925, 510 N.Y.S.2d 74, 502 N.E.2d 989 (N.Y. 1986)
- *Ivax Corp. v. B. Braun of America, Inc.*, 286 F.3d 1309 (11th Cir. 2002)
- *JLM Industries, Inc. v. Stolt-Nielsen SA*, 387 F.3d 163 (2d Cir. 2004)
- *John Wiley & Sons, Inc. v. Livingston*, 376 U.S. 543 (1964)
- *JPD, Inc. v. Chronimed Holdings, Inc.*, 539 F.3d 388 (6th Cir. 2008)
- *Khan v. Parsons Global Servs. Ltd*, 521 F.3d 421 (D.C. Cir. 2008)
- *Klay v. United Healthgroup*, 376 F.3d 1092 (11th Cir. 2004)
- *Knepp v. Credit Acceptance Corp.*, 229 B.R. 821 (Bankr. N.D. Ala. 1999)
- *Konkar Maritime Enterprises v. Compagnie Belge d'Affretement*, 668 F. Supp. 267 (S.D.N.Y. 1987)
- *Kulukundis Shipping Co. v. Amtorg Trading Corp.*, 126 F.2d 978 (2d Cir. 1942)
- *Life Receivables Trust v. Syndicate 102 at Lloyd's of London*, 549 F.3d 210 (2d Cir. 2008)
- *Lloyds v. Lagstein*, 607 F.3d 634 (9th Cir. 2010)
- *Lumbermens Mut. Cas. Co. v. Broadspire Mgmt. Servs.*, 623 F.3d 476 (7th Cir. 2010)
- *Lustfield v. Milne*, 5 Pa. D. & C. 5th 469 (Pa. Ct. Com. Pl. 2008)
- *M & C Corp. v. Erwin Behr GmbH & Co.*, 87 F.3d 844 (6th Cir. 1996)
- *M/S Bremen v. Zapata Off-Shore Co.*, 407 U.S. 1 (1972)
- *Manion v. Nagin*, 392 F.3d 294 (8th Cir. 2004)
- *Marchant v. Mead Morrison Mfg. Co.*, 252 N.Y. 284, 169 N.E. 386 (1929)
- *Marie v. Allied Home Mortgage Corp.*, 402 F.3d 1 (1st Cir 2005)
- *Mastrobuono v. Shearson Lehman Hutton*, 115 S. Ct. 1212 (1995)
- *McDonald v. City of West Branch*, 466 U.S. 284 (1984)
- *Medal Knitwear, Inc. & Hee Soon Wi v. Ji Hoon Jung, JYP Entertainment Co., Ltd., Jin Young Park and Star M. Co. Ltd*, F. Supp. 2d 1, 2011 WL 96522 (E.D.N.Y. 2011) (No. 10-CV-802 FB CLP)
- *Medicine Shoppe International, Inc. v. Turner Investments, Inc.*, 614 F.3d 485 (8th Cir. 2010)
- *Mediterranean Enterprises, Inc. v. Ssangyong Corp.*, 708 F.2d 1458 (9th Cir. 1983)
- *Mercury Telco Group, Inc. v. Empresa de Telecommunicaciones de Bogota*, 670 F. Supp. 2d 1350 (S.D. Fla. 2009)
- *Merrill Lynch, Pierce, Fenner & Smith, Inc. v. Hovey*, 726 F.2d 1286 (8th Cir. 1984)
- *Metallgesellschaft AG v. M/V Capitan Constante*, 790 F.2d 280 (2d Cir. 1986)
- *Michaels v. Mariforum Shipping, SA*, 624 F.2d 411 (2d Cir. 1980)
- *Mitsubishi Motors Corp. v. Soler Chrysler-Plymouth, Inc.*, 473 U.S. 614 (1985)

- *Monegasque de Reassurances SAM (Monde Re) v. Nak Naftogaz of Ukraine*, 311 F.3d 488 (2d Cir. 2002)
- *Montes v. Shearson Lehman Brothers, Inc.*, 128 F.3d 1456 (11th Cir. 1997)
- *Morsey Constructors, LLC v. Burns & Roe Enter., Inc.*, 2008 WL 3833588 (W.D. Ky. 13.08.2008)
- *NBC v. Bear Stearns & Co., Inc.*, 165 F.3d 184 (2d Cir. 1999)
- *Opalinski v. Robert Half Int'l, Inc.*, 2011 U.S. Dist. LEXIS 115534 (D. N.J. 06.10.2011)
- *Ortho Pharma. Corp. v. Amgen, Inc.*, 882 F.2d 806 (3d Cir. 1989)
- *Pacific Reins. Mgmt. Corp. v. Ohio Reins. Corp.*, 935 F.2d 1019 (9th Cir. 1991)
- *Parsons & Whittemore Overseas Co. v. Société Générale de l'Industrie du Papier (RAKTA)*, 508 F.2d 969 (2d Cir. 1974)
- *Perry v. Thomas*, 482 U.S. 483 (1987)
- *Pervel Indus., Inc. v. TM Wallcovering, Inc.*, 871 F.2d 7 (2d Cir. 1989)
- *Prima Paint, Corp. v. Flood & Conklin Mfg. Corp.*, 388 U.S. 395 (1967)
- *Pro Tech Indus., Inc. v. URS Corp.*, 377 F.3d 868 (8th Cir. 2004)
- *Publicis Commun. v. True North Communs. Inc.*, 206 F.3d 725 (7th Cir. 2000)
- *Reichman v. Creative Real Estate Consultants*, 476 F. Supp. 1276 (D.C.N.Y. 1979)
- *Republic of Ecuador v. Chevron Corp.*, 638 F.3d 384 (2d Cir. 2011)
- *Republic of Kazakhstan v. Biedermann Int'l*, 168 F.3d 880 (5th Cir. 1999)
- *Republic of Nicaragua v. Standard Fruit Company*, 937 F.2d 469 (9th Cir. 1991)
- *Roadway Package Sys., Inc. v. Kayser*, 257 F.3d 287 (3d Cir. 2001)
- *Rodriguez de Quijas v. Shearson/American Express, Inc.*, 490 U.S. 477 (1989)
- *Roso-Lino Beverage Distrib. Inc. v. Coca-Cola Bottling Co.*, 749 F.2d 124, 125 (2d Cir. 1984)
- *Sanders v. Forex Capital Markets*, 2011 U.S. Dist. LEXIS 137961 (S.D.N.Y. 29.11.2011)
- *Scherk v. Alberto-Culver Co.*, 417 U.S. 506 (1974)
- *Shearson/American Express v. McMahon*, 482 U.S. 220 (1987)
- *Shell Oil Co. v. CO2 Comm., Inc.*, 589 F.3d 1105 (10th Cir. 2009)
- *Southland Corp. v. Keating*, 465 U.S.1 (1984)
- *Showthemoney Check Cashers, Inc. v. Williams*, 27 S.W. 3d 361 (Ark. 2000)
- *Sperry Int'l Trade v. Government of Israel*, 532 F. Supp. 901 (S.D.N.Y. 1982)
- *Sphere Drake Ins. Ltd. v. All American Life Ins. Co.*, 307 F.3d 617 (7th Cir. 2002)
- *Stanton v. Paine Webber Jackson & Curtis*, 685 F. Supp 1241 (S.D. Fla. 1988)
- *Stedor Enters., Ltd. v. Armtex, Inc.*, 947 F.2d 727 (4th Cir. 1991)
- *STMicroelectronics, NV v. Credit Suisse Securities (USA) LLC*, 648 F.3d 68 (2d Cir. 2011)
- *Stok & Associates, PA v. Citibank, NA*, 387 Fed. Appx. 921 (11th Cir. 2010)

- *Stolt-Nielsen SA v. AnimalFeeds Int'l Corp.*, 548 F.3d 85 (2d Cir. 2008)
- *Stolt-Nielsen SA v. AnimalFeeds International Corp.*, 130 S. Ct. 1758 (2010)
- *Sutter v. Oxford Health Plans LLC*, 2011 U.S. Dist. LEXIS 17123 (D.N.J. 22.02.2011)
- *Termorio SA ESP v. Electrificiadora del Atlantico SA ESP*, 421 F. Supp. 2d 87 (D.D.C. 2006)
- *Thomas v. Union Carbide Agri. Prods. Co.*, 473 U.S. 568 (1985)
- *Thompson v. Zavin*, 607 F. Supp. 780 (C.D. Cal. 1984)
- *Ticknor v. Choice Hotels Int'l.*, 265 F.3d 931 (9th Cir. 2001)
- *Trade & Transport, Inc. v. Nat. Petro. Charterers, Inc.*, 931 F.2d 191 (2d. Cir. 1991)
- *Triangle Constr. & Maint. Corp. v. Our V.I. Labor Union*, 425 F.3d 938 (11th Cir. 2005)
- *Tristar Fin. Ins. Agency, Inc. v. Equicredit Corp.*, 97 F. App'x. 462 (5th Cir. 2004)
- *United Steelworkers of Am. v. Amer. Mfg. Co.*, 264 F.2d 624 (6th Cir. 1959)
- *Virginia Carolina Tools, Inc. v. Int'l Tool Supply, Inc.*, 984 F.2d 113 (4th Cir. 1993)
- *Volt Info.Sciences, Inc. v. Board of Trustees*, 489 U.S. 468 (1989)
- *Westinghouse Elec. Corp. v. NYC Transit Auth.*, 14 F. 3d. 818 (2d Cir. 1994)
- *Wilko v. Swan*, 346 US 427 (1953)
- *Williams v. CIGNA Fin. Advisors Inc.*, 197 F.3d 752 (5th Cir. 1999), cert denied 529 U.S. 1099 (2000)
- *Willoughby Roofing & Supply Co., Inc. v. Kajima Intl, Inc.*, 598 F. Supp. 353 (N.D. Ala. 1984)
- *Wisconsin Auto Title Loans, Inc. v. Jones*, 714 N.W.2d 155 (Wisc. 2006)
- *Wood v. Penntex Res. LP.*, 2008 U.S. Dist. LEXIS 50071 (S.D. Tex. 27.06.2008)
- *Woodland Ltd. P'ship v. Wulff*, 868 A.2d 860 (D.D.C. 2005)
- *Yasuda Fire & Marine Ins. Co. of Europe v. Cont. Cas. Co.*, 37 F.3d 345 (7th Cir. 1994)
- *Zephyros Maritime Agencies, Inc. v. Mexicana De Cobre, SA*, 662 F. Supp 892 (S.D.N.Y. 1987)

# LIST OF ABBREVIATIONS

| | |
|---|---|
| A.2d | Atlantic Reporter, Second Series |
| AAA | American Arbitration Association |
| AC | Law Reports, Appeal Cases (Third Series) |
| ACICA | Australian Centre for International Commercial Arbitration |
| ACM | Appellate Court Mediation |
| ACTSC | Australian Capital Territory Supreme Court |
| ADNDRC | Asia Domain Name Dispute Resolution Centre |
| ADR | Alternative Dispute Resolution |
| ADRLJ | Arbitration and Dispute Resolution Law Journal |
| ADRO | Alternative Dispute Resolution Office |
| AFA | Arbitration Fairness Act |
| AFET | Agricultural Futures Exchange of Thailand |
| Aff'd | Affirmed |
| AFTC | Agricultural Futures Trading Commission |
| AndhLT | Andhra Law Times |
| AIR | All India Reporter |
| AIR-SC | All India Reporter – Supreme Court |
| All ER | All England Reports |
| All ER (Comm) | All England Reports (Commercial Cases) |
| All ER (D) | All England Digest |
| AO | Arbitration Office |
| AP | Andhra Pradesh |
| App. Div. | Appellate Division |
| APPLR | Arbitration, Practice & Procedure Law Reports |
| ArbLR | Arbitration Law Reports and Review |
| Ark. | Arkansas |
| ATF | Receuil des Arrêts des Tribunal Fédéral Suisse |
| Bankr. N.D. Alaska | United States Bankruptcy Court, District of Alaska |
| BLR | Business Law Reports |
| BLR2d | Business Law Reports, Second Series |
| Bom | Bombay |
| BomCR | Bombay Cases Reporter |
| BR | Bankruptcy Reporter |

| | |
|---|---|
| BTT | Board of Trade of Thailand |
| Bus LR | Business Law Reports |
| CA | Court of Appeal |
| C.A.2d | California Appellate Reports, Second Series |
| CACV | Court of Appeal. Civil Appeal. |
| Cal | Calcutta / Calcutta High Court / California |
| CAMCA | Commercial Arbitration and Mediation Center for the Americas |
| CCC | Civil and Commercial Code |
| CCOIC | China Chamber of Commerce |
| CCP | Code of Civil Procedure |
| CCPIT | China Council for the Promotion of International Trade |
| C.D. Cal | Central District of California, United States District Court |
| CEDR | Centre for Effective Dispute Resolution |
| Ch | Law Reports, Chancery Division (Third Series) |
| CIAC | Construction Industry Arbitration Commission |
| CIArb | Chartered Institute of Arbitrators |
| CIETAC | China International Economic and Trade Arbitration Commission |
| Cir | Circuit |
| Civ | Civil |
| CJ | Code Judicaire |
| CLC | CCH Commercial Law Cases |
| CLR | Commonwealth Law Reports |
| CMAC | China Maritime Arbitration Commission |
| CMPD | Conflict Management Promotion Division |
| Comm | Commercial |
| CompLJ | Company Law Journal |
| Con LR | Construction Law Reports (UK) |
| CPC | Code of Civil Procedure |
| CTC | Central Tax Court |
| D | Denison & Pearce's Crown Cases Reserved |
| DB | Division Bench |
| D.C. Cir. | District of Columbia Circuit |
| D.D.C. | United States District Court for the District of Columbia |
| D.N.J. | United States District Court New Jersey |
| D.C.N.Y | United States District Court for the District of New York |
| Del | Delhi |
| DEQP | Department of Environmental Quality Promotion |

| | |
|---|---|
| DIP | Department of Intellectual Property |
| DLT | Delhi Law Times |
| | |
| ECJ | European Court of Justice |
| ECR | European Court Reports |
| ed. | edition; editor |
| E.D. Pa. | United States District Court for the Eastern District of Pennsylvania |
| E.D.N.Y. | Eastern District New York, United States District Court |
| EU | European Union |
| EWCA | England and Wales Court of Appeal |
| EWCA (Civ) | England and Wales Court of Appeal (Civil Division) |
| EWHC | England and Wales High Court |
| EWHC (QB) | England and Wales High Court (Queen's Bench Division) |
| | |
| F.2d | Federal Reporter, Second Series |
| F.3d | Federal Reporter, Third Series |
| FAA | Federal Arbitration Act |
| F. App'x | Federal Appendix: Federal appellate court opinions (not reported in F.3d) |
| F.B. | Full Bench |
| FDRC | Financial Dispute Resolution Center |
| ff | following |
| Fla Dist Ct App | Florida District Court of Appeal |
| FMCS | Federal Mediation and Conciliation Service |
| F.R.D. | Federal Rules Decisions |
| F. Supp. | Federal Supplement |
| F. Supp.2d | Federal Supplement, Second Series |
| | |
| G.R. | General Records |
| Guj LR | Gujarat Law Reporter |
| | |
| HKC | Hong Kong Cases |
| HKEC | Hong Kong Electronic Cases |
| HKFWSMC | Hong Kong Family Welfare Society Mediation Centre |
| HKIAC | Hong Kong International Arbitration Centre |
| HKIArb | Hong Kong Institute of Arbitrators |
| HKLRD | Hong Kong Law Reports & Digest |
| HKMC | Hong Kong Mediation Center |
| HL | House of Lords |
| | |
| IAMA | Institute for Arbitrators and Mediators Australia |
| ICC | International Chamber of Commerce |

| | |
|---|---|
| ICDR | International Centre for Dispute Resolution |
| ICLR | Incorporated Council of Law Reporting (formerly WLR (D)) |
| ICSID | International Centre for the Settlement of Investment Disputes |
| ILPr | International Litigation Procedure |
| JDR | Judicial Dispute Resolution |
| JMHO | Joint Mediation Helpline Office |
| Kar | Karnataka |
| KCAB | Korean Commercial Arbitration Board |
| KOPILA | Korea Private International Law Association |
| KPI | King Prajadhipok's Institute |
| LEADR | Lawyers Engaged in Alternative Dispute Resolution |
| LED | Legal Execution Department |
| Lloyd's Rep | Lloyd's Law Reports |
| LRCHK | Law Reform Commission of Hong Kong |
| LSE | London School of Economics |
| MA | Massachusetts |
| Mah LJ | Maharashtra Law Journal |
| MIGA | Convention Establishing the Multilateral Investment Guarantee Agency |
| MOC | Ministry of Commerce |
| MOJ | Ministry of Justice |
| MP | Madhya Pradesh High Court |
| n. | note |
| NADRAC | National Alternative Dispute Resolution Advisory Council |
| N.D. | Northern District |
| N.D. Ala. | Northern District Alabama, United States District Court |
| N.D. Cal | Northern District California, United States District Court |
| N.D. Ill | Northern District Illinois, United States District Court |
| N.E. | North Eastern Reporter |
| N.E.2d | North Eastern Reporter, Second Series |
| NGO | Non-Governmental Organisation |
| NJA | Nytt Juridiskt Arkiv |
| NLRC | National Labor Relations Commission |
| NMB | National Mediation Board |

| | |
|---|---|
| NSWCA | New South Wales Court of Appeal |
| NSWSC | New South Wales Supreme Court |
| N.W. | North Western Reporter |
| N.W.2d | North Western Reporter, Second Series |
| N.Y. | New York Reports |
| N.Y.2d | New York Reports, Second Series |
| N.Y. App. Division | New York Supreme Court Appellate Division Reports |
| N.Y. Slip Op | New York Reports Official Citation |
| NYC | New York Convention on the Recognition and Enforcement of Foreign Awards, 1958 |
| NZCA | New Zealand Court of Appeal Reports |
| NZLR | New Zealand Law Reports |
| OIC | Office of Insurance Commission |
| OJ | Official Journal of the European Union |
| OJA | Office of the Judicial Affairs |
| ONCA | Ontario Court of Appeal |
| ONSC | Ontario Superior Court of Justice |
| OOJ | Office of the Judiciary |
| p. | page |
| P.3d | West's Pacific Reporter |
| Pa. D. & C. | Pennsylvania District and County Reports |
| PDRCI | Philippine Dispute Resolution Center, Inc. |
| P&H | Punjab and Haryana |
| PILA | Private International Law Act |
| PRC | People's Republic of China |
| QB | Law Reports, Queen's Bench (Third Series) |
| RAJ | Rajdhani Law Reporter |
| RLPD | Rights and Liberties Protection Department |
| RT | Riigi Teataja (Official Journal of Estonia) |
| SCC | Supreme Court Cases, India |
| SCMA | Singapore Chamber of Maritime Arbitration |
| SCMR | Supreme Court Monthly Review |
| S.Ct | Supreme Court Reporter |
| S.D.Fla | Southern District Florida, United States District Court |
| S.D.N.Y. | Southern District New York, United States District Court |
| S.D. Tex. | Southern District Texas, United States District Court |
| SET | Stock Exchange of Thailand |
| SGCA | Singapore Court of Appeal (Neutral Citation) |

| | |
|---|---|
| SGHC | Singapore High Court (Neutral Citation) |
| SI | Statutory Instruments |
| SIAC | Singapore International Arbitration Centre |
| SIArb | Singapore Institute of Arbitrators |
| SLR | Singapore Law Reports |
| SLR(R) | Singapore Law Reports (Reissue) |
| SMC | Singapore Mediation Centre |
| So.2d | Southern Reporter, Second Series |
| SPC | Supreme People's Court of the People's Republic of China |
| Supp. | Supplement |
| Supp. ArbLR | Arbitration Law Reporter Supplement |
| Sup.Ct | Supreme Court Reporter |
| S.W.3d | South Western Reporter Third |
| TCC | Tax Court of Canada |
| TFEX | Thailand Futures Exchange |
| UKHL | United Kingdom House of Lords |
| UKPC | United Kingdom Privy Council |
| UKSC | United Kingdom Supreme Court |
| UNCITRAL Model Law | UNCITRAL Model Law on International Commercial Arbitration |
| UNCITRAL | United Nations Commission on International Trade Law |
| US | United States of America |
| U.S. | United States Supreme Court Reports |
| USCS | United States Conciliation Service |
| U.S. Dist. | United States District Court |
| vol. | volume |
| VSC | Victoria Supreme Court (1998-) |
| W.D. Ky | Western District Kentucky, United States District Court |
| W.D. Tex. | Western District Texas, United States District Court |
| Wis. | Wisconsin |
| WL | Westlaw Transcripts |
| WLR | Weekly Law Reports |
| WLR (D) | Incorporated Council of Law Reporting |
| ZPO | Zivilprozessordnung |

# LIST OF AUTHORS

## ADR MECHANISMS AND THEIR INCORPORATION INTO GLOBAL JUSTICE IN THE TWENTY-FIRST CENTURY: SOME CONCEPTS AND TRENDS

Prof. Dr Dr h.c. Silvia Barona
Silvia Barona is Professor of Procedural Law at the University of Valencia, Spain. She is a member of the Bar and a leading writer on ADR. Her works in this field, both on civil and commercial and on criminal matters, are numerous and have had a high impact in Spain and abroad. Professor Barona was President of the Court of Arbitration and Mediation of Valencia and is a well-known arbitrator and a registered mediator. She has been a member of several official commissions on the restructuration of the judicial system in Spain and holds the Great Cross of Saint Raimundo de Peñafor awarded by the King of Spain.

Prof. Dr Carlos Esplugues, LLM (Harvard), MSc (Edinburgh)
Carlos Esplugues is Professor of Private International Law at the University of Valencia, Spain. He holds Masters degrees from Edinburgh University and Harvard Law School. He is admitted to the Bar and serves regularly as an arbitrator. He is also a registered mediator. Professor Esplugues is a leading Spanish scholar in the field of private international law, international trade law and international dispute resolution. He has been a member of several official commissions on international private law, both in Spain and in Brussels, and lectures regularly in Europe, Latin America and Asia. Professor Esplugues is President of the Spanish Association of International Law Professors.

## AUSTRALIA

Prof. David Bamford
In 2013 David Bamford returned to teaching and research after filling the role of Dean at Flinders Law School, South Australia for five years. His research interests include the workings of the civil and criminal justice system, and the interaction between law and politics. Commissioned research includes government consultancies that evaluate different aspects of the justice system including restorative justice, community justice and therapeutic court

programmes. Recent publications include a book on civil litigation and book chapters on expert witnesses, ADR, and developments in Australian legal education. Professor Bamford has been a visiting professor at universities in Canada, United Kingdom, Finland, Indonesia and South Africa.

## CHINA

Prof. Dr jur. Yuanshi Bu
Yuanshi Bu is Director of the Chair of International Economic Law with special focus on East Asia at the University of Freiburg, Germany. She holds Masters degrees from Nanjing University (2001) and Harvard (2004) and a PhD from the University of Bern (2003). Her main research interests include German and Chinese civil and economic law, international and Chinese investment law, protection of intellectual property rights and technology transfer in East Asia, and arbitration in the People's Republic of China. Professor Bu was admitted to the New York State Bar in October 2005, and is also a member of the Board of the German-Chinese Jurists' Association and an Expert of the Alexander von Humboldt Foundation.

## ENGLAND AND WALES

Prof. Neil Andrews
Neil Andrews is Professor of Civil Justice and Private Law and the University of Cambridge. His main teaching interests are civil justice and procedure (including court litigation, mediation and arbitration), and contract law (both English and transnational). He was called to the English Bar in 1981 and became a Bencher of Middle Temple in 2007. He is a member of the American Law Institute and a Praesidium Member of the International Association of Procedural Law. His main recent works include *Andrews on Civil Processes* (Intersentia 2013; 2 vols: vol 1, Court Proceedings; vol 2, Arbitration and Mediation) and *Contract Law* (Cambridge University Press 2011).

## HONG KONG

Gavin Denton, BBUS, LLB, LLM (Peking), FCIArb
Gavin Denton is the head of Arbitration Chambers Hong Kong, China's first set of chambers dedicated to international arbitration. Gavin is admitted to practice in Hong Kong, England and Australia, and holds business and law degrees from Australia as well as a Masters in Chinese law from Peking University. He specialises in commercial dispute resolution, with significant experience as both counsel and arbitrator in international arbitrations across the Asia-Pacific

region. He is a Fellow of the Chartered Institute of Arbitrators and the Hong Kong Institute of Arbitrators and is Vice Chairman of ICC Australia's Arbitration Committee.

Dr FAN Kun, PhD (Geneva), LLM (NYU, Paris XII)
Fan Kun is Assistant Professor at the Faculty of Law, Chinese University of Hong Kong, and a visiting scholar at the Harvard-Yenching Institute (2012–13). Professor Fan is author of the book *Arbitration in China: A Legal and Cultural Analysis* (Hart Publishing 2013) and has published extensively, with pieces in leading law journals such as the Harvard Negotiation Law Review, the Cardozo Journal of Conflict Resolution, the Yearbook of Private International Law, and the Journal of International Arbitration. Professor Fan is a former Deputy Counsel of the ICC International Court of Arbitration and now practices as a Senior Consultant for Arbitration Asia. She is called to the New York Bar, an Accredited Mediator and a Domain Names Panellist of the Hong Kong International Arbitration Centre.

## INDIA

Darius J. KHAMBATA, LLM (Harvard), SC
Darius J. Khambata practises before the Bombay High Court and the Supreme Court of India. He is currently the Advocate General of Maharashtra and was previously the Additional Solicitor General of India, both distinguished public offices. His practice encompasses commercial and corporate law, constitutional and administrative law, securities law and arbitration. Appearing for the Government, he has successfully defended challenges to the constitutionality of the provisions of several statutes, both Central and State. He has also appeared in several significant domestic and international commercial arbitrations. He is a Vice-President of the London Court of International Arbitration.

Aditya N. MEHTA, LLB (LSE)
Aditya N. Mehta practises as a counsel before the Bombay High Court and various tribunals, where he undertakes a range of corporate, commercial and constitutional litigation. He has also appeared in domestic and international commercial arbitrations. Aditya has significant experience in company law, securities law and tax law matters. Prior to transferring to the Bar, Aditya practised as a commercial solicitor with Linklaters for five years in their London, Singapore and Hong Kong offices. Aditya read law at the London School of Economics and is also a qualified Chartered Accountant.

Naira J. JEJEEBHOY, LLM (Columbia)
Naira Jejeebhoy read law at Government Law College, Mumbai and then earned an LLM from Columbia Law School, where she graduated as a Harlan Fiske

Stone Scholar. Naira practises as an advocate in India and is also qualified to practice in the State of New York. She primarily focuses on commercial and civil dispute resolution. Naira has appeared in *ad hoc* and institutional arbitrations with an Indian or UK seat. She has also appeared before the Supreme Court of India and other Indian courts for the determination of issues arising under the Indian Arbitration and Conciliation Act 1996.

## INDONESIA

Dr Marcella E. Simandjuntak, SH, CN, MHum
Valentinus Suroto
B. Resti Nurhayati, SH, MHum
Dr Marcella E. Simandjuntak, Mr Valentius Suroto and Ms B. Resti Nurhayati are Senior Lecturers at the Faculty of Law, Soegijapranata Catholic University (SCU), Semarang, Central Java, Indonesia. Dr Simandjuntak is currently the Head of the Center for Women's Studies at the SCU Research Institute. She lectures on criminal law, the criminal justice system and criminology. Valentius Suroto and B. Resti Nurhayati are both lecturers in the Civil Law Department. Recently, they have all been actively involved in the Inter-religious Dialogue and Peace Building Initiative Program funded by the United Board for Higher Christian Education in Asia (UBCHEA). One of the programs is to develop a dispute resolution curriculum for law faculty. They are also involved in conducting a multi-year study on Intercultural Dialogue in Encountering Social Conflict with Reconciliation and Peace Building Initiative.

## IRELAND

Prof. Dr Guillermo Palao Moreno
Guillermo Palao Moreno obtained his PhD (with honours) at the University of Valencia where he is a full Professor of Private International Law and International Commercial Law. Professor Palao Moreno is a Fellow of the European Law Institute, an Associate Member of the International Academy of Comparative Law, as well as a correspondent academic of the Spanish Royal Academy of Jurisprudence and Law. He is also a member of the Arbitration and Mediation Centers of the World Intellectual Property Organization (WIPO) and of the Chamber of Commerce of Valencia. He has published extensively and his research has been focused on international contracts and tort law, international company law, international labour law, international litigation and ADR, as well as international intellectual property and IT law. Professor Palao Moreno also has a long teaching experience, at graduate and postgraduate levels, both in European and Latin American universities.

## JAPAN

Prof. Dr Masaaki Haga
Masaaki Haga is a Professor of Law at Keio Law School (Tokyo, Japan). Prior to that, he served as a Research Assistant, Assistant Professor, Associate Professor and Professor at the Faculty of Law of Meiji University (Tokyo, Japan). He has obtained an LLB, LLM and LLD from the Universities of Meiji, Waseda and Keio respectively. He has also held posts as a visiting research fellow at the University of Regensburg (Germany) in 1995–96 (DAAD Scholarship) and in 2003–05 (Humboldt Research Fellowship). His main research is international civil procedural law.

## KOREA

Prof. Gyooho Lee, JSD (Washington), LLM (Washington and Yonsei), LLB (Yonsei)
Gyooho Lee is a Professor of Law at Chung-Ang University School of Law in Seoul, Republic of Korea. He has specialised in civil procedure, arbitration, private international law, intellectual property law, and cultural property law. He obtained an LLB and an LLM from Yonsei University (Seoul, Republic of Korea), an LLM from the University of Washington (Seattle, WA, USA) and a JSD from Washington University (St. Louis, MO, USA). He has also served as a visiting researcher at Georgetown University Law Center (Washington, DC, USA). Currently, he is serving as a Vice President of the Korean Civil Procedure Association, an arbitrator of the Korean Commercial Arbitration Board, and a member of the International Law Association's Committee on Intellectual Property and Private International Law. He is the author of several books including *Failures of American Civil Justice in International Perspective*, co-authored with James R. Maxeiner and Armin Weber (Cambridge University Press 2011).

## PHILIPPINES

Donemark J.L. Calimon
Donemark J.L. Calimon is a Partner at the Litigation and Dispute Resolution Group of Quisumbing Torres Law Offices, a member firm of Baker & McKenzie International. He is a trustee, an officer and an accredited arbitrator of the Philippine Dispute Resolution Center, Inc. (PDRCI); an accredited arbitrator of the Philippine Intellectual Property Office; a Member of the Chartered Institute of Arbitrators, East Asia Branch (Philippine Chapter); and a trustee and officer of the Philippine Institute of Arbitrators. He has acted/acts as counsel or arbitrator in several commercial arbitrations, including arbitrations conducted under the

arbitration rules of the PDRCI and of the International Chamber of Commerce (ICC), and *ad hoc* arbitration under the UNCITRAL Arbitration Rules. He regularly lectures and writes on commercial arbitration. He obtained his law degree at the University of the Philippines in 2000 and was admitted to the Philippine Bar in 2001.

## SINGAPORE

Assoc. Prof. Joel Lee, LLM (Harvard)
Joel Lee is Vice-Dean and an Associate Professor at the Faculty of Law, National University of Singapore. A graduate of Harvard Law School, he runs the faculty's Negotiation and Mediation Workshops. Professor Lee is a consultant with CMPartners (USA) and the Training Director of and a principal mediator with the Singapore Mediation Centre. He is also an adjudicator with the Financial Industry Disputes Resolution Centre, a member of the ADR Advisory Council of the Subordinate Courts of Singapore and a member of the International Mediation Institute's Independent Standards Commission and Intercultural Taskforce. Professor Lee has taught overseas at the University of Copenhagen (Denmark), University of Law, Economics and Science of Aix-Marseille (Aix-en-Provence, France) and Anglia Law School (UK). He is the co-editor and co-author of *An Asian Perspective on Mediation* (Academy Publishing 2009) and the General Editor for the Asian Journal on Mediation. In 2011, Professor Lee received the Outstanding Educator Award, which is the National University of Singapore's highest teaching award.

## THAILAND

Suparb Vongkiatkachorn, LLM (Harvard), LLB (Ramkhamhaeng)
Suparb Vongkiatkachorn holds an LLM from Harvard Law School. He was formerly a co-managing partner of the Bangkok office of Freshfields Bruckhaus Deringer, advising on a wide range of matters, including investment in Thailand, the acquisition of Thai companies, securities and loan transactions, derivatives and other ISDA agreements, corporate formation and joint ventures, dispute resolution, property, and tax matters. He has also been the Deputy Secretary General of the Agricultural Futures Trading Commission of Thailand (AFTC), supervising/assisting in the drafting of futures trading regulations relating to conciliation/arbitration of the AFTC, the Agricultural Futures Exchange of Thailand, and the Thailand Futures Exchange. He is currently a listed arbitrator of the Securities and Exchange Commission of Thailand.

## USA: ARBITRATION

Prof. George A. Bermann
George Bermann is Professor of Law at Columbia Law School, New York, and director of the Center for International Commercial and Investment Arbitration. He teaches and writes in, among other fields, transnational litigation and arbitration, commercial arbitration, investment law and arbitration and European Union law. He has been an active international arbitrator for 30 years, serving in both institutional and *ad hoc* arbitration. He is Director of the American Arbitration Association, and a member of the roster of leading arbitral institutions, including ICDR. In addition, Professor Bermann is the Chief Reporter of the American Law Institute's 'Restatement of the U.S. Law of International Commercial Arbitration', co-author (with Emmanuel Gaillard) of the UNCITRAL Guide to the New York Convention, and editor-in-chief of the American Review of International Arbitration.

## USA: MEDIATION

Shanin Specter
Shanin Specter is a co-founder and partner at Kline & Specter, P.C. in Philadelphia, Pennsylvania. Mr Specter graduated with honors in political science from Haverford College and earned his law degree at the University of Pennsylvania Law School, where he is currently a lecturer at law. He earned his Masters in Law with First Class Honors at Cambridge University. Mr Specter served as a member of a hearing committee on the Disciplinary Board of the Supreme Court of Pennsylvania from 1989 to 1994 and as a chairman from 1994 to 1995. He was a member of the Civil Procedural Rules Committee of the Supreme Court of Pennsylvania from 1995 to 2001. Mr Specter concentrates his law practice on catastrophic personal injury litigation.

Jason L. Pearlman
Jason L. Pearlman is an associate attorney at Kline & Specter, P.C in Philadelphia, Pennsylvania. Mr Pearlman earned a bachelor's degree in economics at the Pennsylvania State University and a law degree with honors at New York Law School. He earned a LLM in trial advocacy at the Temple University James E. Beasley School of Law. Mr Pearlman concentrates his law practice on catastrophic personal injury litigation.

# ADR MECHANISMS AND THEIR INCORPORATION INTO GLOBAL JUSTICE IN THE TWENTY-FIRST CENTURY: SOME CONCEPTS AND TRENDS

Silvia Barona and Carlos Esplugues

'Access to justice in Canada no longer means access just to the public court system. Historically, judges were reluctant to relinquish their grasp on dispute resolution, and they even viewed alternative dispute resolution as antithetical to the parties' interests. This era is gone. It is the role of the legislature, not the courts, to limit access to alternative dispute resolution mechanisms.'

*Seidel v. TELUS Communications Inc.*, 2011 SCC 15 (CanLII),
Lebal and Deschamps JJ (dissenting) [54] p. 50

## Contents

# 1. INCREASING CONFLICTS, GROWING LITIGATION AND EVOLVING RESPONSES: TOWARDS A NEW CONCEPT OF ACCESS TO JUSTICE

## 1.1. 'ACCESS TO JUSTICE' AND 'ACCESS TO STATE COURTS'

The State and State courts have been approached for centuries as almost the only instruments available to ensure access to justice to citizens; that is, to guarantee the right to an effective remedy before an independent and impartial tribunal previously established by law within a reasonable time.[1] A monopoly for the State in the field of dispute resolution has existed to the extent that despite the long presence of non-judicial instruments of dispute resolution in many

1 European Union Agency For Fundamental Rights, *Access to Justice in Europe: An Overview of Challenges and Opportunities*, Publications Office of the European Union, Luxembourg 2011, p. 17.

jurisdictions, they have been traditionally considered as marginal in most countries and have lacked real implementation by citizens and legal actors.

This protagonism of the State and State courts as regards access to justice has superseded the preference for amicable settlement that existed in the Middle Ages all over Europe, before the establishment of nations as we currently understand them.[2] This almost absolute monopoly, which for a long time benefited the State, was the direct consequence of some historical developments that have taken place in the last three centuries in Europe and America. In fact, different political and social changes have directly influenced the configuration, structure and functions of the judiciary in Western countries. For instance, in Europe, the French or Jacobine system of justice, a direct consequence of the French Revolution of 1789, is based on the idea of the existence of a single source of power – the will of the population – and a single way to channel this will – the Parliament. In this scenario, the role played by the judge is limited to the application of the law: 'the judge is the mouth that pronounces the words of the law', according to Montesquieu.[3] Across the Atlantic Ocean, the American system, arising out of the American Revolution of 1776, from which the US was born, takes the old colonial common law as the basis for the acceptance of the role of interpretation of the rules awarded to the judge.[4]

For decades, the situation has been marked by the expansion and strengthening of the jurisdictional power of the State chanelled historically through State courts and State-designed civil procedure. This trend was further accentuated during the twenthieth century, a period that, as a general rule, gave rise to a continuous enhancing of the role of the State, even to the undesirable extent of favouring totalitarian or authoritarian States. From this paradigm it was logical to accept that the best solution for conflicts affecting citizens was the State itself. The State offered 'its' courts and 'its' procedure as the best instrument to reach a solution to any conflict that may arise in the society. It is an obligation for the State to ensure access to justice to citizens and this is done through access to State courts. This premise has been taken to its extreme in many European countries as well as in Latin America, where a truly 'jurisdictional power' understood beyond the specific framework of the system of the administration of justice – the judiciary – is endorsed by the law, and in many cases even by the constitution.

In fact, the idea of social democracy, in which the State assumes responsibility for the protection of citizens by offering policies that protect them and their

---

2 R.L. Keyser, '"Agreement Supersedes Law, and Love Judgment:" Legal Flexibility and Amicable Settlement in Anglo-Norman England' (2012) 30 *Law & Hist. Rev. (Law and History Review)* 37, 41.

3 Ch. De Secondat, Baron de Montesquieu, *Del espíritu de las leyes,* Tecnos, Madrid 1985, Book XI, ch. VI.

4 J.J. Toharia, *Opinión pública y justicia. La imagen de la justicia en la sociedad española,* Consejo General del Poder Judicial, Madrid 2001, pp. 39–40.

rights, has been reflected in the field of justice by the consagration of this jurisdictional power. Significantly, this legal reality underlies some of the developments in the field of access to justice in recent years. It is the analysis of the reasons and grounds that justified this strengthening and leadership of State courts in the field of dispute resolution which favours to some extent the understanding of its current crisis and of the new trends that are increasingly apparent in this area. The monopoly enjoyed by the judiciary, together with other exogenous factors – economic, cultural, social, sociological, technological, etc. – is the basis of the current crisis. The perception of law and legal actors as authoritative and legitimate has declined and this has accelerated the advance of the 'shadow of law' referred to in legal literature since the end of the 1960s.[5] When the legal solution provided by the State proves unsatisfactory for many citizens, alternative methods are necessary.[6]

It is widely accepted that as societies and citizens develop and evolve, conflicts of different kinds – either particular or collective – increase both in number and complexity, thus giving rise to a new sort of litigiousness. This concept has become especially clear in recent decades. Social changes, alongside the technological revolution that the world has undergone, among other factors, have led to the constant increase in the number of disputes that have arisen in modern States. This enlargment of the number of disputes is accompanied by an increase in their complexity. Purely private disputes have increasingly resulted in collective or even social disputes, class actions or disputes involving parties deserving different degrees of protection from the State. From disputes arising from face-to-face relationships between parties, we are now increasingly seeing disputes between parties whose relationships are based upon electronic communication rather than personal contact. Whereas in the past disputes commonly involved citizens of the same jurisdiction, it is now usual for disputes to involve an international element. The object of these disputes has also changed, with an increasing number of them focusing on intangible rights.

The response of the State to this challenge has usually been twofold. On the one hand it broadens the legal system in order to cope with new realities and provide them with legal answers. This has fuelled the growing juridisdictionalisation of life. The law and the legislator aim to cover all aspects of society and social life and this entails as a corollary an overwhelming resort to State legislation and State courts. The only solution for every single dispute is to be taken to court and to be solved in accordance with the law designed by the legislator. On the other hand, this situation has given rise to a budgetary effort of the State over several decades to ensure an efficient and available State court system of justice.

---

5 R.H. McAdams and J. Nadler, 'Coordinating in the Shadow of the Law: Two Contextualized Tests of the Focal Point Theory of Legal Compliance' (2008) 42 *Law & Society Review* 865, 866.

6 Note, J. Paulsson, *Arbitration in Three Dimensions*, LSE Law, Society and Economy Working Papers 2/2010, London School of Economics and Political Science, Law Department, p. 20 <http://papers.ssrn.com/sol3/papers.cfm?abstract_id=1536093> accessed 15.12.2012.

Unfortunately, the situation is not fully satisfactory: courts are perceived as 'expensive, slow and innacurate'.[7] State courts have become more and more inefficient and incapable of offering solutions to the enormous number of disputes of all kinds submitted to them. In the last decades we have witnessed the pervasiveness of the absolute power of State courts in the legal life of citizens, and at the same time the growing sense of its inability to provide them with a quick, sound and affordable solution to their problems. In fact, this extremely broad role granted to the law and to the courts has in certain cases resulted in unexpected solutions, and in too many cases has shown an ineffective legal system. In Europe, for instance, recent figures speak of three main reasons for not using a court to resolve a disagreement or dispute: 'its cost (45%), its duration (27%) and the fear that nothing would come of it (27%)'.[8]

This negative situation and its correlative perception among citizens have encouraged the possibility for citizens to provide fully valid solutions outside the framework of State law. The idea of an 'order without law'[9] has been integrated into society and has been growing steadily ever since.

## 1.2. CRISIS OF THE JUDICIARY AND THE SEARCH FOR NEW HORIZONS

Despite the existing variations among countries, the unstoppable increase in the volume and quality of litigation in modern societies has given rise to such a level of entropy that it favours a deep change in the current situation and understanding of justice in the double meaning of structure of the system of justice – the judiciary – and of the notion of access to justice. The premise is that modern life entails complex problems often requiring complex and multifaceted solutions,[10] and State courts seem unable to provide this response by themselves alone.

This new kind of society – complex, dynamic and with declining paradigms – puts pressure on the traditional means of ensuring access to justice to citizens so far almost linked to the idea of access to State courts' justice. The attempt to achieve better administration of State courts, which underlines the several civil procedure reforms of the last decades, is now accompanied by the search for new tools and ways to ensure a fair and smooth solution to the growing number of disputes arising in the daily life of citizens. It seems that never before has there

7 B.D. Richman, 'Norms and Law: Putting the Horse before the Cart' (2012) 62 *Duke Law Journal* 739, 740.

8 European Commission, *Flash Eurobarometer 347 Business-to-Business Alternative Dispute Resolution in the EU,* 2012, p. 7 <http://ec.europa.eu/public_opinion/flash/fl_347_en.pdf> accessed 30.12.2012.

9 Using the terminology of R.C. Ellickson, *Order Without Law: How Neighbors Settle Disputes*, Harvard Univ. Press, Cambridge MA 1991.

10 C. Menkel-Meadow, 'The Trouble with the Adversary System in a Postmodern, Multicultural World' (1996) 38 *Wm. & Mary L. Rev. (William and Mary Law Review)* 5, 7.

existed such wide awareness of the need for ensuring effective access to justice to citizens as a prerequisite for the achievement of economic development of society and for the consolidation of social peace. The 'third wave' of the access-to-justice movement is well under way.[11]

National courts certainly still play a major role in the search for this paradigm of effective justice. However a growing awareness of the impossibility of fully ensuring it also exists. More and more it has been considered that irrespective of the budgetary effort made by governments, State courts are not sufficient on their own to ensure citizens a smooth, effective and affordable access to redress. Reforms alone seem not to be enough, and alternative ways of ensuring justice for citizens are being explored more and more. This move is based on the blossoming of the ADR movement in recent decades.

This search for alternative ways to ensure access to justice to citizens is nowadays approached as a worldwide trend, although several degrees of acceptance and support in different areas of the world are also apparent. Some very positive attitudes towards ADR coexist with other countries in which this movement receives much more limited support or is approached with caution. In any case, they provide us with a set of several responses to the issue of access to justice in the twenty-first century. Some of these national experiences may be extrapolated to other legal systems while in other cases this possibility is much more limited. But in any case they all enrich the existing worldwide movement in favour of fostering resort to ADR mechanisms. In addition, the existing budgetary constraints that many countries of the world are currently facing may in fact strengthen the recourse to some ADR devices. Thus ADR becomes not only a way to foster access to justice for citizens but also a mechanism to help the State save money.

Of course, as we have already stated, experiences and degrees of development of this movement vary from country to country. Most probably the existing situation in common law systems as well as the experiences of many Asian countries where the effective judicial protection coexists with – and in certain cases is even subsidiary to – other possible available means to solve civil and commercial disputes will serve to enrich many European and Latin American countries where in accordance with the civil legal tradition these two principles – access to justice and due process – are usually understood as primarily connected with State courts.

In any case this vigorous movement in favour of ADR in many areas of the world is said to favour a new approach to the idea of justice, which tries to be much more in accordance with the complex, flexible and changeable social reality in which we are currently living. This modern approach – though not necessarily new, in that many ADR instruments have long been well known in many

11 M. Cappelletti and B. Garth, 'Access to Justice: The Worldwide Movement to Make Rights Effective. A General Report', in M. Cappelleti (gen. ed.), *Access to Justice*, Sijhoof and Noordhoff, Amsterdam 1978, 4 vols., vol. 1: *A World Survey*, book 1, pp. 49 ff. and 54 ff.

jurisdictions – to justice, and consequently to access to justice, stands on the acceptance of the existence of a plurality of ways of access to justice to be chosen by citizens: a sort of multi-rooms civil justice system.[12] Unlike what happened for a long time when access to justice was directly linked to resort to State courts, now this possibility coexists with other available ways for citizens to solve their disputes. It is for them to decide whether to refer their dispute to State courts or to refer it to any of the several available ADR devices, or even to opt for purely self-enforcement schemes in the frame of the already mentioned 'order without law' approach.[13]

## 1.3. THE MOVE TOWARDS ADR

An increasingly complex society exists, a society in which social values tend to prevail in many cases over individual values, where technology is omnipresent and the parameters of behaviour of citizens have widely changed in the last decades, and where an increasing level of legislation in all fields coexists with an enormous amount of litigation, both national and cross-border. All these factors, among others, complicate, in certain cases make impossible, the provision of sound, affordable, rapid and valid solutions to legal disputes in modern societies. In this environment State courts have shown their inability to cope with this situation, as well as all sorts of problems that may arise from maintaining the classic paradigm of binding access to justice solely to State courts. Overworked State courts are unable to offer a valid, specialised and quick response to increasingly complex disputes. More and more they need help from experts and other actors, and this not only increases the duration and cost of access to justice, it also generates a growing dissatisfaction among citizens with the response provided: justice delayed usually means justice denied.[14]

The State is incapable of addressing all claims lodged before national courts. As claims increase in number and complexity and the State is unable to spend more money on justice, judges do not get the specialised training necessary for them to deal with certain categories of cases. The consequence is growing dissatisfaction of citizens with State justice. This has led to a situation in which citizens are more aware of and willing to exercise their rights, irrespective of the financial value or economic or social relevance of their claim. These factors could not have been predicted by the State when the paradigm of access to justice as access to State courts was elaborated.

---

12 '[L]'idea di una giustiszia *in many rooms* non è più una semplice formula dal vago sapore sogiologico, ma l'espressione di un tratto qualificante della moderna amministrazione della giustizia', N. Trocker and A. De Luca, 'Presentazione', in N. Trocker and A. De Luca (eds.), *La mediazione civile alla luce della direttiva 2008/52/EC*, FUP, Florence 2011, p. ix.

13 B.D. Richman, *supra* n. 7, p. 746.

14 W.W. Park, 'Arbitrators and Accuracy' (2010) 1 *J. Int'l Disp. Settlement (Journal of International Dispute Settlement)* 25, 27.

This incapability of State courts to provide a valid and effective response to citizens in the existing pseudo-modern society[15] has given rise on certain occasions to a prima facie rejection by the parties of the possibility of referring their disputes to State courts. The response provided by the State is unsatisfactory and this fact opens several additional options to citizens: to opt for reaching their own solutions completely outside the State framework,[16] or even to leave their dispute unresolved without searching for a solution by any means (this is not unusual: around 25% of all commercial disputes in Europe are left unresolved because citizens refuse to litigate).[17] Citizens may exercise their autonomy and refrain from taking their dispute to any State court. In any case, this behaviour directly reflects the failure of the State to provide citizens with an easy, timely and affordable way of claiming their rights,[18] a fundamental personal right for them and by far one of the most relevant services to be offered by modern States.

The awareness of their failure has forced national legislators to try to find other systems and mechanisms, both within and outside State courts, to raise, discuss, resolve or manage all sorts of disputes and conflicts that can arise in modern societies. Within the scope of State courts, national civil procedures have undertaken many reforms in an attempt to make them quicker and more flexible. Outside State courts, the ADR movement has growing support as a valid way to solve all sorts of disputes.

The support provided to ADR devices has also affected their relationship with State courts. With the passage of time an interesting debate started within the judiciary itself.[19] The awareness of the existence of social dissatisfaction with State-provided justice and with the incorrect functioning of the State system of justice has given rise to a growing concern within the judiciary itself regarding its role, goals and condition. This has generated in some judiciaries an increased sensitivity to ADR, its role and benefits, and has helped certain ADR programs be included within the framework of State courts.[20]

---

15 Note A. Kirby, 'The Death of Postmodernism and Beyond', *Philosophy Now: A Magazine of Ideas* <http://philosophynow.org/issues/58/The_Death_of_Postmodernism_And_Beyond> accessed 07.01.2013.

16 B.D. Richman, *supra* n. 7, p. 746.

17 V. Tilman, *Lessons Learnt From the Implementation of the EU Mediation Directive: The Business Perspective*, Directorate General for Internal Policies. Policy Department C: Citizens' Rights and Constitutional Affairs. Legal Affairs, Brussels 2011, p. 4 <www.europarl.europa.eu/document/activities/cont/201105/20110518ATT19584/20110518ATT19584EN.pdf> accessed 10.12.2012.

18 Note M. Cappelletti, 'Alternative Dispute Resolution Processes within the Framework of the World-Wide Access-to-Justice Movement' (1993) 56 *MLR (Modern Law Review)* 282, 289 ff.

19 L.R. Singer, *Resolución de conflictos. Técnicas de actuación en el ámbito empresarial, familiar y legal*, Paidós, Buenos Aires 1996, p. 20, regarding the 'Pound Conference' called by US SC Justice Warren E. Burger in 1976.

20 Consider, for instance, as regards the US, P. Robinson, 'An Empirical Study of Settlement Conference Nuts and Bolts: Settlement Judges Facilitating Communication, Compromise and Fear' (2012) 17 *Harv. Negot. L. Rev. (Harvard Negotiation Law Review)* 97, 145–146.

In the US for instance, these programs were upheld by way of the reform of the Federal Rules of Civil Procedure in 1983.[21] Rule 16(C) accepted the use of out-of-court mechanisms of dispute resolution. This led after some years to the approval in 1990 of the Civil Justice Reform Act, in which Federal District Courts were invited to create their own plans for reducing costs and delays in the development of civil procedure, and to include ADR programs in those cases in which the subject matter and the circumstances of the case allowed it.[22] This gave rise to so-called court-annexed programs. Nowadays the incorporation of ADR in national models clearly exists in the US, and its development is similar to what has happened in other common law countries, some of which were actually even more radical in certain areas of law, for example Canada,[23] New Zealand[24] and Australia.[25] Some Asian countries have also encouraged resort to ADR devices, though in this case this has been to a great extent due to their idiosyncracies and culture.

All these ideas were developed in the last part of the twentieth century with the clear goal of favouring a valid form of redress for citizens while limiting conflict between the parties; the acceptance of the philosophy of thinking in terms of management of the conflict instead of resolution of the conflict underpins this choice.[26] This is inspired by the notion of social peace instead of violence and the consolidation of the ADR movement.[27]

## 2. THE MULTI-ROOMS JUSTICE SYSTEM

### 2.1. STATE COURTS AND ADR AS COMPLEMENTARY TOOLS

The situation described so far seems to have undergone a quick evolution. The phenomenon of the judicialisation of life and the necessary resort to State courts has reached a turning point. The post-postmodern society that has developed in

21 Note I.R. Kaufman, 'Reform for a System in Crisis: Alternative Dispute Resolution in the Federal Courts' (1990) LIX *Fordham Law Review* 1, 9 ff.

22 *Ibid.*, pp. 7 and 10 ff.

23 The Hon. H.F. Landerkin and A.J. Pirie, 'What's the Issue? Judicial Dispute Resolution in Canada' (2004) 22 *Law in Contexts* 25, 26–27 and 31 ff. (special issue: *Alternative Dispute Resolution and the Courts*, ed. T. Sourdin).

24 See <www.justice.govt.nz/publications/global-publications/a/alternative-dispute-resolution-general-civil-cases/6-adr-and-the-courts-system#6.2> accessed 24.12.2012.

25 Note K. Mack, 'Court Referral to ADR: The Legal Framework in Australia' (2004) 22 *Law in Contexts* 112, 112–113 (special issue: *Alternative Dispute Resolution and the Courts*, ed. T. Sourdin).

26 R. Fisher, *Más allá de Maquiavelo (Herramientas para afrontar conflictos)*, Ed. Garnica, Buenos Aires 1996, p. 21.

27 S. Barona Vilar, *Solución extrajurisdiccional de conflictos. ADR y Derecho Procesal*, Tirant lo Blanch, Valencia 1999, pp. 47 ff.

the last decade in an increasingly globalised world has steadily endorsed the imperative search for new instruments for solution of disputes other than access to State courts. Many of these new instruments try to prevent or avoid conflicts or to learn how, once they have arisen, to manage them in a completely different way, seeking their resolution in the most peaceful and least traumatic way possible for the parties involved. In this new context the evolution of the principle of access to justice has been particularly relevant and profound and has been tailored to provide a valid and sound response to the complex social, economic and political world in which we are currently living. New situations require new solutions, perfectly fitted to them, even if some of these 'new' solutions have long existed in legal systems.

Nowadays the quest for new means of dispute resolution outside the traditional framework of State courts seems unstoppable in many legal systems of the world in which resort to ADR is becoming more and more common. A completely new private dispute resolution scheme is emerging: a system which coexists and interacts with State courts. ADR was first approached as an alternative to State courts but nowadays is increasingly understood as a real complement to the judiciary in the dual sense of these devices being able to require some kind of public enforcement[28] and to the extent that sometimes ADR devices are envisaged within the framework of State courts.[29]

Standing on these ideas, the current situation of access to justice is leaning towards a scenario of justice 'in many rooms'.[30] Instead of a situation of sole and radical reference to State courts and court procedure which has been the usual situation for decades, mainly in some European countries – Spain, Germany, France, Italy, etc. – we face a time in which it is generally considered to be much more interesting to offer a plurality of channels for access to justice to citizens for them to choose freely which is the most valuable and adequate option for them at a given moment and for every dispute. Even the State seems now fully aware of this option. Nevertheless, it must not be forgotten that State courts are still the most habitual way to solve disputes in many countries.[31]

In this paradigm of searching for an efficient access to justice, arbitration, mediation, conciliation and some other institutions embodied in the ADR movement – formerly 'alternative dispute resolution', today 'adequated', not 'alternative', dispute resolution – have an unprecedented relevance. Never before has there existed such an awareness of the possibilities offered by these mechanisms as a complementary, no longer alternative, instrument to State courts, in order to ensure access to justice for citizens: the new paradigm is that

---

28 B.D. Richman, *supra* n. 7, pp. 759–760.

29 Note, C. Glasser and S. Roberts, 'Dispute Resolution: Civil Justice and its Alternatives. Introduction' (1993) 56 *MLR* 277, 278.

30 N. Trocker and A. De Luca, *supra* n. 12, p. ix.

31 For instance, in Europe. Note European Commission, *supra* n. 8, p. 14.

ADR is no longer a substitute for State courts but a complement to them.[32] ADR provides an appropriate instrument to avoid or satisfactorily resolve conflicts both from the perspective of individuals and society as a whole.

## 2.2. PLURAL MEANING OF ADR

Under the reference to ADR several situations and institutions are covered. The reference to ADR may encompass in certain cases the search for a settlement by the parties on their own (negotiation), or a reference to a third person who may help them to reach an agreement (mediation and conciliation) or who is in charge of providing a binding solution to the existing dispute (arbitration).[33]

Thus parties may try to solve their dispute by means of a settlement reached by themselves or their counsellors: they may reach the so-called 'consensus *inter partes*' and thus avoid litigation. Instead of maintaining a purely passive attitude towards the dispute because of the absence of a valid response by the State, the parties try to reach a settlement by themselves. In certain cases the response provided by the other party to the request offers all parties involved in the dispute a high degree of satisfaction that makes it unnecessary to look for an independent third person to solve the dispute.[34] Is this the best solution? Certainly this is not an accurately formulated question in the existing complex world, where there are different available means of dispute resolution. There is not a better solution or a better answer. Rather, there is the solution better tailored to the needs of the parties and the specific dispute at stake.

As a matter of fact, negotiation, or agreement *inter partes*, provides them not only with a quicker way of reaching a solution to their claims but also a tool which allows the parties to obtain a high level of personal satisfaction enabling them to continue with their normal life and their normal relationships. Nevertheless, reality shows that negotiation *inter partes* is not yet the most usual way of solving litigation in modern societies. Its usefulness and affordability depends very much on the specific sort of dispute concerned and on the mindset of the parties involved in it. It can achieve a significant level of success in the field of business, mainly in international business, but this success has not been replicated in other domestic disputes. It is still most usual for citizens to refer their disputes to a

---

32 This happens irrespective of how 'good' or 'bad' State courts are felt to be by citizens. Note in this respect, S. VOIGT, *Does arbitration blossom when State courts are bad?* (2009) Joint discussion paper series in economics, No. 2009–06, pp. 11 ff. and 23 ff. <http://hdl.handle.net/10419/30088> accessed 08.01.2013.

33 Very pertinent in this respect is the title of the book of K.P. BERGER, *Private Dispute Resolution in International Business. Negotiation, Mediation, Arbitation*, 2nd ed., 2 vols., vol. II (Handbook), Wolters Kluwer, Aalphen aan den Rijn 2009, pp. 1, 115 and 301.

34 R.H. MCADAMS and J. NADLER, *supra* n. 5, p. 893. Note the precedent of S. MACAULAY, 'Non-Contractual Relations in Business: A Preliminary Study' (1963) 28 *Am. Sociolog. Rev. (American Review of Sociology)* 55, 61.

neutral third person, generally a judge. The issue of enforcement is also relevant, since alternative dispute resolution has real advantages in terms of speed and ease of enforcement over the courts.[35]

This neutral third person may play one of two very different roles.[36] Parties may turn to an independent third person who will help them to solve their dispute, or they may turn to an independent third person who will definitively solve the dispute by imposing a solution on them.

In the first case, the situation is one of 'self-composition'. Parties involved in the dispute exercise party autonomy as regards their available rights and request a third person to intervene to help them to solve their dispute. This person cooperates with them by maintaining different levels of interaction. However, the final solution is reached by the parties themselves. The type and circumstances of the dispute will favour either a direct or indirect method of resolution. The third person helps them to settle their disputes and no final decision is imposed by him/her upon them. This third person acts as a conduit: it is for the persons involved in the dispute alone to reach a settlement of their dispute. The main idea is that it is always much better to reach an agreement with mutual concessions than have a solution imposed on the parties by a third person, whoever he/she may be.

Obviously this general idea gives rise to several potential positions for the third person involved. He/she may have more or less power according to the will of the parties. He/she may have a more or less active role in the search for an agreement by the parties. This general category would encompass institutions like mediation, conciliation or an ombudsman.

Conversely the parties may agree on the nomination of a third person or persons in charge of rendering a binding solution to the dispute. This so-called 'heterocomposition' implies that an independent third person, who acts *supra partes*, imposes a decision on those who refer a dispute to him/her. The parties involved do not play a leading role in this decision; rather it is the third person who is in charge of reaching a decision and imposing it upon them. The two usual means of heterocomposition known in almost all legal systems are firstly judicial procedure, by which the judge imposes a solution on those who refer their dispute to him/her, and secondly arbitration, where the arbitrator is appointed by the parties for him/her to solve in an imperative manner the dispute submitted to him. In both cases there is an obligation to respect certain basic principles like the adversarial principle or of the equality of the parties.

35 B.D. Richman, *supra* n. 7, p. 762.

36 N. Alcalá-Zamora y Castillo: *Proceso, autocomposición y autodefensa*, UNAM, México 1970, pp. 47 ff.

## 2.3. EXPANSION OF THE ADR MOVEMENT

All these ideas are the basis for the rise of the ADR movement. Certainly its link with Western countries and to the development of the welfare State is clear. Its scope is growing fast and currently a great deal of areas of law in many geographical areas of the world are affected by this movement.

Firstly, an increase in the resort to ADR devices has taken place in many countries of the word. Its admission in unexpected fields of law is growing and its acceptance by citizens and the State is also increasing. From a device applicable solely to private law, it has moved to be referred to certain disputes in the field of public law and to areas of law traditionally closed to private disposition.[37] This resource is now usual even as regards the activity of certain social sectors and involves all ADR devices. Thus, commercial disputes (both national and international), banking and finance, consumer issues, insurance, tourism, energy, construction, telecommunications, aviation, intellectual property and copyright, unlawful competence, corporations, labour relationships, sports, health, leisure, community issues, electoral issues or family disputes including inheritance are, among others, areas currently covered, at least partially, by some of these mechanisms.[38]

In fact, the markedly Anglo-Saxon origin of the ADR movement and its accepted and endorsed evolution in common law systems[39] has not impeded ADR from entering other legal systems of different nature and origin. Despite a much slower implementation in civil law countries, the coexistence of State courts and traditionally State-designed civil procedure with other out-of-court means of dispute resolution is ascertainable in many of them.

All these factors clearly reflect the transcendence of a movement endowed with a generalised geographical and material extension, as well as enjoying an enormous presence and a great legal, social and economic relevance. Nevertheless, its relevance is even higher than shown by those facts so far stated. The current extension of the ADR movement opens a new future for the understanding of access to justice and at the same time generates, logically, a number of inevitable risks.

The expansion of resort to ADR has entailed a certain modification of its goal and understanding. ADR is no longer approached as a purely out-of-court movement, something radically foreign and external to State courts. Nowadays it

---

[37] J.F. Poudret and S. Besson, *Comparative Law of International Arbitration*, 2nd ed., Schulthess, Zurich 2002, pp. 312 ff.

[38] C. Esplugues Mota, *Arbitraje maritime internacional*, Thomson-Civitas, Cizur Menor 2007, pp. 413 ff.

[39] Note W. Twining, 'Alternative to What? Theories of Litigation, Procedure and Dispute Settlement in Anglo-American Jurisprudence: Some Neglected Classics' (1993) 56 *MLR* 380, 380 ff.

is increasingly understood as a flexible movement with many possibilities both within and outside State courts.

Reference to ADR primarily rests on party autonomy, on the will of the citizen not to refer his/her disputes to a judge but to look for other alternative ways to solve, soften or diminish disputes for the sake of individual and social peace. Nevertheless, the economic emergency that many Western countries are currently facing favours the implementation of some compulsory out-of-court dispute resolution schemes which, in some countries, have existed for a long time.[40] The essential path taken is that of the interactive coexistence between jurisdictional and non-jurisdictional solutions. Referring disputes to ADR cannot be approached as a sort of desertion from State courts but as the acceptance of the use of complementary mechanisms as a way to ensure full access to justice for citizens. These complementary mechanisms are capable of acting outside State courts, but also of interacting with them. In this new trend, reference to State courts is always approached as the last option for the parties and always after attempts of self-composition by them, something typical of some Asian cultures.

In this new context, the ongoing process of rethinking the whole idea of access to justice, of reshaping the notion of justice of the twenty-first century, ADR plays a major role in the process of offering citizens a valid instrument for solving their disputes. This role affects the understanding of ADR devices, of their goals and functioning. Thus, as stated, they have been redefined insofar as they are no longer approached as fully isolated from the judiciary. The level of acceptance of these devices and, correlatively, of the caution shown by society and the judiciary towards them vary from country to country depending on each society's specific characteristics, and of the acceptance of the capacity of solution and negotiations by the parties.

Step by step, an interrelation between the traditional notion of access to justice deeply linked to access to State courts and the implementation of ADR devices has taken place to the extent that ADR is blossoming in many nations and looks more and more unstoppable. Such a global awareness of the possibilities that these devices offer as complementary tools to the judiciary has never before existed. This awareness is due not only to citizens' needs and to national initiatives but also to its support by international organisations,[41] for example in Europe by the European Union.[42]

---

40 J.F. Poudret and S. Besson, *supra* n. 37, p. 3.

41 Like UNCITRAL <www.uncitral.org/uncitral/uncitral_texts/arbitration.html> accessed 29.12.2012; or The Hague Academy of Private International Law <www.hcch.net/upload/wop/mediation09_pk.pdf> accessed 29.12.2012.

42 See S. Barona Vilar, 'Reflexiones en torno a la tutela procesal de los consumidores y usuarios. La política de protección de los mismos en la Unión Europea: líneas de presente y de futuro', in S. Barona Vilar (ed.), *Tutela de los consumidores y usuarios en el proceso civil*, Tirant lo Blanch, Valencia 2002; S. Barona Vilar, *Mediación en asuntos civiles y mercantiles*

In most European countries the absence of a clear legal framework for ADR and the absence of a culture of negotiation and agreement until the mid-twentieth century detracted from the use of ADR devices. However, there has now been support for the ADR movement for several decades within the European Union. This support has been focused on certain fields mainly linked to civil and commercial disputes: family law or consumer law are two good examples of this.[43] In addition, a growing acceptance in the area of criminal law is apparent.[44] This support refers in general to any extra-jurisdictional means of dispute resolution, but the main focus has been on mediation.

Such growing support for ADR necessitates a deep reflection on the future of justice and administration of justice by all those involved, including judges, citizens and the legal profession, which must accordingly adapt its attitudes and behaviour.[45]

Almost without being aware of it, we are living in a crucial moment for the understanding of what justice means and its practical articulation. We are no longer facing the classic dilemma of reforming existing rules or designing new mechanisms to reduce the volume of litigation or to alleviate the task of the courts. The current trend and the challenge that it implies goes further. We face a decisive moment in which the real basis is being formed for the future understanding of the meaning of administration of justice – a justice for the twenty-first century that will most probably entail a dramatic variation from what this notion has so far meant in the last two centuries, and in which the ADR movement and ADR devices, as a clear reflection of the global socioeconomic reality of the beginning of the twenthy-first century, will be considered essential elements, with all the changes that this entails.

There are risks. We are living in a time of enormous transformation with important consequences for the role of the State in the life and social relationships of citizens and with a direct influence on the paradigm of

---

*en España. Tras la aprobación de la Ley 5/2012, de 6 de julio, de mediación en asuntos civiles y mercantiles*, Tirant lo Blanch, Valencia 2013.

43 Note G. Palao, 'La mediación y su codificación en Europa: aspectos de Derecho internacional privado', in J.L. Gómez Colomer, S. Barona Vilar and M.P. Calderon Cuadrado (eds.), *El Derecho Procesal español del Siglo XX a golpe de tango. Juan Montero Aroca Liber Amicorum, en homenaje y para celebrar su LXX cumpleaños*, Tirant lo Blanch, Valencia 2012, pp. 1339 ff.

44 See Directive 2012/29/EU of the European Parliament and of the Council of 25.10.2012 establishing minimum standards on the rights, support and protection of victims of crime, and replacing Council Framework Decision 2001/220/JHA, *OJ* L 315 of 14.11.2012. Note S. Barona Vilar, *Mediación penal. Fundamento, fines y régimen jurídico*, Tirant lo Blanch, Valencia 2011.

45 Note, as regards Spain, A. Huergo Lora, 'El arbitraje en el Derecho Administrativo', in S. Barona Vilar, *Arbitraje y Justicia en el Siglo XXI*, Thomson Civitas, Cizur Menor 2007, pp. 271 ff. As regards the specific issue of divorce and the collaborative law movement, T. Schneyer, 'The Organized Bar and the Collaborative Bar Movement: A Study in Professional Change' (2008) 50 *Ariz. L. Rev. (Arizona Law Review)* 289, 295 ff.

considering the tools offered by the State as the most suited to offer sound, flexible and affordable solutions to the needs of citizens. A move to a new model in which the State is fully aware of its incapability of ensuring this, and of the need to offer spaces of activity to private justice devices, is under way.

But of course, the risk of favouring a vision of the model primarily based on its efficiency on a purely economic approach may generate enormous doubts insofar as it may entail a sort of privatisation of justice. What is more, the prevalence of the economy in this new globalised world that is to come, in which the criteria of efficiency prevails over any other and where a sort of obsessive budgetary pretension exists may radically affect the understanding of the concept of the right of access to justice. Citizens are now invited to refer first of all to any available ADR mechanism as a way to reach a settlement, even a partial one, as to the dispute at stake. Only when the different ADR devices have proved useless for the citizen should reference to State courts be made. Accordingly, ADR instruments would now become more than new instruments of justice for the State with the benefit that they are free for the State insofar as it is not obliged to finance them, at least on a general basis; they would also be treated as privileged instruments of justice.

Certainly, trying to reach an agreement by ourselves is always positive for individuals and for society in general. But the current trend of support for ADR, strengthened by budgetary constraints in some areas of the world, may end up forcing citizens to accept that reference of their disputes to State courts is increasingly unlikely. In a sense, ADR is no longer really an alternative to the court system: parties will first make use of ADR and then, only as a last resort, be 'invited' to turn to the courts. The State itself may be tempted to foster this approach since it makes it possible to reduce investment in the national justice system. It seems that financial considerations and the need for economy, rather than the search for an efficient response to the needs of citizens, is what is currently causing this new understanding.

## 3. ARBITRATION

### 3.1. INTRODUCTION

Arbitration seems to be the most extensive private legal system of dispute resolution. Though the current blossoming of arbitration may give rise to the false appearance of arbitration being a product of modernity; an institution that was born in the twentieth century, it is a legal institution with a long tradition, at least in continental legal systems.

Certainly its current revival has entailed changes in the approach to the institution, its understanding and implementation, to the extent of creating new types of arbitration or the use of the term arbitration even in certain cases which are actually not arbitration but rather are purely administrative procedures.[46] New arbitration rules have been enacted or reformed in many countries, new arbitration centres are flourishing all over the world, lawyers are getting involved more habitually in arbitration and even public administration has approached arbitration as a way to avoid its own courts. All these factors imply that something has changed in recent times and that this change is ongoing, although this does not allow us to consider that a new legal institution has been born.

Arbitration can be traced back to Rome. In fact, some Romanists have admitted that arbitration is the basis of modern civil procedure.[47] A different question is how and why arbitration and court procedure have evolved in history in a purely parallel way. Nowadays controversies regarding its nature – for example whether it was a contractual institution, and whether it had an abstract condition or, on the contrary, was a reflection of the judiciary – have been fully overcome.[48] Arbitration is approached focusing on the institution, the way it works and the goals to be reached by it.

According to this approach arbitration is an instrument that is included within the system of justice provided by modern societies. It is an institution available for citizens at their request and is respected and coordinated by the State to a very limited extent since it is fully accepted that arbitration directly depends on the will of the parties. Freedom of the parties and guarantee of certain minimum standards of justice are the two basic principles that the State advocates for ADR in general to embody within its legal framework.

Party autonomy is the basis for arbitration. It is for the parties to submit the current or forthcoming dispute to arbitration. Without party autonomy it is not possible to speak of arbitration or of the function of arbitrators to solve the existing dispute and to offer a formal channel – the arbitration proceeding – for it to be solved. Arbitration is flexible and dependent on the parties, but it entails a certain and necessary level of formalism. Arbitration cannot exist without a valid arbitration agreement. Arbitration also cannot exist without an arbitration proceeding which ensures full equality for the parties involved. Arbitration cannot be understood without the exercise of the heterocompositive function of the arbitrator during the proceeding and without giving the award *res judicata* effect, though enforcement of the award rendered may depend on the State in

---

46 For instance, in Spain, many arbitrations are foreseen in several areas – non-discrimination, telecommunications, domain names, tobacco, hydrocarbons, sport events broadcasting and sport – though they cannot properly be called arbitrations. C. Esplugues Mota, 'Artículo 1. Ámbito de aplicación', in S. Barona Vilar, *Comentarios a la Ley de Arbitraje. Ley 60/2003, de 23 de diciembre, tras la reforma de la Ley 11/2011, de 20 de mayo*, 2nd ed., Thomson Reuters, Civitas, Madrid 2011, pp. 118–121.

47 See, S. Barona Vilar, 'Introducción', in S. Barona Vilar, *Comentarios a la Ley de Arbitraje*, *supra* n. 46, p. 60.

48 *Ibid.*, pp. 67 ff.

case of non-voluntary fulfillment. An arbitration is not possible without any of the elements stated. On this basis the ongoing discussion about the legal status of arbitration seems to be pointless, as it cannot be assigned to a single existing legal category: arbitration is an autonomous institution, 'arbitration is arbitration'.[49]

Arbitration has expanded over recent decades in many countries and in many fields of law and social relationships, although a certain amount of caution seems to still exist in certain areas of the world on, for example, religious grounds.[50] This expansion has enhanced the use of arbitration but at the same time has created some problems as to its implementation. Some well-accepted benefits are now in doubt to the extent that arbitration seems to be losing strength when compared to other ADR devices, for example the rising star of mediation.[51]

## 3.2. IS ARBITRATION BECOMING THE NEW LITIGATION?

Arbitration is fashionable. In comparison to State courts and State civil procedure, arbitration provides citizens with a flexible, voluntary and affordable response to their disputes. Arbitration is said to offer them an efficient response – a flexible, specialised, cost-efficient and speedy response. It grants parties predictability, fairness and justice through a confidential proceeding which results in a final and binding award.[52] This trend, which started perhaps with more intensity in some countries in which the legal system responded to a highly flexible conception, like common law countries, has also been gaining ground in civil legal systems.

The popularity of arbitration is shown by the volume of new State legislation on arbitration that has been enacted. Certainly arbitration has long been known in many nations, but in many cases the existing regulation was due more to the national legislator's regulatory inertia than to the acceptance by the legislator of arbitration as a true instrument of rendering justice for the parties with a broad implementation in practice. For instance, in the US statistics speak of an 84%

---

49 *Ibid.*, pp. 71 ff.

50 Generally in Islamic countries. Note in this respect, A. Alkhamees, 'International Arbitration and Shari'a Law: Context, Scope, and Intersections' (2011) 28 *J. Int. Arb. (Journal of International Arbitration)* 255, 257 ff.

51 Note, for instance, as regards the US, T. Eisenberg and G. Miller, *The Flight from Arbitration: An Empirical Study of Ex Ante Arbitration Clauses in the Contracts of Publicly Held Companies*, New York University Law and Economics Working Papers, 2006, pp. 20 ff. <http://lsr.nellco.org/cgi/viewcontent.cgi?article=1074&context=nyu_lewp> accessed 29.12.2012.

52 T.J. Stipanowich, 'Arbitration: The "New Litigation"' (2010) 1 *U. Ill. L. Rev. (University of Illinois Law Review)* 53; P.J.W. Sherwin and D.C. Rennie, 'Interim Relief Under International Arbitration Rules and Guidelines: A Comparative Analysis' (2009) 20 *ARIA (The American Review of International Arbitration)* 317, 319–320.

decline in federal civil cases between 1962 and 2002. This decline is said to be due to the high costs of civil litigation and of the delays it involves,[53] and a large percentage has now been referred to ADR, primarily arbitration.

New regulations tend to clearly assert that arbitration is based on party autonomy and that it can only commence following a free choice. But at the same time they try to ensure certain minimum standards of fairness for the parties involved in the proceedings; to make clear that, as has already been stated, the award is reached through a real adversarial proceeding, where there is equality between the parties. A third party, the arbitrator, who acts *supra partes*, imposes a final and binding decision on the parties with *res judicata* effect. In addition, modern legislation usually tries to offer a new perspective on the institution and its relationship with State courts, as well as to encourage its use by way of the standardisation of the rules on arbitration, strengthening its position as an additional tool for the judiciary. This wave of new regulation has fuelled the idea of a restructuring of the systems of access to justice and of its understanding in many countries of the world and has opened real possibilities for arbitration in many places so far closed to it.

In this environment of new regulation and new approaches to arbitration, the UNCITRAL Model Law of 1985 on international commercial arbitration, reformed in 2006, has played a major role. The UNCITRAL Model Law of 1985 has been incorporated in a substantial number of countries, thus harmonising the legal framework of arbitration and facilitating access to it.[54] The Model Law has fostered a culture of arbitration in certain areas very favourable to it. Especially in those countries with a civil legal system the existence of modern and well-drafted legislation ensures certainty and allows this institution to be consolidated and applied. In this new legal scenario, arbitration is approached as a valid device to solve prospective disputes in a way much more favourable for the parties – in all possible aspects – than submitting it to the unknown and unpredictable State courts.[55] In this sense, an approach to these new reforms and the proliferation of arbitrations is more than enough to confirm what has been said.[56]

This trend of national reform comes accompanied by two other relevant elements, the flourishing of new arbitration centres worldwide and the continuous reform and adaptation of their arbitration regulations with the goal of ensuring a sound, quick and affordable solution to the dispute at stake.

---

53 Note T.J. Stipanowich, *supra* n. 52, p. 1.

54 Note <www.uncitral.org/uncitral/en/uncitral_texts/arbitration/1985Model_arbitration_status.html> accessed 07.01.2013.

55 Note in this respect, N. Chappe, 'Non-exécution du contrat: le choix de l'arbitrage' (2010) 131 *Revue d'économie industrielle* 9, 20–21.

56 Note C. Esplugues Mota, 'Líneas generals de la regulación del arbitraje en Europa en las últimas décadas: paralelismos y divergencias con el proceso latinoamericano', in A. Zapata De Arbelaez, S. Barona Vilar and C. Esplugues Mota, *El arbitraje interno e internacional en Latinoamérica. Regulación presente y tendencias del futuro*, Universidad Externado de Colombia, Bogotá 2010, pp. 39 ff.

Unfortunately, the growing use of arbitration has led to the reoccurrence of many of the problems and setbacks that State courts encounter daily, to the point that arbitration is now referred to as the 'new litigation'.[57] State courts remain costly, lengthy and inefficient, but arbitration also seems increasingly to emulate these defects, thus creating some concerns about its future development.[58] These concens arise not only because other ADR devices are also becoming highly fashionable – like mediation – but also because of the fact that the expansion of arbitration to almost every kind of dispute, both in the domestic and international realm, has allowed a certain degree of 'contamination' of arbitration by certain specific types of arbitration – mainly by investment protection arbitration – thus generating an attack against the institution in certain parts of the world such as South America.[59]

## 3.3. SOME EXISTING TRENDS IN ARBITRATION

The fact that many national regulations on arbitration share the same legal basis – the UNCITRAL Model Law of 1985 – does not prevent the existence of differences among countries as regards some relevant points which are left untreated, contingency fee agreements being one of them.[60] Nevertheless, there are still certain common trends in this institution. They deserve analysis insofar as their study may provide a global vision of where arbitration currently stands and what its future looks like. Certainly some of these trends are nowadays seen mainly in

---

57 T.J. Stipanowich, *supra* n. 52, p. 4.

58 *Ibid.*, pp. 5–6.

59 For instance, in 2007 the Government of Bolivia thought of the possibility to derogate from the Act on Arbitration and Conciliation of 1997. A draft bill on the derogation of this Act was prepared ('Anteproyecto de Ley Abrogatoria de la Ley No. 1770 de Arbitraje y Conciliación de 10 de marzo de 1997', unreported) although it did not go through. The second paragraph of the Exposition of Principles of this draft bill clearly shows the referred contamination: 'Thus, the Act no. 1770 of Arbitration and Conciliation of March 10, 1997, following the guidelines set forth by the transnational corporations of a neoliberal approach, provides that the national arbitration applies with total absence of the State, in violation of national sovereignty. Consequently, entities that hear arbitrations disputes have fulfilled that role violating collective interests to the detriment of State interests, maintaining absolute confidentiality and developing their acts arbitrarily with the appointment of arbitrators or arbitral tribunals that have become a small circle that has benefited from the high costs of the arbitration proceedings.'

60 In England this possibility has been accepted regarding arbitration in *Bevan Ashford (a firm) v. Geoff Yeandle (Contractors) Ltd (in liquidation)* [1998] All ER (D) 138. In fact, a voluntary Code of Conduct for Litigation Funders has been prepared in England (available at: <www.judiciary.gov.uk/about-the-judiciary/advisory-bodies/cjc/third-party-funding> accessed 28.12.2012), whereas in other arbitration-friendly places like Hong Kong, in accordance with *Canonway Consultants Ltd v. Kenworth Engineering Ltd* (1997 ADRLJ 95), this is considered unacceptable as regards arbitration. Note on this issue, and in general, L.B. Nieuwveld and V. Shannon, *Third-Party Funding in International Arbitration*, Kluwer Law International, The Hague 2012.

international commercial arbitration, but most probably they will also be apparent in domestic arbitration in the near future; we will therefore deal with them jointly.

### *3.3.1. Expansion and specialisation of arbitration*

Arbitration is an expanding institution as regards the scope of disputes it covers and its use worldwide.

One of the main ideas that accompanies arbitration nowadays is its application to almost all sorts of disputes. Arbitration has steadily expanded in recent decades like never before and now covers many fields that could previously only be litigated before State courts. Disputes that can now be submitted to arbitration tend to be much more complex: class actions, multi-party actions, multiple contract disputes, etc.[61] This creates uncertainty and growing costs. Concern about this problem has led to increasing regulation to deal with the issue, which has had differing levels of success;[62] in fact in some cases, because of the complexity of the dispute, there is a growing trend to reach partial settlements within the arbitration framework.[63]

This expansion of arbitration has been accompanied by specialisation. A significant number of national legal systems embody a common set of rules for arbitration, both domestic and international. But this general legislation coexists with an increasing number of specialist arbitration systems applicable to a specific group, sector, or a certain number or kind of persons. This possibility offers specialised responses to specific problems that are not available in State courts. Certainly, arbitration has reached all areas of life, with the exception of some instances where the case is of public interest or relates to public policy, and is thus not available for submission to arbitration. New sectors of arbitration have arisen in almost all areas of law in many countries of the world: transport, insurance, consumer, commercial, corporations, telecommunications, professional responsibility, sport, administration, etc. This has helped arbitration to become a device tailored to the specific interests of the sector and one which provides a sound and more specialised response. This specialisation shows the flexibility of arbitration and encourages its existence

61 This also happens in investment arbitration cases. The pending ICSID case on *Abaclat and others v. Argentine Republic* is very relevant in this respect insofar as some thousands of Italian investors were allowed to file a claim against Argentina because of the Argentinian default of a decade ago (available at: <https://icsid.worldbank.org/ICSID/FrontServlet> accessed 27.12.2012).

62 e.g., Articles 7 and 10, ICC International Arbitration Rules 2012.

63 e.g., in Canada, the judgment of the Superior Court of Justice, Ontario, of 15.02.2012, on *Moore v. Bertuzzi*, 2012 ONSC 597 at [41] ff., endorsing a 'Mary Carter Agreement' (note in this respect, *Booth v. Mary Carter Paint Co.*, 202 So2d 8 (Fla Dist Ct App 1967)). Also note the judgment of the same Court of 30.8.2012 in *Rains v. Molea* 2012 ONSC 4906. In both cases the level of disclosure of the settlement reached was at stake.

but, at the same time, forms the basis of some of the problems that arbitration nowadays encounters.

This specialisation is very much dependent on the arbitrators who intervene in the resolution of these disputes and who are usually very close to these sectors; maritime arbitration, for example, is significant in this respect.[64]

Correlatively to these two facts, the spread of arbitration has led to the consolidation of certain historical places for arbitration – London, mainly – and at the same time the emergence of certain new arbitration seats in other areas of the world, especially in Asia, for instance Hong Kong and Singapore.

### *3.3.2. Arbitrability*

The global expansion of arbitration implies the acceptance of the growing number of topics and issues that can be subject to it. This has the direct effect that arbitrability seems not to be a major issue in arbitration nowadays, at least in international commercial arbitration. More and more areas that were previously excluded from arbitration are being treated as arbitrable. Insolvency[65] or competition law[66] are paradigmatic in this respect. The generally accepted principle is that all rights and relationships that are capable of settlement by the parties can be referred to arbitration. This trend has now been made even more flexible in some new national arbitration legislation, where the usual reference to the 'availability of the rights at stake in the dispute' is now changed to a global reference to the 'economic nature' of the dispute.[67]

Conversely, this attitude is limited in certain fields or relationships that involve a State-protected principle, for example consumer protection.[68] However,

64 C. Esplugues Mota, 'The Role of Arbitrators in International Maritime Arbitration', in R. Stürner, H. Matsumoto, W. Lüke *et al.*, *Festschrift für Dieter Leipold zum 70. Geburstag*, Mohr Siebeck, Tübingen 2009, pp. 869 ff.

65 For instance, in Singapore, the Singapore Court of Appeal Judgment of 11.05.2011, *Larsen Oil and Gas Pte Ltd v. Petroprod Ltd (in official liquidation in the Cayman Islands and in compulsory liquidation in Singapore)* [2011] SGCA 21 set forth three basic rules as regards those aspects of insolvency that are referable to arbitration. Note also the previous case of 16.08.2006 in the case *Ho Wing On Christopher and ors v. ECRC Land Pte Ltd (in liquidation)* [2006] SGCA 25. Also in Switzerland, note the recent Supreme Court ruling of 15.10.2012 on the case 4A_50/2012, *X. Lda., Administradora de Insolvencia v. Y* (available at: <www.polyreg.ch/d/informationen/bgeunpubliziert/Jahr_2012/Entscheide_4A_2012/4A.50__2012.html> accessed 31.12.2012). As regards the arbitrability of arbitration issues, note D. Jones, 'Arbitration Insolvency and Arbitration: An Arbitral Tribunal's Perspective' (2012) 78 *Arbitration* 123, 126, or J. Sutcliffe and J. Rogers, 'Effect of Party Insolvency on Arbitration Proceedings: Pause for Thought in Testing Times' (2010) 78 *Arbitration* 277, 281 ff., where a comparative study of different jurisdictions is done.

66 T. Zuberbühler and Ch. Oetiker, *Practical Aspects of Arbitrating EC Competition Law*, Schulthess, Zurich 2007, pp. 12 ff.

67 Article 1(1), Voluntary Arbitration Act 2011.

68 Even in arbitration-friendly States. That is the case in Canada with the Supreme Court judgment on *Seidel v. TELUS Communications Inc.* (2011 SCC 15) and this despite the fact

the mere existence of imperative rules in a specific area of law is increasingly said not to mean that the dispute is not arbitrable.[69] In fact, in certain specific fields, for example religion, arbitration may be used to override the application of State law.[70]

### 3.3.3. *Ensuring respect for the will of the parties: a revitalised approach to arbitration clauses*

The elements that categorise arbitration are party autonomy and the freedom of citizens to refer their disputes to arbitration. If citizens have party autonomy, allowing them to develop, modify and extinguish their available private rights, there is no obstacle preventing them from trying to solve their dispute otherwise than by referring it to State courts.

This desire of the parties to take their dispute out of State courts and to refer it to arbitration is reflected in the arbitration agreement they reach. The modification of the UNCITRAL Model Law of 1985 focuses on arbitration clauses and the need for them to be in writing, a requirement embodied in the original text, which runs against social and trade reality and which is interpreted differently even within the same jurisdiction.[71] Two options are now included in Article 7 of the Model Law in relation to requirements of formality.[72] These two options are reproduced in certain modern national legislation which still maintains different solutions regarding the written form of the arbitration clause.[73]

---

that overall the judgment endorses the validity of arbitration. On the US, note T. Eisenberg, G.P. Miller and E. Sherwin, 'Arbitration's Summer Soldiers: An Empirical Study of Arbitration Clauses in Consumer and Non-Consumer Clauses' (2007–08) 41 *U. Mich. J.L. Reform (University of Michigan Journal of Law Reform)* 871, 873–877.

69 J.-B. Racine, 'Droit Économique et Lois de Police' (2010) XXIV *Revue internationale de droit économique* 61, 73 ff. In other jurisdictions note, for instance in Sweden, the judgment of the Svea Court of Appeal of 07.10.2011, Case No. T 6798–10 (available at: <www.arbitration.sccinstitute.com/dokument/Court-Decisions/1023105/Judgment-of-the-Svea-Court-of-Appeal-7-October-2011-Case-No-T-6798–10?id=95791> accessed 28.12.2012).

70 See, A.M. Baker, 'A Higher Authority: Judicial Review of Religious Arbitration' (2012) 37 *Vermont Law Review* 157, 184 ff.

71 Note S.I. Strong, 'What Constitutes an "Agreement in Writing" in International Commercial Arbitration? Conflicts Between the New York Convention and the Federal Arbitration Act' (2012) 48 *Stan. J. Int'l. L. (Stanford Journal of International Law)* 47, 52 ff.

72 Also, a Recommendation regarding the interpretation of Article II(2) and Article VII(1) of the New York Convention of 1958 was elaborated in 2006. <www.uncitral.org/pdf/english/texts/arbitration/NY-conv/A2E.pdf> accessed 23.12.2012.

73 Taking into account four pieces of legislation on arbitration enacted in 2011; France (Articles 1442 and 1507 CPC) does not compel the arbitration clause to be in written form, whereas in Costa Rica (Article 7(2) International Commercial Arbitration Act), Hong Kong (Section 19 Arbitration Ordinance) and Portugal (Article 2(1) Voluntary Arbitration Act) the arbitration agreement must be written.

The arbitration clause is the very core of arbitration. In any case the arbitration clause is envisaged as fully dependent on the will of the parties.[74] It is for them to decide to enter arbitration, to fix its duration and viability,[75] and also, in some cases, to modify this option and to waive submission of their dispute to arbitration.[76] The arbitration clause sets forth the scope of the dispute at stake and of the arbitration as a whole and consequently directly affects the possible setting aside of the award rendered.[77] What is more, because it has been agreed on by the parties, some moves are apparent in certain jurisdictions towards parties being awarded damages for breach of the arbitration clause should the national court decline jurisdiction.[78]

The relevance of party autonomy in arbitration and the extension of the institution to almost any sort of dispute creates some specific problems which merit special responses. One of them is the extension of effects generated by the clause to third non-signatory persons and the existence of some *de facto* compulsory arbitration schemes. For instance, in certain areas of activity, the fact of belonging to a certain category of persons (for example athletes) supposes the obligation to submit disputes to arbitration and to do it without having explicitly consented to it and, correlatively, the inability to submit disputes to State courts. This poses some concerns about the existence of a clear consent and

---

74 As regards what this actually means and implies, note E. Onyema, *International Commercial Arbitration and the Arbitrator's Contract*, Routledge, Abingdon 2010, pp. 9 ff.

75 The issue of time-barred claims subject to arbitration has been dealt with in depth in certain jurisdictions, e.g. the US: *Bechtel do Brasil Construções Ltda. v. UEG Araucária Ltda.*, 638 F.3d 150. This is said to be a question for the arbitrators and not for the judges to establish.

76 Regarding the tacit waiver of arbitration note in the US, *Ivax Corp. v. B. Braun of America, Inc.*, 286 F.3d 1309 (11th Cir. 2002); *Green Tree Fin. Corp.-Alabama v. Randolph*, 531 U.S. 79, 80 (2000); *Cabinetree of Wisconsin, Inc. v. Kraftmaid Cabinetry, Inc.*, 50 F.3d 388, 391 (7th Cir. 1995) and more recently the USC judgment of 02.07.2011 in *Stok & Associates, P.A. v. Citibank*, N.A 387 Fed. Appx. 921 (11th Cir. 2010). The petition for a writ of certiori was dismissed on 02.06.2011 because the parties settled (available at: www.supremecourt.gov/Search.aspx?FileName=/docketfiles/10-514.htm, accessed 26.12.2012). Nevertheless, in some other jurisdictions a clear position in favour of arbitration is maintained to the extent that the parties are referred to arbitration in case a valid clause exists which renders exclusive jurisdiction upon a court or an arbitral tribunal even when a response on the merits has been submitted. That is, for instance, the case of Canada: e.g., the Supreme Court judgment of 15.03.2012 in *Momentous.ca Corp. v. Canadian American Association of Professional Baseball Ltd*, 2012 SCC 9 or of 01.05.2003 in *Z.I. Pompey Industrie v. ECU-Line N.V.*, 2003 SCC 27.

77 Note for instance, the judgments of the Singapore High Court of 06.03.2007 in *Ng Chin Siau v. How Kim Chuan* [2007] 2 SLR (R) 789 or of 19.07.2011 in *Kempinski Hotels SA v. PT Prima International Development* [2011] SGHC 171. This scope is not always easily ascertainable, mainly in cases of arbitration clauses with a narrow scope. Note in this respect, *Lombard North Central plc and another v. GATX Corporation* [2012] EWHC 1067 (Comm) rendered by the English Commercial Court on 25.04.2012.

78 That is the case in England. Note the judgment of the Commercial Court of 04.04.2012 in *West Tankers Inc. v. Allianz SpA and another* [2012] EWHC 854 (Comm). The same issue underlines the judgment of the Swiss Federal Court of 11.2.2011 in the case 4A_444/2009, *X v. Y* (available at: <www.polyreg.ch/d/informationen/bgeunpubliziert/Jahr_2009/Entscheide_4A _2009/4A.444__2009.html> accessed 28.12.2012).

also as to access to justice.[79] In addition, the growing use of arbitration in certain specific kinds of actions, specifically class actions which have moved from State courts to arbitration, is under increasing scrutiny in certain jurisdictions.[80]

In any case, a trend towards respecting submission by the parties to arbitration seems to exist in many countries. This trend favours the validity of the arbitration clause agreed on by the parties[81] and has even led to the recognition of the jurisdiction of the arbitrator on the basis of an arbitration clause that has been procured by bribery.[82] Nevertheless, despite this general principle, some problems exist in certain jurisdictions as regards asymmetrical clauses: those that allow one of the parties to choose between referring the dispute to State courts or arbitration.[83]

---

79 Switzerland plays an important role in this field because of the location of many international sports federations in its territory. The Swiss Courts tends to uphold its validity: e.g. Federal Supreme Court judgments of 22.12.2008, case 4A_392/2008/ech, *Union des Associations Européennes de Football (UEFA) v. Association Z.*; of 09.01.2009, case 4A_460/2008 len/, *A. v. Fédération Internationale de Football Association (FIFA)* or of 20.2.2009, case 4A_600/2008, *X v. Y* (available at: <www.polyreg.ch/d/informationen/bgeunpubliziert/index.html> accessed 27.12.2012). Although these negative feelings are ousted by way of a valid 'enforcement' approach in certain cases, note J. Paulsson, *supra* n. 6, pp. 24 ff.

80 For instance in the US; note *Green Tree Financial Corp. v. Bazzle*, 539 U.S. 444 (2003) or *AT&T Mobility LLC v. Concepcion*, 131 S. Ct. 1740 (2011), relating to consumer law, which actually seems to put the discussion to an end (note the recent case of the US Court of Appeal (9th Cir.) of 5.3.2012, *In re Checking Account Overdraft Litigation* MDL No. 2036 (available at: <www.ca11.uscourts.gov/opinions/ops/201114317.pdf> accessed 30.12.2012). More recently, the decision of the National Labour Relations Board of 03.01.2012 in *D.R. Horton, Inc. and Michael Cuda*, Case 12-CA-25764, 357 NLRB No. 184, renders invalid certain clauses that employees were obliged to sign preventing them from joining other employees to pursue claims related to employment either before State courts or arbitration. This same scrutiny regarding arbitration clauses included in consumer contracts is ascertainable in the EU. The ECJ has rendered several relevant judgments on this issue. Note in this respect, the ECJ judgment of 26.10.2006 in case C-168/05, *Mostaza Claro* [2006] ECR I-10421 or of 06.10.2009 in case C-40/08, *Asturcom Telecomunicaciones* [2009] ECR I-9575 regarding the power of the court that is in charge of the action for setting aside an arbitration award to ascertain *ex officio* the validity of the clause embodied in the contract. Note on this issue, T.J. Stipanowich, 'The Third Arbitration Trilogy: Stolt-Nielsen, Rent-a-Center, Concepcion and the Future of American Arbitration', (2011) 22 *ARIA (The American Review of International Arbitration)* 324, 407 ff. on the relationships of employees and consumer contracts with arbitration clauses in some selected jurisdictions.

81 Note the Swiss Supreme Court judgement of 07.11.2011 in Case 4A_246/2011, *X v. Y* (available at: <www.polyreg.ch/d/informationen/bgeunpubliziert/Jahr_2011/Entscheide_4A_2011/4A.246__2011.html> accessed 27.12.2012).

82 Consider *Westacre Investments Inc. v. Jugoimport-SDRP Holding Co. Ltd* [1999] APP.L.R. 05/12 as a very relevant precedent. New cases have arisen ever since. Very important too is the ICSID award of 04.10.2006 in *World Duty Free Co. Ltd v. Republic of Kenya* (ICSID Case No. ARB/00/7) (available at: <https://icsid.worldbank.org/ICSID/FrontServlet> accessed on 27.12.2012).

83 This is the case in the Russian Federation. Note that the Supreme Arbitrazh Court has issued Decree No. 831/12 of 19.06.2012 in the case A40-49223/11-112-401, *Sony Ericsson Mobile Communications Rus v. Russian Telephone Co.* rejecting this possibility in international commercial arbitration due to its unfairness, insofar as this choice is only open to one of the parties (note D. Galagan, 'The Presidium of the Russian Supreme Arbitrazh Court Interprets

The issue of the existence and interpretation of the scope of arbitration agreements is often raised before national courts. These issues have given rise to a certain amount of case law in some countries, putting the role played by State courts as regards arbitration under pressure. Different responses can be seen to the question of the existence of the arbitration clause[84] and of its interpretation,[85] and they reflect the attitude maintained in relation to arbitration in the different jurisdictions. The idea of the minimum intervention of State courts in arbitration seems to be fully accepted in those arbitration-friendly jurisdictions.

Finally, in international arbitration it is also for the parties to select the law applicable to arbitration clauses, something that they do not usually do.[86]

### 3.3.4. *Flexibility of arbitration proceedings*

Arbitration is neither as technical as judicial procedure nor as rigid and preclusive. Arbitration offers a greater flexibility in its development, combining a minimum level of legal security and certainty with a great degree of flexibility, something that in too many cases State court procedures impedes.

Party autonomy allows the parties to opt for a formal or informal arbitration, for an arbitration in which a law is applied to its substance or to *ex aequo et bono* arbitration, to an institutional or an *ad hoc* arbitration. They can also choose the law applicable to both the substance and the procedure of the arbitration. As regards this last issue, some arbitration institutions accept party autonomy to the point of allowing them to refer their procedure to a set of rules different to that set

---

"Sole Option" Clause', *AIA Arbitration-adr.org*, August 2012, pp. 6–7 <www.arbitration-adr.org/documents/?i=245> accessed 30.12.2012). This opposition is also maintained in other major and clearly arbitration-friendly jurisdictions like the US as regards domestic disputes: note *Gonzalez v. West Suburban Imp., Inc.*, 411 F. Supp. 2d 970 (N.D. III 2006); *Wisconsin Auto Title Loans, Inc. v. Jones*, 714 N.W.2d 155 (Wisc. 2006); *Ticknor v. Choice Hotels Int'l.*, 265 F.3d 931 (9th Cir. 2001); *Armendariz v. Found Health PsychCare Sers., Inc.*, 6 P.3d 669 (Cal. 2000) or *Showthemoney Check Cashers, Inc. v. Williams*, 27 S.W. 3d 361 (Ark. 2000), among others.

84 e.g. the jugment of the Irish Supreme Court of 11.11.2010 in *Barnmore Demolition and Civil Engineering Ltd v. Alandale Logistics Ltd, et al.* [2010] No 5910P.

85 In Singapore, for instance, an arbitration-friendly State, State courts maintain the principle of minimum judicial intervention in arbitration and that has entailed a broad interpretation of the meaning of the arbitration clause. Note *Tjong Very Sumito v. Antig Investments Pte Ltd* [2009] SGCA 41; *ALC v. ALF* [2010] SGHC 231, referred to domestic arbitration, or *Equinox Offshore Accommodation Ltd v. Richshore Marine Supplies Pte Ltd* [2010] SGHC 122 as regards the power of granting pre-arbitration process discovery by judges, which was rejected. The same position of minimum intervention is maintained in other jurisdictions, like in England in *Fiona Trust & Holding Corporation and others v. Yuri Privalov and others* [2007] EWCA Civ 20. On the contrary, Pakistan is considered a clear example of State courts' intervention in arbitration where a long tradition against international arbitration seems to have been maintained: note the Supreme Court of Pakistan judgments of 2000 in *HUBCO v. WAPDA* (see (2000) 16 *Arb. Int.* 469), and of 2002 in *SGS v. Federation of Pakistan*, SCMR 1694.

86 This creates some problems when a clear response is lacking. Note, in England, the judgment of the Court of Appeal of 16.05.2012 in *Sulamerica CIA Nacional de Seguros SA v. Enesa Engenharia SA* [2012] EWCA Civ 638.

forth by the institution itself.[87] This wide degree of flexibility has the advantage of shaping the arbitration procedure to the needs and conveniences of the parties. But conversely, extreme flexibility may make the arbitration unpredictable and foster legal uncertainty until the arbitration procedure is under way.

In addition, in many arbitrations the use of legal assistance or legal representatives is not necessary due to the nature of the dispute. Parties are free to attend the arbitration alone and to act on their own behalf. This is not considered to mean a lesser protection for the citizen. Rather, it is a manifestation of the lack of technicality and of the greater flexibility that the arbitration institution inspires.

Arbitration is thus deemed a flexible tool fully dependent on the will of the parties and easily tailored to their needs. Nevertheless, the expansion of arbitration, objectively a positive fact, has entailed more detailed regulation in many cases and has given rise to longer proceedings, and at the same time has encouraged reproduction of the 'zealous advocacy' that lawyers employ before State courts.[88] Within this global reference, and especially as regards common law countries, the availability of certain procedural devices like anti-suit injunctions becomes a relevant issue.[89]

In fact, a certain sense of arbitration becoming more and more akin to litigation is spreading all over the planet and this makes it costly and, at the same time, generates a certain dissatisfaction with the functioning of the system as a whole. One of the undesirable consequences this feeling generates is the existence of certain signs of alarm relating to the relationship between State courts and

---

87 This is the case, for instance, in China at the CIETAC. Article 4.2 of the CIETAC Rules allows parties to the arbitration to select any other arbitration rules as the applicable rules of the arbitration. Nevertheless, this flexibility may run against certain national solutions where the legislation of a certain State is applicable even to arbitration held outside that country. This is a very common reference, though in certain cases is applied on a very broad basis. For instance, in India the court in *Bhatia International v. Bulk Trading SA* (2002) 4 SCC 105 upheld the application of Part I of the Indian Conciliation and Arbitration Act, which according to its wording was only applicable to arbitrations whose seat is in India, to arbitrations whose seat is outside the country. In its judgment of 11.05.2011 in the case *Videocon Industries Ltd v. Union Of India and another* (2011) 6 SCC 161, the Supreme Court maintained this position, although it considered that certain behaviour and agreements by the parties may lead to an implicit agreement on the exclusion of this legislation. This situation seems to have now changed after the ruling of the Indian Supreme Court of 09.06.2012 in *Bharat Aluminium v. Kaiser Aluminium* (Civil Appeal No. 7019 of 2005) (available at: <http://supremecourtofindia.nic.in/outtoday/ac701905p.pdf> accessed 27.12.2012).

88 T.J. Stipanowich, *supra* n. 52, p. 11.

89 See the well known ECJ judgment of 10.02.2009, in case C-185/07, *Allianz (formerly Riunione Adriatica di Sicurtà)* [2009] ECR I-663. Note, E. Gaillard, 'Anti-suit Injunctions Issued by Arbitrators', in A.J. van den Berg, *International Council for Commercial Arbitration. International Arbitration 2006: Back to Basics? Vol. 13 ICCA International Arbitration Congress*, Kluwer Law International, Alphen aan den Rijn 2008, pp. 237 ff., and G. Fisher, 'Anti-Suit Injunctions to Restrain Foreign Proceedings in Breach of an Arbitration Agreement' (2010) 22 *Bond Law Review* 1, 4 ff. or Ch. Debatissta, 'Arbitrators' Powers to Order Interim Measures Including Anti-Suit Injunctions' (2012) 78 *Arbitration* 421.

arbitration. Despite the usually arbitration-friendly atmosphere existing in many Western and Asian countries, certain signs of tension, still minor, are ascertainable both in international and domestic arbitration. The very specific use of EU Regulations and torpedo actions to prevent arbitration[90] or the much more general fact of claiming before State courts certain issues that have been rejected at the arbitration stage[91] reflect this tension created by the parties and their legal counsels.

### 3.3.5. *The quest for effectiveness: provisional measures*

Very much related to the arbitration proceedings and the succesful outcome of the arbitration is the issue of provisional measures. The creation of the Model Law on international commercial arbitration in 1985 is considered a landmark in the evolution of arbitration worldwide. As stated, the Model Law has been applied or taken into account in many of the new arbitration regulations. Though it refers to international arbitration, the Model Law favours a monistic approach to the regulation of the institution. This solution simplifies the regulation and favours a culture of arbitration. The Model Law thus fulfils the double task of offering certainty in the regulation of arbitration and of favouring the enactment of new legislation on arbitration in many countries of the world.[92]

The Model Law was modified in 2006 mainly with regard to arbitration agreements and provisional measures. The goal was to introduce a more flexible approach to arbitration agreements and to accept alternatives to the requirement that agreements should be in writing. Focusing on provisional measures, it was very important to allow the possibility for arbitrators to adopt them and to

90 *Supra* n. 89. See C. Azcarraga Monzonis, 'Heidelberg, West Tankers, Endesa. La revisión del Reglamento Bruselas I en materia arbitral ¿reformar para mejorar?' (2011) 4 *Arbitraje: Revista de Arbitraje comercial y de inversiones* 405, 435 ff. As regards the proposal for reform of the Brussels I Regulation, see B. Hess, 'The Brussels I Regulation: A Recent Case Law of the Court of Justice and the Commission's Proposed Recast' (2012) 49 *Common Market Law Review* 1075, 1100 ff. or V. Lazic, 'The Commission's Proposal to Amend the Arbitration Exception in the EC Jurisdiction Regulation: How "Much Ado About Nothing" Can End Up in a "Comedy of Errors" and in Anti-suit Injunctions Brussels-Style' (2012) 29 *J. Int. Arb. (Journal of International Arbitration)* 19. The final recast version of the Brussels I Regulation has now been published at the *OJ* with a completely different wording to that of the recast version proposed by the Commission: Regulation (EU) No. 1215/2012 of the European Parliament and of the Council of 12.12.2012 on jurisdiction and the recognition and enforcement of judgments in civil and commercial matters (recast) *OJ* L 351 of 20.12.2012.

91 Note the High Court judgment of 21.09.2012 in *Michael Wilson & Partners v. Sinclair* [2012] EWHC 2560.

92 However differences are still ascertainable. Just taking into consideration 2011, Hong Kong, for instance, enacted a new Arbitration Ordinance based on the Model Law enshrining a monistic solution, just as in Portugal with the Voluntary Arbitration Act 2011, which was also based on the Model Law. On the contrary, France also enacted new regulation on international commercial arbitration in January 2011, which coexists with a whole set of rules devoted to internal arbitration. This dualistic position is maintained in other parts of the world, like in Costa Rica as of April 2011.

design a preliminary order that avoids the 'aggression' that provisional measures eventually entail for the party suffering them. Without being a panacea, they aim to complement, in a preliminary form, provisional measures granting them *inaudita parte debitoris* and without enforcement, and leaving its fulfillment to the will of the parties.[93]

Provisional measures are critical for arbitration and to some extent their regulation shows the level of friendliness towards arbitration of a specific jurisdiction,[94] specifically the capacity of courts to cooperate with national and foreign arbitrators on a friendly basis.[95] This idea is broadly shared worldwide.[96] In fact, the need to allow the adoption of provisional measures has led certain arbitration institutions to embody specific rules on this topic. For instance, emergency arbitrators have been accepted by the Arbitration Institute of the SCC for some years,[97] and the ACICA updated its ACICA Arbitration Rules in 2011, setting forth certain Arbitration Emergency Provisions enabling the appointment of an emergency arbitrator and the granting of Emergency Interim Measures of Protection.[98] The same trend is also followed by the ICC International Arbitration Rules 2012.[99]

### 3.3.6. *Introducing new technologies in arbitration*

The application of a new generation of technologies to the administration of justice is an unquestionable reality in many countries of the world. This has also

93 Note S. Barona Vilar, *Medidas cautelares en el arbitraje*, Thomson-Civitas, Cizur Menor 2006, pp. 93 ff., or T. Clay, 'Les mesures provisoires demandées a l'arbitre', in J.-M. Jacquet and E. Jolivet, *Les mesures provisoires dans l'arbitrage commercial international. Évolutions et innovations*, Litec, Paris 2007, pp. 12 ff.

94 However, this assertion runs against figures that show very low use of them by counsels in arbitration; note Queen Mary University of London/White & Case, *2012 International Arbitration Survey. Current and Preferred Practices in the Arbitral Process*, p. 16 < www.whitecase.com/files/Uploads/Documents/Arbitration/Queen-Mary-University-London-International-Arbitration-Survey-2012.pdf> accessed 29.12.2012. Nevertheless, its relevance as regards arbitrations is stressed by the ECJ in its judgment of 17.11.1998 in Case C-391/95, *Van Uden Maritime v. Kommanditgesellschaft in Firma Deco-Line and others* [1998] ECR I-7091.

95 For instance, in the US, consider the judgment of the New York Supreme Court, Appellate Division in *Sojitz Corp. v. Prithvi Information Solutions Ltd*, 2011 N.Y. Slip Op. 1741; 2011 N.Y. App. Div. LEXIS 1709, ordering the attachment of property in connection with an arbitration seated in Singapore. National legislators also take this into account. Thus the French arbitration regulation of 2011 clarifies the issue of the competence to render these measures before the arbitration has started or after its commencement, as well as its scope (Article 1468 CPC).

96 P.J.W. Sherwin and D.C. Rennie, *supra* n. 52, pp. 320 ff.

97 ACICA Arbitration Rules 2010, appendix 2 – Emergency Arbitrators.

98 Schedule 2(3), ICC International Arbitration Rules 2012.

99 Article 29 and Appendix V. A comparative approach may be found at: R. Bose and I. Meredith, 'Emergency Arbitration Procedures: A Comparative Analysis' (2012) 15 *Int. ALR (International Arbitration Law Review)* 186, 187 ff.

entailed the use of new technologies in the agile, flexible and malleable world of arbitration and, in general, of ADR. In fact, new technologies are considered in certain cases to be a sort of 'fourth part' with a relevant role to play in the development of the proceedings and the solution of the dispute.[100]

New technologies are applicable to arbitration proceedings which can be fully or partially carried out online.[101] The introduction of new technologies in arbitration favours the existence of arbitration proceedings online; that means that not only are some procedural acts developed or guaranteed by way of these electronic means, but the whole arbitration proceeding may be performed online from the very beginning, with the interpretation of certain requirements that necessarily should be taken into account with the goal of ensuring the validity of certain specific acts and of the procedure as a whole. New technologies also have a special relevance in the field of serving of documents and in the area of probation both as regards the method of making it available and as to the incorporation into the arbitration of electronic documents. At the same time, national rules on arbitration have accepted the possibility for the arbitration award to be rendered making use of these electronic methods, even to the point of it being rendered online, as long as a record of its content is available and easy to access.

New technologies are also relevant as regards the formation of the arbitration agreement. In this respect, legislation embodies rules relating to evidence for the existence of the arbitration agreement, which may be in any form that can be reproduced or verified, including electronic format (the evidence does not have to be only on paper). In fact, the introduction of new technologies also poses the issue of whether of the consent of the parties to refer their dispute to arbitration can be verified. This is clear as regards the validity of the incorporation of arbitration clauses by reference, the extension of the effects of the arbitration clause towards non-signatory parties and also in relation to the required form of the agreement, at least in international commercial arbitration.[102]

### *3.3.7. Arbitrators in the eye of the storm*

Arbitration is the heterocompositive tool by means of which the parties in the exercise of their freedom refer their dispute to the arbitrator, who is subject to the arbitration regulation chosen by the parties. Arbitrators, whose activity is

---

100 B. Deffains and T. Gabuthy, 'La resolution électronique des litiges favorise-t-elle le développement de nouvelles strategies de négociation?' (2008) 10 *Négociations* 9, 10.

101 UNCTAD, *Dispute Settlement. International Commercial Arbitration. 5.9 Electronic Arbitration*, 2003 <http://unctad.org/en/docs/edmmisc232add20_en.pdf> accessed 31.12.2012.

102 The modern regulation of this issue in France is a good example of this concern. Article 1507 CPC: '*La convention d'arbitrage n'est soumise à aucune condition de forme*'. In other recent EU Member States' reforms, reference to a certain form is embodied: either a reference to the written condition is included (like in Article 9 of the Spanish LA) or Section 583 of the Austrian ZPO which refers to the validity of arbitration clauses embodied, for instance, in an exchange of emails. Note *infra* section 3.3.3.

governed by party autonomy (though it subject to the conditions in those legal limits imposed by the applicable compulsory rules), will decide the dispute by rendering an award which is imposed on the parties after the arbitration proceedings. That decision is fully enforceable and it has *res judicata* effect.

The role played by the arbitrator is very important: 'the quality of arbitration proceeding depends to a large extent on the quality and skill of the arbitrators chosen'.[103] This pre-eminence of the role played by the arbitrator has meant that his/her power grows in modern arbitration in parallel to the power of the parties.[104] Party autonomy is recognised as the basis for arbitration, but correlatively the arbitrator is granted more power than ever. This major role in the arbitration increasingly puts the arbitrator under public scrutiny, though no tension seems to exist between the growing power of the parties and the similarly growing power of the arbitrators. This last point directly depends on the parties, to the extent that an agreement between the parties on the subject of the dispute clearly makes them become *functus officio*.[105]

In the absence of choice by the parties, the arbitrator may determine the legal regime applicable to the procedure and substance of the dispute. Under the so-called *kompetenz-kompetenz* principle, arbitrators may also determine whether they are competent to hear the dispute. Although in some countries, such as Switzerland, there is still a big debate over this issue, the doctrine of negative *kompetenz-kompetenz* seems to be alive and well.[106]

Thus, arbitrators are in certain cases subject to some criticism concerning their involvement in the increasing costs of arbitration. Their tolerance of excessive procedures or their lack of diligence that signifies their non-fulfillment of their obligation to render awards within a reasonable period may give rise to higher costs. Of course it can be said that seeking truth is always the most relevant issue even if this entails lengthy procedures.[107] This criticism favours, for instance, a trend towards reducing the number of arbitrators, at least as a general rule.[108] In case of absence of determination of the number of

---

103 J.D.M. Lew, L.A. Mistelis and S.M. Kroll, *Comparative International Commercial Arbitration*, Kluwer Law International, The Hague 2003, p. 232.

104 C. Esplugues Mota, 'Sobre algunos desarrollos recientes del arbitraje comercial internacional en Europa', in S. Barona Vilar, *Arbitraje y Justicia en el Siglo XXI, supra* n. 45, p. 195.

105 And this is for the arbitrator himself to establish. This position is implicit in almost all modern jurisdictions. Some case law also exists: in England, for instance, there is the English High Court decision in *Martin Dawes v. Treasure & Son Ltd* [2010] EWHC 3218, or in Singapore, another leading place for arbitration, there is the Singapore High Court decision in *Doshion Ltd v. Sembawang Engineers and Constructors Pte Ltd* [2011] SGHC 46.

106 Federal Supreme Court Judgment of 06.08.2012, case 4A_119/2012, c. 3, *AG v. Y.* (2012) *ASA Bulletin (Association Suisse de l'Arbitrage Bulletin)* 30, p. 864.

107 W.W. Park, *supra* n. 15, p. 26.

108 See J. Kirby, 'With Arbitrators Less Can Be More: Why The Conventional Wisdom of Having Three Arbitrators May Be Over-Rated' (2009) 26 *J. Int. Arb. (Journal of International Arbitration)* 337, 342 ff. Nevertheless, this approach does not fit with results embodied in the *2012 International Arbitration Survey, supra* n. 94, p. 5.

arbitrators by the parties some jurisdictions now uphold the single arbitrator choice.[109]

Arbitrators undertake a professional task for which they are paid some fees by the parties involved in the arbitration. Non-payment by one of the parties is relevant in certain jurisdictions to the extent that it may lead to the party losing the benefit of the arbitration clause. This is the case in Switzerland in domestic arbitrations.[110]

Arbitrators are requested to remain independent and neutral and fully committed to the resolution of the dispute at stake in an expeditious manner.[111] Independence requires a high duty of disclosure towards the parties involved in the arbitration.[112] The relevant role played by arbitrators poses the question of his/her relationship with the parties[113] and, additionally, of the application to him/her of certain mandatory provisions of national character, for instance, as regards sex or religious discrimination.[114] It also raises the issue of their appointment with a growing discussion as regards the acceptance of appointment of arbitrators from outside arbitration institutions' lists as way to tackle certain endogamic practices.[115] In fact, arbitrators are requested to be impartial, but this impartiality runs against reality. Practice shows that in many cases, the same arbitrator is appointed by the same party many times and this creates some doubts as to his impartiality in several arbitration-friendly countries.[116] The issue

---

109 A good example is, in England, the recent judgment of 24.07.2012 in *Itochu Corporation v. Johann M.K. Blumenthal GmbH & Co. KG and another* [2012] EWCA Civ 996.

110 Article 30 of the Concordat on Arbitration and, as of 01.01.2011, Article 378 of the Swiss Federal CCP, and judgment of the Swiss Federal Supreme Court of 21.03.2011, Case 4A_574/2010, *A v. B, C, D* (available at: <www.polyreg.ch/d/informationen/bgeunpubliziert/Jahr_2010/Entscheide_4A_2010/4A.574__2010.html> accessed 27.12.2012).

111 As regards the expected duration of the arbitration, note *2012 International Arbitration Survey, supra* n. 94, p. 32.

112 Consider, for instance, in France, *S.A.J. & P. Avax v. Société Tecnimon* (Cour d'appel de Reims, cour de renvoi, 02.11.2011, no. 10/02888, (2012) *ASA Bulletin* 189), or Civ. 1, of 01.02.2012, Case No. 11-11084 (*Bulletin* 2012, I, no. 14); in both cases the award was set aside because of lack of disclosure of all relevant factors by the arbitrator. Note J.-Ch. Honlet, B. Legum and A.-S. Dufêtre, 'France', in J.A. Carter, *The International Arbitration Review*, 3rd ed., Law Business Research Ltd, London 2012, pp. 195–197, nn. 19 and 20. A similar position has been achieved in the US in *STMicroelectronics, NV v. Credit Suisse Securities (USA) LLC*, 648 F.3d 68 (2d Cir. 2011) taking into account the specialisation of the dispute submitted to arbitration which actually affects the understanding of the duty of disclosure.

113 Note *2012 International Arbitration Survey, supra* n. 94, pp. 6 ff.

114 Note in England the Supreme Court judgment of 27.07.2011 in the case of *Jivraj v. Hashwani* [2011] UKSC 40, where the Supreme Court considered that the relationship between the parties and the arbitrator may not give rise to considering the arbitrator as an employee as regards the application of anti-discrimination labour law legislation.

115 As regards sport arbitration, note A. Rigozzi, 'Challenging awards of the Court of Arbitration for Sport' (2010) 1 *J. Int'l Disp. Settlement (Journal of International Dispute Settlement)* 217, 237–238.

116 In Sweden, for instance, a pro-arbitration approach to this issue was set forth by the Supreme Court on 06.09.2010 in Case No. T 10321-06 (NJA 2010 p. 317, *Korsnäs AB v. AB Fortum*

of independence is so relevant that it has even led to the questioning of an arbitrator on the basis that he belonged to the same religious group as one of the parties.[117]

Last, but not least, a gender issue does exist in arbitration, at least in international commercial arbitration, where only a small percentage of arbitrators are women.[118]

## 3.4. SOME MAJOR VIRTUES OF ARBITRATION UNDER SCRUTINY

Some of the advantages of arbitration and ADR in comparison with State courts have already been stated. Among other virtues, arbitration has traditionally been said to preserve confidentiality, and to be more speedy and less costly. Unfortunately, as the use of arbitration expands, some of these virtues now seem to be under pressure.

### *3.4.1. Confidentiality*

One of the big advantages of ADR and arbitration is confidentiality.[119] This is understood as an element of privacy that entails that all information provided during the development of the arbitration cannot be known, as a matter of principle, beyond the arbitration institution, the parties and the arbitrator, although this also raises the issue of the information as regards third parties that may be involved in the arbitration.[120] Confidentiality refers also to the existence and development of the arbitration itself.

Because of this crucial relevance of confidentiality, national legislators have tried to ensure its protection and the determination of a certain number of guarantees. These guarantees include sanctions for the non-fulfilment of the

*Värme*) and in Case No. T 2448-06, of 19.11.2007 (NJA 2007 p. 841, *Jilkén v. Ericsson*). On the contrary, an arbitration award was set aside by the Court of Appeal in its judgment of 27.09.2011 in Case No. T 1085-11 (*Profilgruppen v. KPMG*, available at: <www.arbitration.sccinstitute.com/files/102/1023796/T%201085-11_eng.pdf#search="KPMG"> accessed 22.12.2012). Note M.C. Rivera, 'Repeat Appointment of Arbitrators by the Same Party or Counsel: A Brief Survey of Institutional Approaches and Decisions' (2012) 15 *Spain Arbitration Review / Revista del Club Español del Arbitraje* 103, 103 ff.

117 P. Rescigno, 'Rapporti associative, indipendenza e ricusazione dell'arbitro (il caso dell'Opus Dei)' (2012) XXII *Rivista dell'Arbitrato* 263, 269 ff.

118 See L. Greenwood and C.M. Baker, 'Getting A Better Balance on International Arbitration Tribunals' (2012) 28 *Arbitration International* 653, 653 ff.

119 A.B. Badawi, 'Interpretative Preferences and the Limits of the New Formalism' (2008–09) 6 *Berkeley Bus. L.J.* (*Berkeley Business Law Journal*) 1, 52.

120 Note S. Azzali, 'Intervento alla Tavola rotunda "Transparency *vs* Confidentiality: la riservatezza dell'arbitrato e i diritti di informazione dei terzi"' (2012) XXII *Rivista dell'Arbitrato* 819, 821 ff.

obligation (or duty, depending on who breaches it), and ensuring that the arbitrator cannot be compelled to give evidence in further proceedings. Unfortunately, in practice, the preservation of confidentiality is difficult and entails many perils for the institution.[121]

### *3.4.2. Speediness*

The speediness of arbitration is one of the great benefits of the institution in comparison to State courts. This is particularly important in relation to certain categories of dispute, and it is for this reason that most national legal texts emphasise the need for speed.

The length of the proceedings will be determined by the parties, who can agree on the maximum duration of the procedure and set forth certain specific activities or steps of the proceedings. In the absence of an agreement *inter partes* regarding the deadline, it will usually be established by the arbitration institution or the arbitrator.[122]

Speediness is additionally promoted by the fact that arbitration proceedings have a single instance. The arbitration award is final and fully enforceable from the moment it is rendered. The only possibility of avoiding the award is by entering an action of nullity, which in no way may be understood as an appeal against the award. This is one of the big benefits of arbitration, though by certain sectors it is also considered one of the biggest criticisms. Some practice also shows this fact.[123]

---

121 In England, for instance, confidentiality is considered an implied obligation of the parties (note *Emmott v. Michael Wilson & Partners Ltd* [2008] EWCA Civ 184), though it seems not to be unanimously accepted (*Associated Electric and Gas Insurance Services Ltd v. European Reinsurance Co. of Zurich* [2003] UKPC 11). In France this implied obligation also seems to exist (*Aïta v. Ojjeh* (1986) *Revue de l'Arbitrage* 583; *Bleustein v. Société True North et Société FCB International* (2003) *Revue de l'Arbitrage* 189). The situation in France is somewhat different after the enactment of the new International Arbitration Regulation of 2011. In domestic arbitration, this implicit obligation exists in accordance with Article 1464(4) CPC, whereas it does not exist as regards international arbitration (Article 1506 CPC). In comparison with the previous two situations, in Singapore the need for confidentiality has been fully endorsed by the Singapore High Court in its judgment of 15.06.2009 in *AAY v. AAZ* [2011] 1 SLR 1093 and more recently in the case in *AZT v. AZV* [2012] SGHC 116 (note M. Hwang SC and N. Thio, 'A Contextual Approach to the Obligation of Confidentiality in Arbitration in Singapore – An Analysis of the Decision of the Singapore High Court in AAY and Others v. AAZ' (2012) 28 *Arbitration International* 225, 227 ff.). This debate over the existence of this implicit obligation exists in many other jurisdictions. In Hong Kong, section 18(1) of the Arbitration Ordinance 2011 ensures this obligation of confidentiality for the parties and in the Phillipines, it is ensured by Section 23 of the Alternative Dispute Resolution Act 2004.

122 Average duration is said to be 1720 months. Note *CIArb Costs of International Arbitration Survey 2011*, p. 12 <www.ciarb.org/conferences/costs/2011/09/28/CIArb%20costs%20of%20 International%20Arbitration%20Survey%202011.pdf> accessed 27.12.2012).

123 Some very interesting cases as regards the power of the court to vacate the award because the arbitrator did not reach a certain result are found in the US: from the rather flexible approach

### 3.4.3. *Reduced costs*

Cost efficiency is usually referred to as one of the cornerstones of arbitration as a method of dispute resolution. Nevertheless, as practice increasingly shows, this is not always that clear. In certain sectors, the development of arbitration has led to growing costs, which must be paid by those who refer their dispute to arbitration. This fact raises concerns about the impact that the inability of one of the parties to bear its part of these costs has on his/her right of access to justice.[124]

These costs usually include the fees of the arbitrator and the costs incurred in the administration of the arbitration and its development. Against this general reflection it is said that the matter of reduced costs is more a question of relativity than of the value of the money spent during the arbitration in absolute terms.[125]

However, the whole idea of arbitration as an affordable device is now under some criticism.[126] Growing reference to arbitration has entailed a major degree of formalism in its development, mainly regarding the proceedings: jurisdictional issues are almost a general rule, pre-hearing discovery, post-hearing problems[127] and an increasing feeling of unauthorised practice of law, which has given rise, for instance, to a growing number of awards under scrutiny before State courts. These, among other reasons, imply an increase in costs.[128] Some of this increase seems to be due to the costs involved in the taking of evidence. Evidentiary excess may entail higher costs for the parties. The arbitrator has an important role to play in this area mainly as regards the handling of requests for production of documents by the parties. However, a mutual effort by all those involved in arbitration is necessary to overcome this peril.[129]

---

followed in *Wilko v. Swan*, 346 US 427 (1953), to a much more strict position maintained in *Lloyds v. Lagstein*, 607 F.3d 634 (9th Cir., 2010), 9 U.S.C. §9, *Hall Street Associates LLC v. Mattel, Inc.*, 552 US 576 (2008), *Stolt-Nielsen S.A. v. AnimalFeeds International Corp.*, 130 S. Ct. 1758 (2010), or *Medicine Shoppe International, Inc. v. Turner Investments, Inc.*, 614 F3d 485 (8th Cir. 2010). An interesting analysis of this last decision may be found in S.I. Strong, 'Does Class Arbitration "Change the Nature" of Arbitration? Stolt-Nielsen, AT&T, and a Return to First Principles' (2012) 17 *Harv. Negot. L. Rev. (Harvard Negotiation Law Review)* 201, 202 ff.

124 See F.-X. Train, 'Impécuniosité et accès à la justice dans l'arbitrage international (à propos de l'arrêt de la Cour d'appel de Paris du 17 novembre 2011 dans l'affaire *LP c/ Pirelli*)' (2012) *Revue de l'Arbitrage* 267, 299 ff.

125 *CIArb Costs of International Arbitration Survey 2011*, *supra* n. 122, pp. 11 ff.

126 Note, for instance, H.S. Noyes, 'If You (Re)Build It They Will Come: Contracts To Remake The Rules Of Litigation in Arbitration's Image' (2007) 30 *Harv. J.L. & Pub. Pol'y (Harvard Journal of Law & Public Policy)* 579, 585 ff.

127 *2012 International Arbitration Survey*, *supra* n. 94, pp. 20 ff.

128 T.J. Stipanowich, *supra* n. 52, pp. 9–22.

129 Note T.J. Stipanowich (editor-in-chief), C.E. Von Kann and D. Rothman (ass. eds.), *The College of Commercial Arbitrators Protocols for Expeditious, Cost-Effective Commercial*

Unpredictable and unforeseen costs also always arise. The fact is that the costs associated with arbitration have been escalating for a long time, which implies a growing lack of efficiency. The truth is that the issue of costs becomes more and more relevant when the seat of the arbitration is to be selected by the parties.[130] A sort of race to the most favourable arbitration seat may exist because of the fact that for the same dispute costs can vary depending on the seat of the arbitration.[131]

The costs of arbitration are allocated between the parties. Figures state that in a significant number of cases (80%), arbitrators tend to allocate costs in accordance with the result of the arbitration. Two methods are said to be used: '"costs follow the event" (i.e., the unsuccessful party pays all) (50%) or "apportionment of costs by the tribunal" (30%)'.[132] The first of these two methods is the most usual in Asia and Europe, whereas in other areas of the world responses seem to vary.[133] This approach appears to be broadly accepted by those involved in arbitration.[134]

## 3.5. CONTROL OF ARBITRATION BY NATIONAL COURTS

The analysis of arbitration nowadays shows an important change in the attitude of State courts towards arbitration in many jurisdictions. A growing number of countries consider themselves to be arbitration friendly. This involves at least two general conditions: firstly, a flexible regulation of arbitration embodied in national law; and secondly, a positive attitude towards arbitration maintained by national courts. A certain paradox is said to exist insofar as arbitration 'seeks the cooperation of the very public authorities from which it wants to free itself'.[135]

This positive attitude towards arbitration implies, on the one hand, that a cooperative attitude towards arbitration is now apparent in many courts and leads, on the other, to the preservation of the principle of the minimum intervention of State courts in arbitration. This positive attitude towards arbitration is very much apparent at the stage prior to the rendering of the

---

*Arbitration Key Action Steps for Business Users, Counsel, Arbitrators and Arbitration Provider Institutions*, 2010, p. 13 (available at: <www.thecca.net/CCA_Protocols.pdf> accessed 23.12.2012).

130 In practice, it is interesting to realise that the cost of arbitration tends to be higher in civil law countries than in common law nations – around 13% higher – and in the specific case of Europe, arbitration in the UK is said to be 18% lower than in the continent. *CIArb Costs of International Arbitration Survey 2011*, *supra* n. 122, p. 2.

131 *Ibid.*, p. 14.

132 *2012 International Arbitration Survey*, *supra* n. 94, p. 40.

133 *Ibid.*, p. 40.

134 *Ibid.*, p. 40.

135 J. Paulsson, *supra* n. 6, p. 2.

arbitration award as regards two different but interrelated areas: the setting aside of arbitration awards and the recognition of foreign arbitration awards.

As regards the first issue, it is usually accepted that the award rendered can be solely challenged on very limited grounds which, in addition, are procedural grounds (they do not refer to the merits of the award), are interpreted in a very restrictive manner, and usually leave open enforcement of the arbitration award while the action is pending. Arbitration is a single instance procedure. There is no appeal feasible. Only the action of annulment for setting aside awards is available and exclusively on the basis of certain limited procedural grounds; and this is a different procedure to arbitration, with a different object and with a court hearing as the action. Understanding arbitration as a single-stage proceeding promotes speediness and, consequently, entails a smaller cost for the parties.[136] The existence of a single 'shot' thus becomes one of the elements on which arbitration stands and one of the facts that favour speediness, though a request for limitation of the length of annulment proceedings and a more detailed procedure for appeal of arbitral awards seems to exist.[137]

But this seems to be starting to change. The principle of finality seems to be under some pressure in some countries. Despite its general acceptance in an extremely arbitration-friendly country like England,[138] section 69 of the English Arbitration Act 1996 provides (on an opt-out basis) for a limited right of appeal on certain points of English law.[139] With the same philosophy (on an opt-in basis) but with a much broader scope, the Arbitration Rules of the Spanish Court of Arbitration of March 2011 set forth provisions on an internal appeal mechanism: Article 39 is entitled '*Segunda instancia arbitral*' (second arbitration instance). This appeal mechanism vests an appellate arbitral tribunal with the

136 Nevertheless, interpretation of these grounds – in many cases in line with Article 34 of the Model Law – is in the end dependent on the court. And this may give place to different interpretations. Note for instance the judgment of the Ontario Court of Appeal of 04.10.2011 in *The United Mexican States v. Cargill Inc.*, 2011 ONCA 622, which is interesting insofar as it refers to the *Dallah* case (*infra* n. 146); see paras. [36] to [38].

137 For instance, some countries have not objected to an appeal entered after the expiration of the deadline for the exercise of the action: e.g. judgment of the Swiss Federal Court of 18.06.2012 in Case 4A_488/2011, *X v. UCI, CONI & FCI* in (available at: <www.polyreg.ch/d/informationen/bgeunpubliziert/Jahr_2011/Entscheide_4A_2011/4A.488__2011.html> accessed 28.12.2012).

138 Consider for instance the judgment of the Commercial Court of 11.10.2012 in *Petrochemical Industries Co. (KSC) v. Dow Chemical Co.* [2012] EWHC 2739 (Comm).

139 Note for instance, *Wuhan Ocean Economic & Technical Cooperation Co. Ltd and another v. Schiffharts-Gesselschaft 'Hansa Murcia' mbH & Co. KG* [2012] EWHC 3104; *Mary Harvey v. Motor Insurers' Bureau* (QBD (Merc) (Manchester), Claim No: 0MA40077, 21.12.2011, unreported) and *Shell Egypt West Manzala GmbH v. Dana Gas Egypt Ltd* [2009] EWHC 2097 (Comm). And never as regards factical issues, even if the parties so agree, note in England, *Guangzhou Dockyards Co. Ltd v. ENE Aegiali I* [2010] EWHC 2826. In Singapore, on the contrary, the wrong application of choice-of-law rules has been considered not to be a sufficient ground to set aside an arbitration award: see *Quarella SpA v. Scelta Marble Australia Pty Ltd* [2012] SGHC 166.

power to review the award rendered, which now should be considered as a sort of first instance award; it also accepts, under certain circumstances, the possibility of hearing new evidence. Of course, the parties could accept this in their contract, stating the possibility for review by certain courts in specific circumstances, but this seems to be fully rejected as a matter of principle.[140]

Not necessarily in contradiction with this discussion, there is a growing amount of legislation that endorses the right of the parties to waive their right to set aside an arbitration award.[141] This issue is also considered in national case law.[142]

The second issue refers to the recognition and enforcement of foreign arbitration awards. In this realm the New York Convention of 1958 is the basic text to be taken into account. Though the Convention has gained broad application worldwide,[143] some problems still remain: 'diverging solutions to questions such as the requirements applicable to a request for enforcement, fees, levies, taxes or duties to be paid in connection with such an application, correction of defects in the applications, the time period for applying for recognition and enforcement, and the procedures and competent courts for recourse against a decision refusing to enforce an arbitral award'.[144] Furthermore, in some major jurisdictions, some misinteraction between the New York Convention and national rules is said to exist.[145] In addition, some divergences also appear as regards the existing attitude towards enforcement of foreign arbitration awards: either because the grounds embodied in the

---

140 For instance, in the US, *Hall Street Associates LLC v. Mattel Inc.* (2008) 552 US 576 (Sup. Ct.). See I.M. Ten Cate, 'International Arbitration and the Ends of Appellate Review' (2012) 44 *New York University Journal of International Law and Politics* 1109, 1111 and 1156 ff.

141 This is the case, for instance, of Article 1522 CPC in France which actually states that: 'The parties may, by specific agreement, waive at any time their right to challenge the award'. Unlike in Belgium (Article 1717(4) CJ), Switzerland (Article 192(1) PILA) and Sweden (Article 51 AA), this possibility is not only reserved for foreigners.

142 Note in the US, *Hoeft v. MVL Group*, 343 F.3d 57 (2003) (2d Cir US). Also note in Canada, *Noble China Inc. v. Lei* (1998) 42 O.R. (3d) 69; 42 BLR (2d) 262; and in New Zealand, *Methanex Motunui Ltd & Methanex Waitara Valley Ltd v. Joseph Spellman* [2004] 1 NZLR 95 (NZCA).

143 UNCITRAL, *Report on the survey relating to the legislative implementation of the Convention on the Recognition and Enforcement of Foreign Arbitral Awards (New York, 1958)*, Docs. A/CN.9/656 (available at: <http://daccess-dds-ny.un.org/doc/UNDOC/GEN/V08/541/11/PDF/V0854111.pdf?OpenElement> accessed 28.12.2012) and A/CN.9/656/Add.1 (available at: <http://daccess-dds-ny.un.org/doc/UNDOC/GEN/V08/541/30/PDF/V0854130.pdf?OpenElement> accessed 28.12.2012).

144 *Ibid.*, p. 7, n. 33.

145 Like in the US as regards the NYC and the FAA. See *Monegasque de Reassurances S.A.M. (Monde Re) v. Nak Naftogaz of Ukraine*, 311 F.3d 488 (2d Cir. 2002), *Termorio S.A. E.S.P. v. Electrificiadora del Atlantico S.A. E.S.P.*, 421 F. Supp. 2d 87, 103–04 (D.D.C. 2006) or *Figueiredo Ferraz e Engenharia de Projecto Ltda. v. Republic of Peru*, 2001 WL 6188497 (2d Cir. Dec. 14, 2011). That may give rise to *forum non conveniens* dismissals of actions seeking enforcement of foreigna arbitration awards.

Convention are interpreted in a different way by national courts[146] or due to the fact that grounds not included in the Convention are accepted by courts to deny recognition. In any case, the Convention has worked rather well and it is precisely this fact which has fuelled a trend for the parties wishing to circumvent arbitration to obtain a default judgment from a court and then seek its enforcement.[147]

In addition to these puzzling elements, a clear pro-arbitration signal has been sent in certain jurisdictions by endorsing the enforcement of purely declaratory awards, something not accepted until recently.[148] This can further be seen by the existence of a trend in certain jurisdictions to recognise arbitration awards which have been set aside in their country of origin.[149]

---

146 Consider A.G. Maurer, *The Public Policy Exception under the New York Convention*, Juris, Huntington 2012, pp. 73 ff. A paradigmatic example of the existing conflicting views as to the enforcement of foreign awards is the English Supreme Court judgment of 03.11.2010 in *Dallah Real Estate and Tourism Holding Co. v. The Ministry of Religious Affairs, Government of Pakistan* [2010] UKSC 46 which rejected enforcement of a French arbitration award on the grounds of section 103(2)(b) of the Arbitration Act 1996 (drafted in terms similar to the Article V(1)(a) *in fine* of the New York Convention), considering that Pakistan was not party to the arbitration agreement. On the contrary, several months later, on 17.02.2011, the Cour d'appel of Paris (Pôle 1 – Ch. 1 in *Gouvernement du Pakistan, Ministère des affaires religieuses v. Société Dallah Real Estate and Tourism Holding Company* (2011) *Revue de l'Arbitrage* 286), ruled that the arbitration panel was competent to render the award and granted enforcement to it in France. See J. Grierson and M. Taok, 'Dallah: Conflicting Judgments from the U.K. Supreme Court and the Paris Cour d'Appel' (2011) 28 *J. Int. Arb. (Journal of International Arbitration)* 407, 414 ff. Whereas England and France are clearly arbitration-friendly States and situations like this may appear rather uncommon, in other countries lacking that label the situation may be highly confusing. Russia is one of those countries in which, for instance, the public policy exceptions have been interpreted in a rather convoluted manner. Note in this respect, D.V. Tapola, 'Enforcement of Foreign Arbitral Awards: Application of the Public Policy Rule in Russia' (2006) 22 *Arbitration International* 151, 160. Similar problems as regards the understanding or public policy are found in certain Asian countries; see F. Junita, 'Public Policy Exception in International Commercial Arbitration – Promoting Uniform Model Norms' (2012) 5 *Contemp. Asia Arb. J. (Contemporary Asia Arbitration Journal)* 45, 53 ff. New challenges may arise in the future in other integrated areas like the EU; see in this respect, G.A. Bermann, 'Navigating EU Law and the Law of International Arbitration' (2012) 28 *Arbitration International* 397, 425 ff.

147 Note, for instance, the High Court of Singapore decision of 18.04.2012 in *Giant Light Metal Technology (Kunshan) Co. Ltd v. Aksa Far East Pte Ltd* [2012] SGHCR 2.

148 Consider the English Commercial Court judgment of 29.09.2011 in *African Fertilizers and Chemicals NIG Ltd (Nigeria) v. BD Shipsnavo GmbH & Co Reederei KG* [2011] EWHC 2452 (Comm), or the Court of Appeal decision of 24.01.2012 in *West Tankers Inc v. Allianz SpA v. Generali Assicurazione Generali SpA* [2012] EWCA Civ 27, at [36]. See on this, A. Moody and C. Forsaith, 'Enforcing Declaratory Awards as a Judgment of the English Court – An Effective Weapon If Fighting in Multiple Jurisdictions' (2012) 28 *Arbitration International* 567, 570–571.

149 For instance, in France, note the judgment of the Cour de Cassation, 1st Civil Chamber, of 23.03.1994, *Hilmarton* (1994) *Revue de l'Arbitrage* 327, with note by Ch. Jarosson; and Cour de Cassation, 1st Chamber, of 29.06.2007, *Putrabali* (2007) *Revue de l'Arbitrage* 507, with note by E. Gaillard. Similar acceptance is found in the Netherlands: e.g. the Amsterdam Court of Appeal judgment of 29.04.2009 in *Yukos Capital v. Rosneft*, referred to in the English Court of Appeal judgment of 27.06.2012 in *Yukos Capital SARL v. OJSC Rosneft Oil Co. (No 2)* [2012] EWCA Civ 855, [2012] WLR (D) 186, at [19] to [22].

## 4. THE WAY AHEAD FOR ADR: MEDIATION AND CONCILIATION

As has already been mentioned, several different devices coexist under the umbrella of the ADR movement, mediation, conciliation and arbitration being the most well known in many countries.[150] Arbitration has so far been the most usual one but as a result of the increase in costs and duration of arbitration proceedings and the accompanying increasing level of formalism, we seem to have reached a turning point in favour of mediation.[151] Thus, in Europe where only 11% of all EU companies have ever used an ADR scheme – with 18% having used a court – '[m]ediation style ADR schemes (23%) have been more widely used than arbitration style schemes (10%)'.[152] Reasons for this shift are mainly cost and speed. For instance, a domestic business dispute in Europe needs an average of 17.8 months for courts to resolve it, whereas it takes 10 months with arbitration and only 7.3 via mediation. These figures are similar in cross-border cases: the court needs 15.2 months, arbitration 8 months and mediation 5.8 months.[153]

The same pattern reappears as regards costs. Whereas a domestic dispute before national courts costs €11,500, only €5,500 is needed if the same dispute is taken to arbitration and only €2,700 when referred to mediation. In the case of cross-border business disputes, companies spend an average of €13,000 when they use a court, €6,100 when they refer the dispute to mediation and €21,300 when they use arbitration to solve their dispute.[154] This is clearly one of the factors that has led to the current blossoming of mediation.

The support given by national and international legislators to mediation has grown steadily and permits us to assert, without any doubt, that mediation is nowadays becoming the most fashionable ADR device. But, as happened with arbitration some time ago, mediation is now at a crossroads, facing both opportunities and perils.[155]

---

150 See F. Ben Mrad, 'Définir la médiation parmi les modes alternatifs de régulation des conflits' (2012) 170 *Informations sociales* 11, 13 ff.

151 As regards the comparison between mediation and arbitration, note E. Carroll and K. Mackie, *International Mediation – The Art of Business Diplomacy*, 2nd ed., Kluwer Law International / Tottel Publishing, Alphen aan den Rijn / West Sussex 2006, pp. 69–70.

152 European Commission, *supra* n. 8, p. 7.

153 *Ibid.*

154 *Ibid.*, p. 8.

155 J. Nolan-Haley, 'Mediation: The "New Arbitration"' (2012) 12 *Harv. Negot. L. Rev. (Harvard Negotiation Law Review)* 61, 91 ff.

### 4.1. MEDIATION AND CONCILIATION? OR CONCILIATION AND MEDIATION?

For many centuries arbitration was maintained either as the only alternative to the judicial process or coexisted with conciliation. In many jurisdictions no reference to using mediation to solve or manage disputes was made for a long time. Additionally, conciliation showed that it could easily coexist, at least in theory, with State civil procedure. We stress 'in theory' because despite its historical roots, in too many cases conciliation became a sort of first step preceding and necessary to the initiation of civil procedure before State courts, one that did not really give rise to any true deal between the parties due to the general absence of a culture of negotiation in many Western societies.

Nowadays, this situation seems to have changed. The rising star in the ADR firmament is mediation. Because of its enormous flexibility and the strong support that it receives from national and international institutions, mediation is taking the lead as the main device to solve or manage any kind of dispute. The EU provides a good example of this support for mediation. The enactment of the Directive 2008/52/EC of the European Parliament and the Council of 21 May 2008 on certain aspects of mediation in civil and commercial matters[156] aims to combine the establishment of a clear and broad legal framework for mediation in Europe with the necessary flexibility for enhancing the proper functioning of the institution: the so-called 'diversity-consistency' dilemma.[157] In the following pages we will take the EU as the reference when approaching the institution of mediation.[158]

Mediation and conciliation tend to be confused in many legal systems. Mediation may be similar in some aspects to conciliation but in fact it is a different institution. It could be said that conciliation and mediation are two species within the same genus. Mediation is an informal way of solving disputes notwithstanding that it has only recently been accepted in many jurisdictions. Not for nothing it could be said that mediation implies a certain modernisation and improvement of the old institution of conciliation, with the incorporation of certain specific parameters that refer, among other facts, to the formation of the mediator and his/her role, and to the absence of formalism and the extreme flexibility for the parties that it entails.[159]

---

156 *OJ* L 136, of 24.05.2008. Note on the Directive, C. Esplugues, J.L. Iglesias and G. Palao, *Civil and Commercial Mediation in Europe. National Mediation Rules and Procedures*, vol. 1, Intersentia, Cambridge 2013.

157 N. Alexander, *International and Comparative Mediation Legal Perspectives*, Wolters Kluwer, Alphen aan den Rijn 2009, pp. 75–76.

158 The use of the institution in Europe varies steadily from country to country; see European Commission, *supra* n. 8, p. 12.

159 F. Ben Mrad, *supra* n. 150, p. 13.

This confusion is basically due to the fact that both of them are ultimately dependent on the will of the parties, in that it is up to them to engage in mediation and conciliation, to stick with those processes, and finally to reach a settlement. In both mediation and conciliation, the parties ask a third person to help them to resolve their dispute, and it is the role played by this person that actually differentiates these institutions. The mediator works with techniques to bring the parties closer together. He/she intervenes, helps, cooperates and collaborates with them, but makes no suggestion to the parties as regards the solution to be reached. As a matter of fact it is not possible for the mediator to offer solutions to the parties, unless so requested by them. The best solution is the one reached by the parties and which, among other benefits, is more likely to be voluntarily fulfilled. On the other hand, the conciliator hears the parties and makes settlement proposals to them. A voluntary settlement between the parties is also reached, but their level of involvement in its achievement is much more limited than in mediation.[160]

In many EU Member States, for instance, a clear understanding about what mediation is and what it implies for the parties and the legal system as a whole has long been lacking. In too many EU countries no clear boundaries have historically been drawn by the legislator or in practice between mediation and other institutions like conciliation or transaction. Even today, after the implementation of Directive 2008/52/EC in Member States, this confusion still remains in some jurisdictions. A very significant fact is, for instance, that in Estonia the law transposing the Directive into national law is called the Act 'on conciliation procedure'.[161]

France is historically an excellent example of this situation of confusion.[162] Until the implementation of Directive 2008/52/EC in 2012, mediation and conciliation had traditionally been used as synonymous,[163] and even nowadays some doubts and misunderstanding seem to persist.[164] This is not an isolated situation in Europe. This absence of a clear-cut concept of mediation is also reproduced in some other EU Member States such as the Czech Republic, where even today differences between mediation and conciliation are not clearly established,[165] or Greece, where confusion between mediation and other ADR

160 *Ibid.*, pp. 13–15.

161 Law no. 562 of 03.12.2009, on conciliation procedure (*Lepitusseadus*), passed 18.11.2009, published in RT I No. 2009, 59, 385.

162 Note J. Joly-Hurard, *Conciliation et médiation judiciaires*, PU Aix-Marseille, Aix-en-Provence 2003, p. 19 ff.

163 E. Guinchard and M. Boucaron-Nardetto, 'France', in C. Esplugues, J.L. Iglesias and G. Palao, *supra* n. 156, p. 132.

164 *Ibid.*, p. 134.

165 M. Pauknerová, J. Brodec and M. Pfeiffer, 'Czech Republic', in C. Esplugues, J.L. Iglesias and G. Palao, *supra* n. 156, p. 102.

devices like conciliation existed historically.[166] Furthermore, there are some countries, for example Scandinavian countries, where the presence of a long-lasting and fully consolidated tradition of conflict management is apparent, but it is not clear that the legislator has fully understood what mediation is, or the institution of mediation actually receives a somewhat negative meaning or is infrequently used. What is more, mediation is in too many cases considered synonymous with conciliation or other ADR devices.[167]

This situation is also apparent in other jurisdictions and texts. For instance, the wording of Article 1(3) of the UNCITRAL Model Law on International Commercial Conciliation clearly shows existing difficulties in relation to the verification of the exact meaning of mediation as opposed to other ADR devices like conciliation, and the presence of different legal understandings of it.[168]

Consequences arising out of this confusion may vary from country to country depending on several different factors: their legal tradition, the existence of a pro-mediation position, or the awareness of judges, lawyers and other legal operators of mediation and of its potential. In any case, in recent years the support of mediation has to some extent overshadowed conciliation. It seems that such an expansion of support may also affect arbitration in the future.

## 4.2. NOTION OF MEDIATION

Mediation is a device based on the intervention of a neutral third person, external to the dispute, who assumes the role of meeting the parties and helping them to solve their disagreements. Article 3(a)(I) of Directive 2008/52/EC on mediation states that mediation must be understood as 'a structured process, however named or referred to, whereby two or more parties to a dispute attempt by themselves, on a voluntary basis, to reach an agreement on the settlement of their dispute with the assistance of a mediator'.[169]

The success of mediation directly relies on party autonomy. It is for the parties involved to decide to actually refer their dispute to mediation before a claim is lodged before a State court (out-of-court mediation), and it is for them to take the dispute to mediation once the procedure has been started with or without

166 V. Kourtis and E. Sivena, 'Greece', in C. Esplugues, J.L. Iglesias and G. Palao, *supra* n. 156, pp. 194 and 196 ff.

167 L. Ervo and L. Sippel, 'Scandinavian Countries', in C. Esplugues, J.L. Iglesias and G. Palao, *supra* n. 156, pp. 376 ff.

168 '1.3. For the purposes of this Law, "conciliation" means a process, whether referred to by the expression conciliation, mediation or an expression of similar import, whereby parties request a third person or persons ("the conciliator") to assist them in their attempt to reach an amicable settlement of their dispute arising out of or relating to a contractual or other legal relationship. The conciliator does not have the authority to impose upon the parties a solution to the dispute.'

169 Recital 10 Directive 2008/52/CE.

invitation by the court to do so (court-annexed mediation). It is also for the parties to ensure its success and to reach an agreement after the exchange of information between them and the mediator has taken place, assuming that, as a general rule, the negotiation arises from an absence of trust between the parties. Mediation offers a high level of control by the parties and consequently enhances certainty and legal security[170] and because of that it favours a high level of voluntary enforcement of the settlement reached by the parties.[171] At the same time the facilitative condition that accompanies mediation makes easier the preservation of 'an amicable and sustainable relationship between the parties'.[172] All these benefits, which are manifest even when it comes to purely domestic mediations, 'become even more pronounced in situations displaying cross-border elements'.[173]

Only in certain situations which are directly linked to certain specific matters in which there is either a weak party or a relevant public interest, are compulsory schemes of mediation envisaged. Thus this direct link between the will of the parties and mediation is sometimes superseded in certain countries where compulsory schemes of mediation have existed or exist as regards some very specific disputes or areas of law: Austria,[174] Germany,[175] Romania[176] and Malta[177] are examples of such schemes.

## 4.3. PRINCIPLES OF MEDIATION

Mediation rests on several basic principles that shape the institution. Among them, voluntariness, disposition, equality, confidentiality or impartiality and neutrality of mediators may be stressed as being very important for both understanding mediation and enhancing its future development.

### *4.3.1. Voluntariness*

Despite the existence of certain mandatory schemes, voluntariness is one of the basic principles on which the institution rests; mediation depends on party

170 M. Cover and E. Lecchi, 'Mediating Competition Law Cases' (2008) 74 *Arbitration* 121, 122 ff.
171 Recital 6 Directive 2008/52/EC.
172 *Ibid.*
173 *Ibid.*
174 U. Frauenberger-Pfeiler, 'Austria', in C. Esplugues, J.L. Iglesias and G. Palao, *supra* n. 156, p. 9.
175 §15a EGZPO. I. Bach and U.P. Gruber, 'Germany', in C. Esplugues, J.L. Iglesias and G. Palao, *supra* n. 156, p. 163.
176 Article 2(3) Act 192/2006 on Mediation and Organization of the mediator profession, *Official Monitor* no. 441 of 22.05.2006.
177 T. Sciberras Camilleri, 'Malta', in C. Esplugues, J.L. Iglesias and G. Palao, *supra* n. 156, pp. 294–295.

autonomy. That means that as a matter of principle no one must be compelled to take their dispute to mediation, nor to remain in the mediation or to reach a settlement on the dispute at stake.[178]

### *4.3.2. Disposition*

Mediation is linked to party autonomy and refers to all disputes over relationships that involve rights available for the parties. Consequently, parties to a dispute can withdraw from the mediation at any point. Disposition also signifies that the parties are themselves in charge of the process and that they can organise it as they wish and terminate it at any time without any obligation to reach an agreement.[179] This flexibility favours mediation as an easily tailored device fully adapted to the needs and expectations of the parties involved.[180]

### *4.3.3. Equality*

Certainly parties can organise the mediation the way they wish, but those persons who refer their dispute to mediation and who intervene in the proceedings must have their equality of opportunities fully guaranteed for its entire duration. Additionally, the parties must always have available the opportunity to take their disputes to State courts in case the mediation does not succeed for any reason. In fact one of the big concerns that mediation has traditionally faced is to what extent it poses a threat to the value of justice.[181] These two previously stated ideas tend to run against this feeling.

### *4.3.4. Confidentiality*

One of the basic principles on which mediation rests is confidentiality. It is generally accepted as 'an essential ingredient in mediation',[182] but its exact meaning, content and level of exigence is not homogenous and well understood and can generate a significant level of controversy.[183]

---

178 See on this last issue, the judgment of the English Court of Appeal of 23.04.2012 in *Swain Mason & others v. Mills & Reeve (a firm)* [2012] EWCA Civ 498.

179 Recital 13 Directive 2008/52/EC.

180 R.A.B. Bush and J.P. Folger, 'Mediation and Social Justice: Risks and Opportunities' (2012) 27 *Ohio St. J. on Disp. Resol. (Ohio State Journal on Dispute Resolution)* 1, 4 and 7 ff.

181 *Ibid.*, pp. 3 ff.

182 Note J.J. Alfini, S.B. Press, J.R. Sternlight *et al.*, *Mediation Theory and Practice*, 2nd ed., LexisNexis, Newark 2006, p. 205.

183 In this respect, J. Coben and P. Thompson, 'Disputing Irony: A Systematic Look at Litigation about Mediation' (2006) 11 *Harv. Negot. L. Rev. (Harvard Negotiation Law Review)* 43, 57 ff. For instance, in England, see *Smith v. Weiss* [2002] All ER (D) 356; *Venture Investment v. Hall* [2005] EWHC 1227 (Ch); *Cumbria Waste Management Ltd v. Baines Wilson* [2008] EWHC 786 (QB) (HH Judge Frances Kirkham sitting as a High Court Judge); *Carleton v. Strutt & Parker* [2008] EWHC 424 at [72]; noted on this point by J Sorabji (2008) 27 CJQ 288, 291–2; or

Confidentiality is important for the parties and is also essential for the mediator.[184] Mediation must be confidential and that has a double consequence that is not always very well developed in the several national mediation acts. Firstly, for the sake of achieving a settlement of the dispute submitted to mediation, everybody involved in the process must be free to state and defend his/her position in the process of achieving an agreement. That necessarily entails that all those who are involved in mediation must be silent as regards the mediation and its content and development, both during the mediation and once it has come to an end,[185] that is, as regards the information generated within the mediation. The principle of confidentiality of mediation proceedings refers both to out-of-court and court-annexed mediation. It enables the parties to explore a settlement without any additional distress. The fear of undesired use of information or of one's own settlement proposals or any other statements usually prevents the parties from free expression. Owing to the guarantee of confidentiality, the parties may discuss their matters freely, without fear that their arguments might potentially be availed of in other situations. Secondly, this raises the issue of 'the competence and compellability of mediators as witnesses in formal legal proceedings'[186] – of mediators and other participants in the mediation procedure, we could say. In any case, there are concerns about the meaning of confidentiality in the several jurisdictions, in that what confidentiality means, covers and signifies may vary from one country to another.[187]

The effectiveness of this principle of confidentiality makes it necessary to clearly know when the mediation starts, since the confidentiality obligation refers to the future (once the mediation is finished) but not to the moment prior to the commencement of the mediation.[188]

---

*Brown v. Rice* [2007] EWHC 625 (Ch), Stuart Isaacs QC, which deal with different aspects of this issue and which does not always maintain a similar rationale. Note too, stressing its dependence on party autonomy, *Farm Assist Limited (in liquidation) v. The Secretary of State for the Environment, Food and Rural Affairs (No 2)* [2009] EWHC 1102 (TCC); [2009] BLR 399; 125 Con LR 154.

184 Note E.M. Henke, *Confidentiality in the Model Law and the European Mediation Directive. A Comparison of Solutions Offered in the Mediation Directive and the Model Law on Conciliation with Examination of the Actual Situation in Selected Civil and Common Law Countries*, Grin, Munich 2011, pp. 44 ff.; Ph. Howell-Richardson, 'The European Mediation Directive and Some Thoughts on the Principles Involved in Dealing with the Problems Surrounding Mediation Confidentiality', in Association for International Arbitration (ed.), *The New EU Directive on Mediation. First Insights*, Maklu, Apeldoorn 2008, pp. 47 ff.

185 N. Alexander, *supra* n. 157, p. 246.

186 N. Andrews, 'The Duty to Consider Mediation: Salvaging Value from the European Mediation Directive', in N. Trocker and A. De Luca, *supra* n. 12, p. 33.

187 See, as regards the specific situation in California, R. Callahan, 'Mediation Confidentiality: For California Litigants: Why Should Mediation Confidentiality be a Function of the Court in Which the Litigation is Pending?', (2012) 12 *Pepp. Disp. Resol. L.J. (Pepperdine Dispute Resolution Law Journal)* 66, 66 ff.

188 N. Alexander, *supra* n. 157, p. 295.

In any case, the duty of confidentiality is a key principle of mediation and also raises some relevant questions as regards the relationship between mediation and due justice. The impossibility of using certain relevant information before a national court or arbitration provided during the previous mediation, or the inability of the participants in the process of mediation to be summoned as witnesses in a future procedure or arbitration, may affect the viability of the prospective civil procedure or arbitration and thus, in an indirect manner, the effectiveness of the principle of access to justice.[189]

#### *4.3.5. Neutrality or impartiality of mediators*

As a general principle, the mediator must conduct the mediation in a neutral, impartial and competent manner. In addition to that, and also as a consequence of that, he/she has towards the parties a duty of disclosure of any circumstances which may generate a conflict of interest or affect his/her neutrality and impartiality.

The principle of neutrality and impartiality requires that mediators should not adopt any position in favour of any of the parties, assuming an active role that makes the parties collaborate, without giving preference to any of them. That function obliges the mediator to refrain from maintaining any relationship with the dispute or with the parties. This is the so-called equidistant role to be played by the mediator to ensure the effectiveness of the proceedings as well as to guarantee the full confidence of the parties in the model and in the mediator.

However, resting on this common basis, there are several approaches within the EU, an integrated legal area, to the role played by the mediator, his/her degree of involvement in the solution reached or his/her capacity to advise the parties as regards the content of the dispute and the possible settlement to be reached. For instance, there are some countries in which it is explicitly accepted that the mediator is not allowed to make settlement proposals to the parties. This is the position maintained in Bulgaria[190] and the Czech Republic.[191] But this attitude towards the position maintained by the mediator during the mediation process is also subject to certain exceptions. In some countries the mediator may go further than the mere facilitative role and make some proposals to the parties as regards the content of the dispute, as is the case in Slovenia.[192]

Nevertheless, within this debate over the role played by the mediator during the development of the mediation procedure, there is a special issue regarding the mediator's capacity to provide legal advice to the parties during the

189 *Ibid.*, pp. 252 and 280.

190 Article 10(1), Mediation Act, *State Gazette* no. 110 of 17.12.2004. Note N. Natov, B. Musseva, V. Pandov *et al.*, 'Bulgaria', in C. Esplugues, J.L. Iglesias and G. Palao, *supra* n. 156, p. 81.

191 M. Pauknerová, J. Brodec and M. Pfeiffer, *supra* n. 165, p. 180.

192 Article 14(1), Mediation in Civil and Commercial Matters Act, *Official Journal of the Republic of Slovenia*, no. 56/2008 of 06.06.2008.

mediation. The solution is not clear, though the issue is dealt with in certain jurisdictions[193] and gets contradictory responses in some national legislation regarding the involvement of the mediator in the final settlement and the level of justice of this agreement.[194]

### 4.3.6. *Enforceability of the settlement reached*

The Directive on Mediation of 2008 stresses the necessity of preventing mediation from being considered 'a poorer alternative to judicial proceedings in the sense that compliance with agreements resulting from mediation would depend on the good will of the parties'.[195] It is necessary to ensure that the parties to 'a written agreement resulting from mediation'[196] can have the content of such agreement made fully enforceable. This enforcement should be general and should only be rejected on certain specific and limited grounds. This enforceability should be ensured as regards both purely domestic agreements and agreements reached in cross-border disputes.[197] However, at the same time it needs to be combined with the protection of confidentiality in cases of unclear settlements, unfortunately a situation which is not that unusual.[198]

Practice shows that, unlike the arbitration award which is rendered by an independent third person and has *res judicata* effect, the settlement reached by the parties is considered a contract between them and lacks direct enforceability in the case of non-voluntary fulfilment. In most jurisdictions, enforceability will depend on its homologation by a judge or public authority.

## 5. A NEW UNDERSTANDING OF ACCESS TO JUSTICE IN THE TWENTY-FIRST CENTURY

Modern societies are very much linked to the idea of litigation. A hidden rule seems to exist in the sense that the more advanced a society is, the higher the level of litigation it suffers. This increase in the level of litigation amounts to a sort of 'litigation explosion'[199] that in general terms has been traditionally approached as

---

193 Belgium is a good example of this. The mediator is said to '*reste neuter au sens où il n'est habilité à gére la crise en structurant le debt entre eux et en rétablissant un mode efficace de dialogue. Il ne prend pas position sur le fond des questions abordées done le contenu reste à la maitrise des parties, mais il est, en revanche, responsable de la conduit du processus*' (J. Cruyplant, M. Gonde and M. Wagemans, *Droit et pratique de la médiation*, Bruylant, Brussels 2008, p. 3).

194 R.A.B. Bush and J.P. Folger, *supra* n. 180, pp. 11 ff.

195 Recital 19, Directive 2008/52/EC.

196 *Ibid.*

197 Note Recital 20, Directive 2008/52/EC.

198 J.J. Alfini, S.B. Press, J.R. Sternlight *et al.*, *supra* n. 182, p. 315.

199 This expression was designed by W.K. Olson, *The Litigation Explosion: What Happened When America Unleashed the Law Suit*, Truman Talley Books, New York 1991.

mainly linked to State courts.[200] This explosion puts the whole judicial system under pressure because as the volume of disputes brought before State courts increases, the proceedings become more and more lengthy and the costs incurred by such proceedings also rise.[201] The budgetary effort made by many countries in the world seems not enough to offer citizens an efficient justice in the broad sense of affordability, quality and effectiveness of the system of justice. Despite the money expended, civil and commercial procedures tend to be lengthy and costly and they do not in the end ensure a smooth implementation of the decisions reached.

The goal of tackling this explosion underpins many of the reforms of modern national procedural laws in many countries for the last two decades,[202] as well as the growing support for ADR devices in many parts of the world,[203] in an effort to make the procedural system more efficient and affordable for the parties.[204] In fact, despite differences as to its level of implementation, the use of ADR devices is a growing trend worldwide. Resort to ADR devices to solve disputes is considered an excellent instrument to reach at least three goals:

(a) firstly, ADR devices may supply citizens with a 'cost-effective tool that provides increased access to justice';[205]
(b) secondly, resort to ADR instruments 'alleviates the burdens on over-crowded court systems',[206] thus encouraging judicial efficiency in resolving both domestic and cross border disputes;[207] this becomes highly relevant in times of economic crisis and budgetary constraints; and

---

200 A critical approach to this idea may be found in A.R. Miller, 'The Pretrial Rush to Judgment: Are the "Litigation Explosion," "Liability Crisis," and Efficiency Cliches Eroding our Day in Court and Jury Trials Commitments?' (2003) 78 *NYULR (New York University Law Review)* 982, 985 ff.

201 European Commission, *Green Paper on Alternative Dispute Resolution in Civil and Commercial Law*, Brussels, 19.04.2002, COM (2002) 196 final, p. 7, n. 5 (available at: <http://eur-lex.europa.eu/LexUriServ/site/en/com/2002/com2002_0196en01.pdf> accessed 20.12.2012).

202 European Commission for the Efficiency of Justice (CEPEJ), *European Judicial Systems. Edition 2010 (data 2008): Efficiency and Quality of Justice*, 2010, p. 279 ff. (available at: <https://wcd.coe.int/com.instranet.InstraServlet?command=com.instranet.CmdBlobGet&InstranetImage=1694098&SecMode=1&DocId=1653000&Usage=2> accessed 20.12.2012).

203 See J.J. Alfini, S.B. Press, J.R. Sternlight *et al.*, *supra* n. 182, pp. 13 ff.

204 A critical response to Olson and his proposals for procedure reforms in the US may be found in R.M. Mastro, 'The Myth of the Litigation Explosion' (1991) 60 *Fordham Law Review* 199, 216.

205 G. De Palo, A. Feasley and F. Orecchini, *Quantifying the Cost of Not Using Mediation – A Data Analysis*, European Parliament, Directorate-General for Internal Policies. Policy Department Citizen's Rights and Constitutional Affairs, Brussels 2010, p. 3 (available at: <www.europarl.europa.eu/document/activities/cont/201105/20110518ATT19592/20110518ATT19592EN.pdf> accessed 10.08.2012).

206 *Ibid.* p. 3.

207 Note The International Bank for Reconstruction and Development / The World Bank, *Doing business in a more transparent world*, IBRD/WB, Washington 2012, p. 56 (available at: <www.doingbusiness.org/~/media/fpdkm/doing%20business/documents/annual-reports/english/db12-fullreport.pdf> accessed 28.12.2012).

(c) thirdly, resort to ADR provides the parties with the opportunity to greatly reduce the length and cost of litigation: existing figures are very clear in this respect, at least as regards the specific institution of mediation, which is highly cost effective.[208]

From a purely access to justice approach, points (a) and (c), but not (b), should be stressed. ADR cannot be approached any longer as a radical alternative to State courts nor as a way to decrease the workload of courts; on the contrary it is an instrument that increasingly interacts with State courts, offering citizens several possibilities for solving their disputes in a quick, affordable and specialised manner.[209]

The benefits of the use of ADR devices seem to be objectively clear for everybody: for the parties who have an affordable, flexible and easy tailored way of solving their disputes;[210] for the judge who reduces his workload; for the State which can afford to reduce investment in the judicial system; and for the system of justice as a whole in that it ensures full access to justice to citizens.

Nevertheless ADR is not a unitary notion. A range of several forms of dispute resolution exists within this global notion: arbitration, conciliation, mediation, negotiation, etc.[211] Though they share the common goal of solving disputes and the fact of being non-judicial means of dispute resolution, many differences exist between them and reality shows a variation in the popularity and use of each of these devices. In fact, the success of ADR has an additional effect: it gives rise to a new relationship between arbitration and the other ADR devices. The expansion of the interaction between the different ADR devices is increasingly apparent – med-arb, mini trial, etc. – to the point that it is not always easy to differentiate between them.[212] In fact, mixed approaches are gaining growing support in many countries; for instance, arb-med and med-arb schemes are more and more accepted as a result of the capacity they afford parties to tailor the procedure to their needs and also the possibility to foster a quick solution and to reduce costs.[213] The acceptance of escalation clauses and of their construction – for example the transcendence of the previous step, negotiation or mediation – varies from country to country and from one kind of arbitration to another.[214] The case of protection of investments arbitrations is rather

---

208 N. Alexander, *supra* n. 157, p. 49, n. 118.

209 N. Trocker and A. De Luca, *supra* n. 12, p. ix.

210 Note, T. Relis, *Perceptions in Litigation and Mediation. Lawyers, Defendants, Plaintiffs, and Gendered Parties*, Cambridge Univ. Press, Cambridge 2009, pp. 65–67.

211 N. Alexander, *supra* n. 157, pp. 8 ff.

212 *Ibid.*, pp. 10–12.

213 This possibility is explicitly admitted in Sections 32 and 33 of the the Hong Kong Ordinance of 2011. Nevertheless, the judgment of 12.04.2011 in *Gao Haiyan and Xie Heping v. Keeneye Holdings Limited* [2011] 3 HKC 157 raises concerns about the viability of this possibility.

214 An evolving situation exists in England as regards tiered clauses: negotiation and, in case of its failure, mediation and afterwards resort to state courts, were envisaged in the clause. Case

interesting. Different arbitration panels have tended to accept that the existence of previous negotiations is a question of procedure and not of jurisdiction. That means that the arbitration panel can continue with its work.[215]

In any case we should be well aware that the development in favour of the ADR movement is neither neutral nor exempt from risk. It raises at least two relevant issues regarding the future of dispute resolution and the understanding of access to justice.

Firstly, endorsement of ADR devices, mainly of mediation, may directly lead to reshaping the principle of access to justice which would now be understood in a broad sense; that is, as embracing both reference to national courts and to ADR devices either working alone or together.[216] This directly implies a new understanding of the notion of dispute resolution and leads to the creation of a multi-option civil justice system[217] for citizens. Consequently, mediation, or any other ADR device, should no longer be approached 'as an alternative to court proceedings; it is rather one of several dispute resolution methods available in a modern society and which may be the most suited for some, but certainly not all, disputes'.[218]

Secondly, this option in favour of upholding resort to ADR devices as a way to ensure access to justice to citizens may also be seen as opening windows for a certain level of privatisation of justice. Alternative dispute resolution tools would then be renamed 'private tools for dispute resolution'[219] and would actually appear as a way to settle disputes in a quicker, safer, smoother and sometimes less

---

law concerning mediation clauses stresses their contractual nature and consequently their binding character for the parties to it. The leading case is *Cable & Wireless v. IBM United Kingdom Ltd* [2002] 2 All ER (Comm) 1041, Colman J. A different solution was reached in *Clyde & Co v. Bates van Winkelhof* [2011] EWHC 668 (QB), Slade J.

215 See, for instance, and as a matter of principle, *SGS Société Générale de Surveillance SA v. Islamic Republic of Pakistan* (ICSID Case no. ARB/01/13); *Bayindir Insaat Turizm Ticaret Ve Sanayi AS v. Islamic Republic of Pakistan* (ICSID Case no. ARB/03/29); *Occidental Petroleum Corporation and Occidental Exploration and Production Company v. Republic of Ecuador* (ICSID Case no. ARB/06/11) or *Salini Costruttori SpA and Italstrade SpA v. Kingdom of Morocco* (ICSID Case no. ARB/00/4). All of them are available at: <https://icsid.worldbank.org/ICSID/FrontServlet> accessed 27.12.2012.

216 Recital 5, Directive 2008/52/EC clearly states that the 'objective of ensuring better access to justice […] should encompass acces to judicial as well as extrajudicial dispute resolution methods'. As to this change of understanding of the notion of 'access to justice' see S. Barona Vilar, 'De como la incorporación de las ADR convierte el Derecho Procesal en Derecho de los medios de tutela del ciudadano', in J.L. Gómez Colomer, S. Barona Vilar and M.P. Calderon Cuadrado (eds.), *supra* n. 43, 193, at pp. 214 ff.

217 We refer to the notion set forth at the end of the twentieth century. See Canadian Bar Association, *Systems of Civil Justice Task Force Report*, CBA, Ottawa 1996, p. 27.

218 European Commission, *Proposal for a Directive of the European Parliament and of the Council on certain aspects of mediation in civil and commercial matters*, SEC(2004) 1314, Brussels, 22.10.2004, COM(2004) 718 final 2004/0251 (COD), p. 4 <http://eur-lex.europa.eu/LexUriServ/LexUriServ.do?uri=COM:2004:0718:FIN:EN:PDF> accessed 23.12.2012.

219 Note G. Wagner, 'Harmonization of Civil Procedure – Policy Perspective', in X.W. Kramer and C.H. van Rhee, *Civil Litigation in a Globalising World*, Springer, Heidelberg 2012, p. 112.

expensive manner than referring the dispute to State courts. The creation of a sort of ADR industry would imply the transformation of the understanding of the notion of access to justice by limiting access to State courts as much as possible and, at the same time, increasing resort to ADR devices on every possible occasion.

This trend in favour of opening spaces for private justice could be embodied within the global trend of upholding the privatisation of other previously stated-owned services.[220] However, the 'provision of services' by the State in the field of justice is not comparable to the provision of services by the State in other areas of life. Despite the issues that the privatisation of justice may entail, there is a real risk that it may happen in times of budgetary constraints. In fact, in the EU, the European legislator seems clearly against equating resort to ADR devices with anti-State courts movements.[221] However, the admonition of the European Commission that acceptance of fostering resort to ADR devices 'cannot in any way detract from the obligation of Member States to maintain an effective and fair legal system that meets the requirements of the European Convention of Human Rights, which forms one of the central pillars of a democratic society'[222] shows that the risk does exist and that the Commission is fully aware of it.

The temptation to foster private justice and at the same time to reduce the interest of the State – and, of course, its investment – in maintaining a well-prepared and affordable system of public adjudication exists and most probably will grow in the future. This could lead to a situation in which private and public adjudication will not be approached as the two interrelated faces of the same coin for citizens, but as two fully separated realities competing each against each other in a marketplace of provision of justice services. This discourse is both dangerous and tricky and could eventually affect the quality of justice in the national courts and affect the viability of access to justice for citizens.

ADR seems to be the future – perhaps not the whole future but a large part of it. In any case, the current ADR movement is faced with two big problems. Firstly, despite the benefits that this movement entails for the parties, it is still not sufficiently used. A paradox exists: 'The paradox is that while [... its use] yields highly successful results, mediation is rarely used in a systematic way by disputants and lawyers'.[223] The lack of awareness of the existence of ADR and of what it offers citizens as regards almost any dispute hampers its development. Secondly, the expansion of the use of ADR may favour the extrapolation to ADR devices of certain procedural tricks, as has increasingly happened in arbitration, generating an increase in costs and duration. Time will tell!

---

220 N. Alexander, *supra* n. 157, p. 54.

221 N. Trocker and A. De Luca, *supra* n. 12, p. ix.

222 European Commission, *Proposal...*, *supra* n. 218, p. 4.

223 See G. De Palo, A. Feasley and F. Orecchini, *supra* n. 205, p. 3.

# AUSTRALIA

David Bamford

**Contents**



## 1. INTRODUCTION

While contemporary interest in ADR in Australia began in the late 1970s, ADR has a long-established presence in the world of Australian conflict management. Indigenous societies in Australia have long had a range of dispute resolution methods.[1] The English settlers on arrival in 1788 brought with them the English legal system. This included the relevant provisions in English law relating to arbitration.[2] While this was originally developed to deal with commercial disputes, by the late nineteenth century, conciliation and arbitration had been

---

1 Australian Law Reform Commission, *Recognition of Aboriginal Customary Law*, Report No. 31, Canberra 1986.

2 H. Astor and C. Chinkin, *Dispute Resolution in Australia*, 2nd ed., LexisNexis, Sydney 2002, p. 12.

widely recognised in another field – industrial disputes. Many of the colonies that then made up Australia were heavily influenced by developments in the United Kingdom where conciliation and arbitration were growing as a response to employment-related disputes. This was hastened by a deep depression in the Australian economy in the 1890s that led to numerous major employment disputes and the growth of organised labour as employers reduced wages and dismissed employees. The resultant disruption and hardship fostered a broad acceptance that such disputes would be better managed and resolved through use of an independent decision-maker who was an expert in the area of industrial relations. The 1890s was also the period in which the political leadership in the six Australian colonies was campaigning for the creation of a national government that resulted in the enactment by the British Parliament of the Australian Constitution. In distributing legislative powers between the States and the Commonwealth of Australia, the founders specifically incorporated ADR in the constitution – for industrial disputes. Section 51(xxxv) gave the Australian Parliament power to make laws with respect to 'conciliation and arbitration for the prevention and settlement of industrial disputes extending beyond the limits of any one State'.

Accompanying the introduction of conciliation and arbitration schemes for industrial disputes, the 1890s saw the introduction of workers' compensation schemes, again influenced by British and earlier German schemes. When the national government was established in 1900, workers' compensation remained a matter left with the States, a situation that has continued ever since. The State-based workers' compensation schemes often included an ADR process for managing disputes. The South Australian legislation, for example, provided that disputes were to be arbitrated by a committee 'representative of the employer and his workmen' or, if that did not exist, by a single arbitrator agreed upon by the parties.[3] While for some periods in the last century, workers' compensation disputes in some jurisdictions were moved into the court system, over the last thirty years conciliation and/or arbitration have become the most common dispute resolution methods for workers' compensation disputes.

As a result of its widespread use in industrial and employment related disputes, Australia has over a hundred years of formal recognition of non-adjudicatory dispute resolution that has led to extensive experience and acceptance of ADR as a legitimate and useful response to disputes. This history facilitated the broader wave of ADR that began in the 1980s – the growth of ADR in general dispute resolution.

The 1980s saw ADR advance on many fronts. In the Australian commercial disputes context, the 1980s saw the enactment of uniform commercial arbitration legislation that was intended to help revitalise commercial arbitration. Associated with this was the development of two dedicated

3 The Workmen's Compensation Act 1900, Schedule 2. The current version of this legislation continues to use conciliation as its primary dispute resolution process.

independent commercial dispute resolution services – the Australian Centre for International Commercial Arbitration in 1984 and the Australian Commercial Disputes Centre in 1986. The former, based in Melbourne, was created to promote arbitration as a dispute resolution method and to provide a venue and arbitration services for international commercial disputes. The latter, based in Sydney, was established in 1986 and focused more on domestic commercial disputes and the promotion of mediation as a dispute resolution method.

The Australian Commercial Disputes Centre, while created as an alternative to courts, was the product of two influential judges who had become active proponents of the ADR concept. In 1985 Justice Andrew Rogers, Head of the Commercial List in the Supreme Court of New South Wales, spent six months in New York. During that time he attended an ADR course at Columbia University that convinced him of the benefits of mediation in the context of commercial disputes. On returning to Australia, he quickly persuaded his Chief Justice, Sir Laurence Street, that promotion of ADR was highly desirable. The Chief Justice personally lobbied the New South Wales government who in 1986 agreed to support the formation of the Australian Commercial Disputes Centre.[4]

Domestic arbitration was also championed by another organisation, the Institute of Arbitrators (named the Institute for Arbitrators and Mediators Australia, or IAMA, since 1997) formed in 1975. This provided training for arbitrators and promoted the services of arbitrators. Also actively promoting arbitration since 1995 is the Australian Branch of the Chartered Institute of Arbitrators.

On the mediation front, various organisations developed mediation services in the 1980s. One early adopter of mediation was the community justice movement that had its Australian origins in a New South Wales pilot project established in 1980. Focusing particularly on family and neighbour disputes, the community justice model was expanded in New South Wales in 1983 and subsequently adopted by other Australian states.

Prominent sponsors of mediation include LEADR. Established in 1989 it was initially created by lawyers interested in promoting mediation. Although LEADR stands for Lawyers Engaged in Alternative Dispute Resolution, it has long since become an organisation representing dispute resolvers generally. Its objectives, as set out in its Constitution are:

'(a) the acceptance and use of ADR;
(b) the provision of education, training and research in ADR;
(c) the development and maintenance of high standards of practice in ADR;
(d) the active role of LEADR Members in the practice of ADR; and
(e) the use of ADR to prevent, manage and resolve conflict and disputes.'[5]

---

4 See Sir L. Street, 'Evolution of Commercial ADR in Australia' (2005) 79 *Australian Law Journal* 765.

5 LEADR, Constitution, Clause 1; available online at: <www.leadr.com.au>.

It has played an active role in the development of training and accreditation of mediators and the provision of mediators but now provides the complete suite of ADR services. It has State chapters in Australia and has a New Zealand division that has had a strong presence since 1990.

Another catalyst for the development of mediation as a recognised dispute resolution method in Australia has been the Family Court of Australia. Family law is a matter that falls within the legislative competence of the national government and since 1976 there has been a national Family Court of Australia established by the Family Law Act 1975. While the Family Court has always been a strong advocate of ADR within family disputes, in 1995 the Family Law Act 1975 was amended to reinforce the importance of ADR by designating the ADR methods the 'Primary Dispute Resolution' method for the Court and incorporating a comprehensive regulatory framework for mediation practice in the Family Court Regulations.[6] In addition to in-court services, a wide range of private or non-government family dispute resolution providers quickly grew through the 1980s and 1990s. The national government and the State legal aid agencies also funded a range of family dispute resolution services. In 2006, as part of major changes to the Family Law Act 1975, parents are required 'to attend family dispute resolution before filing a court application, except in certain circumstances, including where there are concerns about family violence and child'.[7] The reform package included the establishment of 65 Family Relationship Centres and increased services for a wide range of dispute resolution and support services.

As with many other overseas jurisdictions, the ADR theory and governance has largely followed practice. Different organisations or individuals developed and experimented with ADR models during the 1980s and 1990s. However by the mid-1990s sufficient experience had been gained to realise that some form of regulation was required to ensure appropriate standards were applied and that the public and ADR practitioners were protected. In 1994 a major report, *Access to Justice* by Justice Ronald Sackville, recommended the establishment of a national body to advise the national government on ADR issues. The national government agreed and in October 1995 created an independent non-statutory body, the National Alternative Dispute Resolution Advisory Council (NADRAC) to advise the national Attorney-General on ways to ensure high-quality, efficient non-court dispute resolution. This role was expanded in 2006 to require NADRAC to 'promote and raise the profile of ADR' more broadly.[8] NADRAC

---

6 T. Altobelli, 'Mediation in the Nineties: The promise of the past' (2000) *Macarthur Law Review* 106.

7 R. Kaspiew *et al.*, *Evaluation of the 2006 family law reforms*, Australian Institute for Family Studies, 2009, p. 4.

8 Justice M. Kellam (Chair of NADRAC), *ADR in Government Forum*, speech delivered 4 June 2008 (copy with author but also available at <www.nadrac.gov.au/Documents/TheHonJusticeMurrayKellamAO.doc>).

has been prominent in the development and introduction of ADR standards and accreditation procedures that now govern aspects of ADR practice.

Having provided this broad overview of the development of ADR in the Australian context, the remainder of this chapter will examine some of the major dispute resolution methods separately to provide a more detailed analysis of their development and to identify future trends. In this context, the scope of the chapter is largely determined by the definition of ADR adopted by NADRAC:[9]

> '[those] processes, other than judicial determination, in which an impartial person assists those in a dispute to resolve the issues between them.'

As with other jurisdictions, definitional issues have bedevilled ADR. Altobelli refers to the 'terminological turmoil' that has surrounded dispute resolution.[10] These have become more than academic issues. Increasingly legislation requires specific dispute resolution methods to be used, necessitating clearer definitions. Some commentators would suggest that the NADRAC definition does not include arbitration – Sir Laurence Street, for example, argues that there is a distinction between resolving disputes with a consensual agreement being the outcome and those disputes finalised by some form of decision.[11] However, this chapter takes a wider view and includes arbitration within its coverage.

For the purposes of this chapter conciliation is distinguished from mediation in that the impartial person 'will provide advice on the matters in dispute and/or options for resolution'. Within mediation, the impartial person (the mediator) has no advisory role with respect to the content or outcome of the dispute, providing advice only on the dispute resolution processes. Common to both is the identification of the issues, the generation of options and the exploration of possible solutions.[12]

## 2. ARBITRATION

The arrival of arbitration with the first white settlers in the late eighteenth century has already been noted. They brought with them the English Arbitration Act 1698 and adopted subsequent English legislation in 1839 and 1857. One of the first major attempts at local legislation was the New South Wales Arbitration Act 1867. English developments continued to strongly influence Australian law

---

9 NADRAC, Glossary, <www.nadrac.gov.au/what_is_adr/GlossaryOfADRTerms/Pages/default.aspx> accessed 12.07.2012.

10 T. Altobelli, 'A Generational Change in Family Dispute Resolution in Australia', (2006) 17 *Australasian Dispute Resolution Journal* 140, 144.

11 Sir L. Street, *supra* n. 4, p 767.

12 NADRAC, *supra* n. 9.

and the English Arbitration Act 1899 became the foundation for arbitration legislation across most of the Australian colonies (which became states following the creation of the Commonwealth of Australia in 1900). Queensland took a different path with its Interdict Act 1867, maintaining in essence the English Arbitration Act 1698 until 1973 when it enacted the Arbitration Act 1973 (based in large part on the English Arbitration Act 1950).[13]

However by the 1970s it was clear that arbitration had fallen into disfavour. In part this was due to the ongoing tension over the proper relationship with courts and the degree to which courts could or should intervene or supervise arbitrations. It was also due to the lack of expertise in recognising what cases were appropriate for arbitration, and in managing arbitrations. Arbitrations had become procedurally rigid and were manifesting many of the deficiencies that accompanied litigation. It was this situation that prompted the establishment of the Institute of Arbitrators in 1975.[14]

The principles and legislation had enabled it to develop a strong active presence. A number of Australian states commissioned enquiries into the state of arbitration that led to proposals for legislative reform that was to be consistent across Australia.[15] The Bill, drafted as part of the New South Wales Law Reform Commission's Report, became the basis for similar legislation across Australia. Between 1984 and 1990 all the Australian States and Territories enacted Commercial Arbitration Acts that were part of this move towards uniformity.

The uniform legislation did much to improve some of the uncertainties that had held back the development of arbitration. Despite its name, the provisions of the Act were not limited to commercial disputes – it operated where there was an arbitration agreement that effectively meant 'an agreement in writing to submit present or future disputes to arbitration'.[16] The Act promotes party autonomy with many of its provisions filling the vacuum if the parties have not agreed on procedural and other aspects. Arbitrators were empowered to conduct arbitrations as they saw fit[17] and were to reach determinations according to law unless the parties had otherwise agreed. In this context arbitrators were empowered to act as 'amiable compositeurs' determining a case on what was fair and reasonable and not strictly according to law.[18] The Acts also provided for mediation and conciliation of disputes and authorised the arbitrator to act as a mediator or conciliator before and during an arbitration. The arbitrator is not prevented from continuing to arbitrate should the dispute proceed to

---

13 D. Jones, *Commercial Arbitration in Australia*, Law Book, Sydney 2011, pp. 10–1.

14 Law Reform Commission of New South Wales, *Report on Commercial Arbitration*, No. 27, Sydney 1976, p. 39.

15 These included Law Reform reports from South Australia (1969), Queensland (1970), Western Australia (1971), Victoria (1974) and New South Wales (1976).

16 Section 4, Commercial Arbitration Act 1986 (Tas).

17 Section 14, *ibid.*

18 Section 22, *ibid.*

arbitration.[19] While the Acts provide that unless the parties have decided otherwise, the arbitrator's determination or award is final and binding and enforceable and limits the grounds for appealing against arbitral awards, the reality is that there was continued scope for court intervention and supervision of arbitrations.

The hopes of the proponents of the uniform commercial arbitration legislation for a dramatic expansion in arbitration were never realised. As with other common law jurisdictions, the courts have significantly limited the utility of arbitrations. Ranging from decisions about the standard of reasons needed to support arbitral decisions to the need to provide natural justice and at times an expansive interpretation of the grounds needed to justify judicial intervention in arbitrations, this has diminished the flexibility and efficiency of the arbitral process.[20] Added to this was the development of inconsistent decisions across the Australian jurisdictions. The uniform commercial arbitration legislation consists of Acts of State Parliaments and is thus subject to interpretation by the different State Supreme Courts.[21] Whilst the High Court of Australia, as the ultimate appellate court, can ensure consistency, many of these matters remained unclear.

By 2004 the Law Institute of Victoria wrote in a submission to an inquiry into the uniform commercial arbitration legislation:[22]

> 'It is noted that arbitration is a rarely used process in the Australian jurisdiction and the likely reason for that is that the current system under review is no more efficient or cost effective than the court system and it may be considered "overly legalistic".'

Adding to the arbitration malaise was the fact the dispute resolution environment had become much more competitive. The civil courts had in the previous twenty years embarked on a major procedural reforms[23] and had set up special procedures for commercial disputes including fast-tracking, commercial lists, and specialist judges. Mediation and other forms of dispute resolution have become well established[24] including within the construction industry, traditionally one of the major users of arbitration.

---

19 Section 27, *ibid.*

20 H. Astor and C. Chinkin, *supra* n. 2, pp. 305–06; NADRAC, *supra* n. 9, p. 14.

21 A.A. De Fina, 'Swings and roundabouts – developments in arbitration in Australia' (2012) 28 *Building and Construction Law Journal*, 169; NADRAC, *supra* n. 9, p. 14.

22 Law Institute of Victoria, *Submission on Australia's uniform commercial arbitration legislation*, 24 June 2004 <www.liv.asn.au/getattachment/401acea3-c159-47f7-b827-e6363f4ff88d/Australias-uniform-commercial-arbitration-legisla.aspx> p. 3, accessed 18.09.2012.

23 D. Bamford, 'Litigation Reform 1980–2000: A Radical Challenge?', in W. Prest and S. Roach Anleu (eds), *Litigation: Past and Present*, UNSW Press, Sydney 2004, p. 176.

24 H. Astor and C. Chinkin, *supra* n. 2, p. 169.

These challenges led to a further round of legislative reform for commercial arbitration – the new uniform commercial arbitration legislation. Following a long period of lobbying and consultation, in 2009 the Standing Committee of Attorneys-General (made up of the Attorneys-General of the Commonwealth, the States and the Territories) agreed to adopt new uniform commercial arbitration legislation and between 2010 and 2012 almost all Australian States and Territories had enacted this legislation.

The major reform has been the adoption of the 2006 UNCITRAL Model Law as the basis for domestic commercial arbitrations. This provides increased opportunity for harmonisation and efficiency as arbitrators are able to use the same jurisprudence and experience for all commercial arbitrations, irrespective of whether they are international or domestic. Among the other major changes was increasing the prospects of a court granting a stay of proceedings when an arbitration agreement exists. With limited exceptions consistent with the Model Law, courts must grant stays of proceedings on the request of a party where the parties have agreed to refer the dispute to arbitration. Also limiting court intervention was the removal of the grounds of 'error of law' and increased limitations on the ability to challenge or seek the removal of arbitrators. Whereas previously these grounds were available for 'misconduct', 'undue influence' or 'incompetence', or 'unsuitable' arbitrators, under the new legislation challenge is only possible if there are 'justifiable doubts as to the arbitrator's impartiality or independence, or if the arbitrator does not possess qualifications agreed to by the parties'. The Act further provides that justifiable doubts as to the impartiality or independence of a person arise only if there is a 'real danger of bias on the part of the person in conducting the arbitration'.[25]

The UNCITRAL Model Law had been adopted for international commercial arbitration in Australia in 1989 following amendment to the International Arbitration Act 1974 (Cth).[26] This 1974 Act incorporated the 1958 New York Convention on the Recognition and Enforcement of Arbitration Awards into domestic law. Until recently this Act left open the possibility of having international arbitrations proceed under the State-based uniform commercial arbitration legislation if the parties so decided, rather than the Model Law.[27] In 2010 following legislative amendment, the International Arbitration Act 1974 (Cth) became the exclusive law governing international commercial arbitrations,[28] and it adopted the 2006 version of the UNCITRAL Model Law, ending the possibility of opting out of the Model Law. The amendments provide

25 Section 12, Commercial Arbitration Act 2010 (NSW).

26 The Australian Constitution provides the Commonwealth Parliament with legislative power to make laws governing international affairs including treaties.

27 See R. Garnett, 'International Commercial Arbitration in Australia: Legal Framework and Problems' (2008) 19 *Australasian Dispute Resolution Journal* 249, 254.

28 Section 21, International Arbitration Act 1974 (Cth).

greater certainty but were also intended 'to encourage courts to become more arbitration friendly and to limit the circumstances in which courts refuse to stay proceedings in the face of an arbitration agreement, or set aside or refuse to enforce a foreign award.'[29] However jurisdiction under the International Arbitration Act 1974 (Cth) was vested concurrently in the Federal Court and the state courts contrary to the recommendations of many of those arguing for reform.

The effect of all this was to make 2010 and 2011 major milestones in the history of arbitration in Australia. Following the new State uniform commercial arbitration legislation and the major amendments to the International Arbitration Act 1974 (Cth), the 2006 UNCITRAL Model Law applies to all commercial arbitrations, domestic and international. This reinforces the primacy given to party autonomy within the arbitration framework and this has been complemented by institutional developments. The Australian Centre for International Commercial Arbitration had developed new rules for arbitration in 2005, supplemented by additional provisions in 2008 and 2011. Its role was further enhanced in 2011 when, by Regulation, it was made the sole appointing authority for arbitrators in international commercial arbitrations when the parties have failed to provide for appointment of arbitrators or have been unable to do so effectively.[30]

The gaggle of arbitration services and bodies managed to bring some commonality (and common sense) to the arbitration scene with the establishment of the Australian International Disputes Centre in Sydney in 2010. It brings together the Australian Commercial Disputes Centre, the Australian Maritime and Transport Arbitration Commission (established in 2007 to promote service maritime disputes), the Chartered Institute of Arbitrators, and the Australian Centre for International Commercial Arbitration.[31] Whether this round of recent reform will see the expansion in arbitration that its supporters desire remains to be seen. Within the Asian region Singapore has become the leading centre for international commercial arbitration, followed by Hong Kong. While doubt remains whether Australia will become a significant player internationally, the legislative change, institutional re-alignments and the judicial and governmental support shown demonstrate the serious commitment that has been made to promote arbitration as an alternative dispute resolution option.

---

29 A. Moschino, 'International Arbitration in Australia – 2010/11 in Review' (2011) 22 *Australasian Dispute Resolution Journal* 215, 215.

30 D. Jones, 'Australia', in Global Arbitration Review, *The Asia-Pacific Arbitration Review 2013*, Law Business Research, London 2012, p. 22.

31 A. Moschino, *supra* n. 29.

## 2.1. CONCILIATION AND MEDIATION

The relationship between conciliation and mediation is one of the most difficult within the ADR framework. Whilst the NADRAC definitions set out earlier distinguish between the two, the reality is that in practice they overlap. Indeed development of models of mediation, like evaluative mediation, blurs the difference between conciliation and mediation. This is particularly so if, as some evidence suggests, evaluative mediation is the more common.[32] Similarly conciliators in practice may do little more than engage in facilitative mediation. Yet because legislation uses the terms as separate concepts, this section examines each separately.

### *2.1.1. Conciliation*

As already discussed, conciliation has long played a role in Australian dispute resolution, especially in the area of industrial relations, employment law and workers' compensation law. A number of states also provided for conciliation more broadly – in Queensland for neighbourhood disputes from 1892 and in South Australia more generally from 1929. However these Acts were not greatly used, although the South Australian Act was used on occasion in family law cases when South Australian courts still exercised a family law jurisdiction.[33]

Conciliation beyond the industrial and employment arena gained new life in the 1970s with its introduction into the Family Law Act 1975 (Cth). The Family Court of Australia, from its creation, was intended to operate in a less formal way, maximising consensual resolution of family disputes. This in part overlapped with the provision of counselling services within the court, and while the Family Law Act 1975 did not refer to conciliation when first enacted, amendments in 1983 and subsequently made specific reference to conciliation and by 1986 it had become mandatory for custody and property disputes.[34] While more recent amendments to the Act have removed some of the references to conciliation, it still remains as a statutorily recognised form of family dispute resolution and the Family Law Rules 2004 provide for the conduct of conciliation conferences.[35]

Conciliation was also mandated by the anti-discrimination legislation enacted by the different States and Commonwealth. The Sex Discrimination Act 1985 (Cth), for example, provided for compulsory conciliation and the Australian Human Rights Commission Act 1986 (Cth) provides that one of the

32 See T. Peisley, 'Blended Mediation: Using Facilitative and Evaluative Approaches to Commercial Disputes' (2012) 23 *Australasian Dispute Resolution Journal* 26.

33 H. Zelling, 'Judges as Arbitrators' (1993) 15 *Adelaide Law Review* 25, 25.

34 E. Evatt, 'Conciliation in Australian Law' (1986) 11 *Sydney Law Review* 1, 1.

35 D. Spencer and S. Hardy, *Dispute Resolution in Australia*, 2nd ed., Lawbook, Sydney 2009, p. 112.

functions of the Australian Human Rights Commission is to 'to inquire into, and attempt to conciliate, complaints of unlawful discrimination'.[36]

Courts and tribunals involved in administrative reviews including planning and environmental disputes have also had a relatively long history of using conciliation. The Land and Environment Court Act 1979 (NSW) incorporated the use of conciliators, as did the Planning Act 1982 (South Australia).[37] In the Land and Environment Court (NSW), while a complete range of dispute resolution methods are available, conciliation and, since 2006, conciliation–arbitration are the primary ADR methods adopted. Between 2005 and 2010 the number of conciliations rose from 17 to 632.[38] Both the Administrative Appeals Tribunal (Cth) and some of the state administrative review tribunals also use conciliation.

Various tribunals involved in consumer and residential tenancy matters also have conciliation as a statutorily based dispute resolution method. Two examples of large volume tribunals using conciliation are the Consumer Trader and Tenancy Tribunal in NSW that dealt in 2011–12 with over 60,000 cases and the Residential Tenancies Authority in Queensland that dealt with over 21,000 cases.[39]

### *2.1.2. Mediation*

However, much more prominent has been the growth in mediation as a concept and a reality. The first formal adoption of mediation in Australia is commonly said to be the New South Wales community mediation project. In 1980 the New South Wales Parliament enacted legislation[40] that enabled the establishment of a trial community justice centre. Following an evaluation by the Law Foundation of New South Wales, further legislation was passed to continue the programme and it expanded to provide services across New South Wales. Its brief was to resolve neighbourhood disputes through use of mediation. Neighbourhood disputes continue to make up the bulk of its work but its remit has been broadened to mediate disputes where parties are in an ongoing relationship.[41]

The New South Wales experience provided a model for similar programmes in other Australian states. Some jurisdictions have special legislation to enable this to happen (e.g. Queensland and the Australian Capital Territory); others

---

36 Section 11, Australian Human Rights Commission Act 1986 (Cth).

37 W. Faulks, 'The Modern Development of Alternative Dispute Resolution in Australia' (1990) 1 *Australasian Dispute Resolution Journal* 61.

38 B. Preston, 'The use of alternative dispute resolution in administrative disputes' (2011) 22 *Australasian Dispute Resolution Journal*, 144, 153.

39 See F. Gibson, 'Alternative Dispute Resolution in Residential Cases' (2007) 18 *Australasian Dispute Resolution Journal* 101.

40 Community Justice Centres (Pilot Project) Act 1980 (NSW).

41 Attorney-General & Justice (NSW), *Community Justice Centres: The Year in Review 2010/11*, Sydney, undated, p. 8.

have simply established community mediation services through administrative and financial agreements.[42] A hybrid form has developed in Victoria with the establishment of community mediation services in the early 1990s that were centralised as the Dispute Settlement Centre Victoria within the Department of Justice in 1993.[43] Amendments were made to the Evidence Act 1958 (Vic) to provide some protection for approved mediators but provide no statutory framework for community or neighbourhood mediation services generally. This community-focused mediation is seen by governments as playing an important role in the access to justice strategy as well as helping reduce pressure on courts. In some jurisdictions structural arrangements exist to enable referral of cases by courts to such services.

Mediation in commercial disputes also evolved in the 1980s and the role of Justice Andrew Rogers and Chief Justice Laurence Street in this regard has already been described.[44] Initially progress was slow – in its first three years (1986–89) the Australian Centre for Commercial Disputes had undertaken 150 mediations or conciliations and had 250 on its books awaiting finalisation.[45] However, since then it has been much more heavily promoted. The work of institutions like LEADR, the Australian Commercial Disputes Centre, and the Institute of Arbitrators and Mediators Australia, to mention just a few, has done much to advance the profile and acceptance of private mediation. The very nature of private mediation means that the extent to which it is occurring, or the processes that are used, are not easily identified.

#### 2.1.2.1. Court-annexed mediation

More discernible is the growth in court-annexed mediation. By 1993 most major courts included references to mediation in their court rules, with South Australia having made the most comprehensive provision.[46] In the federal jurisdiction, mediation pilots had begun as early as 1987 in the Federal Court, and in 1991 the Commonwealth Parliament enacted the Courts (Mediation & Arbitration) Act 1991 which created a statutory framework for mediation in both the Federal Court and Family Court. It would be difficult to find an Australian court that does not now provide in its Act or Rules for referral to mediation.

---

42 Law Commission Of New South Wales, *Community Justice Centres*, IP 23, Sydney 2003, pp. 9–10.

43 H. Astor and C. Chinkin, *supra* n. 2, p. 15.

44 *Supra* p. 55.

45 J. Rickeret, 'Alternative Dispute Resolution in Australian Commercial Disputes: Quo Vadis?' (1990) 1 *Australasian Dispute Resolution Journal* 31, 35.

46 B. Sordo, 'Australian Mediation Initiatives to Resolve Matters Awaiting Trial' (1994) 5 *Australasian Dispute Resolution Journal* 62, 66.

As an example, New South Wales has incorporated in its Civil Procedure Act 2005 a series of provisions governing court-annexed mediation. This includes:[47]

> '(1) If it considers the circumstances appropriate, the court may, by order, refer any proceedings before it, or part of any such proceedings, for mediation by a mediator, and may do so either with or without the consent of the parties to the proceedings concerned.
> (2) The mediation is to be undertaken by a mediator agreed to by the parties or appointed by the court, who may (but need not be) a listed mediator.'

The Civil Procedure Act 2005 covers such matters as immunity from liability, confidentiality and enforcement. A Practice Note that sets out the procedures for cases referred to mediation supplements the Act.[48] The Court can appoint a registrar or other approved court official to mediate and in such cases the mediation is provided free of charge. The court may order that mediator is to be chosen by the parties and failing that appointed by the court.

One of the most recent comprehensive studies of Australian court-annexed mediation was the 2008 study of the Victorian Supreme Court and County Court. The researchers reviewed all the civil cases finalised in a three-month period and found that 33% of the cases in the Supreme Court sample had undergone some form of mediation. Of this group, some 10% had been mediated by court officials and the remainder by external mediators.[49] A real question raised by the research was whether what was happening was in fact mediation. Less than half the mediators had followed the generally accepted model of the mediation process. Much of what occurred appeared to conciliation conferences or 'shuttle negotiation' with a 'mediator' facilitating the process.[50]

Tribunals also make extensive use of mediation. Illustrative of this is the National Native Title Tribunal. Following the landmark High Court of Australia decision in *Mabo v. State of Queensland (No 2)*,[51] for the first time Australian courts recognised Aboriginal ownership of land and allowed for its continued existence in situations where it had not been extinguished by government action or legislation. The native title rights protected the traditional uses of the land, which meant it often gave rise to conflict with competing uses, e.g. mines or sheep or cattle stations on government leases. With the passage of history, different Aboriginal groups might claim rights over the same land as well as face claims by occupiers that native title had been extinguished. To deal with these

47 Section 26.
48 Supreme Court General Practice Note No 6 – Mediation.
49 T. Sourdin, *Mediation in the Supreme and County Courts of Victoria*, Department of Justice, undated, pp. 10 and 15.
50 *Ibid.*, p. 48.
51 (1992) 175 CLR 1.

complex and sensitive issues, the Native Title Tribunal was established and it has adopted mediation as its primary dispute resolution method.[52]

The acceptance of mediation in the litigation process is illustrated by the fact that mediation is now regarded as part of the ordinary costs of the litigation that can be recovered by the winning party unless other costs orders have been made.[53]

The advantages of court-annexed mediation include statutory protection of the mediators and of the confidentiality of the mediation.[54] Another advantage is the capacity to convert settlement agreements into judgments of the court so that they become enforceable immediately. The statutes or court rules that empower a court to order mediation usually include provisions enabling a settlement agreement 'to be embodied in a judgment'[55] or a party 'may apply to the court for an order giving effect to an agreement reached at or after a mediation'.[56] The conversion of a settlement agreement to a judgment is not automatic as the courts have discretion but in the ordinary course, parties can and would expect to have any settlement become orders of the court.

2.1.2.2. Pre-action mediation

Among the various measures that have promoted mediation over the last ten years has been the introduction of pre-litigation requirements by both courts and legislatures. In an increasing number of jurisdictions, legislatures are requiring parties to have attempted some form of dispute resolution before commencing proceedings.[57] The New South Wales and Federal Parliaments have all enacted legislation requiring parties to take genuine or reasonable steps to resolve the dispute before commencing proceedings. The Civil Dispute Resolution Act 2011 (Cth) requires parties in the Federal Court and Federal Magistrates Court to file, when commencing proceedings, a 'genuine steps' statement that outlines the steps taken to resolve the dispute. 'Genuine steps' means a 'sincere and genuine attempt to resolve the dispute, having regard to the person's circumstances and the nature and circumstances of the dispute.'[58] Failure to comply does not invalidate the proceeding but can be taken into the account by the court during the conduct of the case and also when deciding questions of costs.[59] The other major federal trial court, the Family Court has

---

52 Native Title Act 1993 (Cth).

53 *Newcastle City Council v. Paul Wieland* [2009] NSWCA 113.

54 See *infra*, pp. 70–71.

55 Section 65(7), Supreme Court Act 1935 (SA).

56 Section 50(1), Civil Proceedings Act 2011 (Qld).

57 See T. Sourdin, 'Making an attempt to resolve disputes before using courts: We all have obligations' (2010) 21 *Australasian Dispute Resolution Journal* 255.

58 Section 4, Civil Disputes Resolution Act 2011 (Cth).

59 *Supra* n. 51, section 12.

long made participation in mediation a preliminary requirement before litigation.[60] In New South Wales the Civil Procedure Act 2005 (NSW) requires parties to take reasonable steps to resolve the dispute before commencing proceedings.[61]

Even more significant to the growth in mediation has been State legislation that requires certain types of disputes to undergo mediation before litigation can commence. In around the year 2000 Australia experienced an insurance panic – one of the leading insurance companies went into liquidation. This provided a vehicle for vested interests to argue that the insurance crisis was, in large measure, due to excessive litigation and excessively plaintiff-friendly tort law. As tort law is a matter of State law, different States responded to the perceived crisis in different ways. One response was to alter the substantive law of tort with legislative provisions limiting damages, standards of care and in some cases, duty of care. Another response was to minimise the transaction costs involved in bringing tort claims.

One of the best examples is the Personal Injuries Proceedings Act 2002 (Qld). The major purpose of the Act was to 'assist the on-going affordability of insurance through appropriate and sustainable awards of damages for personal injury'. This was to be achieved by:[62]

> '(a) providing a procedure for the speedy resolution of claims for damages for personal injury to which this Act applies;
> (b) promoting settlement of claims at an early stage wherever possible; and
> (c) ensuring that a person may not start a proceeding in a court based on a claim without being fully prepared for resolution of the claim by settlement or trial.'

The Act creates extensive and comprehensive pre-litigation procedures that fall into two broad categories – maximising pre-litigation information collection and exchange, and a compulsory pre-litigation conference. While the compulsory conference does not require the use of mediators, the Act does provide for their use. It certainly has created greater interest and scope for mediation.[63] One consequence has been a collapse in personal injuries litigation in Queensland:[64]

> 'Most personal injury litigation has disappeared because of the compulsory pre-action negotiation imposed as a condition precedent to the plaintiff's entitlement to sue.

---

60 See *supra*, p. 56.

61 Part 2A, Civil Procedure Act 2005 (NSW).

62 Section 4, Personal Injuries Proceedings Act 2002 (Qld).

63 See R. Baer, 'Occupational therapists as mediators in personal injury compulsory conferences' (2007) 18 *Australasian Dispute Resolution Journal* 44.

64 B. Cairns, 'A review of some innovations in Queensland civil procedure' (2005) 26 *Australian Bar Review* 158, 184.

> With very few exceptions, any personal injury claims that do result in a court proceeding tend to be referred to mediation.'

Australian family law has always emphasised processes for minimising adjudication. Counselling and conciliation were part of the initial strategy to achieve this but mediation was quickly added to that strategy in the 1980s and 1990s. In 2006 the national Family Law Act 1975 underwent major amendments including the adoption of pre-action requirements. With a few exceptions, no action can be commenced in the Family Court unless a family dispute resolution practitioner certifies that the parties have made genuine attempts at resolving the dispute that have been unsuccessful. A national network of family dispute resolution centres was established and mediation seen as the primary dispute resolution method. This has mainstreamed mediation and made it familiar to a significant proportion of the population. In the three years after the 2006 amendments, use of existing dispute resolution services grew by 57% and use of Family Relationship Centres grew by 336%.[65]

#### 2.1.2.3. Compulsory mediation

Implicit in the development of mandatory pre-action mediation is the rejection of the argument that mediation is underpinned and defined as being a consensual process. Astor, amongst others, has long argued that this distinguishes mediation from formal justice:[66]

> 'Mediation must therefore derive its legitimacy from other sources, most notably consensuality and neutrality. Consensuality in mediation involves the idea that the parties have chosen a process that allows them to arrive at an agreement to which both (or all) consent and which may involve a choice to avoid the formal justice system in favour of a process that better meets their needs. Clearly the reality of consensuality is crucially affected by the reality of the consents made by the parties.'

This argument has not prevailed and mandatory mediation has continued to develop as part of the dispute resolution framework. It is exists both pre-action and can be ordered by a court any stage in the litigation. While a party's objection to court imposed mediation is a relevant factor to be taken into account by a court in deciding whether to order mediation, it is not determinative. In developing the factors to be taken into account when considering whether the court should order mediation, the English decision of

---

65 L. Moloney *et al.*, 'Mandatory dispute resolution and the 2006 family law reforms; use, outcomes, links to other pathways, and the impact of family violence' (2010) 16 *Journal of Family Studies* 192.

66 H. Astor, 'Rethinking Neutrality – a theory to inform practice' (2000) 11 *Australasian Dispute Resolution Journal* 73, 73.

*Halsey v. Milton Keynes General NHS Trust*[67] has been influential and the factors outlined in that case adopted:[68]

> '(a) the nature of the dispute; (b) the merits of the case; (c) the extent to which other settlement methods have been attempted; (d) whether the costs of ADR would be disproportionately high; (e) whether any delay in setting up and attending the ADR would have been prejudicial; and (f) whether the ADR had reasonable prospects of success.'

Courts have suggested that even if parties do not wish to participate, mediation can still be effective. Even if the dispute is not resolved, often mediation may narrow issues, saving time and cost in any on-going litigation.[69] There does not appear to be compelling evidence that mandatory mediation leads to worse outcomes than consensual mediation.[70] Certainly there has been significant support for mandatory mediation.[71]

### 2.1.2.4. Issues in mediation

With almost thirty years of history, mediation has become a well-established component of the justice system. It has reached the stage where there is sufficient common experience to start to develop standards and to deal with practical concerns that accompany a nascent profession. It has been almost completely unregulated. As Sourdin wrote in 2008, 'In this regard it is clear that the current regulation of mediation in Australia is marked by a degree of fragmentation, duplication and confusion.'[72]

Anyone can claim to be a mediator and offer his or her services to the public. Courts and other organisations involved in the delivery of dispute resolution services use 'approved' mediators and often this is defined as requiring completion of a recognised mediation training course. LEADR had introduced a system of accrediting mediators in 1998. A number of other organisations also accredited mediators who undertook their training courses. Where mediators are members of an established profession, often the profession has adopted standards and accreditation requirements. The legal profession has been a leader in this regard.

A 2001 inquiry by NADRAC had recommended against the introduction of a statutorily imposed regulatory framework preferring to rely on self-regulation

---

67 [2004] 4 All ER 920.

68 *Ezekiel-Hart v. Law Society (ACT)* [2012] ACTSC 135.

69 See *Idoport Pty Ltd v. National Australia Bank* [2001] NSWSC 427.

70 K. Mack, *Court Referral to ADR: Criteria and Research*, National Alternative Dispute Resolution Advisory Council, Melbourne 2003, p. 54.

71 M. McIntosh, 'A step forward – mandatory mediation' (2003) 14 *Australasian Dispute Resolution Journal* 280.

72 T. Sourdin, *Australian National Mediator Accreditation System*, NADRAC, 2009, p. 8.

using a set of voluntary standards developed in consultation with stakeholders. Under the auspices of NADRAC, extensive consultations led to the introduction in 2008 of the National Mediation Accreditation System. This involved the creation of a National Mediation Accreditation Committee that in 2010 set up the Mediation Standards Board. The system provides for voluntary accreditation and this is granted by Recognised Mediation Accreditation Bodies. The Mediation Standards Board has set standards for these Bodies including having at least ten accredited mediators, a capacity to provide training and supervision, a recognised complaints handling mechanism, and being a member of the Mediation Standards Board. These Bodies ensure that mediators accredited by them meet national standards. These include at least 38 hours of training delivered by more than one experienced and qualified mediator that includes participation in at least nine mediation simulations. In addition to the practical component, trainees must satisfactorily complete a written component. To maintain their accreditation a mediator must do at least 25 hours of mediation over a two-year period and at least twenty hours of professional development.[73] This is a higher standard than that required of lawyers by the regulatory framework for lawyers.

A further set of issues complementing the question of appropriate regulatory frameworks is questions of mediator immunity and confidentiality. The lack of protection for mediators and of information disclosed in the mediation process has given rise to much discussion within the dispute resolution community. Where mediation is based on private agreement, these issues can largely be managed as terms of the mediation agreement. The New South Wales Bar Association model agreement includes a clause that excludes any liability to the parties except in the case of fraud and requires the parties to indemnify the mediator for 'all liability of any kind whatsoever'.[74]

Cases against mediators are rare. In *Tapoohi v. Lewenberg (No 2)*[75] a senior barrister who had mediated a dispute over a deceased estate was joined to proceedings when one party failed to comply with the settlement agreement. It was alleged that the party had wanted tax advice on the settlement and had not wanted to settle at that time without it. The mediator was alleged to have pressured the parties to finalise the agreement and the final settlement agreement did not include this condition. The mediator sought to have the claim against him dismissed summarily and failed to do so. The court indicated that the matters were arguable and should go trial.[76]

---

73 D. Spencer and S. Hardy, *supra* n. 35, pp. 236–38.

74 New South Wales Bar Association, Mediation Agreement, clauses 27–8.

75 [2003] VSC 410. See M. Shirely and T. Cockburn, 'When Will a Mediator Operating Outside the Protection of Statutory Immunity be Liable' (2004) 32 *University of Western Australian Law Review* 83.

76 The claim against the mediator was subsequently withdrawn before trial.

The potential for liability has given rise to new professional indemnity insurance products. As part of the approval process for accreditation under the Mediation Standards Board, the mediator must satisfy the Board it has satisfactory insurance cover. Where the mediator is a member of recognised profession, they will usually have compulsory professional indemnity insurance and may not need separate insurance. Where the mediator is appointed by the court or is undertaking a court ordered mediation, many jurisdictions provide the mediator with the protection enjoyed by judges or judicial officials.[77]

NADRAC has recently reported on the issue of immunity and confidentiality to the Commonwealth Government. It distinguished between mandatory ADR and private ADR and recommended different approaches for each of these. Where the ADR was mandatory, which was defined as where required by legislation or ordered by a court, legislation should be enacted requiring the parties to act in good faith and to adhere to prescribed conduct standards. Legislation should provide immunity to the mediators and protect the confidentiality of the mediation.

For private ADR, NADRAC recommended that no statutory immunity should be provided nor should statutorily enforced confidentiality exist. The importance in enabling parties in private mediation to agree to the manner and form of the mediation was thought to be essential to preserve the flexibility, accessibility and informality that are the essence of ADR. Creating statutory provisions was thought to increase the prospect of court intervention and supervision and bring ADR and mediation closer to coercive, public processes of courts.[78]

## 2.2. CASE APPRAISAL AND NEUTRAL EVALUATION

Case appraisal and neutral evaluation involve using a third party to provide the parties with advice on desirable and possible outcomes in the dispute. In 1990 Sir Laurence Street, one of the early promoters of mediation and alternative dispute resolution in Australia noted that 'expert appraisal' was increasingly used as an ADR mechanism.[79] In this chapter 'expert appraisal' and case appraisal are treated as being synonymous although NADRAC does distinguish the latter from the former on the basis that case appraisal is undertaken by a non-expert dispute resolution practitioner.[80]

---

77 See for example, section 65, Supreme Court Act 1935 (SA); section 52, Civil Proceedings Act 2011 (Qld); section 33, Civil Procedure Act 2005 (NSW).

78 National Alternative Dispute Resolution Advisory Council, *Maintaining and Enhancing the Integrity of ADR Processes: From Principles to Practice through People*, Commonwealth of Australia, 2011.

79 Sir L. Street, 'Binding and Non-binding Expert Appraisal', (1990) 1 *Australasian Dispute Resolution Journal* 133.

80 D. Spencer and S. Hardy, *supra* n. 35, p. 268.

During the 1990s a number of Australian jurisdictions began introducing case appraisal or neutral evaluation into their litigation process. In 1994 New South Wales introduced neutral evaluation as an option in the pre-trial process although it was removed in 2004 because it had not been useful.[81] Queensland chose to use the term 'case appraisal' when it introduced its scheme in 1995. Subsequently Tasmania, the Australian Capital Territory and Victoria adopted neutral evaluation as their descriptors when they introduced similar provisions.[82]

The Queensland provisions enable a court to refer any case to a case appraiser who will adopt such procedures as are necessary to reach a 'sound opinion of the likely outcome of the dispute'. This can in special circumstances include taking evidence on oath and examining witnesses. The parties are free to not to accept the advice of the case appraiser but if they continue with litigation and do not do better than the advice of the case appraiser, they incur significant costs penalties.[83] If they do not elect to proceed with the litigation within 28 days of the case appraiser's 'decision', that decision becomes final and is effectively converted to equivalent to a judgment of the court.[84]

The capacity to convert the appraisal into a binding judgment distinguished the Queensland scheme from other Australian schemes. In Tasmania, the Australian Capital Territory and Victoria the neutral evaluation is advisory only. The Victorian scheme is a pilot scheme in the Magistrates Court that commenced in 2010 but has been extended. Its distinguishing feature is that it requires the evaluator to be a magistrate experienced in civil litigation. It also places procedural limits on the process, e.g. a three-hour time limit for the evaluation hearing with each side limited to one hour.[85] Rankin argues that the Queensland model is to be preferred, being more procedurally rigorous and having greater capacity to lead to resolution, although the increased credibility that comes from having a judicial officer undertake the evaluation that occurs in Victoria is a significant advantage.[86]

What little data there is suggests that these procedures have not been greatly used. In Queensland for example, in the five years between 1998 and 2002 there were some 56 referrals to case appraisal.[87] To place this in context during that time approximately 1300–1400 matters were commenced in the court at that time.[88]

---

81 D. Spencer and S. Hardy, *supra* n. 35, p. 278.

82 D. Bamford, *Principles of Civil Litigation*, LawBook, Pyrmont 2010, p. 216.

83 Sections 41 and 45, Civil Proceedings Act 2011 (Qld).

84 Rule 341, Uniform Civil Procedure Rules 1999 (Qld).

85 Magistrates Court Of Victoria, Practice Note 4 of 2010.

86 M. Rankin, 'Case Appraisal and Neutral Evaluation: The creation of objection standards for resolving protracted civil disputes' (2012) 1 *Journal of Civil Litigation and Practice* 91, 110.

87 National Alternative Dispute Resolution Advisory Council, *ADR Statistics*, Commonwealth of Australia, 2003, p. 12.

88 Steering Committee For The Review Of Commonwealth/State Service Provision, *Review of Government Services 2002*, Productivity Commission, Table 9a.

## 2.3. COLLABORATIVE PRACTICE

The concept of collaborative practice appears to have first gained ground in Australia in 2005 when some law firms in Canberra adopted it as part of their practice. The principles of collaborative practice are relatively new, spreading from North America to the United Kingdom and now Australia. Lawyers engaged in collaborative practice enter into agreements that stipulate that should the dispute fail to be resolved and need to proceed to litigation, none of the lawyers or experts involved will continue with the case. New lawyers will need to be engaged to manage the litigation. The advantage of this is said to be that all those involved – the parties and the lawyers – will be enticed to act cooperatively and collaboratively to resolve the matter.[89] While collaborative practice would appear to lend itself to the whole range of dispute resolution options, some argue that it is located within the negotiation paradigm. It does not rely on third parties to facilitate or assist but promotes informed party control of negotiation with obligations to negotiate in good faith and within a problem-solving framework.[90]

The Canberra programme focused on family law and lobbied for recognition of collaborative practice by the Family Court of Australia and inclusion of it within the Family Court procedures. To assist with this and the promotion of collaborative practice more broadly, the proponents established a National Centre for Collaborative Practice in Canberra. Ardagh evaluated the Canberra experience and found that the results had not been overly positive. In fact relatively few cases had used collaborative practice and these were largely lawyer-initiated. There continued to be significant mistrust between lawyers and considerable disagreement and confusion about the model to be used. Ardagh concluded that while the experience had not been a resounding success, it had 'led to experimentation with more flexible and different consensual approaches to lawyering'.[91]

Despite this start, the principle of collaborative practice continued to attract interest and in 2007 the Law Council of Australia agreed to establish a Collaborative Practice Committee to promote the concept. In 2011, after considerable deliberation, the Law Council of Australia promulgated the *Australian Collaborative Practice Guidelines for Lawyers*. There are now collaborative practice associations in most Australian states but the extent to which it is actually practiced remains unknown.

---

89 A. Ardgagh, 'Evaluating collaborative practice in Australia – A case study of family lawyers in the ACT' (2010) 21 *Australasian Dispute Resolution Journal* 204.

90 M. Scott, 'Collaborative Practice: Dispute Resolution Competencies for the New Advocacy' (2008) 8 *QUT Law and Justice Journal* 213, 214.

91 National Alternative Dispute Resolution Advisory Council, *supra* n. 78, p. 216.

## 2.4. ADR IN CRIMINAL CASES

While ADR has developed largely in the context of civil disputes, it is also influencing developments in criminal cases. In Australia criminal process is also adopting certain ADR processes. The three most common kinds of process are offender–victim mediation, conferencing, and circle sentencing.

Underpinning all three processes are a mix of philosophies coupled with dissatisfaction with the outcomes from the criminal justice system for both offenders and victims. Taking the latter first, the high rates of recidivism suggest that the rehabilitative and crime prevention goals of criminal justice are not being met and at the same time victims are often left largely unheard and 'unrepaired' by the criminal justice system.

Complementing this is a collection of philosophical approaches ranging from Christie's arguments against the total appropriation of crime by the state[92] to the restitutionary theories of Abel and Frank.[93] Supplementing this is a range of biblically based responses to crime developed by some church groups and psychological literature on the role of shame and forgiveness in undoing the harm caused by crime.[94] By the 1990s these had coalesced under the banner 'restorative justice' which had as its goals minimising the harm suffered by the victim and enabling the offender to deal with some of the causes of the offending.

### 2.4.1. *Offender–victim mediation*

Around the same time in the 1970s and 1980s the Mennonite community began developing offender–victim mediation to provide an alternative and more therapeutic mechanism for dealing with crimes. By the mid-1990s some 500 programmes existed in North America and it had been adopted in parts of Europe and in Australia. In 1992 one of the earliest offender–victim mediation programmes was piloted in Queensland. Known as the Crime Reparation Project, it ran for 12 months and covered minor offences committed by both adults and juveniles. Research showed only a small number of mediations took place but participants were highly satisfied with the process and it was seen as leading to acceptance by offenders of responsibility for their offending and attempts to prevent re-offending.[95]

A current Australian example of victim–offender mediation has been the programme offered by the Western Australian Department of Correctional

---

92 N. Christie, 'Conflict as Property' (1977) 17 *British Journal of Criminology* 1.

93 C. Abel and F. Marsh, *Punishment and Restitution: A Restitutionary Approach to Crime and the Criminal*, Greenwood, Westport 1984.

94 J. Braithwaite, *Crime, Shame and Reintegration*, Cambridge University Press, Cambridge 1989; D. Van Ness and K. Heetderks Strong, *An Introduction to Restorative Justice*, 4th ed., Matthew Bender, New Providence NJ 2010, pp. 15–7.

95 G. Clarke, 'Victim Offender Mediation in Queensland' (1994) 14 *Queensland Lawyer* 169.

Services. It offers two kinds of mediation – a protective mediation that can be initiated by the victim or offender, and a reparative mediation that is ordered by a court. The purpose of the former is to enable victims and offenders to work out how they will interact when they live with an ongoing likelihood of contact e.g. in small rural communities. The latter is part of the sentencing process and if appropriate, a court can order mediation after the entry of a guilty plea to enable some restitutionary outcomes to be explored.

### *2.4.2. Conferencing*

There are several wellsprings for the development of modern conferencing in criminal law. The development of community conferencing for Maori offenders in New Zealand is often regarded as a starting point for restorative conferencing. In 1989 New Zealand restructured its youth justice legislation to enable new ways of dealing with young offenders. Maori communities had a long history of treating crime and harm caused by a crime as a community issue requiring resolution by the community. The Children, Young Persons and their Families Act 1989 (NZ) introduced the concept of Family Group Conferencing as an alternative to courts. This brought together the offender and his or her family, the victim and his or her family, and the police or other public officials to attempt to reach the best outcomes for victims and offenders.[96]

In 1992 this approach had crossed the Tasman Sea to Australia where police in New South Wales were experimenting on an ad hoc basis with the use of conferencing for young offenders. Very quickly other Australian states began trialling programmes of youth conferencing. South Australia was the first to place this on a statutory basis with the Young Offenders Act 1993 (SA). This has continued to be the primary mechanism for dealing with minor crime committed by young offenders. By 2001 all jurisdictions had some form of conferencing for young offenders and all but two jurisdictions were doing so under legislation.

The conference has three stages. In the introduction the ground rules of the conference are outlined and the participants introduced. In the second phase the police outline the offence and the victim explains the consequences of the crime for them and the offender is invited to explain how or why the offence occurred. In the third phase the conference deals with how the harm can be made good and any the chances of any re-occurrence of criminal behaviour minimised.[97]

---

96 G. Maxwell and A. Morris, *Family, Victims and Culture: Youth Justice in New Zealand*, Social Policy Agency and Institute of Criminology, Wellington 1993.

97 H. Hayes and K. Daly, 'Youth Justice Conferencing and Re-Offending' (2003) 20 *Justice Quarterly* 725, 727.

Ongoing and significant research into the effects of restorative justice conferencing continue in Australia. The results have been consistent in generally showing high satisfaction with the process. Participants feel that they are treated fairly and are happy with the outcomes. The research on recidivism has been inconsistent and the results not as promising as some restorative justice advocates had hoped.[98]

### *2.4.3. Circle sentencing*

Circle sentencing is an alternative process for sentencing indigenous defendants. It seeks to involve the offender's community in the sentencing process. It also gives victims an active role in the sentencing process. Said to have first developed in Canada in 1992, the approach was quickly adopted in Australia. While Australian jurisdictions adopted circle sentencing in different ways, the basic approach was similar.

The defendant must have pleaded guilty to the offence. At the sentencing hearing a more inclusive court environment was created – either on an ad hoc basis or more recently with permanent facilities. The judicial officer would no longer sit in an elevated position remote from the other participants but would be part of a circle or roundtable which included the offender and his or her family, the victim and his or her family, elders from the relevant indigenous community, police, and legal representatives. The elders may speak frankly to the offender and strategies for dealing with the offender are discussed. This can include restitution or reparation for the offender and includes elements of the shaming and re-integration model advocated by Braithwaite and used in the restorative justice conferencing model. The judicial officer alone decides the sentence but takes into account the information gained from the circle sentencing process.

While these can take place within the context of ordinary criminal courts, the most common approach in Australia is to create a specialised Indigenous Court. South Australia was the first to do so in 1999 and most Australian jurisdictions have now followed. By 2009 there were over 50 indigenous courts operating across Australia. These are undergoing continued evaluations but the research again shows limited if any impact on recidivism. However they enjoy high satisfaction rates from a procedural perspective and are seen as building bridges between a disempowered indigenous community and the courts.[99]

---

98 H. Hayes *et al.*, 'Explaining Continuity and Change in Offending Behaviour after a Restorative Justice Conference' (2011) 23 *Current Issues in Criminal Justice* 127, 128.

99 E. Marchetti, *Indigenous Sentencing Courts*, Indigenous Justice Clearinghouse, Research Brief No. 5, 2009.

## 2.5. ADR: EMBEDDED AND EMBODIED

ADR has become embedded in the Australian community. It is to be found at all levels of the community, be it internal family disputes, disputes between neighbours, business disputes, disputes with government and indeed even international disputes. Increasingly sophisticated understandings of conflict management and dispute resolution are converting ADR from a fall-back option to fill a vacuum created by the perceived failings of the formal civil justice system to a set of processes that have intrinsic value in their own right.

ADR exists in the public and the private sphere. It has been present long enough for it now to experience the challenges of 'institutionalisation'. This can be seen in the work of NADRAC that has, for much of the last decade, been grappling with issues of definition, of professional standards, and the development of and regulation of specialised dispute resolution practitioners. Nevertheless tensions inherent in ADR continue to exist. ADR proponents are divided on the degree to which the sector should be regulated. There are those for whom the lack of structures and obligations that have accompanied the evolution of ADR are critical to its capacity to respond to the needs of individuals and the particular circumstances of any dispute. This tension is exacerbated by the increasing involvement of the legal profession in ADR. Judges and lawyers have played a prominent role in promoting ADR and easing its acceptance. But judges and lawyers may bring to ADR the mindset and skills developed during years of legal practice that can be different from ADR practitioners with other backgrounds.

With civil litigation diminishing, increasing numbers of lawyers are becoming mediators, arbitrators, and neutral evaluators. There have been extensive calls for law schools to better prepare law graduates for the new world of dispute resolution.[100] Law schools are now broadening the curriculum to ensure law students are provided with better understandings of ADR. All Australian law schools offer courses in ADR and in many of them, the course (either on its own or combined with another course) is compulsory.[101] One of the competencies required of a law graduate seeking admission to practice is being able to 'assess the merits of the case and identify the dispute resolution alternatives' which are listed as including negotiation, mediation, arbitration,

---

100 K. Douglas, 'Shaping the future: The discourses of ADR and legal education' (2008) 8 *QUT Law & Justice Journal* 118; J. Gutman *et al.*, 'Why Teach Alternative Dispute Resolution to Law Students – Part One' (2006) 16 *Legal Education Review* 125; M. Townes O'Brien, 'Facing Down the Gladiators: Law Schools' Hidden Adversarial Curriculum' (2001) 37 *Monash University Law Review* 43.

101 K. Mack, 'Integrating Procedure, ADR and Skills: New Teaching and Learning for New Dispute Resolution Processes' (1998) 9 *Legal Education Review* 83; K. Douglas, 'The teaching of ADR in Australian law schools: Promoting non-adversarial practice in law' (2011) 22 *Australasian Dispute Resolution Journal* 49.

litigation and case appraisal. The admission requirements also include 'negotiating settlements' and under Lawyers' Skills repeat the need to be able to negotiate settlements and facilitate early resolution of disputes.[102]

Illustrating the acceptance of the growing importance of ADR within the legal practice has been the change to the legal profession's conduct rules. These rules set the standards of legal practice and any breach can lead to disciplinary action being taken against the lawyer. Under the new Australian Solicitors Conduct Rules 2011 solicitors must inform their clients of the 'alternatives to fully contested adjudication of the case which are reasonably available to the client'.[103] This, when combined with the growth of mandatory pre-action requirements intended to promote settlement, means that no practicing lawyer involved in disputes can fail to consider ADR options and properly inform their clients of those options.

102 These competency standards apply across Australia although are enacted by each jurisdiction. See for example, Legal Practitioners Education and Admission Council Rules 2004 (SA), Appendix B.

103 Rule 7(2).

# CHINA

Yuanshi Bu*

## Contents



* The author would like to thank her assistant Mr Daniel Metzger for his effective assistance in preparing the first draft.

# 1. ORIGIN, EVOLUTION AND CURRENT SITUATION OF ADR IN CHINA

## 1.1. OVERVIEW

### *1.1.1. Types of ADR instruments*

In the Chinese legal setting, ADR is a concept borrowed from foreign law, particularly from US law. The most popular ADR instruments include mediation and arbitration. Mediation can be further divided into court-annexed mediation and extra-judicial mediation, which includes people's mediation, administrative mediation, institutional mediation and industry-based mediation.[1]

As the traditional ADR mechanism in China,[2] mediation is often connected with arbitration and treated as the first step preceding arbitration proceedings, as illustrated by the Law on Labor Dispute Mediation and the Law on Mediation and Arbitration of Rural Land Contract Disputes. In the past, the China International Economic and Trade Arbitration Commission (CIETAC) combined mediation and arbitration in its practice despite the lack of explicit mediation rules.[3] The combination of mediation and arbitration has now been incorporated into the current CIETAC arbitration rules. The law on arbitration also contains several provisions which allow for mediation in arbitration proceedings. If the parties thereafter reach a consensus via negotiation, the arbitral tribunal can render a so-called conciliation statement which has the same legal effect as a binding arbitral award. Due to this special feature, some authors see mediation in arbitration proceedings as a distinct subcategory of mediation.

Petition[4] also plays a significant role in addressing grievance,[5] but is not regarded as an ADR instrument in this chapter, because petition offices are only

---

1 Cf. W. Wang, 'The Role of Conciliation in Resolving Disputes: A P.R.C. Perspective' (2005) 20 *Ohio State Journal on Dispute Resolution* 421; some authors see mediation in arbitration proceedings as a subcategory of mediation.

2 Y. Fan, 'Development of ADR in Contemporary China' (2002) *ZZP Int* 533, 534.

3 W. Wang, 'Distinct Features of Arbitration in China – A Historical Perspective' (2006) 23 *Journal of International Arbitration* 74.

4 Petitioning (also known as letters and calls, correspondence and reception, *xinfang* or *shangfang*) is the administrative system for hearing complaints and grievances from individuals in the PRC. Definition from Wikipedia.

5 For a detailed description of the working mechanism of the petition system in China see: C. Minzer 'Xinfang: An Alternative to Formal Chinese Legal Institutions' (2006) 42 *Stanford Journal of International Law* 103.

empowered to forward the petitions to the responsible government agencies after they have examined and confirmed the merits of petitioners' submissions, instead of adjudicating or mediating the disputes themselves.

It should be noted that ADR instruments may also be divided based on their nature or carrier into subtypes such as non-governmental ADR, specialised ADR, industrial ADR and administrative ADR.[6] Non-governmental ADR refers to ADR conducted by grassroots organisations or other non-governmental institutions such as community autonomy organisations. Specialised ADR describes mediation specialised for a certain type of dispute, such as mediation and arbitration of labour, medical or consumer disputes, traffic accidents as well as disputes over intellectual property. Administrative ADR is just another name for administrative mediation, which is used to handle damages resulting from personal or property damage by the competent administrative authority (*infra* at 1.2.4.).

To a certain degree, one ADR instrument can fall into more than one category. For instance, labour arbitration is at the same time both a specialised arbitration as well as an administrative arbitration.

### *1.1.2. Factors affecting the development of ADR*

To understand the evolution and current situation of ADR in China, one must be aware of the interaction between the traditional legal culture, the ideology and guiding policy of the Communist Party, the influence of foreign law, the court mechanism in China and the efficiency as well as neutrality of the ADR instruments. Of course, other factors mentioned in the literature such as the state of the social structure and the awareness of ordinary Chinese people of their legal rights also play a certain role.[7]

Although there is no unity of opinion as to whether Chinese people had the same tendency to avoid formal legal proceedings before the court as the Japanese, it is generally acknowledged that one salient feature of the Chinese traditional legal culture is the official discouragement of the resort to courts.[8] Litigation was somewhat perceived as a disturbance to the harmony of the community and a threat to the stability of society. In contrast, mediation was the channel of dispute settlement favoured by the feudal rulers.

The traditional legal culture has undergone significant – sometimes even entirely opposite – revaluation as the Communist Party ideology changed over time after the foundation of the PRC. In the 1980s, when the primary goal of the Party was to rebuild the legal order, the traditional culture of suppressing

---

6 Y. Fan, *supra* n. 2, pp. 548–549.

7 Y. Fan, *supra* n. 2, p. 550.

8 K. Bernhard and P.C.C. Huang, *Civil Law in Qing and Republican China*, Stanford University Press, Palo Alto 1994, pp. 9 ff.

litigation came under criticism[9] and citizens were encouraged to assert their rights through formal legal channels. In the following period, the political elite felt overstrained by the citizens' activism in pursuing their rights and the positive side of the traditional culture was rediscovered and highlighted. In the last decade China has been experiencing a revival of ADR. This development appears to be in line with the global trend, but is actually brought about by the new orientation of Party policy, which is not surprising in a country like China where Party policy dominates the entire society and the State is sufficiently powerful to determine the direction of the development of the judiciary.[10]

The influence of foreign law on the reconstruction of the legal system in China after the adoption of the reform and opening policy in 1978 has been enormous.[11] One often cited argument for enhancing the employment of ADR in dispute settlement is that ADR represents the international trend that had its origin in the US. However, this argument is debatable. Some have rightfully pointed out that China distinguishes itself from other Western countries in its overall legal environment and the level of development of the rule of law. As China has not yet completed the modernisation of its legal system, while industry nations have already entered a post-modern era, it would be a mistake to diminish the role played by ordinary courts in dispute settlements instead of attaching more importance to it.[12] Obviously, the latter opinion prevails in academic circles.

The attitude towards ADR also depends on the way courts function in China. It should be noted that Chinese judges are subject to regular internal and external performance review. Since a settlement is regarded as a party act, a judge is unlikely to make mistake there. Furthermore, a settlement is not appealable and the parties to a settlement generally have no reason to go to petition, therefore, resolving disputes through settlement is also encouraged by the court. Generally speaking, judges tend to suggest a settlement, or sometimes are even inclined to force the parties into one, in particular in cases which may result in a controversial judgment. In addition, given the significant caseload that has been steadily rising in recent years and the slow growth of the number of judges, most judges would also prefer to close a case through parties' settlement, because this in most cases will reduce the workload of the responsible judge. It is therefore understandable that the court has put more emphasis on mediation in court proceedings in recent years, which has somehow reduced the appeal of non-court annexed mediation to disputing parties.

---

9 For a summary of the critical opinions see H. Chen, 'Mediation, Litigation and Justice: Confucian Reflections in a Modern Liberal Society' (2001) 3 *Modern Law Science* 7–8.

10 In this respect see H. Lu, 'State Channeling of Social Grievances: Theory and Evidence in China' (2011) 41 *Hong Kong Law Journal* 547.

11 Y. Fan, *supra* n. 2, p. 534.

12 C. Zhang, 'Zivilprozess und Durchsetzung privater Ansprüche', in Y. Bu (ed.), *Recht und Rechtswirklichkeit in Deutschland und China*, Mohr Siebeck, Tübingen 2011, pp. 16–18.

Last but not least, the development of mediation in China is also, to a certain degree, restrained by the question of neutrality of the mediators and problems related to the enforceability of mediation agreements. In the latter regard, the People's Mediation Law takes a moderate view: it does not grant enforceability directly to all settlement agreements, but only to those settlement agreements which have been checked and confirmed in judicial ratification proceedings. While the enforcement of people's mediation agreements is explicitly regulated, the issue is still unsettled with regard to administrative mediation, commercial mediation and industrial mediation (*infra*).

The following parts seek to give a more detailed description of the origin, evolution and current situation of each ADR mechanism.

## 1.2. MEDIATION

### *1.2.1. Definition*

The term mediation (调解) is not defined in a statute in China; thus, it is not easy to provide a precise and generally accepted definition thereof. Moreover, English translations of Chinese laws sometimes translate the Chinese term for mediation as 'conciliation', which results in even more confusion. In a broader sense, it can be said that the Chinese term for mediation stands for a process in which the parties voluntarily come to an arrangement about contested rights or obligations under the guidance of a third party.[13] On the one hand, the elements of voluntariness as well as the element of the process not being institutionalised are typical for mediation. On the other hand, in certain areas such as foreign trade or people's mediation, one can observe a high degree of legislative regulation and tightly controlled institutions, which are more typical of arbitration or conciliation. This leads some authors to assume that in China, there is no distinction between 'mediation' and 'conciliation'.[14] Whatever the solution for the linguistic side of the distinction may be, it has to be kept in mind that the Chinese term 'mediation' does not fully correspond to mediation as known in most Western jurisdictions.

### *1.2.2. Court-annexed mediation*

Court-annexed mediation refers to mediation by the courts in ongoing litigation. As a part of civil proceedings, it is governed by Articles 93–99 of the Civil

[13] B. Pissler, 'Mediation in China' in Hopt and Steffek (eds.), *Mediation*, Mohr Siebeck, Tübingen 2007, p. 607.

[14] L. Cao, 'Combining Conciliation and Arbitration in China: Overview and Latest Developments' (2006) 9 *International Arbitration Law Review* 85.

Procedure Law. Court-annexed mediation is the form of mediation that is most similar to mediation in Western jurisdictions.

Mediation has long been used by the courts as a preferred form of dispute resolution, as it existed even prior to the founding of the PRC in the areas ruled by the Communist Party.[15] However, in today's China – unlike in Western countries generally – mediation is not always considered an esteemed tradition, but is sometimes characterised by a negative image, in particular in the last twenty years of the twentieth century. In everyday language, mediation settlements are compromises, in which right and wrong are blurred and the innocent party must sacrifice a portion of its right to restore peace with the more demanding party. The concept of 'judgment instead of mediation' characterised the twenty-year judicial reform in China, which started in the early 1980s.

In the first PRC Civil Procedure Law, enacted in 1982 as a provisionally implemented statute, the 'priority of mediation over trial' (Article 6) was a principle. This was replaced by the principle of 'voluntariness and lawfulness of mediation' (Article 9) in the 1991 Civil Procedure Law. Moreover, it was established that trial must be commenced or resumed if the mediation attempt fails. Thus, the practice of continuing futile mediation attempts is supposed to be put to an end. This shift in attitude towards court-annexed mediation in civil proceedings occurred at a time when China experienced a kind of 'access to justice' movement. In the 1990s, new judge positions were created, imposing courthouses were built and the jurisdiction of the courts was expanded. The motto of this era was 'every village should build a branch office of the Court'. This was accompanied by the departure of mediating activities of judges for the sake of the supremacy of law. However, mediation has experienced a strong revival since the turn of the millennium. As described above, there are many reasons for this change. The crucial one was the new Party line of a 'harmonious society'.[16]

### *1.2.3. People's mediation*

A unique form of mediation is the so-called people's mediation – the only form of mediation to have found entry into the Chinese constitution in 1982.[17] It evolved from its heritage in traditional Chinese conciliation and was first set up in the 1940s in the areas ruled by the Communist Party. In the period from the

---

[15] J. Liang, 'The Enforcement Of Mediation Settlement Agreements in China' (2008) 19 *American Review of International Arbitration* 499.

[16] To understand 'harmonious society' see Kleining, 'In search of harmony' <www.kas.de/db_files/dokumente/laenderberichte/7_dokument_dok_pdf_12235_1.pdf> accessed 24.04.2012.

[17] For a detailed summary of the evolution of people's mediation in China in Chinese see S. Jiang, *Mediation, Rule by Law and Modernization: A Survey on Chinese Mediation Systems*, Chinese Legal Publishing House, Beijing 2001; S. Lubman, *Bird in a Cage: Legal Reform After Mao*, Standford University Press, Palo Alto 1999, pp. 40–71.

foundation of the PRC in 1949 until the beginning of the Cultural Revolution in 1966, people's mediation played an important role in dispute settlement in both rural and urban areas. Although restored in 1978, people's mediation began to decline after reaching its peak between 1986 and 1990.[18] In spite of attempts by the government and legislature to revive people's mediation by enacting an impressively large number of guiding policy documents since 2002[19] and ultimately the People's Mediation Law in 2010, people's mediation has not recovered from the trend of marginalisation.[20] In particular, being perceived rather as a political tool and not a professional dispute resolution instrument, people's mediation does not appeal to the younger, affluent and educated generation.[21] The fact that the revival of people's mediation depends to a large extent on state power and not primarily on party preference suggests the declining acceptance of this dispute resolution mechanism in society.[22]

Some commentators have noticed that the tension between the institutionalisation and the flexibility of people's mediation actually curtails its development in contemporary Chinese society.[23] One advantage of people's mediation is believed to be its flexibility, meaning the mediator may suggest a settlement that better suits the needs of the parties, but is not completely in line with the legal position of the parties according to the law. In this sense, people's mediation is not a right-based mediation, as in Germany, but rather an interest-based mediation. In the past, however, people's mediators were required to mediate according to the law,[24] which significantly confined mediators' room for operation and thereby diminished the attractiveness of people's mediation.[25] This tension has not yet been solved by the People's Mediation Law, which takes an ambiguous attitude by freeing mediators from the strict obligation to abide by the law (Article 22) and at the same time, imposing the duty to stick to principles and to clarify the legal positions of the parties (Articles 3 and 21).

The people's mediation committees are structured to be mass organisations (Article 7). Villagers' committees and residents' committees are required to establish people's mediation committees. Enterprises and public institutions may also choose to establish such mediation committees (Article 8). However, people's mediation committees are subject to the guidance produced by the

18 For a detailed description of the historical development of people's mediation in China see Y. Fan, *supra* n. 2, pp. 537–538.

19 Y. Fan, *supra* n. 2, p. 534.

20 W. Zhou, 'People's Mediation in Transformation: Three Contradictions – Review On The People's Mediation Law' (2011) 10 *Journal of Social Science* 100–101.

21 A. Halegua, 'Reforming the People's Mediation in Urban China' (2005) 35 *Hong Kong Law Journal* 715.

22 W. Zhou, *supra* n. 20, p. 103.

23 W. Zhou, *supra* n. 20, pp. 103–105.

24 Article 1 of the Several Provisions on People's Mediation of 2002 and Article 1 of the Ordinance on the Organization of People's Mediation Committees.

25 W. Zhou, *supra* n. 20, p. 105.

Ministry of Justice, which has resulted to a certain degree in the much criticised bureaucratisation of people's mediation. Until 2008, a nationwide network existed of more than 800,000 people's mediation organisations employing in total about 4 million people's mediators.[26] People's mediation is generally available for all kinds of civil disputes, with the majority of the cases being in practice family, community and non-commercial cases between natural persons, in certain regions also covering disputes between natural persons, legal persons or other social organisations.

The lack of a clear delineation of the scope of application is alleged to be a deficit of the People's Mediation Law. This problem had been recognised in the course of deliberation on the People's Mediation Law, but was ultimately left out in the final legal text for fear of delaying the enactment of this law, which could have caused controversy among the delegates.[27] Currently, it remains to be seen whether some established forms of mediation such as administrative mediation will be merged into people's mediation.[28]

### *1.2.4. Administrative mediation*

In the common understanding, administrative mediation does not primarily refer to mediation in public law, but mainly to mediation in certain areas of civil or commercial law conducted by specific government agencies, whereby the administrative authority acts as mediator, witness and enforcement authority at the same time.[29] The legitimacy for government agencies to intervene in civil and commercial disputes is said to be that the civil/commercial disputes subject to administrative mediation frequently involve administrative law at the same time. For example, a defective product does not only give rise to civil quality disputes but may also trigger administrative fines. Due to their special technical expertise, such agencies may allegedly settle these disputes more rapidly and accurately.

Similar to people's mediation, administrative mediation also emerged prior to the foundation of the PRC in the so-called revolution bases of the Communist Party.[30] Administrative mediation usually precedes some form of litigation with the goal of avoiding lawsuits. The result of such administrative mediation is in essence an agreement between the parties. Due to the lack of enforceability of mediation agreements, administrative mediation is often perceived as a waste of time and resources. In this setting, neither parties nor the mediators are genuinely motivated to go through the mediation procedure. The responsible

26 Explanations on the Draft People's Mediation Law dated 01.07.2010, <www.npc.gov.cn/npc/xinwen/lfgz/flca/2010-07/01/content_1580323.htm> accessed 24.04.2012.

27 Y. Fan, 'An Analysis of the People's Mediation Law of the PRC' (2011) 2 *Jurist* 3.

28 *Ibid.*, p. 3.

29 Y. Fan, *supra* n. 2, p. 549.

30 Y. Fan, *Study on ADR Mechanism*, Renmin University Publishing House, Beijing 2000, p. 76.

government agencies used to express strong reluctance to continue offering this service. However, the current policy of the central government is unambiguous: administrative mediation is a component of the rule of law and has to be strengthened correspondingly.[31] A national regulation dedicated to this form of mediation has already been put under deliberation by the State Council.

Until the national regulation comes into force, administrative mediation is mainly regulated by local regulations and widely scattered single provisions in national statutes and administrative regulations such as the Marriage Law, the Road Traffic Safety Law, the Law on Public Security Administration and Sanction, the Law on Prevention of Air Pollution, the Regulations on Handling Medical Accidents, and the Implementation Regulations of the Road Traffic Safety Law. The subject matter jurisdiction of administrative mediation covers primarily civil disputes and to a limited extent administrative disputes (*infra* at 2.4). The former includes (a) verification of certain rights such as the right to use ocean territory, rights of ownership and use of forests; (b) ascertainment of women's rights to use land of maritime disputes or liability for compensation; and (c) mediation regarding the amount of compensation in medical or traffic accidents or environmental pollution cases or infringement of intellectual property or consumer disputes. In local regulations, the subject matter jurisdiction is extended to almost all civil disputes and administrative disputes arising from administrative activities.[32] Currently, administrative mediation has still many deficits to overcome: the existing rules on administrative mediation are too simplistic and vary significantly from city to city,[33] and the professional qualification of the mediators is often not guaranteed.

### *1.2.5. Institutional mediation*

Institutional mediation refers to mediation conducted by professional mediation centres and is often also called commercial mediation. An example is the Conciliation Center of CCPIT (China Council for the Promotion of International Trade)/CCOIC (China Chamber of Commerce). Most of the disputes solved using this mechanism are concerned with commercial law.[34]

### *1.2.6. Industry-based mediation*

Industry-based mediation refers to mediation conducted by autonomous industrial organisations for industrial professionals in or related to a specific

---

31 Opinions of the State Council on Strengthening the Construction of Rule of Law Governments issued in October 2010.

32 Z. Zhang and Q. Gu, 'A Study on "Administrative Mediation in Chinese Legal Documents"' (2011) 5 *Jiang Huai Forum* 126–127.

33 Z. Zhang and Q. Gu, *supra* n. 32, pp. 128–129.

34 See more details: J. Liang, *supra* n. 15, pp. 502–505.

industry such as accountancy, insurance, banking, logistics, medical services, transportation, real estate or the tourism industry. The legal basis for industry-based mediation is the regulation 'Some Provisions Concerning the Work of People's Mediation' issued by the Ministry of Justice in China in September 2002. Some of the industry-based mediation committees have been set up by the relevant industry associations, and others are established by or under the supervision of the relevant government bureaus.

The status of industry-based mediation committees has also been recognised in Article 34 of the People's Mediation Law, according to which, 'if it is necessary, social groups or other organisations may establish people's mediation committees to mediate disputes among the people.' The Ministry of Justice issued the 'Opinions of the Ministry of Justice on Strengthening the Building of Industry-based and Profession-based People's Mediation Committees' in May 2011 in an effort to further promote industry-based mediation. The general advantage of industry-based mediation is that the mediator normally has sufficient professional know-how and experience. On the other hand, as mediators are selected by the industry association, their neutrality is sometimes questionable.

## 1.3. GRAND MEDIATION

With the adoption of the People's Mediation Law, people's mediation has been given a fresh lease of life. Thus, the new catchword 'grand mediation' was coined with the support of the Supreme People's Court in 2008. 'Grand mediation' (大调解) brings together people's mediation, mediation by administrative bodies and judicial mediation. This is done under the auspices of the Party, the government and the leadership of the Committee of the Party for Politics and Law with the cooperation of the courts, prosecutors, police, petition authorities, real estate supervisory authorities and labour authorities, etc. In concrete terms, people's mediation bodies have been established in courts, petition offices, the traffic police and the labour mediation authorities. One-third of the disputes in Shanghai in 2009 reportedly could be resolved by 'grand mediation' and filtered out of the litigation channel. Despite such potential for success, the superiority of 'grand mediation' has apparently failed to convince all judges and litigants.[35] The advantages and disadvantages of mediation and judgment are often compared and weighed. However, there has been an excessive emphasis on mediation. This is disturbing given that it was introduced on the basis of proposals of some authors as a necessary correction of the supremacy of the law (唯法治论) and the supremacy of legal protection (司法救济至上).[36] If one views

[35] C. Zhang, *supra* n. 12, pp. 13–14.

[36] Y. Fan takes that view in *Theory and Practice of Conflict Settlement*, Tshinghua University Publishing House, Beijing 2007, pp. 293–298.

the legitimacy of the courts solving disputes by mediation as based on principles of self-determination of the parties,[37] one will be disappointed to realise that forced court settlements are common. Even with respect to judges, a free choice between mediation and judgment is not guaranteed, because the mediation rate is a factor in the evaluation of their working performance.[38]

A problematic special feature of 'grand mediation' is that the mediator lacks neutrality. In some cases, such as expropriation cases, the party liable to pay damages, namely the government, is also the mediator.[39] The court merely plays the role of a legally qualified adviser, who fosters a pragmatic solution, both compatible with the legal framework as well as taking social stability into account.[40]

In the overhaul of the Chinese Civil Procedure Law in 2012, a shift of attitude was not in sight. Rather, the coordination between mediation and adjudication has been optimised and the enforceability of settlement agreements has been secured.

## 1.4. ARBITRATION

The Chinese arbitration system began to evolve in the early 1900s with the opening of the Business Arbitration Office in 1912.[41] It was the first arbitration institution in China and was responsible for the settlement of business disputes. However, settlement agreements were weak as they relied on the consent of both parties to be legally binding.[42] After the founding of the PRC in 1949, China began establishing both domestic and foreign-related systems of arbitration that included labour arbitration, contract arbitration and real estate arbitration.[43] In the 1950s and 1960s, the Chinese government began actively promoting arbitration as the preferred means of economic conflict resolution. It was in these years that the systems of domestic and foreign-related arbitration began drifting apart, mainly because of China developing a mandatory domestic administrative arbitration system for the resolution of economic contract disputes. Starting in the 1980s, under the regime of the Economic Contract Law and further regulations, China began developing specific economic contract arbitration commissions at various levels. These arbitration commissions were

---

37 R. Stürner, 'Richterliche Vergleichsverhandlung und richterlicher Vergleich aus juristischer Sicht', in I. Meier, *Recht und Rechtsdurchsetzung: Festschrift für Hans Ulrich Walder zum 65. Geburtstag*, Schulthess, Zürich 1994, p. 280.

38 For a detailed description compare C. Minzner, 'China's Turn Against the Law' (2011) 59 *American Journal of Comparative Law* 956 ff.

39 J. Ai, '"Big Mediation" Under the Logic of Social Stabilization and Its Problems' (2011) 1 *Studies in Law and Business* 24.

40 *Ibid.*, p. 21.

41 J. Tao, *Arbitration Law and Practice in China*, Kluwer, London/New York 2004, p. 1.

42 L. Kniprath, *Die Schiedsgerichtsbarkeit der CIETAC*, Heymanns, Köln/Berlin 2004, p. 20.

43 J. Tao, *supra* n. 411, p. 1.

each specialised in the arbitration of disputes arising in a specific field, such as contracts, labour or intellectual property. These commissions were strictly hierarchical under the State Administration for Industry and Commerce, and jurisdiction was adopted by way of territorial jurisdiction so that parties could not choose arbitration commissions themselves. Arbitral awards did not have a binding effect on the parties.

All changed with the enactment of the Arbitration Law on 1 September 1995. The Arbitration Law introduced party autonomy, the independence of the arbitration commissions and was overall characterised by the effort of bringing domestic arbitration in line with international practice. Moreover, it stipulated that arbitral awards were now legally binding, with courts not being allowed to accept cases that had already been handled by arbitration commissions. From that point on, the evolution of the Chinese arbitration system was harmonised towards the internationally recognised principles of arbitration.

Following China's accession to the New York Convention in 1987, China's foreign-related system of arbitration received an impetus towards conformity with international standards, which was implemented into national law by the provisions of the Civil Procedure Law (1991), the Arbitration Law (1995) and the CIETAC Rules (1994 and 1995).[44] By then, arbitral awards rendered by international arbitral tribunals could be enforced in China, which encouraged the international business community to submit disputes for arbitration between these institutions.[45] The first enforcement of a Chinese arbitral award in a foreign country following the New York Convention was executed in 1989; and the first application of the New York Convention in China occurred in 1990.[46] In particular, the Supreme People's Court has by way of issuing several judicial interpretations ensured that the development of foreign-related and international arbitration in China follows international standards.[47] It can thus be inferred that as regards foreign-related arbitration, Chinese judges see arbitration as a supplement to their own work. Furthermore, as far as domestic arbitration is concerned, courts provide necessary assistance to arbitration, for example deciding on the jurisdiction of an arbitral tribunal if this is disputed (Article 20 of the Arbitration Law) or the preservation of evidence.[48] The most important function of the courts with respect to arbitration, however, is the scrutinising of awards to determine the recognisability and enforceability. In spite of protectionism of some local Chinese courts concerning the enforcement of Chinese arbitral awards, studies have shown that in practice the rejection of arbitral awards by Chinese courts is a rare phenomenon.[49]

---

44 L. Knipráth, *supra* n. 422, pp. 25 ff.

45 J. Tao, *supra* n. 411, p. 12.

46 L. Kniprath, *supra* n. 422, p. 24.

47 J. Tao, *supra* n. 411, p. 13.

48 *Ibid.*, p. 32.

49 L. Kniprath, *supra* n. 422, p. 179.

As regards the qualification of arbitrators, Article 13 of the Arbitration Law stipulates several qualifications necessary for being able to work as an arbitrator in a Chinese arbitration commission. These requirements are subdivided into moral and professional qualifications, such as being just and upright persons and having a minimum of eight years of professional experience in relevant areas.[50] Article 67 of the Arbitration Law allows the appointment of foreign specialists to foreign-related arbitration panels. However, there are no rigid qualification requirements for the appointment of arbitrators to an international panel.[51] It can be concluded that this makes it attractive for foreign nationals to act as arbitrators in a foreign-related arbitration commission (like CIETAC), perhaps even outweighing the relatively low salary. Once appointed, arbitrators appear on a list of the arbitration commissions like the List of Arbitrators of Domestic Cases and the List of Arbitrators of International Cases of CIETAC. The List of Arbitrators of Domestic Cases contains only Chinese arbitrators, whereas in international cases, parties can additionally chose arbitrators from Hong Kong, Macau or other countries.[52]

According to the Arbitration Law, institutions providing arbitration services for cases based in China must be registered with PRC judicial and administrative departments.[53] As foreign arbitration institutions such as the International Chamber of Commerce (ICC) are usually not registered with the PRC judicial and administrative departments, arbitration proceedings are mainly dominated by domestic arbitration institutions. The most prominent institution is CIETAC, alongside the China Maritime Arbitration Commission (CMAC).

CIETAC was established in 1957 under the name 'China Council for the Promotion of International Trade' and was renamed CIETAC in 1988. Since then, CIETAC has developed under the above-mentioned favourable circumstances to become one of the busiest arbitration institutions worldwide. Aside from CIETAC, more than 200 local arbitration institutions exist throughout mainland China.[54] Regarding the competency of these institutions, there are no differences between CIETAC and the local institutions; however, due to its head start in 1957, CIETAC can use its extensive experience especially with regard to international arbitrations as a virtual advantage. CIETAC has furthermore increased its attractiveness to international parties by frequently amending its rules in order to achieve a higher convergence with international best practices and to allow more autonomy and flexibility for the participating parties.[55]

---

50 *Ibid.*, p. 104.

51 J. Tao, *supra* n. 41, p. 98.

52 *Ibid.*, pp. 90–91; L. Kniprath, *supra* n. 42, p. 100.

53 F. Hess, 'The ICC and China' (2010) 15 (2) *IBA Arbitration News* 28.

54 <www.china-arbitration.com> accessed 24.04.2012.

55 R. Peerenboom and X. He, 'Dispute Resolution in China: Patterns, Causes And Prognosis' (2009) 4 *East Asia Law Review* 28; J. Zhu, 'China's CIETAC arbitration – new rules under review' (2011) 15(5) *International Arbitration Law Review* 34.

Nevertheless, recent factors such as the opening of ICC offices in Hong Kong and Singapore in 2008 have strengthened the role of the ICC in the region, thus leading to an increased number of international arbitration cases being dealt with pursuant to ICC rules in Hong Kong and Singapore, yet not in mainland China.[56]

## 2. AREAS OF LAW AFFECTED AND DEVICES USED IN EACH OF THEM

### 2.1. CIVIL LAW

In the area of family law, mediation is a mandatory proceeding mostly envisaged for divorce cases. According to Article 32 of the Marriage Law 2001, courts are obliged to perform mediation prior to trying the case in a divorce suit. Furthermore, mediation is stipulated as the primary legal avenue in cases of domestic violence and abandonment of family members.

Article 15 of the Inheritance Law stipulates that successors shall negotiate a settlement in the spirit of compromise as well as peaceful harmony. If these negotiations fail, the successors can call upon the people's mediation committee for mediation or file a lawsuit with the competent court.

In the area of contract and tort law, mediation may be conducted for certain types of contract disputes such as electricity disputes and disputes about the quality of vehicle repairs or tort liability for medical malpractice or traffic accidents. In this regard, the Ministry of Justice issued an opinion on 12 May 2011 on Strengthening the Building of Industry-based and Profession-based People's Mediation Committees (*supra* at 1.2.6.).

### 2.2. COMMERCIAL LAW

Parties to Chinese-foreign joint ventures are often recommended to hold a number of 'amicable negotiations' before beginning an arbitration proceeding or filing a lawsuit. In the field of foreign trade, arbitration also plays a key role.

### 2.3. LABOUR LAW

Numerous regulations exist regulating proceedings in labour disputes. Chinese labour law envisages a system with multiple steps – voluntary negotiation,

---

56 F. Hess, *supra* n. 53, p. 28.

mandatory mediation, arbitration and trial. After voluntary negotiation has failed, arbitration proceedings can be invoked with the arbitration committee at corporate level or directly with the labour arbitration committee. Mediation is a mandatory proceeding preceding labour arbitration, which in turn must precede a trial before court.

### 2.4. PUBLIC LAW

In the field of administrative law, mediation is prohibited except for cases concerning government liability. An exception is possible when minor disputes between citizens at the same time constitute administrative offences. In that case, police departments can mediate the dispute between citizens, and in the case of a successful mediation the penalty imposed by administrative law will be dropped. Likewise, mediation is permitted in the area of criminal law in private actions.

### 2.5. AREAS OF LAW EXCLUDING ARBITRATION

According to Article 3 of the Arbitration Law, matters relating to family law, inheritance law and administrative law cannot be resolved by way of arbitration.

## 3. GOVERNING RULES AND SOURCES

### 3.1. MEDIATION

The legal framework governing mediation in China consists of a large number of national statutes, administrative regulations, judicial interpretations and local provisions. Below are the most important ones:

National statutes:
- People's Mediation Law (人民调解法), promulgated on 28 August 2010 and effective on 1 January 2011;
- Law on Mediation and Arbitration of Rural Land Contract Disputes (农村土地承包经营纠纷调解仲裁法), promulgated on 27 June 2009 and effective on 1 January 2010;
- Law on Labor Dispute Mediation and Arbitration (劳动争议调解仲裁法), promulgated on 29 December 2007 and effective on 1 May 2008.

Administrative regulations:
- Provisions on the Negotiation and Mediation of Enterprise Labour Disputes (企业劳动争议协商调解规定), promulgated by the Ministry of Human

Resources and Social Security on 30 November 2011 and effective on 1 January 2012;
- Provisions on the Mediation of Electricity Disputes (电力争议纠纷调解规定), promulgated by the State Power Regulatory Commission on 30 September 2011 and effective on 1 January 2012;
- Some Provisions Concerning the Work of People's Mediation (人民调解工作若干规定), promulgated by the Ministry of Justice on 26 September 2002 and effective on 1 November 2002;
- Procedures of Mediation of Disputes about the Rights of Sea Area Use (海域使用权争议调解处理办法), promulgated by the State Oceanic Administration on 28 April 2002 and effective on 28 April 2002;
- Measures on Mediation of Disputes about the Quality of Vehicle Repairs (汽车维修质量纠纷调解办法), promulgated by the Ministry of Communications (dissolved) on 12 June 1998 and effective on 1 September 1998;
- Measures on Administrative Mediation of Contracts Disputes (合同争议行政调解办法), promulgated by the State Administration for Industry and Commerce on 3 November 1997 and effective on 3 November 1997.

Judicial interpretations:
- Several Provisions of the Supreme People's Court on the Judicial Ratification Procedure for the People's Mediation Agreements (最高人民法院关于人民调解协议司法确认程序的若干规定), promulgated by the Supreme People's Court on 23 March 2011 and effective on 30 March 2011;
- Provisions of the Supreme People's Court about Several Issues Concerning the Civil Mediation Work of the People's Court (最高人民法院关于人民法院民事调解工作若干问题的规定), promulgated by the Supreme People's Court on 16 September 2004 and effective on 1 November 2004;
- Some Provisions of the Supreme People's Court on Trying Civil Cases Involving the People's Conciliation Agreements (最高人民法院关于审理涉及人民调解协议的民事案件的若干规定), promulgated by the Supreme People's Court on 16 September 2002 and effective on 1 November 2002.

## 3.2. ARBITRATION

The primary source of law for Chinese arbitration is the Arbitration Law, which was issued in 1994 and entered into effect in 1995. Despite numerous proposals from the academic community and arbitration practitioners, the Arbitration Law has not yet been amended since its enactment and the scheduled overhaul is making slow progress.[57] Aside from the Arbitration Law, other binding

57 M. Chi, 'Drinking Poison to Quench Thirst: The Discriminatory Arbitral Award Enforcement Regime under Chinese Arbitration Law' (2009) 39 *Hong Kong Law Journal* 542.

regulations exist in the Civil Procedure Law as well as a great number of replies issued by the Supreme People's Court. The most prominent example hereof is the 'Interpretation of the Supreme Court on Some Questions on the Application of the Arbitration Law'.

Since 1987, China has been a contracting State to the New York Convention on the Recognition and Enforcement of Foreign Arbitral Awards.

## 4. COOPERATION BETWEEN NATIONAL COURTS AND THE DIFFERENT ADR INSTRUMENTS

### 4.1. MEDIATION

In principle, mediation agreements made by the parties do not qualify as directly enforceable titles, but as conventional contracts. To give a mediation agreement the effect of direct enforceability, the parties may initiate judicial ratification proceedings before a competent court or have the mediation agreement notarised by a public notary, if it deals with a simple debt.

#### *4.1.1. Enforcement of mediation agreements reached in court-annexed mediation proceedings*

The rapid and voluntary compliance with settlement agreements is praised as an advantage of mediation. The efforts of the Supreme People's Court (SPC) to make rescission from judicially drafted settlement awards difficult, actually argues against this assumption. According to Article 97(1) of the Civil Procedure Law 2012, a mediation award will be made in which the submissions, the facts and the mediation results are documented where both parties reach a settlement agreement. A mediation award becomes final and enforceable upon being served on the parties. Article 99 of the Civil Procedure Law allows each party to withdraw from the settlement award made by the court without any objective reason prior to its service. Often one party feels ripped off by the other and refuses to accept the delivery of the settlement award once the peaceful atmosphere generated by the mediation discussion fades and the party gives further thought to the law and facts. This is considered a waste of judicial resources. As a countermeasure, the SPC stipulates *contra legem* that the refusal of service does not contradict the enforceability of the settlement award if the parties agreed to a settlement, the court confirmed its content and the parties and judges have signed the corresponding court record.[58] That means, once the settlement agreement has been signed, the parties are bound by the declaration.

58 Article 13 of the Provisions of the Supreme People's Court about Several Issues Concerning the Civil Mediation Work of the People's Court.

#### *4.1.2. Enforcement of an agreement reached in a people's mediation proceeding*

The enforcement of mediation agreements has been controversial since the people's mediation system was restored. The Ministry of Justice issued the Measures for Handling People's Disputes in 1990 and sought to give compulsory effect to mediation agreements and decisions reached by local governments.[59] However, in 1993 the SPC made it clear in the Notice on How to Deal with Civilian Disputes Handled by Township People's Governments that courts may invariably hear disputes covered by people's mediation agreements and are not bound by the mediation results while adjudicating the cases.[60] The legally binding nature of the people's mediation settlements was reaffirmed by the Supreme People's Court in 2002. Again, the 'binding nature' of the settlement agreement only refers to it being 'binding' like any other civil contract, but does not say anything as regards enforceability.

Generally speaking, a distinction is to be made between the enforcement of a mediation agreement itself and a judicially ratified mediation. A plain mediation agreement without judicial ratification is nothing more than a normal contract, which does not qualify as an enforcement order. Therefore, if one party refuses to perform a mediation agreement, the other party has to obtain an executory title either by suing the non-performing party for breach of contract or by filing a suit with the court for the underlying dispute settled by the mediation agreement. Numerous commentators have tried to confer on a plain mediation agreement the effect of direct enforceability, which was rejected by the judiciary due to lack of support in the black letter law and legal theory. The wording of the pertinent provision in the People's Mediation Law actually does not suggest the direct enforceability of people's mediation agreements.[61] In effect, mediation agreements are not enforceable until judicial ratification by the courts has taken place.

Judicial ratification of people's mediation agreements has been officially established by the People's Mediation Law. Previously, several judicial interpretations already introduced and implemented this legal concept. Judicial ratification proceedings are regarded as a declaratory action and deal with non-contentious matters; they are therefore to be classified as special proceedings.[62] In the case of a successful judicial ratification, the ratification certificate, accompanied by the original mediation agreement, constitutes the enforcement title.[63] It is however still subject to discussion whether a judicially ratified mediation agreement is able to bring about the effect of *res judicata*.[64]

---

59 Y. Fan, *supra* n. 2, p. 538.

60 Y. Fan, *supra* n. 2, p. 539.

61 Y. Fan, *supra* n. 27, p. 10. The wording is: 'The mediation agreement reached through the mediation of the civil mediation committee shall be legally binding and the parties shall perform in light of the stipulations'.

62 G. Xiang, 'The Improvement and Development of the Judicial Ratification Proceeding of Mediation Agreement' (2011) 7 *Journal of Law Application* 14.

63 *Ibid.*, p. 15.

64 *Ibid.*, p. 16.

In pursuance of Article 33 of the People's Mediation Law, the two parties may jointly apply to the court for ratification within thirty days of the mediation agreement taking effect if they deem it necessary. After the court confirms the validity of the mediation agreement in accordance with the law, the other party may apply to the people's court for enforcement, if one party refuses to perform or fails to properly perform. If the court determines that the mediation agreement is invalid, the parties may alter the original mediation agreement or reach a new mediation agreement or may also file a lawsuit to the people's court.

Another highly controversial issue is the standard of examination to be applied by courts to judicial review of people's mediation agreements. The SPC has addressed this issue in several judicial interpretations, but each time the approach has been slightly amended.

For example, according to Article 7 of 'Certain Provisions on Procedures for Judicial Ratification of People's Mediation Agreements' issued by the SPC on 23 March 2011, the mediation agreement is subject to a substantive review in the judicial ratification proceedings. That means the consulted court is allowed to examine the mediation agreement with a view to its compliance with mandatory statutory provisions, compliance with the interests of the state, the public and with third party rights, compliance with public policy and social order as well as the clarity of the contents. This provision deviates from a guideline set out in 'Several Opinions on Establishing and Improving Resolution System in the Disputes in the Link of Litigation and Non-litigation Cases' in that the latter allows the court to even examine whether the mediation is conducted voluntarily and there is no violation of professional ethic rules by the mediator and the mediation organisation. In addition, in contrast to 'Certain Provisions on Procedures for Judicial Ratification of People's Mediation Agreements', the 'Several Opinions on Establishing and Improving Resolution System in the Disputes in the Link of Litigation and Non-litigation Cases' still follow the principle that party autonomy prevails, meaning the court is to ratify the validity of the mediation agreement if the parties are fully aware of the agreement's non-compliance with the above mentioned validity requirements and forfeit the right to challenge the validity. It is safe to assume that this principle has been abandoned since the later-issued 'Certain Provisions on Procedures for Judicial Ratification of People's Mediation Agreements' does not contain a comparable provision. The provision in the 'Certain Provisions on Procedures for Judicial Ratification of People's Mediation Agreements' corresponds more to the common understanding of this issue in the judiciary.[65] Being the latest pertinent rule, it overrides all other relevant deviating older provisions.

---

65 *Ibid.*, p. 15.

#### 4.1.3. *Enforcement of agreements reached in administrative mediation proceedings*

There is no explicit regulation on the enforceability of administrative mediation agreements. Thus, mediation agreements resulting from administrative mediation are not enforceable *per se,* but rather resemble a civil contract as is the case with people's mediation. If a party repudiates the settlement agreement, the other party has to seek an enforceable title either by applying for arbitration (as long as there is an arbitration clause) or directly filing a lawsuit.[66] The non-enforceability of administrative mediation has a significant negative impact on the parties and the mediation bodies (*supra* at 1.2.4.).

In the 'Several Opinions on Establishing and Improving Resolution System in the Disputes in the Link of Litigation and Non-litigation Cases', the SPC opened the possibility of judicial ratification to other forms of mediation such as administrative mediation. However, this document does not qualify as a judicial interpretation and has therefore limited authority.

### 4.2. ARBITRATION

According to Article 62 of the Arbitration Law, arbitral awards can be enforced in China by the courts. When determining a court's competence for enforcing a certain arbitral award, Chinese law differentiates between three types of arbitral awards: 'domestic awards', 'foreign-related awards' and 'foreign awards'. In doing so, the Chinese Arbitration Law deviates from the international common practice (as specified by the New York Convention) of only separating into two categories based on the concept of nationality and territoriality.[67] While it is easy to define 'foreign awards' under Chinese law as awards rendered outside China and 'domestic awards' as awards rendered by Chinese institutions without foreign relevance, it is harder to clearly define the term 'foreign-related award'. Based on a judicial interpretation of the SPC issued in 1992, it can be summed up that 'foreign-related awards' are awards that are rendered by Chinese institutions, but where the underlying case itself has elements that can be considered as 'foreign', such as non-Chinese parties or the underlying relationship between the parties and/or subject matter taking place in a foreign country.[68]

Under the Chinese Arbitration Law, the District Courts at the place of domicile of the debtor and the location of the assets are competent for enforcing 'domestic awards', whereas Intermediate Courts at the place of domicile of the

66 J. Liang, *supra* n. 15, pp. 4 ff.
67 M. Chi, *supra* n. 57, p. 544.
68 *Ibid.*, p. 545.

debtor and the location of the assets are competent for enforcing 'foreign-related awards' and 'foreign awards'.[69]

This differentiation between the three types of awards is especially important for the question of judicial review of arbitral awards. Both the Arbitration Law and the Civil Procedure Law contain special provisions only applicable to 'foreign-related awards' as opposed to 'domestic awards'. This is why the Chinese system is also referred to as a 'dual-track system'.[70]

Concerning 'domestic awards', all the grounds for revocation listed in Article 58 of the Arbitration Law are also grounds for not enforcing an award. Additionally, according to Article 213 I no. 5 of the Civil Procedure Law, the incorrect application of law is also a ground for not enforcing an award. This opens the possibility for courts to examine the award for legal errors, which means that the enforcement court virtually has the power to reopen the whole case.[71] This results in a de facto 'appeal' and is thus under the suspicion of wasting scarce judicial resources.[72]

For the enforcement of 'foreign-related awards', the grounds for not enforcing awards are spelled out in the Arbitration Law and the Civil Procedure Law (Article 71 of the Arbitration Law and Article 274 of the Civil Procedure Law).[73] However, special rules apply to the enforcement of awards rendered in Hong Kong, Macau and Taiwan, which in effect lead to those awards being treated like 'foreign awards'. The enforcement of 'foreign awards' follows the New York Convention, as long as the award was rendered in a contracting State of the Convention. As Article 237 of the Civil Procedure Law is inapplicable to 'foreign-related awards' and 'foreign awards', courts can only scrutinise these awards on procedural issues. This significantly differs from the review of 'domestic awards', as they can be scrutinised on both procedural and material issues.[74] This is regarded as the core difference in the 'dual-track system'.[75] In practice, Chinese courts are extremely cautious with the refusal of enforcement of 'foreign awards'. According to a notification of the SPC from 1995,[76] the SPC has to confirm any judgment of non-enforcement of a 'foreign-related award' and a 'foreign award' before the issuance of such a judgment by a lower court (the so-called reporting system).[77]

Special attention especially for practical reasons needs to be paid to the arbitration clause. The arbitration clause is a prerequisite for the arbitral

69 L. Kniprath, *supra* n. 42, pp. 144, 155 ff.
70 M. Chi, *supra* n. 57, pp. 545–547.
71 L. Kniprath, *supra* n. 42, p. 156.
72 M. Chi, *supra* n. 57, p. 547.
73 L. Kniprath, *supra* n. 42, p. 146.
74 *Ibid.*, p. 143.
75 M. Chi, *supra* n. 57, p. 547.
76 Notice of the Supreme People's Court on the Treatment of Foreign-Related and Foreign Arbitration Award by People's Court dated 28.08.1995.
77 L. Kniprath, *supra* n. 42, pp. 153 ff.

proceedings, and consequently also for the enforcement of arbitral awards. Thus, the focus of judicial review in enforcement proceedings lies on the validity of the arbitration clause. Next to the mandatory written form, further prerequisites need to be met according to the Arbitration Law. According to Article 16 of the Arbitration Law, parties must express their wish to conduct arbitral proceedings as well as the expected scope and must also name the competent arbitral commission. In the past, the missing or incorrect naming of the competent arbitral commission was often the reason for an invalid arbitration clause. Today, however, a less strict view regarding the naming of the arbitral commission has been developed, with acknowledged groups of circumstances under which an arbitral clause remains valid.[78]

## 5. FUTURE PROSPECTS FOR DEVELOPMENT

To predict future development of ADR in China, one must once again take the factors mentioned at the beginning of this chapter as the starting point.

It is clear that the incumbent political leaders attach great importance to the maintenance of social stability and see the revival of mediation as an effective tool helping to reach this goal. The personnel shift in the highest political circle that happened in 2012 is unlikely to bring about a radical change in this regard.

The recent development of ADR in China is to a certain degree worrying in that the advantages of mediation are often overstated and disputants, government agencies, enterprises and social institutions are under a great pressure to follow the Party's preference for mediation. In this sense, in spite of the objections from trade unions arguing that mediation is not a function born by enterprises, the Ministry of Human Resources and Social Security promulgated the 'Provisions on the Negotiation and Mediation of Enterprise Labor Disputes', which require the establishment of people's mediation committees within each enterprise. The State Power Regulatory Commission established the mediation mechanism for electricity disputes, although it is reasonable to believe that the mediation body, namely the State power regulatory authorities, has a bias in favour of electricity enterprises and lacks neutrality in such disputes.

As has already been illustrated during the deliberation process of the People's Mediation Law, the legislator strived for formalisation and institutionalisation of the people's mediation to justify its legitimacy and to accommodate the citizens' rising desire for rule of law, which may undermine its flexibility – the most striking and effective feature of this rather informal form of community mediation. Nonetheless, one could clearly notice the antipathy to the forced

---

78 Details: Y. Bu, *Einführung in das Recht Chinas*, Beck Verlag, München 2009, §27 Marginal Number 5.

ADR in the course of framing the People's Mediation Law. As a consequence, the legislator gave up the idea of making people's mediation a compulsory proceeding preceding litigation.[79] The general trend towards litigation in China should not be construed as a superstitious belief in the omnipotence of litigation, but rather reflects reasonable choices made by the disputants and judges after considering the relevant circumstances such as costs, professional qualification and procedural guarantee.

One point is certain: as long as there is no genuine informed free choice for the parties or the judges, free from the influence of manipulation or coercion, mediation will not receive genuine acceptance by society. Even though ADR currently appears to be booming in China, the top-down approach is neither efficient nor sustainable. This has already become a consensus among people who care about the rule of law in China.[80]

---

79 Y. Fan, *supra* n. 27, pp. 2–3; Q. Yang, 'The Right of Choice of Civil Procedure and the Leading Procedure of the People's Mediation' (2007) 3 *Jurist* 122–123.

80 H. Lu, *supra* n. 10, pp. 569 ff.; C. Minzner, *supra* n. 38.

# ENGLAND AND WALES

Neil Andrews

**Contents**

# 1. INTRODUCTION[1]

Mediation has become popular in England and Wales. It can operate as a complete substitute for civil litigation, or it can supplement that formal process after court proceedings have begun, and even after judgment has been given but an appeal is pending. The English court system encourages pursuit of mediation; the courts can direct litigants in pending actions or appeals to consider mediation if the parties, or one of them, requests, or if the court itself suggests. Leverage to consider and to pursue mediation takes the form of a 'stay' upon current proceedings or the threat of an adverse costs order. An English court will enforce a mediation agreement by ordering a stay of litigation brought in violation of that agreement. The government has a strong interest in promoting ADR because it is less expensive than civil litigation. In short, civil proceedings before the courts are becoming a system of last resort to be pursued only when more civilised and 'proportionate' techniques have failed or could never be made to work.

Arbitration continues to flourish in England and Wales. In this short discussion, it will be possible only to outline, from an English perspective, the main characteristics of this 'behind closed doors' process.

In section 2, we will consider mediation. In section 3 attention turns to arbitration.

# 2. MEDIATION

## 2.1. MEDIATION'S GROWTH IN ENGLAND AND WALES

Mediation is now better understood by businesses and organisations. In England resort to mediation has increased, including within the heartland of commercial disputes.[2] The Ministry of Justice for England and Wales (2010) reported on this:[3] 'the market for mediation in the UK continues to grow. A recent mediation audit carried out by the Centre for Effective Dispute Resolution (CEDR) showed that there had been nearly 6,000 civil and commercial mediations carried out in

---

1 For more detailed discussion by the author, see N. Andrews, *Civil Processes*, Intersentia, Cambridge 2013, vol. II, ch. 1; N. Andrews, *The Three Paths of Justice: Court Proceedings, Arbitration, and Mediation in England*, Springer, Dordrecht/Heidelberg/London/New York 2011; N. Andrews, *The Modern Civil Process*, Mohr Siebeck, Tübingen 2008; N. Andrews, *Contracts and English Dispute Resolution*, Jigakusha Publishing, Tokyo 2010; and his General Report on Arbitration for the World Congress of the International Association of Procedural Law, Heidelberg, 2011, N. Andrews, 'Global Perspectives on Commercial Arbitration, Part 1' (2011) 201 *Revista de Processo* 249–298, and 'Global Perspectives on Commercial Arbitration, Part 2' (2012) 202 *Revista de Processo* 293–338.

2 K. Mackie, D. Miles, W. Marsh and T. Allen, *The ADR Practice Guide*, 3rd ed., Tottel, London 2007, especially chs. 5, 6 and 7.

3 Ministry of Justice, 'Implementation… Paper', London 2010 (a consultation paper), at [10].

2009.[4] Based on the outcome of the 2007 Mediation Audit, the 2009 figure showed there was a doubling of mediation activity since 2007.'

The Government announced in March 2011 (press release of 29 March 2011 by the Ministry of Justice, London)[5] that it would like to expand resort to mediation. Its statement proposes this change:

> 'Increasing the use of mediation: We are proposing introducing automatic referral to mediation in small claims cases, automatic referral to mediation awareness sessions in higher-value cases and consulting on making mediated settlements enforceable by courts. This is to help people avoid the anxiety and expense of court where possible, although court will still be an option for those who mediation cannot help. [...] Last year, more than three quarters of claims in the civil system were settled after allocation, but before trial. This represents 87,000 cases which could potentially have been resolved earlier if mediation had been used more widely.'[6]

The rise of mediation, not just in England, is largely attributable to six factors: (a) the perception (nearly always also the reality) that court litigation is unpredictable; (b) the court-based adjudicative process (and extensive preparation for the final hearing) is a source of expense, delay, and anxiety; (c) court litigation offers little scope for direct participation by the parties, as distinct from legal representatives; (d) final judgment normally awards victory to only one winner; (e) trial is open-air justice, visible to mankind in general; and (f) litigation is private war – even if judges pretend that it is governed by elaborate rules and conciliatory conventions designed to take the sting out of the contest. In a general and vague sense, the European mediation directive sits well with this national and, of course, global trend. But one hardly needs this instrument to underscore the reality of modern dispute resolution.

## 2.2. MEDIATION AGREEMENTS[7]

Many companies now prefer to use international arbitration in combination with other ADR mechanisms. Such a combination of techniques will be specified in a 'multi-tiered' dispute resolution clause.[8] The leading English decision concerning

[4] <www.cedr.com/index.php?location=/news/archive/20100513_347.htm>.

[5] <www.justice.gov.uk/news/press-release-290311a.htm>.

[6] A consultation paper of 2011 supplies details: 'Solving disputes in the county courts: creating a simpler, quicker and more proportionate system' (CP 6/2011: Ministry of Justice: Cm 8045) (29.03.2011).

[7] D. Joseph, *Jurisdiction and Arbitration Agreements and their Enforcement*, 2nd ed., Sweet & Maxwell, London 2010; K. Mackie, D. Miles, W. Marsh and T. Allen, *The ADR Practice Guide*, 3rd ed., Tottel, London 2007, ch. 9; Centre for Effective Dispute Resolution at: <www.cedr.co.uk/library/documents/contract_clauses.pdf>; D. Spencer and M. Brogan, *Mediation: Law and Practice*, Cambridge University Press, Cambridge 2006, ch. 12 for Australian material.

[8] The School of International Arbitration, Queen Mary, University of London, report (2005), available online at: <www.pwc.com/Extweb/pwcpublications.nsf/docid/0B3FD76A8551573E8

mediation clauses[9] is *Cable & Wireless v. IBM United Kingdom Ltd* (2002).[10] In this case the relevant clause was a so-called 'tiered' provision. It initially required the parties to endeavour to negotiate a resolution by considering the relevant dispute within their own organisations. The clause stated that mediation would be obligatory if these negotiations collapsed.[11] Thereafter, the parties to this clause contemplated that, if the dispute were still unresolved, proceedings before a court could take place. After negotiation had failed, one party decided to bypass the stipulated stage of mediation, and prematurely brought a claim before the English High Court. The other party challenged this.

Colman J found that there had been a breach of the dispute resolution agreement, because a party had 'jumped' the mediation stage and proceeded straight to litigation. To remedy this, the judge placed a 'stay' upon those formal court proceedings. The stay would be lifted if a party returned to court and demonstrated that the mediation attempt had been unsuccessful. But, although the stay was appropriate in this case, the judge said that this would not always be so:

> 'For example, there may be cases where a reference to ADR would be obviously futile and where the likelihood of a productive mediation taking place would be so slight as not to justify enforcing the agreement. Even in such circumstances ADR would have to be a completely hopeless exercise.'

However, in some contexts, statute invalidates contracts which purport to exclude formal recourse to State-administered courts or tribunals. For example, in *Clyde & Co v. Bates van Winkelhof* (2011)[12] Slade J considered a clause[13] within a

---

5257168005122C8>. I am grateful to Stephen York for this reference.

9 D. Joseph, *Jurisdiction and Arbitration Agreements and their Enforcement*, 2nd ed., Sweet & Maxwell, London 2010; K. Mackie, D. Miles, W. Marsh and T. Allen, *The ADR Practice Guide*, 3rd edn., Tottel, London 2007, ch. 9; Centre for Effective Dispute Resolution at: <www.cedr.co.uk/library/documents/contract_clauses.pdf>; D. Spencer and M. Brogan, *Mediation: Law and Practice*, Cambridge University Press, Cambridge 2006, ch. 12 for Australian material.

10 [2002] 2 All ER (Comm) 1041, Colman J.

11 Generally, K. Mackie, D. Miles, W. Marsh and T. Allen, *The ADR Practice Guide*, 3rd ed., Tottel, London 2007, 9.6.4.

12 [2011] EWHC 668 (QB), Slade J.

13 The relevant clauses stated: '41.1 If at any time there is a dispute, difference or question that shall arise between the Members or between the LLP and the Members (including any Outgoing Member or his personal representatives), or any of them, touching the membership of the LLP or the rights and liabilities of the Members (together "Referred Matters"), then the Member or Members involved in such dispute, difference or question ('parties') shall deal with it as provided in this clause and clause 41.2 below. The matter shall be immediately referred by any of the parties to the Management Board requiring it to meet and to make a decision on the relevant matter within 28 days of the matter being so referred to the Management Board ("Decision Period"). The Management Board shall meet and discuss the relevant matter with a view to resolving the issue in a sensible and fair manner. If the Management Board reaches agreement with the parties within the Decision Period the Members agree that such agreement be promptly implemented. If the Management Board fails to agree on any matter within the Decision Period or if the dispute is with the Management Board itself then clause 41.2 below shall apply.
41.2 If a dispute still remains after the application of 41.1 above, including any question regarding the Referred Matters or the application of this dispute resolution procedure, then the

partnership deed requiring a partner in a law firm to refer any disputes or differences arising from her work for the firm to mediation and then to arbitration. The partner had brought complaints to an Employment Tribunal alleging various statutory breaches by her law firm of equality law, and seeking compensation. Slade J concluded that the High Court could not grant an injunction compelling her to desist from pursuing these Employment Tribunal proceedings. Statute[14] clearly precluded 'contracting out' of this tribunal system of rights.

## 2.3. PRE-ACTION DUTY OF PARTIES TO CONSIDER ADR

The Civil Procedure Rules (CPR) state that:

> 'the courts increasingly take the view that litigation should be a last resort, and that claims should not be issued prematurely when a settlement is still likely. Therefore, the parties should consider whether some form of alternative dispute settlement would be more suitable than litigation, and if so, endeavour to agree which form to adopt.'[15]

There is also a general 'tick box' invitation in the Allocation Questionnaire, enabling each party to indicate whether mediation might be an option.

## 2.4. OCCASIONS FOR JUDICIAL ENCOURAGEMENT OF MEDIATION[16]

The English courts' overall responsibility to administer civil justice includes 'helping the parties to settle the whole or part of the case'[17] and 'encouraging the

---

parties agree first to refer the matter to the Centre for Dispute Resolution (CEDR) in an attempt to settle the dispute in good faith by Alternative Dispute Resolution (ADR). If the dispute is not settled within 30 days of the request to CEDR by one of the parties, or such further period as the parties shall agree in writing, either party may require that the dispute be referred to and finally resolved under the Rules of the London Court of International Arbitration, which Rules are deemed to be incorporated by reference into this clause 41.2, save that the parties preserve the right to appeal or to refer to the English Courts on questions of law which shall have jurisdiction in such circumstances. The Members and the LLP reserve all their respective rights in the event that no agreed resolution shall be reached in the ADR procedure and none of them shall be deemed to be precluded from taking such interim formal steps as may be considered necessary to protect such person's position while the ADR procedure is pending.'

14 Section 120, Equality Act 2010, and section 203, Equality Rights Act 1996.

15 'Practice Direction: Protocols' 4.7.

16 For a typology of court-assisted modes of ADR, W.D. Brazil and J. Smith, 'Choice of Structures…' (1999) 6 *Dispute Resolution Magazine* 8, cited in O. Fiss and J. Resnik, *Adjudication and Its Alternatives*, Foundation Press, New York 2003, p. 468: court employs full-time in-house neutrals; or contracts with non-profit making organisations for such a programme; or directly pays firms to serve as neutrals; or orchestrates voluntary mediations; or refers parties to neutrals (whether selected by the court or by the parties) who charge; this last is the general English model, and furthermore, the parties select the neutral.

17 CPR 1.4(2)(f).

parties to use an alternative dispute resolution procedure if the court considers that appropriate.'[18] In addition to the 'tick box' mechanism contained in the Allocation Questionnaire (see preceding paragraph), resort to mediation is a question of direct communication between a judge and the parties (notably during the pre-trial stages, but occasionally after judgment during the process of giving permission to appeal). From 1 April 2013,[19] Allocation Questionnaires were replaced by Directions Questionnaires.[20]

In the Commercial Court (a part of the Queen's Bench Division, in the High Court), the practice is that a judge will not require the parties to mediate unless one party makes such a request and the suggestion seems to the judge to be reasonable. Parties to litigation in that court are regarded as 'sophisticated'. They enjoy legal advice concerning the range of dispute-resolution available to them. It would be unduly heavy-handed, therefore, for a judge to insist on a stay if neither party has an interest in mediation.[21] However, wider language appears in the *Admiralty and Commercial Court Guide* (2011), which does not rule out judicial initiative:[22] 'The Commercial Judges will in appropriate cases invite the parties to consider whether their dispute, or particular issues in it, could be resolved through ADR.' Where mediation seems appropriate, the court has devised a formula (rather misleadingly called an 'ADR Order') designed to achieve consensus on the nomination of a mediator, and to require reasons to be given to the court for failure to proceed to mediation.[23]

---

18 CPR 1.4(2)(e); Chancery Guide (2005), ch. 17; *The Admiralty and Commercial Courts Guide*, 9th ed., 2011, section G and appendix 7 (available on the CPR webpage under 'Guides').

19 CPR 26.2A, CPR 26.3; PD (5A); PD (5C); PD (15); PD (26); PD (27); PD (28); PD (29).

20 PD (5A); PD (5C); PD (15); PD (26); PD (27); PD (28); PD (29).

21 Author's 2009 conversation with a Commercial Court judge.

22 *The Admiralty and Commercial Courts Guide*, 9th ed., 2011, at G1.3.

23 *Ibid.*, Appendix 7. It provides: 'On or before [*] the parties shall exchange lists of 3 neutral individuals who are available to conduct ADR procedures in this case prior to [*]. Each party may [in addition] [in the alternative] provide a list identifying the constitution of one or more panels of neutral individuals who are available to conduct ADR procedures in this case prior to [*]. On or before [*] the parties shall in good faith endeavour to agree a neutral individual or panel from the lists so exchanged and provided. Failing such agreement by [*] the Case Management Conference will be restored to enable the Court to facilitate agreement on a neutral individual or panel. The parties shall take such serious steps as they may be advised to resolve their disputes by ADR procedures before the neutral individual or panel so chosen by no later than [*]. If the case is not finally settled, the parties shall inform the Court by letter prior to [disclosure of documents/exchange of witness statements/exchange of experts' reports] what steps towards ADR have been taken and (without prejudice to matters of privilege) why such steps have failed. If the parties have failed to initiate ADR procedures the Case Management Conference is to be restored for further consideration of the case.' In *Halsey v. Milton Keynes General NHS Trust* [2004] EWCA Civ 576; [2004] 1 WLR 3002, at [30], Dyson LJ explained: 'An ADR order made in the Admiralty and Commercial Court in the form set out in Appendix 7 to the Guide is the strongest form of encouragement. It requires the parties to exchange lists of neutral individuals who are available to conduct "ADR procedures", to endeavour in good faith to agree a neutral individual or panel and to take "such serious steps as they may be advised to resolve their disputes by ADR procedures before the neutral individual or panel so chosen". The order also provides that if the case is not settled, "the

To sum up this aspect: the English position involves selective judicial recommendation of mediation, normally after one party has requested mediation.[24]

## 2.5. JUDICIAL ORDER TO 'STAY' COURT PROCEEDINGS TO FACILITATE MEDIATION[25]

Even in the absence of a mediation agreement, an English court can direct that the proceedings be stayed for a month at a time[26] while the parties pursue ADR or other settlement negotiations.[27] A stay merely places the proceedings in a state of suspense. Proceedings can be resumed when this becomes appropriate. The stay can be issued either at the parties' request or on the initiative of the court. The matter is subject to the court's discretion. There is no automatic right to a stay.

## 2.6. COSTS SANCTIONS FOR FAILURE TO PURSUE MEDIATION

English courts are prepared, where appropriate, to register censure of a party's unreasonable refusal to engage in mediation. That refusal might be failure to accede to the opponent's call for mediation, or the court's own suggestion, that mediation be contemplated. Indeed the Court of Appeal in the *McMillan* case (2004) said that if both parties to an appeal spurn the judicial recommendation that mediation be considered, and instead they proceed straight to appeal without attempting mediation, each party will bear its own costs for that stage of the proceeding, with no opportunity for costs-shifting in favour of the victorious party to the appeal.[28]

parties shall inform the court [...] what steps towards ADR have been taken and (without prejudice to matters of privilege) why such steps have failed". It is to be noted, however, that this form of order stops short of actually compelling the parties to undertake an ADR.'

24 For sceptical discussion of any form of mandating or coercing resort to mediation, M. Brunsdon-Tully, 'There is an A in ADR but Does Anyone Know What it Means Anymore?' (2009) *CJQ* 218–36.

25 For a typology of court-assisted modes of ADR, W.D. Brazil and J. Smith, 'Choice of Structures...' (1999) 6 *Dispute Resolution Magazine* 8, cited in O. Fiss and J. Resnik, *Adjudication and Its Alternatives*, Foundation Press, New York 2003, p. 468: court employs full-time in-house neutrals; or contracts with non-profit making organisations for such a programme; or directly pays firms to serve as neutrals; or orchestrates voluntary mediations; or refers parties to neutrals (whether selected by the court or by the parties) who charge; this last is the general English model, furthermore, the parties select the neutral.

26 CPR 26.4(3).

27 CPR 3.1(2)(f); CPR 26.4(1)(2).

28 *McMillan Williams v. Range* [2004] EWCA Civ 294; [2004] 1 WLR 1858, *per* Ward LJ: '[29] Tuckey LJ gave this [direction] to the parties when he granted permission to appeal: "The costs of further litigating this dispute will be disproportionate to the amount at stake. ADR is strongly recommended." [...] The parties should have written to each other along the lines that, "Lord Justice Tuckey has very sensibly suggested ADR. My client thinks that is a splendid idea. Please can we get on with it as soon and as cheaply as possible?"[... 30] In my

In determining the unreasonableness of a party's refusal to pursue mediation, the Court of Appeal in *Halsey v. Milton Keynes General NHS Trust* (2004) listed the following criteria:[29]

> 'the nature of the dispute; the merits of the case; the extent to which other settlement methods have been attempted; whether the costs of the ADR would be disproportionately high; whether any delay in setting up and attending the ADR would be prejudicial; whether the ADR had a reasonable prospect of success.'

It will be more common to apply a costs sanction against a party who not only refused to consider mediation but who also lost the substantive case (or appeal). This type of 'refusenik' might be ordered[30] to pay the other side's costs on an 'indemnity basis' rather than 'standard basis'[31] (indemnity costs, although not punitive, are a full measure of compensatory costs; whereas standard basis costs are a substantial but incomplete measure of such compensation; and the difference between the two measures can be very large, given the high levels of costs incurred by parties in England).

As for costs sanctions against a party who has clearly won the relevant court proceedings, the 'mediation offeror' (who has lost the case) will bear the burden of showing on the balance of probabilities that the mediation would have had a reasonable prospect of success, assuming the mediation offeree (who eventually won the case) would have participated in the mediation in a co-operative manner.[32] Satisfying this burden of proof will be an uphill task.

And so the question of a costs sanction against a victorious party is more likely to arise when the party to be sanctioned has rejected a judicial recommendation for mediation (as distinct from a suggestion made by the other side). In this context, robust costs sanctions are likely to be applied if the court (notably the Court of Appeal), when granting permission to appeal, has indicated that the parties should consider mediation. If one party fails to respond positively to such a judicial recommendation, the appeal court, when considering the question of costs at the conclusion of the appeal, might deny that party the costs of the appeal even if he has been successful on the merits of the appeal. In both *Dunnett v. Railtrack plc* (2002)[33] and *McMillan Williams v. Range* (2004)[34] a member of the Court of Appeal (Schiemann LJ in the *Dunnett* case, and Tuckey

---

judgment this is a case where we should condemn the posturing and jockeying for position taken by each side of this dispute and thus direct that each side pay its own costs of their frolic in the Court of Appeal. I would allow the appeal with no order for costs.'

29 [2004] EWCA Civ 576; [2004] 1 WLR 3002, at [16] ff.; for a strong application of this costs regime, in which the *Halsey* criteria were fully considered, *P4 Ltd v. Unite Integrated Solutions plc* [2006] EWHC 2924 (TCC), Ramsey J.

30 *Virani Ltd v. Manuel Revert y Cia SA* [2003] EWCA Civ 1651; [2004] 2 Lloyd's Rep 14.

31 On the difference between standard basis and indemnity costs, N. Andrews, *The Modern Civil Process*, Mohr Siebeck, Tübingen 2008, para. 9.12.

32 *Halsey v. Milton Keynes General NHS Trust* [2004] EWCA Civ 576; [2004] 1 WLR 3002.

33 [2002] 1 WLR 2434, CA, at [13] ff.

34 [2004] EWCA Civ 294; [2004] 1 WLR 1858, at [29] and [30].

LJ in the *McMillan* case) issued an unsolicited recommendation that, instead of proceeding straight to appeal, both parties should pursue mediation. Dyson LJ in the *Halsey* case (2004) also noted the special status of a judicial recommendation:[35]

> 'Where a successful party refuses to agree to ADR despite the court's encouragement, that is a factor which the court will take into account when deciding whether his refusal was unreasonable. The court's encouragement may take different forms. The stronger the encouragement, the easier it will be for the unsuccessful party to discharge the burden of showing that the successful party's refusal was unreasonable.'

It is submitted that costs sanctions are unjustified if the relevant party to the appeal convinces the court that he has considered properly the opportunity to mediate but he has then chosen to bring or respond to the appeal for objectively satisfactory reasons. Once the court is satisfied that the party did properly consider the mediation option, there should be no scope for sanctions. The party who succeeds in the appeal (the appellant if the appeal is successful, or the respondent if the appeal fails) should receive the costs of that appeal from the defeated opponent, in accordance with the costs-shifting principle: to 'sanction' him for failure to attend or participate in a mediation is too heavy-handed and unprincipled. Similarly, the defeated opponent should be ordered to pay costs on the standard basis, and not (by way of 'sanction') on the higher indemnity basis.

## 2.7. PRIVILEGED MEDIATION DISCUSSION[36]

It has long[37] been recognised that non-mediated settlement negotiations can be privileged. This is known as 'without prejudice' privilege.[38] The sibling doctrine

---

35 *Halsey v. Milton Keynes General NHS Trust* [2004] EWCA Civ 576; [2004] 1 WLR 3002, at [29].

36 Literature concerning *privilege in the context of mediation or conciliation*: N. Andrews, *English Civil Procedure*, Oxford University Press, Oxford 2003, paras. 25.45 to 25.48; N. Andrews, *The Modern Civil Process*, Mohr Siebeck, Tübingen 2008, paras. 11.49 to 11.61; N. Andrews, *Contracts and English Dispute Resolution*, Jigakusha Publishing, Tokyo 2010, paras. 22.20 ff; H. Brown and A. Marriott, *ADR Principles and Practice*, 3rd ed., Sweet & Maxwell, London 2011; *Cross and Tapper on Evidence*, 12th ed., Oxford University Press, Oxford 2010, p. 475; K. Mackie, D. Miles, W. Marsh and T. Allen, *The ADR Practice Guide*, 3rd ed., Tottel, London 2007, paras. 7.2 ff.; B. Thanki (ed.), *The Law of Privilege*, Oxford University Press, Oxford 2006, paras. 7.24, 7.38 to 7.39; for USA and Australian sources, P. Newman, in M. Liebmann (ed.), *Mediation In Context*, Jessica Kingsley Publishers, London/Philadelphia 2000, p. 188; D. Spencer and M. Brogan, *Mediation: Law and Practice*, Cambridge University Press, Cambridge 2006, ch. 9, noting esp. at p. 329, Australian legislation on this topic; for general comment, Scottish Law Commission's Report, 'Evidence: Protection of Family Mediation' [1992] SLC 136 (Report) (June 1992) (containing notes on the draft Bill); the Civil Evidence (Family Mediation) (Scotland) Act 1995; symposium in (1988) 12(1) *Seton Hall Legis J.*

37 On the development of this privilege, D. Vaver, '"Without Prejudice" Communications – Their Admissibility and Effect' (1974) *Univ. Brit. Col. L. Rev.* 85 (cited by Robert Walker LJ in *Unilever plc v. The Proctor & Gamble Co.* [2000] 1 WLR 2436, 2445, CA).

38 N. Andrews, *English Civil Procedure*, 2003, ch. 25; H. Brown and A. Marriott, *ADR Principles and Practice*, 3rd ed., Sweet & Maxwell, London 2011; *Cross and Tapper on Evidence*,

of privilege concerns 'mediation secrecy'. Here is a summary of this subtle and developing topic.

In this context of mediation, the parties normally adopt such protection by express agreement, but sometimes privilege rests merely upon implicit consensus.[39]

In *Cumbria Waste Management Ltd v. Baines Wilson* (2008) it was held that mediated settlement discussions between parties X and Y remain privileged if X or Y is unwilling to waive privilege.[40] It follows that in subsequent litigation between X and D, the third party D cannot obtain disclosure of the mediation discussions between X and Y unless both X and Y waive their privilege.

Conversely, the parties might waive privilege in their mediation communications. If so, when the court is required to assess costs in litigation subsequent to an unsuccessful mediation, Jack J in *Carleton v. Strutt & Parker* (2008) has declared that the courts will consider the 'unreasonableness' of positions taken during the mediation.[41]

However, the mediator possesses no independent immunity against being required to supply information to a court concerning the circumstances of a mediation. Instead the true analysis is that evidential privilege in this context is controlled by the parties to the mediation. Thus in *Farm Assist Limited (in liquidation) v. The Secretary of State for the Environment, Food and Rural Affairs (No 2)* (2009)[42] Ramsey J upheld a witness summons requiring a mediator to give evidence on the question whether a settlement achieved during the relevant mediation had been procured by duress by a party to that settlement. He distinguished:[43] (a) an express confidentiality clause, including a right of confidentiality in favour of a mediator (not the same as a head of privilege); (b) implied rights of confidentiality (not the same as a head of privilege); (c) 'without prejudice' communication privilege (a privilege held by the parties, but not by the mediator); and (d) an express clause precluding the parties from

12th ed., Oxford University Press, Oxford 2010, 470 ff; D. Foskett, *The Law and Practice of Compromise*, 7th ed., Sweet & Maxwell, London 2010, ch. 22; C. Hollander, *Documentary Evidence*, 10th ed., Sweet & Maxwell, London 2009, ch. 16; M. Iller, *Civil Evidence: The Essential Guide*, Sweet & Maxwell, London 2006, paras. 8-88 to 8-104; P. Matthews and H. Malek, *Disclosure*, 3rd ed., Sweet & Maxwell, London 2010, ch. 11; *Phipson on Evidence*, 17th ed., Sweet & Maxwell, London 2010, paras. 24-18 ff; C. Passmore, *Privilege*, 2nd ed., XPL Law 2006, ch. 10; B. Thanki (ed), *The Law of Privilege*, Oxford University Press, Oxford 2006, ch. 7; *Zuckerman on Civil Procedure*, 2nd ed., Sweet & Maxwell, London 2006, ch. 16; A.F.C. Koo, 'Confidentiality of Mediation Communications' [2011] *CJQ* 192; J. McEwan, '"Without Prejudice": Negotiating the Minefield' (1994) 13 *CJQ* 133.

39 *Reed Executive plc v. Reed Business Information Ltd* [2004] EWCA Civ 887; [2004] 1 WLR 3026; *Aird v. Prime Meridian Ltd* [2006] EWCA Civ 1866; *Bradford & Bingley plc v. Rashid* [2006] UKHL 37; [2006] 1 WLR 2066; *Barnetson v. Framlington Group Ltd* [2007] EWCA Civ 502; [2007] 1 WLR 2443, at [34].

40 [2008] EWHC 786 (QB) (HH Judge Frances Kirkham sitting as a High Court Judge).

41 [2008] EWHC 424 at [72]; noted on this point by J. Sorabji (2008) 27 *CJQ* 288, 291–292.

42 [2009] EWHC 1102 (TCC); [2009] BLR 399; 125 Con LR 154.

43 *Ibid.*, at [45] ff.

calling the mediator as a witness (this was held not to create a separate head of privilege or immunity). None of these was effective to shield the mediator.

*Brown v. Rice* (2007) confirms that a party to a mediated settlement, no less than an unmediated settlement, can adduce the contents of settlement negotiations both to prove whether a settlement was reached and to ascertain its terms.[44] The court will apply contractual principles to determine whether a binding settlement agreement has arisen during mediation.

Mediation agreements, as in *Brown v. Rice*, often prescribe that a binding settlement must be reduced to writing and signed by the parties, or by their authorised representatives. Such a formality clause also governs acceptance of an offer made during the conclusion of the mediation meeting(s) but expressed to be open for acceptance within a specified period after the meeting has ended (unless the need for writing and signature has been varied, waived or consensually overridden by another provision).

The UK Supreme Court in *Oceanbulk Shipping and Trading SA v. TMT Asia Ltd* (2010)[45] held that 'without prejudice' negotiations, which resulted in a settlement agreement, can be admitted for the purpose of ascertaining the factual matrix of the relevant agreement. In light of that background material, the court could then interpret the terms of the settlement. To decide otherwise would be to create an unprincipled distinction between interpretation of all other commercial contracts and interpretation of settlement agreements.

## 2.8. MEDIATION AND SETTLEMENT SCEPTICISM

There are two arguments. The first is the sound and incontestable argument that mediation has its limits. The second is the bolder and controversial assertion that mediation should be treated with distrust.

As for the first argument, it must be accepted that mediation is possible only if both parties are willing to discuss their dispute, to examine the merits of their position in good faith, and ultimately to consider making concessions, whether tactical or magnanimous. Traditional court litigation will continue because it offers a strong form of dispute resolution. The court's coercive powers are indispensable in some contexts, especially in claims against fraudulent or uncooperative persons. Moreover, court litigation also embodies many values, notably the principle of publicly accessible proceedings and reasoned decisions.

---

44 [2007] EWHC 625 (Ch), Stuart Isaacs QC.

45 [2010] UKSC 44; [2010] 3 WLR 1424 (reversing [2010] EWCA Civ 79; [2010] 1 WLR 1803 (Longmore and Stanley Burnton LJJ; Ward LJ dissenting). For another recent discussion *R v. K (A)* [2009] EWCA Crim 1640; [2010] QB 343, at [44] to [73].

But then one must address the second argument. Banging the kettle drums of 'rights', 'entitlement', and 'perfect procedural justice', some oppose the growth of mediation. The gist of their opposition is the suggestion that mediation is an insidious phenomenon, that the government is promoting it for reasons of parsimony (saving expenditure on the more expensive system of court justice), and that it is apt to undermine people's true rights.[46]

Colleagues in, for example, Germany and Italy are surprised by the Anglo-American tradition of very high levels of pre-trial settlement and the relative paucity of adjudication by courts on the merits. And within the Anglo-American academic community, there have been strong criticisms of the trend towards privatised methods of promoting settlement by ordinary negotiation or procuring such compromises following mediation.

In particular, in her 2008 Hamlyn Lectures, Hazel Genn[47] criticised the assumption that mediation delivers 'justice'. She prefers the view that mediation involves loss of the opportunity to receive substantive justice through the court system:[48] 'What mediation is offering is simply the opportunity to discount [legal claims] in order to be spared the presumed misery and uncertainty of the adjudication process.' Genn questions whether it should be government policy to augment the business of mediators and to reduce court lists. This is her important conclusion:[49]

> 'there is an interdependency between courts as publicisers of rules backed by coercive power, and the practice of ADR and settlement more generally. Without the background threat of coercion, disputing parties cannot be brought to the negotiating table. Mediation without the credible threat of judicial determination is the sound of one hand clapping. A well-functioning civil justice system should offer a choice of dispute resolution methods.'

And she adds:

> 'We need modern, efficient civil courts with appropriate procedures that offer affordable processes for those who would choose judicial determination. This is not impossible. But it requires recognition of the social and economic value of civil justice, an acknowledgement that some cases need to be adjudicated, and a vision for reform that addresses perceived shortcomings rather than simply driving cases away.'

---

46 H. Genn, *Judging Civil Justice*, Cambridge University Press, Cambridge 2010, chs. 1–3; H. Genn, 'Understanding Civil Justice' (1997) 50 *CLP* 155, 186–7, and P.L. Murray, 'The Privatization of Civil Justice' (2007) 12 *ZZP Int. (Zeitschrift für Zivilprozess International)* 283–303; P.L. Murray, 'Mediation and Civil Justice: A Public-Private Partnership?' (2009) 14 *ZZP Int.* 241; E. Thornburg, 'Reaping What We Sow: Anti-Litigation Rhetoric, Limited Budgets, and Declining Support for Civil Courts' (2011) 30 *CJQ* 74.

47 H. Genn, *Judging Civil Justice*, Cambridge University Press, Cambridge 2010, ch. 3.

48 *Ibid.*, p. 119.

49 *Ibid.*, p. 125.

Another vigorous and long-standing opponent of the modern rush towards privatised justice is Owen Fiss. In his polemic, 'Against Settlement' (1984), he wrote:[50] 'Settlement is for me the civil analogue of plea bargaining: consent is often coerced; the bargain may be struck by someone without authority [...] Although dockets are trimmed, justice may not be done.' He added: 'Like plea bargaining, settlement is a capitulation to the condition of mass society and should be neither encouraged nor praised.'

Certainly, the process of settlement is not perfect. Possible objections to settlement (including mediated settlements) are:[51] (a) parties to settlement might not fully understand their respective positions; (b) the parties might be significantly unequal in various ways; (c) a party might have procured the settlement by underhand dealing;[52] (d) a party's full civil entitlement should not be reduced by compromise;[53] (e) assessment of the 'merits' must be measured, precise, and exacting;[54] and (f) the public search-light at trial should be shone upon serious wrongdoing.

As for factors (a) to (e), Hazel Genn has said: 'studies highlight [...] the ways in which power influences the outcome of settlement negotiations [...] Factors which are important are: legal intelligence – getting the right lawyers and experts; financial resources-paying for the [same]; and having the psychological, social, and economic ability to endure litigation.'[55]

---

50 [1984] *Yale LJ* 1073; reprinted in D. Galligan (ed.), *Procedure*, Dartmouth, Aldershot 1992, ch. 16; see also O. Fiss, *The Law As It Could Be*, NYU Press, New York 2003. For references to the debate which Fiss's 1984 article engendered in the US, O. Fiss and J. Resnik, *Adjudication and Its Alternatives*, Foundation Press, New York 2003, pp. 481 and 488; and see J. Resnik, 'For Owen M Fiss: Some Reflections on the Triumph and Death of Adjudication' (2003) 58 *Miami U. L. Rev.* 173.

51 For a convenient collection of literature addressing these points, H. Genn, 'Understanding Civil Justice' (1997) 50 *CLP* 155, 186–7.

52 e.g., an aggrieved party to a compromise 'threw the contractual book' at the opponent, in an attempt to overturn the compromise: *Halpern v. Halpern (No 2)* [2007] EWCA Civ 291 (distribution of estate among family members; allegation that not all relevant assets were revealed and that the compromise should be regarded as vitiated on numerous suggested grounds; the report at [2007] 3 All ER 478 concerns a specific aspect of the case; consult the online version at [1] ff for the numerous contractual challenges); cf also for an allegation that a mediated settlement had been procured by duress, *Farm Assist Limited (in liquidation) v. The Secretary of State for the Environment, Food and Rural Affairs (No 2)* (2009) [2009] EWHC 1102 (TCC); [2009] BLR 399; 125 Con LR 154.

53 One of Jeremy Bentham's anxieties: S. Roberts, 'Settlement as Civil Justice' (2000) 63 *MLR* 739, 743 n. 11, W. Twining, 'Alternatives to What?...' (1993) 56 *MLR* 380, 384 (examining various theorists' accounts of the civil process, notably Bentham, Llewellyn, Fuller and Damaska).

54 For a stimulating account of accuracy and legality, J.A. Jolowicz, 'The Dilemmas of Civil Litigation' in Id. (ed.), *On Civil Procedure*, Cambridge University Press 2000, ch. 4.

55 H. Genn, 'Understanding Civil Justice' (1997) 50 *CLP* 155, 179; see also H. Genn, *Hard Bargaining: Out of Court Settlement in Personal Injury Actions*, Oxford University Press, Oxford 1987 (reviewed N. Andrews [1989] *CLJ* 506) and other studies cited in Genn (1997) *ibid.*; see also H. Genn, *The Paths to Justice: What People Do and Think About Going to Law*, Hart, Oxford 1999; H. Genn, 'Court-Based ADR Initiatives for Non-Family Civil Disputes:

As for the sixth of these considerations, the openness of civil trial, an American commentator, Paul Carrington, has said: 'what people bring to court is the refuse of our national and community life. Mendacity, greed, brutality, sloth, and neglect are the materials with which we work'.[56]

Sir Jack Jacob, writing in 1985, before the ADR movement had made a serious impact in mainstream English civil justice, endorsed the ideal of open access to courts for the widest range of disputes:[57] 'It should be a fundamental aim of civil justice to open wide the gates of the Halls of Justice and to provide adequate and effective methods and measures, practices and procedures, reliefs and remedies, to deal with all justiciable claims and complaints.' He added: 'Such an aim would produce greater harmony and concord in society and increase the understanding and respect of the community for law and the system of civil justice.'

But this court-centred view seems debatable. England has not adopted Jacob's aim. Avoidance of litigation and encouragement of pre-trial settlement are the bedrock assumptions of the modern civil system of justice.

Nevertheless, one must acknowledge that it would be regrettable if matters could always be conveniently swept under the carpet by a last-minute settlement designed to avoid adverse publicity. Here are some examples taken from modern Britain: a senior female police-woman complains that her rise within the hierarchy has been obstructed by sexual discrimination;[58] a family wishes to complain that their son's suicide within the British armed forces was the result of bullying by fellow soldiers;[59] a car-dealer's standard-term warranty for repair of

---

The Commercial Court and the Court of Appeal', Department for Constitutional Affairs Research Reports 1/2002, 2002 <www.hmcourts-service.gov.uk/docs/adr_initiatives.pdf> (this last piece in examined briefly in Section 5 of the author's paper on the Commercial Court and case management).

56 P.D. Carrington, 'Teaching Civil Procedure: A Retrospective View' (1999) 49 *Jo. of Leg. Educ.* 311, 328.

57 J.I.H. Jacob, 'Justice Between Man and Man' (1984) 34 *Jo. of Leg. Educ.* 268 (cited H. Genn, 'Understanding Civil Justice' (1997) 50 *CLP* 155, 185–186); Genn suggests that 'our future prosperity has more to do with what is going on in offices and factories in the Far East than with whether Lord Woolf's fast track will achieve its objectives.' Cf. also Jacob's statement in 'Access to Justice in England', by the same author, *The Reform of Civil Procedural Law*, Sweet & Maxwell, London 1982, pp. 125–127: 'In a civilised society, there should be no room for barriers to justice, no second-class access to justice, just as there should be no second-class justice' (reprinting of his contribution to M. Cappelletti and B. Garth, *Access to Justice, a World Survey*, vol. 1, bk. 1, Guiffrè and Sijthoff, Italy 1978; and Jacob's later statement in *The Fabric of English Civil Justice*, Sweet & Maxwell, London 1987, p. 277, 'there should be, not only equality before the law, but equality of access to the law and legal services [...] alike for rich and poor and those of moderate means, and that such access should extend to all civil claims and defences at all levels of the judicial process, without regard to the nature of the dispute or complaint or the relief or remedy claimed.'

58 See the 'Halford' affair, July 1992, discussed in N. Andrews, *Principles of Civil Procedure*, Sweet & Maxwell, London 1994, p. 26.

59 Such complaints have received publicity: for Parliamentary comment in 2006 on a QC's report into one set of incidents, <www.publications.parliament.uk/pa/ld199900/ldhansrd/pdvn/lds06/text/60329-05.htm>.

new vehicles is mischievously declared to have been 'forfeited' for a reason which is no longer tenable under competition law;[60] a tenant has failed for many years to induce his landlord, a large charity, to satisfy its repair obligations, and it appears that there have been similar complaints by other tenants against this landlord.[61]

Sometimes statute prohibits exclusion of formal recourse to State-administered courts or tribunals. Thus in *Clyde & Co v. Bates van Winkelhof* (2011)[62] the (English) High Court refused to uphold a clause requiring a partner in a law firm to refer any disputes or differences arising from her work for the firm to mediation and then to arbitration. The partner had brought complaints to an employment tribunal alleging various statutory breaches by her law firm of equality law, and seeking compensation. Statute[63] clearly precludes 'contracting out' from this open and public system of adjudication before a tribunal. By contrast, in *Fulham FC (1987) Ltd v. Richards* (2010)[64] Vos J held that a wide arbitration agreement could cover a dispute arising from a transfer of a footballer. The agreement to arbitrate did not infringe any element of public policy. Therefore, Vos J decided to stay related court proceedings, commenced under the Companies legislation to challenge the activities of the relevant company officials.

## 2.9. CONCLUDING REMARKS ON MEDIATION

The main points have been as follows.

(a) Mediation is an 'alternative' form of 'civil justice'. It can operate as a complete substitute for civil litigation, or it can supplement that formal process after court proceedings have begun or even after judgment has been given but an appeal is pending.
(b) Civil proceedings before the courts are becoming a system of last resort to be pursued only when more civilised and 'proportionate' techniques have failed or could never be made to work.
(c) The process of mediation has become popular in England, and this is likely to increase for two reasons.
(d) First, many disputants now recognise that mediation is often more attractive than the formal processes of court adjudication or arbitration. These are the

---

60 Typically, customer's garage failing to fit replacement mechanical part bearing manufacturer's logo, even though part in fact fitted has same objective specification as the manufacturer's named part; facts told to the author: for the legal background to this, see the Office of Fair Trading's comments at <www.oft.gov.uk/News/Press+releases/2003/PN+170-03.htm>.

61 Examples must be legion; e.g., *English Churches Housing Group v. Shine* [2004] EWCA Civ 434.

62 [2011] EWHC 668 (QB), Slade J.

63 Section 120, Equality Act 2010, and section 203, Equality Rights Act 1996.

64 [2010] EWHC 3111 (Ch); [2011] 2 All ER 112.

private vectors which drive demand for mediation. Because these are spontaneous responses by disputants, based on their private assessment of the merits of this style of dispute resolution, these factors can be called 'organic'.

(e) However, second, reinforcing these private and organic factors are the various forms of institutional support for the movement towards mediation.
(f) Government has a strong interest in promoting ADR because it is less expensive than civil litigation.
(g) Government is now actively promoting mediation. This is the process of official proselytising and cajoling. However, mediation should not be imposed on parties if it is evident that there is insufficient shared willingness to engage in constructive discussion. Thus mediation is possible only if both parties are willing to discuss their dispute, to examine the merits of their position in good faith, and ultimately to consider making concessions, whether tactical or magnanimous (however, a court might sometimes be justified in suggesting mediation even if both parties seem initially opposed to this).
(h) State-controlled courts can support and promote the private processes of mediation and arbitration.
(i) An English court will enforce a mediation agreement by ordering a stay of litigation brought in violation of that agreement
(j) The court system encourages pursuit of mediation. In England direct judicial encouragement of mediation involves selective judicial recommendation of mediation. The courts can direct litigants in pending actions or appeals to consider mediation if the parties, or one of them, requests, or if the court itself suggests.
(k) Leverage to consider and to pursue mediation takes the form of a 'stay' upon current proceedings or the threat of an adverse costs order. The English courts also subject disputants to the general threat of adverse costs awards if parties unreasonably spurn sensible mediation overtures made by the opponent or by the court.
(l) Mediation is not undertaken by judges in cases but by mediators outside the judicial system or by mediators who have been employed or hired by the official court system to assist disputants.
(m) Confidential communications during mediation are privileged against compulsory production in legal proceedings. However, the mediator does not enjoy any personal evidential immunity against being compelled by a court to provide information or give evidence concerning a mediation.
(n) Traditional court litigation will continue because it offers a strong form of dispute resolution. The court's coercive powers are indispensable in some contexts, especially in claims against fraudulent or uncooperative persons.

(o) Court litigation also embodies many values, notably the principle of publicly accessible proceedings and reasoned decisions.

# 3. ARBITRATION

## 3.1. NATURE OF ARBITRATION IN ENGLAND AND WALES

An arbitration tribunal's power to reach a binding decision on the merits is to be contrasted with mediation (or conciliation). A mediator, although neutral, is not empowered or expected to give a binding decision. A mediator is instead mandated to facilitate a consensual resolution of the parties' dispute.

Arbitration shares with court adjudication two core procedural values or principles: impartiality of the arbitrator, and a duty to hear the other's case.[65] However, arbitration does not embody the principle of publicity (for the confidential nature of arbitration proceedings.[66] The arbitrator should give reasons in support of his award,[67] unless the parties have 'contracted out' of this requirement.[68] In fact most awards are reasoned. There is a (heavily qualified) power to challenge the award before the court on the basis of an error of law.[69]

The arbitral award on the merits becomes *res judicata*. And so it is binding on the parties and their successors in title.[70] The award can be made a judgment and enforced within the English judicial system of enforcement. Alternatively, the award can be enforced outside England under the New York Convention 1958 to which many nations are party.[71]

Arbitration in England rests on the Arbitration Act 1996 (England and Wales). The 2006 'Report on the Arbitration Act 1996 (England and Wales)' reveals that the English legislation is perceived as effective.[72] No changes were

---

65 For detailed examination of these fundamental procedural principles, N. Andrews, *English Civil Procedure*, Oxford University Press, Oxford 2003, paras. 4.28 ff., 5.01 ff.

66 On this principle, in the context of English civil court proceedings, N. Andrews, *ibid.*, paras. 4.49 ff.; generally on English arbitration, N. Andrews, *Civil Processes*, Intersentia, Cambridge 2013, vol. II.

67 *Ibid.*, paras. 5.39 ff.

68 Section 69, Arbitration Act 1996; if 'reasons' are dispensed with, by agreement, there is no such right of appeal: section 69(1), 1996 Act: 'An agreement to dispense with reasons for the tribunal's award shall be considered an agreement to exclude the court's jurisdiction under this section'; and section 45(1), 1996 Act.

69 Section 69, Arbitration Act 1996.

70 Section 58(1), Arbitration Act 1996.

71 New York Convention on the Recognition and Enforcement of Foreign Arbitral Awards 1958; for the process in England of recognition and enforcement of a New York Convention award, section 101, Arbitration Act 1996.

72 'Report on the Arbitration Act 1996 (England and Wales)', 2006; report prepared for the Commercial Court Users' Committee, the British Maritime Law Association, the London Shipping Law Centre, and other bodies (the authors were various barristers, solicitors, and

recommended. A 2005 London report stated that companies gave four reasons for preferring international commercial arbitration to court proceedings:[73] (a) the confidential nature of the process; (b) flexibility and party control; (c) speed and efficiency; and (d) swift enforcement of awards including enforcement in foreign jurisdictions, applying the New York Convention 1958. In fact arbitration business is booming in England.

Commercial parties opt for arbitration primarily to achieve the following: (a) confidentiality; (b) party selection of the panel, governing norms, and the arbitral procedure (notably selection of a 'neutral' panel for the arbitration of disputes between parties who are based in different jurisdictions); (c) speediness and efficiency; and (d) finality.

## 3.2. ARBITRATION CLAUSES[74]

The English Arbitration Act 1996 requires the arbitration agreement to be in writing.[75] The arbitration clause *might be valid* even though the main contract might not be. This notion, the so-called principle of 'separability' (contained in section 7 of the Arbitration Act 1996 (England and Wales)), entails that the main transaction, the substantive source of the dispute, normally a contractual document, is separate from the arbitration agreement, even though that clause is (nearly always) included in the same document. In short, the invalidity of the main contract does *not necessarily* entail the invalidity of the arbitration agreement (see the remarks of Lord Hoffmann in *Fiona Trust and Holding Corporation v. Privalov* (2007)).[76] This detachment of the contract for decision-

---

other arbitration specialists – see Appendix A of report for details); for the text, see <www.idrc.co.uk/aa96survey/Report_on_Arbitration_Act_1996.pdf>.

73 Available online at <www.pwc.com/Extweb/pwcpublications.nsf/docid/0B3FD76A8551573E85257168005122C8>.

74 D. Joseph, *Jurisdiction and Arbitration Agreements and their Enforcement*, 2nd ed., Sweet & Maxwell, London 2010; an agreement to arbitrate is subject to the traditional analysis of repudiatory breach and 'acceptance' by the innocent party: J. Levy [2007] *NLJ* 1036, noting *Bea Hotels NV v. Bellway LLC* [2007] EWHC 1363 (Comm), Cooke J; and *Downing v. Al Tameer Establishment* [2002] EWCA Civ 721, at [21], [25] and [26], also noting the seminal 'contractual' analysis of arbitration agreements in *Bremer Vulcan v. South India Shipping Corporation Limited* [1981] AC 909, HL; '*The Hannah Blumenthal*' [1983] 1 AC 854, HL; '*The Splendid Sun*' [1981] QB 694, CA, and '*The Leonidas D*' [1985] 1 WLR 925, CA (on this stream of authority, MB (2001), pp. 503 ff.). Selected journal comments: J. Lew, 'Achieving the Dream: Autonomous Arbitration' (2006) 22 *Arb. Int.* 179; R. Park, 'Determining Arbitral Jurisdiction: Allocation of Tasks Between Courts and Arbitrators' (1997) 8 *Am. Rev. Int'l Arb.* 133.

75 Section 3, Arbitration Act 1996 (England and Wales); MB (2001), pp. 16, 258 ff.; for an important discussion of arbitration clauses affecting sovereign States, *Svenska Petroleum Exploration AB v. Government of the Republic of Lithuania (No 2)* [2006] EWCA Civ 1529; [2007] QB 886, considering section 9(1), State Immunity Act 1978.

76 [2007] UKHL 40; [2007] 4 All ER 951, notably Lord Hoffmann's speech at [17] to [19]; otherwise known as *Premium Nafta Products Ltd v. Fili Shipping Co Ltd.* Considered in *JSC*

making (the arbitration clause) from the principal contract enables 'one stop' arbitration to occur: the arbitral panel are competent to determine the validity of both the arbitration clause and the main transaction; so-called *kompetenz-kompetenz*. Thus the principle of separability operates alongside the related principle of *kompetenz-kompetenz*.

## 3.3. ANTI-SUIT INJUNCTIONS CONCERNING OFFENDING PROCEEDINGS OUTSIDE THE EUROPEAN UNION

The English courts have a long-established jurisdiction to compel a defendant, over whom the court has jurisdiction, to refrain from commencing, or continuing, foreign civil proceedings, or from participating in arbitration. Such an injunction will be granted if, in particular, that litigious activity will involve a breach of either an exclusive jurisdiction clause nominating England as the only chosen forum or breach of an arbitration clause. In the House of Lords' reference to the European Court of Justice, in *Turner v. Grovit* (2001),[77] Lord Hobhouse made these trenchant points concerning the English courts' power to grant an anti-suit injunction:

> '22 [...] Certain preconceptions and misunderstandings still tend to persist as to the nature of the type of restraining order made in the present case and the grounds upon which it can be applied for. It is important not to be misled by these misconceptions.
> 23 The present type of restraining order is commonly referred to as an 'anti-suit' injunction. This terminology is misleading since it fosters the impression that the order is addressed to and intended to bind another court. It suggests that the jurisdiction of the foreign court is in question and that the injunction is an order that the foreign court desist from exercising the jurisdiction given to it by its own domestic law. None of this is correct. When an English court makes a restraining order, it is making an order which is addressed only to a party which is before it. The order is not directed against the foreign court [...] The order binds only that party, in personam, and is effective only in so far as that party is amenable to the jurisdiction of the English courts so that the order can be enforced against him.'

---

*BTA Bank v. Ablyazov* [2011] EWHC 587 (Comm), Christopher Clarke J (granting a stay of English civil proceedings because an arbitration clause had been shown to exist by the party seeking the stay, and the party seeking to oppose the stay had not shown that this clause had been avoided on the ground of non-disclosure).

77 [2001] UKHL 65; [2002] 1 WLR 107; N. Andrews, 'Injunctions in Support of Civil Proceedings and Arbitration', in R. Stürner and M. Kawano (eds.), *Comparative Studies on Enforcement and Provisional Measures*, Mohr Siebeck, Tübingen 2011, pp. 319–344; and see now the *AES* case [2013] UKSC 35.

The English Commercial Court in *Shashoua v. Sharma* (2009)[78] and the English Court of Appeal in *Midgulf International Ltd v. Groupe Chimiche Tunisien* (2010)[79] have confirmed that the European Court of Justice's decision in the *West Tankers* case (*Allianz SpA etc v. West Tankers, 'The Front Comor'* (2009))[80] does not preclude use of anti-suit injunctions against parties contemplating bringing, or already actively pursuing, proceedings in the courts of a country which is not a Member State of the European Community or a Contracting State within the Lugano system.

## 3.4. ANTI-SUIT INJUNCTIONS CONCERNING OFFENDING PROCEEDINGS WITHIN THE EUROPEAN UNION

The decision of the European Court of Justice in *Allianz SpA etc v. West Tankers, 'The Front Comor'* (2009)[81] has established that English courts can no longer issue 'anti-suit injunctions' to restrain a party to an arbitration from continuing such wrongful judicial proceedings in the courts of a Member State within the EU jurisdictional zone (that is, the Members States governed by the Brussels Jurisdiction Regulation (2001)).[82]

A proposed EU change (now withdrawn) would have provided (in Draft Article 29, section 4, of the Jurisdiction Regulation):[83] 'Where the agreed or designated seat of an arbitration is in a Member State, the courts of another Member State whose jurisdiction is contested on the basis of an arbitration agreement shall stay proceedings once the courts of the Member State where the

78 [2009] EWHC 957, at [39].

79 [2010] EWCA Civ 66; [2010] 1 CLC 113.

80 *Allianz SpA etc v. West Tankers* (C-185/07) [2009] 1 AC 1138; [2009] 1 All ER (Comm) 435; [2009] 1 Lloyd's Rep 413; [2009] 1 CLC 96; [2009] ILPr 20; *The Times*, 13 February 2009; noted E. Peel (2009) 125 *LQR* 365.

81 *Allianz SpA etc v. West Tankers, 'The Front Comor'* (C-185/07) [2009] 1 AC 1138; [2009] 1 All ER (Comm) 435; [2009] 1 Lloyd's Rep 413; [2009] 1 CLC 96; [2009] ILPr 20; *The Times*, 13 February 2009; noted E. Peel (2009) 125 *LQR* 365; C. Consolo, 'Arbitration and EC Law: an Italian reaction to the Heidelberg Colloquium' (2009) *Lis Int'l* 102–108; H. Seriki, 'Declaratory Relief and Arbitration: the Aftermath of "*The Front Comor*"' (2010) 7 *JBL* 541–555 H. Seriki, 'Anti-Suit Injunctions, Arbitration and the ECJ: An Approach Too Far?' (2010) 7 *JBL* 24; P. Schlosser, 'Europe – Is it Time to Reconsider the Arbitration Exception from the Brussels Regulation?' [2009] *Int. ALR* 45; A. Mourre and A. Vagenheim, 'The Arbitration Exclusion in Regulation 44/2001 after *West Tankers*' [2009] *Int. ALR* 75; P. Clifford and O. Browne, 'Lost at Sea or a Storm in a Tea Cup? Anti-suit Injunctions after *West Tankers*' [2009] *Int. ALR* 19; A. Pullen, 'The Future of International Arbitration in Europe: *West Tankers* and the EU Green Paper' [2009] *Int. ALR* 56.

82 Council Regulation 44/2001 of 22.12.2001 on jurisdiction and the recognition and enforcement of judgments in civil and commercial matters.

83 The EU Commission's 'Proposal for a Regulation of the European Parliament and of the Council on jurisdiction and the recognition and enforcement of judgments in civil and commercial matters', Brussels 14/12/2010 COM (2010) 748 Final 2010/0383 (COD).

seat of the arbitration or the arbitral tribunal is located have been seised of proceedings to determine, as their main object or as an incidental question, the existence, validity or effects of that arbitration agreement. This paragraph does not prevent the court whose jurisdiction is contested from declining jurisdiction in the situation referred to above if its national law so prescribes. Where the existence, validity or effects of the arbitration agreement are established, the court seised shall decline jurisdiction.'

How would this have worked? Suppose P and D's contract states that disputes concerning it will be arbitrated in London. In breach of this, P sues D in a Paris court. D will be able to bring court proceedings in London (the 'seat' of the ostensible arbitration) seeking a declaration that the arbitration clause is binding, the Paris court will be obliged to stay its proceedings. The English court's declaration will be binding on all Member State courts. It will be noted that, although the arbitrators nominated by the relevant clause are free to decide to begin the arbitration, having made their own assessment of the arbitration clause's validity and effect, nevertheless, for the purpose of the proposed amendment, the arbitrators' determination of their jurisdiction is not the legal event which triggers the Paris court's duty to place its proceedings in suspense. The upshot of the proposed amendment would have been that the *kompetenz-kompetenz* principle (arbitrators' provisional capacity to determine whether an arbitration clause exists, is valid, and to fix its scope) would have been eroded. Instead, the courts would have become the main actors determining the validity of arbitration agreements.

## 3.5. FREEZING RELIEF AND ARBITRATION

In *Mobil Cerro Negro Ltd v. Petroleos De Venezuela SA* (2008)[84] Walker J emphasised that English worldwide freezing orders[85] should be made 'only sparingly' in support of arbitration and, usually, only where there is 'compelling evidence of serious international fraud'.[86]

## 3.6. CONFIDENTIALITY

The Court of Appeal's decision in *Emmott v. Michael Wilson & Partners Ltd* (2008)[87] confirms that an obligation of confidentiality arises as a matter of law

84 [2008] EWHC 532 (Comm); noted A. Johnson [2008] *CJQ* 433–444.

85 N. Andrews, *The Modern Civil Process*, Mohr Siebeck, Tübingen, Germany 2008, paras. 4.03 ff.

86 *Ibid.*, at [5].

87 [2008] EWCA Civ 184; [2008] Bus LR 1361; [2008] 1 Lloyd's Rep 616; noted H. Dundas, 'Confidentiality in English Arbitration: The Final Word? *Emmott v. Michael Wilson &*

(on the basis of an 'implied term in law') in arbitration references conducted in accordance with English law. This implied term governs all documents 'prepared for', 'used', and 'disclosed during' arbitration proceedings governed by English law. The English courts recognise various exceptional contexts in which arbitral confidentiality will not prevail. Lawrence Collins LJ summarised the position as follows:[88]

> 'the principal cases in which disclosure will be permissible are these: the first is where there is consent, express or implied; second, where there is an order, or leave of the court (but that does not mean that the court has a general discretion to lift the obligation of confidentiality); third, where it is reasonably necessary for the protection of the legitimate interests of an arbitrating party;[89] fourth, where the interests of justice require disclosure, and also (perhaps) where the public interest requires disclosure.'

He added:[90]

> 'The interests of justice are not confined to the interests of justice in England. The international dimension of the present case demands a broader view.'

*Emmott v. Michael Wilson & Partners Ltd* (2008)[91] shows that the English courts will be prepared to relax confidentiality in order to prevent another court, whether in England or elsewhere, from being misled concerning an issue, provided the parallel court proceedings arise from similar events and there is a sufficient connexion between the parties to the relevant arbitration and the

---

*Partners'* (2008) 74 *Arbitration* 458–466; for background discussion of this topic in the following: (only (a) contains reference to this recent case): (a) A. Redfern and M. Hunter, *International Commercial Arbitration*, 5th ed., Oxford University Press, Oxford 2009, paras. 2.145 to 2.176; (b) *Russell on Arbitration*, 23rd ed., Sweet & Maxwell, London 2007, paras. 5-172 to 5-180; (b) M. Mustill and S. Boyd, *Commercial Arbitration: 2001 Companion Volume*, Sweet & Maxwell, London 2001, pp. 112–113; (c) N. Andrews, *Civil Processes*, Intersentia, Cambridge 2013, vol. II, ch. 8. For background journal articles: various authors, (1995) 11 *Arb. Int.* 3, 319; F. Dessemontet, 'Arbitration and Confidentiality' (1996) 7 *Am. Rev. Int'l Arb.* 299; P. Neill, 'Confidentiality in Arbitration' (1996) 12 *Arb. Int.* 287; A. Rogers and D. Miller, 'Non-Confidential Arbitration Proceedings' (1996) 12 *Arb. Int.* 319; M. Pryles, 'Confidentiality', in L.W. Newman and R.D. Hill (eds.), *The Leading Arbitrators' Guide to International Arbitration*, Juris Publishers, Bern, Switzerland 2004, ch. 19; K. Noussia, *Confidentiality in International Commercial Arbitration*, Springer, Heidelberg 2010.

88 *Emmott v. Michael Wilson & Partners Ltd* [2008] EWCA Civ 184; [2008] Bus LR 1361, at [107].

89 *Ibid.*, at [101], *per* Collins LJ: '[disclosure is] permissible when, and to the extent to which, it was reasonably necessary for the establishment or protection of an arbitrating party's legal rights *vis-à-vis* a third party in order to found a cause of action against that third party or to defend a claim, or counterclaim, brought by that third party. It would be this exception which would apply where insurers have to be informed about the details of arbitral proceedings.'

90 *Ibid.*, at [111].

91 [2008] EWCA Civ 184; [2008] Bus LR 1361; [2008] 1 Lloyd's Rep 616.

parties to the relevant parallel litigation. In the *Michael Wilson* case (2008) MWP, a law firm specialising in international commercial arbitration, was a party to arbitration in London and party to court litigation in several jurisdictions (Jersey, Colorado, the British Virgin Islands (BVI), and New South Wales (NSW)) involving former associates of MWP, namely E (Emmott), N (Nicholls) and S (Slater). All this litigation concerned the same basic claim by MWP that these former members of its staff had conspired to steal business from MWP. There was an obvious inconsistency, and hence relevance, in the fact that, in the London arbitration, MWP had abandoned allegations of fraud committed by these three, but MWP retained this allegation on the same facts in the NSW and BVI court litigation. The English Court of Appeal held that these facts justified permitting E, one of the parties to the English arbitration, to disclose material generated during that arbitration. Such disclosure was justified because of the danger that the NSW and BVI courts might otherwise be misled. It did not matter that E was not party to the relevant foreign court proceedings. It was enough that those proceedings concerned the same 'substratum of facts' as the arbitration.

## 3.7. PARTY AUTONOMY

Party autonomy extends to procedural matters. Thus the procedure adopted in individual arbitration references can be tailor-made to suit the dispute's specific features. It has been suggested that, where necessary, 'every case demands its own procedure'.[92] But arbitration clauses seldom prescribe detailed matters of procedure.

One of arbitration's main attractions is that disputants can select the panel. In *Jivraj v Hashwani* (2011)[93] the United Kingdom Supreme Court held that the appointment of arbitrators is not governed by the European provisions prohibiting selection by reference to religious belief. Lord Clarke did not dispute that an arbitrator was appointed under a contract and that his services were rendered pursuant to that contract; but the central issue was whether an arbitrator is employed 'under a contract personally to do any work'.[94] He said: 'There is in my opinion some significance in the fact that the definition does not simply refer to a contract to do work but to "employment under" such a contract [… T]he role of an arbitrator is not naturally described as employment under a

92 The need for arbitrators not simply 'to copy the CPR' (or Commercial Court Guide) is echoed in a recent report on the operation of the Arbitration Act, 'Report (2006) on the Arbitration Act 1996 (England and Wales)', at [43] to [45]; report prepared for the Commercial Court Users' Committee, the British Maritime Law Association, the London Shipping Law Centre, and other bodies; accessible at <www.idrc.co.uk/aa96survey/Report_on_Arbitration_Act_1996.pdf>.

93 [2011] UKSC 40; [2011] 1 WLR 1872.

94 *Ibid.*, at [23].

contract personally to do work. That is because his role is not naturally described as one of employment at all.' Since the 2003 Regulations implemented an EU Directive, Lord Clarke considered the case law of the Court of Justice of the European Union[95] on this issue. He found[96] that the Court 'draws a clear distinction between those who are, in substance, employed and those who are "independent providers of services who are not in a relationship of subordination with the person who receives the services"' and he held that this same distinction should be drawn for the purposes of the 2003 Regulations. He continued:[97]

> 'The arbitrator is in critical respects independent of the parties. His functions and duties require him to rise above the partisan interests of the parties and not to act in, or so as to further, the particular interests of either party. As the International Chamber of Commerce ('the ICC') puts it, he must determine how to resolve their competing interests. He is in no sense in a position of subordination to the parties; rather the contrary. He is in effect a 'quasi-judicial adjudicator' [...] In England his role is spelled out in the Arbitration Act 1996. By section 33, he has a duty to act fairly and impartially as between the parties and to adopt procedures suitable to the circumstances of the particular case so as to provide a fair means of determination of the issues between the parties [...] Once an arbitrator has been appointed, at any rate in the absence of agreement between them, the parties effectively have no control over him. Unless the parties agree, an arbitrator may only be removed in exceptional circumstances.'

## 3.8. SPEED AND EFFICIENCY

Parties to arbitration hope that the process will be swifter and cheaper, but no less accurate, than English court litigation. The Arbitration Act 1996 (England and Wales) injects the discipline of time-management and cost-effectiveness into the arbitral process, while respecting the parties' interest in gaining a fair result. It states: 'The tribunal shall [...] adopt procedures suitable to the circumstance of the particular case, avoiding unnecessary delay or expense, so as to provide a fair means for the resolution of the matters falling to be determined.'[98] It is likely that this arbitral 'mission statement' exerted an intellectual influence on the drafting of a similar 'Overriding Objective' in the Civil Procedure Rules of 1998 (it should be recalled that Lord Woolf's reports, providing the blueprint for the CPR (1998), were composed in 1995 and 1996, when the Arbitration Bill, as it then was, was being debated). However, the arbitral process can be 'hijacked'

95 The main cases being: *Allonby v. Accrington and Rossendale College* (Case C-256/01) [2004] ICR 1328; *Lawrie-Blum v. Land Baden-Württemberg* (Case 66/85) [1987] ICR 483; and *Kurz v. Land Baden-Württemberg* (Case C-188/00) [2002] ECR I-10691.

96 [2011] UKSC 40; [2011] 1 WLR 1872, at [27].

97 *Ibid.*, at [41] to [43].

98 Section 33(1)(b), Arbitration Act 1996 (England and Wales).

cynically, or it can become bogged down, as a result of improper commencement of court proceedings, in violation of the contractual commitment to arbitrate.

## 3.9. FINALITY OF THE AWARD

There is a (heavily qualified) power to challenge the award before the High Court (a) on the basis of an error of (English) law.[99] Here the High Court acts as the 'gate-keeper': unless both parties agree to an appeal on a point of law, the court will apply the restrictive criteria of the statutory 'filter' to determine whether to grant permission for such an appeal.[100] Other possible grounds of challenge before the court are (b) lack of jurisdiction,[101] and (c) the assertion that the arbitral panel has been guilty of 'serious irregularity affecting the tribunal, the proceedings or the award'.[102] The last is regarded as 'a long stop, only available in

---

99 Section 69(2)(3), Arbitration Act 1996 (England and Wales); there are many cases on this provision, for example, Flaux J in *ASM Shipping Ltd of India v. TTMI Ltd of England ('The Amer Energy')* [2009] 1 Lloyd's Rep 293, at [17] to [19]; the report by V.V. Veeder and A. Sander (2009) notes that the Commercial Court, in London, considered 36 applications in 2006, and granted leave in 9; in 2007, 58, leave granted in 13; in 2008, 57, leave granted in 14; disclosing an average of 50 a year, with leave granted in 12 (noted M. O'Reilly, 'Provisions on Costs and Appeals: An Assessment from an International Perspective', paper delivered at the British Institute of International and Comparative Law conference, London, February 2010).

100 Section 69, Arbitration Act 1996 (England and Wales).

101 Section 67, Arbitration Act 1996 (England and Wales) states: '(1) A party to arbitral proceedings may (upon notice to the other parties and to the tribunal) apply to the court – (a) challenging any award of the arbitral tribunal as to its substantive jurisdiction; or (b) for an order declaring an award made by the tribunal on the merits to be of no effect, in whole or in part, because the tribunal did not have substantive jurisdiction. A party may lose the right to object (see section 73) and the right to apply is subject to the restrictions in section 70(2) and (3). (2) The arbitral tribunal may continue the arbitral proceedings and make a further award while an application to the court under this section is pending in relation to an award as to jurisdiction. (3) On an application under this section challenging an award of the arbitral tribunal as to its substantive jurisdiction, the court may by order – (a) confirm the award, (b) vary the award, or (c) set aside the award in whole or in part. (4) The leave of the court is required for any appeal from a decision of the court under this section.'

102 Section 68, Arbitration Act 1996 (England and Wales) 1996; section 68(2) specifies: 'Serious irregularity means an irregularity of one or more of the following kinds which the court considers has caused or will cause substantial injustice to the applicant – (a) failure by the tribunal to comply with section 33 (general duty of tribunal); (b) the tribunal exceeding its powers (otherwise than by exceeding its substantive jurisdiction: see section 67); (c) failure by the tribunal to conduct the proceedings in accordance with the procedure agreed by the parties; (d) failure by the tribunal to deal with all the issues that were put to it; (e) any arbitral or other institution or person vested by the parties with powers in relation to the proceedings or the award exceeding its powers; (f) uncertainty or ambiguity as to the effect of the award; (g) the award being obtained by fraud or the award or the way in which it was procured being contrary to public policy; (h) failure to comply with the requirements as to the form of the award; or (i) any irregularity in the conduct of the proceedings or in the award which is admitted by the tribunal or by any arbitral or other institution or person vested by the parties with powers in relation to the proceedings or the award.'

extreme cases where the tribunal has gone so wrong in its conduct of the arbitration that justice calls out for it to be corrected.'[103]

There is no power to appeal from a finding or application of a point of foreign law.[104] Furthermore, as the Court of Appeal decided in *C v. D* (2007),[105] if the seat of the arbitration is England and Wales, a party cannot evade this last limitation by seeking a declaration from a foreign court that the English award on a point of foreign law involves a misunderstanding or misapplication of that foreign law.

It is possible to contract out of the curial appeal process concerning points of law, but careful wording must be adopted (see end of this paragraph). Thus Gloster J in *Shell Egypt West Manzala GmbH v. Dana Gas Egypt Ltd* (2009) held that the formula 'final, conclusive and binding', contained in the arbitration clause, and clearly intended to bestow some form of finality on an award, did not render an arbitration award secure from appeal to the High Court on a point of law.[106] The words 'final, conclusive and binding' merely indicated that the award would be final and binding as a matter of *res judicata*: that is, findings of fact are binding, with the result that there should be no further litigation on the same factual matters between the same parties. This still leaves the door open to the award being subject to appeal to the High Court on a point of law (if permission to appeal to the High Court can be obtained from a judge under section 69(2)(3), Arbitration Act 1996 (England and Wales)). To exclude this possibility of appeal on a point of English law, it would be necessary explicitly to state that the award would not be subject to appeal or other recourse. Thus the rules of the London Court of International Arbitration (LCIA), Article 26.9, provide: 'The parties also waive irrevocably their right to any form of appeal, review or recourse to any State court or other judicial authority, insofar as such waiver may be validly made.'

## 3.10. RECOGNITION AND ENFORCEMENT OF ARBITRATION AWARDS UNDER THE NEW YORK CONVENTION 1958[107]

If an award falls for recognition or enforcement under New York Convention principles, English case law establishes that the court where recognition or

103 Lord Steyn in *Lesotho Highlands Development Authority v. Impreglio SpA* [2006] 1 AC 22, HL.

104 This is the result of the definition of 'question of law' in section 82(1), Arbitration Act 1996 (England and Wales); affecting scope of section 69, Arbitration Act 1996 (England and Wales) (appeal to court on a 'question of law arising out of an award made in the [arbitration] proceedings'; choice of substantive law covered by section 46(1), 1996 Act.

105 *C v. D* [2007] EWCA Civ 1282; [2008] 1 Lloyd's Rep 239.

106 [2009] EWHC 2097 (Comm).

107 Selected journal comments: E. Gaillard, 'Enforcement of Awards Set Aside in the Country of Origin' (1999) 14 *ICSID Rev.* 16; J. Paulsson, 'May or Must Under the New York Convention: An Exercise in Syntax and Linguistics' (1998) 14 *Arb. Int.* 227; S. Wilske,

enforcement is sought can re-open the disputed issue of law/fact to determine whether the 'losing party' in the arbitration was truly a party to the relevant arbitration agreement. This is provided the party resisting such recognition has consistently opposed the arbitrators' jurisdiction.

The UK Supreme Court in *Dallah Real Estate & Tourism Holding Co v. Pakistan* (2010)[108] held that a Paris award could not be recognised in England, under the New York Convention, because the French arbitration tribunal had incorrectly determined that the Pakistan Government was a party to the relevant arbitration agreement. The Pakistan Government had neither signed the arbitration agreement, nor had it been named as a party to that agreement. Instead that Government had structured the relevant substantive transaction (including the literal terms of the arbitration clause) by using a trust. The English court held that the arbitration award was flawed because the tribunal had not applied French law to determine whether the Pakistan Government was in fact a party to the arbitration agreement (this being the applicable law to the construction of the arbitration agreement, in default of party choice of another system). The *Dallah* case (2010), above, shows the extensive scope during foreign enforcement proceedings under the New York Convention for the enforcing court to rehear the question concerning the validity of the arbitration agreement.

But it is somewhat embarrassing that a French court (Paris *Cour d'appel*) has recently reached the opposite conclusion: that this award was satisfactory, according to French arbitration principles and that the Pakistan Government should be regarded as a party to the arbitration agreement.[109] This decision was made pursuant to Article 1502(1) of the French Code of Civil Procedure. This permits the court to refuse to enforce an award 'if the arbitrator has ruled upon the matter without an arbitration agreement or [the putative arbitration agreement is in fact] a void and lapsed agreement'. The French court then focused on the parties' dealings between the parties. It noted that the Pakistan Government negotiated the contract, and that the trust created by the Government was merely a signatory. The Paris *Cour d'appel* also noted that the Government was involved in the performance of the contract, and that it effectively controlled the same transaction's termination. It concluded that the trust was 'purely formal' and that the Government was the true Pakistani party to the transaction. By contrast the English courts had given very considerable weight to the legal separateness of the trust and had endeavoured to reflect its perception that the arbitration agreement had not merely been signed by the

L. Shore and J.-M. Ahrens, 'The "Group of Companies Doctrine" – Where is it heading?' (2006) 17 *Am. Rev. Int'l Arb.* 73.

108 [2010] UKSC 46; [2010] 3 WLR 1472.

109 *Gouvernement du Pakistan v. Société Dallah Real Estate & Tourism Holding Co.*, Cour d'appel de Paris, Pôle 1, Ch. 1, no. 09/28533 (17 February 2011) <www.practicallaw.com/8-505-0043>. On which see the comment by White & Case: <www.whitecase.com/insight-03022011/>.

trust, and made no mention of the Government as an additional party, but that there was no true consensus between the members of this triangle that the Government should be treated as a party to the arbitration agreement.

## 4. CONCLUSION

I have examined the English legal system's attempt to maintain harmonious relations between the State-administered court system and the systems of arbitration or mediation. The marriage at times can be tempestuous, at other times harmonious, but it is always interesting. The marriage has not broken down: too many depend on its success.

Already mediation has become popular in England. Its popularity is likely to increase because it is widely recognised that it can often be more attractive than the formal processes of court adjudication or arbitration. But these private vectors (so-called 'organic' factors) are also reinforced by institutional support for the same popular and commercial movement towards mediation. England has moved beyond any sense that mediation is an impoverished or 'second-best' form of civil justice. Within a mature system of civil justice there is a place for both formal and informal processes. State-controlled courts can support and promote the private processes of mediation and arbitration.

Arbitration continues to prosper as a highly attractive alternative form of dispute resolution. The English courts are keen to foster it, not only because commercial judges have often gained valuable pre-judicial experience of the system during their time at the Bar (acting both as advocates and as arbitrators), but because retired judges – although unable to act as advocates – often hope to return to arbitration as arbitrators.

To express the interaction between the public and private forms of civil justice, the author has elsewhere suggested, in lectures given in Pavia (2009),[110] Sao Paulo, Curitiba (2010) and Rio (2011), that a helpful metaphor might be that of 'Civil Justice's Double Helix'.[111] The metaphor expresses the idea that one strand – consisting of ADR, including arbitration and mediation – and the other strand – the court process – are complementary and entwined. Together the two strands of the public court process and the alternative forms of private dispute resolution have considerable strength.

---

110 N. Andrews, 'The Modern Civil Process in England: Links between Private and Public Forms of Dispute Resolution' (2009) 14 *ZZP Int.* 3–32; also translated as 'La "Doppia Elica" della Giustizia Civile: I Legami tra Metodi Privati e Pubblici di Risoluzione delle Controversie', in *Rivista Trimetrale di Diritto e Procedura Civile* (2010) 529–548 (I am grateful to Elisabetta Silvestri, Pavia, for this excellent translation).

111 The 'double helix' structure of DNA was discovered by Francis Crick and James Dewey Watson (Nobel Prize 1962); the latter is an Honorary Fellow of Clare College, Cambridge, where the author is a Fellow; and there is a sculpture of the Double Helix within the college's grounds.

# HONG KONG

Gavin DENTON and FAN Kun*

'The time, costs, acrimony and uncertainty involved in traditional litigation raise hard issues as to whether the present dispute resolution process is adequate to meet the needs of justice and efficiency.'
Wong Yan Lung SC, HKSAR former Secretary of Justice

## Contents



* The authors would like to thank Stephanie Poon and Vincent Chan for their useful research assistance.

## 1. ARBITRATION IN HONG KONG

Hong Kong is one of the leading centres for international commercial arbitration in Asia, and increasingly one of the leading centres in the world. On 1 July 1997, mainland China resumed sovereignty over Hong Kong from Britain and Hong Kong was designated a Special Administrative Region (SAR) of the People's Republic of China.[1]

[1] Hong Kong Island was ceded in perpetuity from China to the United Kingdom in 1842 following the First Opium War and the southern part of Kowloon Peninsula was ceded in 1860, following the Second Opium War. A 99-year lease over the New Territories was then entered into between the UK and China on 1 July 1898. On 19 December 1984, the Sino-

Under the principle of 'one country, two systems', the Hong Kong SAR will retain a different political and legal system to that of mainland China for 50 years following handover in 1997 (i.e. until 2047). Hong Kong has an independent judiciary and its system of law is based on the common law, which was adopted following Hong Kong's cession to Britain in 1841.[2] The Basic Law of the Hong Kong SAR, enshrines the important concepts of 'one country, two systems' and was adopted on 4 April 1990 by the Seventh National People's Congress (NPC) of the People's Republic of China (PRC). The Basic Law came into effect on 1 July 1997 and states that 'the Hong Kong Special Administrative Region [shall] exercise a high degree of autonomy and enjoy executive, legislative and independent judicial power, including that of final adjudication', except in relation to foreign relations and defence.

The Hong Kong SAR is located on the south coast of mainland China and is bordered by the Pearl River Delta and South China Sea. Hong Kong is a city of just over 7 million people and is recognised as a leading financial and trade centre. Its location makes it an ideal hub for international arbitration as it is four hours or less to Korea, mainland China, the Philippines, Vietnam, Singapore, Japan, Thailand, and Malaysia and within six hours of Indonesia and India. In total, nearly half the world's population lives within a six hour flight of Hong Kong.

Hong Kong has firmly established itself as one of the, if not the, leading arbitration centre in Asia. In 2011 Hong Kong introduced its new Arbitration Ordinance (Cap. 609) and in 2012 the Hong Kong International Arbitration Centre (HKIAC) doubled in size and modernised its facilities to become a world-class venue for the conduct and administration of arbitrations and mediations. Furthermore, in 2012 the China International Economic and Trade Arbitration Commission (CIETAC) opened its first office outside of mainland China in Hong Kong and joined the HKIAC and the ICC International Court of Arbitration's (ICC) Asian Secretariat to make Hong Kong the only city in the world where all three leading arbitration institutions have offices. Hong Kong is also home to the largest branch of the Chartered Institute of Arbitrators (CIArb) outside of England, as well as the Hong Kong Institute of Arbitrators (HKIArb). A further strength of Hong Kong is the array of leading professionals including legal, engineering, financial, architectural and consultancy firms, etc., that provide support services to arbitrations seated in Hong Kong. Finally, Hong Kong is also home to the Vis (East) Moot, which supports the promotion and

---

British Declaration was signed acknowledging that China would resume sovereignty of Hong Kong Island, Kowloon and the New Territories on 1 July 1997. The Declaration was ratified by the United Kingdom and China on 27 May 1985 and registered with the United Nations on 12 June 1985.

2 The Letters Patent of 5 April 1843 defined the constitutional structure of Hong Kong as a Crown Colony and 'Royal Instructions' designated how the region should be established and governed.

study of international commercial arbitration and runs a leading international mooting competition for students from law schools from all over Asia and around the world. Hong Kong has recently established 'Hong Kong International Arbitration Week', which takes place each year in October and brings together organisations from around the world to host conferences and events, including the Hong Kong Arbitration Charity Ball.

## 1.1. THE DEVELOPMENT OF ARBITRATION IN HONG KONG

### *1.1.1. Legal framework*

Hong Kong became a common law jurisdiction following its cession to Britain in 1841. As stated above, Hong Kong has remained a common law jurisdiction following the return of sovereignty to mainland China in 1997. The common law tradition in Hong Kong is enshrined in the Basic Law of Hong Kong and has been the cornerstone of the historical development of arbitration in Hong Kong. With an international and independent judiciary, a financial and legal system underpinned by the rule of law, and a pro-enforcement jurisdiction of arbitral awards, Hong Kong retains its position as one of the leading jurisdictions for the resolution of cross-border commercial disputes across Asia.

#### 1.1.1.1. 1843 to 1997: Colonial period

When the colony of Hong Kong was established, a system of civil litigation was not immediately implemented.[3] Hong Kong's first Arbitration Ordinance was enacted in 1844 not as a distinct dispute resolution mechanism presented as an alternative to litigation, but rather because there was no British court system in place at the time.[4] The purpose of the 1844 Arbitration Ordinance was to allow the Governor to direct civil disputes to arbitration during the early days of Britain's colonial presence in preparation for the establishment of the Hong Kong Supreme Court.[5] This ordinance was subsequently repealed because there was concern the power extended to the Governor was too broad.

In 1855, Hong Kong enacted the Common Law Procedure (Amendment of the Civil Administration of Justice) Ordinance, which imported into Hong Kong law the civil procedure rules of England at the time. This included provisions

---

3 G. Ma, N. Kaplan *et al.*, *Arbitration in Hong Kong: A Practical Guide*, 1st ed., Sweet & Maxwell/Thomson Reuters, Hong Kong 2003, p. 79.

4 See generally Kathryn Sanger's overview of Hong Kong Arbitration online: [2007] *Asia-Pacific Arbitration Review* <www.globalarbitrationreview.com>.

5 No. 6 of 1844 [20 March 1844] <http://oelawhk.lib.hku.hk/exhibits/show/oelawhk/searchresult?stext=*:*&sfield=ZZ&edition=1890&no_result=10>.

empowering the court to direct parties to arbitration regarding matters that it could not 'conveniently try'.[6]

From 1960 until the handover in 1997, arbitration law and procedure in Hong Kong generally mirrored the developments in England.[7] In the early 1960s, a working party was set up with representatives from the construction and engineering industry because of a need to reform the law on arbitration after the enactment of the UK's 1950 Arbitration Act. As a result, the first formal arbitration law in the form of the Arbitration Ordinance (Cap. 341) was enacted on 5 July 1963, which was largely based on the 1950 Arbitration Act.[8] The Arbitration Ordinance (Cap. 341) was split into two regimes: an international regime, which was governed by the UNCITRAL Model Law, and a domestic regime governed under provisions set out in the Ordinance itself.

Two notable amendments were made to the Arbitration Ordinance (Cap. 341) in 1982 and in 1996. In 1982, the Law Reform Commission of Hong Kong (LRCHK) published its Report on Commercial Arbitration, which made recommendations, *inter alia,* in relation to the consolidation of arbitrations and dismissal of claims for want of prosecution. These recommendations were implemented by the Arbitration (Amendment) Ordinance No. 10 of 1982.[9] The 1996 amendment gave legal effect to those provisions of the UNCITRAL Model Law that were applicable to Hong Kong by promoting greater party autonomy and limiting the scope of court intervention.

#### 1.1.1.2. 1997 to 2012: Current legal framework

The reversion of sovereignty of Hong Kong back to China in 1997 had significant implications for arbitrations under the Arbitration Ordinance (Cap. 341) involving mainland Chinese parties. The principal problem was that, with the return of sovereignty to the PRC, the New York Convention no longer applied to cross-border enforcement of arbitral awards, as Chinese awards were no longer

6 No. 6 of 1855 [25 August 1855] Common Law Procedure (Amendment of the Civil Administration of Justice) Ordinance <http://oelawhk.lib.hku.hk/items/show/91> (found at s. II).

7 M.J. Moser and T.Y.W. Cheng SC JP, *Hong Kong Arbitration: A User's Guide*, 2nd ed., CCH Hong Kong, Hong Kong 2008, p. 49.

8 L. Raymond, *Hong Kong Mediation Handbook*, Sweet & Maxwell, Hong Kong 2009, p. 35. See also X.B. Xu and G.D. Wilson, 'One Country, Two – International Commercial Arbitration – Systems' (2000) 17(6) *J. Int'l Arb.* 47, and M.J. Moser and T.Y.W. Cheng SC JP, *supra* n. 7. G. Ma, D. Brock *et al.*, *Arbitration in Hong Kong: A Practical Guide Hong Kong*, 2nd ed., Sweet & Maxwell/Thomson Reuters, Hong Kong 2011. See also Hong Kong Law Reform Commission, Report on Commercial Arbitration (topic 1) (1981): <www.hkreform.gov.hk/en/docs/rcarbitration_e.pdf> at para. 7.2 and Hong Kong Department of Justice, Consultation Paper on the Reform of the Law of Arbitration in Hong Kong and Draft Arbitration Bill (2008): <www.gov.hk/en/residents/government/publication/consultation/docs/2008/arbitration.pdf> at para. 7 of Introduction.

9 X.B. Xu and G.D. Wilson, *supra* n. 8, p. 59.

deemed 'foreign' awards.[10] Similarly, there was doubt as to whether such awards could be classified and enforced as 'domestic' awards in the mainland given Hong Kong's status as a Special Administrative Region of the People's Republic of China and thus a separate and distinct legal jurisdiction.

In *Ng Fung Hong Ltd v. ABC*[11] the Hong Kong courts dealt with an application for the enforcement of a China International Economic and Trade Arbitration Commission (CIETAC) arbitral award in Hong Kong. Findlay J held that an arbitral award made in the mainland was no longer an award enforceable in Hong Kong, either by means of the New York Convention or under the Arbitration Ordinance (Cap. 341). Accordingly, the application to enforce the CIETAC award was denied. The decision triggered retaliatory actions by the People's Courts in mainland China, which following *Ng Fung Hong* refused to enforce Hong Kong awards. The impasse was not resolved until 21 June 1999 when the Arrangement Concerning Mutual Enforcement of Arbitral Awards Between the Mainland and the Hong Kong Special Administrative Region (the 'Arrangement') was signed.

Described as embodying the 'spirit of the New York Convention',[12] this Arrangement was reflected in the amended Part IIA of the Arbitration Ordinance (Cap. 341) by the Arbitration Amendment Ordinance 2000, which came into effect on 1 February 2002. Section 2GG of the Arbitration Ordinance (Cap. 341) was amended to clarify that the summary procedure for enforcement of awards, orders, and directions under Section 2GG of the Ordinance applied to awards, orders and directions made either '*in or outside Hong Kong*'. This change gave the High Court the power to summarily enforce awards published in jurisdictions not covered by the New York Convention (Part IV) or the Arrangement (Part IIIA), such as Taiwan.

Additionally, the Legislative Council deemed it necessary to further respond to Findlay J's holding in *Ng Fung Hong*, asserting that section 2GG applied only to those arbitrations conducted in Hong Kong was deemed necessary.[13] This came in the form of the Arbitration (Amendment) (No. 2) Ordinance 2002, which clarified that '[n]otwithstanding anything in this Ordinance, [section 2GG] applies to an award, order and direction made or given *whether in or outside Hong Kong*' (emphasis added).[14]

In 1996, a Report by the Hong Kong International Arbitration Centre (HKIAC) Committee on Arbitration Law, proposed that Hong Kong establish a unified system of law based on the UNCITRAL Model Law for both international and domestic arbitrations. The same goal was reiterated as one of the main

10 D. Sandborg, 'Arbitration in Hong Kong', in P.J. McConnaughay and T.B. Ginsburg (eds.), *International Arbitration in Asia*, 2nd ed., US JurisNet 2006, p. 56.
11 [1998] 1 HKC 213.
12 Hong Kong Legislative Council LC Paper No. CB(4)228/12-13(04), p. 2.
13 Hong Kong Legislative Council LC Paper No. CB(2)2486/99-00.
14 Arbitration (Amendment) (No. 2) Ordinance 2000 subsection 2GG(2).

recommendations in a Report of the Hong Kong Institute of Arbitrators Committee on Hong Kong Arbitration law in 2003.[15] The 2003 Report also took things one step further by recommending that Hong Kong's Arbitration Ordinance should also follow the order and chapter headings of the Model Law[16] which would result in a 'unitary regime that is drafted with as user-friendly a structure as possible'.[17]

Following these reports, an Arbitration Bill was drafted, and in June 2005 the Department of Justice consulted the Legislative Council Panel on Administration of Justice and Legal Services (AJLS Panel), which lent its support to the proposed reforms. A working group was set up in September 2005 to examine the details of the legislative proposals and the draft bill.

After many years of consideration and consultation, the Arbitration Ordinance (Cap. 609) was eventually passed in November 2010, and became effective on 1 June 2011. The new Arbitration Ordinance (Cap. 609) now provides a uniform regime for arbitration in Hong Kong based on the UNCITRAL Model Law.[18] The Arbitration Ordinance (Cap. 609) is seen as a significant and welcome development for arbitrations conducted in Hong Kong, because it reduces judicial supervision and limits potential intervention. More importantly, it removes the distinction between domestic and international arbitrations and is seen as more user-friendly as it effectively extends the application of the updated 2006 UNCITRAL Model Law to all arbitrations in Hong Kong.

However, the 'old' Arbitration Ordinance (Cap. 341) is not yet entirely obsolete. All contracts entered into before the Arbitration Ordinance (Cap. 609) came into effect will still be governed under the old regime, thus recognising the need to respect the contractual intention of parties at the time they entered into their contracts and the importance of party autonomy in arbitration.

Despite the removal of the bifurcated regime, parties may still opt in to certain provisions previously applicable to domestic arbitration only, which are listed in Schedule 2 of the Arbitration Ordinance (Cap. 609).[19] These 'opt-in' provisions allow parties to retain all the provisions that previously applied to domestic arbitrations.[20] If an existing arbitration agreement, or any future agreement made within six years of the commencement of the Arbitration Ordinance (Cap. 609) refers to domestic arbitration, the opt-in provisions will automatically apply.[21] Yet it is worth noting that parties may

15 Hong Kong Institute of Arbitrators, *Report of Committee on Hong Kong Arbitration Law* (2003): <www.hkreform.gov.hk/en/docs/runcitral-e.pdf> at para. 3.7 [2003 Report].

16 *Ibid.*, para. 5.12.

17 *Ibid.*, para. 5.14.

18 G. Ma, D. Brock *et al.*, *supra* n. 3.

19 See Hong Kong Arbitration Ordinance (Cap. 609), section 99.

20 *Ibid.*

21 *Ibid.*, sections 100(a), (b).

always choose to opt out of the provisions listed in Schedule 2, even if they automatically apply.[22]

The opt-in provisions were implemented mainly to cater for the construction industry, which often requires a consolidation of disputes between various parties. The opt-in provisions will automatically apply to sub-contracts of any 'construction contracts' (as defined by section 2(1) of the Construction Industry Council Ordinance (Cap. 587)).[23] However, parties can specifically exclude the opt-in provisions in either the main contract or sub-contract. In addition, the automatic opt-in provisions will not apply to a sub-contract if it does not include an arbitration agreement, or the sub-contractor is not resident in Hong Kong, or the sub-contracted work is to be performed outside of Hong Kong.

### *1.1.2. Governing rules and sources: UNCITRAL*

The UN General Assembly established the United Nations Commission on International Trade Law (UNCITRAL) in 1966. UNCITRAL was founded as a result of the recognition that disparities in national laws governing international trade created obstacles to the flow of trade. The UN General Assembly regarded UNCITRAL as the vehicle by which the UN could play a more active role in reducing or removing these obstacles.

The historical and dominant trend in the development of Hong Kong's arbitration law since the enactment of the Civil Administration of Justice (Amendment) Ordinance of 1855, had been to mirror the developments and amendments made to English legislation.[24] Yet the Hong Kong International Arbitration Centre established an Arbitration Law Committee in 1992 to contemplate reform proposals in light of simultaneous reform efforts in jurisdictions such as England, the Netherlands and Singapore.[25] One of the goals of the Committee was to harmonise the procedure for domestic and international arbitrations with the objective of having the Model Law regime apply to both.[26]

The historical tendency of following English arbitral legislation changed, however, upon the enactment of the Arbitration (Amendment) (No. 2) Ordinance 1989 (64 of 1989), which designated the UNCITRAL Model Law as the applicable law for international arbitrations seated in Hong Kong, albeit that Part II of the Arbitration Ordinance (Cap. 341) enabled parties to an international arbitration the option to choose whether they wanted the UNCITRAL Model Law or the domestic regime to apply to their international arbitration.[27]

---

22 *Ibid.*, section 102.
23 See also *ibid.*, section 101.
24 *Supra* n. 8.
25 X.B. Xu and G.D. Wilson, *supra* n. 8, p. 55.
26 M.J. Moser and T.Y.W. Cheng SC JP, *supra* n. 7, p. 57.
27 Section 2M of the Arbitration Ordinance.

The promulgation of the Arbitration Ordinance (Cap. 609) marks a further step away from its English origins by eliminating the distinction between international and domestic arbitrations and adopting the UNCITRAL Model Law with only minor changes.

## 1.2. ARBITRATION SERVICE PROVIDERS

### *1.2.1. Hong Kong International Arbitration Centre*

The Hong Kong International Arbitration Centre (HKIAC) was established in 1985 to assist parties to resolve their disputes by arbitration or other alternative dispute resolution methods. It was established by a group of leading businessmen and professionals in Hong Kong to be a focal point for dispute resolution across Asia. Although the HKIAC was originally funded by the business community and the Hong Kong Government, it is independent from the Hong Kong SAR Government and is financially independent.[28]

The HKIAC maintains a panel of experienced arbitrators as well as a list of less experienced practitioners, for use by parties looking to appoint an arbitrator. It also maintains a list of qualified mediators and administers the mediation service for Hong Kong Government contracts.[29]

#### 1.2.1.1. HKIAC Rules

The HKIAC has formulated several sets of rules, including rules for domestic arbitrations, 'short form' proceedings, small claims, documents-only proceedings, and electric transaction disputes.

The HKIAC also has Short Form Arbitration Rules for use by parties wishing to expedite the resolution of their dispute. For disputes of less than US $50,000, parties may adopt the Small Claims Procedure and can opt for a matter to be determined on the documents (i.e. without an oral hearing). The HKIAC also has Procedures for the Administration of International Arbitration for parties seeking the assistance of an administered arbitration while also taking advantage of the flexibility of the UNCITRAL Arbitration Rules. And in January 2002, the HKIAC issued the Electronic Transaction Arbitration Rules. These rules are intended to provide a framework for fast-track, administered arbitrations arising from e-commerce transactions.

---

28 M.J. Moser and T.Y.W. Cheng SC JP, *Hong Kong Arbitration: A User's Guide*, Kluwer Law International, The Hague 2004, p. 11.

29 Hong Kong International Arbitration Centre <www.hkiac.org/index.php/en/hkiac/about-us> accessed 06.06.2012.

### 1.2.1.2. HKIAC's Administered Arbitration Rules

In 2008, the HKIAC introduced the HKIAC Administered Arbitration Rules (HKIAC Rules), which superseded the 2005 HKIAC Procedures for the Administration of International Arbitration. Save to the extent that the parties have agreed to adopt the 2005 Procedures in an agreement made prior to 1 September 2008, the 2008 Rules took effect from 1 September 2008 and are intended to be a 'light touch' set of procedures to facilitate the parties in the course of their arbitration.[30]

In 2012, the HKIAC's Rules Revision Committee was tasked with reviewing its Administered Arbitration Rules and recommending changes to ensure it maintains a modern set of arbitral rules designed to deal effectively with increasingly complex cross-border disputes.

Following discussions by the committee, a draft Consultation Paper was released in October 2012 for public comment.

The proposed changes to the 2008 Rules included:

(a) joinder of additional parties;
(b) consolidation of arbitrations;
(c) fees of arbitral tribunals;
(d) interim measures of protection; and
(e) emergency arbitrators.

These changes have been incorporated into HKIAC's new Administered Arbitration Rules, which will become effective as of 1 November 2013.[31] Additional issues addressed by the revised rules include: HKIAC's prima facie power to proceed with arbitrations; arbitrations involving multiple contracts; and the broadening of the circumstances in which parties may apply for their dispute to be determined on an expedited basis.

### 1.2.1.3. HKIAC's new powers under the Arbitration Ordinance

Under section 23 of the Arbitration Ordinance (Cap. 609), the HKIAC now has the power to decide the number of arbitrators in a tribunal where there is no agreement between the parties. In performing this function, the HKIAC is bound to follow the Arbitration (Appointment of Arbitrators and Umpires) Rules (Cap. 609B). Furthermore, in accordance with section 24 of the Arbitration Ordinance (Cap. 609), the HKIAC has been vested with the statutory authority to appoint arbitrators, where the parties have not agreed on a mechanism for

30 Guide to Arbitration in Hong Kong <www.hkiac.org/show_content.php?sec=1> accessed 17.01.2011, cited in G. Ma, D. Brock *et al.*, *supra* n. 8, p. 176.

31 The revised HKIAC Rules can be found at: <www.hkiac.org/index.php/news/479>.

making appointments or where the agreed mechanism has broken down. Prior to the introduction of the Arbitration Ordinance (Cap. 609), both these powers were the purview of the High Court.

### *1.2.2. ICC International Court of Arbitration*

The International Chamber of Commerce International Court of Arbitration (ICC) is a leading provider of dispute resolution services globally and opened the 'Secretariat of the ICC International Court of Arbitration – Asia Office' in Hong Kong in November 2008. This was the first Secretariat opened outside of Paris, France to administer arbitrations and to service Asia and the Middle East.

The ICC also opened the ICC Regional Office in Singapore in 2009, which is tasked with business development, training and education across East and South Asia and Australia. Significantly, on 1 January 2012 the ICC introduced its new rules, which replaced those of 1998.

### *1.2.3. China International Economic and Trade Arbitration Commission*

On 24 September 2012, the China International Economic and Trade Arbitration Commission (CIETAC) opened its first sub-commission outside of mainland China in the Hong Kong SAR. This is a significant step for CIETAC in its evolution from a domestic Chinese arbitral institution into potentially a leading regional player. It is also a very welcome development in Hong Kong, as CIETAC is now the busiest arbitral institute in the world based on the number of cases. In 2011, CIETAC accepted a total of 1,435 new arbitration cases, including 470 foreign-related cases (an increase of 12% on the previous year), and 965 domestic cases. The total claims totalled RMB 15.6789 billion, an increase of 14% over 2012.[32]

Importantly, all CIETAC disputes seated in Hong Kong will be governed by Hong Kong's Arbitration Ordinance (Cap. 609), and by having a sub-commission based in Hong Kong it is likely that the number of international arbitrations administered by CIETAC will increase.

The introduction of CIETAC's new arbitration rules is also likely to have a positive impact. On 1 May 2012, CIETAC also introduced its new arbitration rules (the 2012 Rules), which replaced its 2005 version. It is worth noting that some of the new rules will apply where CIETAC arbitrations are seated in Hong Kong. The 2012 Rules contain provisions for the granting of interim measures by an arbitral tribunal where the seat of the arbitration is outside of the PRC and may therefore be used in CIETAC arbitrations seated in Hong Kong (Article 21.2). Furthermore, where the parties fail to agree on the language of their arbitration, under Article 71.1 of the 2012 Rules, Chinese is no longer the default language. The 2012 Rules allow CIETAC to choose 'Chinese or any other

---

32 Working Report of 2011 and Working Plan of 2012 (Excerpt) (5 January 2012, Beijing).

language [...] having regard to the circumstances of the case'. This may be useful for parties that have chosen to seat their arbitrations in Hong Kong.

In addition, where the parties fail to stipulate the seat of their arbitration, under Article 7.2 of the 2012 Rules CIETAC may nominate the seat of arbitration to be somewhere other than 'the domicile of CIETAC or its sub-commissions' taking into account all the circumstances of the case. As CIETAC now has a sub-commission in Hong Kong, it is entitled to seat future arbitrations there anyway, but under the 2012 Rules it may also select any other jurisdiction that it determines to be most appropriate.

Given that CIETAC has established its first sub-commission outside of mainland China, there is growing optimism that mainland China may eventually allow other international arbitral institutions, such as the HKIAC, the ICC and the Singapore International Arbitration Commission (SIAC), to operate within mainland China. That said, any such change is likely to require amendments to China's Arbitration Law and at present the authors are not aware of any plans for legislative change.

### *1.2.4. Asia Domain Name Dispute Resolution Centre*

The HKIAC and CIETAC in Beijing are joint venture partners in the dispute settlement facility known as the Asia Domain Name Dispute Resolution Centre (ADNDRC). The ADNDRC is one of the four domain name dispute resolution providers approved by the Internet Corporation for the Assignment of Names and Numbers (ICANN) to provide dispute resolution services in respect of general top level domain names such as .com, .net and .org.

## 1.3. ENFORCEMENT OF ARBITRAL AWARDS IN HONG KONG

### *1.3.1. New York Convention*

The New York Convention on the Recognition and Enforcement of Foreign Arbitral Awards lays down a detailed framework for the recognition and enforcement of arbitration awards. Hong Kong adopted the New York Convention on 21 April 1977 by virtue of the United Kingdom having acceded to it on behalf of Hong Kong. It was incorporated as Part IV of the Arbitration Ordinance (Cap. 341) by the Arbitration (Amendment) Ordinance 1975, allowing for reciprocal enforcement of arbitral awards between Hong Kong and other parties to the Convention. This amendment to the Ordinance took effect in 1977, following the UK's ratification of the New York Convention and its declaration that the application of the Convention would extend to the territories it then regarded as its colonies.

The Hong Kong courts recognise and enforce arbitration awards made in other countries that are signatories to the New York Convention in accordance with the terms of the New York Convention. Similarly, Hong Kong awards can generally be enforced through the courts of other signatories to the Convention. Hong Kong remains a member to the New York Convention because China signed the New York Convention on 22 January 1987 and extended the applicability of the New York Convention to Hong Kong after 1997. The Arbitration Ordinance (Cap. 609) also provides for Hong Kong courts to enforce awards made in non-Convention countries.[33]

### *1.3.2. 1985 Foreign Judgments (Reciprocal Enforcement) Ordinance*

It is possible for parties who have arbitral awards that have been enforced in designated foreign countries to have these foreign judgments enforced in Hong Kong. Under the 1985 Foreign Judgments (Reciprocal Enforcement) Ordinance, judgments of countries to which the Ordinance's provisions are extended can be registered in Hong Kong provided that they are final and conclusive and a sum of money that is not fines or other penalties, is payable.

In addition, the judgment must have been made after the coming into effect of the order extending the Ordinance's provisions to that country.[34] After registration, these judgments are enforceable in the same way as Hong Kong judgments.[35] However, under the Ordinance, foreign judgments of the designated countries are simply registered with the High Court in Hong Kong and subsequently enforced as Hong Kong judgments. There are a total of 15 designated countries including parts of the Commonwealth, namely Australia, Bermuda, Brunei, India, Malaysia, New Zealand, Singapore and Sri Lanka, as well as other non-commonwealth countries including Belgium, France, Germany, Italy, Austria, the Netherlands and Israel. Interestingly, the Ordinance has not been amended after the handover to include the UK as a country whose judgments can be enforced under the Foreign Judgments (Reciprocal Enforcement) Ordinance. If an arbitral award has been recognised and enforced in one of the aforementioned countries, it may be more time- and cost-effective to have the judgment enforced in Hong Kong rather than to try to enforce the arbitral award by way of the New York Convention.

---

33 See Hong Kong Arbitration Ordinance (Cap. 609) Part 10, Division 1.

34 Foreign Judgments (Reciprocal Enforcement) Ordinance (Cap. 319), section 3(2), Laws of Hong Kong, cited in M. Pryles, *Dispute Resolution in Asia*, 3rd ed., Kluwer Law International, The Hague 2006, p. 117.

35 *Supra* n. 15, sections 3–4.

## 1.4. JUDICIAL SUPPORT FOR ARBITRATION

Hong Kong's High Court is comprised of two courts: the Court of First Instance and the Court of Appeal. The Court of First Instance is a court of record with unlimited jurisdiction in both civil and criminal matters and it is also an appellate court that hears appeals from the Magistrates' Courts, Small Claims Tribunal and other tribunals and adjudication boards. The Court of Appeal is the second most senior court in Hong Kong and deals with appeals of all civil and criminal cases from the Court of First Instance and the District Courts of Hong Kong.

The Court of Final Appeal of Hong Kong is the superior court of Hong Kong. Importantly, in order to maintain trust in the independence of Hong Kong's judiciary, under the Basic Law, judges from other common law jurisdictions may be appointed to the bench in accordance with Article 92 of the Basic Law. At present the Court of Final Appeal has four permanent judges and a larger pool of non-permanent judges drawn from the United Kingdom, Australia, South Africa and New Zealand.

The Court of Final Appeal has the power of final interpretation with regard to all laws in force in Hong Kong, except for the Basic Law. Under Article 158 of the Basic Law, the Standing Committee of the National People's Congress has the power to interpret the Basic Law. That said, Article 158 of the Basic Law also delegates such power to the courts of Hong Kong for interpretation while handling court cases.

As provided by the Basic Law, and in accordance with the common law, precedent is still applicable as persuasive authority in the courts of Hong Kong and before arbitral tribunals for procedural and substantive matters that are governed by Hong Kong law.

The Hong Kong courts are very pro-arbitration and Order 73 of the Rules of the High Court governs the way in which all applications are made to the High Court under the Arbitration Ordinance (Cap. 609) including, for example, applications for interim measures of protection, appeals against an award, and enforcement of an award made in Hong Kong or overseas. Practice Directions are also applicable in circumstances where an application is made to the Hong Kong courts in connection with arbitration.

In April 2009 Hong Kong introduced the Civil Justice Reform (CJR), which introduced reforms to civil proceedings before the High Court and District Court. The underlying objectives of the CJR were to increase the cost-effectiveness and efficiency of any practice and procedure regarding civil proceedings before the courts; to ensure fairness between the parties; facilitate the settlement of disputes and distribute the resources of the courts fairly (see section 2.2. below).

Order 1A Rule 4(2) of the rules of the High Court deals with the duty of the court in implementing active case management in addition to the Rules of High Court and the Rules of District Court. As a result, ADR is increasingly encouraged to help with case settlement and it may even be considered a duty, as part of active case management, for courts to encourage parties to use an ADR procedure.[36]

## 1.5. RECENT DEVELOPMENT AND FUTURE PERSPECTIVES

### 1.5.1. *Enforcement of Hong Kong SAR/Chinese awards in India*

Both China and India are signatories to the New York Convention, which requires that contracting States recognise and enforce arbitral awards made in all other contracting States, subject to any declarations and reservations of those States. The most common reservation is that of 'reciprocity' whereby States only agree to recognise and enforce awards made in other States where that State affords reciprocal treatment to their awards.[37]

Under the Indian Arbitration and Conciliation Act 1996, which governs the enforcement of 'foreign awards' by Indian courts, the Indian government is required to identify (by way of the Government Gazette) those States whose awards the Indian courts are required to recognise and enforce. Unfortunately, many of the signatories to the New York Convention have not been gazetted and there remains considerable concern that awards from non-gazetted States may not be enforceable in India. It is of concern that of the 146 States Parties to the New York Convention, less than a third have been gazetted in India.

Until 2012, China was absent from the list of gazetted States, which had the potential to prevent awards made in China or Hong Kong from being enforced in India. It also had the potential for China to reciprocate and to refuse to enforce Indian awards in China. Given the enormous and rapidly increasing trade between the world's two most populous nations, this was a matter that required urgent attention. Therefore, on 19 March 2012 the Department of Legal Affairs of the Indian Government Ministry of Law and Justice, issued a notification under section 44(b) of the Arbitration Act, which declared that China (including the Special Administrative Regions of Hong Kong and Macau) is now a territory to which the New York Convention applies.[38] As such, any awards made in China, Hong Kong

---

36 Civil Justice Reform, Practice Direction 31, Part A at para. 1.

37 See reciprocity reservation in Article I(3) of the New York Convention (entered into force 7 June 1959).

38 Schedule I of the Indian Arbitration Act.

or Macau on or after 19 March 2012 ought to be recognised and enforced by the Indian courts, subject to the provisions of the New York Convention.

### *1.5.2. Case law: recent leading cases*

#### 1.5.2.1. *Democratic Republic of Congo v. FG Hemisphere Assocs. LLC*

In 2010 the Hong Kong Court of Appeal (HKCA), on appeal from a decision by the Court of First Instance (CFI),[39] heard the case of *FG Hemisphere Associates LLC v. Democratic Republic of Congo (DRC).*[40] The HKCA was asked to consider whether the restrictive doctrine of state immunity applied in Hong Kong (which is the approach followed by the English common law) or whether the mainland Chinese position of absolute immunity applied following the handover of Hong Kong back to mainland China on 1 July 1997.

In a split decision, the HKCA (by a two-to-one majority) upheld the CFI decision that the restrictive approach to state immunity still applied in Hong Kong. However, unlike the CFI decision, the contracts giving rise to the arbitrations were held by the HKCA to be commercial in nature, which prevented the DRC from asserting immunity from suit.

The decision appeared to reaffirm Hong Kong's unique political and legal position as prescribed by the Basic Law, which, as of 1 July 1997, has operated under the 'one country, two systems' whereby Hong Kong's common law legal system will remain in place until at least 2047. Prior to the Handover, the common law of Hong Kong recognised the doctrine of restrictive immunity; however, following 1 July 1997 it was unclear what the position would be.

However, the HKCA decision was appealed to Hong Kong's highest court, the Court of Final Appeal (CFA). The CFA's judgment was handed down on 8 June 2011[41] and overturned the earlier decision of the HKCA. In reaching its decision, the CFA dealt with the following issues:

(a) sovereign immunity – whether the restrictive doctrine applies (as it did prior to the handover in July 1997), or whether the doctrine of absolute immunity from suit and execution applies, as is the case in mainland China; and
(b) waiver of immunity – whether the DRC had waived any immunity from suit and execution to which it might otherwise have been entitled by having agreed to refer its dispute to ICC arbitration.

The two doctrines of state immunity are 'absolute immunity' and 'restrictive immunity'. In 'absolute immunity', the national courts of one State would *not*

39 *FG Hemispheres Associates LLC v. Democratic Republic of Congo (DRC)* [2009] 1 HKC 111.
40 [2010] 2 HKC 487, CA.
41 *Democratic Republic of Congo v. FG Hemisphere Assocs. LLC* [2011].

*normally* have jurisdiction to determine matters in which another State is named as defendant. This is subject only to the exception where the defendant State waives immunity before the forum State. 'Restrictive immunity' recognises a commercial exception, including (a) in the context of immunity from jurisdiction, States do not enjoy immunity from suit where they are engaged in purely commercial transactions and (b) in the context of immunity from execution, if the relevant assets are used for a commercial purpose they will not be immune from the process of execution.[42]

The decision of the CFA, which was also a split decision (three to two), overturned the decision of the HKCA and found that Hong Kong, as a matter of legal and constitutional principle, must adhere to the same doctrine of state immunity as that of mainland China (i.e. absolute immunity).[43]

The decision is of limited application and applies only in the context of enforcement of arbitral awards or court judgments against a foreign State's assets held in Hong Kong. In this respect, a foreign State's assets are immune from execution in Hong Kong, unless the foreign State is found to have waived both immunity from suit and from execution.

An effective waiver of immunity can be established where the defendant State waives its immunity by submitting to the jurisdiction of the Hong Kong court when the suit and execution actions are pursued against that defendant State. In this case it was held at first instance, on appeal and again on final appeal that the DRC had not waived its immunity in the face of the court.[44]

Note that this case does not change the position in respect of enforcement against Chinese 'crown' assets in Hong Kong. In the case of *Hua Tian Long*[45] it was determined that sovereign immunity does not apply as between mainland China and Hong Kong. Following 1 July 1997, mainland China enjoys 'crown' immunity in Hong Kong, which is also absolute.[46] Nonetheless, the common law principles on waiver of that crown immunity, as discussed in the *FG Hemisphere* case, will apply.

---

42 C. Hassle, 'The practical implications of the CFA's decisions in Democratic Republic of Congo v. FG Hemisphere Associates LLC', June 2011.

43 The judgment was handed down on a provisional basis, as the CFA took the unusual step of referring specific questions relating to state immunity to the Standing Committee of the National People's Congress (SCNPC) for interpretation. However, it is extremely likely that the SCNPC will affirm the CFA's provisional decision. The CFA's decision referral of specific questions to the SCNPC is consistent with the procedure set out in the Basic Law and does not affect the independence of Hong Kong's judiciary.

44 Written waiver clauses acceded to by foreign States in contracts (including arbitration clauses) are not sufficient to establish an effective waiver at the enforcement stage and will not confer jurisdiction upon the Hong Kong courts. *Supra* n. 3.

45 A decision of the Court of First Instance.

46 By contrast, the Hong Kong Government of the HKSAR does not enjoy absolute immunity and proceedings can be brought against the Hong Kong Government in accordance with the provisions of the Crown Proceedings Ordinance (Cap. 300).

While an agreement to arbitrate does not amount to an effective waiver when seeking to enforce an arbitration award against sovereign or crown assets in Hong Kong, the CFA did not overturn the HKCA's finding that an agreement to arbitrate operates to remove state immunity in respect of the jurisdiction of the arbitral tribunal over the State. It has been noted that:

> 'The effect of this is that by agreeing to arbitrate (rather than litigate) in Hong Kong, the foreign State cannot later claim to be immune from the jurisdiction of the arbitral tribunal. A Hong Kong arbitral award against the State will continue to be enforceable against that State's commercial assets in other jurisdictions which are signatories to the New York Convention and which adopt restrictive (rather than absolute) immunity, in accordance with the law of the jurisdiction in which enforcement is sought.'[47]

### 1.5.2.2. *Pacific China Holdings Ltd v. Grand Pacific Holdings Ltd*

Hong Kong's Arbitration Ordinance is based on the UNCITRAL Modal Law and on 29 June 2011, Hong Kong's Court of First Instance (CFI) set aside an arbitral award in favour of Grand Pacific Holdings, due to breaches of Article 34(2)(a)(ii) and (iv) of the UNCITRAL Model Law.[48]

Article 34(2)(a) provides that a court may set aside an arbitral award for a variety of reasons, including where a party can show that it has been prevented from presenting its case, or that the arbitral procedure was not in accordance with the agreement of the parties.

Pacific China Holdings (PCH) claimed that it was denied the opportunity to fully present its case for the following reasons:

(a) the tribunal refused to allow PCH to rely on three additional submissions that PCH wished to file because the tribunal thought that requiring Grand Pacific Holdings (GPH) to review them a few weeks before an evidential hearing was unfair; and
(b) the tribunal refused to allow PCH an opportunity to respond to submissions by GPH on the relevance of Hong Kong and New York law.

Additionally, PCH alleged that the procedure that was followed did not comply with the procedural timetable as agreed by the parties, which required that pre-hearing submissions be simultaneously exchanged. PCH was required to file its pre-hearing submissions by 20 November 2007, whereas GPH was permitted to file a supplemental submission in reply to a PCH expert statement on 30 November 2007, just prior to the commencement of the hearing.

---

47 G. Ma, N. Kaplan *et al.*, *supra* n. 3.

48 *Pacific China Holdings Ltd v. Grand Pacific Holdings Ltd* (2011) HKCU 1249.

While there may be legitimate reasons for setting aside an award under Article 34(2)(a), it is important that the Courts take a robust approach to the interpretation of any such application, as it could potentially harm the reputation of a jurisdiction that purports to be pro-enforcement.

The case was appealed to the HKCA, and on 9 May 2012 the court reversed the earlier decision of the CFI.[49] The HKCA held that there were no breaches of Article 34(2)(a) and that for a party to establish any such breach, it would need to prove that the tribunal's conduct was of a 'serious' or 'egregious' nature. Furthermore, the Court confirmed that an arbitral tribunal has wide-ranging powers in relation to decisions regarding 'case management', thus confirming the broad authority and discretion of a tribunal. This decision was a welcome one, as it once again demonstrates the supportive approach taken by Hong Kong's courts for international arbitration.

Importantly, the HKCA appeared to accept that even where a breach of Article 34(2)(a) is proven, the Court has a discretion not to set aside an award where it believes that the outcome would have been the same, irrespective of the breach.

Finally, in determining costs, the HKCA confirmed that where a party fails in its attempt to set aside an award or resist enforcement, costs should be awarded on an indemnity basis, unless there are special circumstances. This approach confirms that taken by lower courts[50] and that of *Gao Haiyan et al. v. Keeneye Holdings Ltd et al.*[51] (see case below) in which the Court of Appeal held that where a party has agreed to arbitrate its dispute, any application to set aside an arbitral award or to resist enforcement should be the exception, not the rule, in order to stop parties that lose their case from appealing as a matter of standard procedure.[52]

PCH subsequently applied for leave to appeal to the CFA, which was denied by the CFA on 21 February 2013. The CFA upheld the decision of the HKCA, emphasising the expansive case management authority of arbitral tribunals and declaring that 'seriousness' or 'egregiousness' of the conduct complained of remains the threshold for challenging an award.

This threshold, as established by Hong Kong's highest court, serves to warn a losing party to an arbitration that Hong Kong courts will be reluctant to interfere with an arbitral tribunal's broad discretion in dealing with procedural matters. The decision also further buttresses the distinct pro-enforcement approach of the Hong Kong courts. Losing parties will need to think hard before attempting to set aside an arbitral award in light of this threshold and the potential cost consequences that may apply to a failed application.

---

49 *Pacific China Holdings Ltd v. Grand Pacific Holdings Ltd* (2012) HKEC 645.
50 *A v. R* [2009] 3 HKLRD 389.
51 [2012] 1 HKC 491.
52 *Pacific China Holdings Ltd v. Grand Pacific Holdings Ltd* (2012) HKEC 645.

### 1.5.2.3. *Gao Haiyan and Xie Heping v. Keeneye Holdings Ltd*

On 12 April 2011, Reyes J, in the case of *Gao Haiyan and Xie Heping v. Keeneye Holdings Ltd*[53] before the CFI, refused enforcement of a mainland Chinese arbitral award on the basis that a mediation carried out during the arbitration by one of the arbitrators was 'tainted' by the appearance of bias.

The arbitration was administered by the Xi'an Arbitration Commission in mainland China. During the arbitration proceedings the parties agreed to arb-med, to try and settle the dispute. Consequently, 'mediation' took place between the Secretary General of the Xi'an Arbitration Commission, the co-arbitrator appointed by Gao, and a representative of Keeneye. The mediation took place over dinner at an international hotel in Xi'an.

At the dinner it was suggested that a settlement be reached whereby Keeneye would pay Gao compensation in the sum of RMB 250 million. The representative of Keeneye was asked to 'work on' Keeneye in order to get it to accept the proposed settlement. However, both Keeneye and Gao refused to accept the proposed settlement and the arbitration continued. The award handed down by the tribunal was demonstrably different to the proposed settlement discussed at the mediation, and made a non-binding recommendation that Gao pay Keeneye compensation in the sum of RMB 50 million.[54]

Keeneye appealed to the Xi'an Intermediate People's Court (Xi'an IPC) to set aside the award on a variety of grounds, including bias on the part of the arbitral tribunal. The Xi'an IPC refused to set aside the award on the basis that it did not find any bias.

However, when enforcement was sought in Hong Kong, Reyes J refused enforcement of the award on the basis that enforcement would be against the public policy of Hong Kong, pursuant to section 40E(3) of Hong Kong's old Arbitration Ordinance (Cap. 341), which was still in force.[55]

While Reyes J accepted, albeit somewhat reluctantly, that the dinner in the hotel amounted to mediation, he stated that the circumstances surrounding the dinner were sufficient to give rise to an apprehension of bias and he refused to enforce the arbitral award. The HKCA allowed an appeal against Reyes J's decision.

The HKCA overturned Reyes J's earlier decision and decided that the award administered by the Xi'an Arbitration Commission did not contravene public policy. The HKCA held that public policy meant 'not contrary to the "fundamental conceptions of morality and justice of the forum"'.[56] In Hong Kong, 'the opportunity of a party to present his case and a determination by an

53 [2011] 3 HKC 157.

54 K. Barton, 'Med-Arb and bias: Gao Haiyan v Keeneye Holdings Ltd', November 2011.

55 Section 40E has been superseded by section 95 of the new Arbitration Ordinance, Cap. 609.

56 Sir A. Mason NPJ in *Hebei Import & Export Corp. v. Polytek Engineering Co. Ltd* (1999) 2 HKCFAR 111.

impartial and independent tribunal which is not influenced, or seen to be influenced, by private communications are basic to the notions of justice and morality'.[57]

The HKCA also emphasised that courts 'should recognise the validity of decisions of foreign arbitral tribunals as a matter of comity.'[58]

The award had already been subject to setting-aside proceedings before the Xi'an IPC, which had refused to set aside the award for bias. As such, the HKCA held that more weight should have been given to the decision of the Xi'an IPC, and that any subsequent enforcing court should be extremely wary in reaching a different conclusion.[59]

Another issue dealt with by the HKCA was that of waiver. In Reyes J's decision before the CFI, His Honour held that Keeneye had not waived its right to object to the impartiality and independence of the arbitral tribunal by providing a supplemental submission and continuing with the arbitration, after the alleged bias (i.e. the mediation) had occurred. He said that Keeneye's fear that an objection to the impartiality and independence of the Tribunal would antagonise the tribunal, and subsequent failure to object was a 'clumsy compromise' instead of waiver of objection. However, the Court of Appeal disagreed and stated that 'failure to raise an issue will result in waiver' and that it is 'not open to a litigant to wait and see how his claims turns out before pursuing his complaint of bias'.[60]

This decision strongly supports international arbitration and prevents parties from waiting to see how a tribunal decides a matter before it raises an issue of bias and that any claim as to bias must be made at the time the bias occurs or a party becomes aware of any such bias.

Importantly, the HKCA also addressed the fact that the Xi'an IPC did not consider that the mediation and the manner in which it was conducted, created any bias.

The Court stated that it should not be too ready to refuse to enforce an award on the basis of an apparent bias, where mediations are carried out differently to Hong Kong. For example, the mere fact that the mediation had been conducted at a hotel and in the presence of a representative of the respondent other than its lawyer, did not automatically create an apprehension of bias. In essence, the Court stressed that it is necessary to take into account the fact that mediations may be conducted differently in jurisdictions outside of Hong Kong, and that this did not automatically result in potential bias. The Court determined that the

57 *Gao Haiyan and Xie Heping v. Keeneye Holdings Ltd* [2011] 3 HKC 157.

58 Quoting Litton PJ in *Hebei Import & Export Corp.*

59 Reminiscent of Reyes J's holding in *Xiamen Xinjingdi Group Ltd v. Eton Properties Ltd & another* [2008] 6 HKC 287 where he held that Hong Kong courts should not second-guess awards and that, regarding enforcement, courts should be as mechanistic as possible.

60 D. Brock, 'Med-Arb and bias: An appeal against Keeneye', September 2011.

Xi'an IPC was in the best position to apply the facts and to decide if any bias, or apprehension of bias existed – and it found that no such bias existed.

### 1.5.3. *Future perspectives*

After the 2007 global financial crisis, there has been increased interest in Asia and, in particular, mainland China. Hong Kong as a Special Administrative Region of China is an increasingly important player in international trade, finance and also in cross-border dispute resolution. The new Arbitration Ordinance (Cap. 609); the expansion and upgrading of the facilities at the HKIAC; the opening of CIETAC's first sub-commission outside of mainland China, combined with Hong Kong's geographic location and array of legal and support services; the adherence to the rule of law and the independence of its judiciary, all make Hong Kong one of the leading arbitration centres in Asia.

So what else can Hong Kong do to improve its attractiveness as a venue for international arbitrations in the face of increasing competition from Singapore, Korea, Malaysia and Australia? One clear advantage that Hong Kong has is its ability to leverage off the success of mainland China and to seek to position itself as the first choice for companies doing business with private companies and State-owned enterprises (SOE) in China. This includes promoting Hong Kong as a venue to regions showing increased trade with mainland China, such as Africa and South America. Hong Kong's arbitration community also needs to continue to advocate the fact that while it is a Special Administrative Region of China, it maintains a neutral and independent judiciary, and has a leading Arbitration Ordinance and a pool of world-class arbitrators from around the world to choose from.

## 2. MEDIATION IN HONG KONG

Mediation offers a quicker, simpler and more cost-efficient way to solve disputes than litigation and arbitration, and takes into account a wider range of interests of the parties, which ensures a greater chance of reaching an agreement that will be voluntarily respected, while preserving an amicable and sustainable relationship between the parties. As a result, mediation is increasingly used in many different jurisdictions around the world to resolve disputes other than through litigation in the courts. In Hong Kong, whether the use of mediation is embraced and prospers is considered to be crucial to Hong Kong maintaining its status as a leading financial and business centre. It is also vital to its efforts to build a more harmonious community.[61] In this section, we will examine the

61 Forward by Secretary of Justice, Report of the Working Group on Mediation, February 2010, available at <www.doj.gov.hk/eng/public/pdf/2010/med20100208e.pdf> accessed 20.10.2012.

development of mediation in Hong Kong in terms of the pilot schemes, civil justice reforms, the regulatory framework, the mediation service providers and mediator accreditation.

## 2.1. PILOT SCHEMES

Prior to the implementation of the Civil Justice Reform on 2 April 2009, Hong Kong's Judiciary had already explored the possibility of mediation in different areas. Various pilot schemes were launched and some of them have been adopted as standard practice. Some of the most important pilot schemes include:

(a) Pilot Scheme on Family Mediation;
(b) Pilot Scheme for the Construction and Arbitration List;
(c) Commercial Mediation Pilot Scheme; and
(d) Pilot Scheme for Building Management.

### *2.1.1. Pilot Scheme on Family Mediation*

Family mediation is well established in Hong Kong. The non-governmental organisations (NGOs) in Hong Kong first started to provide family mediation in the late 1980s. In May 2000, the Judiciary introduced a three-year family mediation pilot scheme[62] and set-up a Mediation Coordinator's Office in the Family Court Building. The Mediation Coordinator conducted information sessions to assist couples to consider mediation in an attempt to resolve their matrimonial disputes. This pilot scheme is voluntary in nature and envisages the possibility of mediation in different situations, including a petition, or a joint application, whether the parties are legally represented or not. The pilot scheme was made permanent when the Judiciary issued Practice Direction 15.10 on Family Mediation on 28 March 2012.[63]

### *2.1.2. Pilot Scheme for the Construction and Arbitration List*

A two-year pilot scheme for voluntary mediation of cases in the construction and arbitration list was carried out from 1 September 2006 to 31 August 2008, in order to encourage parties in construction cases in the Construction and Arbitration List to consider the use of mediation as a possible cost-effective means of resolving their disputes. The pilot scheme was adopted as standard

62 The Evaluation Study on the Pilot Scheme on Family Mediation (Final Report, January 2004) is available on the website of the Judiciary at <www.judiciary.gov.hk/en/publications/hkpu_finalreport.pdf> accessed 20.10.2012.

63 Practice Direction 15.10 on Family Mediation, available at <http://legalref.judiciary.gov.hk/lrs/common/pd/pdcontent.jsp?pdn=PD15.10.htm&lang=EN> accessed 20.10.2012.

practice with minor changes when the Judiciary issued Practice Direction 6.1 on the Construction and Arbitration List on 12 February 2009.[64] Notably, the Practice Direction provides that the court may impose cost sanctions against a party who unreasonably refuses to attempt mediation.

### *2.1.3. Commercial Mediation Pilot Scheme*

The development of commercial mediation is strategically important for Hong Kong to maintain and strengthen its position as an international financial services centre and a regional centre for the resolution of commercial disputes. The Commercial Mediation Pilot Scheme (CMPS) was established and implemented by the Hong Kong Mediation Council from July 2007 to December 2008. The goals of the CMPS are to assist parties in commercial disputes to reach a negotiated settlement of their disputes amicably and economically by mediation; to demonstrate the feasibility and viability of commercial mediation; and to encourage more use of mediation in resolving commercial disputes in Hong Kong. The rules and procedures governing the mediation of commercial disputes have been kept simple and transparent to facilitate access to mediation and the aim is to have mediation take place within a month of the dispute being submitted to the scheme. The Hong Kong Mediation Council (HKMC) has a panel of suitably qualified accredited mediators available under the CMPS and can assist in the selection or appointment of a mediator under this scheme.

### *2.1.4. Pilot Scheme for Building Management*

The Lands Tribunal introduced a pilot scheme to streamline the processing of building management cases on 1 January 2008. The purpose of the scheme was to facilitate the more cost-efficient, expeditious and fair disposal of building management cases. After evaluation and consultation, the Lands Tribunal decided to adopt the measures in the pilot scheme, with some modifications, as standard practice with effect from 1 July 2009 by issuing the Direction of the President of the Lands Tribunal.[65] The parties are encouraged to resolve their disputes by way of mediation and the scheme is only applicable to cases where both parties have legal representation.

---

64 Practice Direction 6.1 on Construction and Arbitration List, available at <http://legalref.judiciary.gov.hk/lrs/common/pd/pdcontent.jsp?pdn=PD6.1.htm&lang=EN> accessed 20.10.2012.

65 Direction Issued by the President of the Lands Tribunal Pursuant to Section 10(5)(a) of the Lands Tribunal Ordinance (Cap. 17), available at <http://legalref.judiciary.gov.hk/lrs/common/pd/pdcontent.jsp?pdn=LTPD_BM1.htm&lang=EN> accessed 20.10.2012.

## 2.2. CIVIL JUSTICE REFORM

The Honourable Chief Justice appointed the Working Party on Civil Justice Reform (Working Party) in February 2000 to review the rules and procedures of the High Court in civil proceedings and to recommend changes thereto, with a view to ensuring and improving access to justice at reasonable cost and speed. The Working Party completed the review and published its Final Report on 3 March 2004, making a total of 150 recommendations.[66]

In his 2007–08 Policy Address entitled 'Investing for a caring society', Mr Donald Tsang, the then Chief Executive of the HKSAR, made the following remarks:

> 'To alleviate conflicts and foster harmony, we will promote the development of mediation services. On many occasions, interpersonal conflicts need not go to court. Mediation can reduce social costs and help parties concerned to rebuild their relationship. This is a new trend in advanced regions around the world. The cross-sector working group headed by the Secretary for Justice will map out plans to employ mediation more extensively and effectively in handling higher-end commercial disputes and relatively small-scale local disputes.'

Following Mr Tsang's Policy Address, the Secretary for Justice's Working Group on Mediation (Working Group) was set up in 2008 to review the current development of mediation and provision of mediation services in Hong Kong, and to make recommendations on ways to facilitate and encourage a wider use of mediation in Hong Kong and to ensure the quality and standard of mediators. The Final Report of the Working Group was published in February 2010.[67]

The Civil Justice Reform (CJR) was implemented in April 2009 in Hong Kong. The CJR sets out a number of underlying objectives as stated in Order 1A Rule 1 of the Rules of the High Court. These included the following objectives: to increase cost effectiveness of civil procedure; to deal with cases as expeditiously as is reasonably practicable; to promote a sense of reasonable proportionality and procedural economy; and to facilitate the settlement of disputes. The Judiciary issued a Practice Direction on Mediation (PD 31), which became effective as of 1 January 2010. It seeks to provide a framework within which the court can discharge its duty to facilitate the use of mediation when exercising its case management powers and for the parties to make use of mediation in appropriate cases for the settlement of their disputes.[68]

---

66 Final Report of Chief Justice's Working Party on Civil Justice Reform, available at <www.legco.gov.hk/yr06-07/english/bc/bc57/papers/bc570611cb2-1960-e.pdf> accessed 19.10.2012.

67 Report of the Working Group on Mediation, available at <www.doj.gov.hk/eng/public/pdf/2010/medexe20100208e.pdf>.

68 For a discussion on the Civil Justice Reform in Hong Kong and its effects on judicial practice, see, F. Kun, 'Mediation and Civil Justice Reform in Hong Kong' (Winter/Spring 2011) *International Litigation Quarterly* 11–14.

Since 1 January 2010, parties to litigation are required to comply with the PD 31 procedures, including the filing of a Mediation Certificate, a Mediation Notice and a Mediation Response. This procedural requirement ensures that the parties and their legal advisers make genuine efforts to settle their disputes through mediation prior to litigation. The PD 31 also provides a strong disincentive against parties who unreasonably fail to attempt mediation in the form of an adverse costs sanction. In exercising its discretion on costs sanctions, the court takes into account all relevant circumstances, including any unreasonable failure of a party to engage in mediation, where this can be established by admissible evidence.

Article 5 of PD 31 provides that the Court will not make any adverse costs orders against a party on the ground of unreasonable failure to engage in mediation where (a) the party has engaged in mediation to the 'minimum level of participation' agreed to by the parties or as directed by the Court prior to the mediation in accordance with paragraph 13 of the PD; or (b) a party has a reasonable explanation for not engaging in mediation. The High Court of Hong Kong dealt with the question of what constitutes a 'minimum level of participation' in *Hak Tung Alfred Tang v. Bloomberg LP*.[69] It directed that the minimum level of participation should not be construed as the number of hours of mediation, but instead should be focused on the quality. As such, the parties shall participate in the mediation up to and including at least one substantive mediation session with the mediator, as set out in Appendix C of PD 31.

In determining whether a party has 'unreasonably refused to engage in mediation', Hong Kong followed the test in *Halsey*,[70] taking into account the following circumstances:

(a) the nature of the dispute;
(b) merits of the case;
(c) the extent to which other settlement methods have been attempted;
(d) whether the cost of the ADR would be disproportionately high;
(e) whether any delay in setting up and attending the ADR would have been prejudicial; and
(f) whether the ADR has a reasonable prospect of success.

It should be noted that in *Golden Eagle*,[71] the Hong Kong Court of First Instance shifted the burden of proof in determining 'whether the ADR has a reasonable prospect of success.' Instead of placing the burden on the willing party to show that there was a reasonable prospect that mediation would have been successful, as is the approach adopted in *Halsey*, the court held that the burden should be

69 *Hak Tung Alfred Tang v. Bloomberg LP* [2010] HKEC 1227.
70 *Halsey v. Milton Keynes General NHS Trust* [2004] EWCA Civ 576.
71 *Golden Eagle International (Group) Ltd v. GR Investment Holdings Ltd* [2010] 3 HKLRD 273.

placed on the party refusing to mediate to provide a reasonable explanation. By shifting the burden of proof onto the party that refuses to participate to provide a reasonable explanation, the Hong Kong courts have removed the hurdle imposed by *Halsey*, which Lightman J and Lord Phillips criticised as unduly weakening the costs sanctions against a party that unreasonably refuses to mediate.

## 2.3. REGULATORY FRAMEWORK

The Working Group in its Final Report recommended that Hong Kong should introduce legislation for mediation, in order to provide a proper legal framework for the conduct of mediation in Hong Kong. In order to progress this recommendation, the Department of Justice prepared a draft Mediation Bill and conducted two consultation sessions with stakeholders in late June 2011. The Mediation Bill primarily defines the meaning of mediation and mediation communications, and includes provisions on confidentiality of mediation communications. The Mediation Bill was introduced into the Legislative Council on 30 November 2011, and a Bills Committee was established to scrutinise it.[72]

On 15 June 2012, the Mediation Ordinance was passed by Hong Kong's Legislative Council. It will come into operation on a day to be appointed by the Secretary for Justice by notice published in the Gazette.[73] The main objects of the Mediation Ordinance are (a) to promote, encourage and facilitate the resolution of disputes by mediation; and (b) to protect the confidential nature of mediation communications. The Mediation Ordinance largely mirrors the Mediation Bill introduced to the Legislative Council, with some minor changes. For example, the Mediation Ordinance added another exception to confidentiality, when a person may disclose a 'mediation communication', as defined in section 2, as of right (i.e. without needing the prior permission of the court). In addition to the limited circumstances set out in the Mediation Bill, a person may disclose a mediation communication if 'the disclosure is made for the purpose of seeking legal advice'.[74]

The Mediation Ordinance unifies the terminology, and provides a definition of the term mediation:

> 'Mediation is a structured process comprising one or more sessions in which one or more impartial individuals, without adjudicating a dispute or any aspect of it, assist the parties to the dispute to do any or all of the following:
> (a) identify the issues in dispute;

72 See Department of Justice's official website <www.doj.gov.hk/eng/public/mediation.htm>.
73 See Legislative Council's official website <www.legco.gov.hk/yr11-12/english/bc/bc52/general/bc52.htm>.
74 Section 8(2)(f) of the Mediation Ordinance.

(b) explore and generate options;
(c) communicate with one another;
(d) reach an agreement regarding the resolution of the whole, or part, of the dispute.'[75]

The Mediation Ordinance applies to any agreement to mediate if the mediation is wholly or in part conducted in Hong Kong, or if an agreement to mediate provides that the Ordinance or the law of Hong Kong is to apply to the mediation.[76] It does not apply to a process specified in Schedule 1, such as certain Labour Tribunal mediations and labour relations mediations, mediations pursuant to certain discrimination ordinances and 'arb-med' proceedings referred to in the Arbitration Ordinance.[77] The Mediation Ordinance also has retrospective effect, and applies to agreements to mediate entered into before or after the Mediation Ordinance comes into effect and to mediations that are conducted before or after that date.

One of the most important aspects of the Mediation Ordinance is to provide legal certainty regarding confidentiality of mediation communications and the admissibility of mediation communications in evidence. A mediation communication is defined as 'anything said or done; any document prepared; or, any information provided, for the purpose of or in the course of mediation.'[78] Effectively, the legislation puts the confidentiality of mediation communications on a statutory footing (in addition to the contractual confidentiality of the mediation process and the convention of the 'without prejudice' nature of mediation communications as between the parties).

## 2.4. MEDIATION SERVICE PROVIDERS

Various professional organisations are developing mediation services within their own bodies and maintain their own list of mediators. These professional bodies offer a wider range of mediation services, ranging from general mediation services, to specialised mediation services, such as family mediation and financial dispute resolution services, which are tailored to the specific needs of the users.

### *2.4.1. Law Society of Hong Kong*

The Law Society of Hong Kong was incorporated in 1907 and is the professional association for practicing solicitors in Hong Kong. The Law Society has a

75 Section 4(1), *ibid.*
76 Section 5(1), *ibid.*
77 Section 5(2), *ibid.*
78 Section 2(1), *ibid.*

Mediation Coordinator (MCO) who provides updates to their members on the latest case law and best practices in mediation. The MCO coordinates the training and accreditation of solicitors as mediators. The Law Society, through the Academy of Law, has organised and accredited mediator training courses in the general and family categories as well as mediation advocacy courses. It has established its own Accreditation Scheme with its mediation rules and a list of its accredited mediators. The accredited mediators are regulated by an Ethical Code for Mediators and the Code of Practice of the Law Society.[79]

### *2.4.2. Hong Kong Bar Association*

Founded in 1949, the Hong Kong Bar Association is the professional organisation that oversees the regulation of barristers in Hong Kong. The objects of the Hong Kong Bar Association are generally to consider and to take proper action on all matters affecting the legal profession and the administration of justice. The Hong Kong Bar Association is active in promoting mediation within its membership through mediator training courses run by the Centre for Effective Dispute Resolution (CEDR). It maintains a list of mediators.[80]

### *2.4.3. Hong Kong International Arbitration Centre and Hong Kong Mediation Council*

The Hong Kong International Mediation Centre (HKIAC) was established in 1985 by a group of leading business and legal professionals in Hong Kong, with the aim of assisting disputing parties to solve their disputes by arbitration and mediation. The HKIAC accredits suitably qualified persons as mediators and administers mediations pursuant to two sets of rules: the Government of the HKSAR's Mediation Rules and the HKIAC Mediation Rules. The HKIAC Mediation Rules[81] are published by the HKIAC in consultation with the Hong Kong Mediation Council and are similar to the Government of the HKSAR's Mediation Rules, both of which are commonly incorporated by reference into contracts. The Hong Kong Mediation Council is a division of the HKIAC, which was established to promote the use of mediation in the resolution of commercial disputes, either as a stand-alone dispute settlement process or as an adjunct to arbitration. It organises seminars on mediation and other ADR techniques, trains and certifies mediators, and establishes standards of practice for mediators.

79 For more information about the Law Society of Hong Kong's mediation services, see Law Society's website, Mediation Services <www.hklawsoc.org.hk/pub_e/default.asp?> accessed 20.10.2010.

80 See <http://hkba.org/the-bar/mediator-list/index.html> accessed 20.10.2010.

81 HKIAC Mediation Rules, effective as of 1 August 1999, available at <www.hkiac.org/index.php/en/mediation/mediation-rules> accessed 19.10.2012.

The HKIAC has established separate panels of accredited mediators for both general and family mediation. It approves Stage 1 Mediator Accreditation courses conducted by various providers of mediator training in Hong Kong. It does not provide any Stage 1 mediator training as it does not wish to be in a possible conflict position of an organisation which provides both training and accreditation at the same time. It also provides Stage 2 Mediator Accreditation Assessments. This assessment is benchmarked and reviewed independently by an international mediation expert to meet best practice in international mediation assessment. Mediators who have successfully completed Stages 1 and 2 accreditation assessments are eligible to be considered for inclusion on the HKIAC panels of accredited mediators.[82]

### *2.4.4. Hong Kong Mediation Centre*

The Hong Kong Mediation Centre (HKMC) was established in 1999 and has the status of a charitable institution as recognised by Hong Kong's Inland Revenue Department. It is the first non-profit corporate mediation institution with charitable status in Hong Kong. The composition of HKMC is a group of professionals in various fields who are committed to the promotion of mediation to handle disputes in Hong Kong. Since its inception, the HKMC has been actively involved in pro bono mediation services to the general public. The mediation cases are referred by the Home Affairs Department, the Housing Authority, the Social Welfare Department, professional bodies, community organisations and public healthcare institutions, etc. The HKMC has partnered with the Social Welfare Department, the Home Affairs Department, the Police Department and the Hong Kong Federation of Women in various pro bono mediation schemes.

There are substantial similarities in the aims and objectives of the Hong Kong Mediation Council and the HKMC. The two organisations have worked closely together on a number of projects, including the 'Mediate First' Pledge Project and the Pilot Project on Community Venues for Mediation.

### *2.4.5. Centre for Effective Dispute Resolution*

The Centre for Effective Dispute Resolution (CEDR) is a London-based mediation and alternative dispute resolution body founded as a non-profit organisation in 1990 with the support of the Confederation of British Industry and a number of British businesses and law firms, to encourage the development and use of ADR and mediation in commercial disputes.[83] CEDR has an

---

82 For details of the HKIAC mediators' accreditation process and criteria, see <www.hkiac.org/index.php/en/how-to-become-a-mediator> accessed 20.10.2012.

83 See CEDR's official website <www.cedr.com/about_us/> accessed 20.10.2012.

operational base in Hong Kong – CEDR Asia Pacific, an independent organisation with a mission to cut the cost of conflicts and create choice and capability in dispute prevention and resolution in South East Asia.[84] In 2008, CEDR and the HKIAC signed a Cooperation Agreement wherein both organisations committed to the development of efficient methods of resolving commercial disputes and to promoting the use of mediation, conciliation, arbitration and any other appropriate procedures or combinations of procedures.[85] This includes the development of dispute resolution by organising seminars, conferences and educational programs whenever possible. In 2008, CEDR was accredited by the Hong Kong Law Society as an approved training body. To date, CEDR has accredited 335 mediators in Hong Kong and performed 94 mediations.[86]

### 2.4.6. *Hong Kong Family Welfare Society Mediation Centre*

The Hong Kong Family Welfare Society Mediation Centre (HKFWSMC) is a non-governmental welfare agency. Since 1997, it has provided mediation services through its 'Family Mediation Service' scheme, to help couples facing divorce or separation to resolve relevant family disputes. The main purpose of the 'Family Mediation Service' is to preserve the interests of children as much as possible, including financial support and accommodation and to help to alleviate the pain and stress experienced by children as a result of their parents' separation or divorce. Recently, the HKFWSMC has expanded the scope of its mediation services to cover conflicts among family members, parents, peers, colleagues and neighbours.[87]

### 2.4.7. *Joint Mediation Helpline Office*

In 2010, the Joint Mediation Helpline Office (JMHO) was jointly founded by the HKMC, the Hong Kong Bar Association, the Law Society of Hong Kong, the Chartered Institute of Arbitrators (East Asia Branch), the Hong Kong Institute of Arbitrators, the Hong Kong Institute of Architects, the Hong Kong Institute of Surveyors and the HKMC. It was set up as a non-profit-making organisation with a view to promoting the use of mediation as a means of dispute resolution in Hong Kong. The mediation services provided at the JMHO include explaining the basic principles of mediation, answering general enquiries in relation to mediation, and putting users in contact with mediators of one of the

---

84 See CEDR Asia Pacific <www.cedr-asia-pacific.com/cedr/index.php> accessed 20.10.2012.

85 See CEDR's official website, *CEDR's International Mediation Activity* <www.cedr.com/about_us/international/list.php?param=64> accessed 20.10.2012.

86 *Supra* n. 63.

87 For more information about the HKFWSMC, see <www.mediationcentrehk.org/eng_title_01_page_001.htm> accessed 19.10.2012.

participating service providers. The JMHO does not provide mediators for family, community or building management disputes.[88]

### 2.4.8. *Financial Dispute Resolution Centre*

Following the collapse of Lehman Brothers in 2008 and losses incurred by a significant number of people in Hong Kong, the Hong Kong Government set up the Lehman Brothers-Related Investment Products Dispute Mediation and Arbitration Scheme. Due to the success of the scheme, which had an 89% settlement rate, the government established the Financial Dispute Resolution Centre (FDRC) in November 2011, with the support of some financial institutions. The FDRC is an independent organisation, which requires financial institutions who are its members to resolve monetary disputes with their customers through mediation and arbitration. The FDRC's mission is to provide independent and impartial 'mediation first, arbitration next' processes of dispute resolution to facilitate the resolution of monetary disputes between individual customers and financial institutions in Hong Kong. If mediation does not result in settlement, claimants may decide to take their matter to arbitration. The FDRC also maintains its own list of mediators and arbitrators.[89]

## 2.5. MEDIATOR ACCREDITATION

Just as 'arbitration is only as good as the arbitrator(s)',[90] so too 'mediation is only as good as the mediator(s)'. The quality and competence of mediators is of crucial importance to maintaining confidence in the mediation process. Therefore, proper training, appropriate accreditation standards and effective disciplinary procedures are essential to the success of mediation in Hong Kong.

There is currently no single Hong Kong regulatory framework for the regulation of mediators. The 1,600-plus mediators in Hong Kong are accredited by a number of different bodies, each adopting its own training and accreditation criteria.[91] The Working Group recognised that the establishment of a single body for accrediting mediators was desirable to ensure the quality of mediators, consistency of standards, education of the public about mediators and mediation, build public confidence in mediation services and maintain the credibility of

---

88 For more information about the JMHO, see <www.jointmediationhelpline.org.hk/> accessed 20.10.2012.

89 For more information about the FDRC, see <www.fdrc.org.hk/en/html/aboutus/aboutus_role.html> accessed 20.10.2010.

90 This phrase has been so widely cited that it has become a proverb in the arbitration community. For a list of references, see T. Clay, *L'arbitre*, Dalloz, Paris 2001, p. 11, n. 3.

91 Opening remarks by the then Secretary for Justice, Mr Wong Yan Lung, SC, at the 'Mediate First' conference at the Hong Kong Convention and Exhibition Centre on 11.05.2012.

mediation.[92] However, in view of the diversity of existing service providers and the obvious challenge to persuade them to surrender jurisdiction without legislative backing, the Working Group considered that the time was not right to prescribe a standardised system for accrediting mediators.[93] As such, the Mediation Ordinance does not provide for a single accreditation body for mediators in Hong Kong.

Recently, with the joint efforts of the Accreditation Group of the Secretary for Justice's Mediation Task Force and that of the major mediation bodies, broad consensus has been reached among the major mediation bodies regarding the establishment of a new accreditation body. The Accreditation Group is now working towards the establishment of the Hong Kong Mediation Accreditation Association Limited (Association), which will be governed by a council made up of representatives of key mediation service providers in Hong Kong. The Association will perform the role of the premier accreditation body for mediators in Hong Kong, discharging accreditation and disciplinary functions. According to the former Secretary for Justice, Mr Wong Yan Lung SC, 'the current thinking is that the four major mediation service providers, namely the Law Society, the Bar Association, the HKIAC and the HKMC, will be the founding members of the Association, as well as the anchor members of its Council which would include elected and co-opted members. It is also proposed that a body which joins the Association will have to terminate its own existing accreditation system.'[94] It is expected that the Memorandum and Articles of Association of the Association will be finalised and registered with the Companies Registry shortly.[95]

## 3. CONCLUSION

To conclude, since the implementation of the Civil Justice Reform on 2 April 2009, the litigation culture in Hong Kong has undergone a fundamental change. One important aspect of such change is the proactive encouragement and support by the judiciary for the use of mediation as a form of alternative dispute resolution. Furthermore, since the implementation of PD 31 on 1 January 2010, a strong disincentive has been provided in the form of an adverse costs sanction against parties who unreasonably refuse to attempt mediation. The enactment of the Mediation Ordinance is certainly another positive step in the right direction. It provides a basic statutory framework for the conduct of mediations and is expected to fortify Hong Kong's status as an international dispute resolution centre.

---

92 Recommendation 25, Working Group Report.

93 Recommendation 26, Working Group Report.

94 *Supra* n. 32.

95 *Supra* n. 32.

As the Secretary for Justice, Mr Rimsky Yuen SC, recently noted:

'The promotion of mediation is not the end but the beginning of the transformation of our dispute resolution culture. One key feature of traditional dispute resolution is that the process is normally only engaged after a dispute has arisen. This should not be the only way to handle conflicts or disputes. Rather, in many contexts, there are good reasons to implement an efficient concept of conflict management which involves a well-designed mechanism that can prevent, identify, address and defuse conflicts at the earliest possible stage. How mediation, either as a process of its own or combined with other means of ADR, can be developed and modified to achieve this end will have to depend on the continuous support of the community as a whole.'[96]

96 Keynote Speech on 'Mediation in Hong Kong: The Road Ahead' by Rimsky Yuen SC, now Secretary for Justice, delivered at the 'Mediation First' Conference at the Hong Kong Convention and Exhibition Centre on 11.05.2012.

# INDIA

Darius J. Khambata,* Aditya N. Mehta and Naira J. Jejeebhoy

**Contents**



---

* This paper is co-authored with two young and talented lawyers who practice before the Bombay High Court. I am deeply indebted to them for the first draft and for their valuable contribution.

## 1. INTRODUCTION

Alternative dispute resolution is one of the means by which the overburdened justice delivery system in India reduces the number of outstanding cases. There are several ways in which this is achieved:

(a) diversion of a substantial number of cases to specialised tribunals and regulatory authorities established by statute, conferred with far-reaching quasi-judicial powers and dealing with specialised subjects such as industrial disputes, excise and customs, securities markets, telecoms, electricity, etc.;
(b) the Arbitration and Conciliation Act 1996 (the 1996 Act) covering the consensual remedies of arbitration and conciliation (or mediation);
(c) statutory arbitrations: several statutes provide for arbitration and imply the existence of an arbitration agreement governed by the provisions of the 1996 Act;
(d) a traditional forum of judicial settlement known as the *Lok Adalat* (Peoples' Court) established under the Legal Services Authorities Act 1987 (the LSA Act);
(e) section 89 of the Code of Civil Procedure 1908 (the CPC): section 89 empowers a court to refer the parties to arbitration, conciliation, judicial settlement or mediation.

## 2. ARBITRATION: THE STATUTORY FRAMEWORK

Traditional forms of community and *panchayat* arbitration have long existed in India and are referred to in the Upanishads.[1] With the arrival in India of the East India Company we find the first reference to arbitration in the Bengal Regulations of 1772. Act VIII of 1859 passed by the Legislative Council for India contained provisions for arbitration (sections 312 to 325). It was, however, only in the Indian Arbitration Act 1899 that the recognisable common law form of

1 Philosophical discourses (dating back to earlier than 1200 BCE) that explained the Vedas, ancient Hindu religious texts.

arbitration came to be introduced into Indian law as a consolidated statute. For the better part of the twentieth century three statutes governed the law and practice of arbitration in India:

(a) the Arbitration Act 1940 (the 1940 Act), which contained the general law of arbitration;
(b) the Arbitration (Protocol and Convention) Act 1937 (the Protocol Act), which was enacted to give effect to the Protocol on Arbitration Clauses 1923 and the Convention on the Execution of Foreign Arbitral Awards 1927 (the Geneva Convention); and
(c) the Foreign Awards (Recognition and Enforcement) Act 1961 (the Foreign Awards Act), which was enacted to give effect to the New York Convention on the Recognition and Enforcement of Foreign Arbitral Awards 1958.

The 1940 Act resulted in a struggle for supremacy between the autonomy of arbitrations and judicial intervention and review of awards.[2]

Each of these three Acts was repealed by the 1996 Act,[3] which was enacted to consolidate and amend the law relating to domestic arbitration, international commercial arbitration and enforcement of foreign arbitral awards in India as well as to define Indian law relating to conciliation and for matters connected therewith or incidental thereto.[4] The legislative intent behind the 1996 Act was to minimise the supervisory role of the Court in the arbitral process, to facilitate enforcement of domestic awards, make arbitration laws more responsive to contemporary requirements and to provide a speedy alternative method for resolution of disputes.[5] The 1996 Act was modelled on the UNCITRAL Model Law and the UNCITRAL Conciliation Rules. The Act is divided into three parts. Part I deals with domestic arbitration proceedings and is a complete code providing for arbitration agreements, the conduct of the arbitration and awards made in India. Part II provides for the recognition and enforcement of foreign awards under the New York Convention and the Geneva Convention. Part III contains provisions for conciliation of disputes.

---

2 *Guru Nanak Foundation v. Rattan Singh* (1981) 4 SCC 634, 635 ('the way in which the proceedings under the Act are conducted and without an exception challenged in Courts, has made lawyers laugh and legal philosophers weep. Experience shows and law reports bear ample testimony that the proceedings under the Act have become highly technical accompanied by unending prolixity, at every stage providing a legal trap to the unwary. Informal forum chosen by the parties for expeditious disposal of their disputes has by the decisions of the Courts been clothed with "legalese" of unforeseeable complexity.').

3 Section 85, 1996 Act.

4 Preamble, 1996 Act.

5 *Food Corpn of India v. Indian Council of Arbitration* (2003) 6 SCC 564, 572; *Fuerst Day Lawson Ltd v. Jindal Exports Ltd* (2001) 6 SCC 356, 370.

## 2.1. DOMESTIC ARBITRATION, INTERNATIONAL COMMERCIAL ARBITRATION AND FOREIGN ARBITRATION

Part I of the 1996 Act differentiates between two types of arbitration, namely, one where both contesting parties are Indian and the other (called 'international commercial arbitration') where at least one of the parties is a foreign citizen, a body corporate or entity whose central management and control is exercised from outside India or a foreign government.[6] An international commercial arbitration can be held either within India or outside. For convenience the term 'domestic arbitration' is used in this paper to describe an arbitration between two Indian parties where the seat of arbitration is in India, and the term 'international commercial arbitration' is used to describe all other arbitrations involving at least one foreign party and which could be held either in India or outside. If held outside India the arbitration is referred to as a 'foreign arbitration'.

## 2.2. LIMITS OF JUDICIAL INTERVENTION

Section 5 of the 1996 Act is one of its most important provisions and contains an interdiction against judicial intervention.[7] Section 5 represents the primary object of the 1996 Act. It seeks to clearly define the limits of judicial intervention and to restrict it to the express provisions of Part I of the 1996 Act. This minimises the supervisory role of the courts.[8] The expression 'judicial authority' is far wider than the word 'court' (defined in section 2(1)(e)) and includes quasi-judicial tribunals such as the State and National Consumer Forums, the Company Law Board, and the Board for Industrial and Financial Reconstruction.[9] Coupled with section 16, section 5 represents the determination of Parliament to autonomise the arbitration process. The actual experience however has sometimes belied this will.

---

6 Section 2(1)(f), 1996 Act.

7 Section 5 provides 'Notwithstanding anything contained in any other law for the time being in force, in matters governed by this part, no judicial authority shall intervene except where so provided in this part.'

8 *P. Anand Gajapathi Raju v. P.V.G. Raju* (2000) 4 SCC 539, 541; *C.D.C. Financial Services (Mauritius) Ltd v. BPL Communications Ltd* (2003) 12 SCC 140, 144.

9 *Morgan Securities and Credit (Private) Ltd v. Modi Rubber Ltd* (2006) 12 SCC 642, 661–662.

## 2.3. ARBITRATION AGREEMENTS

Section 7 of the 1996 Act defines what constitutes an 'arbitration agreement' for the purposes of Part I.[10] Section 7 is modelled on Article 7 of the UNCITRAL Model Law and contains a broader definition than that in the 1940 Act.

### *2.3.1. Requirements of an arbitration agreement*

An arbitration agreement must relate to a present or future dispute in connection with some contemplated affair; it must be the intention of the parties to settle such a dispute by a private tribunal; the parties must agree in writing to be bound by the decision of such tribunal and the parties must be *ad idem*.[11]

Under the 1940 Act an arbitration agreement was not required to be in any particular form,[12] although it had to be written, and whether the parties labelled an arbitration agreement as such was held to be non-conclusive.[13] There is nothing in section 7 which suggests that the position under the 1996 Act is different. The parties are free to agree on any provisions so long as the arbitration agreement does not militate against the provisions of the 1996 Act.[14]

### *2.3.2. Intent to arbitrate essential*

Where there is a specific and direct expression of intent by the parties to have the dispute settled by arbitration, an arbitration agreement exists even if the attributes of an arbitration agreement are not all set out. However, a clause relating to settlement of disputes will not be an arbitration agreement where it contains words that exclude the attributes of an arbitration agreement or there is anything in it that detracts from an arbitration agreement.[15] A clause in a contract providing that disputes arising during the partnership are to be

---

10 '7. Arbitration agreement. (1) In this Part, 'arbitration agreement' means an agreement by the parties to submit to arbitration all or certain disputes which have arisen or which may arise between them in respect of a defined legal relationship, whether contractual or not. (2) An arbitration agreement may be in the form of an arbitration clause in a contract or in the form of a separate agreement. (3) An arbitration agreement shall be in writing. (4) An arbitration agreement is in writing if it is contained in – (a) a document signed by the parties; (b) an exchange of letters, telex, telegrams or other means of telecommunication which provide a record of the agreement; or (c) an exchange of statements of claim and defence in which the existence of the agreement is alleged by one party and not denied by the other. (5) The reference in a contract to a document containing an arbitration clause constitutes an arbitration agreement if the contract is in writing and the reference is such as to make that arbitration clause part of the contract.'

11 *Bihar State Mineral Development Corpn v. Encon Builders (I) (P) Ltd* (2003) 7 SCC 418, 423.

12 *Rukmanibai Gupta v. Collector, Jabalpur* (1980) 4 SCC 556, 560.

13 *K.K. Modi v. K.N. Modi* (1998) 3 SCC 573, 584.

14 *C.M.C. Ltd v. Unit Trust of India* (2007) 10 SCC 751, 754.

15 *Jagdish Chander v. Ramesh Chander* (2007) 5 SCC 719, 724–725.

mutually decided by the partners or are to be referred to arbitration if the parties so determine has been held to lack the main attribute of an arbitration agreement, viz consensus *ad idem*.[16] Similarly, if the clause merely indicates a hope of the parties or a tentative arrangement to explore arbitration it does not constitute an arbitration agreement.[17] The mere use of the word 'arbitrator' or 'arbitration' is not conclusive and it is the meeting of minds between the parties in relation to referring the dispute to arbitration that is essential. The court may examine correspondence with a view to determining whether there was any meeting of minds between the parties which could create a contract between them.[18] Although ambiguity in a clause may cause it to be regarded as merely an agreement to agree, the court may also look at surrounding circumstances and correspondence in determining whether it constitutes an arbitration agreement.[19] Once the intention of the parties to refer disputes to arbitration becomes clear from the agreement and other material available before the court, mere inartistic drafting of the arbitration clause cannot be taken advantage of to avoid arbitration.[20] In order to constitute an arbitration agreement, the clause should not be one that merely provides for a mechanism to avoid future disputes.[21]

### 2.3.3. *Writing requirement*

Section 7(3) requires an arbitration agreement to be in writing and section 7(4) defines exactly what is meant by the term 'in writing'. A signed document which is faxed fits within the requirements of section 7(4)(b).[22] An arbitration agreement can also arise from the correspondence exchanged between parties.[23] If there is no agreement in writing as contemplated by section 7, an arbitration agreement cannot be implied even if a contract between the parties can be implied. However, if the party opposing arbitration had acknowledged or confirmed in any correspondence or other agreement or document that it was a party to an arbitration agreement, that is sufficient to constitute an arbitration agreement under section 7(4)(b) or section 7(5) of the 1996 Act.[24]

16 *Ibid.*, pp. 725–726.
17 *Ibid.*, p. 725.
18 *Rickers Verwaltung GmbH v. Indian Oil Corpn Ltd* (1999) 1 SCC 1, 8.
19 *Powertech World Wide Ltd v. Delvin International General Trading LLC* (2012) 1 SCC 361, 368.
20 *Visa International Ltd v. Continental Resources (USA) Ltd* (2009) 2 SCC 55, 64.
21 *K.K. Modi v. K.N. Modi, supra* n. 13.
22 *Great Offshore Ltd v. Iranian Offshore Engineering & Construction Co.* (2008) 14 SCC 240, 256–257: fax was held to be a means of telecommunication under section 7(4)(b).
23 *Dresser Rand SA v. Bindal Agro Chem Ltd* (2006) 1 SCC 751, 765.
24 *Indowind Energy Ltd v. Wescare (I) Ltd* (2010) 5 SCC 306, 315, *Smita Conductors Ltd v. Euro Alloys Ltd* (2001) 7 SCC 728, 736.

### 2.3.4. *Non-signatory may be bound by arbitration agreement*

Under certain circumstances even a non-signatory to the arbitration agreement can be bound by the arbitration agreement.[25]

### 2.3.5. *Arbitration agreement by acquiescence in the statement of defence or reply*

The words 'statements of claim and defence' occurring in section 7(4)(c) of the 1996 Act are not restricted to pleadings before the arbitral tribunal but also cover situations where any suit, petition or application filed before any court asserts the existence of an arbitration agreement and there is no denial thereof in the defence, counter or written statement filed by the other party.[26]

### 2.3.6. *Incorporation of arbitration clause by reference: general conditions and standard forms*

Section 7(5) provides for incorporation of an arbitration clause in another document. The Supreme Court has held that section 7(5) requires a conscious acceptance of the arbitration clause in another document. Hence: (a) the contract should contain a clear reference to the documents containing the arbitration clause; (b) the reference to the other document should clearly indicate an intention to incorporate the arbitration clause into the contract; (c) the arbitration clause should be appropriate, that is, capable of application in respect of disputes under the contract, and should not be in conflict with any term of the contract; and (d) a general reference to another contract does not have the effect of incorporating the arbitration clause from the other contract; however, (e) where parties stipulate that conditions of the contract framed by one of the parties shall form a part of their contract or where the contract provides for incorporation of a standard form of terms and conditions of trade or professional associations or institutions which publish or circulate such standard terms and conditions, then if such conditions of the contract or standard form contain an arbitration clause it stands incorporated.[27]

### 2.3.7. *Connected contracts*

Where a party has a claim jointly against two separate parties arising out of two separate agreements, both of which contain an arbitration clause governed by the rules of the same institution, the joint claim may be referred to a single arbitration in order to avoid multiplicity of proceedings, conflicting decisions

---

25 *Chloro Controls (I) (P) Ltd v. Severn Trent Water Purification Inc. and others* (2013) 1 SCC 641, paras. 102–109: such as parties by implied consent, third party beneficiaries, guarantors, assignees, and by theories of agency, apparent authority, piercing of the veil, joint venture, estoppel and succession.

26 *S.N. Prasad v. Monnet Finance Ltd* (2011) 1 SCC 320, 325–326.

27 *M.R. Engineers & Contractors (P) Ltd v. Som Datt Builders Ltd* (2009) 7 SCC 696, 707.

and injustice.[28] However such contracts should be interconnected in such a way as to render it natural for the disputes under both agreements to be covered under the one arbitration clause.[29] However the presence of an arbitration clause in a housing loan contract will not entitle the flat purchaser to join the bank as a party in an arbitration initiated by him against the developer, if there is no arbitration clause in the tripartite agreement.[30] Arbitration agreements in the main contract can be extended to disputes in relation to contracts arising out of and which are incidental to the main contract since the purpose and spirit of arbitration required the reference of all disputes between the parties for final adjudication before an adjudicating authority of their choice.[31] As a question of construction of the contract it has also been held that where there is no privity between the sub-contractor and the principal, it would not be open to the sub-contractor to claim the benefit of the arbitration clause in the main contract.[32]

### *2.3.8. Present dispute essential*

The right to demand arbitration and the jurisdiction of the arbitral tribunal is contingent on the existence of a genuine dispute between the parties.[33] A dispute can be said to arise when one party to an arbitration agreement makes or asserts a claim against the other party to the arbitration agreement and the other party denies such a claim.[34] However, even where a claim is not followed by a denial, a party invoking an arbitration clause may proceed on the basis that the other party to the contract has denied or disputed his claim if the matter is referred to the arbitrator within reasonable time.[35] Section 7(1) of the 1996 Act does not require that the dispute be contractual. It has been held that the 1996 Act applies to both civil and commercial disputes.[36]

## 2.4. APPOINTMENT OF ARBITRATORS

### *2.4.1. Autonomy in appointment*

Section 11 of the 1996 Act gives the parties to arbitration agreements autonomy in selecting a procedure for appointing an arbitral tribunal. A party entrusted

---

28 *P.R. Shah Share & Stock Brokers v. BHH Securities* (2012) 1 SCC 594, 600.

29 *Olympus Superstructures Pvt Ltd v. Meena Vijay Khetan* (1999) 5 SCC 651, 665–666.

30 *Deutsche Post Bank Home Finance Ltd v. Taduri Sridhar* (2011) 11 SCC 375, 382.

31 *Ispat Industries Ltd v. Baby Samuel & Co.* (2009) 1 Mah LJ 1000, 1002.

32 *Maintech Engineers v. Jotindra Steel Tubes Ltd* (1993) 51 DLT 463, 467.

33 *Ramesh Kumar v. Furu Ram* (2011) 8 SCC 613, 634: a sham dispute to procure an award to avoid stamp duty payable on an agreement to sell property.

34 *Deutsche Post Bank Home Finance Ltd v. Taduri Sridhar* (2011) 11 SCC 375, 382–383.

35 *McDermott International Inc. v. Burn Standard Co. Ltd* (2006) 11 SCC 181, 226.

36 *H. Srinivas Pai v. H.V. Pai* (2010) 12 SCC 521, 522–523.

with the duty of nominating an arbitrator cannot nominate a person that a reasonable person would not consider independent and impartial. The responsibility to nominate an arbitrator has been held to be a solemn fiduciary obligation and therefore only an unbiased and fair arbitrator can be nominated.[37]

### *2.4.2. Number of arbitrators*

The parties are free to determine the number of arbitrators provided this number is not an even number. In the absence of such determination the tribunal shall consist of a sole arbitrator.[38]

### *2.4.3. Where the agreed procedure fails*

Where there is no agreement as to the appointment procedure or where the procedure agreed to by the parties fails, section 11 of the 1996 Act provides for appointment of the arbitrator(s) by the Chief Justice.[39] The 'Chief Justice' under section 11 is not a *persona designata*.[40] In the case of domestic arbitrations the Chief Justice of the High Court is the appointing authority, but for international commercial arbitrations the appointing authority is the Chief Justice of the Supreme Court of India.[41] Regard is to be had to the qualifications required of the arbitrator by the agreement and other considerations likely to secure the appointment of an independent and impartial arbitrator.[42]

### *2.4.4. Delegation of section 11 power*

In *Patel Engineering* the Supreme Court held that the Chief Justice performs a judicial function when exercising powers under section 11(6). The earlier view of the Supreme Court that the power was administrative in nature,[43] was

37 *Alcove Industries Ltd v. Oriental Structural Engineers* (2008) 1 ArbLR 393 (Del), 423.

38 Section 10, 1996 Act.

39 The UNCITRAL Model Law uses the term 'Court' instead. The purpose of replacing that term with the expression 'Chief Justice' is to confer the power of appointment on the highest courts, i.e. the Supreme Court and the High Courts, and to exclude the jurisdiction of the District Courts which would otherwise also be covered by the definition of 'Court' in section 2(1)(e) of the 1996 Act. Section 2(1)(e) defines Court as 'the principal Civil Court of original jurisdiction in a district and includes the High Court in exercise of its ordinary original civil jurisdiction having jurisdiction to decide the questions forming the subject matter of the arbitration if the same had been the subject matter of a Suit.' District Courts are subordinate to the relevant High Court.

40 *S.B.P. & Co. v. Patel Engineering Ltd* (2005) 8 SCC 618, 645–646.

41 Section 11(12)(a) and (b), 1996 Act. Each State has a High Court as its highest Court. The Supreme Court is the highest court in India. All High Courts are subject to the appellate jurisdiction of the Supreme Court.

42 Section 11(8), 1996 Act.

43 *Konkan Railway Corporation Ltd v. Rani Construction Pvt Ltd* (2002) 2 SCC 388.

overruled. Since the power under section 11 is a judicial power, the Chief Justice is entitled to delegate the power only to another judge of the High Court or the Supreme Court as the case may be. The power exercised by this delegate judge is the power of the Chief Justice.[44] A non-judicial body or institution cannot exercise judicial powers and cannot be delegated the power of appointment under section 11. Hence designation of any person or institution (such as a Chamber of Commerce or an Institute of Engineers) under section 11(6) is only for the purpose of nominating to the Chief Justice the name of a suitable person if an arbitrator is to be appointed.[45]

### *2.4.5. Matters to be considered*

Whilst considering an application under section 11(6) the court is required to consider certain issues touching upon the merits of the case, such as the existence and validity of the arbitration agreement, the existence of a live claim and the territorial jurisdiction of the court.[46] However, whilst appointing an arbitrator a court is not required to draw up a list of disputes referred to the arbitrator, and the appointment is an implied reference in terms of the arbitration agreement. The arbitrator will have jurisdiction to entertain issues even though they were not raised during the section 11 application.[47]

### *2.4.6. Preliminary issues under section 11*

In a later decision,[48] the Supreme Court has identified and categorised the preliminary issues that usually arise in a section 11 application. The first category consists of issues that the court must decide, such as the territorial jurisdiction of the court and the existence and validity of an arbitration agreement in relation to the contract in question, including any allegation of fraud which would vitiate the arbitration agreement.[49] The second category consists of issues that the court may decide, such as prima facie satisfaction that the claim is not time barred.[50] The decision on the issue of limitation is only to be taken when the claim is evidently and patently time barred and where there is no need to consider detailed evidence on the issue.[51] The third category consists of issues that the court cannot decide and must leave exclusively to the arbitrator, such as whether the claim falls within the scope of the arbitration agreement,

[44] *Patel Engineering, supra* n. 40, pp. 662–663.
[45] *Patel Engineering, supra* n. 40, pp. 647–648, 662.
[46] *Patel Engineering, supra*, n. 40, pp. 642, 643, 653, 660–661, 663.
[47] *State of Goa v. Praveen Enterprises* (2011) 3 Arb LR 209, 222.
[48] *National Insurance Co. Ltd v. Boghara Polyfab Pvt Ltd* (2009)1 SCC 267, 283–284.
[49] *Bharat Rasiklal Ashra v. Gautam Rasiklal Ashra* (2012) 2 SCC 144, 147, 149.
[50] *Shree Ram Mills Ltd v. Utility Premises (P) Ltd* (2007) 4 SCC 599, 608.
[51] *Indian Oil Corpn v. SPS Engg. Ltd* (2011) 3 SCC 507, 514.

whether the claim is barred on the ground of *res judicata*[52] and the merits of the claim. The court will not embark upon an examination of the issue of arbitrability or appropriateness of adjudication by a private forum.[53] However, in some cases where claims clearly do not fall within the scope of the arbitration clause courts have rejected section 11 applications, on the ground that it is futile to appoint an arbitrator in such matters.[54] Although the Chief Justice has the judicial power to determine certain preliminary issues between the parties, those issues cannot be considered by the Chief Justice in an application under section 11 where an arbitrator has already been appointed without judicial intervention.[55]

### *2.4.7. Finality of a decision under section 11*

The decision of the Chief Justice on preliminary matters is final and the power of the arbitrator to determine those issues stands excluded.[56] If an issue is decided by the Chief Justice at the time of appointing an arbitrator under section 11, that issue cannot be raised subsequently in order to challenge the arbitrator's award under section 34 of the 1996 Act.[57] However, where the Chief Justice only arrives at a prima facie view on a preliminary issue, the substantive determination on the merits of the issue would be left open to be determined by the arbitrator.[58] Where on a prima facie examination the Chief Justice is of the view that the defence raised by a party is not genuine or bona fide, the Chief Justice may conclude that it is not necessary to refer the dispute to arbitration and may instead chose to settle the issue finally.[59]

### *2.4.8. Challenging an order under section 11*

It is not possible to appeal the order of a Chief Justice under section 11. As the order passed by a Chief Justice of a High Court under section 11(6) is a judicial order it can only be challenged by recourse to the residuary and extraordinary power of the Supreme Court under Article 136 of the Constitution of India.[60] The order cannot be challenged before the High Court by invoking its writ

---

52 *Ibid.*, p. 515.

53 *Booz Allen & Hamilton v. SBI Home Finance Ltd* (2011) 5 SCC 532, 545.

54 *Harjit Singh v. Delhi Development Authority* (2009) 2 Arb LR 349 (Del-DB), 350, 354.

55 *Oriental Instruance Co. Ltd v. Unitech Ltd* (2008) 1 Arb LR 187 (Del), 194.

56 Section 11(7), 1996 Act; *Patel Engineering, supra* n. 40, pp. 644 and 649, *National Insurance, supra* n. 48, p. 282.

57 *Food Corporation of India v. A.M. Ahmed & Co.* (2006) 13 SCC 779, 787.

58 *Shree Ram Mills Ltd v. Utility Premises Pvt Ltd* (2007) 4 SCC 599, 608.

59 *Union of India v. Master Construction* (2011) 12 SCC 349, 355.

60 Article 136 of the Constitution of India confers jurisdiction on the Supreme Court to grant 'special leave to appeal from any judgment, decree, determination, sentence or order in any cause or matter passed or made by any court or tribunal in the territory of India.'

jurisdiction under Article 226 of the Constitution of India.[61] The order under section 11 by the Chief Justice of the Supreme Court can be reviewed only under Article 137. Review under Article 137 is exceptional.[62]

### *2.4.9. Named arbitrators and qualifications of arbitrators*

The Supreme Court has resolved a conflict of decisions between various High Courts by holding that parties should be directed as far as possible to appoint an arbitrator in the manner provided in the arbitration agreement, but in exceptional circumstances (e.g. where the impartiality of the arbitrator to be appointed under the terms of the agreement is in doubt) the Chief Justice can make alternative arrangements for appointment of an arbitrator having due regard to the qualifications and other conditions prescribed in the agreement.[63] If the independence of the named arbitrator is questionable then the Chief Justice may appoint an independent arbitrator even if the arbitrator has been named.[64]

### *2.4.10. Forfeiture of contractual right to appoint an arbitrator*

Section 11(6) does not provide for the expiry of any particular time period before a party can approach the Chief Justice under section 11. Where an appointment is not made as per the contractually agreed procedure after a request from a party and thereafter that party files an application under section 11(6), then the right of the other party to appoint an arbitrator is forfeited when the section 11 application is made.[65] Once a party forfeits its right to appoint an arbitrator, a court is not required to grant that party an opportunity to appoint an arbitrator before it makes an appointment under section 11.[66] Where an appointment is made by a party after a valid section 11(6) application has been made by the other party, the appointment is null and void. The Supreme Court has held that a period of thirty days from the receipt of a request for appointment from the opposite party was adequate and failure to appoint thereafter entitled the

61 Article 226 of the Constitution of India recognises the power of High Courts to issue directions, orders and writs to any person, or authority for the purpose of enforcement of fundamental rights and for any other purpose.

62 *Jain Studios v. Shin Satellite Public Co. Ltd* (2006) 5 SCC 501, 505; Article 137 provides for review by the Supreme Court of its own judgments and orders.

63 *Ace Pipeline Contracts Pvt Ltd v. Bharat Petroleum Corporation Ltd* (2007) 5 SCC 304, 315; *Northern Railway Administration, Ministry of Railways v. Patel Engineering Co. Ltd* (2008) 10 SCC 240, 245.

64 *Denel (Pty) Ltd v. Ministry of Defence* (2012) 2 SCC 759, 767; *Northern Railway Administration, Ministry of Railways v. Patel Engineering Co. Ltd* (2008) 10 SCC 240, 245.

65 *Datar Switchgears Ltd v. Tata Finance Ltd* (2000) 8 SCC 151, 157.

66 *Dakshin Shelters (P) Ltd v. Geeta S. Johari* (2012) 5 SCC 152, 156.

opposite party to invoke section 11.[67] However, the Bombay High Court has interpreted that decision as merely laying down the need to wait a reasonable time and that therefore the right to file an application under section 11(6) does not automatically arise on the expiry of thirty days, but instead only arises upon the expiry of a reasonable period.[68]

### *2.4.11. When the appointment is complete*

There is no requirement of formal acceptance by an arbitrator in order for his appointment to be complete.[69] The Bombay High Court has taken the view that the appointing authority is not required to communicate the acceptance of the nomination by the arbitrator to the parties in order for the appointment to be complete.[70] The Delhi High Court has held that the appointment of an arbitrator is complete only when it is communicated and received by the arbitrator.[71] On the other hand, the Bombay High Court has taken the view that it is only necessary that communication of his appointment has been sent to (even if not yet received by) the arbitrator in order for the appointment to be complete.[72]

## 2.5. ORDER OF REFERENCE TO ARBITRATION

### *2.5.1. Mandatory reference*

A judicial authority is mandatorily required to refer the parties before it to arbitration if the action brought before it is the subject of an arbitration agreement.[73] Such reference has to be on the application of one of the parties. section 8 is stricter than the corresponding provision in Article 8 of the UNCITRAL Model Law.[74] The judicial authority has to decide whether there is

67 *Datar Switchgears, supra* n. 65, p. 155.

68 *Voltas Ltd v. Rolta India Ltd* (2011) 113 BomLR 393, 415–426.

69 *Keshav Singh Dwarkadas Kapadia v. Indian Engineering Co.*, AIR 1969 Bom 227, 228–230; affirmed by the Supreme Court in *Keshav Singh Dwarkadas Kapadia v. Indian Engineering* Co. (1971) 2 SCC 706.

70 *Voltas Ltd v. Rolta India Ltd* (2011) 113 BomLR 393, 402–403.

71 *R.S. Avatar Singh and Co. v. Indian Tourism Development Corporation Ltd*, AIR 2003 Del 249, 251.

72 *Voltas Ltd v. Rolta India Ltd* (2011) 113 BomLR 393, 403–404.

73 Section 8, 1996 Act. *Magna Leasing & Finance Ltd v. Potluri Madhavilata* (2009) 10 SCC 103, 114–5.

74 The UNCITRAL Model law introduces a qualification that does not require a reference to arbitration if the court finds that the arbitration agreement 'is null and void, inoperative or incapable of being performed'. Section 8 applies to Part I arbitrations which are essentially arbitrations seated in India, whether between two Indian parties or international commercial arbitrations. If the arbitration is a foreign arbitration governed by Part II than the

an arbitration agreement, whether all the parties to the suit are parties to such agreement, whether the dispute in the action is arbitrable and whether the defendant had applied before submitting its first statement on the substance of the dispute.[75] To be maintainable the application must be filed not later than the submission by the applicant of the first statement on the substance of the dispute, that is to say his first statement on the merits.[76]

### *2.5.2. No reference where all parties to action are not parties to agreement*

The Supreme Court has however held that it is not possible under section 8 to bifurcate legal proceedings into different causes of action, some against those who are party to the arbitration agreement and some against those who are not.[77] Consequently the Supreme Court refused to refer a suit to arbitration where some of the parties to the suit were not parties to the arbitration agreement. The Supreme Court did not determine whether the parties to the action who were not parties to the arbitration agreement were necessary for determination of the dispute in the action before it.[78] The Supreme Court also made no distinction between the addition of necessary or even proper parties and unnecessary ones added only for the purpose of escaping arbitration. The *Sukanya Holdings* principle has also been extended to foreign arbitrations by the Bombay High Court although the Court noted the possibility of an application to delete unnecessary parties prior to an application under section 45 of the 1996 Act in respect of an action filed before an Indian court covering the same subject matter as that of the foreign arbitration.[79] The Supreme Court has refused to reconsider *Sukanya Holdings* in a matter that arose before it under section 45. Recognising that it was open to a court to strike out unnecessary parties if they were added to the action before the court, the Supreme Court held that where such parties could not be struck off, the proceedings must continue only before the court.[80]

---

corresponding provision under section 45 of the 1996 Act includes the aforementioned UNCITRAL qualification.

75 *Booz Allen & Hamilton*, *supra* n. 53, p. 542.

76 *Rashtriya Ispat Nigam Ltd v. Verma Transport Co.* (2006) 7 SCC 275, 289.

77 *Sukanya Holdings (Private) Ltd v. Jayesh H. Pandya* (2003) 5 SCC 531, 535; *S.N. Prasad v. Monnet Finance Ltd* (2011) 1 SCC 320, 324.

78 Order 1, Rule 10 of the Code of Civil Procedure makes a distinction between a necessary party without whom no order can be effectively passed and a proper party whose presence is necessary for a complete and final decision of the question involved in the proceedings. Whereas a suit can be dismissed for non-joinder of a necessary party it cannot be dismissed merely because a proper party has not been joined.

79 *Novartis Vaccines and Diagnostics Inc. v. Aventis Pharma*, judgment dated 3 October 2007 in Arbitration Petition No. 302 of 2007, Bombay High Court.

80 *Chloro Controls (I) Pvt Ltd v. Severn Trent Water Purifications Inc.* (2013) 1 SCC 641, para. 90. Also see *supra* n. 26.

## 2.6. CHALLENGING AN ARBITRATOR

### 2.6.1. *Disclosures by arbitrator*

Under section 12 of the 1996 Act, prior to being appointed and even thereafter, an arbitrator is required to disclose circumstances that are likely to raise doubts as to his independence or impartiality. A party can challenge the appointment of an arbitrator if that party becomes aware, after the appointment is made, of circumstances that raise doubts as to the arbitrator's independence or impartiality or regarding his lack of qualification. It is not essential that the challenge should establish that the arbitrator is not, in fact, independent or impartial. It is sufficient if the party establishes circumstances which are likely to give rise to justifiable doubts as to his independence or impartiality.[81] The Supreme Court earlier required a real likelihood or reasonable apprehension that the arbitrator was biased and not a mere suspicion of bias.[82] In a later decision the Supreme Court changed its approach and preferred the 'real danger' test to the 'reasonable apprehension' test.[83] Although these decisions were under the 1940 Act, there is nothing in the 1996 Act to suggest that the position under it is different.

### 2.6.2. *Relationship between the arbitrator and a party: employee arbitrators*

Section 12 of the 1996 Act requires an arbitrator to be independent in addition to being impartial. The Supreme Court has nevertheless upheld the appointment of employees of public sector undertakings as arbitrators in respect of disputes involving their employer, provided that the employee was not associated with the relevant contract.[84] Where a party acquiesced in the appointment of an arbitrator with full knowledge that the arbitrator was the chief engineer of the other party, the arbitrator's appointment could not later be challenged as there was nothing to indicate the occurrence subsequently of something prompting a reasonable apprehension of bias.[85] However, an employee arbitrator would be disqualified if he had earlier expressed a view or taken a decision on the matter that suggested that he lacked an impartial mindset.[86] The Supreme Court has also observed that government authorities and companies should phase out the appointment of their employees as arbitrators, having regard to the insertion of the requirement of 'independence' in the 1996 Act.[87] The position of an

---

81 *Yashwitha Constructions (P) Ltd v. Simplex Concrete Piles India Ltd* (2008) 4 Andh LT 266.

82 *International Airports Authority of India v. K.D. Bali* (1988) 2 SCC 360, 368.

83 *Kumaon Mandal Vikas Nigam Ltd v. Girja Shankar Pant* (2001) 1 SCC 182, 201.

84 *Indian Oil Corporation Ltd v. Raja Transport (P) Ltd* (2009) 8 SCC 520, 532.

85 *Ladli Construction Co (P) Ltd v. Punjab Police Housing Corpn Ltd* (2012) 4 SCC 609, 616–618.

86 *Bharat Sanchar Nigam Ltd v. Motorola India Pvt Ltd* (2009) 2 SCC 337, 347; *OPBK Construction Pvt Ltd v. Punjab Small Industries* (2008) 3 ArbLR 189 (P&H), 196.

87 *Indian Oil Corporation Ltd v. Raja Transport (P) Ltd* (2009) 8 SCC 520, 534; *Union of India v. Singh Builders Syndicate* (2009) 4 SCC 523, 528.

employee of a private corporation as an arbitrator is different from that of a public sector employee and it may be reasonable to apprehend bias in view of his interest in the company.[88]

### *2.6.3. Procedure for challenging an arbitrator*

Where the parties do not agree to any specific procedure to challenge an arbitrator, the challenge must be made before the arbitral tribunal itself within fifteen days of the party becoming aware of the circumstances giving rise to doubts about the independence or impartiality of the arbitrator.[89] If the challenge to the arbitrator's appointment is not successful, the arbitral tribunal is required to continue with the matter and make an award. Until the award is made the party challenging the appointment of the arbitrator cannot move a court to challenge the appointment or remove the arbitrator.[90] Once the award is made, the award can be challenged under section 34 of the 1996 Act, including in respect of a rejection of challenge under section 13.

## 2.7. INTERIM MEASURES

### *2.7.1. By courts*

Section 9 of the 1996 Act empowers the court, before or during arbitral proceedings or at any time after the making of the award but before it is enforced, to grant a wide spectrum of interim measures of protection and other interim relief. Any interim relief required during the period before or after the arbitral proceedings can only be obtained from a court.[91] Whilst claiming relief prior to commencing arbitral proceedings the applicant must satisfy the court that arbitral proceedings are actually contemplated or manifestly intended.[92]

### *2.7.2. By the arbitral tribunal*

Section 17 empowers the arbitral tribunal subject to an agreement to the contrary between the parties, to take any interim measure or protection which it may consider necessary '*in respect of the subject matter of the dispute.*'

---

88 *Indian Oil Corporation Ltd v. Raja Transport (P) Ltd* (2009) 8 SCC 520, 533.

89 Section 13, 1996 Act.

90 *Tata Industries Ltd v. Grasim Industries Ltd* (2011) 3 Bom CR 326, 330.

91 *Firm Ashok Traders v. Gurumukh Das Saluja* (2004) 3 SCC 155, 169.

92 *Sundaram Finance Ltd v. NEPC India Ltd* (1999) 2 SCC 479, 488; *Firm Ashok Traders, supra* n. 91, p. 168.

### 2.7.3. *Differences between section 9 and section 17*

The relief under section 9 can be granted on an *ex parte* basis and can, depending on the circumstances, even be against a person who is not a party to the arbitration agreement.[93] Further, whilst the relief under section 17 can only be granted to protect the subject matter of the dispute, the measures under section 9 can be wider.[94] Whilst parties can contractually agree to exclude the applicability of section 17 they cannot exclude the application of section 9.[95] An arbitrator's orders under section 17 are not executable as decrees of a court, unlike awards which are. Orders under section 9 are passed by a court and carry all the sanction and force of orders of a court.[96]

### 2.7.4. *Nature of relief available under section 9*

Courts have wide powers under section 9 and can order a variety of interim measures such as preservation, interim custody or sale of goods that are the subject matter of arbitration;[97] securing the disputed amount where there is a real danger of an award made in favour of the applicant being defeated;[98] conditional attachment of property belonging to the respondent;[99] restraining the sale of property to maintain the status quo;[100] preservation of evidence;[101] or appointing a receiver.[102] On the other hand, it is not possible to obtain interim measures under section 9 in respect of the arrest of a vessel;[103] preventing revocation or breach of a contract which is not specifically enforceable;[104] specific performance of contracts of personal service;[105] or preventing the invocation of a bank guarantee, unless the beneficiary has committed a fraud of which the bank has notice or where there are special equities in favour of granting such an injunction.[106]

---

93 *Nandos Indage v. Nando's Resources BV* (2009) 4 BomCR 139, 141; *Girish Mulchand Mehta v. Mahesh S. Mehta* (2010) 1 BomCR 31, 38–9 (DB).

94 *Maharashtra State Electricity Board v. Datar Switchgears Ltd* (2003) 2 BomCR 81, 105–6.

95 Section 17, 1996 Act.

96 *M.D., Army Welfare Housing v. Sumangal Services Pvt Ltd* (2004) 9 SCC 619, 646, 649.

97 Section 9(ii)(a), 1996 Act.

98 *Global Co. v. National Fertilizers Ltd*, AIR 1998 Del 397, 400.

99 *Yenepoya Minerals & Granites P Ltd v. Maharashtra Apex Corpn Ltd* (2004) 2 ArbLR 47 (Kar), 51.

100 *N. Srinivasa v. Kuttukaran Machine Tools Ltd* (2009) 5 SCC 182, 190.

101 Section 9(ii)(c); *Prima Developers v. Lords Co-operative Group Housing Society Ltd* (2009) 2 ArbLR 387, 390.

102 Section 9(ii)(d); *Firm Ashok Traders v. Gurumukh Das Saluja* (2004) 3 SCC 155, 156.

103 *J.S. Ocean Liner LLC v. M.V. Golden Progress* (2007) 2 BomCR 1, 8.

104 *Arvind Construction Co. Pvt Ltd v. Kalinga Mining Corpn* (2007) 6 SCC 798, 804.

105 *Percept D'Mark (India) Pvt Ltd v. Zaheer Khan* (2006) 4 SCC 227, 246.

106 *BSES Ltd v. Fenner India Ltd* (2006) 2 SCC 728, 733–4.

## 2.8. JURISDICTION OF THE ARBITRAL TRIBUNAL

### 2.8.1. *Incorporation of the doctrine of kompetenz-kompetenz*

Under the 1940 Act the arbitral tribunal was not empowered to decide disputes regarding the existence or validity of the parent contract or facts which rendered it illegal.[107] Disputes pertaining to the existence, validity and effect of the arbitration agreement or the arbitrability of disputes could be decided by the arbitral tribunal if the agreement was wide enough but this was subject to final determination by a court.[108] Section 16 of the 1996 Act, which is modelled on Article 16 of the UNCITRAL Model Law, has removed this restriction and confers on the arbitral tribunal the competence to decide questions affecting its own jurisdiction, including in relation to the existence and validity of an arbitration agreement.[109] The authority of the arbitral tribunal under section 16 of the 1996 Act is not confined to the width of its jurisdiction but goes to the very root of its jurisdiction.[110]

### 2.8.2. *Arbitration not interrupted*

Section 16(1)(a) of the 1996 Act recognises that an arbitration clause in a contract is a collateral term or an independent agreement.[111] Section 16(1)(b) also provides that a decision by the tribunal that the contract is null and void shall not entail *ipso jure* the invalidity of the arbitration clause.

Section 16(5) emphasises the need for the tribunal to continue its adjudication uninterrupted by objections to its jurisdiction. If the tribunal holds that it has jurisdiction, it is required to proceed with the arbitral proceedings to their conclusion by making a final award. It is only if the tribunal accepts that it has no jurisdiction that it must then make an immediate order terminating the arbitration. In the case of an order rejecting jurisdiction a direct appeal to the court is provided under section 37(2).[112] No second appeal is permitted from an order passed by a court under section 37.

---

107 *Wellington Associates Ltd v. Kirit Mehta* (2000) 4 SCC 272, 281.

108 *Renusagar Power Co. Ltd v. General Electric Co.* (1984) 4 SCC 679, 703–704, 731–732.

109 *National Insurance*, *supra* n. 48, pp. 279–280, 282–283.

110 *Gas Authority of India Ltd v. Keti Construction (I) Ltd* (2007) 5 SCC 38, 51.

111 *National Insurance*, *supra* n. 48, pp. 279–280, *National Agricultural Co-op. Marketing Federation India Ltd v. Gains Trading Ltd* (2007) 5 SCC 692, 695–696.

112 This is a rare departure from the UNCITRAL Model Law which offers an appeal even from an order upholding jurisdiction. Parliament apparently did not provide for such an appeal to simplify and hasten the arbitral process.

### 2.8.3. *Arbitrability*

In *Booz Allen & Hamilton Inc. v. SBI Home Finance Ltd*[113] the Supreme Court held the different facets of the term 'arbitrability' in relation to the jurisdiction of the arbitral tribunal to be: (a) whether the disputes are capable of adjudication and settlement by arbitration; (b) whether the disputes are covered by the arbitration agreement; and (c) whether the parties have referred the disputes to arbitration. Well-recognised examples of non-arbitrable disputes were enumerated in the decision in *Booz Allen & Hamilton Inc.* as including (a) disputes relating to rights and liabilities which give rise to or arise out of criminal offences; (b) matrimonial disputes relating to divorce, judicial separation, restitution of conjugal rights or child custody; (c) guardianship matters; (d) insolvency and winding up matters;[114] (e) testamentary matters (grant of probate, letters of administration and succession certificate);[115] (f) eviction or tenancy matters governed by special statutes where the tenant enjoys statutory protection against eviction and only the specified courts are conferred jurisdiction to grant eviction or decide the disputes; and (g) disputes relating to mortgages.[116]

The Supreme Court has also held that matters involving serious allegations of fraud and malpractices where detailed evidence is required cannot be decided in arbitration.[117]

### 2.8.4. *Waiver of objection*

Section 16(2) of the 1996 Act requires that a challenge to the jurisdiction of the arbitral tribunal be raised not later than the submission of the statement of defence. The plea is required to be raised by this point so that remedial measures may be immediately taken and one can avoid the time and expense involved in the hearing of the matter before a tribunal which may ultimately be found to be

113 (2011) 5 SCC 532, 546.

114 *Haryana Telecom Ltd v. Sterlite Industries (India) Ltd* (1999) 5 SCC 688, 689.

115 *Chiranjilal Goenka v. Jasjit Singh* (1993) 2 SCC 507, 519–520.

116 *Natraj Studios (P) Ltd v. Navrang Studios* (1981) 1 SCC 523, 537.

117 *N. Radhakrishnan v. Maestro Engineers* (2010) 1 SCC 72, 77; *Ivory Properties & Hotels Pvt Ltd v. Nusli Wadia* (2011) 2 BomCR 559, 563–564. The decision in *N. Radhakrishnan* is, it is submitted, erroneous. The Supreme Court reached its conclusion based on the judgment in *Abdul Kadir v. Madhav Oak*, AIR 1962 SC 406, 411, a decision under the 1940 Act. The Supreme Court overlooked that the reference to arbitration under the 1940 Act was discretionary, unlike under section 8 of the 1996 Act under which reference to arbitration is mandatory once it is found there is an express provision for arbitration: *Magna Leasing & Finance Ltd v. Potluri Madhavilata* (2009) 10 SCC 103, 114–115, a case under section 8 of the 1996 Act.

not properly constituted or lacking in jurisdiction.[118] The jurisdictional question is, therefore, to be determined as a preliminary issue.[119]

Section 4 of the 1996 Act clarifies that a party who carries on an arbitration without raising, in a timely manner, any objection to non-compliance with any provision of the Act or requirement of the arbitration agreement, is deemed to have waived his right to so object. It has been held that a challenge to the composition of the tribunal is not an absolute right and if a party chooses not to object within the prescribed time there is a deemed waiver under section 4.[120] If the plea of jurisdiction is not raised before the arbitral tribunal in accordance with section 16 of the 1996 Act, such a plea cannot be raised in proceedings to set aside the award unless good reason is shown.[121] However, mere participation in the proceedings is not tantamount to acceptance of the jurisdiction of the arbitral tribunal[122] and once a party objects to the jurisdiction of the tribunal, the party does not waive his rights by proceeding with the arbitration under protest.[123]

## 2.9. CONDUCT OF THE ARBITRATION

### 2.9.1. *Tribunal not bound by strict rules of procedure and evidence*

The conduct of arbitral proceedings can be decided by agreement between the parties and failing such agreement, it is left to the arbitral tribunal to conduct proceedings in the manner it considers appropriate.[124] The arbitral tribunal is not bound by the provisions of the Code of Civil Procedure 1908 or the Indian Evidence Act 1872.[125] The arbitral tribunal has the power to determine the admissibility, relevance, materiality and weight of any evidence.[126] Although not bound by strict rules of procedure or evidence, the arbitral tribunal cannot disregard rules founded on principles of natural justice and public policy.[127]

---

118 *Gas Authority of India Ltd v. Keti Construction (I) Ltd* (2007) 5 SCC 38, 53.

119 *McDermott International Inc. v. Burn Standard Co. Ltd* (2006) 11 SCC 181, 205.

120 *Narayan Prasad Lohia v. Nikunj Kumar Lohia* (2002) 3 SCC 572, 582–583.

121 *Gas Authority of India Ltd v. Keti Construction (I) Ltd* (2007) 5 SCC 38, 53–54.

122 *Travancore Devaswom Board v. Panchamy Pack (P) Ltd* (2004) 13 SCC 510, 512.

123 *Rambaksh Lachmandas v. Bombay Cotton Co.*, AIR 1931 Bom 81, 82; *Chetandas Daga v. Radhakissen Ramchandra*, AIR 1927 Bom 553, 555–556; *Babubhai Tansukhlal v. Madhavji Govindji & Co.*, AIR 1931 Bom 343, 346.

124 Section 19(2) and (3), 1996 Act.

125 Section 19(1), 1996 Act.

126 Section 19(4), 1996 Act.

127 *Aboobakar Latif v. Reception Committee*, AIR 1937 Bom 410, 416; *Chandrabhan Bilotia v. Ganpatrai & Sons*, AIR 1944 Cal. 127, 130; *Maharashtra State Electricity Board v. Datar Switchgear Ltd* (2003) 2 BomCR 81, 98.

### *2.9.2. Form and content of arbitral award, interest and costs*

An arbitral award has to be in writing and signed by the members of the tribunal. As long as the signatures of the majority of the members are present and a reason for the omission to sign by any other member is stated, the award will be valid.[128] The award is required to state reasons unless the parties have agreed to the contrary or the award is on agreed terms.[129] The arbitral tribunal has the power to make an interim arbitral award and to award interest at such rate as it deems reasonable between the date on which the cause of action arose and the date of the award.[130] Unless otherwise agreed any sum directed to be paid by an award shall carry interest at 18% per annum from the date of the award to the date of payment.[131] Unless otherwise agreed by the parties, the arbitral tribunal is empowered to award costs which mean reasonable costs relating to the fees and expenses of the arbitrators and witnesses, legal fees and expenses, administration fees of the supervising institution and any other expenses in connection with the proceedings and the award.[132]

## 2.10. CHOICE OF LAW

The 1996 Act allows a choice of substantive law to parties in international commercial arbitration whether seated in or outside India.[133] This is not permissible for a domestic arbitration where Indian substantive law is mandatory.[134] An arbitral tribunal can decide *ex aequo et bono* or as *amiable compositeur* only if the parties authorise it to do so.[135]

## 2.11. JURISDICTION OF COURTS: CONFERMENT OF EXCLUSIVITY

Where two or more courts would have ordinarily had jurisdiction to decide the question forming the subject matter of the arbitration, the court before which an application is first made will be conferred with exclusive jurisdiction and any subsequent applications in respect of that arbitration cannot be made before any

128 Section 31(1) and (2), 1996 Act.
129 Section 31(3), 1996 Act.
130 Section 31(6) and (7), 1996 Act.
131 Section 31(7)(b), 1996 Act.
132 Section 31(8), 1996 Act.
133 Section 28(1)(b), 1996 Act. See above under Statutory Framework, for the meaning of 'international commercial arbitration' under the 1996 Act.
134 Section 28(1)(a), 1996 Act.
135 Section 28(2), 1996 Act.

other court.[136] There are limited exceptions to section 42.[137] The venue of arbitration is not relevant in determining the jurisdiction of a 'court', under section 2(1)(e) of the 1996 Act.[138] The definition of 'court' includes the High Court.[139]

## 2.12. CHALLENGE OF AN AWARD

### *2.12.1. Grounds of challenge*

The grounds for challenging an award are in section 34 of the 1996 Act[140] (corresponding to Article 34 of the UNCITRAL Model Law). Interpretation of this provision has however led to a more intrusive judicial review than envisioned by Parliament.

### *2.12.2. Composition and procedure of tribunal*

Where the composition of the tribunal or its procedure is in conformity with the agreement of the parties, there is no right to challenge the award unless the

136 Section 42, 1996 Act, *Deepak Mitra v. D.J. Allahabad*, AIR 2000 All 9, 18.

137 *P. Anand Gajapathi Raju v. P.V.G. Raju* (2000) 4 SCC 539, 543, *Pandey & Co. Builders Pvt Ltd v. State of Bihar* (2007) 1 SCC 467, 474.

138 *GE Countrywide Consumer Financial Services Ltd v. S.S. Bhatia* (2006) 2 ArbLR 170 (Del), 175; *Apparel Export Promotion Council v. Prabhati Patni* (2005) 3 ArbLR 518 (Del), 530. However for a contrary view see *Paramita Constructions Pvt Ltd v. UE Development India Pvt Ltd* (2008) 3 ArbLR 522 (AP), 530–1.

139 Section 2(1)(e), 1996 Act, *Sundaram Finance Ltd v. M.K. Kurian*, AIR 2006 Mad 218, 220 (DB), *Fountain Head Developers v. Maria Arcangela Seqieura* (2007) 3 Bom CR 393, 399–400.

140 '34. Application for setting aside arbitral award. [...] (2) An arbitral award may be set aside by the Court only if – (a) the party making the application furnishes proof that – (i) a party was under some incapacity, or (ii) the arbitration agreement is not valid under the law to which the parties have subjected it or, failing any indication thereon, under the law for the time being in force; or (iii) the party making the application was not given proper notice of the appointment of an arbitrator or of the arbitral proceedings or was otherwise unable to present his case; or (iv) the arbitral award deals with a dispute not contemplated by or not falling within the terms of the submission to arbitration, or it contains decisions on matter beyond the scope of the submission to arbitration: Provided that, if the decisions on matters submitted to arbitration can be separated from those not so submitted, only that part of the arbitral award which contains decisions on matters not submitted to arbitration may be set aside; or (v) the composition of the arbitral tribunal or the arbitral procedure was not in accordance with the agreement of the parties, unless such agreement was in conflict with a provision of this Part from which the parties cannot derogate, or, failing such agreement, was not in accordance with this Part; or (b) the Court finds that – (i) the subject-matter of the dispute is not capable of settlement by arbitration under the law for the time being in force, or (ii) the arbitral award is in conflict with the public policy of India. Explanation. Without prejudice to the generality of sub-clause (ii), it is hereby declared, for the avoidance of any doubt, that an award is in conflict with the public policy of India if the making of the award was induced of affected by fraud or corruption or was in violation of section 75 or section 81.'

agreement is in conflict with a mandatory provision of the 1996 Act. Accordingly, holding the number of arbitrators prescribed in section 10 of the 1996 Act to be a provision which can be derogated from, the Supreme Court refused to set aside an award on the ground that it had been passed by a tribunal consisting of only two arbitrators.[141]

### *2.12.3. Public policy*

The term 'public policy of India' used in section 34(2)(b)(ii) is undefined. In *Renusagar Power Co Ltd v. General Electric Co.*,[142] construing an identical provision contained in section 7(1)(b)(ii) of the Foreign Awards Act, the Supreme Court held that the term 'public policy' meant more than mere contravention of law. It was held that a foreign award would not be enforced on the ground that it was contrary to the public policy of India if its enforcement would be contrary to (a) a fundamental policy of Indian law; (b) the interests of India; or (c) justice or morality. In a later decision the Supreme Court clarified that the term 'public policy' in section 7(1)(b)(ii) meant 'public policy of India' and could not be extended to include the public policy of any foreign country.[143]

### *2.12.4.* Saw Pipes*: wider review of awards*

Although the language of section 34(2)(b)(ii) was identical, in *Oil & Natural Gas Corporation Ltd v. Saw Pipes Ltd*,[144] while considering a challenge to an award under section 34 of the 1996 Act, the Supreme Court interpreted the words 'public policy' widely and held that, in addition to the grounds enumerated in *Renusagar*, an award could be set aside if it was patently illegal and such illegality went to 'the root of the matter' or was so unfair and unreasonable that it shocked the conscience of the court. The expansive meaning given to the phrase 'public policy' by the Supreme Court in *Saw Pipes* has been criticised on the basis that it converts the proceedings under section 34 of the 1996 Act into a fully fledged appeal and frustrates the very purpose of the 1996 Act. Even under Indian law public policy is to be invoked only '*in clear and incontestable cases of harm to the public*'.[145]

In *McDermott International Inc. v. Burn Standard Co. Ltd*[146] the Supreme Court clarified that courts only had a limited supervisory role under the 1996

141 *Narayan Prasad Lohia v. Nikunj Kumar Lohia* (2002) 3 SCC 572, 582–583.

142 1994 Supp (1) SCC 644, 681–682.

143 *Smita Conductors Ltd v. Euro Alloys Ltd* (2001) 7 SCC 728, 738.

144 (2003) 5 SCC 705, 727–728; A better approach was that adopted by the Bombay High Court in *Vijaya Bank v. Maker Development Services Pvt Ltd* (2001) 3 BomCR 652, 666, wherein the narrower concept of international public policy was preferred even under section 34(2)(b)(ii) of the 1996 Act. This decision is no longer good law after *Saw Pipes, supra*.

145 *Ghetulal Parekh v. Mahadeodas Mauja*, AIR 1959 SC 781, 795.

146 (2006) 11 SCC 181, 208.

Act and the intervention of courts was to be of a minimal level and in limited circumstances only, e.g. in the case of fraud or bias by the arbitrators, violation of natural justice, etc. Nevertheless the Supreme Court did not reconsider *Saw Pipes*,[147] and in fact added two new heads under which an award could be set aside, viz where the reasons given were vitiated by perversity in evidence and whether the award was vitiated by internal contradictions.

In *Saw Pipes* it was clarified that an illegality must go to the root of the matter for it to be considered as in conflict with public policy and accordingly a mere error of law or a trivial illegality, even though it may be apparent on the face of an award, cannot be made a ground of interference under section 34(2)(b)(ii).[148] Further, public policy cannot be invoked to set aside an award on the ground that the reasons given by an arbitrator are not reasonable.[149] Despite the foregoing and the clarification in *McDermott* that only a minimal level of intervention by courts was permissible, several courts in India have given the term 'patent illegality' a wide interpretation and have effectively re-introduced the ground of 'error of law apparent on the face of the award' into the 1996 Act.[150] In *Numaligarh Refinery Ltd v. Daelim Industrial Co. Ltd*,[151] despite accepting that courts will generally not interfere with findings of fact and will not substitute their interpretation of the contract for that of the arbitrator, the Supreme Court on the facts and circumstances of that case went into the merits of the case like an appellate court. It has been held that an award which is against the terms of the contract violates section 28(3) of the 1996 Act and is patently illegal and thus is contrary to the public policy of India.[152] It has also been held that an arbitral award can be set aside even if it is tainted with any material or patent irregularity, such as the failure to join a party that a court considers a necessary party.[153]

Though the Supreme Court has not overruled the decision in *Saw Pipes*, it has taken note of the criticism of the expansive meaning given to 'public policy'

---

147 It could not have, since the Bench hearing *McDermott* was of equal strength to that which had decided *Saw Pipes*: the Indian Supreme Court sits in benches of two or three or more judges, but not *en banc*. The largest bench of the Supreme Court has thus far been of thirteen judges.

148 *M.R. Power Projects v. State of Arunachal Pradesh* (2009) 4 Gau LR 154; *National Highways Authority of India v. Afcons Infrastructure Ltd* (2008) 3 ArbLR 56, 63; *Centrotrade Minerals & Metals Inc. v. Hindustan Copper Ltd* (2006) 11 SCC 245, 280.

149 *Moradabad Development Authority v. VR Construction & Engineering Co.* (2007) Supp ArbLR 80.

150 *Jagmohan Singh Gujral v. Satish Ashok Sabnis* (2004) 1 BomCR 307, 316; *Bharat M. Nagori v. Satish Ashok Sabnis* (2003) 6 BomCR 257, 260–261; *Damodar Valley Corporation v. Central Concrete & Allied Products Ltd* (2007) 3 Arb LR 531 (Cal), 542; *Vishal Exports Overseas Ltd v. Ind Agro Synergy Ltd* (2007) 3 ArbLR 502 (MP), 504.

151 (2007) 8 SCC 466, 483.

152 *J.G. Engineers (P) Ltd v. Union of India* (2011) 5 SCC 758, *Hindustan Zinc Ltd v. Friends Coal Carbonisation* (2006) 4 SCC 445, 450.

153 *Chief Signal v. Hytronics Enterprises* (2006) 2 ArbLR 343 (AP), 352; *Hindustan Shipyard Ltd v. Essar Oil Ltd* (2005) 1 RAJ 132 (AP), 147–148.

and has left the issue of reconsidering *Saw Pipes* to a larger bench of the Supreme Court.[154]

*Saw Pipes* construed section 28(1)(a) of the 1996 Act in a similar way to Article 28 of the UNCITRAL Model Law, both of which are essentially choice of law provisions, as imposing a mandate on arbitrators to apply substantive law without mistake. *Saw Pipes* is unclear as to whether the new head of 'patent illegality' is akin to an error of law. Indeed *Saw Pipes* recognises that an error of law is not an available ground of challenge under the 1996 Act.[155] The addition of the prefix 'patent' is not of much consequence since under the 1996 Act the award must state the reasons on which it is based and all reasoning will be patent.[156]

### *2.12.5. Partial setting aside of the award*

Where an award deals with and decides several claims separately and distinctly, the court may set aside the award in relation to some items and uphold the award to the extent that it is valid.[157]

### *2.12.6. Effect of the time limit in section 34(3)*

By virtue of section 34(1), an application for setting aside an award cannot be made beyond the time stipulated in section 34(3) of the 1996 Act.[158] However new grounds can be added by an amendment even though a fresh claim would be barred by limitation.[159]

## 2.13. EASY ENFORCEABILITY OF THE AWARD

Section 36 of the 1996 Act provides that an award becomes enforceable in the same manner as a decree of the court as soon as the limitation period under section 34 expires or if no application has been made thereunder. This makes available in the enforcement of an award, the full array of measures provided in law for execution of a decree of a court.

---

154 *McDermott International Inc. v. Burn Standard Co. Ltd* (2006) 11 SCC 181, 211; *Centrotrade Minerals & Metals Inc. v. Hindustan Copper Ltd* (2006) 11 SCC 245, 283.

155 *Saw Pipes, supra* n. 144, p. 736.

156 Section 31(3), 1996 Act.

157 *J.G. Engineers Pvt Ltd v. Union of India* (2011) 5 SCC 758, 775; *R.S. Jiwani v. Ircon International Ltd* (2010) 1 BomCR 529 (FB), 552–553.

158 *Union of India v. Popular Construction Co.* (2001) 8 SCC 470, 475.

159 *State of Maharashtra v. Hindustan Construction Co. Ltd* (2010) 4 SCC 518, 530.

## 2.14. RIGHT TO APPEAL UNDER SECTION 37

Section 37 of the 1996 Act enables a party aggrieved by an order of the arbitral tribunal accepting a plea under section 16(2) or 16(3), that it has no jurisdiction or is exceeding the scope of its authority, to immediately prefer an appeal to the court against this decision of the tribunal.[160] There is no right to appeal where such a plea is rejected. Under section 37, an appeal also lies against an order of the arbitral tribunal granting or refusing to grant an interim measure under section 17 of the 1996 Act. A second appeal from the decision of the court under section 37 to the High Court is not available. The High Court retains its supervisory and revisional jurisdiction under the CPC.[161]

## 2.15. PART I OF THE 1996 ACT AND ARBITRATIONS SEATED OUTSIDE INDIA

### *2.15.1. Position under the repealed Foreign Awards Act*

Under the 1940 Act read with the Foreign Awards Act, the Supreme Court had recognised the importance of the seat of an arbitration and held that in the absence of a specific choice of law to govern the conduct and procedure of the arbitration, the *lex arbitri* or the curial law of the arbitration proceedings (the law which governed the conduct of the arbitration) was the law of the country in which the arbitration was held and the courts of the seat would have jurisdiction in this regard.[162] It also held that the law governing the arbitration agreement would, in the absence of an intention to the contrary, follow the proper law of the main contract and all matters in respect of the arbitration agreement would be within the competence of the courts of the country whose laws so governed the arbitration agreement. In another case under the same Acts the Supreme Court held that the curial law operates during the continuance of proceedings before an arbitrator while the law governing the agreement to arbitrate would apply to the question of whether the dispute was arbitrable and for giving effect to the resultant award.[163]

These were decisions based on section 9(b) of the Foreign Awards Act which provided that the Foreign Awards Act would not apply to 'any award made on an arbitration agreement governed by the law of India'. Consequently, it was held that where the law governing the arbitration agreement was Indian, it was the

160 *Patel Engineering, supra* n. 40, p. 641; *McDermott International Inc., supra* n. 35.

161 *ITI Ltd. v. Siemens Public Communications Network Ltd* (2002) 5 SCC 510, 520; *Nirma Ltd v. Lurgi Lentjes Energietechnik GmbH* (2002) 5 SCC 520, 521.

162 *NTPC v. Singer Co.* (1992) 3 SCC 551, 564.

163 *Sumitomo Heavy Industries Ltd v. ONGC Ltd* (1998) 1 SCC 305, 313–314.

1940 Act that would apply for the purpose of enforcing or setting aside the award and not the Foreign Awards Act.

*2.15.2. The 1996 Act*

Section 2(2) of the 1996 Act provides that Part I of the 1996 Act applies where the place of arbitration is in India. There are no provisions in the 1996 Act that are akin to the provisions of section 9(b) of the Foreign Awards Act which stands repealed. Under the 1996 Act the Supreme Court initially held (in a case under section 11) that in the absence of an express choice of law governing the contract as a whole or the arbitration agreement, a rebuttable presumption arises that the parties had intended these laws to be the same as the law of the country where the arbitration was seated.[164]

*2.15.3.* Bhatia International: *Part I extended to foreign arbitrations*

However subsequently the issue of which law was to apply and which court had jurisdiction in an international commercial arbitration again arose under the 1996 Act. In *Bhatia International v. Bulk Trading SA*,[165] the Supreme Court rejected the contention that the provisions of Part I were restricted only to arbitrations in India.[166] The Supreme Court held that where the arbitration was in India, the provisions of Part I could not be derogated from and compulsorily applied, but in international commercial arbitrations held outside India parties were free to derogate from all or any of the provisions of Part I either by an express or implied agreement. The Supreme Court held that Indian Courts could grant interim relief under section 9 (in Part I of the 1996 Act) although the arbitration was in Paris.

In *Venture Global Engg. v. Satyam Computer Services Ltd*,[167] the Supreme Court interpreted the decision in *Bhatia International* to mean that absent an express or implied agreement to the contrary, parties could challenge an award under section 34 of Part I before an Indian court despite the fact that the arbitral proceedings had been conducted outside India. Although the agreement provided that the governing law was the law of the State of Michigan (USA), it also had a clause which provided that notwithstanding anything to the contrary in the agreement, the parties would at all times act in accordance with Indian law. This clause was held by the Supreme Court to override other clauses of the agreement including the clause relating to the settlement of disputes by arbitration and, therefore, it was found that enforcement of the award necessarily

164 *Shreejee Traco (I) Pvt Ltd v. Paperline International Inc.* (2003) 9 SCC 79, 82.

165 (2002) 4 SCC 105, 117, 123.

166 The Supreme Court relied on the fact that section 2(2) had omitted the word 'only' which appeared in Article 1(2) of the UNCITRAL Model Law, 119–121.

167 (2008) 4 SCC 190, 207–208.

had to be in India. Thus indirectly the provisions of section 9(b) of the Foreign Awards Act were resurrected and applied notwithstanding their repeal.

Following *Bhatia International*, it has been held that mere choice of a foreign seat or a foreign law to govern the main contract does not *ipso facto* exclude Part I of the 1996 Act, if other factors indicated that the parties intended that Part I of the 1996 Act was to apply.[168] Nevertheless, where the contract clearly elucidated an intention to exclude all or any of the provisions of Indian law, such agreement has been respected by Indian courts, which have held that Part I of the 1996 Act did not apply to such arbitrations. Parties may be held to have agreed to exclude Part I of the 1996 Act by their choice of a foreign law to govern the arbitration agreement or by their choice of a foreign curial law.[169]

168 *National Agricultural Coop. Marketing Federation India Ltd v. Gains Trading Ltd* (2007) 5 SCC 692, 697: Hong Kong but the clause referred to the 1996 Act. *Indtel Technical Services Pvt Ltd v. W.S. Atkins Rail Ltd* (2008) 10 SCC 308; *Citation Infowares Ltd v. Equinox Corpn* (2009) 7 SCC 220.

169 *Aurohill Global Commodities Ltd v. MSTC Ltd* (2007) 7 SCC 120, 124: foreign seat and arbitration governed by foreign law, meant that Part I was impliedly excluded; *Dozco India Pvt Ltd v. Doosan Infracore Co. Ltd* (2011) 6 SCC 179, 186: parties had agreed all three of these laws would be Korean law and that the seat of the arbitration would be Seoul, Korea, hence Part I was excluded; *Hardy Oil & Gas Ltd v. Hindustan Oil Exploration Co. Ltd* (2006) 1 GujLR 658 (Gujarat High Court): English law as the law governing the arbitration, London as the place of the arbitration and English as the language amounted to an agreement that the entire arbitral proceedings are to be governed by English law and Part I of the 1996 Act was excluded, although Indian law governed the main contract; *Videocon Industries Ltd v. Union of India* (2011) 6 SCC 161, 178: where the seat of the arbitration is not India, the express choice of a foreign law to govern the arbitration agreement will be sufficient to exclude the applicability of Part I of the 1996 Act notwithstanding a choice of Indian law as the proper law of the contract; *Yograj Infrastructure Ltd v. Ssang Yong Engg. & Construction Co. Ltd* (2011) 9 SCC 735, 750: although parties had agreed that their contract would be subject to the laws of India, the Supreme Court held that Part I of the 1996 Act would not apply since parties had agreed that the arbitration proceedings (i.e. the seat) would be in Singapore in accordance with the Singapore International Arbitration Centre Rules; *Prima Buildwell Pvt Ltd v. Lost City Developments LLC* (2011) 3 ArbLR 350 (Delhi): the curial law of an arbitration is determined by the seat of the arbitration and that choice of a seat of arbitration is akin to an exclusive jurisdiction clause, excluding Part I of the Indian Act; *Eitzen Bulk A/S v. Ashapura Minechem Ltd* (2012) 2 BomCR 168 (Bombay High Court): a clause providing for arbitration in London which stated that English law was to apply meant that the whole of Part I of the Indian Act was 'impliedly excluded' rejecting the contention that the clause was only restricted to the curial law; *Sakuma Exports Ltd v. Louis Dreyfus Commodities* (2012) 1 BomCR 547 (Bombay High Court), upheld on 6 August 2013 (Appeal No. 337 of 2013 in Arbitration Petition No. 636 of 2011): the arbitration was subject to the Rules of the Refined Sugar Association, London, the seat of the arbitration was England and the substantive law of the contract was English law, consequently it was held that the law governing the arbitration agreement was English law and the choice of an English seat excluded Part I of the 1996 Act.

### *2.15.4.* Bharat Aluminium: *Part I restricted to arbitrations in India*

In its judgment dated 6 September 2012, in *Bharat Aluminium Co. v. Kaiser Aluminium Technical Services,*[170] the Supreme Court prospectively overruled *Bhatia International* and *Venture Global* and held as follows:

(a) Part I of the 1996 Act applies only to arbitrations which have their seat in India – neither the venue of the hearings (which could be for convenience) nor any reference to the 1996 Act in the agreement affect this;
(b) there is complete segregation between the provisions of Part I and Part II of the 1996 Act;
(c) the provisions of section 9 in Part I are limited in their application only to arbitrations which are seated in India; they cannot be extended to international commercial arbitrations seated outside India; and
(d) no action for interim relief is available in India on the basis of an international commercial arbitration seated outside India.

The Supreme Court in *Bharat Aluminium* however declared the above law to apply only prospectively to arbitration agreements executed after its judgment.[171] Consequently, the law laid down in *Bhatia International* and *Venture Global* will continue to apply to pre-6 September 2012 arbitration agreements. This will lead to two different classes of foreign arbitrations and awards requiring differing treatment under the 1996 Act.[172]

## 2.16. RECOGNITION AND ENFORCEMENT OF FOREIGN AWARDS

Part II of the 1996 Act deals with the recognition and enforcement of foreign arbitration awards that are recognised under the New York Convention or the Geneva Convention, both conventions being schedules to the 1996 Act.

### *2.16.1. New York Convention awards*

In order for a foreign award to be recognised under the 1996 Act it must be on differences between persons arising out of legal relationships, whether contractual or not, considered as commercial under the law in force in India.[173] The award must also have been made pursuant to an agreement for arbitration to

170 Judgment of a five-judge Bench. (2012) 9 SCC 552.

171 The Supreme Court is the only court in India empowered to apply the doctrine of prospective overruling. It does so by the plenary power conferred on it by Article 142 of the Constitution of India to pass any order or decree, in any cause before it, to do complete justice.

172 Hence this paper contains commentary on the earlier position in law as well.

173 Section 44, 1996 Act.

which the New York Convention applies and it must be made in a territory to which the central government declares the New York Convention applies.[174] Not all arbitration agreements under the New York Convention are recognised, but only those that are on disputes considered 'commercial'. The term 'considered as commercial' has been given a very broad interpretation.[175] Nevertheless a matrimonial, family, cultural, social or political relationship would not be a commercial dispute, unless it is a dispute between family members in relation to a commercial venture.[176]

### *2.16.2. Conditions for enforcement of foreign awards*

Under section 48 of the 1996 Act (equivalent to Articles V and VI of the New York Convention), a court may refuse to enforce a foreign award against a party if the party proves to the court that:

(a) the parties to the arbitration agreement were under some incapacity or that the agreement is not a valid agreement under the law to which the parties have subjected it or failing any indication under the law of the country where the award was made;[177]
(b) proper notice of appointment of the arbitrator or of the arbitral proceedings were not given to him or that he was unable to present his case;
(c) the award deals with issues beyond the scope of the arbitration;
(d) the composition of the arbitral tribunal is not in accordance with the agreement or the law of the seat of the arbitration; or
(e) the award is not binding on him or has been set aside or suspended in the country in which the award was made.

In addition, the enforcement of the award can be refused if it would be contrary to the public policy of India or if its subject matter is not capable of being settled by arbitration in India. The expression 'public policy of India' used in section 48 is to be given a narrow meaning as in *Renusagar* and not that given in *Saw Pipes*.[178]

---

174 Section 44, 1996 Act, *National Ability SA v. Tinna Oil and Chemicals Ltd* (2008) 3 ArbLR 37 (Del), 4748.

175 *R.M. Investments & Trading Co. P. Ltd v. Boeing Co.* (1994) 4 SCC 541, 546–547.

176 *Mukesh H. Mehta v. Harendra H. Mehta* (1995) 5 CompLJ 517 (Bom) 525, upheld by the Supreme Court in *Harendra H. Mehta v. Mukesh H. Mehta* (1999) 5 SCC 108, 137.

177 This corresponds to Article V(1)(e) of the New York Convention. It has been held that the words 'under the law' refer to the procedural law governing the arbitration and not the substantive law: *International Electric Corporation v. Bridas Sociedad Anonima Petrolera Industrial y Commercial*, 745 F.Supp 172 (S.D.N.Y.) 1990, a view accepted by the Supreme Court in *Bharat Aluminum*, *supra* n. 170, paras. 150–157.

178 See n. 142. In *Phulchand Exports Ltd v. O.O.O. Patriot* (2011) 10 SCC 300, 309, the Supreme Court applied the *Saw Pipes* wider meaning of the term 'public policy' even to determine

### 2.16.3. *Prima facie approach whilst referring parties to arbitration*

When a court is seised of an action in respect of which the parties have made a New York Convention arbitration agreement, then at the request of either party the court may refer the proceedings to arbitration, unless the court finds that the agreement is null and void, inoperative or incapable of being performed.[179] Section 45 operates notwithstanding the provisions of Part I of the 1996 Act. Hence greater deference is given to arbitral proceedings in the case of a New York Convention arbitration and a judicial authority can intervene only where the arbitration agreement is 'null and void, inoperative or incapable of being performed'.

With a view to hearing matters at the pre-reference stage expeditiously, only a prima facie review by the court is required to determine whether the arbitral agreement is valid.[180] A final finding on the issue is reserved for the arbitral tribunal, which may need to make its decision based on foreign law. Where the court is of the prima facie view that the arbitration agreement is null and void, inoperative or incapable of being performed, it must afford full opportunity to the parties to lead evidence, then decide the question like a trial on the preliminary issue and pass a reasoned order, so that the affected person may challenge the order by way of an appeal under section 50(1)(a) of the 1996 Act.[181] However where the Court determines that the objections to the reference are not tenable and that the arbitration agreement is not null and void, inoperative or incapable of being performed, such determination attains finality and is not open to question by the arbitral tribunal. The Supreme Court has however now held that the ratio of *Patel Engineering* as regards finality under section 11(7) applies with equal force under section 45 as it does under section 8 of the 1996 Act.[182] To that extent the ratio of *Shin-Etsu* stands overruled.

### 2.16.4. *Geneva Convention awards*

Pursuant to sections 53–60 of the 1996 Act, foreign awards made under the Geneva Convention in relation to disputes considered to be commercial disputes under Indian law are recognised in India and can be enforced by Indian courts. Section 57 of the 1996 Act which provides for enforcement of Geneva Convention

enforceability of a foreign award. However, the *Renusagar* concept has been reinstated by the Supreme Court in *Shri Lal Mahal Ltd v. Progetto Grano SpA* (3 July 2013 in Civil Appeal No. 5085/2013) in which it was accepted by the Supreme Court that its decision in *Phulchand* was erroneous and that there was no ground of 'patent illegality' to reject enforcement of a foreign award.

179 Section 45, 1996 Act (corresponding to Article II(3) of the New York Convention).

180 *Shin-Etsu Chemical Co. Ltd v. Aksh Optifiber Ltd* (2005) 7 SCC 234, 266.

181 *Ibid.*, pp. 277–278 (*per* Dharmadhikari J concurring).

182 *Chloro Controls (I) P. Ltd v. Severn Trent Water Purification Inc. and others* (2013) 1 SCC 641, para. 130.

awards is similar to section 48 (applicable to New York Convention awards) except that enforcement can be refused not only if the award is contrary to the public policy of India but also if it is contrary to Indian law.

### 2.17. STATUTORY ARBITRATIONS

Several statutes provide for the settlement of claims or disputes by arbitration. Even if the statute makes no reference to the 1996 Act, section 2(4) of the 1996 Act deems such enactments to be arbitration agreements under the 1996 Act. Examples are found in sections 86(1)(f) and 158 of the Electricity Act 2003, section 11 of the Securitisation and Reconstruction of Financial Assets and Enforcement of Security Act 2002, section 6 of the Interest on Delayed Payments to Small Scale and Ancillary Industrial Undertakings Act 1993, and section 7B of the Indian Telegraphs Act 1885.

## 3. CONCILIATION

Conciliation requires a contract (by invitation and acceptance) between the parties.[183] The conciliator may be appointed by agreement between the parties or by an institution requested by the parties.[184] Under Part III of the 1996 Act, a conciliator can not only assist the parties to arrive at a settlement but is also permitted to make proposals for a settlement and to formulate or re-formulate the terms of a possible settlement.[185] Although provision is made for filing of statements and the broad procedure to be followed, a conciliator is not bound by the strict rules of procedure or evidence.[186] Confidentiality attaches to the proceedings and to the settlement agreement[187] and there are bars on the use of the content of conciliation proceedings as evidence in other proceedings.[188]

The settlement agreement signed by the parties has the same status and effect as an award on agreed terms under section 30.[189] Conciliation proceedings are terminated by the signing of a settlement agreement or by a written declaration of the conciliator or of both the parties.[190] No arbitral or judicial proceedings can be initiated during conciliation proceedings.[191] The conciliator is barred

183 Section 62, 1996 Act.
184 Section 64, 1996 Act.
185 Sections 72 and 73, 1996 Act, *United India Insurance Co. Ltd v. Ajay Sinha* (2008) 7 SCC 454, 463–464.
186 Sections 65, 66, 69 and 70, 1996 Act.
187 Section 75, 1996 Act.
188 Section 81, 1996 Act.
189 Section 74, 1996 Act.
190 Section 76, 1996 Act.
191 Section 77, 1996 Act.

from acting as arbitrator or representative of any party or from being called as a witness in any arbitral or judicial proceedings.[192]

## 4. PROPOSED AMENDMENTS

The Ministry of Law and Justice of the Union of India is in the process of considering several substantial amendments to the 1996 Act necessitated by the problems that have arisen in its implementation and by the recommendations contained in the 176th Report of the Law Commission of India.

## 5. *LOK ADALATS*: COURT AND MEDIATOR

The LSA Act provides for settlement of disputes by *Lok Adalats* or 'Peoples Courts', a form of adjudication that was prevalent in ancient India.[193] The benefits of the *Lok Adalat* system have been enumerated by the Supreme Court as follows:[194]

> '1. There is no Court fee and if Court fee is already paid the amount will be refunded if the dispute is settled at *Lok Adalat* according to the rules.
> 2. The basic features of *Lok Adalat* are the procedural flexibility and speedy trial of the disputes. There is no strict application of procedural laws like the Civil Procedure Code and Evidence Act while assessing the claim by *Lok Adalat*.
> 3. The parties to the dispute can directly interact with the Judge through their Counsel which is not possible in regular Courts of law.
> 4. The award by the *Lok Adalat* is binding on the parties and it has the status of a decree of a Civil Court and it is non-appealable which does not cause the delay in the settlement of disputes finally.'

The method of settlement followed by the *Lok Adalat* is to guide and persuade the parties, with reference to principles of justice, equity and fair play, to compromise and settle their disputes by explaining the pros and cons, strengths and weaknesses, and advantages and disadvantages of their respective claims.[195] The *Lok Adalats* have powers similar to a Civil Court, although not identical.[196] An award passed by the *Lok Adalat* is conclusive, binding and has the same effect as a decree on compromise between the parties.[197] Section 20(5) of the LSA

---

192 Section 80, 1996 Act.
193 *P.T. Thomas v. Thomas Job* (2005) 6 SCC 478, 485–486.
194 *Ibid.*
195 *State of Punjab v. Jalour Singh* (2008) 2 SCC 660, 665.
196 Section 22, LSA Act.
197 Section 21 and 22E, LSA Act; *P.T. Thomas*, *supra* n. 193.

Act recognises the right of a party whose case is not settled before the *Lok Adalat* to have his case continued before the court and obtain a decision on the merits.[198] While functioning as members of *Lok Adalats*, judges are merely statutory conciliators and ought not to find fault with any particular litigant or make a record of the conduct of any litigant during negotiations in their failure report which might prejudice the mind of the court while hearing the case.[199] *Lok Adalats* are organised for such areas, at such intervals and with such jurisdiction as certain specified authorities (such as the Supreme/High Court Legal Services Committee) think fit.[200] Additionally the Central or State Authorities can establish permanent *Lok Adalats*.[201]

The jurisdiction of *Lok Adalats* has been extended to settlement of certain criminal matters and to cases referred by various courts and tribunals such as the family court (matrimonial disputes), consumer forum (consumer complaints), motor accident tribunal (accident claims), and the rent control court (disputes between landlord and tenant).[202] The award passed by the *Lok Adalat* based on a compromise has to be treated as a decree capable of execution by a civil court.

## 6. REFERENCE TO ADR BY A COURT

Section 89 and Order 10, Rule 1-A of the CPC enables a court to refer parties to alternative dispute resolution processes to settle their disputes.[203] Where it appears to the court that elements of a settlement which may be acceptable to the

198 *B.P. Moideen Sevamandir v. A.M. Kutty Hassan* (2009) 2 SCC 198, 204.

199 *Ibid.*

200 Section 19, LSA Act.

201 Section 22B, LSA Act.

202 *K.N. Govindan Kutty Menon v. C.D. Shaji* (2012) 2 SCC 51, 59–60.

203 'Section 89. Settlement of disputes outside the Court. (1) Where it appears to the court that there exist elements of a settlement which may be acceptable to the parties, the court shall formulate the terms of settlement and give them to the parties for their observations and after receiving the observation of the parties, the court may reformulate the terms of a possible settlement and refer the same for – (a) arbitration; (b) conciliation; (c) judicial settlement including settlement through *Lok Adalat*; or (d) mediation. (2) Where a dispute had been referred – (a) for arbitration or conciliation, the provisions of the Arbitration and Conciliation Act, 1996 shall apply as if the proceedings for arbitration or conciliation were referred for settlement under the provisions of that Act; (b) to *Lok Adalat*, the court shall refer the same to the *Lok Adalat* in accordance with the provisions of sub-section (1) of section 20 of the Legal Services Authority Act, 1987 and all other provisions of that Act shall apply in respect of the dispute so referred to the *Lok Adalat*; (c) for judicial settlement, the court shall refer the same to a suitable institution or person and such institution or person shall be deemed to be a *Lok Adalat* and all the provisions of the Legal Services Authority Act, 1987 shall apply as if the dispute were referred to a *Lok Adalat* under the provisions of that Act; (d) for mediation, the court shall effect a compromise between the parties and shall follow such procedure as may be prescribed. Order X, Rule 1A. Direction of the Court to opt for any one mode of alternative dispute resolution. After recording the admissions and denials, the court shall direct the parties to the suit to opt either mode of the settlement outside the court as specified

parties exists, the parties, at the instance of the court, are to be made to apply their minds so as to opt for one of the ADR methods mentioned in the section and if the parties do not agree then the court will itself refer them.[204] There cannot, however, be a reference to arbitration or conciliation under section 89 unless there is mutual consent of the parties for such a reference.[205] As a result the ADR process in section 89 has been 'a non-starter with many courts'.[206] If the parties agree to arbitration, the provisions of the 1996 Act will apply after the stage of reference and the case will move outside the stream of the court.[207] However, if the matter is referred to conciliation, mediation or judicial settlement and an amicable settlement is not arrived at despite efforts being made, the dispute will ultimately go to trial.[208]

In *Salem Advocates Bar Association*,[209] the Supreme Court considered the operation of section 89 of the CPC and recommended model rules which may be adopted by the High Courts to give effect to it. Pursuant thereto model rules have been framed.[210] These have been adopted by several High Courts. Many High Courts have also established mediation centres with infrastructure for conducting mediations on a formal basis. The Supreme Court has framed a detailed procedure as guidelines for courts under section 89 which requires the mutual consent of litigants for a settlement to be concluded or for a reference to arbitration.[211] Thus the essentially consensual nature of arbitration is not affected by section 89.

## 7. CURRENT SITUATION

Recalling his days as a young lawyer, Mohandas Karamchand Gandhi wrote that 'the true function of a lawyer was to unite parties riven asunder [...] a large part of my time during the twenty years of my practice as a lawyer was occupied in bringing about private compromises of hundreds of cases. I lost nothing thereby – not even money, certainly not my soul'.[212] That dream has been slow to take root in India, but ADR is now here to stay. Perhaps the greatest success has been achieved by the *Lok Adalats* which have resolved millions of smaller disputes. Until the proposed amendments are made to the 1996 Act, it is

in sub-section (1) of section 89. On the option of the parties, the court shall fix the date of appearance before such forum or authority as may be opted by the parties.'

204 *Salem Advocates Bar Association v. Union of India* (2003) 1 SCC 49.

205 *Afcons Infrastructure Ltd v. Cherian Varkey Construction Co. (P) Ltd* (2010) 8 SCC 24, 48.

206 *Ibid.*

207 *Salem Advocates Bar Association*, *supra* n. 204, p. 55.

208 *Ibid.*, p. 41; *Afcons Infrastructure*, *supra* n. 205.

209 *Supra* n. 204, pp. 55–57.

210 Civil Procedure Alternative Dispute Resolution & Mediation Rules, 2006.

211 *Afcons Infrastructure*, *supra* n. 205, pp. 45–47.

212 M. Gandhi, *The Story of My Experiments with Truth*, 1927, reprint June 1996, p. 112.

expected that the arbitration experience in India will continue to yield mixed results. What is cause for optimism is the widespread recognition amongst litigants and lawyers that dispute resolution, and not litigation, is the preferred option in the Indian legal system.

# INDONESIA

Marcella Elwina Simandjuntak, Valentinus Suroto and B. Resti Nurhayati

**Contents**

## 1. INTRODUCTION

The development of alternative dispute resolution in Indonesia started with the enactment of Act No. 30 of 1999 on Arbitration and Alternative Dispute Resolution (the Arbitration Act). Before the enactment of the Act, dispute resolution was commonly done only in court through the litigation process. The purpose of this chapter is to describe how ADR has developed in Indonesia since the enactment of the Arbitration Act. In addition, this chapter also describes the regulation and various kinds of alternative dispute resolution. First and foremost, however, this chapter will discuss the development of dispute resolution in court. It should be noted that in Indonesia, methods of ADR such as reconciliation and mediation are integrated in the court process. ADR is used to avoid the courts being flooded with cases, and to help break deadlock between the parties. This is in line with the nature of the Indonesian judicial system, i.e. fast, simple, and inexpensive.[1]

In the past few years, there has been significant development and progress in out-of-court dispute resolution. It is true that at present, out-of-court dispute resolution is mainly focused on civil cases, especially those cases related to trade. Although there are many ways to resolve criminal cases using ADR, in Indonesia, these methods have not been adopted. However, the government recently enacted Act No. 11 of 2012 on Juvenile Justice, based on the concept of restorative justice. The Act provides for the possibility for children or juveniles who are charged with crimes to have their trials outside the court without undergoing the process of litigation.

Even though ADR has become increasingly popular in the past few years, if we trace its history, it is clear that indigenous and rural societies have used ADR mechanisms like mediation for a long time, and still today they use this mediation to resolve personal disutes and minor criminal cases. This will be discussed further in the following sections.

---

1 Before discussing this further, it is important to categorise various types of disputes. While ADR can be used in both civil and criminal disputes, in criminal disputes it is limited to indigenous societies. We could distinguish between several types of disputes depending on the kind of legal personality involved in the dispute. The first type covers private law disputes between legal personalities, namely natural persons and legal entities. This type of dispute is commonly referred to as a private dispute and is characterised by the absence of public authorities. The second type covers disputes between legal personalities under criminal law and can be referred to as a public-initiated dispute or, more popularly, a criminal case. This kind of dispute concerns an individual brought to trial on the initiative of the State. The third type of dispute is dispute between legal personalities under constitutional law; this kind of dispute involves institutions of the State. The fourth type is a dispute between the State as defendant and an individual as plaintiff, which some scholars refer to as a public defendant dispute. The final type is a dispute between legal personalities under international law, which is referred to as an international dispute to which the resolution, mechanism and institutions are completely different from other types of dispute. See also H. Juwana, *Dispute Resolution Process in Indonesia*, IDE Asian Law Series No. 21, Institute of Developing Economies (IDE-Jetro), Japan 2003, pp. 1–2.

# 2. DISPUTE RESOLUTION MECHANISMS IN INDONESIA

As already mentioned, in Indonesia, legal disputes, especially in civil cases, can be examined and decided both in court (litigation) and outside court (non-litigation). As a country formerly colonised by the Dutch for more than 300 hundred years, it must be understood that the Indonesian judicial system has many things in common with the judicial systems of the European countries that use the civil law system.

## 2.1. DISPUTE RESOLUTION IN COURT

The legal basis of dispute resolution through litigation in Indonesia is Article 10 of Act No. 48 of 2009 on Judicial Powers. The Article states that:

> '(1) The court cannot deny the investigation, trial and decision of any case by stating that there is no legal basis for a particular case or that the legal basis is not clear; instead, the court must investigate and and hold the trial for the case.
> (2) The provision as stated in article (1) does not prevent any efforts to resolve the civil case by reconciliation.'

Some legal experts argue that this means that whatever the case, the dispute 'should' be examined in court and the use of reconciliation should be considered as an 'exception'. But since the enactment of the Supreme Court Regulations No. 1 of 2008 on Court-Annexed Mediation Procedure (PERMA), every process of dispute resolution in the court should first be aimed at achieving reconciliation.

Based on Article 18 of Act No. 48 of 2009 on Judicial Powers, there are five types of courts or tribunals in Indonesia. The courts and tribunals have their own jurisdictions called *peradilan*. The five courts are divided on the basis of absolute competence of the court to examine or execute a case. Article 18 clearly states that: 'the judicial power in Indonesia consists of the Supreme Court and the courts under the Supreme Court such as the General Court, Religious Court, Military Court, Administrative Court, and Constitutional Court.'

The General Court has the right to investigate and decide civil and criminal cases. This includes any cases related to family law such as a child custody, divorce, division of wealth between husbands and wives, etc. In terms of familial cases, the General Court applies to non-Muslim families. In addition, the General Court has the right to investigate and decide criminal cases and cases related to trade and business disputes. One of the departments in the General Court, for example, is the Trade Court which has the right to investigate and decide bankcruptcy cases based on Act No. 37 of 2004 on Bankruptcy and Postponement of Debt Payment and Intellectual Property Rights cases. Under the General Court there is also the Children's Court whose purpose is to investigate children's criminal cases, the Human Rights Court which has the power to investigate and decide cases involving violations of human rights (based on Act No. 26 of 2000 on the Human Rights Court), and the Corruption Court which is in charge of investigating and deciding corruption cases.

The role of the Religious Court is to decide cases related to family disputes such as the custody of children, inheritance, divorce and the division of wealth between husbands and wives or the wealth accumulated during marriage for Muslims. The Military Court has the right to decide offences committed by military personnel or the army and police. This includes both military cases based on the Military Penal Code and cases which are not fully related to military cases but which have a connection with military issues. However, since the enactment of Act No. 48 of 2009, even the General Court has the right to investigate and decide any cases related to military personnel, depending on the types of violation. In this case, the General Court has a broader scope as it possesses the right to investigate civil cases involving non-Muslims and criminal cases other than those involving military personnel which should be examined and decided under the Military Penal Code.

The Administrative Court has the authority to investigate any disputes in State administration between natural or legal persons and agencies or officials of State administration as a result of a decision which is considered to violate the rights of the natural or legal person. The Administrative Court was created to protect those who are disadvantaged by a decision of State administration. Another court is the Constitutional Court which is responsible for the judicial review of acts or regulations which are considered to be unconstitutional.

In addition to the types of courts above, Aceh, based on the special autonomous nature of the Nanggroe Aceh Darussalam Province, has a Shari'ah Court. This court has the right to investigate and decide cases resulting from violation of the Shari'ah law as already regulated in certain Qanun (a compliation of several provisions) which applies only in this province. Cases that can be solved by the Shari'ah Court are gambling cases (*maisir*), liquor cases (*khmer*), and seclusion cases – based on the Qanun, a man and a woman who are not married must not be together in a secluded place without a third person.

In order to regulate the court in detail, Act No. 2 of 1986 was enacted. This Act is on the General Court, and was later amended by Act No. 8 of 2004. In addition, Act No. 14 of 1985 on the Supreme Court was enacted, and was updated and amended by Act No. 5 of 2004 and Act No. 3 of 2009.

Hierarchically, the resolution or investigation of a case in court is executed in two levels. The first level is the State Court; if any parties in dispute want to appeal, they can go to the second level or High Court. This applies to any Court under the General Court and the Religious Court. In general, the State Court and High Court examine the facts or what is usually referred to as *judex factie*.

Further, any disadvantaged parties in the High Court can appeal to the Supreme Court (known as a cassation). The cassation examination is often called as *judex juris*. There are various reasons why cassation examinations may overturn the decision of the lower court: (a) the court is considered not to have the right or to have gone beyond its right to examine and decide the case; (b) the court incorrectly applies the enacted law or is against the enacted law; and (c) the court does not fulfil all the requirements as regulated in an act or regulation. Thus, according to their hierarchies, vertically every court is divided into three categories (levels), i.e. State Court, High Court, and Supreme Court.

Legal practitioners understand that the resolution of a case in court has many weaknesses. Nevertheless, it avoids vigilantism (*eigenrichting*). The weaknesses of dispute resolution in court, especially for civil cases in Indonesia, are that it is time consuming, costly, and moreover difficult to enforce. Another weakness is severe delay in the investigation of cases due to too many cases in court. The following table demonstrates the number of cases in the State Court, High Court, and Supreme Court for the period of 2010–2011 based on the Annual Report of the Supreme Court of the Republic of Indonesia.[2]

Based on this Annual Report, the total number of cases received by all courts all over Indonesia in 2011 was 5,319,522. There were 113,300 unresolved cases from 2010 plus 5,206,222 new cases. There was a 70.60% increase in the number of cases from 2010 in which the total number was 3,051,717. The number of cases received by State Courts and High Courts throughout Indonesia in 2011 was as follows:

**Table 1. Details of incoming cases in every type of Court**

| Types of Courts | Unresolved Cases 2010 | Incoming Cases 2011 | Number | Resolved | Unresolved |
|---|---|---|---|---|---|
| General | 37,307 | 4,816,804 | 4,854,111 | 4,808,881 | 45,230 |
| Religious | 62,959 | 363,249 | 426,208 | 353,933 | 72,257 |
| Military | 497 | 2,932 | 3,429 | 3,000 | 429 |
| Administrative | 438 | 1,432 | 1,870 | 1,428 | 442 |
| Tax (uder the General Court) | 9,466 | 7,065 | 16,531 | 7,724 | 8,807 |
| **Total** | 110,667 | 5,191,482 | 5,302,149 | 5,174,996 | 127,183 |

2 Supreme Court of the Republic of Indonesia, Annual Report 2011, Executive Summary, Jakarta 2011, pp. 8–29.

**Table 2. Total number of cases that had to be resolved by the State Court and High Court in 2011**

| Level of Court | Unresolved Cases 2010 | Incoming Cases 2011 | Number | Resolved | Unresolved |
|---|---|---|---|---|---|
| State Court | 110,667 | 5,191,482 | 5,302,149 | 5,174,966 | 127,183 |
| High Court | 2,633 | 14,740 | 17,373 | 14,300 | 3,073 |
| **Total** | 113,300 | 5,206,222 | 5,319,522 | 5,189,266 | 130,256 |

Table 2 shows the total number of cases that had to be resolved by the State Court and High Court in 2011. From Table 3, it can be seen that the number of incoming cases in the Supreme Court in 2011 was 12,990 (in all types of courts, i.e. General, Religious, Military and State Administration). Surprisingly there was a 4.04% decrease in the number of cases compared to 2010. This is the first decrease in the number of cases in the last decade. In the past, the number of cases that came to the Supreme Court of the Republic of Indonesia increased every year. However, the phenomenon is in contrast with the number of the incoming cases to the State Court and High Court which increased significantly.

**Table 3. Cases based on authority in the Supreme Court of the Republic of Indonesia in 2011**

| No. | Types of Authority | Unresolved Cases 2010 | Incoming Cases 2011 | Load of Cases | Resolved | Unresolved |
|---|---|---|---|---|---|---|
| A. | Cases | | | | | |
| 1. | Cassation | 6,479 | 10,336 | 16,815 | 10,968 | 5,805 |
| 2. | Revision/*Herziening* | 1,935 | 2,540 | 4,475 | 2,648 | 1,827 |
| 3. | Pardon/*Gratie* | 10 | 64 | 74 | 57 | 17 |
| 4. | Judicial Review | – | 50 | 50 | 46 | 4 |
| | **Total** | 8,424 | 12,990 | 21,414 | 13,719 | 7,695 |
| B. | Non-cases | | | | | |
| | Petition of Fatwa | – | 221 | 221 | 221 | 0 |
| | **Total** | | 221 | 221 | 221 | 0 |

To avoid the delay in resolving cases – in line with the idea that 'justice delayed is justice denied' – ADR was introduced as one of the efforts to give justice to those in need. The increase in the number of cases and the delay in the cases' investigation in court as discussed above gives us an idea of the importance of ADR in overcoming the weaknesses of the litigation process.

## 2.2. TYPES OF ADR

In the 'modern law' era, arbitration was the first method of ADR introduced in Indonesia, and appeared before other alternatives such as mediation. Before and after independence, arbitration was regulated and used as a method of resolution for civil and trade disputes as regulated in Articles 615–651 of the Civil Procedure Regulations (*Reglement op de Rechtsvordering, Staatblad 1847:52*), Article 377 of the Revised Regulations of Indonesia (*Het Herziene Indonesische Reglement, Staatblad 1941:44*), and Article 705 of the Regulations for Territories Outside Java and Madura (*Rechtsreglement Buitengewesten, Staatblad 1927:227*). All of those were created and enforced when Indonesia was still under Dutch colonial rule. Article 377 HIR and/or Article 705 RBg emphasise that the disputing parties can resolve their cases through an arbitrator or an arbitration in which the arbitration has the function of and the right to resolve cases in the form of decision (decree).[3] In addition, there was also a regulation stating that the disputing parties or arbitrators are subject to procedural law applied to Europeans (Dutch colonists). But since 1999, the legal basis of dispute resolution through arbitration and other methods of ADR is Act No. 30 of 1999 on Arbitration and Alternative Dispute Resolution.

Some experts state that the name of Act No. 30 of 1999 on Arbitration and Alternative Dispute Resolution causes confusion because it differentiates arbitration from other methods of ADR. In fact, arbitration is only one of many types of the available methods of ADR. Moreover, Act No. 30 of 1999 contains more regulation concerning arbitration compared to other methods of ADR. The other methods of ADR mentioned in the Act are consultation, mediation, conciliation, and expert judgement.

### *2.2.1. Arbitration*

According to Act No. 30 of 1999, arbitration is a way of resolving civil/private disputes outside of the general court which is based on a written arbitration agreement between the parties involved in the dispute. Arbitration as regulated in Act No. 30 of 1999 covers both national and international disputes relating to trade, banking, finance, investment, industry and intellectual property rights. All of these are based on Article 5 which states that the disputes that can be resolved with arbitration are those related to trade and in which the parties in dispute, according to the law, have absolute ownership. The cases that cannot be resolved by arbitration agencies are cases which, according to the law, cannot be resolved with reconciliation.

According to Article 3 of the Arbitration Act, the High Court or State Court has no right to resolve any dispute between parties that already have an

3 M.Y. Harahap, *Arbitrase*, Pustaka Kartini, Jakarta 1991, p. 22.

arbitration agreement. This demonstrates the power of the arbitration institution; where the parties have chosen arbitration, the State will not intervene. This respects party autonomy and freedom to pursue different methods of dispute resolution. In addition, the speed of decision-making and the privacy and confidentiality associated with arbitration have led to its popularity amongst the business community.

Resolution through arbitration requires an arbitration agreement between the parties involved in the dispute. An arbitration agreement is an agreement in the form of an arbitration clause in a written agreement signed by the parties before the dispute occurs, or it is in itself an arbitration agreement signed by the parties after the dispute happens. Therefore, based on the time when an agreement is made, in practice there are two kinds of arbitration in Indonesia, i.e. *pactum de compromittendo* and deed of compromise. The difference between the two lies in the time when the agreement is made. A *pactum de compromittendo* is created before the dispute occurs, whereas a deed of compromise is created after the dispute arises. The requirement of a written arbitration agreement is stated in Article 7: 'In the event that a dispute arises, or has arisen, the parties agree to resolve the dispute with arbitration by means of a written agreement signed by the parties involved in the dispute.'

In practice, an arbitration agreement is executed by writing an arbitration clause into the agreement. The use of the term 'arbitration clause' means that the primary agreement is followed or supplemented by an agreement about how to carry out the arbitration in resolving disputes between the parties.[4] According to Suyud Margono, arbitration clauses regulate the particular arbitration bodies to be appointed when disputes arise, the location where the arbitration will take place, the law and regulations that will be used, the qualification of the arbitrators, and the language which will be used in the arbitration process.[5]

In practice, there are two types of arbitration in Indonesia. The first is ad hoc arbitration or, as it is often called, voluntary arbitration. This type of arbitration is used to resolve or decide a particular case. The second type is institutional arbitration, which is arbitration by a permanent arbitral body. The arbitral body is an institution which is created for the purpose of hearing disputes following an agreement between the parties for their dispute to be dealt with outside the court.[6] One of the permanent arbitration institutions in Indonesia is BANI, or Badan Arbitrase Nasional Indonesia (Indonesian National Arbitration Body). Even though permanent arbitral bodies like BANI have existed for a long time in Indonesia, the number of cases investigated and resolved by BANI is still relatively small compared to the number of cases investigated and resolved by

---

4 S. Margono, *Penyelesaian Sengketa Bisnis Alternative Dispute Resolution: Teknik dan Strategi dalam Negoisasi, Mediasi dan Arbitrase*, Ghalia Indonesia, Jakarta 2010, p. 147.

5 As stated by Suyud Margono in F.H. Winarta, *Hukum Penyelesaian Sengketa Arbitrase Nasional Indonesia dan Internasional*, Sinar Grafika, Jakarta 2010, p. 42.

6 M.Y. Harahap, *supra* n. 3, p. 151.

the court. The following table shows the number of cases investigated and resolved by BANI from 2008 to 2011 as reported by the Board of BANI Arbitration Centre, Krisnawenda:

**Table 4. Number of cases registered, revoked, struck out and resolved by BANI**

| Year | Cases Registered | Cases Revoked | Cases Erased | Cases Resolved |
|---|---|---|---|---|
| 2008 | 19 | 1 | 5 | 13 |
| 2009 | 44 | 5 | 4 | 35 |
| 2010 | 41 | 4 | 4 | 33 |
| 2011 | 58 | 3 | 5 | 40 |
| 2012–July | 36 | 3 | – | 2 |

Arbitration procedure begins with the filing of the dispute with the Arbitration Panel chosen by the parties. Subekti points out that the filing should include at least (a) the complete names and addresses of the parties in dispute; (b) a short description of the dispute; and (c) what the parties in dispute claim.[7] In the filing, they must attach a copy of the agreement or the deed of agreement which particulary includes the arbitration clause. If the filing is done by the representatives of the parties, the person lodging the claim must have a special power of attorney for that purpose. After examining the case, the arbitration panel will decide the case based on the provision of law or based on justice and appropriateness.

The Arbitration Act states that the arbitration decision is final and legally binding on the parties. This means that if one of the parties does not comply with the decision willingly, the other party can ask the State Court to re-examine the decision.

### *2.2.2. Other types of ADR*

Although the Arbitration Act mentions other methods of ADR such as consultation, negotiation, mediation, conciliation and expert judgement, it does not define these terms (except arbitration, as discussed above). Other types of dispute resolution other than arbitration are only regulated in one chapter and one article of the Act, i.e. Chapter II, Article 6. Therefore their meaning or their definition can only be understood from legal doctrine or expert opinion. Further, this chapter only explains mediation but does not explain other types of dispute resolution. Chapter II, Article 6(1) of Act No. 30 of 1999 states that civil disputes or disagreements can be solved by the parties involved with alternative

---

7 As stated by Subekti in F.H. Winarta, *Hukum Penyelesaian Sengketa Arbitrase Nasional Indonesia dan Internasional*, Sinar Grafika, Jakarta 2011, p. 50.

dispute resolution based on the good faith to avoid litigation in the State Court. This particular part of the Act also states that ADR should be conducted by a face-to-face meeting of the parties within 14 days and the result of the meeting should be set forth in a written agreement.

#### 2.2.2.1. Consultation

Because the Arbitration Act does not explain the meaning of consultation, the meaning of this term can only be understood from experts' opinions. According to Gunawan Wijaya, consultation is a personal act between one party, the client, and another party, the consultant, who is able to meet the needs of the client. There is no regulation concerning the obligation to follow or comply with the opinions of the consultants. There is always a possibility that the clients will do what the consultants say; however, the clients are free to decide what is best for their own interests. This means that in a consultation, the role of the consultant in dispute resolution is not significant. The consultant only expresses his or her opinions then formulates the possible forms of dispute resolution the parties want if they ask the consultant to do so.[8]

#### 2.2.2.2. Negotiation

Negotiation is an ADR mechanism executed outside the court. In general, this type of dispute resolution is informal. There is no obligation for the parties to meet directly at the time the negotiation is being conducted. Through negotiation, the parties in dispute perform a re-assessment of their rights and obligations and expect a win-win solution by making a concession on their particular rights based on reciprocity. The agreement achieved in the negotiation is usually set forth in a written agreement and signed and executed by the parties involved in the dispute.[9] This agreement is final and binds the parties. Article 6(7) of the Arbitration Act, requires that this written agreement is registered at the State Court within 30 days of the date of the signing of the agreement. It also requires that the agreement must be executed within 30 days from the date that the agreement is registered at the State Court. Idrus Abdullah gives another opinion about negotiation: according to him, negotiation is a personal approach between the two parties in dispute to negotiate to resolve the dispute without involving a third party.[10]

---

8 G. Wijaya, *Alternatif Penyelesaian Sengketa*, Seri Hukum Bisnis, Raja Grafindo Persada, Jakarta 2005, pp. 86–87.

9 G. Wijaya, *supra* n. 8, p. 89.

10 I. Made Sukadana, 2012, *Mediasi Peradilan: Mediasi dalam Sistem Peradilan Perdata Indonesia dalam Rangka Mewujudkan Proses Peradilan yang Sederhana, Cepat, dan Biaya Ringan*, Prestasi Pustaka Publisher, Jakarta 2012, p. 17.

The Arbitration Act does not limit the scope of negotiation. But according to Gunawan Wijaya, based on Article 5, it is appropriate to say that anything which is in accordance with law and which can be resolved with an 'agreement' can be negotiated. Because it is an agreement between two parties, the result of negotiation cannot be denied due to the oversight of the law or because of another reason such as that one of the parties has been harmed. It may be possible to renege on the agreement if there is proof that key elements of the dispute have not been properly considered, or there has been fraud or coercion, or the agreement has been achieved based on fraudulent documentation.[11]

### 2.2.2.3. Mediation

Mediation is regulated in Article 6(3) of the Arbitration Act. This Article explains that if the dispute or the disagreement cannot be resolved with the agreement of the two parties, it may be resolved with the involvement of one or more expert advisors through a mediator. If in this way agreement is still not achieved, or the mediator fails to invite the two parties, the two parties can contact an arbitration body or an ADR body to appoint a mediator.

After the appointment of the mediator by an arbitration body or an ADR body, the mediation must start within seven days. An effort to resolve the dispute through a mediator is executed by upholding confidentiality, and within 30 days there must be a written agreement signed by all the parties involved in the dispute.

A written agreement to resolve disputes or disagreement is final and binds the two parties who execute it. The agreement must be registered at the State Court within 30 days of it being signed and the agreement must be executed within 30 days of its registration at the State Court. If agreement is not achieved, the two parties, based on the written agreement, can file a claim to resolve the dispute through arbitration body or ad hoc arbitration.

Before the enactment of the Arbitration Act, the Supreme Court of the Republic of Indonesia issued the Circular No. 1 of 2002 to empower the State Court to put the reconciliation into effect. This Circular aims at, among other things, limiting cassation and ordering all judges in charge of trying the cases to really try to resolve the dispute by applying the provisions of Article 130 HIR or Article 154 RBg, and not only offer suggestions to achieve an agreement between the two disputing parties.[12]

The Circular No. 1 of 2002 was then revoked and replaced with Peraturan Mahkamah Agung (PERMA) No. 2 of 2003 on the Procedure of Mediation in Court. PERMA No. 2 of 2003 is expected to become an effective instrument in reducing the caseload of the court. According to Made Sukadana, the reason

11 G. Wijaya, *supra* n. 9, pp. 88–90.
12 I. Made Sukadana, *supra* n. 10, p. 8.

behind this Supreme Court Regulation is clear because mediation is one of the fastest and least expensive methods of ADR compared to the litigation process which can take a very long time. To follow up the execution of PERMA, the Supreme Court decided that some of the State Courts should take part in a pilot project to develop dispute resolution by way of agreement or settlement. Batu Sangkar State Court (West Sumatra) and Bengkalis State Court (Bengkalis Regency) developed the execution of mediation with a focus on indigenous issues; meanwhile, in Jakarta Pusat State Court and Surabaya State Court, the focus of mediation was on business cases (with written mediation agreements).[13]

PERMA No. 2 of 2003 was replaced with PERMA No. 1 of 2008 on Court-Annexed Mediation Procedure which became effective on 31 July 2008. Substantially, the material/content of the two regulations is similar. PERMA No. 1 of 2008 emphasises that if the process of dispute resolution in court is not preceded by mediation procedure, the decision is 'null and void'. Even judges in their decision have to mention that they have tried to resolve the dispute through mediation.

This PERMA also prolonges the mediation process from 22 to 40 business days. With the agreement of the parties in dispute, this process can also be prolonged for a second time to the maximum of 14 business days. In the past, the mediation process was only 22 business days if the mediator was a court mediator and 30 business days if the appointed mediator was from outside the court. Another change is that the scope of mediation is broader in the new PERMA. In the old PERMA, mediation could only be executed by the General Court in the State Court. With the enactment of PERMA No. 1 of 2008 the scope of mediation is broadened into the Religious Court. The new PERMA also provides that the process of mediation must be executed in every level of court, which includes the High Court, cassation and case review or *herziening*.

Thus, even though the Arbitration Act, especially in Article 6(1) states clearly that ADR should be executed outside the court; the Supreme Court integrates mediation into the process or procedure of the court. Some legal experts are critical of such integration of the mediation process into the court. This Supreme Court regulation is considered to be confusing both from normative and practical perspectives. From the normative perspective, this regulation is confusing because based on the hierarchy of legislation, by imposing an obligation and reducing the rights of citizens, PERMA goes beyond the limits of its authority. In order for such content to be legitimate, it should be contained in a regulation of at least the same level as an Act. Even Article 2(3) of PERMA mentions that any parties who do not execute the mediation procedure in accordance with PERMA are acting contrary to the provision of Article 130 HIR and/or Article 154 RBg which can result in the withdrawal of the verdict. The Supreme Court Regulation No. 1 of 2008 plays down the regulation of peace

13 I. Made Sukadana, *supra* n. 10, pp. 19–20.

agency as regulated in HIR/RBg which has the same level as an Act. Therefore, it is evident that the validity of this Supreme Court Regulation is debatable. But on the other hand, the Supreme Court is of the opinion that, based on Article 79 of Act No. 3 of 2009 about the Second Amendment of Act No. 14 of 1985 on the Supreme Court, the Regulation is valid. Article 79 of the Act determines that the Supreme Court has the right to issue a Regulation of the Supreme Court to fill in or supplement the procedural law. From a practical perspective, there is confusion because PERMA No. 1 of 2008 insists that mediation is to be integrated in court procedings. Moreover, the Supreme Court threatens that a court's decision will be 'null and void' if mediation is not conducted prior to the court procedings. Experts state that this integration slows down the process of resolving disputes as it prolongs the process of examination. It is also contrary to the Indonesian judicial principle that access to justice should be simple, fast and low cost.[14]

In line with the above opinion, it is stated in the preamble of the PERMA No. 1 of 2008 that the integration of mediation into the process of dispute resolution in court can be an effective instrument to solve the overwhelming number of cases in the court. It could strengthen and maximize the function of the court in resolving disputes in addition to the judicial court process. From a practical perspective, regarding the confusion about the integration of mediation into the litigation procedure in court, it is explained in the preamble that based on Article 130 HIR and Article 154 RBg, this is aimed at intensifying and pushing the parties in dispute to always undertake the alternative process of resolution first. In this vein, it is clear that, practically speaking, the purpose of the PERMA is to guarantee the certainty, order, and the smoothness of the resolution process before the issuance of other regulations of the same level as Acts.[15]

If in Act No. 30 of 1999 we cannot find the meaning of the definition of mediation, we can find such a definition in the PERMA No. 1 of 2008. Mediation is a way of resolving disputes through the process of negotiation to achieve an agreement between the two parties with the help of a mediator. A mediator is a neutral party who helps the parties in dispute in the process of negotiation to seek many possibilities of resolving the dispute without deciding or forcing an agreement. In this meaning or definition, the significant differences between the mediation and arbitration processes is that in mediation a mediator does not have the right to decide or force an agreement; but in arbitration, an arbitrator has the right to decide and force a resolution.

How about cases which can be resolved through mediation? Article 4 states that except cases which are to be resolved through the procedure of the trade court or industrial relations court, and appeals of decisions of the Consumer Dispute Settlement Body and the Business Competition Supervisory

---

14 I. Made Sukadana, *supra* n. 10, pp. 27–28.

15 I. Made Sukadana, *supra* n. 10, p. 28.

Commission, all civil disputes submitted to the State Court must first be resolved through an agreement with the help of a mediator. The exceptions exist because there is already a dispute resolution agency particularly for cases related to industrial relationships, consumer disputes, and business competition.

Mediation is basically executed in private unless the two parties agree otherwise. As a consequence of the integration of mediation in court proceedings, on the first day of trial the judge strongly requests the two parties to resolve the dispute through mediation. Even where there are co-defendants in the dispute, this does not prevent the mediation process. Therefore, from the beginning the judge must try to delay the process of the court proceedings so that the parties in dispute have the chance to resolve their dispute through mediation. Furthermore, at the start of proceedings the judge has to explain the mediation procedure to the two parties.

The two parties can choose any or a combination of any of the following as their mediator: a judge who is not responsible for investigating the case; an advocate or law professor; a non-legal professional who the parties feel has sufficient knowledge or experience in the subject matter of the dispute; or a judge panel of examiners. If the two parties fail to choose a mediator on the appointed day, the judge will appoint a certified judge who is not responsible for investigating the case. If no qualified judge can be found to act as a mediator, the trial judge must appoint another judge who is not responsible for the case to act as a mediator.

The parties involved in the dispute must undertake the mediation process with good faith. One of the parties may withdraw from the mediation process if the opposing party does not undertake the mediation in good faith. The mediator has to declare that the mediation has failed if one or both of the parties or the representatives of the parties do not come to the mediation meeting twice in a row according to the mediation schedule which the two parties have agreed, or have not come to the mediation meeting twice in a row without any reason even though they have been invited. If, during the mediation process, it becomes apparent that the dispute concerns the interests of a third party who is not mentioned in the lawsuit or mediation, the mediator must inform the parties and the judge in charge of the case that the case cannot be mediated because the parties are not complete.

If mediation is succesful, the two parties with the help of the mediator must formulate in writing the resolution that they have achieved, which must be signed by the two parties and the mediator. If during the mediation process the two parties are represented by their lawyers, the parties must formulate in writing the resolution that they have achieved. Before the parties sign the resolution, the mediator examines the content of the resolution to avoid any part of the resolution which is against the law or which cannot be executed or which is in bad faith. The parties must appear before the judge again on the appointed day to submit the resolution to him. The parties can submit the resolution to the judge to be strengthened in the form of deed of resolution. If the parties do not want the dispute resolution to be strengthened in the form of deed of resolution, the resolution they have achieved must include a clause revoking the lawsuit and/or a clause stating that the case has been resolved.

The mediation process is said to fail if after the limit of the maximum length of time, i.e. 40 business days, the disputing parties fail to produce a dispute resolution. If this happens, the mediator must declare in writing that the mediation process has failed and inform the judge of this failure. Upon receiving the information about the failure, the judge continues to investigate the case in accordance with the applicable procedural law. At every stage of investigating the case, the presiding judge still has the right to push for resolution before he pronounces the verdict. This resolution effort lasts for a maximum of 14 business days from the date that the disputing parties express to the presiding judge their wish to achieve resolution.

PERMA states that if the disputing parties fail to achieve a resolution, the statements and confessions of the parties in the mediation process cannot be used as evidence in the process of the trial of the case or another case. In addition, the notes taken by the mediator must be destroyed and the mediator cannot become a witness in the process of the trial of the case. The mediator is also not subject to civil and criminal liability over the content of the resolution as the result of the mediation process.

Except in the State Court, the parties may agree to mediate disputes that are currently in the process of appeal, cassation or case review as long as the verdict of the disputes has not been decided. The agreement of each party to mediate should be put into writing to the Head of the State Court which is in charge of the dispute. The Head of the State Court in charge of the case should notify the Head of the Court of Appeal or the Head of the Supreme Court about the wish of the parties to find a resolution. If the case is being examined in the Court of Appeal or Cassation, the judge can delay the investigation of the dispute for as long as 14 business days from the day he receives the information that the parties want to achieve resolution. If the case file and the review material have not been sent to the higher court, the Head of the State Court must delay the process to give the parties a chance to achieve resolution.

Even though there has been a regulation about mediation and mediation has been integrated into court proceedings for the purpose of overcoming the backlog of cases in court, in reality only few justice seekers prefer to use mediation. The success of mediation in dispute resolution, unfortunately, is also relatively poor. Table 5 below shows the results of a study by Made Sukadana describing the low success rate of the court mediation process:[16]

[16] I. Made Sukadana, *supra* n. 10, pp. 174–175.

**Table 5. Percentage of success of mediation in some State Courts**

| Court Location | Year | Number of Cases | Successful Mediation | Percentage of Success |
|---|---|---|---|---|
| Bandung | 2006 | 370 | 19 | 5.14 |
| | 2007 | 360 | 16 | 4.44 |
| | 2008 | 425 | 45 | 1.58 |
| | 2009 | 305 | 26 | 8.25 |
| Jakarta Selatan | 2006 | 2173 | 12 | 0.55 |
| | 2007 | 2439 | 14 | 0.57 |
| | 2008 | 1663 | 10 | 0.60 |
| | 2009 | 1479 | 13 | 0.87 |
| Bogor | 2006 | 83 | 3 | 3.52 |
| | 2007 | 105 | 6 | 5.71 |
| | 2008 | 127 | 3 | 2.36 |
| | 2009 | 92 | 26 | 28.26 |
| Depok | 2006 | 90 | 2 | 2.22 |
| | 2007 | 137 | 3 | 2.18 |
| | 2008 | 141 | 5 | 3.54 |
| | 2009 | 105 | 3 | 2.85 |

From the Table, we can see that the percentage of success of mediation is not yet significant. This lack of success, according to Made Sukadana, is because the courts have not taken mediation seriously. Besides, this is caused by the abundance of cases submitted to the courts. The number of mediator-judges is also very small. For this reason, litigation is prioritised above mediation.

In his study, Made Sukadana concluded that unsuccessful mediation is primarily caused by the limited amount of time mediator-judges have. In order for mediation to be successful, judges need to have more time to dedicate to it. Furthermore, judges have to pay more attention to the mediation process because it is hard to find a resolution that is acceptable to all of the parties involved in the dispute.[17]

2.2.2.4. Conciliation

In essence, conciliation is a type of dispute resolution based on agreement between the parties. Like consultation, negotiation and mediation, the Arbitration Act does not contain the meaning and definition of conciliation.

[17] I. Made Sukadana, *supra* n. 10, pp. 176–177.

The term 'conciliation' can only be found in Article 1(10) and in paragraph 9 of the general explanation of the Act. According to Made Sukadana, conciliation is a process in which a third party (the conciliator) provides assistance by offering and suggesting a way of resolving the dispute between the two parties. The conciliator must be neutral in the sense that he cannot direct the decision in favour of the interests of one of the parties.[18] According to Gunawan Wijaya, any dispute which is going to be resolved through conciliation is subjected to the provisions of Articles 1851–1864 of the Civil Law Act. In accordance with Article 6(7) of the Arbitration Act, the written agreement as the result of conciliation must be registered in a State Court within 30 days of it being signed and must be executed within 30 days of its registration at the State Court. The written agreement of conciliation is final and binds each party. Furthermore, Gunawan Wijaya states that conciliation can be attempted before the litigation process begins. Hence, conciliation can not only help avoid the litigation process altogether, but can also be initiated by either party in every level of court, both inside and outside the court proceedings, with the exception of disputes in which a legally enforceable verdict has already been given.[19]

#### 2.2.2.5. Expert judgment or legal opinion by arbitration body

According to Gunawan Wijaya, in addition to resolving disputes that happen between parties who have agreed to use ADR, an arbitration body can also offer consultation in the form of a legal opinion upon the request of every party in need; not only for parties bound in an agreement but also for other parties. He states:

> 'A legal opinion is an input for each party in composing or drafting an agreement. This will regulate the rights and obligations of each party in the agreement. In giving the legal opinion, the legal expert can interpret or give explanation to the provisions in the agreement which have been written by each party. In this case, the legal opinion by an expert will make the provision clear for each party to execute it.'[20]

Made Sukadana explains that expert judgment can be defined as a resolution reached by the two parties in dispute with the help of an expert. The role of the expert is to assess a loss (usually in tort cases) or to assess a condition.[21] The legal basis of expert judgment or legal judgment is the formulation of Article 52 of the Arbitration Act. This Article states that each party in an agreement has the right to ask for a binding opinion from an arbitration body in the context of certain legal relationships. Therefore an arbitration body can offer a binding

---

18 I. Made Sukadana, *supra* n. 10, p. 9.
19 G. Wijaya, *supra* n. 8, pp. 93–94.
20 G. Wijaya, *supra* n. 8, p. 95.
21 I Made Sukadana, *supra* n. 10, p. 9.

opinion about a certain legal relationship before the dispute arises.[22] Gunawan Wijaya also explains that an opinion given by an arbitration body is binding because the opinion offered will become an inseparable part of the body of agreement. Any violation of the given legal opinion means a violation of the agreement or default. In addition, this legal opinion is final for each party as regulated in Article 53 of Act No. 30 of 1999 which states that any party should not violate a legal opinion through any legal efforts.[23]

## 3. DEVELOPMENT OF ALTERNATIVE DISPUTE RESOLUTION IN VARIOUS LEGAL FIELDS AFTER THE REFORMATION ERA

It is unarguable that the trend of the use of ADR has increased after the reformation era with the fall of the New Order regime under Soeharto, in 1998. After the fall of the regime, many civil movements appeared. Alongside the civil movements, various NGOs also appeared that offered help for the society in seeking justice. Before the reformation, Soeharto did not give enough space for civil movement and NGOs in Indonesia. The interference of the executive (the government) in judicial authority was very significant. Thus we can say that the reformation was one of the factors which opened the way for the development of ADR in Indonesia.

### 3.1. ENVIRONMENTAL DISPUTE RESOLUTION

The first Act in the Republic of Indonesia to introduce non-litigation dispute resolution during the enactment of Act No. 14 of 1970 on the Basic Principles of Judicial Power was Act No. 23 of 1997 on Environmental Management which was then replaced by Act No. 32 of 2009 on the Protection and Management of the Environment.

Act No. 23 of 1997 on Environmental Management states that environmental dispute resolution can be executed through the court or outside the court based on the voluntary choice of the parties to the dispute. If the parties choose out-of-court dispute resolution, court proceedings can only be commenced if one or all of the parties declare that the preferred process has failed. In this case, the court does not have the right to investigate and try the case, except where the dispute resolution outside the court has been considered to fail.

---

22 G. Wijaya, *supra* n. 8, p. 95.

23 G. Wijaya, *supra* n. 8, pp. 95–96.

Environmental dispute resolution outside the court can be resolved with the help of a third party which may or may not have the authority to make a binding decision.

The provision of environmental dispute resolution which can be found in Act No. 23 of 1997 on Environmental Management did not change in Act No. 32 of 2009. The difference, however, lies in the phrase that clearly mentions the term mediator and/or arbitrator as this third party.

For more details, the definition of environmental dispute as regulated in Act No. 32 of 2009 on the Protection and Management of the Environment is a 'dispute between two or more parties as the result of any activity which potentially and/or which already has an impact on the environment.'

Article 85(3) of Act No. 32 of 2009 states that 'environmental dispute resolution can make use of a mediator and/or an arbitrator to help resolve the environmental dispute'. According to Takdir Rahmadi, there are three ways (not just two) to resolve environmental disputes outside the court, i.e. through negotiation, mediation, and arbitration.[24] Out-of-court dispute resolution may help achieve an agreement in respect of (a) the form and amount of compensation, (b) recovery actions as a result of contamination and/or destruction, (c) particular actions to guarantee that there will be no more contamination and/or destruction, and (d) actions to prevent a negative impact on the environment. Article 85(2) of Act No. 32 of 2009 only prohibits the use of mediation and arbitration in the category of environmental criminal cases.

Due to the possibilities of environmental dispute resolution outside the court, the Government of the Republic of Indonesia issued Government Regulation No. 54 of 2000 on the Institute for Providing Services for Out-of-Court Environmental Dispute Resolution. Based on this government regulation, an institution or a third party can offer services in environmental dispute resolution through mediation and/or arbitration.

## 3.2. FORESTRY DISPUTE RESOLUTION

The legal basis of forestry dispute resolution is Act No. 41 of 1999 on Forestry as amended by Act No. 1 of 2004. Article 74(1) of Act No. 41 of 1999 states that: 'Conflicts pertaining to forestry can be resolved in a court or outside a court, depending on the options that are voluntarily selected by the parties involved.' It is further stated in paragraph 2 that: 'When conflict resolution is selected to be outside a court, claims can then be made in a court if consensus is not achieved among the parties involved.' Forestry dispute resolution outside the court does not apply to forestry crime as regulated in the Forestry Act.

---

24 T. Rahmadi, *Mediasi: Penyelesaian Sengketa melalui Pendekatan Mufakat*, Raja Grafindo Persada, Jakarta 2010, pp. 57–58.

Article 75(2) states that out-of-court dispute resolution in relation to forestry disputes aims to achieve an agreement in relation to (a) return of a right, (b) the amount of compensation, and/or (c) specific actions necessary for recovering the functions of forests. This Act also regulates that the parties can appoint and make use of the services of a third party. It is also stated that an NGO can help in forestry dispute resolution. Hence NGOs can become a mediator or offer their services to the parties involved in a forestry dispute.

As already mentioned, forestry dispute resolution can take place both in and out of court. This regulation is a big step forward. In the past, even though forestry disputes between the State and the people were common, in Act No. 5 of 1967 on Basic Forestry Law, there was no regulation on this matter. In Article 17 of the Basic Forestry Law for example it is stated that:

> 'The implementation of the rights of indigenous communities and the rights of its members and the rights of individuals, to directly or indirectly benefit from the forest, as far as (these rights) are based on provision in the law and still exist in reality, may not disturb the goals stipulated in this law.'[25]

According to Adriaan Bedner and Stijn van Huis, this Article has the potential to prejudice the rights of the indigenous community. In the explanation of the Article, the rights of the indigenous community are reduced to only consist of the use of forest land for livestock, hunting, and the collection of forest products. In the past, the existence of the indigenous society was considered to have the potential to disturb national policy goals of conservation and production. However, the most important 'disturbance' that might be caused by indigenous communities according to the old *rezim* was their obstruction to development projects. This restriction according to Bedner and Huis impacted the lives of *adat* law communities in a more fundamental way. The Basic Forestry Law granted power to the State to define land as forest area. Indigenous communities tilling land in areas designated as forests suddenly had to comply with national forestry policies. In practice, this meant that their rights to farm land within forest areas had suddenly been replaced by the right to collect forest products. As they could no longer sufficiently support themselves, they were often forced to turn to agriculture elsewhere or to work in the forestry sector.[26]

---

25 A. Bedner and S. van Huis, 'The Return of the Native in Indonesian Law' (2008) 164(2/3) *Bijdragen tot de Taal-, Land- en Volkenkunde* 182.

26 A. Bedner and S. van Huis, *supra* n. 25, p. 182.

## 3.3. WATER RESOURCES DISPUTE RESOLUTION

Water resources dispute resolution is regulated in Act No. 7 of 2004 on Water Resources. A water resources dispute is a dispute relating to the management of water resources and/or a dispute about the right to use water or the right to lease water, such as a dispute between consumers, a dispute between businessmen, between consumers and businessmen, between territories or areas, and between upstream and downstream.

Based on Article 88 of Act No. 7 of 2004, the first step in resolving the dispute is the deliberations to reach consensus. If the parties cannot achieve a consensus or agreement, they can obtain dispute resolution through the court or outside the court. Out-of-court dispute resolution methods include arbitration as well as other types of ADR. Water resources dispute resolution can be done through consultation, negotiation, mediation, conciliation, and expert judgment.

## 3.4. LABOUR OR INDUSTRIAL RELATIONS DISPUTE RESOLUTION

Act No. 2 of 2004 on Industrial Relations Disputes (LN 2004, No. 6) also regulates the use of mediation as a method of industrial relations dispute resolution. Article 1(11) defines industrial relations mediation as the resolution of disputes over rights and interests or termination of employment, and disputes between workers/labour associations in a company, through discussion which is mediated by one or more neutral mediators.[27]

Further, Article 1(12) formulates the definition of mediator as an official in a government institution who is responsible for employment, who meets the requirements of a mediator as regulated by the minister for labour affairs, and who has the responsibility to produce a written suggestion to the parties in dispute as to how to solve their industrial relations dispute. The second part of the Article contains commonly known elements of the definition of a mediator, i.e. they must be neutral and not show bias towards a party. But, according to Takdir Rahmadi, there is no clear statement in this Act that the mediator does not have the right to decide the case. The mediator's role could then be confused with the duty of an arbitrator who has the right to decide a case.[28]

Based on Act No. 2 of 2004, mediation can be commenced after the parties have failed to achieve a resolution through bipartite negotiation and do not then choose to attempt resolution through conciliation or arbitration within seven business days. Article 4(4) of Act No. 2 of 2004 states:

---

27 T. Rahmadi, *supra* 24, p. 62.
28 T. Rahmadi, *supra* 24, p. 63.

> 'In case the disputing parties do not choose to resolve the dispute through conciliation or arbitration within seven business days, the government institution in charge of employment delegates the dispute resolution to the mediator.'

From the wording of Article 4(4) it is not really clear whether the mediation is mandatory or voluntary. However, if we pay close attention to the words 'institution in charge of employment delegates the dispute resolution to the mediator', it seems that mediation is mandatory if the disputing parties do not choose conciliation or arbitration. Furthermore if we relate this to Article 83(1) of Act No. 2 of 2004, we have a better understanding that labour dispute resolution is mandatory. Article 83(1) of Act No. 2 of 2004 states: 'The petition submitted without attachment of the minutes of settlement through mediation or conciliation, should be returned by the judge of the Industrial Relations Court to the plaintiff.' The statement of Article 83(1) implies that the Industrial Relations Court does not have the authority to investigate the dispute if the parties have not tried to resolve the dispute through mediation and conciliation.[29]

## 3.5. CONSUMER DISPUTE RESOLUTION

In Article 45(2) of Act No. 8 of 1999 about Consumer Protection (LN 1999, No. 22) it is stated that: 'Consumer dispute resolution can be done through the court or outside the court based on the voluntary preference of the disputing parties'. In paragraph 4 it is stated that if the disputing parties choose out-of-court consumer dispute resolution, court proceedings can only be commenced if one or both of the parties declare that their efforts to resolve the case have failed.

Act No. 8 of 1999 on Consumer Protection regulates the use of mediation as an out-of-court method to resolve consumer disputes. The use of consensus in consumer dispute resolution is reflected in Article 47 of Act No. 8 of 1999 which, among other things, states: 'Consumer dispute resolutions outside the court are executed in order to reach an agreement as regards the form and amount of the compensation and certain actions to guarantee that there will be no more losses on the consumers' side.'[30] Mediation, arbitration and conciliation, as regulated in Article 52(a), are carried out by the Consumer Dispute Settlement Body (Badan Penyelesaian Sengketa Konsumen, BPSK). BPSK is a particular body which was created pursuant to the Consumer Protection Act. The primary task of BPSK is to resolve any disputes between consumers and businessmen.[31] Therefore the task and authority of BPSK includes handling and resolving consumers' disputes, by making use of mediation, arbitration or conciliation.

---

29 T. Rahmadi, *supra* 24, pp. 63–64.

30 T. Rahmadi, *supra* n. 24, p. 59.

31 G. Wijaya, *supra* n. 8, p. 73.

But according to Gunawan Wijaya, consumer disputes may be resolved by other methods, such as peaceful settlement (agreement) between the disputing parties. At every stage of the dispute, the parties should consider reaching a peaceful settlement. This means that according to the Act of Consumer Protection, there are three methods of dispute resolution, namely through the court, through BPSK, and through ADR and/or arbitration as regulated in Act No. 30 of 1999 on Arbitration and Alternative Dispute Resolution.[32]

Article 54(3) states that the decision of BPSK is final and binding. BPSK must issue their decision within 21 business days of proceedings being commenced. Within seven business days of receiving the decision of BPSK, the parties must comply with the decision. The disputing parties may submit an objection to the State Court within 14 business days of receiving the notification of the decision. If the parties do not submit an objection during the appointed time they are deemed to agree with the decision of BPSK.

## 3.6. PUBLIC INFORMATION DISPUTE RESOLUTION

Resolution of public information disputes according to Act No. 14 of 2008 on Public Information Disclosure (LN 2008, No. 61) can be achieved through the litigation and non-litigation processes. As regards the litigation process, the lawsuit must be submitted to the Administrative Court if the defendant is a State public agency and to the State Court if the defendant is a public agency other than a State public agency.

A public information dispute is a dispute between a public agency and users of public information which is related to the rights of obtaining and using information based on legislation. The legal basis of public information dispute resolution which is submitted to the court is Article 4(4) which states that: 'Every applicant of public information has the right to submit a lawsuit to the court if he or she encounters any obstacle in receiving information or he or she cannot receive certain information as regulated in the legislation.' This is based on the consideration that everybody has the right to: (a) see and know about public information; (b) go to a public meeting which is open to everybody to gain public information; (c) gain a copy of public information through a petition as regulated in the provision of the legislation; and/or (d) spread public information as regulated in the legislation.

Not all public information can be disclosed. Therefore a public agency has the right to withhold public information if it is against the provisions of the legislation. Public information which cannot be disclosed by a public agency is the following: (a) information that can harm the State; (b) information which is related to the protection of business interests from unfair competition; (c) information related

[32] G. Wijaya, *supra* n. 8, p. 76.

to personal rights; (d) information related to confidentiality of position; and/or (e) public information that is not known or documented completely.

Public information dispute resolution outside the court can be done via mediation and adjudication. Mediation as explained in Act No. 14 of 2008 is a dispute resolution between the parties with the help of an Information Commission mediator.

The Information Commission is an independent agency which is in charge of executing legislation along with its implementation, establishing standard technical guidance of public information services and resolving public information disputes through mediation and/or non-litigation adjudication. If mediation is used, the members of the Information Commission are the mediators. The Information Commission consists of the National Information Commission which is in the capital of Indonesia, the Provincial Information Commission, and if needed, the Information Commission can be established at the regional level.

One of the roles of the Information Commission is to invite and/or unite the disputing parties and ask for relevant notes or materials owned by the related public agency to make a decision in resolving public information disputes. The dispute has to be resolved within 100 business days at the latest. Article 39 states that the Information Commission decision resulting from the agreement through mediation is final and binding. The agreement of each party in the process of mediation is set forth in the form of the mediation decision of the Information Commission.

Dispute resolution through mediation can be applied to any dispute when there is no timely information, when there is no response to an information request, when there is no sufficient response to an information request, when there is an imposition of unreasonable fees, and/or when information is delivered after the period stipulated in the Act.

## 3.7. DISPUTE RESOLUTION IN BANKING

The use of mediation to resolve banking disputes is not based on law, but on Bank Indonesia's policy as stipulated in Bank Indonesia Regulation No. 8/5/PBI/2006. The use of mediation in the context of banking disputes as stated in Bank Indonesia Regulation No. 8/5/PBI/2006 is voluntary.

Bank Indonesia through Bank Indonesia Regulation No. 3/5/PBI/2006 on 30 January 2006 and Circular Letter of Bank Indonesia No. 8/14/DPNP on 1 June 2006 issued a policy that strongly encourages bank customers and banks to pursue mediation as a means of dispute resolution. The Regulation specifies the criteria of disputes that can be resolved through mediation, namely: (a) civil disputes arising from financial transactions; (b) disputes arising from the results of the bank's settlement of customer complaints; and (c) disputes that carry financial claims with a maximum value of Rp 500,000,000 (rupiahs). The deadline for filing dispute resolution according to the Regulation should be no later than 60 days from the date of settlement completion. It should be written and sent to the banking agency mediation.[33]

## 3.8. LAND DISPUTE RESOLUTION

Under the provisions of Article 23(c) of the Presidential Decree of the Republic of Indonesia No. 10 of 2006 on National Land Agency, it is stated that the Deputy Minister of Research and Treatment Dispute and Conflict is in charge of alternative problem, dispute, and conflict resolutions through mediation, facilitation, etc.

The provisions of Article 23 of Presidential Decree No. 10 of 2006 show the government's policy to use mediation as a way to resolve land disputes. Prior to the enactment of Presidential Decree No. 10 of 2006, the usual approach to settling land disputes was by way of consensus agreement. However, the new use of the term mediation is explicitly stated in Presidential Decree No. 10 of 2006. This results from the increasing popularity of the term mediation within the field of law, in Indonesian laws and regulations, and among Indonesian policy makers. Detailed legal provisions on the use of mediation in the context of land disputes do not exist. The existing provisions are only in the form issued by the Technical Guidelines of National Land Agency No. 05/Juknis/DV/2007 on the Mechanism of Mediation Implementation. The preamble of the Technical Guidelines states that one of the laws that becomes the legal basis of mediation is Act No. 30 of 1999 on Arbitration and Alternative Dispute Resolution. The Act firmly stipulates that the use of arbitration and alternative dispute resolution is voluntary. Thus, the use of mediation to resolve land disputes is also voluntary.[34]

## 3.9. DISPUTE RESOLUTION IN JOURNALISM

Article 15(2)(d) of Act No. 40 of 1999 on the Press (LN 1999, No. 166) regulates the functions of the Press Council, such as giving consideration to and solving complaints from the public over cases dealing with the news in the press. Alamudi Abdullah states that although the function of the Press Council as defined in Article 15(2)(d) is general and does not specifically mention the function of mediation, in practice, the Press Council has taken on the function of mediation for disputes between the press and those who feel aggrieved by the news.[35]

---

33 T. Rahmadi, *supra* 24, p. 65.

34 T. Rahmadi, *supra* 24, p. 66.

35 T. Rahmadi, *supra* 24, p. 73.

Mediation by the Press Council is mediation outside the courts and done voluntarily or by the choice of the parties. Thus, the Press Council is able to run the mediaton if the press broadcasting the news and those who are reported so request or agree. If the parties, with the help of the Press Council, reach agreement, the dispute ends with a peace agreement out of court. If the parties fail to reach an agreement, and those who were reported are not satisfied, they can submit a lawsuit to the court on the basis of tort. In addition to its mediating function, the Press Council also performs the role of the keeper of the journalism code of ethics. As the keeper of the code of conduct, the Press Council has the authority to issue Statements of Assessment and Recommendations. Conceptually, these are similar to a combination of expert judgment and fact-finding.

As a follow up to the implementation of the dispute resolution function, the Press Council issued Regulation Press Council No. 1/Peraturan-DP/J/2008 about the complaints procedure to the Press Council. The provision in the Press Council relating to the mediation function is listed in Article 7(1) which states: 'The Press Council seeks a settlement through deliberation and consensus which is set forth in peace statements'. The formulation of Article 7(1) does not contain the word 'mediation' or 'mediator', but rather has the words 'seek resolution through deliberation and consensus which is set forth in peace statements'. Conceptually, these words reflect the role or function of mediation that is run by the Press Council.[36]

## 3.10. DISPUTE RESOLUTION IN INDIGENOUS SOCIETY

Even though the term mediation derives from English and is an English word, conceptually the essence of mediation has been practiced by the people of Indonesia long before the term mediation became popular within the scope of law. '*Adat* law' or customary law is a phenomenon in Indonesia. The presence of *adat* law in the community has a special meaning because it is a reflection of the culture and way of life of the people. *Adat* law has a distinctive character. It is believed to be bound to the society where it was born and has grown, and is a form of phenomenological juridical community.[37] According to Iman Sudiyat, *adat* law is concrete, real and empirical. The division of all material governed by *adat* law is made in accordance with the inductive nature of the object or objects being handled. So its existence is not in the abstract as it is for the modern law whose formulations are often far from reality. Other characteristics of *adat* law are that it is religious, communal, democratic, closely connected to the local culture, able emphasise feelings rather than what is rational, able to prioritise moral and

36 T. Rahmadi, *supra* 24, p. 74.

37 M. Syamsudin, E. Kumoro, A. Rachiem F. and M. Tabrani (eds.), *Hukum Adat dan Modernisasi Hukum*, FH UII, Yogyakarta 1998, p. v.

spiritual values, unpretentious and simple. *Adat* law in Indonesia has never distinguished between public law (or criminal law) and private law. At least according to Iman Sudiyat, the boundary between the two is rather vague.[38] Philosophically and culturally *adat* peoples do have a different character, nature and characteristics to urban communities characterised by their understanding of modern law. *Adat* peoples in Indonesia are communalistic. The phrases '*urip bebarengan*' (live peacefully together), '*padha-padha*' (togetherness) and '*rukun agawe santosa*' (harmony brings happiness) in Javanese society, for example, can illustrate that they emphasise the importance of harmony.[39] Therefore, indigenous or *adat* communities place great importance on 'consensus and agreement' in decision-making. By their nature, these people think that bringing a case to court is sometimes considered taboo and will not solve the problem at hand, as the nature of court settlement is winning and losing. Maintaining harmony is considered more important by the *adat* peoples with their kinship attachment.

Mediation in *adat* communities is used to resolve family, inheritance, land boundary and other types of disputes. In addition, mediation is also used to settle some minor crimes such as fighting, petty thefts, etc. Thus, in *adat* communities, peace settlement through 'consensus agreement' is not confined to civil matters only, but also for criminal matters. According to the principle of State law, a criminal offence should not be settled between parties in conflict; however, in reality, community leaders in *adat* communities often resolve criminal offences through mediation. The above example highlights the differences in approach to conflict settlement between the State law and the law of society (folk law, non-State law).[40]

Almost all of the disputes in indigenous societies in the past were settled by a consensus agreement or '*musyawarah-mufakat*' which is very similar to mediation. Besides Indonesia, some indigenous societies in several Asian countries such as Malaysia, Thailand and the Philippines also used mediation to settle disputes. Joel Lee and Teh Hwee Hwee suggest:

> 'Mediation is also practised in Malaysia, Indonesia, Thailand and the Philippines. [...] In the neighbouring country of Indonesia, consensual procedures for decision-making and dispute resolution have traditionally been used. Disputes have been handled by judicial procedures in which an authorative decision-maker met with the disputing parties to negotiate a settlement with his advice, using customary standards and criteria. In addition, group consensual-based deliberative procedures

38 I. Sudiyat, 'Perkembangan Beberapa Bidang Hukum Adat sebagai Hukum Klasik Modern', in M. Syamsudin, E. Kumoro, A. Rachiem F. and M. Tabrani (eds.), *Hukum Adat dan Modernisasi Hukum*, FH UII, Yogyakarta 1998, pp. 20–21 and pp. 29–31.

39 M. Koesno, 'Menuju kepada Penyusunan Teori Hukum Adat', in M. Syamsudin, E. Kumoro, A. Rachiem F. and M. Tabrani (eds.), *Hukum Adat dan Modernisasi Hukum*, FH UII, Yogyakarta 1998, pp. 62–63.

40 T. Rahmadi, *supra* n. 24, pp. 69–70.

known as *musyawarah*, which aim to achieve an acceptable solution for all involved, have traditionally been employed.'[41]

Although Indonesian *adat* law is very important for the people of Indonesia and varies greatly because of the diversity of tribes and customs in Indonesia, Sukanto argues that Indonesian people have to be careful because *adat* law contains outdated or inapplicable rules, and customs that are influenced by Western religion or law.[42] Therefore, we suggest that case settlements in *adat* communities should be thoroughly investigated as to whether they are still applicable.

As previously described, in *adat* law there is no clear difference in the method of resolving criminal and civil matters. In *adat* law, the cases that were categorised as criminal law according to State law can also be resolved by consensus agreement or through the peace efforts. In relation to this issue, Bagir Manan says:

> 'Peace in *adat* law is not limited only to civil disputes. Peace is also prevalent in criminal offences. Often, criminal cases that require imprisonment are resolved peacefully. In cases of death caused by a fight or quarrel, the resolution is achieved through the compensation to families of the victims. The compensation is not only material, but can also be immaterial such as paying *adat* fines or carrying out certain obligations to restore the spiritual balance. Even statements of regret and sincere apology that are accepted by the victim's family can sometimes be an important foundation for peace. [...] Moreover, this kind of peace efforts should bring about legal consequences, which is closing the case once peace is achieved. The doctrine which states that the criminal nature remains intact and thus the offences will still be pursued should be abolished.'[43]

Within the scope of *adat* communities, *adat* functionaries act as mediators in resolving disputes between members of the *adat* communities. The members of *adat* communities often ask religious leaders to help resolve disputes or family and inheritance conflicts. However, within *adat* communities, those *adat* functionaries often play dual roles as mediators as well as arbitrators. In early stages, functionaries use a persuasive approach and give suggestions for dispute settlement, but if one or both parties reject their proposal, the dispute will be resolved through court. Those who are dissatisfied with the decision of *adat* functionaries can take their case to the local court.[44]

There are even written rules of dispute and conflict resolution by *adat* functionaries in Aceh Province (where Shari'ah law is enforced). The regulation

---

41 J. Lee and H.H. Teh, 'The Quest for an Asian Perspective on Mediation', in J. Lee and H.H. Teh (eds.), *An Asian Perspective on Mediation*, Academy Publishing, Singapore 2009, pp. 5–6.

42 Soekanto, *Meninjau Hukum Adat Indonesia: Suatu Pengantar untuk Mempelajari Hukum Adat*, Edisi 3, Raja Grafindo Persada, Jakarta 1996, pp. 62–63.

43 T. Rahmadi, *supra* n. 24, p. 71.

44 T. Rahmadi, *supra* n. 24, pp. 71–72.

of dispute resolution by *adat* functionaries in the province of Aceh (which has a special autonomy to apply part of Islamic law) has even been made in writing. This written form of rules is called Qanun No. 7 of 2000 on the Implementation of *Adat* Life. In this Qanun it is stated that *adat* law, customs and practices that still prevail and thrive in Acehnese society must be maintained as long as they are not in conflict with Islamic Shari'ah law. Islamic Shari'ah in this case is the benchmark of the carrying out of *adat* life in Aceh. *Adat* institutions serve as a means of control of security, peace, harmony and public order, to solve social problems and to mediate (justice of the peace) the disputes that arise in the community. In this Qanun it is also stated that in resolving the dispute, law enforcement officials first give the chance to Keuchik (village-level traditional leaders) and Imum Mukim (subdistrict level traditional leaders) to resolve disputes in Gampong and Mukim respectively. Keuchik have the authority to resolve disputes and problems that occur in Gampong. The disputes and problems include problems in families, between families, and social issues that arise in society. Keuchik should try to resolve those problems peacefully through deliberation in a Gampong *adat* meeting. If within a period of two months the dispute can not be resolved in Gampong, and the parties to the dispute do not accept the *adat* decision at Keuchik level, the dispute will be resolved by Imum Mukim in a Mukim *adat* meeting. All disputes and controversies that Keuchik and Imum Mukim have reconciled in a traditional meeting are binding on the parties. Those who do not follow the *adat* decision at the Keuchik or Imum Mukim level will receive a severe penalty according to *adat* customs because they damage the agreement and disrupt the balance of living in the community. Furthermore, the Qanun also expresses that if within the period of one month Imum Mukim cannot resolve the case or the parties to the dispute are not satisfied with the *adat* decision at Mukim level, then the parties can submit the case to law enforcement officials. Law enforcement officials can take into consideration the *adat* decision that has been imposed upon disputing parties when solving the case. The minutes of the meetings for each settlement made by Keuchik and Imum Mukim are recorded and announced to the public.

Based on the rules in this Qanun, the *adat* institution led by Keuchik or Imum Mukim will first attempt to resolve any disputes (either civil or criminal cases), before the parties in such disputes submit their case to the court. In this case Imum Mukim or Keuchik serve as mediators (justices of the peace) of the disputes that community. The total time for the process of dispute resolution allowed in the village level by Keuchik is two months whereas the time allowed at the district level by Imum Mukim is one month. We can conclude that the dispute resolution process as set forth in the Qanun is a process of mediation which is conducted before parties to a dispute bring their cases through a formal channel that is dispute resolution by means of State law. Any legal decision given at the level of the Gampong and Mukim *adat* meeting will be recorded and announced for the public.

However, in reality, there are disputes in *adat* communities that have been resolved by *adat* functionaries that are then submitted to the State Court. According to Takdir Rahmadi, this could be evidence of the problems of the dispute resolution process by *adat* functionaries. Thus, we need to examine the problems. One of the causes he mentions is the decline of the kinship system and social attachment which results from the increase of materialism and individualism in society as well as the weakening of the power of *adat* functionaries. The increasing popularity and prestige of advocacy professions might also constitute an important factor in the decrease of dispute resolution through consensus agreement. The general public is no longer interested in consensus agreement because they are more familiar with advocacy professions. Thus, during a conflict, people tend to seek assistance from lawyers even though legal professions in Indonesia are more litigation-oriented. In addition, the curriculum in law departments in universities tends to direct their graduates to view court as the only means of resolving a dispute. However, in recent years, a number of law schools in Indonesia have offered courses such as 'a choice of dispute resolution' or 'alternative dispute resolution' that among other things includes learning about negotiation and mediation that are based on a consensus approach to dispute resolution.[45]

## 4. FINAL REMARKS

The above discussions show that at least in the past decade, alternative dispute resolution in Indonesia has experienced rapid growth, especially within the area of the making of policy or laws and regulations. The political will of the Supreme Court to use alternative dispute resolution is also evident through the issuance of the Supreme Court Regulation No. 1 of 2008 on Court-Annexed Mediation Procedure. It stipulates that parties to a dispute should seek peace efforts and/or mediation; otherwise, a court decision would be considered 'null and void' or annulled by law. The Supreme Court has even integrated mediation into the process or events in court. However, as previously stated, in reality the success rate of peacemaking or reconciliation, mediation and arbitration is very low. Training for new judges to serve as mediators is critical so that all judges in the State Court or even in higher courts can conduct the mediation process to reduce the backlog of cases in courts. Under the present conditions, this is an extremely challenging endeavour.

---

45 T. Rahmadi, *supra* n. 24, p. 72.

# IRELAND

Guillermo Palao Moreno*

'There is no nation of people under the sun that doth love equal and indifferent justice better than the Irish.'
Sir John Davies, Attorney General in Ireland to James I, 1606.

## Contents



* I am grateful to Mr William Aylmer (Solicitor and Mediator, Partner, Compton Aylmer), Mr Timothy Bouchier-Hays (Solicitor and Arbitrator, Partner, McCann Fitzgerald) and Mr Brian Hutchinson (Senior Lecturer, University College Dublin), for their advice; and to Mr John Doyle and Mr Jon O'Riordan (Solicitors and Arbitrator, Partners, Dillon Eustace) and Ms Patricia Boyd (Solicitor and Mediator) for reading a previous version of this paper and offering valuable comments. My gratitude also goes to Ms Mary Gaynor (Director of the Library, Law Society, Dublin) for the outstanding service provided during my research visit in Dublin and to Mr T.P. Kennedy (Director of Education, Law Society, Dublin) for opening to me the doors of the Law Society and facilitating access to relevant Irish practitioners. Any opinion and mistakes are the sole responsibility of the author. This article has been drafted in the framework of the R+D Projects: 'MEC/SEJ2007–64594. Hacia una cultura de las ADRs: De la mediación al arbitraje' and 'Proyecto de la Generalitat Valenciana PROMETEO/2010/095 para grupos de investigación de excelencia sobre: Mediación y arbitraje: piezas esenciales en el modelo de justicia del Siglo XXI'.

# 1. ORIGIN AND EVOLUTION OF ADR MECHANISMS

ADR is a term that generally embraces processes such as arbitration, mediation and conciliation. However, in Ireland there is no uniform consensus on the scope of the term ADR.[1] It is most commonly used as an umbrella term to refer to only mediation and conciliation, and does not cover arbitration,[2] a process which enjoys a long legislative tradition and a great degree of autonomy in Ireland. In this respect, the Rules of the Superior Courts (Mediation and Conciliation) 2010 define ADR process to mean 'mediation, conciliation or another dispute resolution process approved by the Court, but does not include arbitration'.[3] However, in this text and unless otherwise specified, the term ADR will be taken to cover all three methods of complementary dispute resolution.

Ireland has historically shown a great interest in ADR, both from a practical as well as from a legislative perspective. However, when analysing its origin and evolution, a distinction must be drawn between arbitration on the one hand and mediation and conciliation on the other. While arbitration has enjoyed a very long tradition in Ireland, mediation and conciliation were introduced in Irish practice only recently, although they have gained a great deal of popularity and have spread to several areas of practice since then.

## 1.1. ARBITRATION

Before English rule in Ireland in the twelfth century, and even before the arrival of Christianity on the island, arbitration was an habitual method of resolving disputes according to the ancient *Brehon* Laws, administered by *Brehons* (or *brithem*).[4] The English involvement in Ireland from the twelfth century also had a great influence. However, to a certain extent, the *Brehon* arbitral practice still

---

1 J. Madigan (plus a team of specialist contributors), *Appropriate Dispute Resolution (ADR) In Ireland. A Handbook for Family Lawyers and their Clients*, Family Law, Dublin 2012, pp. 61–63.

2 See B. Hutchinson, *Arbitration and ADR in Construction Disputes*, Round Hall/Thomson Reuters, Dublin 2010, p. 10.

3 SI No. 502/2010. Available at <www.irishstatutebook.ie/2010/en/si/0502.html> accessed 23.10.2012.

4 M.M. Collins, 'Foreword to the first issue' (2012) ix-x *European International Arbitration Review* ix; M.J. Gorman, 'The Ancient *Brehon* Laws of Ireland' (1913) 61 *University of Pennsylvania Law Review* 217, 220 and 227; C. Ó Hoisín, 'Ireland as a Venue for International Arbitration' (2001)

took place until the seventeenth century.[5] During that period Irish legislation was very much influenced by English legislative developments, leading to a confluence of both legal systems in many aspects before the countries drifted apart in 1921.

From a legislative point of view, the first piece of Irish legislation regulating arbitration dates from the seventeenth century. The Act for Determining Differences by Arbitration[6] was introduced in 1699, following the English Act of 1698.[7] For more than two centuries, arbitration was governed by that Act in Ireland and enjoyed a wide practical application, with remarkable examples like the Arbitration Court known as the Ouzel Galley Society (the forerunner of the present day Dublin Chamber of Commerce).[8] It is worth mentioning in relation to this that Ireland was excluded from the English Arbitration Act that was enacted in 1889.[9]

Modern arbitration legislation appeared in the middle of the twentieth century in Ireland after its independence in 1922, when several Acts were passed in order to establish a much clearer and succinct legal framework for this institution. The starting point for that legal process can be found at Article 40.3 of the *Bunreacht na hÉireann* or the Constitution of Ireland of 1937, a provision which foresees the right of access to justice of all citizens.

In that respect, it is worth mentioning the Arbitration Acts 1954, 1980 and 1998.[10] On the one hand, the Arbitration Act 1954, which was heavily influenced by the English Arbitration Act 1950, regulated domestic arbitration. On the other hand, the Arbitration Act 1980 (which amended the previous Act) was passed in order to provide legal effect to both the Washington Convention 1958[11] and the New York Convention 1958,[12] also following the amendments of the English Arbitration Acts of 1975 and 1979. Further, in order to promote Ireland as an adequate venue for international commercial arbitrations and adapt to the

---

29 *Int'l J. Legal Info.* 244, 247. See also <www.courts.ie/Courts.ie/library3.nsf/pagecurrent/3CBAE4FE856E917B80256DF800494ED9?opendocument> accessed 23.10.2012.

5 M.M. Collins, *supra* n. 4, p. ix.

6 9 William 111 Act c15. C. Ó Hoisín, *supra* n. 4, pp. 246–247. See <www.qub.ac.uk/ild/?func=display_bill&id=786> accessed 23.10.2012.

7 10 William 111 Act c14.

8 C. Ó Hoisín, *supra* n. 4, pp. 247–249.

9 In that respect, see C.A. Stanuell, 'The extension to Ireland of the Arbitration Act, 1889' (1910), pp. 371–387, electronic document available at <www.tara.tcd.ie/bitstream/2262/6179/1/jssisiVolXII371_387.pdf> accessed 23.10.2012.

10 See *inter alia* M.W. Carrigan, *Handbook on Arbitration in Ireland*, Law Society of Ireland, Dublin 1998; A. Dowling-Hussey and D. Dunne, *Arbitration Law*, Thomson Round Hall, Dublin 2008; E. Stewart, *Arbitration: Commentary and Sources*, First Law, Dublin 2003.

11 Available at <https://icsid.worldbank.org/ICSID/StaticFiles/basicdoc/CRR_English-final.pdf> accessed 23.10.2012.

12 Available at <www.uncitral.org/uncitral/en/uncitral_texts/arbitration/NYConvention.html> accessed 23.10.2012.

challenges of the globalisation process, in 1998 the Arbitration (International Commercial) Act was passed, resembling the English Arbitration Act 1996.

As a result of that codification process, Ireland produced separate pieces of legislation which were differently applicable to national and international arbitrations. While the Acts of 1954 and 1980 governed domestic arbitration, international arbitrations were governed by the 1998 Act.

The current situation is governed by the Arbitration Act 2010,[13] which provides the general and default system in Ireland (as stated in its section 29), repealing the 1954–98 Acts (section 4).[14] The origin of this Act can be traced back to 2008, when the International Council for Commercial Arbitration (ICCA) Conference took place in Dublin.[15] The Act, which gives force to the United Nations Commission on International Trade Law (UNCITRAL) Model Law 1985, on International Commercial Arbitration for Ireland (with its amendments as adopted in 2006) adds some provisions which supplement the articles of the Model Law, to allow not only a sound application of that text, but also a coordination between arbitral institutions and courts in Ireland.

Pursuant to the aim of the UNCITRAL Model Law, the Act follows the so-called 'monistic' approach and is therefore applicable to domestic as well as to international arbitrations. Thus the new Act clearly departs from the previously accepted approach in Ireland. However, it also has to be taken into consideration that other legal instruments provide for statutory arbitration.[16] In addition to this, it is also important to underline that several pieces of Irish legislation have been amended to be adapted to the new statutory framework after 2010.[17]

Besides and from an international perspective, Ireland was an early, as well as an active, participant in the international codification process of arbitration law, which has taken place mainly in UNCITRAL, but also in the framework of the World Bank.[18] Firstly, Ireland acceded to the New York Convention 1958, on the Recognition and Enforcement of Foreign Arbitral Awards, in 1959. Secondly, Ireland ratified the Washington Convention on the Settlement of Investment Disputes between States and Nationals of Other States, in 1981.[19] Thirdly, Ireland adopted the UNCITRAL Model Law on International Commercial Arbitration of 1985, in 1998 and more recently in 2012 (with its amendments as adopted in 2006).

---

13 Available at <www.irishstatutebook.ie/2010/en/act/pub/0001/index.html> accessed 23.10.2012.

14 A comparison of the two systems can be found at: N.G. Bunni, 'The Arbitration Act 2010' (2010) 76(4) *Arbitration* 582, 582–585.

15 N.G. Bunni, *supra* n. 14, p. 586.

16 See *infra* at section 2.2.1.

17 For example, the Statute of Limitations 1957, the Landlord and Tenant (Ground Rents) Act 1967, the Patents Act 1992, and the Copyright and Related Rights Act 2000. See B. Mansfield, *Arbitration Act 2010 and Model Law: A Commentary*, Clarus Press, Dublin 2012, pp. 73–76.

18 See <www.uncitral.org/uncitral/uncitral_texts/arbitration.html> accessed 23.10.2012.

19 See <https://icsid.worldbank.org/ICSID/ICSID/RulesMain.jsp> accessed 23.10.2012.

## 1.2. MEDIATION AND CONCILIATION

The introduction of mediation and conciliation in Ireland is relatively novel as compared with arbitration. However both methods have rapidly evolved and have gained popularity in Ireland, where they have become commonplace.[20] The first examples of mediation in Ireland can be traced back to 1986, when the Legal Aid Board offered mediation services for families and to 1989, when the Judicial Separation and Family Law Reform Act 1989[21] established that spouses should try to mediate their dispute before seeking judicial separation.[22] However, it was from the beginning of the twenty-first century that mediation and conciliation started to gain support and popularity. From that moment, both public institutions and private organisations have taken decisive steps to promote the use of mediation and conciliation in Ireland.

The first to react were private institutions like the Mediator's Institute of Ireland (MII)[23] and the Irish Commercial Mediation Association (ICMA),[24] which started to work on an *ad hoc* basis.[25] In support of this, it is also worth mentioning the importance of the training courses organised in Dublin by organisations like the Centre for Effective Dispute Resolution (CEDR),[26] as well as the specialised mediation and conciliation schemes which started to be developed for particular sectors of industry and public services.[27]

Besides this, mediation and conciliation also started to attract the attention of public institutions. First of all, as mentioned before, particular mediation schemes in relation to some public services were developed (i.e. health, discrimination and consumer complaints).[28] Secondly, it is also worth mentioning the support and direction provided from some courts (in particular, the Commercial Division of the High Court). Thirdly, and from a legislative perspective, by the normative process started by the Houses of the *Óireachtas*

---

20 N. Dunleavy and G. Carey, 'Ireland', in *The International Comparative Legal Guide to: International Arbitration 2011*, Global Legal Group, London, p. 265; electronic document available at <www.mop.ie/__data/assets/pdf_file/0006/7962/International-Comparative-Legal-Guide-International-Arbitration-2011.pdf> accessed 23.10.2012.

21 See <www.irishstatutebook.ie/1989/en/act/pub/0006/index.html> accessed 23.10.2012.

22 W. Aylmer, 'Ireland', in C. Esplugues, J.L. Iglesias and G. Palao (eds.), *Civil and Commercial Mediation in Europe*, Intersentia, Cambridge 2012, p. 235. See also S. Conneely, *Family Mediation in Ireland*, Ashgate/Dartmouth, Aldershot 2002, pp. 4 ff.; K. Liston, *Family Law Negotiations. An Alternative Approach*, Round Hall/Thomson Reuters, Dublin 2005, p. 8.

23 See <www.themii.ie/> accessed 23.10.2012. J. Madigan, *supra* n. 1, pp. 182–188.

24 See <www.icma.ie/> accessed 23.10.2012. J. Madigan, *supra* n. 1, pp. 200–201.

25 W. Aylmer, *supra* n. 22, p. 236.

26 At <www.cedr.com/>. In particular, see <www.cedrsolve.ie/> and <www.cedr.com/?location=/news/archive/20030120.htm> accessed 23.10.2012.

27 See *infra* at section 2.2.2.

28 See *infra* at section 2.2.2.

(the National Parliament) in 2010, to create a general and default legal framework for mediation and conciliation in Ireland.

As far as the legislative process is concerned, 2010 was a significant year for mediation and conciliation in Ireland. The first step to be mentioned is the seminal Report of the Law Reform Commission (LRC), 'Alternative Dispute Resolution: Mediation and Conciliation' of 2010.[29] This was a complete analysis of mediation and conciliation in Ireland which included 108 recommendations, covering significant aspects like: the scope of both dispute resolution mechanisms, the general principles applicable to them, the relationship between ADR and the courts, accreditation and training of mediators and conciliators, as well as their application to disputes related to employment and industrial relations, family relationships, personal injuries, commercial law, consumer affairs and property law. Following the LRC Report, a Draft Mediation and Conciliation Bill was published as an Appendix with 38 sections, focusing on a facilitative model.[30] Also in that year, the Rules of the Superior Courts (Mediation and Conciliation) 2010 were introduced.

However, the legislative process is not yet finished. The Irish Government has shown great support for mediation in its Programme for Government for 2011–16, where it was highlighted that '[w]e will encourage and facilitate use of mediation to resolve commercial, civil and family disputes in order to speed up resolution of disputes, reduce legal costs and ameliorate the stress of contested court proceedings'.[31]

In 2012 a Draft Scheme of Mediation Bill was published[32] (which did not cover conciliation), establishing 20 sections based on the LRC Report which cover all aspects of the mediation process and constitutes the basis of the future Mediation Act. More recently, in June 2012 the Joint Committee on Justice, Defence and Equality of the Houses of the *Óireachtas* delivered a Report in relation to the Scheme welcoming the proposed legislation and highlighting some of the main elements of the Scheme (i.e. public awareness, regulation of mediators, Code of Conduct, national register, confidentiality and withdrawal of mediators) to turn Ireland into a centre for international mediation.[33] In that respect, a new Bill is expected to be published shortly.

Furthermore, it must be underlined that, as a Member State of the EU, the approval of the Directive 2008/52/EC of the European Parliament and of the

29 Hereinafter, LRC Report 2010. Available at <www.lawreform.ie/_fileupload/Reports/r98ADR.pdf> accessed 23.10.2012.

30 See M. Twomey, 'The Mediation and Conciliation Bill 2010 – Proposed Changes to Alternative Dispute Resolution' (2011) 4 *IBL* 22.

31 Available at <www.socialjustice.ie/content/programme-government-2011–2016-full-text> accessed 23.10.2012.

32 Available at <www.justice.ie/en/JELR/MedBillGSFinal.pdf/Files/MedBillGSFinal.pdf> accessed 23.10.201. See B. Hutchinson, 'Editorial. Draft Mediation Bill Published' [2012] *CLP* 19.

33 Available at <www.oireachtas.ie/parliament/media/committees/justice/mediation-bill-report.pdf> accessed 23.10.2012.

Council of 21 May 2008 on certain aspects of mediation in civil and commercial matters,[34] has been a decisive element to be taken into account for the evolution of mediation in Ireland. In relation to this, the European Communities (Mediation) Regulations 2011[35] transposed the Directive into Irish law.

## 2. CURRENT STATE OF ADR

ADR enjoys a healthy and promising situation in Ireland. Both arbitration and mediation and conciliation currently enjoy a thriving practice, and a balanced intervention from courts. In spite of the different levels of regulation, all ADR schemes have been taken seriously by the legislature, in order to create modern legal frameworks to support them.

### 2.1. LEGAL FRAMEWORK

#### *2.1.1. Arbitration*

As mentioned earlier, the current relevant text in the field of arbitration in Ireland is the Arbitration Act 2010, in force from 8 June 2010. Besides, and complementing that Act, it is also worth mentioning the Rules of the Superior Courts (Arbitration) Act 2010,[36] defining the possibilities of application to the Court in relation to arbitral proceedings.[37]

The Arbitration Act 2010 modernises Irish arbitration law by replacing the existing legislation and by providing a comprehensive new legal framework, based on the UNCITRAL Model Law of 1985 (with its amendments as adopted in 2006). The primary purpose of the Arbitration Act 2010 is to give force to and apply the Model Law to all arbitrations which take place within Ireland, regardless of their character (national or international) as well as to adapt and supplement the existing Irish legal environment and arbitral practice.

The Arbitration Act 2010 is divided into three Parts and contains 32 sections. Part 1 (Preliminary and General) provides, *inter alia,* definitions to ease its

34 *OJ* L 136, 24.5.2008, pp. 3–8.

35 SI No. 209/2011. Available at <www.irishstatutebook.ie/pdf/2011/en.si.2011.0209.pdf> accessed 23.10.2012. See J. Heneghan and C. Byrne, 'Ireland implements Mediation Directive' (2011) 3 *Accountancy Plus* 18–19; B. Holohan, '"Free at last, free at last. Thank God Almighty, we are free at last". Judges' powers under the new European Communities (Mediation) Regulations 2001' (2011) 1 *Arbitration and ADR Review* 3.

36 SI No. 361/2010. Available at <www.irishstatutebook.ie/2010/en/si/0361.html> accessed 23.10.2012.

37 See *infra* at section 3.1.

interpretation (section 2),[38] as well as determining the application of the Act (section 3), and the repeal of the 1954–98 Acts (section 4). Part 2 (Arbitration) is the longest and contains the most relevant provisions. Finally, Part 3 (Reference to Arbitration where Proceedings are Pending before Court) relates to the power of the High Court and Circuit Court to stay proceedings to facilitate arbitration (section 32).[39]

In relation to its scope of application, the 2010 Act is the general and default system for arbitrations in Ireland (section 29). It covers arbitration agreements to which a State authority is a party (section 28);[40] however most of the Act is not applicable in proceedings pursuant to the Washington Convention (section 25). The Act is also not applicable to questions related to the employment relationship or arbitration under the Industrial Relations Act 1964 (section 30). Consumer arbitration is not be covered in the case of an agreement with a consumer (but not including an amateur sportsman) where the term has not been individually negotiated[41] and if the dispute amounts to less than €5,000 (section 31).[42] However, according to some authors, this economic limit is not always in the best interest of consumers.[43] The non-application of the Act is fully compatible with 'private' arbitrations and the possible intervention of the High Court in those arbitral proceedings.[44]

There are several aspects of Part 2 and 3 of the Arbitration Act 2010 which are worth mentioning. However, specific questions related to the relationship between the courts and arbitration will be covered later.[45] The most decisive Part of the Act is Part 2, which starts by adopting the Model Law to either domestic or international arbitrations (section 6), which turns into a directly applicable text (Schedule 1 of the Act). After this important assertion, which will favour Ireland as an attractive venue for arbitration,[46] the rest of the provisions introduce significant clarifications and provide for particular solutions to fit the Model Law within the Irish legal system.

The Model Law and arbitration clauses will be construed taking into account the *travaux préparatoires* of UNCITRAL, according to section 8. That means that unless otherwise provided, most of the Model Law will be of direct

---

38 Note the 'curious' definition of arbitration, which covers international or not international commercial arbitrations, based on previous drafts of the Act. See B. Hutchinson, 'The New Irish Arbitration Act' (2010) *Int. ALR* 15, 15–16.

39 See B. Mansfield, *supra* n. 17, pp. 81–84. *Bord na Mona v. John Sisks & Son Ltd* (unreported), provides the authority on the approach taken by the court in relation to the extension of time. See A. Dowling-Hussey and D. Dunne, *supra* n. 10, pp. 399–400.

40 In that respect, see *Byrne v. Ireland* [1972] 1 IR 241.

41 To be proved by the non-consumer. B. Mansfield, *supra* n. 17, p. 80.

42 Unless the parties agree after the dispute has arisen.

43 B. Hutchinson, *supra* n. 38, pp. 16–17.

44 B. Mansfield, *supra* n. 17, p. 77.

45 See *infra* at section 3.1.

46 B. Hutchinson, *supra* n. 38, p. 17.

application. This mainly affects aspects of the arbitration agreement, the composition of the arbitral tribunal, the granting of interim measures and preliminary orders, conduct of arbitral proceedings, the creation of the award and the termination of arbitral proceedings. This legal regimen fully respects party autonomy as regards the different aspects of the arbitration agreement and the conduct of arbitral proceedings.[47]

Additionally, section 24 specifies that the New York Convention (interpreted in accordance with the recommendation of 2006), the Geneva Convention and the Geneva Protocol will have force of law in Ireland.[48]

The Arbitration Act 2010 provides for particular solutions related to the composition of the arbitral tribunal, arbitral proceedings and the award. Section 7 determines the commencement of the arbitral proceedings for the purposes of this Act and also for the purposes of section 496 of the Merchant Shipping Act 2010, referring to the moment agreed by the parties or the day 'on which the respondent received a written communication containing a request for the dispute to be referred to arbitration'.[49]

Sections 13 to 22 regulate the arbitral tribunal and its powers. Section 13 departs from the position in section 10 of the Model Law, by establishing one (rather than three) as the default number of arbitrators,[50] in order to reduce the costs of arbitral proceedings.[51] The arbitral tribunal may examine parties or a witness, and administer oaths or affirmations (section 14),[52] as well as take evidence in aid of a foreign arbitration (section 15).[53] Concurrent arbitrations can be consolidated by agreement of the parties (section 16).[54] That agreement will also be taken into account when interpleader is granted by a court (section 17).[55] The arbitral tribunal's power regarding the award of interest is regulated under section 18,[56] while section 19 refers to the possibility of providing security for the costs of the arbitration and section 21 to the recovery of costs, fees and

---

47 An analysis of the effects of the Model Law on Ireland can be found in N.G. Bunni, *supra* n. 14, pp. 586–592.

48 Schedules 2, 3 and 4 of the Arbitration Act 2010.

49 See B. Mansfield, *supra* n. 17, pp. 22–26.

50 In that respect and departing from the previous system, the High Court is not able to direct an arbitrator to a particular case. N.G. Bunni, *supra* n. 14, p. 592.

51 See B. Mansfield, *supra* n. 17, pp. 38–39.

52 *Ibid.*, p. 40.

53 *Ibid.*, pp. 40–41.

54 *Ibid.*, pp. 41–42.

55 According to Mansfield: 'Interpleader is a civil process whereby a person in possession of property or owning money that is or may be claimed adversely by two or more persons (to one or other of whom he can be liable) is enable, subject to certain conditions, to be relieved from liability to the claimants or either of them with regard to the disposition of property or money'. See B. Mansfield, *supra* n. 17, p. 43.

56 This question is however not covered by the Model Law. N.G. Bunni, *supra* n. 14, p. 584.

expenses of the tribunal,[57] leaving plenty of room for party autonomy even before the dispute takes place.[58]

In relation to the arbitral award and according to section 20, the arbitral tribunal can make an award requiring specific performance of a contract (other than a contract for the sale of land).[59] Section 22 grants arbitrators immunity for acts or omissions during the arbitration proceedings, extending their immunity to all civil liability and not only from liability for negligence.[60] The award will be enforceable and binding on the parties, according to section 23, a provision which will not affect its recognition or enforcement under the Geneva and New York Conventions.[61]

Moreover, while section 26 determines the survival of the arbitration agreement and the authority of the arbitral tribunal in the event of death,[62] section 27 clarifies that an arbitration agreement forming part of a contract to which a bankrupt is a party will be enforceable for those disputes related to that contract and therefore treated like other contracts.[63]

### *2.1.2. Mediation and conciliation*

Mediation and conciliation enjoy a fruitful practice in Ireland. This is partly due to the support of certain institutions and organisations and, more importantly, the active involvement of the High Court.[64] Further, the current economic situation also supports the use of this ADR mechanism.[65] However, in spite of the current great interest and practice, a general Act on mediation or conciliation has not yet been enacted in Ireland.[66] However, there are several pieces of legislation which include these methods, for diverse purposes, as well as diverse State bodies which use either mediation or conciliation in specific dispute areas.[67]

---

57 Costs will be awarded 'as it sees fit' and not expected to 'follow the event', shifting from the traditional model, unless parties otherwise provide. B. Hutchinson, *supra* n. 38, p. 16.

58 N. Dunleavy and G. Carey, *supra* n. 20, p. 264.

59 See B. Mansfield, *supra* n. 17, pp. 49–50.

60 See B. Mansfield, *supra* n. 17, p. 57. As for domestic arbitration, the question of arbitrator's immunity was already established as for the prior system in *Redahan v. Minister for Education* [2005] IEHC 271.

61 In a recent judgment the High Court (Commercial) considered that, in the application of that section, it did not had 'jurisdiction to give leave to enforce' a partial award (delivered at Vienna) and granted and adjournment on enforcement. *Danish Polish Telecommunication Group I/S v. Telekomunikacja Polska SA* [2011] IEHC 369.

62 See B. Mansfield, *supra* n. 17, pp. 67–70.

63 *Ibid.*, p. 69.

64 J. Behan, 'A Focus on Ireland: Introduction and Overview' (2010) 76(4) *Arbitration* 580, 581.

65 In that respect, M. Quinn and N. White, 'Mediation –The answer to legal costs critics?' (May 2011) *Law Society Gazette* 20; available at <www.lawsociety.ie/Documents/Gazette/Gazette%202011/May2011.pdf> accessed 23.10.2012.

66 See *supra* at section 1.2.

67 See *infra* at section 2.2.2.

In that respect, the following pieces of legislation provide for mediation in relation to several fields of litigation. First of all, mediation and conciliation were referred to in relation to family disputes in the Judicial Separation and Family Law Reform Act 1989, the Family Law (Divorce) Act 1996,[68] the Children Act 1997[69] and the Civil Partnership and Certain Rights and Obligations of Cohabitants Act 2010.[70] Discrimination disputes can also be managed through ADR, thanks to the Employment Equality Act 1998[71] or the Equal Status Act 2000.[72] Moreover, personal injury cases may be solved by those methods as contemplated in the Personal Injuries Assessment Board Act 2003,[73] the Civil Liability and Courts Act 2004,[74] and the Medical Practitioners Act 2007.[75] Finally, it is also worth mentioning the Multi-Unit Development Act 2011.[76]

Additionally, several statutory provisions of a procedural character refer to ADR, attempting to coordinate court activities and ADR proceedings. In that respect, the following should be mentioned: the Enforcement of Court Order (Amendment) Act 2009,[77] the Circuit Court Rules (Case Progression (General)) 2009,[78] the Rules of the Superior Courts (Mediation and Conciliation) 2010[79] and the European Communities (Mediation) Regulations 2011.

Apart from that, it is worth mentioning that the Mediators' Institute of Ireland has developed a Code of Ethics and Professional Conduct.[80]

The Draft General Scheme of Mediation Bill 2012 does not provide for a comprehensive set of rules, but 20 Heads which aim at guiding the future Mediation Act. Head 2 defines mediation as 'a facilitative and confidential process in which a mediator assists parties to a dispute to attempt by themselves, on a voluntary basis, to reach a mutually acceptable and voluntary agreement to resolve their dispute'. According to Heads 4 and 5 of the Draft, parties must be informed about mediation by solicitors and barristers before starting a judicial

68 See <www.irishstatutebook.ie/1996/en/act/pub/0033/index.html> accessed 23.10.2012.

69 See <www.irishstatutebook.ie/1997/en/act/pub/0040/index.html> accessed 23.10.2012.

70 Available at <www.irishstatutebook.ie/2010/en/act/pub/0024/index.html> accessed 23.10.2012.

71 See <www.irishstatutebook.ie/1998/en/act/pub/0021/index.html> accessed 23.10.2012.

72 See <www.irishstatutebook.ie/2000/en/act/pub/0008/index.html> accessed 23.10.2012.

73 See <www.irishstatutebook.ie/2003/en/act/pub/0046/index.html> accessed 23.10.2012.

74 See <www.irishstatutebook.ie/2004/en/act/pub/0031/index.html> accessed 23.10.2012.

75 Available at <www.irishstatutebook.ie/pdf/2007/en.act.2007.0025.pdf> accessed 23.10.2012. See W. Aylmer, *supra* n. 22, p. 238.

76 Available at <www.justice.ie/en/JELR/Pages/Multi_Unit_Act> accessed 23.10.2012. Section 27 of this Act refers to the possibility of a 'mediation conference' in the framework of a judicial proceeding provided for in section 24.

77 Available at <www.irishstatutebook.ie/pdf/2009/en.act.2009.0021.pdf> accessed 23.10.2012.

78 Available at <www.irishstatutebook.ie/2009/en/act/pub/0021/index.html> accessed 23.10.2012.

79 See <www.irishstatutebook.ie/2010/en/si/0502.html> accessed 23.10.2012.

80 See <www.themii.ie/documents/CoE.pdf> accessed 23.10.2012. See J. Madigan, *supra* n. 1, p. 163.

procedure, and sign a statement after the information has been received.[81] They should also receive information concerning the costs of the proceedings.[82]

Head 6 refers to mediation conditions and establishes the possibility for the parties to engage in mediation and their autonomy in respect of the terms of the agreement they may reach. If that happens, Head 15 determines the possibility for the Court to facilitate the mediation process. The standards required of mediators are dealt with in Heads 7 to 9, thus underlining the importance of the quality of the mediation proceedings.[83] The first, Head 7, relates to the role of the mediators, *inter alia* by requiring a written agreement between the parties and informing the parties of their duties and the consequences of their engagement in mediation. Unless otherwise agreed by the parties, mediators should not make proposals to resolve the dispute during the mediation process. The duty to provide information on training and experience is mentioned in Head 8. Head 9 relates to Codes of Practice (conduct) for mediators.

Head 10 provides for the highly controversial and important issue of confidentiality, establishing that all communications between the parties will remain confidential. In that respect, it should be mentioned that, according to Regulation 4 of the European Communites (Mediation) Regulations 2011, confidentiality will be preserved but may exceptionally be limited for public policy reasons.[84] According to Head 11, agreements to submit the dispute to mediation create obligations for the parties and thus are considered enforceable as contracts, especially where there is a procedure which has already been defined.[85] In that respect, the settlement must be considered as a contract between the parties.[86] However, mediation agreements will only be enforceable after an order of the court.[87]

In line with current practice in Ireland, Head 12 enables the court to invite parties to consider mediation. After the mediation process has ended, the mediator shall report to the court, without comment or recommendation, as determined by Head 13. As established in Head 14, the mediation process will have an effect on limitation and prescription periods, from the moment the dispute is referred to mediation until 30 days after the process ends. Costs are dealt with in Head 16. In principle, costs and fees will be equally shared by the parties.[88] However, and taking Head 17 into consideration, when costs must be

---

81 W. Aylmer, *supra* n. 22, p. 243. Section 6 of the Guide to Professional Conduct of Solicitors in Ireland also refers to this obligation. Available at <www.lawsociety.ie/Documents/committees/conduct2.pdf> accessed 23.10.2012.

82 J. Madigan, *supra* n. 1, p. 68.

83 B. Hutchinson, *supra* n. 32.

84 J. Madigan, *supra* n. 1, pp. 160–161.

85 *Health Service Executive v. Keogh, trading as Keogh Software* [2009] IEHC 419. See W. Aylmer, *supra* n. 22, p. 239; B. Hutchinson, *supra* n. 2, pp. 115–116.

86 B. Hutchinson, *supra* n. 2, pp. 127–128; J. Madigan, *supra* n. 1, p. 175.

87 W. Aylmer, *supra* n. 22, p. 241.

88 *Ibid.*, p. 243.

awarded, any unjustified refusal of one of the parties to attend the information session or even to consider the use of mediation should be taken into account.[89]

The Draft General Scheme of Mediation Bill 2012 also contemplates particular issues such as the involvement of children in mediation related to family law disputes (Head 18). Mediator immunity is also an important issue and, in relation to this, the projected system contemplates in Head 19 that mediators will not be liable for damages,[90] except in cases of bad faith with malicious purpose, or when human rights or the welfare of children are disregarded.[91] Finally, Head 20 also allows the court to direct parties to mediation in personal injury actions.[92]

## 2.2. AREAS OF PRACTICE

Nowadays, ADR covers several diverse areas of dispute resolution practice in Ireland.

### *2.2.1. Arbitration*

In relation to arbitration, there are several pieces of Irish legislation which contemplates recourse to statutory arbitration. In that respect, the following Acts can be mentioned:[93] the Wildlife Act 1976 (amended in 2000), Derelict Sites Act 1990, National Lottery Act 1986, Bankruptcy Act 1988, Patents Act 1992, Merchant Shipping (Salvage and Wreck) Act 1993, Statistics Act 1993, Roads Act 1993, Dublin Docklands and Development Authority Act 1997, Credit Union Act 1997, Universities Act 1997, Air Navigation and Transport Act 1998, Copyright and Related Rights Act 2000, Transport (Railway Infrastructure) Act 2001, Industrial Designs Act 2001, Communication Regulation Act 2002, Broadcasting (Major Events Television Coverage) Act 2005.

Arbitration is commonly used for commercial disputes, as well as for construction disputes. In that respect, the Rules for use with Public Works and Construction Services Contracts 2008 should be mentioned.[94] Further, Engineers Ireland launched a Dispute Resolution Board in 2009,[95] establishing a

89 J. Fox, 'Order 56A and the Cost implications of refusal to engage in ADR' (2011) *Bar Review* 22; J. Madigan, *supra* n. 1, p. 179; B. Mansfield, 'The cost implications for refusing to avail of ADR in civil litigation in the Superior Courts' [2011] *CLP* 8.

90 J. Madigan, *supra* n. 1, p. 180.

91 B. Hutchinson, *supra* n. 32.

92 *Ibid.*

93 See A. Dowling-Hussey and D. Dunne, *supra* n. 10, p. 55; B. Mansfield, *supra* n. 89, p. 73.

94 Available at <http://constructionprocurement.gov.ie/arbitration-rules/> accessed 23.10.2012. See B. Hutchinson, *supra* n. 2, pp. 17 and 25; R. Sherlock, 'Dispute Resolution Provisions in the (Irish) Public Works Contracts' (2010) 76(4) *Arbitration* 636, 639–640.

95 See <www.engineersireland.ie/services/dispute-resolution.aspx> accessed 23.10.2012.

new Arbitration Procedure in 2011.[96] Arbitration is also a mechanism to solve consumer disputes, for example holiday disputes.[97] In that respect, an arbitration scheme for tour operators has been developed, within the framework of the Chartered Institute of Arbitrators – Irish Branch. Another example can be found in the Advertising Standards Authority of Ireland.

### *2.2.2. Mediation and conciliation*

Mediation and conciliation have gained much popularity and have spread to diverse areas of practice in Ireland during the last two decades. There are several reasons for this development and for the good expectations for the future in Ireland. They relate not only to their benefits, but also to the more common use by the courts, the existence of experienced professionals and the increased awareness of businesses.[98] Additionally, the high success rate of ADR, particularly mediation, must be highlighted.[99] Originally, ADR mechanisms developed on an out-of-court and *ad hoc* basis.[100] However, both State intervention and support from private organisations led to these significant developments.

First of all, several State bodies currently offer mediation and conciliation services. In that respect, the relevant bodies include the Equality Tribunal,[101] the National Disability Authority,[102] and the Conciliation Service of the Labour Relations Commission.[103] In relation to family disputes, a Family Mediation Service has been developed, acting through the Family Support Agency,[104] and since 2012 there has been a service annexed to the Dublin Metropolitan District Family Court.[105] Collaborative practice can also be mentioned, as it is gaining popularity in Ireland to cope with family disputes.[106]

---

96 Available at <https://www.engineersireland.ie/EngineersIreland/media/SiteMedia/services/employment-services/Arbitration-Procedure-2011.pdf> accessed 23.10.2012. On the history and development of the Dispute Resolution Board, see C. Fahy, 'The Role of Engineers Ireland in Dispute Resolution' (2010) 76(4) *Arbitration* 620. In relation to the application of the Arbitration Act 2010 to those arbitration procedures, see C. Fahy, 'Dispute Resolution in the Irish Construction Industry: Future Trends' (2012) 78(2) *Arbitration* 163, 166–167.

97 N. Dunleavy and G. Carey, *supra* n. 20, p. 265.

98 See the Irish Commercial Mediation Association (ICMA) article published in 2011, 'ADR gaining ground in Ireland'; available at <www.icma.ie/_fileupload/ADR%20gaining%20ground%20in%20Ireland.pdf> accessed 23.10.2012.

99 LRC Report 2010, *supra* n. 29, p. 9. Also J. Doyle, 'Mediation in Commercial Disputes', Dillon Eustace, Dublin 2010, pp. 4 and 7; available at <www.dilloneustace.ie/download/1/Mediation%20in%20Commercial%20Disputes.pdf> accessed 23.10.2012.

100 W. Aylmer, *supra* n. 22, p. 238.

101 See <www.equalitytribunal.ie> accessed 23.10.2012.

102 See <www.nda.ie> accessed 23.10.2012.

103 See <www.lrc.ie/docs/Welcome/4.htm> accessed 23.10.2012. See J. Madigan, *supra* n. 1, pp. 188–195.

104 See <www.fsa.ie> accessed 23.10.2012.

105 W. Aylmer, *supra* n. 22, p. 238. See <www.courts.ie/courts.ie/library3.nsf/16c93c36d3635d5180256e3f003a4580/3a8061a30c8f0f46802578ee003e24f9?OpenDocument> accessed 23.10.2012.

106 J. Madigan, *supra* n. 1, p. 80.

Other initiatives of interest are the Private Residential Tenancy Board,[107] the Advertising Standards Authority of Ireland,[108] the Financial Services Ombudsman's Bureau,[109] the Office of the Pensions Ombudsman,[110] and the Direct Selling Association of Ireland.[111]

Secondly, nowadays many organisations provide services in the field of ADR in Ireland. In that respect, the following can be mentioned: the Mediator's Institute of Ireland,[112] the Irish Commercial Mediation Association,[113] Friarylaw,[114] the Mediation Forum Ireland,[115] Mediate Ireland,[116] the Law Society of Ireland,[117] the Bar Council,[118] the Chartered Institute of Arbitrators – Irish Branch,[119] and the Dublin International Arbitration Centre.[120]

As mentioned above, construction disputes have attracted a great deal of interest for the use of ADR schemes.[121] In relation to this, the Royal Institute of the Architects of Ireland, as part of its standard contract,[122] has developed a mediation system[123] based on the Building Control Act,[124] as well as a conciliation procedure.[125] Engineers Ireland[126] also established a conciliation procedure in 2007[127] and a mediation procedure in 2011.[128] Finally, the Construction Industry Federation[129] has established mandatory mediation in one of its standard contracts.[130]

---

107 See <https://www.prtb.ie> accessed 23.10.2012.

108 See <www.asai.ie> accessed 23.10.2012.

109 See <www.financialombudsman.ie> accessed 23.10.2012.

110 info@pensionsombudsman.ie.

111 See <http://dsai.ie/index.php> accessed 23.10.2012.

112 See <www.themii.ie> accessed 23.10.2012.

113 See <www.icma.ie> accessed 23.10.2012.

114 See <www.friarylaw-mediation.ie> accessed 23.10.2012.

115 See <www.mediationforumireland.com> accessed 23.10.2012.

116 See <http://mediateireland.com> accessed 23.10.2012.

117 See <www.lawsociety.ie> accessed 23.10.2012.

118 See <www.lawlibrary.ie/viewdoc.asp?DocID=4> accessed 23.10.2012.

119 See <www.arbitration.ie> accessed 23.10.2012.

120 See <www.dublinarbitration.ie> accessed 23.10.2012.

121 B. Hutchinson, *supra* n. 2, pp. 17–18 and 120–129.

122 *Ibid.*, p. 120.

123 See <www.riai.ie/register/resolving_disputes> accessed 23.10.2012.

124 Available at <www.oireachtas.ie/viewdoc.asp?fn=/documents/bills28/acts/2007/a2107.pdf> accessed 23.10.2012.

125 Available at <www.riai.ie/uploads/files/Conciliation_Procedures_as_referred_to_in_the_relevant_clauses_of_the_RIAI_Agreements.pdf> accessed 23.10.2012.

126 See <www.engineersireland.ie/services/dispute-resolution.aspx> accessed 23.10.2012.

127 Available at <www.engineersireland.ie/EngineersIreland/media/SiteMedia/services/employment-services/Conciliation-Procedure-2007.pdf> accessed 23.10.2012.

128 Available at <www.engineersireland.ie/EngineersIreland/media/SiteMedia/services/employment-services/Mediation-Procedure-2011.pdf> accessed 23.10.2012.

129 See <www.cif.ie> accessed 23.10.2012.

130 J. Behan, *supra* n. 64, p. 580.

## 3. THE COURT PROCESS AND ADR

Irish legislation has recognised the significant importance of the relationship between the ADR process and the courts. This question has undergone a significant evolution during the legislative process. Current regulation is most heavily focused on arbitration. However, in line with the growing importance of mediation and conciliation, the legislature has increased its focus in this area.

### 3.1. ARBITRATION

Irish courts supported arbitration under the application of the 1954–98 Acts.[131] The Arbitration Act 2010 (partly thanks to the influence of the Model Law) has clarified this relationship, has increased the powers of the arbitral tribunal and has also imposed more restrictions on courts as regards the possibility of intervening in arbitral proceedings, which has been dramatically minimised compared with the previous system.[132]

First of all, the 2010 Act has specified the possible situations of court intervention in arbitration.[133] The High Court will be competent in relation to all aspects referred to by the Model Law in Articles 6 and 9 – performed by its President (section 9) – and will also exercise powers in support of arbitral proceedings (section 10).[134] Thus, the High Court will be the competent authority in relation to questions as to interim measures or taking of evidence, as well as security for costs orders or discovery if agreed by the parties. In that respect it is important to state that the High Court has traditionally played this role in respect of arbitration in Ireland and, thus, this provision will enhance the specialisation of the judges.[135] Besides, the decision of the High Court will be final and shall not be appealed to the Supreme Court (section 11). This will be a major benefit for parties who will avoid the long delays and increase in costs which would be inevitable if parties could appeal to the Supreme Court.[136] The award will also be enforceable by leave of the High Court (section 23(1)). Finally

---

131 In this respect, *Keenan v. Shield Insurance Company* [1988] *IR* 89. See. R. Murphy, 'The Courts and Alternative Dispute Resolution' (2010) 76(4) *Arbitration* 600, 602; C. Ó Hoisín, *supra* n. 4, p. 253.

132 B. Mansfield, *supra* n. 89, p. 3. Also, J. Doyle, *A New Era for Arbitration in Ireland*, Dillon Eustace, Dublin 2010, pp. 4 and 7; available at <www.dilloneustace.ie/download/1/A%20New%20Era%20for%20Arbitration%20in%20Ireland.pdf> accessed 23.10.2012.

133 B. Hutchinson, *supra* n. 2, pp. 22–24.

134 See B. Mansfield, *supra* n. 89, pp. 28–36.

135 B. Hutchinson, *supra* n. 38, p. 16. In that respect, the importance of the commercial division of the High Court and the role played by Kelly J must be underlined. See R. Murphy, *supra* n. 131, p. 603.

136 See B. Mansfield, *supra* n. 89, pp. 36–37.

and according to section 32, the High Court and Circuit Court will have the power to stay proceedings to facilitate arbitration.

Secondly, it is important to underline that the current system (as regulated by Article 34 of the Model Law) limits the possibilities to set aside the arbitral award.[137] This solution contrasts with the previous regime, which provided for more possibilities of court intervention in arbitration proceedings. The application to set aside the arbitral award must generally be brought within three months, or 56 days if the ground is public policy (section 12).[138] In relation to the restriction of the powers of the courts, it will no longer be possible, as it was in the past, to refer questions of law to the High Court which may appear during the arbitration proceedings.[139]

Thirdly, section 32 enables the High Court and the Circuit Court to stay proceedings to facilitate arbitration proceedings. This provision permits a healthy and collaborative legal relationship between courts and arbitration proceedings and it enables the court to refer a case to arbitration. However, the Act does not contemplate penalties for those parties who do not agree to refer the dispute to arbitration following the stay.[140]

Finally, sections 23 and 24, when referring to the effects of awards and the enforcement of foreign awards by an Irish court, have clarified that the court must respectfully facilitate enforcement. Further, in accordance with Article 5 of the Model Law, a court is not able to set aside an award based on an error in law, as under the previous system in Ireland.[141] In that respect, it is also significant to note that Irish courts have traditionally shown a very collaborative attitude, when the enforcement of an award has been at stake.[142]

Therefore and due to the adoption of the Model Law, the Arbitration Act 2010 offers the parties a great degree of autonomy when compared with previous instruments (the 1954–98 Acts)[143] and limits the possibility for court intervention (as will be analysed later). However, it also envisages that courts can

---

137 This provision has been analysed under the prior system with deceptive results by the High Court (*Broström Tankers AB v. Factorias Vulcano SA* [2004] 2 IR 191) and more recently by the Supreme Court (*Galway City Council v. Samuel Kingston Construction Ltd* [2010] IESC 18). In relation to the second judgment, T. Wren, 'All is Not Well with Irish Arbitration: The Grey Clouds of Galway City Council v Samuel Kingston Construction Ltd' (2011) 77(3) *Arbitration* 387; A. Sahnley, '*Galway City Council v Samuel Kinston Construction Ltd*: A Response to Tom Wren' (2012) 78(2) *Arbitration* 203.

138 See B. Mansfield, *supra* n. 89, p. 38.

139 M.W. Carrigan, 'Arbitration Acts Spells' (Nov. 2010) *Law Society Gazette* 14, 15; available at <www.lawsociety.ie/Documents/Gazette/Gazette%202010/November 2010.pdf> accessed 23.10.2012.

140 B. Hutchinson, *supra* n. 38, p. 17.

141 B. Mansfield, *supra* n. 89, p. 3.

142 N. Dunleavy and G. Carey, *supra* n. 20, pp. 263–264. However the High Court refused to enforce a New York Convention award on public policy grounds in *Broström Tankers AB v. Factorias Vulcano SA* [2004] IR 191.

143 M.W. Carrigan, 'Arbitration Acts Spells', *supra* n. 139, p. 14; B. Mansfield, *supra* n. 89, p. 3.

refer disputes to arbitration.[144] This approach affects cost reduction and also positively affects the efficacy of the arbitration award.

On the other hand, attention must also be paid to Order 56 of the Rules of the Superior Courts,[145] as amended by the Rules of the Superior Courts (Arbitration) Act 2010. These Rules regulate and clarify the possibilities of application to the court concerning arbitration proceedings. According to section 3 of the Rules, the following orders may be made by request to the Court:[146]

> '(a) for any interim measure of protection in relation to an arbitration or an intended arbitration under Article 9 of the Model Law; or (b) to appoint an arbitrator pursuant to Article 11(3)(a) or 11(3)(b) of the Model Law; or (c) to take the necessary measure pursuant to Article 11(4) of the Model Law in the event of a failure to act, an inability to reach agreement or a failure to perform a function under an appointment procedure agreed upon by the parties; or (d) to decide on a challenge to an arbitrator pursuant to Article 13(3) of the Model Law (provided that the application is made within the period prescribed in that Article); or (e) to decide on the termination of the mandate of an arbitrator pursuant to Article 14(1) of the Model Law; or (f) to decide on a plea that the arbitral tribunal does not have jurisdiction pursuant to Article 16(3) of the Model Law (provided that the application is made within the period prescribed in that Article); or (g) to recognize or to recognize and enforce an interim measure issued by an arbitral tribunal in accordance with Article 17H(1), but subject to the provisions of Article 17I, of the Model Law; or (h) to issue any interim measure in relation to arbitration proceedings in accordance with Article 17J of the Model Law; or (i) to make an order in accordance with Article 34 of the Model Law (provided, in a case to which section 12 of the Act applies, the application is made within the period prescribed in that section); or (j) for the leave of the Court to enforce or to enter judgment in respect of an award pursuant to section 23(1) of the Act; or (k) to enforce an award in accordance with Article 35(1), but subject to the provisions of Articles 35 and 36, of the Model Law; or (l) to enforce the pecuniary obligations imposed by an award, within the meaning of section 25 of the Act, under that section; or (m) for any other relief under or in pursuance of the Act, for which provision is not otherwise made in this Order.'

## 3.2. MEDIATION AND CONCILIATION

Ireland has enacted significant pieces of legislation to allow an appropriate relationship between courts and ADR proceedings. As mentioned by some authors, these legislative initiatives aim at moving 'Irish civil procedure into the

144 This possibility already existed in the Commercial Court under the prior legal framework. See E. Stewart, 'A View From the Bar: Arbitration in Ireland 2010' (2010) 76(4) *Arbitration* 607, 607.

145 In relation to the practice and procedure of arbitration proceedings in the High Court prior to 2001, A. Dowling-Hussey and D. Dunne, *supra* n. 10, pp. 395–418.

146 See R. Murphy, *supra* n. 131, p. 602.

21st Century by integrating mediation into the civil justice system', as long as the 'intention is to make mediation a factor to be considered at all stages of a legal case'.[147] In the words of the LRC Report 2010, 'an integrated civil justice process includes a combination of ADR processes, such as mediation and conciliation, and the court-based litigation process'.[148]

Along these lines, the European Communities (Mediation) Regulations 2011 and the Rules of the Superior Courts (Mediation and Conciliation) 2010, which provide a new Order 56A to be inserted into the Rules of the Superior Courts, should be mentioned. The Draft Scheme of Mediation Bill 2012 deals with this relationship in Heads 11 to 15 and 20. The current legal framework implements decisive features of the Directive and preserves high standards for mediation in Ireland.[149]

First of all, Rule 2 of the 2010 Rules and Regulation 3 of the 2011 Regulations make it possible for the court, on its own initiative, to stay as well as to invite parties to take ADR into consideration, 'when it considers it appropriate and having regard the circumstances of the case' and 'where the parties consent'.[150] Those possibilities are also provided for by Heads 11 to 15 of the Draft Scheme of Mediation Bill 2012.

Secondly, according to those provisions, limitation periods can also be extended when the parties decide to use an ADR process, in order to facilitate the use of ADR. This possibility has also been considered in Heads 6 and 15 of the Draft Scheme of Mediation Bill 2012. In relation to this and in accordance with Rule 4 of the 2010 Rules, parties shall apply for that order 28 days before the date on which the proceedings are first listed for hearing. Further, the court may refuse to make an order for discovery when parties already have agreed to use an ADR mechanism.[151]

It is significant to note that non-engagement in ADR can involve financial consequences to the litigants and a collaborative attitude can lead to no order as to costs being made.[152] Finally and as mentioned in Regulation 5 of the 2011 Regulations, the parties can agree to apply to court to obtain an Order which will make the agreement enforceable.[153]

---

147 B. Hutchinson, *supra* n. 2, and J. Madigan, *supra* n. 1, p. 173.

148 LRC Report 2010, *supra* n. 29, p. 3.

149 Directive 2008/52/EC of the European Parliament and of the Council of 21 May 2008 on certain aspects of mediation in civil and commercial matters. See J. Madigan, *supra* n. 1, p. 160.

150 W. Aylmer, *supra* n. 22, pp. 237 and 242; B. Hutchinson, *supra* n. 2, p. 116; J. Madigan, *supra* n. 1, p. 175. On the limits of the judge's encouragement, B. Holohan, *supra* n. 35, p. 4. See *Charlton v. Kenny*, The High Court Record No. 2006/4266P; *Six Mile Investment [Unlimited] and others v. Companies Acts 1963 to 2001*, No. 2012/63 COS.

151 *Mandraki Associates Ltd v. Shell International Petroleum Company Ltd and others* [2006] IEHC 216. See B. Hutchinson, *supra* n. 2, p. 119.

152 In that respect, *Kay-El (Hong Kong) Ltd v. Musgrave Ltd* [2005] IEHC 418. See R. Murphy, *supra* n. 131, p. 604.

153 W. Aylmer, *supra* n. 22, p. 242; J. Heneghan and C. Byrne, *supra* n. 35, p. 19.

# 4. FUTURE PROSPECTS

As underlined in this work, ADR currently enjoys a fruitful practice and also has a promising future in Ireland.

## 4.1. ARBITRATION

Arbitration has enjoyed a very long tradition and now enjoys a flourishing practice in Ireland in many areas, particularly in the fields of construction, consumer and commercial disputes. Ireland has experienced significant recent legal developments that have taken place from 2010, updating the system. Ireland benefits from being an English-speaking common law country with highly qualified legal and other support professionals, and a supportive legislative and judicial framework based on the internationally accepted Model Law; Ireland also has modern communications facilities and infrastructure and is strategically located for both the USA and Europe. Taking all these circumstances into account, it can be anticipated that Ireland can become an appropriate venue for international commercial arbitration. Apart from that and in relation to the areas of practice, it is significant to note that construction disputes – a traditional field for arbitration – are now moving towards adjudication, as reflected in sections 6 and 9 of Construction Contracts Bill 2010.[154]

## 4.2. MEDIATION AND CONCILIATION

Mediation and conciliation has been practiced in Ireland since the late 1980s, especially in respect of family, equality and personal injuries disputes. Apart from the existing legislation devoted to specific sectors of practice, several Draft Bills and a General Scheme have been produced in Ireland in order to create a general and default legal system for mediation from 2010 to 2012 (leaving conciliation aside, however). This projected legislation is deeply rooted in an extensive practice and in the support of authorities (jurisdictional as well as legislative), practitioners and particulars. However, the enactment of a new Bill (and future Act) will clarify the current legal status of mediation and it will definitely increase its use in Ireland.[155] Apart from that, it can be noted that new methods, like collaborative practice, have been incorporated in order to manage family disputes.

---

154 Available at <www.oireachtas.ie/documents/bills28/bills/2010/2110/b21a10s.pdf> accessed 23.10.2012. See C. Fahy (2012), *supra* n. 96, p. 168; A. Hussey, 'Statutory Adjudication for Ireland' (2010) 76(4) *Arbitration* 613.

155 W. Aylmer, *supra* n. 22, p. 244.

# JAPAN

Masaaki HAGA*

## Contents



* The author thanks Ms Urayoshi for her support in translating into English. This work was supported by JSPS KAKENHI Grant No. 24530102.

# 1. INTRODUCTION

When discussing an ADR system as part of the civil-affairs dispute settlement mechanisms of Japan, it is useful to also have an understanding of the court system. A brief introduction to the court system will therefore be provided in section 1 before ADR is discussed in more detail in sections 2 to 4. In the last sections some future prospects of ADR in Japan are given.

## 1.1. COURTS

In Japan, there are one Supreme Court, eight high courts (with six branches), 50 district courts (203 branches) and 50 family courts, and 438 summary courts. The family court handles cases on disputes concerning family issues and has the same rank as district courts. Unlike many other countries, Japan does not have a Constitutional Court (subordinate judicial review system). The general court makes a constitutional judgment when judging a concrete case. Establishment of extraordinary tribunals is forbidden by the Constitution (Constitution Act, Article 76(2)).

The summary court and the district court take the role of a court of first instance. As for subject matter jurisdiction, a summary court handles a case when the amount in dispute is equal to or less than 1,400,000 yen, and a district court handles a case when the amount in dispute exceeds 1,400,000 yen (Court Act, Article 33(1)(1)). When the summary court conducts the first trial of the case, the district court is the court of second instance, and the high court is the court of third instance. When the court of first instance is the district court, the court of second instance is the high court and the third is the Supreme Court.

In civil cases there is no statutory requirement to be presented by a lawyer (see Article 54(1) of the Code of Civil Procedure, the principle that an attorney-at-law must serve as a counsel).

## 1.2. JUDICIAL POPULATION

According to the Japan Federation of Bar Associations the judicial population in 2011 consisted of 2,850 judges (excluding judges of summary courts), 1,816 prosecutors, and 30,518 attorneys.[1] The approximate overall population of Japan is 127,540,000 as of November 2012.[2]

1 Japan Federation of Bar Association (ed.), White Paper on Attorney (Bengoshi Hakusho) (2011), p. 98.

2 Data from the homepage of the Ministry of Internal Affairs and Communications, Statistics Bureau <www.stat.go.jp/data/jinsui/pdf/201211.pdf>.

From an international perspective the Japanese legal population is rather small. According to data on international comparison of judicial populations from 2011,[3] the number of people per one lawyer is 273 in the US, 435 in UK, 525 in Germany, and 1,244 in France, while it is 4,196 in Japan. The number of people per one judge is 9,553 in the US, 15,074 in UK, 4,070 in Germany, and 10,964 in France, while it is 44,932 in Japan. In addition, the number of people per one prosecutor is 9,455 in the US, 17,929 in UK, 15,971 in Germany, and 32,677 in France, while it is 71,500 in Japan.

## 1.3. CASES

It is also helpful to compare the total number of cases in each court (the number of newly accepted cases) and the number of conciliations by comparison.[4] In 2011 the summary court had 554,675 newly accepted cases, and there were 63,009 conciliation cases. In the district court, the number of newly accepted cases was 231,583, and conciliation cases were 11,882. In the high court, the number of newly accepted cases was 28,087, and conciliation cases were 5. In the Supreme Court, the number of newly accepted cases was 5,775. The total number of newly accepted cases of the family court in 2011 was 815,522, and, among those, the number of family conciliation cases was 137,390 for which the family court is also responsible (see further below).[5]

The number of cases newly accepted by a court, especially that of property-related cases, sharply changes according to the social situation of the year. For example the total number of cases newly accepted at the summary court in 2003 was 337,231. There were 613,260 civil conciliation cases at the summary court, and 537,015 of them were specifically conciliation cases regarding a multiple debtor.[6] The number of conciliation cases in 2003 is remarkably higher compared with the statistics in 2011. The high number was caused by the problem of the monetary crisis and unrecoverable debt disposal in Japan that was discussed as an urgent issue. The specific conciliation system that was to deal with the multiple debtor problem was introduced in 2000. The large number of specific conciliations in 2003 tells that this system was widely used. However, the number of family conciliation cases has not changed drastically. The number of family conciliation cases in 2003 was 136,125, and remains mostly unchanged.[7]

---

3 Japan Federation of Bar Association (ed.), *supra* n. 1, pp. 74–76.

4 General Secretariat, Supreme Court, Annual Report of Judicial Statistics for 2011, Vol. 1, Civil Cases (Heisei 23 Nendo Shiho Tokei Nempo Minjigyosei-hen), p. 2.

5 General Secretariat, Supreme Court, Annual Report of Judicial Statistics for 2011, Vol. 3, Family Cases (Heisei 23 Nendo Shiho Tokei Nempo Kaji-hen), p. 9.

6 General Secretariat, Supreme Court, Annual Report of Judicial Statistics for 2003, Vol. 1, Civil Cases (Heisei 15 Nendo Shiho Tokei Nempo Minjigyosei-hen), p. 24, p. 57.

7 General Secretariat, Supreme Court, Annual Report of Judicial Statistics for 2011, Vol. 3, Family Cases (Heisei 15 Nendo Shiho Tokei Nempo Kaji-hen), p. 2, p. 22.

# 2. OVERVIEW OF ADR

## 2.1. HISTORY OF ADR

The early ADR system can be characterised as consisting mainly of judicial type ADR which was responsive to social problems. Before the Second World War, judicial type conciliation was performed in broad fields, such as land and house lease, farm tenancy, labour disputes, and personnel affairs.[8] Back then, private sector type ADR was performed only by the Japan Shipping Exchange, and no governmental type ADR existed.

After the war, governmental type ADR came into the picture.[9] The Central Labour Relations Commission was established immediately after the war, and the Central Construction Work Screening Panel was formed a little later. In 1970, the authoritative governmental type ADR organisations, such as the Central Construction Work Dispute Screening Panel, were established. Many private sector type ADR organisations were formed after the 1990s.[10] For example, the Products Liability Center was founded in 1993 after the enforcement of the Product Liability Law.[11] In addition, the arbitration bodies responsible for handling intellectual property or sports dispute were founded around this time.

Recently, the specific conciliation system dealing with the problem of multiple debtors has been used most frequently. Since most users of the conciliation system had this problem, the law was revised in 2000 and provided a new system focusing on the multiple debtor problem by adding special provisions to the conciliation system.[12]

---

8 For judicial ADR, the following systems were established: land and house lease conciliation in 1922, farm tenancy conciliation in 1924, labour dispute conciliation and commercial affairs conciliation in 1926, monetary claims temporary conciliation in 1932, personal affairs conciliation in 1939, environmental dispute compensation conciliation in 1940, family affairs conciliation in 1948, civil conciliation in 1951, traffic conciliation in 1974, specific conciliation in 2000, and labour tribunal judgment system in 2006.

9 The Central Labour Relations Commission in 1946, the Central Construction Work Dispute Panel in 1956, the Consumer Affairs Center in 1965, and the Central Environmental Dispute Panel in 1970.

10 The Japan Commercial Arbitration Association in 1953, the Nichibenren Traffic Accident Consultation Center in 1967, the Traffic Accident Arbitration Committee in 1974, the Japan Center for Settlement of Traffic Accident Disputes in 1978, the Products Liability Center in 1993, the Japan Intellectual Property Arbitration Center in 1998, the Housing Dispute Panel in 2001, and the Japan Sports Arbitration Agency in 2003. The Japan Shipping Exchange was already formed in 1926.

11 Act No. 85 of 1994. The Act came into force on 1 July 1995.

12 Study Group on Special Conciliation Act, *Question and Answer – Special Conciliation Act* (Ichimon Itto Tokutei Chotei-ho), 2000, p. 31.

## 2.2. CLASSIFICATIONS OF ADR

As mentioned above, ADR in Japan, especially court-annexed ADR, has played a large role as a civil dispute resolution tool for a long time. It is supposed that ADR has a merit in respect of its simplicity, swiftness, low cost, confidential nature and flexibility when compared with a lawsuit.

Generally, Japanese ADR is classified as judicial type ADR, governmental type ADR, and private-sector type ADR. An overview of the ADR system established in recent years will be given in section 6.

### *2.2.1. Judicial type ADR*

Judicial type ADR is set up by a court. Civil conciliation (based on the Civil Conciliation Act), family conciliation (based on the Family Affairs Procedure Act), and labour dispute adjudication (based on the Labour Tribunal Act) are included in this type. Settlement prior to the filing of an action (Code of Civil Procedure, Article 275) also belongs to judicial type ADR.

### *2.2.2. Governmental type ADR*

For governmental type ADR, it is said that this type of ADR is a feature specific to Japanese ADR. The reason administrative organs use ADR is to realise more efficient control and raise the level of policy performance about the matter of which that agency is in charge.[13] Administrative organs can specifically perceive the cause of the dispute, frequency, parties' names, and the influence on a third party, etc. through ADR organisations. Moreover, in governmental type ADR, announcing an adversary party's (the trader's) name may be permitted based on a law, and in that case it leads to the effective dispute settlement because of public pressure. The following are examples of governmental type ADR: (a) National Consumer Affairs Center of Japan for consumer disputes (based on the National Consumer Affairs Center Act); (b) consumer service centre for consumer disputes (based on ordinances); (c) Committee on Labour Affairs for labour disputes (Labour Union Act, Article 19); (d) labour trouble processing operating room at the Ministry of Health, Labour and Welfare also for labour disputes; (e) screening panel for construction contract work disputes for disputes related to construction contracts (defective buildings, contractual default, non-payment, etc.) (Construction Business Act, Article 25); (f) Environmental Disputes Coordination Commission for disputes about pollution or environment (National Government Organisation Act, Article 3(2)); and (g) National Tax Tribunal, etc.

---

13 YAMAMOTO and YAMADA, *Law of ADR and Arbitration* (ADR Chusai-ho), 2008, p. 19.

Among these, the most used ADR organisations are the one in the Ministry of Health, Labour and Welfare ((d) above) which handles 7,146 cases and the National Tax Tribunal ((g) above) which handles 2,755 (both according to 2007 statistics).[14]

### *2.2.3. Private sector type ADR*

Private sector type ADR includes ADR other than judicial type and governmental type ADR and can be classified into the following four types. Firstly, there is an industry type of ADR which solves disputes between fellow traders. The Japan Commercial Arbitration Association for disputes arising from international and domestic business transactions and the Japan Shipping Exchange for maritime affairs disputes belong to this type. Secondly, there is a type of ADR which is established and managed by a bar association. This type of ADR uses, for example, terms such as 'conciliation centre' or 'dispute settlement centre'. Thirdly, there are organisations of associated law professionals who deal with disputes in technical fields (paralegals), such as organisations of the judicial scrivener and the registered land and house investigator, etc. Fourthly, there is a type of ADR that is established and managed by an industry group composed of specific business operators. This ADR organisation is aimed at resolving consumer disputes concerning the products and services which these business operators provide. For example, the Products Liability Consulting Center, financial industry, and dealers on the internet have established specific ADR organisations. The screening panel for indemnity liability by the Japan Medical Association also belongs to this type.

As regards private sector type ADR, two serious problems arise. Firstly, securing sufficient funding is an important issue and a very serious problem. If an organisation tries to manage only with the commission from parties to a dispute, commission will become high and the use of such an ADR system will be decreased. The same applies if a specialist provides ADR in a highly specialised area. In addition expenses for investigations can be very high.

Secondly, when an fee is made from persons other than the parties to a dispute, a problem will arise in respect of neutrality. In this regard, the first to third types mentioned above maintain their neutrality. However, since the fourth type is an ADR organisation which one of the parties to a dispute operates, a problem may arise in respect of neutrality. However, as advantages of this type of ADR, we can see the following points: expertise is secured, a prompt action to consumers is possible, and feedback for improvement in a product or service can be passed to business operators quickly because the industry participant is directly in charge of the process. Therefore, there also is a hybrid

---

14 ADR Center of Japan Foundation of Bar Association (ed.), *ADR as the Means for Dispute Resolution* (Funso kaiketsu shudan to shiteno ADR), 2010, p. 12.

model of the second type and the fourth type as another type of ADR to realise both expertise and neutrality. This fifth type of ADR provides services in concert with an industry group, although a bar association participates in the establishment and management of an ADR organisation. The following are examples of this type: the Japan Center for Settlement of Traffic Accident Disputes[15] targeted at traffic accident related disputes, the Automobile Liability Insurance and Mutual Aid Dispute-Settlement Mechanism similarly targeted at traffic accident related disputes (Automobile Liability Security Act, Articles 23–25), and the housing dispute resolution body (Housing Quality Assurance Act, Article 66) targeted at disputes involving defective houses.

The two problems of costs and neutrality cannot be solved easily. On the one hand it is necessary to let the public know that the high quality of the ADR system must be secured and the fee must be enough to continue the system. But if on the other hand trade associations supports the financial background of ADR, the concern for non-neutrality or dissatisfactions level of the party will seriously increase. Another possibility to solve the financial problem is to introduce the legal aid system in the field of ADR, so that the public are able to use the ADR system more easily.[16]

It is also a critical challenge to secure the high quality of dispute resolution supplied by the ADR institutions, especially in the private ADR system. Therefore a certification system was introduced based on the Act on Promotion of Use of Alternative Dispute Resolution[17] for the convenience of the parties concerned when they select one of the ADR institutions. This system aims to certify the ADR institutions that fulfil the requirements specified by the Act. However, the certification is not compulsory, so an ADR institution without certification may operate as an ADR institution.[18]

ADR organisations introduced below are organisations certified according to the Act on Promotion of Use of Alternative Dispute Resolution. The Minister of Justice shall certify the ADR institution which meets the criteria regulated by the Act. Article 6 of the Act on Promotion of Use of Alternative Dispute Resolution describes the requirements of certification:[19] (a) matters which the ADR institution covers must be clarified (para. 1); (b) the specialists must be secured as participants (para. 2); (c) the specialist who presides over the ADR must be fair (para. 3); (d) the institution must be fair (para. 4); (e) the system for getting the advice of an attorney must be secured if a non-attorney presides over the ADR (para. 5); (f) notice of proceedings (paras. 6, 9 and 13); (g) the standards

---

15 7,471 cases were applied in 2007. ADR Center of Japan Federation of Bar Association (ed.), *supra* n. 14, p. 14.

16 Yamamoto and Yamada, *supra* n. 13, p. 397.

17 Act No. 151 of 2004.

18 ADR Center of Japan Foundation of Bar Association (ed.), *supra* n. 14, p. 95.

19 The criteria for certification are mainly related to systematical guarantee for procedural justice. Yamamoto and Yamada, *supra* n. 13, p. 226.

for the proceedings (e.g. duration of process) must be known (para. 7); (h) criteria and formula for application (para. 8); (i) the method to safely keep or return the provided data and the range of confidentiality must be described (paras. 10, 11 and 14); (j) the condition for ending the proceedings must be described (para. 12 and 13); (k) calculation method for fee (para. 15); and (l) complaints procedure (para. 16).

Introducing the certification system brings the effect of:

(a) providing the public the standard for choice between ADR institutions;[20]
(b) a specialist who is not an attorney may preside over the ADR; and
(c) people are more willing to use the ADR system because the prescription period will be interrupted and the civil proceedings may be suspended if ADR is pending (Articles 25 and 26).[21]

As of December 2012 the number of certified organisations was 117 (except for the organisations which have closed business).[22]

For civil disputes there are organisations operated by bar associations, for example the Dispute Settlement Centers of the Bar Associations of Kyoto, Yokohama, Aichi, Hyogo and those operated by judicial scrivener associations, for example the Tokyo Judicial Scrivener Association Conciliation Center, the Kyoto Judicial Scrivener Association Conciliation Center, the Fukuoka Judicial Scrivener Association ADR Center.[23] Other organisations dealing with civil disputes in general are, e.g. public interest incorporated associations, comprehensive dispute settlement centres. Moreover, there is a conciliation centre operated by the Judicial Scrivener Association for civil disputes whose amount in controversy is equal to or less than 1,400,000 yen.

#### 2.2.3.1. Commercial affairs

The ADR organisation that handles commercial cases is the general incorporated association, the Japan Commercial Arbitration Association.[24] Subcontract dealings can be handled by the Juridical Foundation, the National Association of Trade Promotion for Small and Medium Enterprises' Subcontract Proper

20 According to the Act on Promotion of Use of Alternative Dispute Resolution, the Minister of Justice shall certify the ADR institution which meets the criteria regulated by the Act. If a person applies to the certified institution, the prescription will be interrupted and the civil proceedings may be suspended (Articles 25 and 26). The certification system is aimed not only to maintain the credibility of the ADR institution but to give the related person more possibility of choices for dispute resolution. Kobayashi, *Act on Promotion of Use of Alternative Dispute Resolution* (Saibangai funsokaiketsu sokushin-ho), 2005, p. 154.

21 Kobayashi, *supra* n. 20, p. 154.

22 <www.moj.go.jp/KANBOU/ADR/jigyousya/ninsyou-index.html> accessed on 15.12.2012.

23 <www.moj.go.jp/KANBOU/ADR/itiran/funsou002.html> accessed on 15.12.2012.

24 <www.moj.go.jp/KANBOU/ADR/itiran/funsou005.html> accessed on 15.12.2012.

Dealings Promotion Center, and the public interest incorporated association, such as the Tokyo Metropolitan Small Business Promotion Agency's Subcontract Dealings Dispute Settlement Center.[25]

2.2.3.2. Intellectual property

The Japan Intellectual Property Arbitration Center is the relevant ADR organisation for disputes about intellectual property rights in general.[26]

The ADR organisation which handles disputes about software, is the general incorporated association, the Software Information Center's Software Dispute Settlement Center.[27]

The ADR organisation for disputes between the right holder and the business operator regarding infringement of the Trademark Act and Unfair Competition Prevention Act, is the general incorporated association, the Union des Fabricants.[28]

2.2.3.3. Consumer contracts

Disputes about the accommodation contract between a travel agent and consumers concluded in Japan are handled by the Rikkyo University Tourist Center.[29]

The ADR organisations which handle disputes about defective automobiles and home electronics are the Association for Electric Home Appliances, and public interest incorporated associations, such as the Product Liability of Automobile Counselling Center.[30]

The specific non-profit activity corporation, the Study Abroad Support Council's Study Abroad Trouble Solution Mechanism, deals with disputes concerning studying abroad.[31]

The ADR organisation which handles disputes about the sales contract of brand-name goods is the general incorporated association, the Association Against Counterfeit Product Distribution.[32]

For disputes about a specific commercial transaction, there is a public interest incorporated association: the Nippon Association of Consumer Specialists.[33]

---

25 <www.moj.go.jp/KANBOU/ADR/itiran/funsou004.html> accessed on 15.12.2012.
26 <www.moj.go.jp/KANBOU/ADR/itiran/funsou008.html> accessed on 15.12.2012.
27 <www.moj.go.jp/KANBOU/ADR/itiran/funsou006.html> accessed on 15.12.2012.
28 <www.moj.go.jp/KANBOU/ADR/itiran/funsou007.html> accessed on 15.12.2012.
29 <www.moj.go.jp/KANBOU/ADR/itiran/funsou012.html> accessed on 15.12.2012.
30 <www.moj.go.jp/KANBOU/ADR/itiran/funsou010.html> accessed on 15.12.2012.
31 <www.moj.go.jp/KANBOU/ADR/itiran/funsou013.html> accessed on 15.12.2012.
32 <www.moj.go.jp/KANBOU/ADR/itiran/funsou009.html> accessed on 15.12.2012.
33 <www.moj.go.jp/KANBOU/ADR/itiran/funsou011.html> accessed on 15.12.2012.

### 2.2.3.4. Business reorganisation

The ADR organisation responsible for handling disputes about business reorganisation is the Japan Association of Turnaround Professionals.[34]

### 2.2.3.5. Business succession

The ADR organisation responsible for handling disputes about the succession of a business of small and medium-sized enterprises is the general incorporated association, the Institute for Corporate Reconstruction.[35]

### 2.2.3.6. Finance and insurance

The ADR organisation responsible for handling disputes about financial instruments is a specific non-profit activity corporation, the Financial Instruments Mediation Assistance Center.[36]

The ADR organisation responsible for handling disputes about a mutual aid contract is an incorporated association; the Japan Cooperative Insurance Association Incorporated.[37]

### 2.2.3.7. Labour

The ADR organisations responsible for handling labour relationship disputes are the labour trouble solution centres operated by the Japan Federation of Labour Social Security Attorney's Association.[38] Other ADR organisations such as the incorporated association, the Japan Industrial Counsellors Association, a corporation, the Japan Industrial Counsellors Association ADR Center, and a specified non-profit activity corporation; the Individual Industrial Dispute Resolution Center might be competent ADR organisations for labour disputes.

### 2.2.3.8. Medical disputes

The specified non-profit activity corporation, the Medical Dispute Study Group Medical Dispute Counselling Center is responsible for handling medical disputes.[39]

---

34 <www.moj.go.jp/KANBOU/ADR/itiran/funsou014.html> accessed on 15.12.2012.

35 <www.moj.go.jp/KANBOU/ADR/itiran/funsou015.html> accessed on 15.12.2012.

36 <www.moj.go.jp/KANBOU/ADR/itiran/funsou017.html> accessed on 15.12.2012.

37 <www.moj.go.jp/KANBOU/ADR/itiran/funsou016.html> accessed on 15.12.2012.

38 <www.moj.go.jp/KANBOU/ADR/itiran/funsou018.html> accessed on 15.12.2012; 41 of the public consultants on social and labour insurance meetings work.

39 <www.moj.go.jp/KANBOU/ADR/itiran/funsou019.html> accessed on 15.12.2012.

#### 2.2.3.9. Residential environment

Firstly, the ADR organisations responsible for handling disputes about the boundaries of land, are the boundary problem counselling centres operated by the Land and House Investigator Association.[40] Secondly, responsible for handling disputes about the price of real estate is the Real Estate Appraiser Conciliation Center, operated by a public interest incorporated association, the Japan Association of Real Estate Appraisers.[41] Thirdly, disputes about a foreigner's workplace environment etc. are dealt with by Administrative Scrivener (Gyoseishoshi Lawyer) ADR Centers operated by the Administrative Scrivener Associations.[42] Fourthly, for disputes about animal welfare, there are Administrative Scrivener ADR Centers operated by the Administrative Scrivener Associations.[43] Fifthly, for disputes about a condominium, there is a specified non-profit corporation, the Fukuoka Condominium Owner's Association's Condominium Problem-Solving Center.[44] Sixthly, disputes about security deposit refunds etc. are dealt with by Administrative Scrivener ADR Centers operated by the Administrative Scrivener Associations.[45] Finally, for disputes about leasehold, there is the Aichi Judicial Scrivener Conciliation Center.[46]

#### 2.2.3.10. Traffic

Firstly, the ADR organisations responsible for handling disputes about bicycle accidents are the Administrative Scrivener ADR Centers operated by the Administrative Scrivener Associations.[47] Secondly, for disputes about bicycle accidents or traffic accidents resulting in property damage, there are Administrative Scrivener ADR Centers operated by the Saitama Gyoseishoshi Lawyers' Association.[48]

#### 2.2.3.11. Family affairs

Firstly, the ADR organisation responsible for handling issues regarding husband-and-wife and parent-and-child disputes between foreign parties is the dispute

---

40 <www.moj.go.jp/KANBOU/ADR/itiran/funsou024.html> accessed on 15.12.2012; 17 of the land and house investigator meetings work.

41 <www.moj.go.jp/KANBOU/ADR/itiran/funsou025.html> accessed on 15.12.2012.

42 <www.moj.go.jp/KANBOU/ADR/itiran/funsou022.html> accessed on 15.12.2012.

43 <www.moj.go.jp/KANBOU/ADR/itiran/funsou021.html> accessed on 15.12.2012; four of the administrative scrivener meetings work.

44 <www.moj.go.jp/KANBOU/ADR/itiran/funsou020.html> accessed on 15.12.2012.

45 <www.moj.go.jp/KANBOU/ADR/itiran/funsou027.html> accessed on 15.12.2012.

46 <www.moj.go.jp/KANBOU/ADR/itiran/funsou026.html> accessed on 15.12.2012.

47 <www.moj.go.jp/KANBOU/ADR/itiran/funsou028.html> accessed on 15.12.2012; seven of the administrative scrivener meetings work.

48 <www.moj.go.jp/KANBOU/ADR/itiran/funsou029.html> accessed on 15.12.2012.

settlement centre for foreign couples and parent-and-child operated by the Kyoto Gyoseishoshi Lawyers Association.[49] Secondly, for disputes about marital relationships etc., there are an incorporated association, the Japan Industrial Counsellors Association; a public interest incorporated association, the Family Problems Information Center; and the Saitama Gyoseishoshi Lawyers Association.[50] Thirdly, for disputes about inheritance, there is the Saitama Gyoseishoshi Lawyers Association's ADR Center and the Aichi Judicial Scrivener Conciliation Center.[51]

#### 2.2.3.12. Sport

The ADR organisation responsible for handling disputes about sports is a general incorporated association, the Japan Sports Arbitration Agency.[52]

#### 2.2.3.13. Energy

The ADR organisation responsible for handling disputes about the use of an electric power system is a general incorporated association, the Electric Power System Council of Japan.[53]

## 3. ARBITRATION

### 3.1. HISTORY OF THE ARBITRATION SYSTEM[54]

The modernistic development of laws in Japan was caused by the historical situation where pressure from foreign countries forced the national isolation policy to end. Japan had persisted on the national isolation policy for over 200 years, until the middle of the nineteenth century. However, some foreign governments began to ask for commerce with Japan in around the second half of the eighteenth century. Eventually, Japan concluded the Treaty of Amity and Commerce with the United States in 1858, and also concluded similar treaties with the UK, France, the Netherlands, and Russia. However, these treaties stipulated the one-sided most-favoured-nation treatment and approved the consular jurisdiction by foreign countries, meaning that Japan could not judge

49 <www.moj.go.jp/KANBOU/ADR/itiran/funsou030.html> accessed on 15.12.2012.
50 <www.moj.go.jp/KANBOU/ADR/itiran/funsou032.html> accessed on 15.12.2012.
51 <www.moj.go.jp/KANBOU/ADR/itiran/funsou031.html> accessed on 15.12.2012.
52 <www.moj.go.jp/KANBOU/ADR/itiran/funsou033.html> accessed on 15.12.2012.
53 <www.moj.go.jp/KANBOU/ADR/itiran/funsou034.html> accessed on 15.12.2012.
54 Shindo, in Shindo and Kojima (eds.), *Commentary on the Civil Procedure* (Chushaku Minji Sosho-ho), vol. 1, 1991, p. 2; Shindo, Takahashi and Takada, in Kaneko *et al.*, *Commentary on the Civil Procedure* (Jyokai Minji Sosho-ho), 2011, p. 1.

foreigners who committed crimes in Japan. Since Japan could not decide the tariff autonomously, these are generally considered unequal treaties.

Although the Meiji government tried hard to abolish unequal treaties, negotiation ran into difficulties. The government soon realised that adoption of a modernistic legal system was a pressing necessity to improve bargaining power and abolish unequal treaties. Thus, the effort to codify the Japanese Code of Civil Procedure was made under these circumstances. The Meiji government set up the law investigation division of the Department of Justice in 1876, and it started the compilation of the practices and statutes related to a civil action. In 1883, a draft based on the 1806 French Code of Civil Procedure was drawn up by Boissonade who was a French legal scholar participating in the compilation of the Japanese Civil Code and Commercial Code. However, the government decided to edit the Japanese Code based on the 1877 German Code of Civil Procedure, which was the latest code at that time. The draft written by Techow, who was the German counsellor of Prussia, was submitted to the government in 1886. Amendment was made to this draft proposal, and the Code of Civil Procedure was promulgated as Act No. 29 in 1890 and was enforced from 1 January 1891.

The 1890 Code of Civil Procedure consisted of eight Parts and 805 Articles including Part VIII: Arbitration Procedure.

These arbitration procedure provisions (Articles 786–805) were modelled, as already mentioned above, on the 1877 German Code of Civil Procedure Part X: Arbitration Procedure (Articles 851–872), with hardly any change in content. This is considered to have given priority to the completion of the Code rather than fully examining its contents in order to abolish the unequal treaty as soon as possible.[55] Thus, since Japan's arbitration provisions were inherited from the German law mostly word for word, it is hard to say they were thoroughly examined as to whether they would suit the actual conditions in Japan.[56] Moreover, even though the Arbitration Act was revised in Germany in response to requests of the time, Part VIII: Arbitration Procedure in the Code of Civil Procedure in Japan for a long time was hardly revised, since the arbitration proceedings were rarely used. Despite the fully-fledged revision of most of the Code of Civil Procedure in 1926 and then later in 1996 the part on arbitration procedure was never touched, not even in the 1996 revision, and remained under the name Act on Public Notice Procedure and Arbitration Procedure which contained the original provisions, and was left from the trend of the time.

The use of the arbitration law was rare.[57] On the one hand national awareness of arbitration was not sufficient. Practical knowledge on arbitration procedure or arbitration organisations was not common, and people tended to

---

55 Koyama, *Arbitration Law* (Chusai-ho), 2nd ed., 1983, p. 21.
56 Kojima, *Arbitration Law* (Chusai-ho), 2000, p. 56.
57 *Ibid.*, p. 62.

have the impression that arbitration is less reliable, based on the simple fact that a lay person might be involved in arbitration, while a judge plays a part in conciliation.[58] On the other hand, there was an indication that the system of arbitration did not conform with the sentiment of Japanese people toward the legal system. That is, since Japanese people in general are wary of being controlled by legal norms,[59] they prefer the conciliation system which aims for the actual consent by compromise between the parties rather than the arbitration system in which a solution is imposed on the parties based on a legal norm.

When the Code of Civil Procedure was revised in 1996, the provisions for arbitration should also have been revised together with the other parts of the code as they were all included in one Code of Civil Procedure. However, the Legislative Council of the Ministry of Justice shelved revision of the arbitration provisions, in order to realise early revision of the Code of Civil Procedure, and it performed a complete revision of the bankruptcy-related laws after that. So nearly 110 years passed with the arbitration provisions not being substantially amended, although the development of arbitration law progressed quickly in other countries, ignited by the United Nations Commission of International Trade Law having enacted the UNCITRAL Model Law on International Commercial Arbitration in 1985.

However, new recommendations for reform by the Justice System Reform Council were released in June 2001,[60] and the opinion that 'arbitration legislation (including international commercial arbitration) should be improved at an early stage while observing an international trend' was offered as one aspect of expansion and activation of alternative dispute resolution procedure.[61] Then, the Arbitration Investigative Committee was set up by the Task Force on Judicial Reform in December 2001. The members consisted of 11 persons in total: four professors, one judge, one member from the Ministry of Justice, one from a bar association, one from the Ministry of Economy, Trade and Industry, and three from the permanent arbitration organisation. The resulting Bill was submitted to Parliament and enacted in July 2003.[62]

The following problems with the law before 2003 were pointed out.[63] Firstly, it was inadequate for the handling of international arbitration. Japan ratified the New York Convention on Recognition and Enforcement of Foreign Arbitral

58 Mikazuki, *Study on Civil Procedure* (Minji soshoho kenkyu), vol. 9, 1984, p. 160.

59 Kawashima, *The Book Collection of Takeyoshi Kawashima* (Kawashima Takeyoshi Chosakushu), vol. 4, 1982, p. 320.

60 Judicial Reform Council (Shihoseido kaikaku shingikai), 'The Judicial Reform Council Opinion Document' (Shihoseido kaikaku shingikai ikensho) (2001) 1208 *Jurisuto* 185.

61 *Ibid.*, p. 202.

62 Aoyama, 'Looking back to the establishment of the arbitration law' (Chusai-ho no seitei wo furikaette) (Nov. 2003) *JCA Journal* 2.

63 Aoyama, in Miki and Yamamoto (eds.), *The Theory and the Practice of the New Arbitration Law*, 2006, p. 5.

Awards in 1961.[64] Although a Convention shall be applied to the contracting States, the application status of the arbitration provisions in the Code of Civil Procedure (Articles 801 and 802) was not clear when considering the relation with non-contracting States. Secondly, the old law did not require the arbitration agreement to be in a written document. This lacked conformity with the Jurisdiction Agreement provision (Code of Civil Procedure, Article 11(2)) which requires a written document and also deviated from the general understanding in international arbitration. Thirdly, the number of arbitrators was specified as two persons. This provision differed from the international tendency of specifying an uneven number of arbitrators. Fourthly, arbitration proceedings could be terminated in a wide range of circumstances. For example, expiration of an arbitration contract (Article 793) and non-permission of arbitration procedure (Articles 797 and 805) were stipulated. Since the grounds for revocation of an arbitral award were widely defined (Article 801), the legal stability of an arbitral award was not adequately secured. Finally, judgment procedure was required to enforce an arbitral award, so a quick execution was blocked.

## 3.2. THE ARBITRATION ACT

### 3.2.1. *Scope of application*

Although the present Japanese Arbitration Act (2003 Act No. 138, enforced 1 March 2004) was formed basically in accordance with the UNCITRAL Model Law, it includes some provisions specific to Japanese law. One of these is the scope of application of the Arbitration Act. The Model Law is applied to an international commercial arbitration, but the law of Japan shall be applied to a case regardless of whether it is international, domestic, commercial or non-commercial. The reason for this is based on the fact that sometimes the distinction between these is difficult, and the contents of Model Law are applicable to these cases.

### 3.2.2. *Participation of the court*

In general, a court is not involved in the proceedings of ADR. However, there is an exception for arbitration. According to Article 4 of the Arbitration Act, a court may participate in arbitration procedure when required by the Arbitration Act, for example when no agreement between parties exists about an arbitrator's appointment (Arbitration Act, Article 17), an arbitrator is dismissed (Arbitration Act, Article 20), evidence is examined (Arbitration Act, Article 35), the arbitral

[64] Convention No. 10 of 1961.

award is revoked (Arbitration Act, Article 44), and the arbitral award is enforced (Arbitration Act, Article 46).

In these cases, a district court shall have subject matter jurisdiction, and it is specified that the territorial jurisdiction shall also be exclusive jurisdiction (Arbitration Act, Article 5(1)).

### *3.2.3. Arbitration agreement*

The scope of a dispute solvable by arbitration (arbitrability) is considered as a dispute in respect of which the parties can make settlement (Arbitration Act, Article 13(1)). However, divorce and dissolution of adoptive relations cases were excluded. It was considered that the judgment of personal status change should ultimately be left to the person himself instead of to the third party.[65]

The arbitration agreement should be executed in written form. In addition, agreement by e-mail also has effect (Arbitration Act, Article 13(2) and (4)).

The provision to affirm the separability of arbitration agreements is stipulated (Arbitration Act, Article 13(6)). This confirms the position of the commonly accepted theory and precedent in Japan in which neither the nullity nor rescission of a main contract necessarily affected the validity or effect of an arbitration agreement.[66]

When a case is brought regarding a dispute which is the subject of an arbitration agreement, the court in charge of the case shall dismiss the proceedings when a petition is filed by the defendant (Arbitration Act, Article 14(1)). This handling was the traditional position of commonly accepted theory and precedent.[67]

In regard to international arbitration, the applicable law, with which the formation and validity of the arbitration agreement are governed, comes into question. The applicable law solves some problems on several aspects, such as competence of the arbitration court's jurisdiction, the demurrer by the court, and revocation and enforcement of an arbitral award, and others. On this point, the New York Convention and the Model Law set forth the provisions on the grounds of revocation of foreign arbitral awards or the grounds of recognition refusal, without putting forward general provisions about arbitration agreements (New York Convention, Article 5(1)(a); Model Law, Article 34(2)(a) and

---

65 Kondo, 'The point and the explanation of the new arbitration law' (July 2004) *JCA Journal* 54.

66 The Japanese Supreme Court, judgment of 15.07.1975, Minshu vol. 29, no. 6, p. 1061. Kojima, *supra* n. 56, p. 147; Swaki, in Kojima and Takakuwa, *Commentary on the Arbitration Law* (Chushaku Chusai-ho), 1988, p. 215; Koyama, *supra* n. 55, p. 100.

67 The Japanese Supreme Court, judgment of 04.09.1997, Minshu vol. 51, no. 8, p. 3657; Osaka High Court, judgment of 20.02.1974, Hanreijiho no. 746, p. 42; Tokyo High Court, judgment of 09.10.1990, Kin'yu shojihanrei no. 863, p. 42; Kaneko, *System of Civil Procedure Law* (Shinshu Minjisosho-ho Taikei), p. 42 (Supp. ed. 1965); Taniguchi, *Civil Procedure Law* (Kojutsu Minjisosho-ho), 1988, p. 202; Nakamura, *Lecture on New Civil Procedure Law* (Shin Minjisosho-ho Kogi), 2000, p. 151.

Article 36(1)(a)). The law of Japan similarly specifies this as the reason of revocation of the arbitral awards (Arbitration Act, Article 44(1)(2)) or the reason of recognition refusal (Arbitration Act, Article 45(2)(2)), and approves the parties' autonomy for the decision on the applicable law of arbitration agreement.

### *3.2.4. Competence of the arbitration court*

When the existence of arbitration competence becomes an issue in arbitration procedure, the arbitration court itself may judge the problem (Arbitration Act, Article 23(1)). Also, an arbitration court may order provisional measures when it considers it necessary, unless otherwise agreed between the parties (Arbitration Act, Article 24). However, enforceability is not recognised in this provisional measure.[68]

### *3.2.5. Arbitration procedure*

Arbitration procedure may be decided based on the parties' agreement; if there is no agreement of the parties, an arbitration court defines it (Arbitration Act, Article 26(1) and (2)).

Moreover, an arbitration court or a party with permission from the arbitration court may ask the court for the examination of evidence (Arbitration Act, Article 35). The reason for this is that the fact finding by the arbitration court must be of the same level of security as that in a lawsuit, because the arbitral award has the same effect as a final and binding judgment (Arbitration Act, Article 45(1)) and a lawsuit cannot be used when there is an arbitration agreement.[69]

### *3.2.6. Arbitral award*

The applicable law for the arbitral award is decided by the agreement of the parties (Arbitration Act, Article 36(1)). When there is no agreement, an arbitration court applies the law of the country which has the closest relation to the dispute (Arbitration Act, Article 36(2)).

An arbitration court can offer a settlement when there is an agreement of both parties (Arbitration Act, Article 38).

The grounds for revocation of an arbitral award and refusal of recognition or enforcement of an arbitral award were fixed according the New York Convention and Model Law (Arbitration Act, Article 44(1), Article 45(2), and Article 46(8)).

---

68 Kondo and Kataoka, 'The overview of the arbitration law' (Chusai-ho no Gaiyo) (2003) 769 *NBL* 44.

69 Kobayashi, in Kojima and Takakuwa (eds.), *The Notation and the Point at Issue and Arbitration Law* (Chushaku to Ronten Chusai-ho), 2007, p. 198; Kondo and Kataoka, *supra* n. 68, p. 45.

In addition, proceedings for the arbitral award's revocation and the execution permission were changed to decision-procedure from judgment-procedure (Arbitration Act, Article 44(5), and Article 46(7)). This made the simple and quick conclusion of cases possible.

## 4. CONCILIATION

Civil conciliation is a procedure aimed at the resolution of disputes in a reasonable and appropriate manner, realised by the mutual concessions of the parties to the civil dispute concerned (Civil Conciliation Act, Article 1). In conciliation, the judgment by the third party does not bind the parties, so both parties are free to accept or reject the conciliation proposal provided by the conciliation committee (Civil Conciliation Act, Article 16).

### 4.1. OVERVIEW

#### *4.1.1. History of conciliation*

The conciliation system in civil cases was originally developed in answer to the type of case and based on necessity. Conciliation laws enacted before the Second World War were for example:

(a) Land and House Lease Conciliation Law (1922 Act No. 41, enforced 1 October 1922),[70]
(b) Farm Tenancy Conciliation Law (1924 Act No. 18, enforced 1 December 1924),
(c) Commercial Conciliation Law (1926 Act No. 42, enforced 1 November 1926),
(d) Monetary Debt Temporal Conciliation Law (1932 Act No. 26, enforced 1 October 1932),[71], and
(e) Personal Affairs Conciliation Law (1939 Act No. 11, enforced 1 July 1939),[72] etc.

---

70 The conciliation system in Japan is deemed to have been established by the law for the first time. Koyama, *Civil Conciliation Law* (Minji Chotei-ho), 2nd ed., 1977, p. 19.

71 The new system for making a fair division of unpredictable economic change (loss) between the parties was required as a result of the global depression which began in 1929. Therefore, conciliation is used to adjust the debt. This system was often used and the number of applications in 1935 was 84,668. Koyama, *supra* n. 70, p. 30.

72 Some historical background is needed to the establishment of the Personnel Conciliation Act (Jinji Chotei-ho). The Japanese Civil Law is the fundamental law, which covered not only the law of property but also family law, and was in force on July 1897. The codification of civil law was planned in 1866. The draft Japanese Civil Code was modelled on the civil law in France

After the Second World War the conciliation system was organised into two different conciliation systems, namely civil conciliation and family conciliation. After the war, laws relevant to civil conciliation were largely amended. In 1947, the Civil Conciliation Act was enacted as Act No. 222. Following this, the Land and House Lease Conciliation Law, Farm Tenancy Conciliation Law, Commercial Conciliation Law, and Monetary Debt Temporal Conciliation Law were abolished. The reason for having enacted a unified law for civil conciliation is explained as follows: Previous laws relevant to conciliation were enacted one by one according to the demand at the time. They should be consolidated, because they were very complicated from the viewpoint of paperwork at a court and that of the parties concerned.[73]

### *4.1.2. Types and function of conciliation*

Today, conciliation is classified into two types: conciliation performed at a court and conciliation performed at other organisations than a court. Civil conciliation and family conciliation belong to the former. Conciliation by the Committee on Labour Affairs (Labour Union Act, Article 20) and conciliation by the Environmental Disputes Coordination Commission (Act on Settlement of Environmental Pollution Disputes, Article 31) belong to the latter.

At any rate, the conciliation system, regardless of civil conciliation or family conciliation, has played a significant role as a dispute resolution system alongside judicial type ADR. In particular, the specific conciliation system has been used to solve the multiple debtor problem by the method of conciliation and with the mutual concessions of both parties, and it has been functioning as a useful means to avoid bankruptcy of individuals and companies that are debtors. Moreover, in Japan, the Conciliation First Principle is adopted (Family Affairs

---

(1804) which was considered to be the most excellent civil law in the world. In the original plan, the code should have been proclaimed in 1890, and enforced in 1893 (the old civil code). But opinions against the civil code came out, asserting that the code was only an imported system from a Western country and would destroy the traditional Japanese system. The enforcement of the old civil code was then postponed indefinitely. The code investigation committee was established, and the new draft, which was modelled on the draft of German civil code and composed of the former three books (General Provision, Real Rights, Claim) and of the latter two books (Relatives, Inheritance), was published. Both parts were in force on 16 July 1897 (Wagatsuma, Ariizumi and Kawai, *Civil Law* (Mimpo), 3rd ed., vol. 1, 2008, p. 3). However, the provisions of Relatives and Inheritance in the 1897 Code were similar to the old code; therefore many people were not satisfied with the solution in accordance with the Civil Code 1897. Then the Personnel Conciliation Act (Jinji Chote-ho) was established in 1939, with the purpose that family affairs would be resolved not under the Civil Code but the synonymy and the consideration. In 1940, 6,899 new cases were brought, which was far more than expected. 60% of them were ended by the confirmation of conciliation (Koyama, *supra* n. 70, p. 33.). The Personnel Conciliation Act (Jinji Chote-ho) was then substituted for the Domestic Relations Trial Act (Kaji Shimpan-ho) under the new Constitution.

73 The 10th Diet House of Representatives, Committee on Judicial Affairs, No. 20, p. 6 (9 May 1951).

Procedure Act, Article 257), so parties are required to go though the conciliation procedure before bringing an action to a court. One reason for this is that the problems involving family relations inherently do not necessarily aim at rational solution, rather, the necessity of aiming at harmonious solution while adjusting human relations is high, and the structure of a lawsuit (open to the public, adversarial system) is not necessarily suitable for maintenance of healthy family relations.[74] In addition, the conciliation system aims at not only easing the burden on the family court, but also the peaceable solution by talks while urging calm discussion between the parties by providing for a cooling-off period.

## 4.2. CIVIL CONCILIATION PROCEDURE

### *4.2.1. Scope of application*

The civil conciliation court handles disputes related to civil affairs (Civil Conciliation Act, Article 2). However, family conciliation and labour dispute conciliation are excluded from the scope of application

### *4.2.2. Competent court*

The jurisdiction over a conciliation case belongs to a summary court or a district court that has jurisdiction over the location of the general venue of the opponent, or it belongs to a summary court or a district court determined by an agreement (Civil Conciliation Act, Article 3).

### *4.2.3. Presiding official*

Conciliation proceedings are conducted by the conciliation committee (Civil Conciliation Act, Article 5(1)). The conciliation committee is comprised of one conciliation chief and two or more civil conciliation committee members in principle (Civil Conciliation Act, Article 6). The conciliation chief is designated by a district court from among the judges (Civil Conciliation Act, Article 7(1)). A member of a civil conciliation committee is elected based on his specialised knowledge (Civil Conciliation Act, Article 8(1)). However, when the court considers it appropriate, the judge can implement conciliation by himself (Civil Conciliation Act, Article 5(1)).

---

74 Ninomiya, *Family Law* (Kazoku-ho), 2nd ed, 2005, p. 22; Sagami, *Domestic Relations Trial Act* (Kaji Shimpan-ho), 2007, p. 331. Wagatsuma, 'About Family Conciliation' (Kaji Chotei-ron), in *Study on Civil Law*, vol 7–7, 1969, p. 119, has great impact on the theoretical ground for the principle which requires applying for conciliation proceedings before civil procedure. Wagatsuma's article emphasises that family affairs especially are suited for conciliation proceedings because the regulation of family affairs does not depends on rationality.

#### 4.2.4. *Location*

Conciliation is implemented on the date designated by the court. However, the location where the conciliation takes place is more flexible. It can be implemented in an appropriate location outside the court (Civil Conciliation Act, Article 12(4)).

#### 4.2.5. *Actions during the conciliation procedure*

On the date for conciliation, the following actions may be conducted: allegation, investigation of facts, examination of evidence, mediation, preparation and instruction of conciliation agreement, and exchange of opinion. For the hearing of the parties' opinions, a cross-interview system is adopted, so the petitioner and the opponent are heard separately.

#### 4.2.6. *Principles of procedure*

The conciliation committee may gather materials or collection for conciliation (Rules of Civil Conciliation, Article 12(1)). Since the parties in principle have to appear in court on the date conciliation takes place (Civil Conciliation Act, Article 12(3)), the principle of oral argument is guaranteed. In most cases, conciliation takes place over two days or less.[75] Conciliation procedure is performed in hearings closed to the public (Rules of Civil Conciliation, Article 10). When court proceedings are pending in relation to a case which is subject to conciliation, the court in charge of the case may suspend the court proceedings until a conciliation case is concluded (Civil Conciliation Act, Article 20(3)).

#### 4.2.7. *Third party participation*

A third party who has an interest in the results of conciliation can participate in the procedure with the permission of the conciliation committee (Civil Conciliation Act, Article 11).

#### 4.2.8. *Judgment standard*

The committee can judge the case not based on the substantive law but on the logical sequence if the conclusion reached by the substantive law does not stand up to reason under the circumstances (Civil Conciliation Act, Article 1).

[75] There were 66,272 conciliation cases in the summary court in 2011. Among them, there were 9,193 cases without a date of oral arrangement, 27,994 cases with one date of oral arrangement, and 15,470 cases with two dates of oral arrangement. General Secretariat, Supreme Court, *supra* n. 4, p. 62.

### 4.2.9. *Success or failure of conciliation*

When an agreement between the parties is reached and is documented, then conciliation is established. This written record has the same effect as a final and binding judgment (Civil Conciliation Act, Article 16). Since a record of the judicial settlement has the same effect as a final and binding judgment (Code of Civil Procedure, Article 267), a record of conciliation is deemed to be a title of obligation (Civil Execution Act, Article 22(7)).

There is an argument about whether *res judicata* is recognised in respect of a conciliation record. The view accepting *res judicata*[76] argues that in respect of agreement of the parties at a court, a record of conciliation is similar to the record of settlement by judicial settlement;[77] a settlement record as well as a conciliation record are supposed to have 'the same effect as a final and binding judgment', and *res judicata* also is contained in the same effect as a final and binding judgment. On the other hand, the view against *res judicata*[78] argues that the judgment procedure is a compulsory dispute settlement means, but settlement and conciliation are autonomous dispute settlement means; the due process protection in conciliation procedure is weaker than that in adjudication.

When parties do not reach an agreement, the conciliation committee can terminate the case as conciliation has not been established (Civil Conciliation Act, Article 14). In this case, the court can make 'the decision in lieu of conciliation' in consideration of all the circumstances, after hearing the opinion from the members of the conciliation committee (Civil Conciliation Act, Article 17). This procedure gives a solution in the form of a ruling by a court, but gives consideration to the efforts of the conciliation committee in working towards settlement. However, the effect will be lost if the party concerned files an objection (Civil Conciliation Act, Article 18(4)).

When the case is concluded as conciliation failure and the petitioner files an action within two weeks from the date on which he receives the notice of termination of the proceedings as a result of the failure of conciliation, it is considered that an action was filed at the time of the petition (Civil Conciliation

---

76 Yamamoto and Yamada, *supra* n. 13, p. 200.

77 There are divided opinions on whether the procedural settlement has the effect of *res judicata*. The Japanese Supreme Court has admitted the *res judicata* effect of judicial settlement (Japanese Supreme Court, judgment of 5 March 1958, Minshu vol. 12, no. 3, p. 381), but the procedural settlement can be challenged because of mistake (Japanese Supreme Court, judgment of 14 June 1958, Minshu vol. 12, no. 9, p. 1492). Accordingly the theory of the Supreme Court is interpreted as the limited *res judicata* theory: the procedural settlement or conciliation has *res judicata* effect only when the settlement or conciliation is effective under material law (civil law). In academic literature, both the arguments for and against *res judicata* effect have strong support. For *res judicata*: Ito, *Civil Procedure* (Minji Sosho-ho), 4th ed., 2011, p. 466; Kaneko, *supra* n. 67, p. 309. Against *res judicata*: Mikazuki, *Civil Procedure* (Minji sosho-ho), 1959, p. 443; Shindo, *Civil Procedure* (Minji sosho-ho), 5th ed., 2011, p. 372.

78 Komuro, in Ishikawa and Kajimura, *Commentary on the Civil Conciliation Law* (Chukai Minji Chotei-ho), 2nd ed., 1992, p. 219.

Act, Article 19),and the prescription periods are interrupted accordingly (Civil Code, Article 147).

According to statistics from 2011, of the total 66,272 conciliation cases accepted by the summary court, 13,538 cases were settled by conciliation, 13,583 cases were not settled by conciliation, and 24,370 cases were settled by a decision in lieu of conciliation.[79] In addition, in most cases, the conciliation procedure lasted less than three months.[80]

## 4.3. FAMILY CONCILIATION PROCEDURE

The Family Affairs Procedure Act and the Personal Status Litigation Act were enacted to provide a procedure for the resolution of disputes relating to family affairs. The procedures under the Family Affairs Procedure Act can be divided into family conciliation (Family Affairs Procedure Act, Article 244) and domestic relations trial (Family Affairs Procedure Act, Article 39). Whereas the Civil Conciliation Act provides a general procedure rule for the conciliation procedure, the rules for family conciliation in the Family Affairs Procedure Act can be said to be special law related to family affairs. Sometimes it is unclear whether cases fall within the scope of family or civil conciliation cases as they are within the scope of both. A rule regarding the transfer of a case between the family court and the summary court/district court which has jurisdiction over civil dispute conciliation exists in Civil Conciliation Act, Article 4(2), and Family Affairs Procedure Act, Article 9(1).

Family affairs cases are decided by family courts, which are equal to the district courts in rank. The family court is authorised as 'a court which can judge and make a conciliation of a case which is provided by Family Affairs Procedure Act' and 'a court of first instance for a litigation related to personal status which is provided by Personal Status Litigation Act (Court Act, Article 31-3(1)(1) and (2))'.

The main feature of family conciliation, concerning a litigation related to personal status, is that a petitioner has to allege conciliation to a family court (Article 257, Family Affairs Procedure Act). This is called 'the Conciliation First Principle'.

### *4.3.1. Scope of application*

Article 244 of the Family Affairs Procedure Act defines the cases to which the family conciliation procedure can be applied as 'cases about personal status and

---

79 General Secretariat, Supreme Court, *supra* n. 4, p. 62.

80 There were 66,272 conciliation cases in the summary court in 2011. Among them, 16,798 cases ended within one month, 22,991 cases within two months, and 11,951 cases within three months. General Secretariat, Supreme Court, *supra* n. 4, p. 62.

other cases about the family'. Although, it excepts some cases which are described as 'those listed in Appended Table 1'.

First, 'cases about personal status' means cases which are within the scope of personal status litigation.[81] There are four categories (Personal Status Litigation Act, Article 2). The first category consists of cases such as void and annulled marriages, divorce, annulment of divorce by agreement, revocation of divorce by agreement, and confirmation of the existence of marriage. The second consists of cases such as denial of a child born in wedlock, affirmation, annulment of affirmation, rescission of affirmation, the determination of paternity when the presumption of child in wedlock does not apply, and the confirmation of the existence of a real parent–child relationship. The third includes cases such as annulment of adoption, rescission of adoption, dissolution of adoption, annulment of adoption by agreement, rescission of adoption by agreement, and the confirmation of the existence of adoptive parenthood. Finally, the fourth consists of other cases about the formation or existence of status, such as confirmation of the existence of affinity.[82]

As regards 'other cases about the family', this provision covers not only internal family disputes, but also disputes about property and status which widely affect the 'preservation of the peaceful and healthy family lifestyle'.[83] Therefore, for example, disputes over the use of land and buildings, disputes over payment, claims for abatement of legally reserved portion (Civil Code, Article 1031), and claims for recovery of inheritance (Civil Code, Article 884) can be covered by this provision.[84]

Cases in the category of 'those listed in Appended Table 1' are exceptionally brought before the Family Courts. The Family Affairs Procedure Act provides Appended Table 1 and Appended Table 2. The first list includes cases such as the start of guardianship, adjudication of somebody's disappearance, forfeiture of parental authority, acceptance of a qualified acceptance statement, acceptance of renunciation of inheritance statement, probate, and assignment of the executor. The second list includes cases such as division of estate, ruling as to spousal maintenance, rulings as to the share of expenses arising from marriage, rulings as to the distribution of property, and assignment of the person who has parental authority. Those two categories categorise the family affairs cases into two groups: cases which have a high public interest and cases which have a low public interest. It is impossible for parties to resolve through conciliation those cases which have high public interest (Appended Table 1). On the other hand, cases

81 Kajimura and Tokuda, *The Law of Family Affair Proceeding* (Kaji-jiken Testuzuki-ho), 2nd ed., 2007, p. 55.

82 *Ibid.*, p. 55.

83 Yamakido, *The Act on Adjudication of Domestic Relations* (Kaji Shimpan-ho), 1958, p. 83.

84 Matsumoto, *Personal Status Litigation Act* (Jinji Sosho-ho), 3rd ed., 2012, p. 15.

which have low public interest (Appended Table 2) may be resolved with conciliation.[85]

#### 4.3.2. *Competent court*

The jurisdiction over family conciliation cases belongs to the family court which exercises jurisdiction over the area where the opponent maintains an address, or the family court which has been agreed by the parties (Family Affairs Procedure Act, Article 245(1)). If a family court does not have territorial jurisdiction, it can transfer the case to the family court with jurisdiction (Family Affairs Procedure Act, Article 246).

#### 4.3.3. *Presiding official*

A conciliation committee is responsible for the conciliation. A conciliation committee is composed of one judge and two members of the conciliation committee of family affairs (Family Affairs Procedure Act, Article 248(1)). Conciliation will be carried out by the judge only if the family court considers it appropriate (Family Affairs Procedure Act, Article 247(1)). However, if a petition is filed by either of the parties, conciliation has to be carried out by the conciliation committee (Family Affairs Procedure Act, Article 247(2)).

#### 4.3.4. *Actions in the conciliation procedure*

While the family affairs case is pending, the conciliation committee may take such actions as are necessary for the conciliation. For example, during the case for relations adjustment between husband and wife, to make the conflict over the custody of child settle down temporarily, the conciliation committee prohibits the parents taking children away from each other, determines who will be the provisional custodian, and makes an order for the provisional payment of maintenance.[86] This action is called an action prior to the conciliation. The phrase 'prior to the conciliation' means 'prior to the end of the conciliation', as opposed to 'prior to the application'.

However, this action is not enforceable (Family Affairs Procedure Act, Article 266(1) and (3)). Although, if any party fails to comply with the action prior to the conciliation, the family court will charge 100,000 yen or less as a non-penal fine (Article 266(4)). This provisional measure is based on the expectation of both parties' cooperation and voluntary restraint.[87]

---

85 Kaneko (ed.), *Question and Answer – The Law of Family Affair Proceeding* (Ichimon Itto Kaji-jiken Testuzuki-ho), 2012, p. 51.

86 Kajimura and Tokuda, *supra* n. 81, p. 67.

87 Kajimura and Tokuda, *supra* n. 81, p. 68.

#### 4.3.5. *Principles of procedure*

The fact is found by the committee, and the evidence is examined on its authority or on petition (Family Affairs Procedure Act, Articles 56 and 258). The family affairs conciliation procedure is closed to the public (Family Affairs Procedure Act, Article 33).

Any party who wishes to file a lawsuit has to first apply to the family court for conciliation (Conciliation First Principle, Family Affairs Procedure Act, Article 257(1)). If the party files a lawsuit without first applying for conciliation, in principle, the court must refer the case to the family court's conciliation (Family Affairs Procedure Act, Article 257(2)). Also, where it is possible to carry out conciliation in respect of a case pending in court, the court can hear the parties' opinions and has authority to refer the case to conciliation (Family Affairs Procedure Act, Article 274(1)). This provision is based on the idea that it is more appropriate to solve a family dispute by leading both parties to mutual agreement through the conciliation procedure than ending the case by a strong method such as court decision.[88]

#### 4.3.6. *Judgment standard*

Conciliation is based on the parties' mutual agreement, and this idea is applicable to cases such as divorce by conciliation.[89] However, what are the standards required to make an agreement? In the case of conciliation, it is better to aim at finding a valid and acceptable solution for both parties than aiming at legal accuracy, however to make the solution legally enforceable, a qualified person should be involved in the conciliation committee. Therefore, although the standard of the judgment is the substantive law, finding a valid solution not based on the substantive law is the function of family affairs conciliation.[90]

#### 4.3.7. *Success or failure of conciliation*

Regarding the matters which are provided in Family Affairs Procedure Act Appended Table 2 (e.g., division of estate, ruling as to spousal maintenance, ruling as to the share of expenses arising from marriage, ruling as to the distribution of property, and assignment of the person who has parental authority), if conciliation is established, it has the effect of a 'final and binding decision (Family Affairs Procedure Act, art. 39)' (Family Affairs Procedure Act, Article 268(1)). In addition, regarding the family affairs procedure for divorce or

---

88 Matsumoto, *supra* n. 84, p. 15.

89 Wagatsuma, *Family Law* (Shinzoku-ho), 1961, p. 179.

90 Izumi, *Family Law* (Shinzoku-ho), 1997, p. 139; Noda, *Modern Family Law* (Gendai Kazoku-ho), 1996, p. 104.

dissolution of adoption, if there is an agreement between both parties and the contents of the agreement are contained in a written statement, that agreement has the effect of a 'final and binding judgment' (Family Affairs Procedure Act, Article 268(1)). In cases such as dissolution of adoption and divorce, the parties' disposition is acceptable: thus if an agreement is made and contained in a written statement during the procedure of family affair conciliation, the effect of annulling status such as divorce and dissolution of adoption will be accepted.[91]

On the other hand, in family affairs cases other than divorce and dissolution of adoption, the scope of the trial is the status which is outside of the parties' control. Therefore, even if an agreement is made, it does not mean that the establishment of conciliation is accepted. In this case, the family court will conduct the necessary investigations, and after hearing opinions from the members of the family affairs conciliation committee, the family court can make 'a decision corresponding to the agreement', if it is valid (Family Affairs Procedure Act, Article 277(1)).

As mentioned above in relation to civil conciliation, the question of whether a conciliation statement has a *res judicata* effect or not is controversial.[92] Most family affairs cases end within six months.[93]

If there is no possibility of the parties' agreement, the conciliation committee can end the family affairs conciliation and make a notification to this effect (Family Affairs Procedure Act, Article 272(1) and (2)). In that case, if either of the parties file a lawsuit within two weeks, it is treated as a lawsuit which is filed at the time of application (Family Affairs Procedure Act, Article 3): thus the effect of interruption of prescription arises at the time of application (Civil Code, Article 147(1)).

On the other hand, even if the parties do not reach agreement during the conciliation procedure and the conciliation fails, in order not to waste the efforts for the establishment of conciliation, the family court can make a decision (Family Affairs Procedure Act, Article 284(1)). This decision is called 'a decision in lieu of conciliation'. At that time the family court can use its authority to decide to appoint any judge to solve the problem if it is necessary. Also, if the family affairs conciliation procedure is carried out in the conciliation committee, the family court has to listen to the conciliation committee's opinion (Family Affairs Procedure Act, Article 284(2)). By the judgment, the family court may order parties to hand over children, pay money and distribute assets (Family Affairs Procedure Act, Article 284(3)). The purpose of this Article is as follows. Regardless of the civil conciliation or the family conciliation, conciliation must be established by both parties' agreement. However, if the conciliation fails

---

91 Matsumoto, *supra* n. 84, p. 16.

92 See *supra* n. 77.

93 There were 136,292 cases for family conciliation in 2011. Among them, 13,917 cases were ended within one month, 47,039 cases were over within three months and 44,175 cases were over within six months. General Secretariat, Supreme Court, *supra* n. 5, at 16.

because the parties are stuck on one small issue on which they are unwilling to compromise, even where the conciliation committee has developed a conciliation plan, that failure spoils the conciliation committee's effort and also damages social trust in the conciliation system. Therefore, on the premise of annulment of a decision when either of the parties have an objection, a possibility for ending the conflict is provided (Family Affairs Procedure Act, Article 286(1)), and that is the justification for a judge making a decision in lieu of conciliation.[94]

## 4.4. SPECIAL CONCILIATION PROCEDURE

Civil conciliation was originally often used as a debt adjustment method for debtors who were in danger of economic failure. There was a time when disputes over credit loans and money lending businesses occupied three quarters of the number of conciliation cases which were dealt with in summary courts.[95] From that point, civil conciliation has been used, in a broad sense, as a method of insolvency proceedings.

Therefore, as a special rule of civil conciliation and as a special rule of collective rearrangement, the Act on Special Conciliation Proceedings for Expediting Arrangement of Specified Debts, etc., was made, and put into effect from February 1990.

### *4.4.1. Competent court*

In principle, as in the regular civil conciliation procedure, the summary court with jurisdiction over the place of the opponent's address will be the court with jurisdiction (Civil Conciliation Act, Article 3). However, in special conciliation cases, it is rather usual that there is only one debtor and several creditors. In this case, it is more effective to deal with several cases applied by the same applicant (debtor) in one court. Therefore, in an effort to make an efficient trial, the requirements of transfer are loosened (Act on Special Conciliation Proceedings, Article 4), and cases are consolidated as far as possible when several special conciliation cases about the same debtor are pending (Act on Special Conciliation Proceedings, Article 6).

### *4.4.2. Presiding official*

Basically, the conciliation committee plays the same role as that in a civil conciliation. In other words, the conciliation committee is composed of the chief, who is a judge, and at least two members of the conciliation committee

---

94 Matsumoto, *supra* n. 84, p. 19.

95 See *supra* n. 6.

(Civil Conciliation Act, Article 6 and Article 7(1)). Usually, committee members' opinions have to be based on professional knowledge or experience (Civil Conciliation Act, Article 8(1)). However, in the case of special conciliation, as the purpose is a particular debtor's economic rehabilitation more speciality is required. Therefore, the court is required to choose a specialist as a member of the civil conciliation committee depending on the case such as law, finance, corporate finance, evaluation of assets and so on (Civil Conciliation Act, Article 8).

### *4.4.3. Personal scope of application (debtor)*

The personal scope of this procedure, who is called the 'specified debtor', includes not only natural persons, but also legal persons (Act on Special Conciliation Proceedings, Article 2(1)). The specified debtor includes, individuals or artificial persons who are in danger of failure of payment, persons who cannot satisfy debt which is already due, and artificial persons who are in danger of insolvency. In terms of the course of legislation, the main target is a multiple debtor. However, this procedure is actually commonly used in the case of corporate insolvency.

### *4.4.4. Principles of procedure: features of special conciliation*

In special conciliation procedure, considering the debtor's financial resources and the determination of the amount of the remaining debt, the rehabilitation plan is constituted on the basis of the debtor's capacity for payment. If the special conciliation cannot be agreed, the debtor would go bankrupt. In order to make the procedure fast, both parties have to submit materials about the amount of the remaining debt and so on.[96] On this point, the issue of insufficiency of collection of materials has been pointed out before. Therefore, the existing law requires both parties to explain the reasons for the causation or satisfaction of debts (Act on Special Conciliation Proceedings, Article 10). In addition, the conciliation committee can require parties to submit related documents (Act on Special Conciliation Proceedings, Article 12), and if the party refuses to submit the related documents without any reason, they will be charged a maximum non-penal fine of 100,000 yen (Act on Special Conciliation Proceedings, Article 24).

If the execution has started during the time of conversation about the rearrangement of debts by special conciliation, the establishment of special conciliation becomes difficult. For solving this problem, the court may order the suspension of execution proceedings (Act on Special Conciliation Proceedings, Article 7).

96 Study Group on Special Conciliation, *supra* n. 12, p. 82.

### 4.4.5. *Merit of special conciliation*

As special conciliation procedure is one of the conciliation procedures, its binding power works only between both parties. Therefore, it does not bind a creditor who is not a party to the conciliation plan. However, the special conciliation system is an effective method in cases where the number of creditors is small, or where there is no creditor who is against the conciliation plan.

# 5. SETTLEMENT

## 5.1. TYPES OF SETTLEMENT

There are two categories of settlement, out-of-court settlement based on the substantive law and judicial settlement which is made in and authorised by the court; the latter can be further categorised into prompt decision settlement and procedural settlement. Judicial settlement, which is made in and authorised by the court was introduced in the civil procedure law in 1890 and still exists.

Procedural settlement, where both parties come to a compromise during the legal procedure and end the conflict, is also one of the solutions to end the trial which is used as a substitute for the court's judgment.[97] Therefore, it does not belong to ADR. Once the procedural settlement is settled and written on the record, it has the same power as a final decision in that it is possible to carry out the execution (Civil Execution Act, Article 22(7)).

## 5.2. SETTLEMENT UNDER PRIVATE LAW

Settlement based on private law is the contract that both parties enter into to end the conflict (Civil Code, Article 695). The settlement is usually reached as a result of negotiation. However, this is often only possible in cases where the reason behind the conflict is relatively simple and the emotional friction between the parties is not serious. Therefore, if it is not possible for the parties to solve the conflict through agreement, or a party fails to comply with the settlement agreement, the determination of rights through civil procedure becomes necessary.

---

97 In Japan the summary court and the district court are the courts of first instance. The former is competent for cases with a subject matter of an estimated maximum value of up to 1.4 million yen, and the latter is competent for those cases with a value of over 1.4 million yen. Court Act, Article 33(1)(1). About 14% of cases are ended by procedural settlement in the summary court, and 29% in the district court.

## 5.3. SETTLEMENT PRIOR TO FILING OF ACTION

Settlement prior to filing of action is the settlement which is made when both parties attend the summary court (Code of Civil Procedure, Article 275). This settlement is not based on the pending trial, but rather is a security to prevent the case going to trial. In the case of settlement prior to the filing of an action, the contents of the settlement are written on the statement by the clerk in front of the judge, and it will have the same power as a final decision (Code of Civil Procedure, Article 267). Therefore, if the debtor voluntary fulfils his or her duty, execution can be carried out without trial (Civil Execution Act, Article 22(7)).

Settlement prior to the filing of an action is not a civil procedure, so the amount sued for is not taken into account. Therefore, no matter how large or small the sum of money is, any enforceable claim can be subject to that settlement. As an easy way of getting the title of obligation, there is a notarised deed made by a notary public. However, although the notarised deed works only for money or other substitutes, the statement of settlement need not contain the contents of the debt. For this reason, a statement of settlement is preferred in certain cases. Further, a statement of settlement can be used to obtain a right of execution, even before a conflict has arisen.[98]

# 6. FUTURE OF ADR

Recently, the diversity of the civil dispute resolution system has drawn increasing attention, and the development of ADR is sought in many new fields. Among them, I believe it would be beneficial to mention ADR in medical cases and ADR for damages arising out of nuclear affairs, in particular.

In comparison to normal civil cases, medical cases are very complicated and time consuming.[99] As a result, the patient suffers from heavy financial and psychological burdens. On the other hand, the day-to-day business of the medical institution is also affected, with troubled patient relations. Besides, both parties conflict very strictly under civil procedure because in civil procedure the critical theme is whether or not the medical institution has legal responsibility (e.g. negligence) in accordance with substantive law. But this is not at all what the patient desires. He or she expects the honest response of the medical institution or wants to know what actually happened. To realise such purpose, a more

98 Matsuura and Kato, in Kaneko *et al.*, *supra* n. 54, p. 1502.

99 The average duration of civil procedure for medical cases was approximately 34.5 months in 1999. Thereafter, the duration was shortened to 24 months in 2008 because of the establishment of a special branch of medical cases in the court. Ueki, *From Civil Procedure for Medical Cases to ADR for Madical Cases* (Iryo saiban kara Iryo-ADR), 2011, p. 3.

flexible system is sought.[100] Then, the ADR system for medical cases was established by the bar associations, and attorneys with expertise in medical cases have become part of this.[101]

A nuclear accident occurred on 11 March 2011 as a result of an earthquake in eastern Japan. The Nuclear Damage Claim Dispute Resolution Center was publicly established so that disputes arising out of such accident will be resolved quickly and in an integrated fashion. The centre was established based on the Atomic Energy Damage Compensation Law and started operating in September 2011. The proceedings aim at the early resolution of a dispute with the support of an agent (attorney). The task of the centre covers only disputes against the Tokyo Electric Power Company and the damage caused by the nuclear accident. The duration of proceedings is expected to be three months. If settlement is not reached, the dispute will go to court proceedings. Many attorneys are designated at the centre not only as an agent but also as an investigator who searches fact-finding or precedent judgments, to speed up the proceedings.[102] As of 7 December 2012, 4,797 cases have been heard. Among them, 1,683 cases were ended (1,352 cases were agreed by settlement) and 3,114 cases are still pending.[103]

---

100 Ueki, *supra* n. 99, p. 200. The purpose of the plaintiff (patient) for civil procedure is not always to get damages. Yamamoto and Yamada, *supra* n. 13, p. 380.

101 ADR Center of Japan Foundation of Association (ed.), *Medical Dispute and ADR* (Iryofunso to ADR), 2011, p. 46.

102 Idei, *Towards Dispute Resolution arising out of Compensation for Nuclear Affairs* (Genshiryoku songaibaisho no Kaiketsu ni mukete), Niben Frontier, Dec. 2011, p. 26.

103 <www.mext.go.jp/a_menu/anzenkakuho/baisho/1310412.htm> accessed on 15.12.2012.

# KOREA

Gyooho Lee*

## Contents



* My special thanks go to Dr Keon-Hyung Ahn, who works as the Deputy Director at the Dispute Resolution Center of the Korean Commercial Arbitration Board, for providing me with the statistical data shown in this paper.

# 1. INTRODUCTION

Korea is one of the most litigation-prone societies in the world.[1] The overall increase of court filings in civil cases in Korea is the outcome of factors external to the courts, and of the costs the parties incur as they directly use the courts.[2] These external factors include 'the increase in the number of disputes resulting from the Korean economy's rapid growth and the increasing weakness of traditional dispute resolution mechanisms such as family, churches, and neighbourhoods.'[3] Litigation costs can be included as the internal costs, which refers to costs incurred by access to justice.[4] Non-judicial and judicial ADR mechanisms may help the parties autonomously resolve their disputes, reducing those social costs and judicial caseloads.

ADR in Korea includes mediation, conciliation, compromise, and arbitration. In this regard, mediation refers to ADR by which 'the mediator facilitates a discussion between the parties.'[5] The mediator may or may not present his/her opinions on the strength of each party's argument.[6] In either case, the mediator is not empowered to impose his/her opinions on the parties.[7] Conciliation means ADR by which the conciliator facilitates a discussion between the parties and has slightly more power to impose his/her will on both parties than in mediation.[8] In some instances, however, the terms 'mediation and conciliation' are used interchangeably. Conciliation can be divided into judicial conciliation and administrative conciliation. Judicial conciliation can be categorised as civil judicial conciliation and judicial conciliation for family cases only.

As far as an institution which operates ADR is concerned, the types of ADR in Korea can be classified into three categories as follows: (a) ADR conducted by courts; (b) ADR operated by administrative governmental agencies; and (c) ADR operated by private organisations.[9]

The ADR operated by courts is conciliation under the Judicial Conciliation of Civil Disputes Act, conciliation under the Family Litigation Act, compromise in court pending an action, an order to recommend compromise, and compromise

---

1 For more details, see G. Lee, 'Attorney Fee Arrangements Really Matter in Terms of Access to Justice in Korea', in M. Reimann (ed.), *Cost and Fee Allocation in Civil Procedure*, Springer, 2012, pp. 201–202.

2 G. Lee, *supra* n. 1, p. 12.

3 G. Lee, *supra* n. 1, p. 202.

4 G. Lee, *supra* n. 1, p. 202.

5 <www.wisegeek.com/what-is-the-difference-between-conciliation-and-mediation.htm> accessed 30.10.2012.

6 <www.wisegeek.com/what-is-the-difference-between-conciliation-and-mediation.htm> accessed 30.10.2012.

7 <www.wisegeek.com/what-is-the-difference-between-conciliation-and-mediation.htm> accessed 30.10.2012.

8 <www.wisegeek.com/what-is-the-difference-between-conciliation-and-mediation.htm> accessed 30.10.2012.

9 Y.J. Ham, *Introduction to Dispute Resolution*, Jinwonsa, 2010, pp. 324–325.

in court prior to the commencement of an action.[10] The ADR managed by governmental agencies includes mediation, conciliation, ruling, and arbitration of administrative agencies. The ADR carried out by private sectors is KCAB's ADR.

## 2. JUDICIAL ADR

### 2.1. COMPROMISE

Both parties to a lawsuit can reach a compromise before a court. Also, a court may, irrespective of the progress of litigation, recommend a compromise, or have a commissioned judge or an entrusted judge recommend it.[11] In this case, the court, a commissioned judge or an entrusted judge may order the party or his/her legal representative to appear before the court.[12]

When a plaintiff or a defendant has failed to appear on the trial date or failed to dispute the merits of the case despite appearing, it shall be deemed that the matters stated in the written complaint, written reply and other preparatory documents submitted by him/her have been stated, and the other party who has appeared may be ordered to dispute on this basis.[13] In cases where the written reply and the other preparatory documents, which are deemed to have been stated by the parties, contain an indication of intent of a compromise, and are authenticated by a notarial office, it shall be deemed that the compromise has been constituted if the other party himself/herself appears on the date of trial and accepts such indication of intent of compromise.[14]

When a compromise is entered into in the course of trial or preliminary hearing, such compromise shall have the same effect as a final and conclusive judgment.[15]

In principle, litigation costs shall be borne by the losing party.[16] However, where parties reach a compromise in court, including in the case of a ruling to recommend a compromise, each party bears his/her own compromise costs and litigation costs unless there exit any particular provisions as to allocation of those costs.[17]

A court, a commissioned judge or an entrusted judge may, pending the court action, render *ex officio* a ruling recommending a compromise in order to fairly

---

10 Y.J. Ham, *supra* n. 9, p. 324.
11 Article 145(1), Korean Civil Procedure Act.
12 Article 145(2), Korean Civil Procedure Act.
13 Article 148(1), Korean Civil Procedure Act.
14 Article 148(3), Korean Civil Procedure Act.
15 Article 220, Korean Civil Procedure Act.
16 Article 98, Korean Civil Procedure Act.
17 Article 106, Korean Civil Procedure Act.

settle the case by taking account of the parties' interests and all other circumstances, within the scope and spirit of the claim.[18] The junior administrative officer, etc. of the court shall serve on the parties the authentic copy of a compromise or written ruling which contains the recommendations for compromise.[19] The parties may raise an objection against the ruling within two weeks from the date of service of the authentic copy of the relevant compromise or written ruling.[20] Such an objection may be raised even prior to the service of such authentic copy.[21] An objection shall be made by submitting a written objection to the court issuing a ruling recommending a compromise.[22] A written objection must state the names of the parties and, if any, their legal representatives, the details of the ruling recommending a compromise, and the basis of the objection against it.[23] The party who has raised an objection may withdraw his/her objection by obtaining the consent of the other party, not later than the time when a judgment on the case is declared.[24] The right to object to the ruling may be waived before an objection is raised.[25] Any waiver of rights to object the ruling shall be made in a written statement.[26] In case where an objection has not been raised in accordance with methods which conform to laws and regulations, or is found to have been raised subsequent to a lapse of rights to object, the court, the commissioned judge or the entrusted judge shall, if such defects are not rectifiable, reject the objection. When the commissioned judge or the entrusted judge has failed to dismiss the objection, the court of the lawsuit shall dismiss it.[27] An immediate appeal may be raised against the ruling to dismiss an objection.[28]

A ruling recommending a compromise shall take the same effect as a judicial compromise: (a) when there exists no objection within two weeks from the date of service of the authentic copy of the relevant protocol or written ruling; (b) when a ruling dismissing an objection has become final and conclusive; or (c) when the party concerned withdraws his/her objection, or waives his/her right to object.[29] When an objection is lawful, the lawsuit shall return to the same status as prior to the ruling recommending a compromise. In this case, any procedural acts taken earlier shall continue to take effect.[30] A ruling

18 Article 225(1), Korean Civil Procedure Act.
19 Article 225(2), Korean Civil Procedure Act.
20 Article 226(1) Korean Civil Procedure Act.
21 Article 226(1), proviso of the Korean Civil Procedure Act.
22 Article 227(1), Korean Civil Procedure Act.
23 Article 227(2), Korean Civil Procedure Act.
24 Article 228(1), Korean Civil Procedure Act.
25 Article 229(1), Korean Civil Procedure Act.
26 Article 229(2), Korean Civil Procedure Act.
27 Article 230(1), Korean Civil Procedure Act.
28 Article 230(2), Korean Civil Procedure Act.
29 Article 231, Korean Civil Procedure Act.
30 Article 232, Korean Civil Procedure Act.

recommending a compromise shall lose its effect when a judgment has been declared at the instance of court.[31]

As for a civil dispute regarding which a party has not commenced a lawsuit, he/she may file a motion for pre-action compromise with the district court where the general forum of the other party is located, by specifying the gist of the grounds for the claim and the circumstances surrounding the dispute.[32] In this regard, a pre-action compromise before a court differs from an out-of-court compromise contract between the parties. A party cannot delegate the right to appoint a representative for the pre-action compromise.[33] The court, may, if deemed necessary, order the appearance of the party himself/herself or his/her legal representative, in order to examine whether or not the right of representation exists.[34] The provisions relating to the litigation shall apply *mutatis mutandis* to a motion for pre-action compromise, unless they are contrary to the nature of pre-action compromise.[35] When a pre-action compromise is reached, the junior administrative officer, etc. of a court shall indicate in the protocol the parties, their legal representatives, the gist of and grounds for the claim, the terms of the pre-action compromise, the date and the court concerned, and the judge and the junior administrative officer, etc. of the court shall put their names and seals to the protocol.[36] When a pre-action compromise has not been achieved, the junior administrative officer, etc. of a court shall enter the reasons thereof in the protocol.[37] If either party fails to appear on the date for the pre-action compromise, the court may deem that no pre-action compromise has been achieved between them.[38] In the case of failure to achieve pre-action compromise, a party may file a motion for instituting a lawsuit.[39] If lawful grounds for commencing a lawsuit exist, it shall be deemed that the lawsuit has been instituted when a motion for a compromise has been filed. In this case, the junior administrative officer, etc. of the court shall promptly forward the record of litigation to the competent court.[40] Unless otherwise prescribed, court proceedings must be filed within two weeks from the date of service of the certified copy of the protocol.[41] In cases where a pre-action compromise has been achieved, its expenses shall be borne by each party unless otherwise agreed. On the other hand, in cases where a pre-action compromise has not been achieved, the costs shall be borne

31 Article 232, Korean Civil Procedure Act.
32 Article 385(1), Korean Civil Procedure Act.
33 Article 385(2), Korean Civil Procedure Act.
34 Article 385(3), Korean Civil Procedure Act.
35 Article 385(4), Korean Civil Procedure Act.
36 Article 386, Korean Civil Procedure Act.
37 Article 387(1), Korean Civil Procedure Act.
38 Article 387(2), Korean Civil Procedure Act.
39 Article 388(1), Korean Civil Procedure Act.
40 Article 388(2), Korean Civil Procedure Act.
41 Article 388(3), Korean Civil Procedure Act.

by the applicant. However, where a motion for commencing a lawsuit has been filed, the expenses of the pre-action compromise shall consist of part of the costs of the lawsuit.[42]

## 2.2. CONCILIATION

### *2.2.1. Civil conciliation under the Judicial Conciliation of Civil Disputes Act*

The Judicial Conciliation of Civil Disputes Act[43] is designed to settle civil disputes according to a simple procedure based on mutual concessions between the parties, common sense and actual circumstances.[44] A conciliation case shall be under the jurisdiction of the District Court, the Branch Court of the District Court, the Municipal Court or the Provincial Court, which has the jurisdiction over one of the following: (a) the place of the general forum of the defendant under the Civil Procedure Act; (b) the place of business or business office of the defendant; (c) the place of work of the defendant; (d) the location of the subject matter of the dispute; or (e) the place where the damage occurred. Nonetheless, a conciliation case may be placed under the jurisdiction of the court with exclusive jurisdiction to hear the judicial proceedings, or a court determined by agreement of the parties.[45]

A judge in charge of a conciliation case, as designated by the chief judge of the High Court, the chief judge of the District Court or the chief judge of a Branch Court of the District Court, or a judge of a Municipal or Provincial Court in charge of a conciliation case (hereinafter 'conciliation judge'), shall transfer cases to the competent court by means of a ruling, if no jurisdiction exists in his/her court. However, the conciliation judge is allowed not to transfer the case if the respondent makes a statement not contesting the competence of the court in the conciliation procedure, or if the conciliation judge finds that the case particularly needs to be resolved through the conciliation procedure, or if a stay is deemed particularly necessary to resolve a case.[46] A court may, if deemed necessary, refer a case pending therein to conciliation before a judgment in an appellate court is rendered.[47] Cases of conciliation shall be dealt with by the conciliation judge.[48] A conciliation judge may directly conciliate cases or may refer the conciliation to commissioners who regularly deal with affairs related to conciliation (hereinafter 'standing commissioners') under the Judicial Conciliation of Civil Disputes Act

42 Article 388(4), Korean Civil Procedure Act.
43 Act No. 11157, amended on 17.01.2012, effective since 18.04.2012.
44 Article 1, Judicial Conciliation of Civil Disputes Act.
45 Article 3, Judicial Conciliation of Civil Disputes Act.
46 Article 4(1), Judicial Conciliation of Civil Disputes Act.
47 Article 6, Judicial Conciliation of Civil Disputes Act.
48 Article 7(1), Judicial Conciliation of Civil Disputes Act.

and a council of conciliation. A conciliation judge shall allow the conciliation committee to conciliate a case if a party so requests.[49]

Nonetheless, following a conciliation referral the court may directly conciliate cases if it is deemed appropriate to directly handle cases.[50] In this case, the court may have a commissioned judge or an entrusted judge take charge of the conciliation. In such cases, the commissioned judge or the entrusted judge shall have the same power as a conciliation judge.[51]

Standing commissioners and courts that conciliate cases shall also have the same power as a conciliation judge in handling a conciliation case.[52]

A conciliation committee shall be comprised of a chief commissioner and two or more commissioners.[53] A chief commissioner must either be a conciliation judge or a standing commissioner, the chief judge of the court, a commissioned judge or an entrusted judge, or a judge of a Municipal or Provincial Court.[54] A commissioner must have a high level of knowledge and experience, and a high moral reputation, and shall be appointed, in advance, by the chief of a High Court, the chief of a District Court or the chief of a Branch Court.[55] A standing commissioner shall be appointed by the Minister of National Court Administration among persons who have bar licence with certain careers determined by the Supreme Court Rules.[56] The term of office of commissioners shall be two years unless a commissioner is commissioned with his/her term of office fixed within two years under special circumstances.[57] The commissioners, who comprise a council of conciliation, shall be designated under agreement of the parties or a chief commissioner among the qualified persons mentioned above.[58] The conciliation proceedings by the conciliation committee are conducted by the chief commissioner.[59] Conciliation shall have the same effect as a judicial compromise, which has *res judicata* effect on the parties.[60]

Where agreement of conciliation has been reached, expenses incurred therein are borne by each party unless otherwise agreed upon between the parties, and where agreement of conciliation has not been reached, they are

49 Article 7(2), Judicial Conciliation of Civil Disputes Act.
50 Article 7(3), Judicial Conciliation of Civil Disputes Act.
51 Article 7(5), Judicial Conciliation of Civil Disputes Act.
52 Article 7(4), Judicial Conciliation of Civil Disputes Act.
53 Article 8, Judicial Conciliation of Civil Disputes Act.
54 Article 9, Judicial Conciliation of Civil Disputes Act.
55 Article 10(1), Judicial Conciliation of Civil Disputes Act.
56 Article 10(1), proviso of Judicial Conciliation of Civil Disputes Act.
57 Article 10(2), Judicial Conciliation of Civil Disputes Act.
58 Article 10 *bis*, Judicial Conciliation of Civil Disputes Act.
59 Article 11, Judicial Conciliation of Civil Disputes Act.
60 Article 29, Judicial Conciliation of Civil Disputes Act.

borne by the applicant.[61] Filing fees for a conciliation amount to one-fifth of those for an ordinary lawsuit.[62]

Interestingly enough, civil conciliation by jury is available even though civil jury trial is not permitted in Korea. Since 2006 when, for the first time Changhung Branch Court adopted conciliation by jury,[63] civil conciliation by jury has been used by courts nation-wide. For instance, Kwangju District Court and Mokpo Branch Court firstly conducted conciliation by jury in 2012.[64] Conciliation by jury is based on Article 16 of the Civil Conciliation Act, which prescribes that '[a] person or persons interested in the result of conciliation may join the conciliation proceedings upon permission from a conciliation judge' and that '[t]he conciliation judge may, if it is deemed necessary, allow a person or persons interested in the result of conciliation to join the conciliation proceedings.'

Conciliation has the same effect as a compromise in court, which has *res judicata* effect.[65]

The Court Conciliation Centres, which consist of standing commissioners, were established in Seoul and Busan in 2009,[66] and in Daejon, Daegu, and Kwangju in 2011. These five cities are the place where the five High Courts are located in Korea.

In addition to court-annexed conciliation, Seoul Central District Court, which began an early conciliation mechanism in March 2010, allows external court-connected conciliation. The Seoul Central District Court designated the Comprehensive Assistance Centre for Disputes of the KCAB largely in commercial cases and the Arbitration Centre of Seoul Bar Association. A conciliation judge can allot the conciliation cases to the Comprehensive Assistance Centre for Disputes at the KCAB and the Arbitration Centre of Seoul Bar Association. The managing conciliator should report the outcome of the conciliation to the conciliation judge in Seoul Central District Court within 45 days.

Conciliation rates for single judge division cases and collegiate division cases were 5.2% and 9.5% in 2011 respectively.[67] Taking into account the fact that the conciliation rate for single judge division cases was 2.2% in 2008, I think that the adoption of the standing commissioners system in 2009 affected the conciliation rate for the single-judge division cases.

---

61 Article 37(2), Judicial Conciliation of Civil Disputes Act.

62 Article 3, Judicial Conciliation of Civil Disputes Rules.

63 <http://kwangju.co.kr/read.php3?aid=1340636400471091006> accessed 11.10.2012.

64 *Ibid.*

65 Article 29, Judicial Conciliation of Civil Disputes Act.

66 <http://blog.daum.net/nrpark/13745485> accessed 29.11.2012.

67 See *infra* Tables 1 and 2.

Table 1. Single judge division cases before a court of first instance (including small claims cases)

| Classification / Year | Types of case disposition | | | | | | | | | | Appeal | Appeal rate |
|---|---|---|---|---|---|---|---|---|---|---|---|---|
| | Total | Order to dismiss plaintiff's complaint | Judgment | | | | | Concilia-tion | Compro-mise or accept-ance of plaintiff's claim | Plaintiff's voluntary dismissal | Others | | |
| | | | Subtotal | In favour of plaintiff in whole or in part | In favour of defendant | Judgment by dismissal | Others | | | | | | |
| 2007 | 1,177,911 (100.0%) | 11,871 (1.0%) | 740,898 (62.9%) | 715,395 (60.7%) | 24,260 (2.1%) | 1,107 (0.1%) | 136 (0.0%) | 42,445 (3.6%) | 25,218 (2.2%) | 91,086 (7.7%) | 266,393 (22.6%) | 29,381 | 4.0 |
| 2008 | 1,235,550 (100.0%) | 9,488 (0.8%) | 820,840 (66.4%) | 796,106 (64.4%) | 23,256 (1.9%) | 1,272 (0.1%) | 206 (0.0%) | 46,769 (3.8%) | 27,943 (2.2%) | 93,651 (7.6%) | 236,859 (19.2%) | 28,946 | 3.5 |
| 2009 | 1,049,077 (100.0%) | 12,543 (1.2%) | 645,714 (61.6%) | 617,403 (58.9%) | 26,752 (2.6%) | 1,408 (0.1%) | 151 (0.0%) | 46,733 (4.5%) | 29,823 (2.8%) | 100,800 (9.6%) | 213,464 (20.3%) | 31,544 | 4.9 |
| 2010 | 937,971 (100.0%) | 12,210 (1.3%) | 589,792 (62.9%) | 560,933 (59.8%) | 27,023 (2.9%) | 1,697 (0.2%) | 139 (0.0%) | 48,474 (5.2%) | 33,375 (3.6%) | 100,890 (10.7%) | 153,230 (16.3%) | 31,596 | 5.4 |
| 2011 | 914,551 (100.0%) | 11,938 (1.3%) | 594,410 (65.0%) | 564,759 (61.8%) | 27,765 (3.0%) | 1,757 (0.2%) | 129 (0.0%) | 47,518 (5.2%) | 31,965 (3.5%) | 102,410 (11.2%) | 126,310 (13.8%) | 33,407 | 5.6 |

Source: Office of Court Administration, Annual Judicial Report for 2011, p. 630 <www.scourt.go.kr/justicesta/JusticestaListAction.work?gubun=10> accessed 02.12.2012.

**Table 2. Collegiate division cases before a court of first instance**

| Classification / Year | Types of case disposition | | | | | | | | | | | Appeal | Appeal rate |
|---|---|---|---|---|---|---|---|---|---|---|---|---|---|
| | Total | Order to dismiss plaintiff's complaint | Judgment | | | | | Conciliation | Compromise or acceptance of plaintiff's claim | Plaintiff's voluntary dismissal | Others | | |
| | | | Subtotal | In favour of plaintiff in whole or in part | In favour of defendant | Judgment by dismissal | Others | | | | | | |
| 2007 | 44,359 (100.0%) | 449 (1.0%) | 27,580 (62.2%) | 19,597 (44.2%) | 7,404 (16.7%) | 546 (1.2%) | 33 (0.1%) | 4,449 (10.0%) | 25,20 (5.7%) | 7,896 (17.8%) | 1,465 (3.3%) | 11,196 | 40.6 |
| 2008 | 48,880 (100.0%) | 498 (1.0%) | 29,794 (61.0%) | 21,115 (43.2%) | 8,087 (16.5%) | 563 (1.2%) | 29 (0.1%) | 5,189 (10.6%) | 3,517 (7.2%) | 8,137 (16.6%) | 1,745 (3.6%) | 12,305 | 41.3 |
| 2009 | 53,387 (100.0%) | 959 (1.8%) | 33,024 (61.9%) | 23,528 (44.1%) | 8,785 (16.5%) | 690 (1.3%) | 21 (0.0%) | 5,413 (10.1%) | 3,408 (6.4%) | 8,798 (16.5%) | 1,785 (3.3%) | 13,725 | 41.6 |
| 2010 | 51,897 (100.0%) | 911 (1.8%) | 32,022 (61.6%) | 22,416 (43.2%) | 8,847 (17.0%) | 734 (1.4%) | 25 (0.0%) | 5,607 (10.8%) | 3,209 (6.2%) | 8,559 (16.5%) | 1,589 (3.1%) | 13,550 | 42.3 |
| 2011 | 53,437 (100.0%) | 1,040 (1.9%) | 33,662 (63.0%) | 23,578 (44.1%) | 9,250 (17.3%) | 798 (1.5%) | 36 (0.1%) | 5,098 (9.5%) | 3,177 (6.0%) | 8,456 (15,8%) | 2,004 (3,8%) | 14,804 | 44.0 |

Source: Office of Court Administration, Annual Judicial Report for 2011, p. 631 <www.scourt.go.kr/justicesta/JusticestaListAction.work?gubun=10> accessed 02.12. 2012.

### 2.2.2. *Conciliation of family affairs under the Family Litigation Act*

The provisions of the Judicial Conciliation of Civil Disputes Act shall apply *mutatis mutandis* to family conciliation unless the Family Litigation Act provides otherwise.[68] A person who intends to institute a lawsuit or request an adjudication of the family court for family litigation cases of Categories B[69] and C[70] and family non-litigation cases of Category E,[71] must first apply for conciliation.[72] When a lawsuit has been commenced or an adjudication has been requested without first making a request for conciliation, the family court must refer the relevant case to conciliation, unless the court deems it impossible to summon one party or both parties without service by publication or it would be

---

68 Article 49, Family Litigation Act (Act No. 10212, amended on March 31, 2010, effective since March 31, 2010).

69 The cases in Category B under the Family Litigation Act are as follows: (a) confirmation on whether a relation of de facto marriage exists; (b) revocation of a marriage; (c) revocation of a divorce; (d) judicial divorce; (e) determination on fatherhood; (f) denial of a legitimate child; (g) revocation of an affiliation; (h) objection against an affiliation; (i) request for an affiliation; (j) revocation of an adoption; (k) revocation of a breach of adoption; (l) judicial breach of adoption; (m) revocation of full adoption; and (n) breach of full adoption (see Article 2(1)(1)(b), Family Litigation Act).

70 The cases in Category C under the Family Litigation Act are as follows: (a) a claim for damages due to a cancellation of an engagement, or an unlawful annulment of the relation of de facto marriage, including a claim against a third person, and a claim for restitution; (b) a claim for damages caused by a nullity or revocation of a marriage, or that of a divorce, or a divorce, including a claim against a third person, and a claim for restitution; (c) a claim for damages caused by a nullity or revocation of an adoption, or a breach of adoption, or a breach of adoption, including a claim against a third person, and a claim for restitution; and (d) a claim for revocation of a fraudulent act for the preservation of a claim for division of property under Article 839 of the Civil Act and a claim for restitution thereof (see Article 2(1)(1)(c), Family Litigation Act).

71 The cases in Category E under the Family Litigation Act are as follows: (a) disposition concerning the cohabitation, support, cooperation or bearing of living expenses by husband and wife pursuant to Articles 826 and 833 of the Civil Act; (b) disposition as to a change of a property administrator or division of the common property pursuant to Article 829(3) of the Civil Act; (c) disposition as to the fostering of children and alterations thereof, and the restriction or exclusion of visitation rights, pursuant to Articles 837 and 837 *bis* of the Civil Act, including cases where each of the aforementioned provisions is applied *mutatis mutandis* under Article 843 of the Civil Act, and where it has been caused by a revocation of marriage or an affiliation thereof; (d) disposition as to division of the property pursuant to Article 839 *bis* (2) of the Civil Act, including cases applicable *mutatis mutandis* under Article 843 of the Civil Act, and where it has been caused by a revocation of marriage; (e) designation and change of a person with the parental authority pursuant to Article 909(4) and (6) of the Civil Act, including cases which are caused by the annulment of a marriage; (f) adjudication of loss of the parental authority, representative right to legal acts, and property administration right, and that of a recovery of the lost authority or right, pursuant to Articles 924–926 of the Civil Act; (g) objection against a decision of a family council pursuant to Article 972 of the Civil Act; (h) disposition as to support pursuant to Articles 976–978 of the Civil Act; (i) decision on the contributory portion pursuant to Article 1008 *bis* (2) and (4) of the Civil Act; and (j) disposition as to the division of inherited property pursuant to Article 1013(2) of the Civil Act (see Article 2(1)(2)(b), Family Litigation Act).

72 Article 50(1), Family Litigation Act.

impossible to reach a conciliation even if the relevant case was referred to conciliation.[73] A family conciliation case is subject to the jurisdiction of the family court having jurisdiction over family litigation cases or family non-litigation cases corresponding thereto, or of the family court decided upon by agreement of the parties concerned.[74] Family conciliation cases are dealt with by a conciliation committee composed of one chief conciliator and two or more conciliators.[75] A judge in charge of conciliation may, when a proper reason exists, independently make conciliation, unless the parties concerned clearly express their dissenting opinions.[76] A chief conciliator or a judge in charge of conciliation is designated among judges of their competent court by the chief of a family court or of its branch court.[77] Among persons of learning and high moral repute who have been commissioned, in advance, every year by the chief of a family court or of its branch court, or who have been selected by an agreement of the parties concerned, conciliators constituting the conciliation committee are designated by the chief conciliator for each and every case.[78] Along with participating in a conciliation conducted by a conciliation committee, conciliators shall state their opinion based on their expertise on other conciliation cases in compliance with a request from a family court, conciliation committee or judge in charge of conciliation, or hear the opinions of persons interested in the relevant case for a settlement of the dispute.[79] A chief conciliator or judge in charge of conciliation shall, before conducting conciliation, request that a family affairs investigator conduct an investigation into the facts of the case, within a fixed deadline, unless any special circumstance exists.[80] Any claims for family cases of Categories B, C and E may be joined to apply for conciliation.[81] In order to settle several claims between the parties at once, the parties can file a request for conciliation and join any related civil claims by obtaining permission of the conciliation committee or a judge in charge of conciliation.[82] The conciliation committee shall, in conducting its conciliation, persuade the parties concerned by taking account of the benefits of conciliation for all interested persons and the parties concerned, and by devising a scheme capable of achieving a peaceful and final settlement of a dispute.[83] In conciliating the matters directly related to the interests of a minor child, such as the designation and change of a person who is to exercise the parental authority over that minor child and a decision on the method of

73 Article 50(2), Family Litigation Act.
74 Article 51(1), Family Litigation Act.
75 Article 52(1), Family Litigation Act.
76 Article 52(2), Family Litigation Act.
77 Article 53(1), Family Litigation Act.
78 Article 53(2), Family Litigation Act.
79 Article 54, Family Litigation Act.
80 Article 56, Family Litigation Act.
81 Article 57(1), Family Litigation Act.
82 Article 57(2), Family Litigation Act.
83 Article 58(1), Family Litigation Act.

fostering, the welfare of that minor child shall be considered preferentially.[84] The conciliation shall be effectuated by entering in a protocol the matters agreed upon between the parties concerned.[85] Any decision substituting a conciliation or a final conciliation shall have the same effect as a judicial compromise unless it applies to matters not disposable by the parties concerned voluntarily.[86]

## 3. ADMINISTRATIVE ADR

Conciliations made by administrative agencies generally have the same effect as judicial compromise which has *res judicata* effect on the parties only.

The Korea Medical Dispute Mediation and Arbitration Agency[87] was established on 8 April 2012 pursuant to an 'Act on Remedies for Damages Due to Medical Malpractice and Conciliation of Medical Dispute', which was enacted on 7 April 2011 and effective since 8 April 2012.

Under the Environmental Dispute Adjustment Act,[88] the term 'adjustment' means mediation, conciliation, and administrative ruling of environmental disputes.[89] In accordance with the Environmental Dispute Adjustment Act, the central environmental dispute adjustment committee was established in the Ministry of Environment, and local environmental dispute adjustment committees were established in the special metropolitan city, metropolitan city or province (referred to as '*Do*' in Korean) respectively.[90] When there is a request for adjustment, an environmental dispute adjustment committee may advise the parties to agree to environmental damages.[91] This advice will not affect the progress of adjustment.[92] In short, the Environmental Dispute Adjustment Act covers mediation, conciliation, and administrative ruling of environmental disputes.

The Framework Act on Consumers purports 'to prescribe consumers' rights and duties, the duties of the State, local governments and enterprises, the roles of consumer organisations and relationship between consumers and enterprises in free market economy in order to protect consumers' rights and interests, and also to prescribe basic matters necessary for comprehensively facilitating consumer policies and thereby to contribute to the improvement of consumers'

---

84 Article 58(2), Family Litigation Act.
85 Article 59(1), Family Litigation Act.
86 Article 59(2), Family Litigation Act.
87 <www.k-medi.or.kr/Index.do> accessed 20.10.2012.
88 Act No 11267, amended on 01.02.2012, effective since 02.05.2012.
89 Article 2(3), Environmental Dispute Adjustment Act.
90 Article 4, Environmental Dispute Adjustment Act.
91 Article 16 *bis* (1), Environmental Dispute Adjustment Act.
92 Article 16 *bis* (2), Environmental Dispute Adjustment Act.

lives and the development of national economy.'[93] The council of consumer organisations registered with the Fair Trade Commission may autonomously mediate disputes for the settlement of consumers' complaints and damages unless they regard the matter as under the control of a dispute mediation organisation which is established pursuant to the provisions of other Acts, whose business area demands specialisation, as prescribed by the Presidential Decree.[94] The autonomous dispute mediation shall be deemed to have the effect of an agreement with the same contents which is concluded between the parties if they accept it.[95] The Consumer Dispute Mediation Commission pursuant to the Framework Act on Consumers was established in the Korea Consumers Agency so as to mediate disputes raised between consumers and enterprises.[96] When the Consumer Dispute Mediation Commission receives an application for dispute mediation, it shall complete the dispute mediation within 30 days from the date when the application is received.[97] Nonetheless, where it is impossible to complete the dispute mediation within 30 days due to unavoidable circumstances, the Commission may extend the period. In this case, it shall inform the parties and their representatives thereof specifying the reasons and the period.[98] When a dispute mediation is completed within the period mentioned above, the chairperson of the Commission shall promptly notify the parties of the contents thereof.[99] Upon receipt of the notification, the parties must inform the Commission of the acceptance or refusal of the contents of the dispute mediation within 15 days after receiving such notification. If they fail to express their intention within 15 days, they shall be deemed to accept the contents of the dispute mediation.[100] If the parties accept or are deemed to have accepted the contents of the dispute mediation, the contents of the dispute mediation shall have the same effect as a judicial compromise.[101] In any cases where similar damage has been caused to many consumers, the State, a local government, the Korea Consumer Agency, a consumer organisation or an enterprise may make a request or application to the Commission to mediate the disputes collectively.[102]

The request or application for collective mediation of consumer disputes must be made in writing.[103]

---

93 Article 1, Framework Act on Consumers: Act No. 10678, amended on 19.05.2011 and effective since 20.08.2011.

94 Article 31(1), Framework Act on Consumers.

95 Article 31(2), Framework Act on Consumers.

96 Article 60(1), Framework Act on Consumers.

97 Article 66(1), Framework Act on Consumers.

98 Article 66(2), Framework Act on Consumers.

99 Article 67(1), Framework Act on Consumers.

100 Article 67(3), Framework Act on Consumers.

101 Article 67(4), Framework Act on Consumers.

102 Article 68(1), Framework Act on Consumers.

103 Article 57(1), Enforcement Decree of the Framework Act on Consumers.

The institutions which perform administrative ADR, mainly focusing on conciliation, include the Personal Information Dispute Mediation Committee,[104] the Health Insurance Dispute Mediation Committee,[105] the Construction Business Dispute Conciliation Committee,[106] the Internet Address Dispute Resolution Committee,[107] the Conciliation Committee on Electronic Document and Electronic Transaction,[108] and the Korea Copyright Commission.[109]

There is a special arbitration statute that is applicable to the media industry only. It is the Act on Arbitration and Remedies for Damage Caused by Press Reports (Press Arbitration Act).[110] Article 24(1) of the Press Arbitration Act provides that any dispute concerning a request for a report on a corrected statement, etc. or compensation for damage may, at the request of both parties who agree to comply with a final and conclusive decision of the competent arbitral tribunal on that dispute, be submitted to arbitration. An arbitral award under the Press Arbitration Act has the same effect as a final and conclusive judgment rendered by a court.[111]

## 4. ARBITRATION

### 4.1. OVERVIEW

Korea has a strong geographical advantage to be a desirable seat of arbitration in East Asia.[112] In other words, Korea is surrounded by China, Japan, and Russia and can be an ideal arbitral situs for disputes between Chinese and Japanese parties, disputes between Chinese and Russian parties, disputes between Japanese and Russian parties, or disputes between American or European and Chinese or Japanese parties.[113] In fact, the number of disputes settled through arbitration has been on the rapid increase since the revision of the Korean Arbitration Act in 1999.[114] The rapid increase in arbitration in Korea is in part

104 Articles 40–50, Personal Information Protection Act.

105 Article 89, Health Insurance Act.

106 Articles 69–80, Framework Act on Construction Industry.

107 Articles 16–24, Act on Internet Address Resource.

108 Articles 32–37 *bis*, Framework Act on Electronic Document and Electronic Transaction.

109 Articles 112–119, Copyright Act.

110 Law No. 7370 (25.01.2005), last revised by Law No. 10587 (14.04.2011); Kyu Ho Youm, Codified Sources, 1 Media, Advertising, & Entertainment Law Throughout the World §21:3 (2012).

111 Article 25(1), Press Arbitration Act.

112 <www.sidley.com/files/News/f8a224dd-c1ce-428f-a0ab-04a50384903b/Presentation/NewsAttachment/73efc124-bdbf-4611-b82b-04dcf22f78e8/IntlArbMay0307v2.pdf>, p. 4, accessed 20.10.2012.

113 *Ibid.*

114 H.G. Lee, 'Arbitration', in A. Kritzer, S. Eiselen, J. Vanto and J. Vanto, *International Contract Manual*, 2012, §64:4.

due to the active efforts of the Korean Commercial Arbitration Board (KCAB) focusing on improving the fairness, expediency and efficiency of arbitration proceedings carried out under its auspices.[115] In addition, the liberalisation of the Korean legal service market through bilateral free trade agreements with other countries will encourage the consumers of arbitration services to be represented by foreign lawyers or law firms in international arbitrations conducted in Korea when the governing law of the arbitration is Korean law.[116]

In this regard, Korea has concluded negotiations on several bilateral free trade agreements.[117] Those agreements are the Free Trade Agreement between the Republic of Korea and the Republic of Chile,[118] the Free Trade Agreement between the Republic of Korea and the Republic of Singapore,[119] the Free Trade Agreement between the Republic of Korea and the EFTA States,[120] the Framework Agreement on Comprehensive Economic Cooperation Among the Republic of Korea and the Member Countries of the Association of Southeast Asian Nations,[121] the Agreement on Trade in Goods under the Framework Agreement on Comprehensive Economic Cooperation among the Governments of the Republic of Korea and the Member Countries of the Association of Southeast Asian Nations,[122] the Agreement on Dispute Settlement Mechanisms under the Framework Agreement on Comprehensive Economic Cooperation among the Governments of the Republic of Korea and the Member Countries of the Association of Southeast Asian Nations,[123] and the Comprehensive Economic Partnership Agreement between the Republic of Korea and the Republic of India.[124] In addition, the Free Trade Agreement between the Republic of Korea and the United States of America[125] has been ratified by the

115 *Ibid.*

116 <www.sidley.com/files/News/f8a224dd-c1ce-428f-a0ab-04a50384903b/Presentation/NewsAttachment/73efc124-bdbf-4611-b82b-04dcf22f78e8/IntlArbMay0307v2.pdf>, p. 4, accessed 20.10.2012.

117 <www.fta.go.kr/new/index.asp> accessed 20.10.2012.

118 FTA between Korea and Chile, c 16. It was signed on 15.02.2003 and came into effect on 01.04.2004.

119 FTA between Korea and Singapore, c 17. It was signed on 4.08.2005 and came into effect on 02.03.2006.

120 EFTA States refer to the Republic of Iceland, the Principality of Liechtenstein, the Kingdom of Norway, and the Swiss Confederation. See also c 7 of FTA between Korea and EFTA that deals with intellectual property rights, signed on 15.12.2005 and effective on 01.09.2006.

121 Member Countries of the Association of Southeast Asian Nations (ASEAN) refer to Brunei Darussalam, the Kingdom of Cambodia, the Republic of Indonesia, the Lao People's Democratic Republic, Malaysia, the Union of Myanmar, the Republic of the Philippines, the Republic of Singapore, the Kingdom of Thailand, and the Socialist Republic of Vietnam. See Article 3.1(j) of the FTA between Korea and ASEAN. It was signed on 13.12.2005 and ratified on 02.04.2007.

122 Signed on 24.08.2006, ratified on 02.04.2007, and came into effect on 01.06.2007.

123 Ratified on 02.04.2007.

124 FTA between Korea and India, c 12.

125 KORUS FTA, c 18.

Korean and US legislatures after it was signed on 30 June 2007. It has been effective since 15 March 2012. In addition, the Free Trade Agreement between the European Community and its Member States and the Republic of Korea was initialled on 15 October 2009 and signed on 6 October 2010, and came into effect on 1 July 2011. Furthermore, negotiations on the Free Trade Agreement between Korea and Peru were concluded on 30 August 2010 and it became effective on 1 August 2011.[126]

In this context, Korean companies have increasingly used arbitration as a means to resolve cross-border disputes[127] and it is likely to increase with the ratification of the American and EU FTAs.[128]

## 4.2. HISTORY OF KOREAN ARBITRATION LAW

The history of Korean arbitration law dates back to the mid-1960s. The first Korean Arbitration Act was enacted on 16 March 1966. The unique feature of the Korean Arbitration Act of 1966 was that it was not incorporated into the Korean Civil Procedure Act but was enacted as an independent Act, separated from the Korean Civil Procedure Act.[129] Article 14(1) of the Korean Arbitration Act of 1966 merely provided that a compulsory execution based on an arbitral award may be conducted only if a Korean court has confirmed its legality by means of a judgment of execution. Hence, it was doubtful whether an enforcement judgment based on a foreign arbitral award might be enforced in Korea. This doubt was eliminated when Article 39 of the Korean Arbitration Act of 1999 prescribed the recognition and enforcement of a foreign arbitral award. The Korean Arbitration Act of 1999 incorporated various elements of the United Nations Commission on International Trade Law Model Law on International Commercial Arbitration (UNCITRAL Model Law).[130] The 1999 Act did not explicitly state who can take

---

126 <www.fta.go.kr/new/ftakorea/borderpsd_read.asp> accessed 20.10.2012.

127 See, e.g., *Itoman (USA), Inc. v. Daewoo Corp.*, 68 N.Y.2d 925, 510 N.Y.S.2d 74, 502 N.E.2d 989 (1986) (holding that where a broker negotiated a transaction between a Korean seller and American purchaser, the broker's signature on the seller's confirmation of order which provided for arbitration in Korea could have invalidated an implied ratification of broker's notes and could have bound the buyer to arbitrate in Korea if the broker had power to act for the buyer in agreeing to Korean arbitration).

128 <http://asia.legalbusinessonline.com/news/breaking-news/international-arbitration-lawyers-in-demand-in-korea/38359> accessed 30.10.2012.

129 K.-H. Sohn, 'Development in the Korean Law on International Jurisdiction, Studies on the Jurisdiction of International Civil Litigation', in 2012 Sino-Korean Symposium on International Private Law held in Beijing (China), on 03.11.2012, pp. 85, 88.

130 T.F. MacLaren, 'Arbitration-Overview', in *Eckstrom's Licensing: Joint Ventures*, vol 5, 2012, §17:31; J. Tirado, 'Court Support for Arbitration in the Asia Pacific Region' (2008) 13(1) *IBA Arb. News* 8; L. Blomgren Bingham, S. W. Lee and W.K. Chang, 'Participatory Governance in South Korea: Legal Infrastructure, Economic Development, and Dispute Resolution' (2007) 19 *Pac. McGeorge Global Bus. & Dev. LJ* 375, 382.

part in an arbitration. In addition, the 1999 Act prescribed that, unless the parties agree otherwise, all evidence must be translated into Korean.[131]

The revision of the Act in 2010[132] aimed to simplify the legal text in order for lay persons to easily understand the contents of the Act. The revision of the Act in 2010 did not intend to change the meaning of the legal provisions of the Act. The Korean Arbitration Act only is applicable where Korea is designated as the place of arbitration in the arbitration agreement.[133] As mentioned above, the current Arbitration Act in Korea does not contain provisions on confidentiality because it is based largely on the UNCITRAL Model Law.[134] In this regard, the Korean Arbitration Act does not explicitly prescribe the confidentiality obligation of the various participants in the arbitral proceedings and the Korean courts have never interpreted that an arbitration agreement included confidentiality as its implied term.[135] Hence, where one or more parties to an arbitration agreement seated in Korea are concerned about the confidentiality of arbitral proceedings or evidence submitted in the arbitration, he/she or they need to take this into account in the arbitration agreement and the agreed applicable procedural rules.[136]

Separately, the parties may rely on the Commercial Arbitration Rules of the KCAB in private disputes arising out of commercial transactions.[137] The KCAB plays a pivotal role in carrying out arbitration procedure in Korea.[138] Currently, the KCAB is the only approved arbitral institution in Korea.[139] Established in 1966,[140] the KCAB has its own default rules which will apply to arbitration proceedings. KCAB enacted its domestic Arbitration Rules on 16 November 1989 which have been amended six times. The current Arbitration Rules for domestic use are those which were amended by the Supreme Court on 29 June 2011, effective since 1 September 2011.

Article 9 of the KCAB's Arbitration Rules provides that '[t]he arbitration proceedings shall be kept confidential'. There is no further guidance in terms of the ambit of the confidentiality obligation, so the KCAB's Arbitration Rules are silent as to the kind of information required to be kept secret or as to the persons to whom the confidentiality obligation applies.[141]

---

131 T.F. MacLaren, *supra* n. 130, §17:31.

132 Act No. 10207, effective since 31.03.2010.

133 R.B. Han, 'Recognition of Arbitration Agreements' (2003) 12(1) *Intl. Civil Pro. Korea*.

134 B. Hughes, 'Towards a Uniform Approach to Confidentiality in Arbitration: A Role for the New IBA Rules' (2012) 17(1) *IBA Arb. News* 43.

135 *Ibid.*, p. 43.

136 *Ibid.*, p. 44.

137 R.B. Han, *supra* n. 133, p. 1.

138 C.-G. Park, 'A Comparative Analysis of Arbitral Institutions and Their Achievements in the United States and Korea' (2004) 15 *Am. Rev. Int'l Arb.* 475.

139 A.S. Gutterman and R.L. Brown, 'Litigation and Alternative Dispute Resolution-Arbitration' (2012) 3 *Going Global* §39:50.

140 <www.kcab.or.kr/jsp/kcab_eng/kcab/kcab_111_ex.jsp> accessed 25.10.2012.

141 B. Hughes, *supra* n. 134, p. 45.

KCAB enacted the Rules of International Arbitration for the Korean Commercial Arbitration Board (International Arbitration Rules), which were approved by the Korean Supreme Court on 25 January 2007. According to the International Arbitration Rules, the model arbitration clause said that, for future disputes: 'Any dispute, controversy or claim arising under, out of or relating to this contract (including non-contractual claims) and any subsequent amendments of this contract, including, without limitation, its formation, validity, binding effect, interpretation, performance, breach or termination, shall be referred to and finally resolved by arbitration under KCAB International Arbitration Rules,[142] which Rules are deemed to be incorporated by reference into this clause. The number of arbitrators shall be [one/three]. The seat, or legal place, of arbitration shall be [City/Country]. The language to be used in the arbitral proceedings shall be [language]'; and for existing disputes: 'We, the undersigned parties, hereby agree that the following dispute shall be referred to and finally determined by arbitration in accordance with the KCAB International arbitration Rules: [brief description of the dispute]. The number of arbitrators shall be [one/three]. The seat, or legal place, of arbitration shall be [City/Country]. The language to be used in the arbitral proceedings shall be [language].'

KCAB revised the International Arbitration Rules in 2011 to apply by default to the international cases at KCAB arising out of contracts signed following 1 September 2011, where one of the parties is not Korean or the venue of the arbitration is designated outside Korea, unless the parties agree otherwise.[143] The essential features of the 2011 revision of KCAB's International Arbitration Rules provide as follows:

(a) the Rules provide the expedited procedures. Parties may agree to have their arbitration administered pursuant to expedited procedures or, where the amount in dispute does not exceed 200,000,000 Korean Won, the case will automatically be administered by the expedited procedures;[144]
(b) the KCAB has changed its schedule of arbitrator fees in international cases in order to offer proper rates of remuneration for arbitrators;[145]
(c) the Rules enhance the key functions of the Secretariat of the KCAB. The Secretariat can consult the International Arbitration Committee on issues of appointment and challenge of arbitrators.[146]

142 T. Moxham, 'Sweeping Changes at the Korean Commercial Arbitration Board' (2011) 16(2) *IBA Arb. News* 146.
143 <www.kcab.or.kr/jsp/kcab_eng/law/law_02_ex.jsp> accessed 25.10.2012.
144 *Ibid.*
145 *Ibid.*
146 *Ibid.*

The model arbitration clauses administered by the KCAB are that, for future disputes: 'Any disputes arising out of or in connection with this contract shall be finally settled by arbitration in Seoul in accordance with the International Arbitration Rules of the Korean Commercial Arbitration Board. The number of arbitrators shall be [one/three]. The seat, or legal place, of arbitral proceedings shall be [city/country]. The language to be used in the arbitral proceedings shall be [language]'; and for existing disputes: 'We, the undersigned parties, hereby agree that the following dispute shall be referred to and finally determined by arbitration in accordance with the KCAB International Arbitration Rules: [brief description of the dispute]. The number of arbitrators shall be [one/three]. The seat, or legal place, of arbitral proceedings shall be [city/country]. The language to be used in the arbitral proceedings shall be [language].' Notably, Article 52 of the KCAB's International Arbitration Rules, entitled 'Confidentiality', states:

> '1. The arbitration proceedings, and records thereof, shall be closed to the public;
> 2. The members of the Arbitral Tribunal and the Secretariat, the parties and their representatives and assistants shall not disclose facts related to arbitration cases or facts learned through arbitration cases except where disclosure is consented to by the parties, required by law or required in court proceedings.'[147]

Korea became a signatory to the Washington Convention on the Settlement of Investment Disputes between States and Nationals of Other States of 1965 right after the enactment of the Korean Arbitration Act of 1965. Korea acceded to this Convention on 28 January 1967. Korea has become one of the countries which expeditiously adopted the international legal mechanism designed to resolve international investment disputes by arbitration.[148] Also, Korea signed up for the New York Convention on the Recognition and Enforcement of Foreign Arbitral Awards of 1957 so as to vitalise arbitration internationally on 8 February 1973. Korea declared that it would apply the New York Convention only to recognition and enforcement of arbitral awards made in the territory of another contracting State.[149] Also, Korea declared that it would apply the New York Convention only to differences arising out of legal relationships, whether contractual or not, that are considered commercial under the national law.[150] Korean courts generally take a positive position favouring enforcement of foreign arbitral awards and

---

147 B. Hughes, *supra* n. 134, p. 45 (arguing that 'as with the international ad hoc and institutional rules, there is a lack of consistency in approach to confidentiality even as between the two sets of KCAB arbitration rules' and thus 'IBA Rules provide a convenient, consistent, efficient and fair framework for addressing confidentiality and other discovery issues in arbitration').

148 <www.kcab.or.kr/jsp/kcab_eng/law/law_02_ex.jsp> accessed 25.10.2012.

149 New York Convention, Notes (a).

150 New York Convention, Notes (c).

have seldom refused to recognise and enforce a foreign arbitral award on the basis of, for example, lack of basis for arbitration or violation of public policy.[151]

## 4.3. STATISTICAL DATA ON KOREAN ARBITRATION CASES

**Table 3. KCAB statistics (1967–2010)**

| Year | Arbitration | Mediation | Subtotal | Consultation | Total |
|---|---|---|---|---|---|
| 1967–1969 | 17 | 88 | 105 | 0 | **105** |
| 1970 | 7 | 119 | 126 | 0 | **126** |
| 1971 | 2 | 66 | 68 | 0 | **68** |
| 1972 | 4 | 95 | 99 | 121 | **220** |
| 1973 | 5 | 111 | 116 | 164 | **280** |
| 1974 | 13 | 124 | 137 | 462 | **599** |
| 1975 | 11 | 177 | 188 | 413 | **601** |
| 1976 | 15 | 188 | 203 | 464 | **667** |
| 1977 | 32 | 305 | 337 | 395 | **732** |
| 1978 | 38 | 501 | 539 | 215 | **754** |
| 1979 | 20 | 644 | 664 | 320 | **984** |
| 1980 | 26 | 509 | 535 | 1,331 | **1,866** |
| 1981 | 34 | 509 | 543 | 1,328 | **1,871** |
| 1982 | 58 | 494 | 552 | 1,050 | **1,602** |
| 1983 | 66 | 480 | 546 | 798 | **1,344** |
| 1984 | 70 | 566 | 636 | 914 | **1,550** |
| 1985 | 70 | 482 | 552 | 982 | **1,534** |
| 1986 | 57 | 482 | 539 | 1,422 | **1,961** |
| 1987 | 79 | 518 | 597 | 1,585 | **2,182** |
| 1988 | 54 | 574 | 628 | 1,092 | **1,720** |
| 1989 | 56 | 545 | 601 | 1,186 | **1,787** |
| 1990 | 36 | 470 | 506 | 1,466 | **1,972** |
| 1991 | 51 | 560 | 611 | 2,543 | **3,154** |
| 1992 | 71 | 554 | 625 | 2,551 | **3,176** |
| 1993 | 68 | 623 | 691 | 2,422 | **3,113** |
| 1994 | 72 | 621 | 693 | 2,188 | **2,881** |
| 1995 | 79 | 628 | 707 | 2,996 | **3,703** |
| 1996 | 109 | 585 | 694 | 3,237 | **3,931** |

151 H.G. Lee, 'Arbitration', in A. Kritzer, S. Eiselen, J. Vanto and J. Vanto, *International Contract Manual*, 2012, §64:5.

| Year | Arbitration | Mediation | Subtotal | Consultation | Total |
|---|---|---|---|---|---|
| 1997 | 133 | 564 | 697 | 3,911 | **4,608** |
| 1998 | 192 | 520 | 712 | 4,221 | **4,933** |
| 1999 | 150 | 349 | 499 | 5,964 | **6,463** |
| 2000 | 175 | 474 | 649 | 4,336 | **4,985** |
| 2001 | 197 | 446 | 643 | 5,284 | **5,927** |
| 2002 | 210 | 470 | 680 | 5,372 | **6,052** |
| 2003 | 211 | 451 | 662 | 5,221 | **5,883** |
| 2004 | 185 | 474 | 659 | 4,089 | **4,748** |
| 2005 | 213 | 496 | 709 | 4,641 | **5,350** |
| 2006 | 215 | 534 | 749 | 5,063 | **5,812** |
| 2007 | 233 | 552 | 785 | 5,748 | **6,533** |
| 2008 | 262 | 785 | 1,047 | 7,108 | **8,155** |
| 2009 | 318 | 664 | 982 | 7,184 | **8,166** |
| 2010 | 316 | 801 | 1,117 | 6,229 | **7,346** |
| Total | **4,230** | **19,198** | **23,428** | **106,016** | **129,444** |

Source: Performance Report of the Arbitration Department at the KCAB for 2010 (January 2011)

**Table 4. Arbitration cases registered**

| | 2010 | | 2009 | |
|---|---|---|---|---|
| Category | Number of cases | Amount (US$ million) | Number of cases | Amount (US$ million) |
| Domestic | 264 | 462 | 240 | 576 |
| International | 52 | 73 | 78 | 78 |
| Total | **316** | **535** | **318** | **654** |

Source: Performance Report of the Arbitration Department at the KCAB for 2010 (January 2011)

The Korean Commercial Arbitration Board (KCAB) has been providing alternative dispute resolution services since 1967. From 1967 to 2010, the KCAB has administered a total of 4,317 domestic and international arbitration cases. The KCAB also provides a range of other alternative dispute resolution services, such as mediation and consultation. In 2010, the KCAB received a total of 316 requests for arbitration, including 52 international cases.

While there was little change in the total number of registrations between 2009 and 2010, domestic arbitration cases rose by 10% and international registrations returned to their long-term yearly average of around 50 following a record number of registrations in 2009.

**Table 5. Arbitrations by industry**

| | 2010 | | | 2009 | | |
|---|---|---|---|---|---|---|
| Category | Domestic | Int'l | Total | Domestic | Int'l | Total |
| International trade | 12 | 39 | **51** | 5 | 59 | **64** |
| Domestic trade | 98 | 0 | **98** | 122 | 0 | **122** |
| Maritime | 14 | 5 | **19** | 20 | 8 | **28** |
| Construction | 90 | 2 | **92** | 61 | 3 | **64** |
| Technology | 19 | 1 | **20** | 6 | 2 | **8** |
| Finance | 3 | 0 | **3** | 2 | 1 | **3** |
| Intellectual property | 7 | 2 | **9** | 5 | 1 | **6** |
| Labour | 3 | 1 | **4** | 0 | 3 | **3** |
| Real estate | 12 | 0 | **12** | 12 | 0 | **12** |
| Other | 6 | 2 | **8** | 7 | 1 | **8** |
| **Total** | **264** | **52** | **316** | **240** | **78** | **318** |

Source: Performance Report of the Arbitration Department at the KCAB for 2010 (January 2011)

In 2010, 75% (39 cases) of all international arbitrations registered with the KCAB related to international commerce. Other industry sectors to feature in KCAB international arbitrations in 2010 include maritime, intellectual property and construction industries. Cases concerning domestic commercial disputes and the construction industry comprised the two largest groups by industry sector in 2010, with 31% and 29% respectively.

**Table 6. Arbitrations by type of dispute**

| | 2010 | | | 2009 | | |
|---|---|---|---|---|---|---|
| Category | Domestic | Int'l | Total | Domestic | Int'l | Total |
| Product quality (inc. lack of quantity) | 12 | 18 | **30** | 12 | 18 | **30** |
| Delayed or cancelled shipment | 15 | 4 | **19** | 17 | 9 | **26** |
| Payment | 146 | 17 | **163** | 129 | 30 | **159** |
| Transportation | 8 | 1 | **9** | 6 | 2 | **8** |
| Contractual interpretation | 78 | 12 | **90** | 67 | 16 | **83** |
| Intellectual property | 2 | 0 | **2** | 2 | 0 | **2** |
| Other or unknown | 3 | 0 | **3** | 7 | 3 | **10** |
| **Total** | **264** | **52** | **316** | **240** | **78** | **318** |

Source: Performance Report of the Arbitration Department at the KCAB for 2010 (January 2011)

**Table 7. Arbitrations based on amounts in controversy**

| | 2010 | | 2009 | |
|---|---|---|---|---|
| **Amount** | **Domestic** | **Int'l** | **Domestic** | **Int'l** |
| Unquantified claims | 5 | 2 | 5 | 0 |
| up to US$ 10,000 | 34 | 3 | 34 | 6 |
| from US$ 10,000 to US$ 100,000 | 96 | 15 | 86 | 28 |
| from US$ 100,000 to US$ 200,000 | 46 | 14 | 31 | 12 |
| from US$ 200,000 to US$ 500,000 | 22 | 6 | 27 | 11 |
| from US$ 500,000 to US$ 1,000,000 | 21 | 7 | 24 | 9 |
| from US$ 1,000,000 to US$ 5,000,000 | 23 | 3 | 17 | 7 |
| from US$ 5,000,000 to US$ 10,000,000 | 5 | 0 | 9 | 3 |
| over US$ 10,000,000 | 12 | 2 | 7 | 2 |
| Total | 316 | | 318 | |

Source: Performance Report of the Arbitration Department at the KCAB for 2010 (January 2011)

In 2009 and 2010, there were 40 domestic and five international arbitrations registered where the amount claimed exceeded US$ 1 million.

**Table 8. Outcomes**

| | 2010 | | 2009 | |
|---|---|---|---|---|
| | **No. of cases** | **Amount (US$ millions)** | **No. of cases** | **Amount (US$ millions)** |
| Award | 195 | 312 | 173 | 232 |
| Award by consent | 52 | 77 | 57 | 19 |
| Proceedings stopped* | 17 | 28 | 13 | 4 |
| Withdrawal | 54 | 231 | 47 | 8 |
| Total | **318** | **648** | **290** | **263** |

* Request for arbitration was received by KCAB but proceedings did not commence due to failure to submit required fees or documents.

Source: Performance Report of the Arbitration Department at the KCAB for 2010 (January 2011)

**Table 9. Duration of arbitrations***

| | 2010 | | 2009 | |
|---|---|---|---|---|
| | **No. of cases** | **Days** | **No. of cases** | **Days** |
| Domestic | 260 | 139 | 229 | 136 |
| International | 58 | 218 | 61 | 191 |
| **Total** | **318** | **153** | **290** | **148** |

*Time period is calculated from date of the receipt of the Request for Arbitration by the KCAB to the issuing of the final award, or the settlement or withdrawal of the case.

Source: Performance Report of the Arbitration Department at the KCAB for 2010 (January 2011).

**Table 10. Arbitrations by nationality**

| **Nationality** | **2010** | **2009** |
|---|---|---|
| USA | 11 | 12 |
| China | 8 | 14 |
| Japan | 5 | 3 |
| Hong Kong | 3 | 1 |
| Russia | 3 | 3 |
| Thailand | 3 | 1 |
| Panama | 2 | 1 |
| Germany | 2 | 5 |
| Ireland | 2 | 1 |
| Others | 13 | 37 |
| **Total** | **52** | **78** |

Source: Performance Report of the Arbitration Department at the KCAB for 2010 (January 2011).

In 2010, 22 different nationalities registered international arbitrations with the KCAB, with the United States and China accounting for 20% and 18% of the registrations respectively. The largest number of international arbitrations registered with the KCAB in 2010 came from the Asian region, followed by North America and Europe. Other nationalities not included in this table include: Lebanon, Uzbekistan, Mongolia, Taiwan, India, Indonesia, Saudi Arabia, Philippines, Italy, the UK, the UAE, Canada and Singapore.

**Table 11. Mediation cases**

| Category | 2010 | 2009 |
|---|---|---|
| Domestic | 636 | 454 |
| International | 165 | 210 |
| **Total** | **801** | **664** |

Source: Performance Report of the Arbitration Department at the KCAB for 2010 (January 2011).

2010 was a record year for KCAB mediation with 801 cases registered, a rise of 20% from 2009. The KCAB has administered over 19,000 mediations over the last 40 years.

**Table 12. Mediation by most frequent countries (over four arbitrations)**

| 2010 | | 2009 | |
|---|---|---|---|
| **Nationality** | **No. of cases** | **Nationality** | **No. of cases** |
| China | 21 | USA | 31 |
| Japan | 20 | India | 19 |
| USA | 15 | UAE | 11 |
| India | 15 | Turkey | 11 |
| Germany | 8 | Japan | 10 |
| Pakistan | 8 | China | 8 |
| Hong Kong | 6 | UK | 8 |
| Turkey | 6 | Kuwait | 7 |
| UK | 5 | Germany | 7 |
| UAE | 4 | Malaysia | 6 |
| Malaysia | 4 | Thailand | 6 |
| Vietnam | 4 | Jordan | 5 |
| Singapore | 4 | Iran | 5 |
| Egypt | 4 | Hong Kong | 4 |

Source: Performance Report of the Arbitration Department at the KCAB for 2010 (January 2011)

## 4.4. ARBITRABILITY

### *4.4.1. Overview*

The term 'arbitrability' relates to whether a certain dispute is qualified for being resolved by arbitration. A non-arbitrable arbitration agreement is invalid so that arbitrators cannot render an arbitration award pursuant to it. The award will be set aside even after the rendition of the award.[152] Also, the award will not be recognised or enforced.[153]

Article 3(2) of the Korean Arbitration Act provides that '[t]he term "arbitration agreement" means an agreement by the parties to submit to arbitration all or certain disputes which have arisen or which may arise between them in respect of defined legal relationships, whether contractual or not.' Hence, even non-contractual disputes can be settled by arbitration. Article 3(1) of the Korean Arbitration Act prescribes that '[t]he term "arbitration" means a procedure to settle any dispute in private laws, not by the judgment of a court, but by the award of an arbitrator or arbitrators, as agreed by the parties.' In other words, any dispute under private law is arbitrable, whether or not it is contractual.

Also, Article 2(2) of the Korean Arbitration Act stipulates that '[t]his Act shall not affect any other Act by virtue of which certain disputes may not be submitted to arbitration or may be submitted to arbitration only according to provisions other than those of this Act, nor those treaties which are valid in the Republic of Korea.'

With regard to the categories of substantive claims that are capable of resolution by arbitration, disputes related to criminal, constitutional, or administrative law matters are generally regarded not to be arbitrable because the scope of arbitrability under the Korean Arbitration Act is limited to disputes under private laws.[154] In this regard, some critics argue that the limitation is unnecessarily restrictive.[155]

So far, there have been only a few court decisions mentioning the scope of arbitrability in Korea.[156] In 1992, the Korean Supreme Court upheld that tort claims may be settled by arbitration.[157] The special arbitration statute, the Act on Arbitration and Remedies for Damage Caused by Press Reports (Press Arbitration Act), is applicable to the media industry only.[158] Article 24(1) of the Press Arbitration Act provides that any dispute concerning a request for a report

---

152 Article 36(2)(b)(i), Korean Arbitration Act.

153 Article V(2)(a), New York Convention.

154 Y.J. Mok, *Commercial Arbitration*, Pakyoungsa, 2011, p. 65.

155 See, e.g., K.H. Suk, 'Kukje sangsa jungjebeop yeon'gu', *Essays in International Commercial Arbitration*, Vol. 1, Pakyoungsa, 2007, p. 28.

156 Bae, Kim & Lee LLC, *Arbitration Law of Korea: Practice and Procedure*, p. 60.

157 Judgment rendered by the Korean Supreme Court on 14.04.1992 (Case No. 91da17146).

158 Law No. 7370 (25.01.2005), last revised by Law No. 10587 (14.04.2011); Kyu Ho Youm, 'Codified Sources', in 1 *Media, Advertising, & Entertainment Law Throughout the World*, 2012, §21:3.

on a corrected statement, etc. or compensation for damage may, at the request of both parties that agree to comply with a final and conclusive decision of the competent arbitral tribunal on that dispute, be submitted to arbitration. An arbitral award under the Press Arbitration Act has the same effect as a final and conclusive judgment rendered by a court.[159] Recently, the Korean legal community has paid significant attention to the issue of whether disputes about the existence or validity of intellectual property rights whose registration is required to be effective are arbitrable because those issues are of public nature. The arbitrability of intellectual property disputes is discussed below.

### *4.4.2. Intellectual property rights-related disputes*

#### 4.4.2.1. Case law

The term 'intellectual property' refers to knowledge, information, technology, the expression of thoughts or feelings, the indication of business or goods, varieties of organism or genetic resources and other intangibles created or discovered by creative activities, experience, etc. of human beings, the value of property of which may be realised.[160] The Framework Act on Intellectual Property defines the term 'new intellectual property' as 'intellectual property that appears in new fields in line with economic, social or cultural changes or the development of science and technology.'[161] Therefore, the term 'intellectual property right' means 'any right relating to intellectual property recognised or protected according to Acts and subordinate statutes, treaties, etc.'[162] The key issue here is whether the validity of intellectual property rights is arbitrable in an intellectual property infringement action.

In *LG Electronics Inc. v. Daewoo Electronic Corp.*,[163] the Korean Supreme Court unanimously ruled that a Korean court could dismiss a patent injunction or damages claim for lack of non-obviousness even before a patent is formally invalidated by the Intellectual Property Tribunal of the Korea Intellectual Property Office. Prior to the *LG Electronics* case, when a defendant raised a patent invalidity defence and the invalidation action was pending simultaneously, a Korean court could merely review the infringement issues or stay the infringement action pending a decision from a patent invalidation action.[164] However, some critics have argued that it would not be equitable for

159 Article 25 (1), Press Arbitration Act.
160 Article 3(1), Framework Act on Intellectual Property, enacted on 19.05.2011, effective since 20.07.2011 (Law No. 10629).
161 Article 3(2), Framework Act on Intellectual Property.
162 Article 3(3), Framework Act on Intellectual Property.
163 Judgment rendered by the Korean Supreme Court of 19.01.2012 (Case No. 2010da95390) (*en banc*).
164 *Ibid.*

courts to enforce a patent or delay the infringement action for a period of time when a patent was likely to be invalidated.[165] In order to solve this problem prior to the *LG Electronics* case, the Korean Supreme Court has permitted the court to dismiss the infringement action when the patent lacks the 'novelty' requirement.[166] For the first time, the *LG Electronics* case opened the door for a court to decide issues of non-obviousness as well as novelty in civil cases relating to infringement In this regard I can say that the *LG Electronics* case allows the parties to arbitrate disputes related to intellectual property including validity of claims.

In *Taeyeon Medical Co., Ltd v. Medtronic, Inc.*,[167] the Korean High Court ruled that Medtronic's apparatus for Kyphon Balloon Kyphoplasty, in respect of which they later applied for patent, infringed Taeyeon's valid patent and ordered the destruction of the apparatus and materials made by Medtronic. In this case, the patent was for apparatus for forming hole in spongelike bone, comprising a catheter tube, an inflatable structure coupled to the front end portion of the catheter tube, a hub with a fitting unit coupled to the back end portion of the catheter tube, and a probe. The inside of the catheter tube comprises the probe and a lumen formed around the probe. The probe is characterised in that the back end portion is fixed at the hub or the rear side cap of the hub, and the front end portion contacts the inner front end portion of the inflatable structure. In *Kyphon SARL v. Taeyeon Medical Co., Ltd*,[168] on Kyphon SARL's appeal after Medtronic, Inc. had assigned its standing to sue to Kyophon SAPL, the Korean Supreme Court unanimously held that the validity of a patent, including the non-obviousness requirement, can be heard and determined by a court in the patent infringement action for damages and injunction.

The application of the approach taken by the *LG Electronics Inc.* court and the *Kyphon SARL* court in terms of patent infringement actions was extend to trademark cases. In *HIWOOD Inc. v. HIWOOD Inc.*,[169] the *en banc* decision rendered by the Korean Supreme Court on 18 October 2012 (Case No. 2010Da10300 (*en banc*)) held that the court was allowed to hear and determine the validity of trademark registration as a preliminary question where the plaintiff brought an action for injunction or damages. The core holding of the *HIWOOD* Court is as follows:

> '[I]n cases where it is clear that a trademark registration will be invalidated by a ruling of the IPT, an action for injunction or damages due to trademark infringement is not allowed due to the abuse of the trademark right made by the plaintiff unless

165 *Ibid.*

166 Judgment rendered by the Korean Supreme Court 09.12.1986 (Case No. 86do51147).

167 Judgment rendered by the Korean Seoul High Court on 08.07.2010 (Case No. 2009na22763).

168 Judgment rendered by the Korean Supreme Court on 15.03.2012 (Case No. 2010da63133).

169 Judgment rendered by the Korean Supreme Court on 18.10.2012 (Case No. 2010da10300) (*en banc*).

> there are special circumstances which can allow him/her to do it. Hence, the court hearing an action for injunction or damages due to trademark infringement is empowered to hear and adjudicate the invalidity of the trademark registration as the preliminary question to determine whether the defendant's affirmative defense based on the abuse of the trademark right is correct when his/her defense was raised. This rationale is also applicable to service mark.'

Hence, I think that the *LG Electronics Inc.*, *Kyphon SARL* and *HIWOOD Inc.* cases expanded the scope of the subject matter of arbitral disputes in intellectual property cases. In other words, the validity of a patent or a trademark in a patent or trademark infringement action for damages and/or injunction is arbitrable.

#### 4.4.2.2. KOPILA Principles on International Intellectual Property Litigation

The Korean Principles on International Intellectual Property Litigation approved by the Korea Private International Law Association on 26 March 2009 (KOPILA Principles)[170] purport to set forth the rules for international jurisdiction, conflict of laws, recognition and enforcement of foreign adjudication, and arbitration on international intellectual property disputes.[171] According to the Korean Principles, the term 'intellectual property rights' is defined as the rights granted to intellectual assets, which means intangible assets such as inventions, designs, works, trade secrets, trademarks that are derived from intellectual creation, device, or use by human beings.[172] The concept 'intellectual asset' pursuant to the KOPILA Principles is broad enough to cover one protected under unfair competition laws or intangible property, which may be included in intellectual property in the near future.[173]

The KOPILA Principles define registered intellectual property rights as 'Intellectual Property Rights being effective by registration or deposit such as patent', distinguishing registered from non-registered intellectual property rights.[174] In addition, Article 2 of the KOPILA Principles defines the terms

---

170 KOPILA Principles were approved at the general meeting held by the Korean Private International Law Association on 26.03.2010. The Drafting Committee for the Korean Principles consists of five members: Professor Kyung-Han Sohn, Sungkyungwan University School of Law, its chairman Professor Kwang-Hyun Suk, Seoul National University School of Law, Chief Judge Seong Ho Lee, Seoul High Court, Chief Judge Ta Ak Rho, Patent Court, Professor Gyooho Lee, Chung-Ang University School of Law, and Jin-A Park, Ewha Women's University School of Law.

171 Article 1, KOPILA Principles.

172 Article 2(1) and (2), KOPILA Principles.

173 Korean Private International Law Association, *A Commentary to Principles on International Intellectual Property Litigation*, in *Principles on International Intellectual Property Litigation*, 2010.

174 Article 2(3), KOPILA Principles.

'State',[175] 'Registered State',[176] 'Protecting State',[177] 'Habitual Residence',[178] 'International Intellectual Property Disputes',[179] 'Existence/Validity Disputes',[180] 'Non-negotiated Contract',[181] 'Interim Measures',[182] 'Adjudication',[183] 'Preliminary Questions',[184] 'Foreign Adjudication',[185] 'Foreign Arbitral Award',[186] 'Recognition State'[187] and 'Enforcement State'.[188] These KOPILA Principles apply to civil or commercial disputes regarding intellectual assets including existence/validity disputes.[189] Hence, the KOPILA Principles extend their application to administrative trials on disputes regarding the granting, validity, abandonment, or cancellation of intellectual property rights.[190] Also,

175 Article 2(4), KOPILA Principles, prescribing that '"State" means a territory or region that maintains independent legislative and judicial body'.

176 Article 2(5), KOPILA Principles, stating that '"Registered State" means a State in which Intellectual Property Rights are registered or deposited, or in which IPRs are deemed to have been registered or deposited by provisions of a treaty'.

177 Article 2(6), KOPILA Principles, prescribing that '"Protecting State" means a State that grants Intellectual Property Rights or for which their protection is sought. In case of infringement of IPRs, it means the State of infringement regardless of their registrations of the rights. In order to be qualified a place of infringement, its market must be substantially affected by the infringement. If the case is infringement of the moral rights of an author, the rights must be affected within the State'.

178 The term 'Habitual Residence' refers to 'the place where a party habitually resides, including the party's principal place of business. The Habitual Residence also includes the State where it has its statutory seat of legal entity or the State under whose law it was incorporated or formed'. Article 2(7), KOPILA Principles.

179 This denotes intellectual property disputes whose parties have Habitual Residence in a different State, and include disputes related to intellectual property rights that are registered or protected in a foreign State and disputes that occurred by activities related to intellectual property rights in a foreign State. See Article 2(8), KOPILA Principles.

180 This is defined as 'disputes regarding granting, validity, abandonment, or cancellation of intellectual property rights'. See Article 2(9), KOPILA Principles.

181 This means a 'contract that is concluded with the terms and conditions determined in advance by one party for repeated use'. See Article 2(10), KOPILA Principles.

182 This is defined as 'provisional seizure, provisional disposition, and other provisional measures against a party ordered by a judge or arbitrator in reply to a petition of the other party prior to the final judgment or arbitral award'. See Article 2(11), KOPILA Principles.

183 This refers to 'judgments, decisions, orders, etc. rendered by a court or administrative body including interim measures and decisions on disputes between private parties such as invalidity of a patent'. See Article 2(12), KOPILA Principles.

184 These mean 'the problems of which the determination is unavoidable as a prerequisite for the adjudication process, but that need not be explicitly included in the conclusion of an adjudication of a court or, of an arbitral award'. See Article 2(13), KOPILA Principles.

185 This means an adjudication that is not regarded as domestic adjudication. See Article 2(14), KOPILA Principles.

186 It means an arbitral award that is not regarded as one under the law of Enforcement State. See Article 2(14), KOPILA Principles.

187 'Recognition State' is a State that recognises or is requested to recognise a foreign adjudication or a foreign arbitral award. See Article 2(15), KOPILA Principles.

188 'Enforcement State' is a State that enforces or is requested to enforce a foreign adjudication or a foreign arbitral award. See Article 2(15), KOPILA Principles.

189 Article 3, KOPILA Principles.

190 KOPILA, *supra* n. 166, p. 4.

the KOPILA Principles are applied to interim measures, taking into account its importance in intellectual property-related disputes.[191]

As mentioned above, the KOPILA Principles distinguish registered from non-registered intellectual property rights, taking into account the facts that the term 'Protecting State' or the State where protection is sought cannot be clearly defined whereas the term 'Registered State' is straightforward and that a law governing registered intellectual property rights needs to be differentiated from one governing non-registered intellectual property rights in terms of their initial ownership.[192] In other words, initial ownership of registered intellectual property rights is governed by the law of each Registered State while initial ownership of the non-registered intellectual property rights is governed by the law of State in which the intellectual assets are first created or devised, such as the law of the State of habitual residence of the person who created or devised them.[193] If there is more than one person involved in the creation or devise of non-registered intellectual property rights, the law of the State with the closest connection to the creation, devise and the first publication shall govern unless the parties agree otherwise.[194] However, the law of the Protecting States in which the rights are first exploited will govern if the governing law regarding initial ownership of non-registered intellectual property rights does not recognise the intellectual property rights.[195]

Articles 33–49 of the KOPILA Principles govern arbitration. As far as arbitration of intellectual property rights-related disputes is concerned, the matters that are not provided specifically in the KOPILA Principles are determined pursuant to the Model Law on International Commercial Arbitration of UNCITRAL, including its 2006 Amendment.[196] They consist of general provision, arbitrability of intellectual property disputes, arbitration agreements of international intellectual property disputes, arbitral proceedings of international intellectual property disputes, and recognition and enforcement of arbitral awards. In this regard, several features of the KOPILA Principles need to be noted.

In terms of arbitration of intellectual property rights-related disputes, party autonomy is stressed. The arbitrator or court, to the fullest extent, respects the principle of party autonomy in consideration of the purport of the arbitration system, in determining the validity or the subject of the arbitration agreement.[197] In addition, the KOPILA Principles place strong weight on the place of arbitration. Parties can freely select the place of arbitration and can further agree

---

191 Article 2(11), KOPILA Principles; See KOPILA, *supra* n. 166, p. 5.
192 KOPILA, *supra* n. 166, p. 6.
193 Article 24(1) and (2), KOPILA Principles.
194 Article 24(3), KOPILA Principles. The application of this provision is not limited to copyright.
195 Article 24(4), KOPILA Principles.
196 Article 35, KOPILA Principles.
197 Article 33, KOPILA Principles.

to the omission of a place of arbitration. Unless otherwise agreed, the arbitrator determines the location with regard to the circumstances of the intellectual property rights-related disputes in question, inclusive of the convenience of the parties.[198] In addition, the KOPILA Principles provide for an online arbitration procedure.[199]

Article 37(1) of the KOPILA Principles prescribes that disputes on the existence or validity of registered intellectual property rights, such as patent rights and trademark rights, and the defence of their invalidity are arbitrable. However, the arbitral award on the existence or validity of the registered intellectual property rights is effective only pursuant to Article 37(1) proviso of the KOPILA Principles. Article 37(1) of the KOPILA Principles makes it clear that existence or validity issues of registered intellectual property rights are dealt with on merit. On the other hand, the decisions of the Korean Supreme Court seem to imply that existence or validity issues are arbitrable as preliminary questions. With the consent of the parties, the holder of registered intellectual property rights or other interested parties may participate in the arbitration proceedings to argue and prove the existence or validity of registered intellectual property rights.[200] As far as choice of law under the KOPILA Principles is concerned, the issue as to whether the intellectual property dispute in question can be resolved by arbitration shall be determined by the law of the place of arbitration. If there is no place of arbitration for a specific case it shall be determined by the substantive law governing the arbitration agreement.[201] In cases where there is an issue as to whether the intellectual property dispute in question can be resolved by arbitration, the arbitrator or the court shall consider whether or not the law of the States such as the State of habitual residence of the defendant, the State where seizable assets are located, and the State where the upcoming arbitral award may be recognised or enforced would approve the arbitrability of the intellectual property disputes in question.[202]

## 4.5. ARBITRATION AGREEMENTS

Article 3(b) of the Korean Arbitration Act refers to an 'arbitration agreement' as 'agreement between the parties to resolve, by arbitration, all or a part of disputes which have already arisen or which may arise in the future in respect of a defined legal relationship, whether contractual or not.' This definition is in line with that found in Article 7(2) of the UNCITRAL Model Law of 1985.[203] Its fundamental

---

198 Article 34, KOPILA Principles.
199 Article 46, KOPILA Principles.
200 Article 37(2), KOPILA Principles.
201 Article 38(2), KOPILA Principles.
202 Article 38(3), KOPILA Principles.
203 Bae, Kim & Lee, *supra* n. 156, p. 55 and n. 3.

elements are (a) an agreement to resolve all or a portion of present or future disputes by arbitration, (b) a requirement that any such dispute must concern 'a defined legal relationship', and (c) the absence of any requirement that the dispute must be a contract dispute.[204] One party may require another to submit to arbitration only where there is an arbitration agreement between them, inclusive of 'an express submission to arbitration'.[205] Private parties may validly enter into an arbitration agreement at any time in order to submit a pending dispute or future disputes to arbitration.[206] An arbitration agreement binds the parties to it only in terms of their own legal rights and obligations.[207]

An arbitration agreement may be in the form of a separate agreement or in the form of an arbitration clause in a contract.[208] The arbitration agreement must be in writing.[209] An arbitration agreement will be considered to be in writing under the circumstances: (a) where a document signed by the parties contains an arbitration agreement; (b) where a document exchanged by means of letters, telex, telegrams, fax or other means of communication contains an arbitration agreement; or (c) where one party alleges that the content of a document exchanged between the parties contains an arbitration agreement, and the other party does not deny it.[210] So long as a contract is in writing and incorporates an arbitration clause as part of the contract, the arbitration agreement is considered to have been made.[211] When an action is brought before a court with respect to the subject matter of an arbitration agreement and the defendant raises a plea for the existence of the arbitration agreement, the court must dismiss the action unless it finds that the arbitration agreement is non-existent, null and void, inoperative or incapable of being performed.[212] A defendant must raise the plea by no later than his/her first statement on the merits.[213] Even where an action regarding the subject matter of an arbitration agreement is pending before a court, an arbitral tribunal may commence or continue arbitral proceedings, and render an arbitral award.[214] A party to an arbitration agreement may, before the commencement of or during arbitral proceedings, request a court to grant interim measures of protection.[215]

---

204 For more details, see *ibid.*, pp. 55–62.
205 R.B. Han, *supra* n. 133, para. 12.1.
206 *Ibid.*
207 *Ibid.*
208 Article 8(1), Korean Arbitration Act.
209 Article 8(2), Korean Arbitration Act.
210 Article 8(3), Korean Arbitration Act.
211 Article 8(4), Korean Arbitration Act.
212 Article 9(1), Korean Arbitration Act.
213 Article 9(2), Korean Arbitration Act.
214 Article 9(3), Korean Arbitration Act.
215 Article 10, Korean Arbitration Act; K.-R. Kim, 'How Do You Settle Business Disputes with Koreans?: The Advent of a New Amendment to the Korean Arbitration Act' (2002) 15 *Transnat'l Law* 227, 232.

The following foreign cases are good examples which dealt with disputes related to an arbitration clause that subjects the parties to binding arbitration in Korea.

In *In re Kinoshita & Co.,*[216] the court held that when an arbitration clause 'refers to disputes or controversies "under" or "'arising out of" the contract', arbitration is restricted to 'disputes and controversies relating to the interpretation of the contract and matters of performance'. The *In re Kinoshita & Co.* court reasoned that the phrase 'arising under' is narrower in scope than 'arising out of or relating to', the standard language recommended by the American Arbitration Association.[217] So, in *Mediterranean Enterprises, Inc. v. Ssangyong Corporation*[218] the Ninth Circuit Court of Appeals ruled that an arbitration clause containing the phrase any disputes 'arising hereunder' was not intended to cover any dispute between the parties, but rather 'to cover a much narrower scope of disputes, i.e., only those relating interpretation and performance of the contract itself.'[219]

In a dispute over the quality of fabric imported into New York, USA, the New York importer requested arbitration in New York pursuant to the salesnote, and the Korean exporter argued that arbitration should proceed in Korea by virtue of the confirmation order.[220] In *Itoman (USA), Inc. v. Daewoo Corp.*, the Court of Appeals in New York held that granting an order compelling arbitration in New York was required, where the record contained three confirmation orders, each somewhat different, one confirmation order negated implied ratification of the broker's salesnote binding parties to arbitrate in New York, and the New York importer and buyer denied that the broker had authority to bind it to arbitration in Korea.[221] The Court said:

> 'Central to resolving where the arbitration should take place is a determination whether the salesnote or the Confirmation controls. Had there been no Confirmation signed by New, but only the broker's sales note, we would agree with the courts below that arbitration should proceed in New York. When a sale is negotiated by a broker who sends "bought and sold notes" to both parties containing an arbitration clause, the broker is said to act for both parties. Though they do not expressly agree to arbitration and do not sign the broker's notes, the buyer and seller nonetheless are bound to arbitrate in accordance with those documents when they merely retain them and proceed with the transaction.'[222]

---

216 287 F.2d 951, 953 (2d Cir. 1961).

217 *Ibid.*

218 708 F.2d 1458 (9th Cir. 1983).

219 *Ssangyong*, 708 F.2d at 1464.

220 *Itoman (USA), Inc. v. Daewoo Corp.*, 68 N.Y.2d 925, 510 N.Y.S.2d 74, 502 N.E.2d 989 (N.Y., 1986).

221 *Daewoo*, 68 N.Y.2d, at 927, 501 N.Y.S.2d at 76, 502 N.E. 2d at 991.

222 *Daewoo*, 68 N.Y.2d, at 927, 501 N.Y.S.2d at 75–76, 502 N.E. 2d at 990–91.

In other words, the *Daewoo* court stated that in a broker negotiated transaction between a Korean exporter and American importer, the broker's signature on the seller's confirmation of order which set forth arbitration in Korea could have negated an implied ratification of the broker's sales note and could have bound the American importer to arbitrate in Korea if the broker had authority to act for the American importer in agreeing to Korean arbitration.

In *Asoma Corp. v. M/F Faros*,[223] a charterer, Asoma Corporation, brought an action to recover for damage to steel coils shipped pursuant to bills of lading against SK Shipping Co. Ltd, Columbia Shipmanagement Ltd. and Pelagos Shipping Ltd. The United States District Court for the Southern District of New York dismissed the shipper's complaint for improper forum on the ground that bills of lading contained a forum selection clause mandating arbitration in Korea, whereas the shipper argued that the voyage charter party, which designated the Southern District of New York as the proper forum, rather than bills of lading, should determine the issue.[224] On appeal, Asoma court held that the shipper was entitled to amend its complaint to include the charter party.[225]

In *Halide Group, Inc. v. Hyosung Corporation*,[226] where the plaintiff Halide Group, Inc. entered into a contract with the defendant Hyosung Corporation for the design, engineering, and licensing of a fluorine ($F_2$) gas and nitrogen trifluoride ($NF_3$) gas production facility to be constructed in Ulsan, Korea,[227] the plaintiff sought a declaration that it had not breached the contract and that the defendant had an obligation to pay it the remaining balance due under the contract, and sought a preliminary injunction restraining the defendant from the use of the plaintiff's technology pending a resolution of the dispute between the parties. The contract included an arbitration clause stating:

---

223 D.C.N.Y. 2001, 2001 WL 1588929, vacated C.A.2d, 2002, 53 Fed. Appx. 581.

224 2001 WL 1588929 (S.D.N.Y.).

225 D.C.N.Y. 2001, 2001 WL 1588929, vacated C.A.2d, 2002, 53 Fed. Appx. 581.

226 F. Supp. 2d 1, 2010 WL 4456928 (E.D.Pa., 2010) (No. CIV. A. 10-02392).

227 In accordance with Article 2.1 of the contract, 'Hyosung agreed to pay Halide a $1,750,000.00 license fee for "license with the exclusive right in Korea and China to use any intellectual property right and Technical Information in order to construct, operate and maintain the [Ulsan] Plant or Additional Plants, and to produce, sell, and export the Products [F2 Gas and NF3 Gas]" (the "License"). Pursuant to Article 3.1 of the [a]greement Hyosung also agreed to pay Halide a $3,800,000 engineering fee for a Basic Engineering Design Package, a Detail Engineering Design Package, Technical Services, Training, and Procurement Services (all as defined in the [a]greement) and other services if requested by Hyosung and mutually agreed to by the parties. Halide asserts that Hyosung has not yet paid it $741,000 of the engineering fee and $800,000 of the license fee. Hyosung does not deny that it has withheld certain payments from Halide. Instead, Hyosung asserts that Halide breached the [a]greement and that it has properly withheld payment from Halide pursuant to Article 14 of the [a]greement. Halide disputes the allegation that it has breached the Agreement and thus disputes the propriety of Hyosung's withholding of payments. Halide also contends that Hyosung has no right to use the License until Hyosung has paid the remaining balance due for the License under the [a]greement.' See F.Supp.2d 1, 2010 WL 4456928(E.D.Pa., 2010) (No. CIV. A. 10-02392).

'*Arbitration.* The parties shall use best efforts to negotiate and amicably resolve any dispute or claim arising out of or in connection with this Agreement. Any such dispute or claim which cannot be settled amicably by the parties hereto shall be finally resolved by arbitration in the defendant's country. The arbitration proceedings shall be conducted in the English language by a panel of three arbitrators, with one arbitrator selected by each of the parties, and the third arbitrator selected by the two arbitrators selected by the parties. Any award rendered shall be final and binding on the parties and judgment may be entered thereon in any competent jurisdiction. Notwithstanding the foregoing, either party hereto may seek preliminary injunctive relief from any court of competent jurisdiction pending the outcome of such arbitration proceedings.'[228]

Having found that the dispute between Halide and Hyosung as to whether the parties had breached their respective obligations under the contract fell within the scope of the contract's arbitration clause, the *Hyosung* court held that Halide's requested declaratory judgment as to the merits of its claim was 'the province of the arbitrator and not the [c]ourt to interpret a contract where there is a "plausible" claim of arbitrability.'[229] The *Hyosung* court, however, was not persuaded that the plaintiff would suffer an irreparable injury without a preliminary injunction while stating that 'a district court has the authority to grant injunctive relief in an arbitrable dispute, provided that the prerequisites for such relief are satisfied.'[230] Hence, all of the issues in the suit are subject to binding arbitration.

It is at issue whether a party can avoid his or her attorney's agreement to binding arbitration where the attorneys of both parties agreed to binding arbitration in Korea during an appearance before an American court. In *Medal Knitwear, Inc. & Hee Soon Wi v. Ji Hoon Jung, JYP Entertainment Co., Ltd., Jin Young Park and Star M Co. Ltd.*,[231] the plaintiff Hee Soon Wi, appearing *pro se*, moved to reopen his case, which was dismissed on 4 October 2010 as 'the parties agreed to binding arbitration in Korea during an appearance before Magistrate Judge Cheryl L. Pollack.'[232] The plaintiff argued that he did not authorise his attorneys to consent to such arbitration. Stating that '[a]ny other notion would be wholly inconsistent with our system of representative litigation', the *Medal Knitwear* court held that the plaintiff cannot avoid his attorney's agreement to

228 For Article 23.7 of the contract providing for arbitration of disputes, see F.Supp.2d 2, 2010 WL 4456928(E.D.Pa., 2010) (No. CIV. A. 10-02392).

229 *Ibid.*, p. 3.

230 To seek preliminary injunctive relief, a plaintiff must prove: '(1) irreparable injury if relief is not granted to prevent a change in the status quo pending the outcome of an arbitration; (2) a reasonable probability of eventual success on its claims; (3) that the possibility of harm to other interested persons if injunctive relief is granted would not outweigh the harm it will suffer if injunctive relief is denied; and (4) that the injunction it seeks will serve the public interest.' See *Thompson v. Nienaber*, 239 F.Supp.2d 478, 485 n. 9 (D.N.J.2002).

231 F. Supp. 2d 1, 2011 WL 96522 (E.D.N.Y., 2011) (No. 10-CV-802 FB CLP).

232 *Ibid.*, p. 1.

binding arbitration because 'each party is deemed bound by the acts of his lawyer-agent.'[233]

## 4.6. ARBITRAL TRIBUNALS

The number of arbitrators shall be determined by the agreement of the parties.[234] The default rule is that the number of arbitrators is three.[235] The procedure for appointing arbitrators is determined by agreement of the parties. However, arbitrators are appointed as a default rule by virtue of one of the following methods: (a) in an arbitration with a sole arbitrator, an arbitrator shall be appointed, upon request of either party, by a court if the parties are unable to agree on an arbitrator within 30 days after a party has received a request for appointment of an arbitrator from the other party; or (b) in an arbitration with three arbitrators, each party appoints one arbitrator, and the two appointed arbitrators appoint the third arbitrator by agreement. In that case, the appointment shall be made, upon request of either party, by a court if a party fails to appoint an arbitrator within 30 days of receipt of a request to do so from the other party, or if the two arbitrators appointed fail to appoint the third arbitrator within 30 days of their appointment.[236] The arbitrator is appointed by a court upon request of a party regardless of an agreement of the parties on the procedure for appointing arbitrators where a party fails to appoint an arbitrator in accordance with the procedure agreed upon, where the parties or two arbitrators fail to appoint an arbitrator in accordance with the procedure agreed upon, or where an institution or any other third party, to whom appointment of an arbitrator has been delegated, fails to appoint an arbitrator.[237]

A person who has been appointed as an arbitrator or has received a request to become an arbitrator must, without delay, inform the parties of any circumstances likely to give rise to doubts as to such person's impartiality or independence.[238] An arbitrator may be challenged only if any circumstances likely to give rise to doubts as to his/her impartiality or independence exist or the arbitrator does not possess the qualifications agreed to by the parties.[239] However, a party may challenge an arbitrator appointed by that party, or in whose appointment that party participated, only for reasons of which that party became aware after the appointment was made.[240]

233 *Ibid.*
234 Article 11(1), Korean Arbitration Act.
235 Article 11(2), *ibid.*
236 Article 12(3), *ibid.*
237 Article 12(4), *ibid.*
238 Article 13(1), *ibid.*
239 Article 14(2), *ibid.*
240 Article 13(2), proviso of the Korean Arbitration Act.

The procedure for challenging an arbitrator is determined by the parties' agreement.[241] In the absence of the parties' agreement on the procedure for challenging an arbitrator, a party who intends to challenge an arbitrator must submit an application for the challenge in writing to the arbitral tribunal within 15 days of the date on which the arbitral tribunal was constituted or the date on which it became aware of circumstances likely to give rise to doubts as to his/her impartiality or independence.[242] In such cases, the arbitral tribunal shall decide on the challenge unless the challenged arbitrator withdraws from office or the other party agrees to the challenge.[243] If a party fails to successfully challenge an arbitrator by the parties' agreement or the procedure for challenging an arbitrator before the arbitral tribunal, the challenging party may submit an application challenging the relevant arbitrator to a court within 30 days after having received notice of the decision rejecting the challenge. In such cases, the arbitral tribunal may, even while the challenge is pending before court, continue arbitral proceedings or render an award.[244] A decision by the court on challenge of an arbitrator may not be subject to appeal.[245]

If an arbitrator becomes *de jure* or *de facto* unable to perform the arbitrator's duties or delays performance of duties with no justifiable reason, the arbitrator's mandate shall terminate if the arbitrator withdraws from office or if the parties agree on the termination.[246] In the event of a dispute regarding the termination of an arbitrator's mandate, any party may request a court to decide on it.[247] A decision by a court on the termination of mandate following an application for termination of mandate is not subject to appeal.[248] Where the mandate of an arbitrator is terminated and a substitute arbitrator is to be appointed, the substitute arbitrator will be appointed in accordance with the procedure applicable to the appointment of the arbitrator being replaced.[249]

The arbitral tribunal may rule on its own jurisdiction, including on any objections with respect to the existence or validity of the arbitration agreement. In such cases, if the arbitration agreement is in the form of an arbitration clause, the validity of any other clause of the contract does not affect the validity of the arbitration clause.[250] An objection to the arbitral tribunal's jurisdiction must be raised not later than the submission of the statement of defence on the merits. In such cases, a party is not precluded from raising such an objection by the fact that such party has appointed, or participated in the appointment of, an

241 Article 14(1), Korean Arbitration Act.
242 Article 14(2), *ibid.*
243 Article 14(2), *ibid.*
244 Article 14(3), *ibid.*
245 Article 14(4), *ibid.*
246 Article 15(1), *ibid.*
247 Article 15(2), *ibid.*
248 Article 15(3), *ibid.*
249 Article 16, *ibid.*
250 Article 17(1), *ibid.*

arbitrator.[251] An objection that the arbitral tribunal has exceeded the scope of its authority must be raised as soon as grounds for the objection are raised during the arbitral proceedings.[252] The arbitral tribunal may rule, in the case of an objection to its jurisdiction, to admit a later objection if it considers the delay justified.[253] Also, the arbitral tribunal may rule on an objection to its jurisdiction either as a preliminary question or in an arbitral award on the merits.[254] If the tribunal rules as a preliminary question that it has jurisdiction, the party who raised the objection may, within 30 days after having received notice thereof, request the court to review the jurisdiction of the tribunal.[255] Where a party has raised an objection to the arbitral tribunal's jurisdiction, the tribunal may continue arbitral proceedings or render an arbitral award while his/her request for the objection is pending before a court.[256]

Unless otherwise agreed by the parties, the arbitral tribunal may, at the request of a party, render a decision granting such interim measures of protection as the arbitral tribunal may consider necessary in respect of the subject matter of the dispute. In such cases, the arbitral tribunal may determine the amount of security to be provided by the respondent in lieu of such interim measure.[257] The arbitral tribunal may order the party requesting the interim measure to provide appropriate security.[258] The KCAB's International Arbitration Rules can be found at its homepage or in Bae, Kim & Lee, *Arbitration Law of Korea: Practice and Procedure.*

## 4.7. ARBITRATION PROCEDURE

The parties must be treated equally in the arbitral proceedings and each party must be given a sufficient opportunity to present its case.[259] The parties may agree on the arbitral proceedings except when contrary to the mandatory provisions of the Korean Arbitration Act.[260]

The parties may agree on the arbitral proceedings except when contrary to the mandatory provisions of the Korean Arbitration Act. In the absence of the parties' agreement on the arbitral proceedings, the arbitral tribunal may, subject to the provisions of the Korean Arbitration Act, conduct the arbitration in such

251 Article 17(2), *ibid.*
252 Article 18(3), *ibid.*
253 Article 18(4), *ibid.*
254 Article 18(5), *ibid.*
255 Article 18(6), *ibid.*
256 Article 17(7), *ibid.*
257 Article 18(1), *ibid.*
258 Article 18(2), *ibid.*
259 Article 19, *ibid.*
260 Article 20(1), *ibid.*

manner as its deems appropriate. In such cases, the tribunal shall have the power to determine admissibility, relevance, and weight of any evidence.[261]

The place of arbitration shall be determined by the parties' agreement.[262] Where the parties fail to agree on the place of arbitration, the arbitral tribunal determines the place of arbitration, taking into account all circumstances of the case, including the convenience of the parties.[263] Despite the parties' agreement on the place of arbitration or the arbitral tribunal's determination as to the place of arbitration, the arbitral tribunal may, unless otherwise agreed by the parties, meet at any place it deems appropriate for consultation among the arbitrators, for hearing witnesses, experts or the parties, or for inspection of goods, places or documents.[264] Unless otherwise agreed by the parties, arbitral proceedings commence on the date when a request for a dispute to be referred to arbitration is received by the respondent.[265] The request must include the parties, the subject matter of the dispute and details of the arbitration agreement.[266]

The language to be used in the arbitral proceedings is determined by the parties' agreement. When the parties fail to agree on the language to be used in the arbitral proceedings, it shall be designated by the arbitral tribunal. When the arbitral tribunal fails to designate the language for the arbitral proceedings, Korean shall be used.[267] The language to be used in the arbitral proceedings shall, unless otherwise specified, apply to any written statement by a party, any oral hearing and any award, decision or other communication by the arbitral tribunal.[268] The arbitral tribunal may, if it deems necessary, order a party to submit any documentary evidence accompanied by a translation into the language to be used in the arbitral proceedings.[269]

In Korea, a party to an arbitration agreement is not allowed to apply to an emergency arbitrator, or the competent court, as an interim measure before the arbitral tribunal is constituted. To solve this problem, on 1 May 2006 the ICDR for the first time introduced emergency arbitrator proceedings by adding an Article 37 to the ICDR Rules. Article 32 and Appendix II of the Arbitration Rules of the Stockholm Chamber of Commerce (SCC) also set forth an emergency arbitrator mechanism. According to the SCC Arbitration Rules, an applicant for an interim measure must satisfy the following requirements for issuance of an interim measure: (a) the applicant has to demonstrate that it may suffer irreparable or serious harm in a commercially sensitive, not in a strictly literal

261 Article 20(2), *ibid.*
262 Article 21(1), *ibid.*
263 Article 21(2), *ibid.*
264 Article 21(3), *ibid.*
265 Article 22(1), *ibid.*
266 Article 22(2), *ibid.*
267 Article 23(1), *ibid.*
268 Article 23(2), *ibid.*
269 Article 23(3), *ibid.*

sense without the interim measure; (b) the applicant has to persuade the emergency arbitrator that the application is urgent; and (iii) the applicant is required to satisfy the reasonable possibility that it may succeed on the merits of the claim.

The following foreign case is a good illustration of a dispute related to an arbitration clause that subjects the parties to KCAB arbitration rules. In the *Haimalu* case in 2006, a Korean corporation, Haimalu, entered into a development contract and a chain contract in August 2001 with a Chinese corporation, Popeyes. Under the agreement, the Korean company would give an operating license to the Chinese company, who would remunerate royalty to the Korean company and bear the costs of starting shops. The contracts contained an arbitration clause stating 'arbitration according to the Arbitration Rules of the Korean Commercial Arbitration Board.'[270] When the Chinese company failed to pay royalty and other relevant costs to the Korean counterpart, the Korean company brought arbitration before the Korean Commercial Arbitration Board and the KCAB rendered an arbitral award in favour of the Korean company on 22 October 2004. Afterwards, as the Chinese company failed to conform to the award, the Korean company commenced enforcement proceedings against the Chinese company in front of the Harbin IPC in April 2005.[271] The Chinese company argued that enforcement should be refused alleging a violation of the arbitration procedure. The Chinese company showed that the serving of the notice of the arbitration hearing and of the arbitral award had not been made in accordance with the Korea-China MAT of 2005 because it had not been translated into Chinese and was served directly by mail to the Chinese company instead of going through the Ministry of Justice in China.[272] The Harbin IPC was inclined to refuse the enforcement of the arbitral award on basis of the invalidity of the arbitration agreement and the lack of due notification of the Chinese company. It presented the case to the Heilongjiang HPC in compliance with the Prior Reporting System. The Heilongjiang HPC could not reach a unanimous decision and thus presented the case to the SPC for further instructions on 14 October 2005.[273] The SPC held that provisions on service of legal documents in the Korea-China MAT of 2005 applied to service of court documents, and not to service of arbitration documents. It further ruled that per DHL to the Chinese company directly, the way the notices had been served complied with the applicable Koran arbitration law and with the applicable arbitration rules, and that there were no grounds for refusal to enforce the Korean arbitral award under Article V of the New York Convention of

270 C. von Wunschheim, *Enforcement Com. Arb. Awards China*, 2012, Appendix M §46.
271 *Ibid.*
272 *Ibid.*
273 *Ibid.*

1958.[274] Hence, it ordered that the arbitral award be enforced on 3 March 2006.[275]

## 4.8. INTERNATIONAL COMMERCIAL ARBITRATION AND INTERNATIONAL LITIGATION

According to Article 3(2) of the Korean Arbitration Act, the term 'arbitration agreement' is defined as an 'agreement between the parties to settle, by arbitration, all or some disputes which have already occurred or might occur in the future with regard to defined legal relationships, whether contractual or not.'

It has become more common in international commercial arbitration cases for the respondent to seek a strategic advantage by filing a competing action in a foreign country, effectively disavowing its agreement to arbitrate. If the action is instituted in the same jurisdiction where the arbitration is pending, the party seeking to arbitrate may ask the court to stay the litigation and compel arbitration. For example, the *Ssangyong* court affirmed a stay of the entire action in California, USA in favour of arbitration of some claims in Korea.[276]

In accordance with Article 9(1) of the Arbitration Act, a court before which an action is brought in a matter which is the subject of an arbitration agreement shall dismiss the action when the respondent presents an affirmative defence for the existence of the arbitration agreement. But litigation is usually commenced in a country outside the jurisdiction where the arbitration is proceeding. When it comes to this kind of situation, the best course of action for the party seeking to enforce the agreement to arbitrate may be to petition the court with jurisdiction to issue an order prohibiting the parties from continuing with the foreign lawsuit – an 'anti-suit' injunction, because the *lis pendens* doctrine is not used to block the commencement of a lawsuit in a foreign country per se.

The Korean Arbitration Act encompasses both domestic and international arbitration. Article 6 of the Act prescribes that '[i]n matters governed by this Act, no court shall intervene except as provided in this Act.' Article 9 of the Act also stipulates that:

> '(1) A court before which an action is brought in Korea in a matter which is the subject of an arbitration agreement shall, when the respondent raises a plea for the existence of an arbitration agreement, reject the action: *Provided* that this shall not apply in cases where it finds that the agreement is null and void, inoperative or incapable of being performed.
>
> (2) The respondent shall raise a plea under paragraph (1) not later than when submitting his first statement on the substance of the dispute.

274 *Ibid.*

275 *Ibid.*

276 *Mediterranean Enterprises, Inc. v. Ssangyong Corp.*, 708 F.2d 1458 (9th Cir. 1983).

(3) Where an action referred to in paragraph (1) has been brought, arbitral proceedings may nevertheless be commenced or continued, and an award may be made, while the issue is pending before the court.'

In addition, Article 10 of the Act provides that '[a] party to an arbitration agreement may request, before or during arbitral proceedings, from a court an interim measure of protection and for a court to grant such measure.' Furthermore, Articles 9 and 10 shall apply even in cases where the place of arbitration has not yet been determined or is not in Korea.[277] A court before which an action is brought in a matter which is the subject of an arbitration agreement shall, when the respondent raises a plea for the existence of an arbitration agreement, dismiss the action pursuant to Article 9 of the Korean Arbitration Act. In this regard, the legal nature of an arbitration agreement can be defined as a procedural act rather than a substantive act.

When both international arbitration and litigation are pending with regard to the same parties and claim, anti-suit injunctions, anti-arbitration injunctions, pro-arbitration injunctions, and actions for damages due to breach of an arbitration agreement need to be discussed.

First, a Korean court is not allowed to issue an anti-arbitration order. In cases where the issue is whether a provisional measure seeking suspension of arbitration proceedings is permitted on the basis of the illegality of the arbitration proceedings, the Korean Supreme Court held that '[i]n light of the tenor of Article 10 of the former Korean Arbitration Act[278] prescribing that

---

277 Article 2, Korean Arbitration Act.

278 Article 17 of the current Korean Arbitration Act provides that:
'(1) The arbitral tribunal may rule on its own jurisdiction, including any objections with respect to the existence or validity of the arbitration agreement. For that purpose, an arbitration clause which forms part of a contract shall be treated as an agreement independent of the other terms of the contract.
(2) A plea that the arbitral tribunal does not have jurisdiction shall be raised not later than the submission of the statement of defence. A party shall not be precluded from raising such a plea by the fact that he has appointed, or participated in the appointment of, an arbitrator.
(3) A plea that the arbitral tribunal is exceeding the scope of its authority shall be raised as soon as the matter alleged to be beyond the scope of its authority is raised during the arbitral proceedings.
(4) The arbitral tribunal may, in either case of paragraphs (2) and (3), admit a later plea if it considers the delay justified.
(5) The arbitral tribunal may rule a plea referred to in paragraph (2) or (3) either as a preliminary question or in an arbitral award on the merits.
(6) If the arbitral tribunal rules as preliminary question that it has jurisdiction under paragraph (5), any party who is dissatisfied with that ruling may request, within thirty days after having received notice thereof, the court to decide on the jurisdiction of the arbitral tribunal.
(7) While a request under paragraph (6) is pending, the arbitral tribunal may continue the arbitral proceedings or make an arbitral award.
(8) A decision of the court under paragraph (6) shall be subject to no appeal.'

arbitrators can proceed with arbitration and grant an arbitration award even though a party to an arbitration agreement argues that arbitration proceedings are not permissible, he or she is not allowed to seek an interim measure staying proceedings pending arbitration before a Korean court on the basis of the illegality of the arbitration proceedings. In this regard, it calls for a separate discussion as to whether a party to an arbitration agreement can seek a declaratory judgment which confirms the illegality of the arbitration proceedings or whether he or she can argue the illegality of the arbitration proceedings following the grant of an arbitration award even in the cases where the court finds that the arbitration proceedings are prohibited.'[279] Moreover, another Korean Supreme Court case upheld that an action seeking a declaratory judgment which confirms illegality of arbitration proceedings is illegal.[280] The rationales supported by the latter case are as follows:

(a) in cases where a party proceeds with arbitration in the absence of an arbitration agreement, the other party can raise a plea that the arbitral tribunal does not have jurisdiction before a court pursuant to Article 17(1) to (3) of the Korean Arbitration Act;[281]
(b) there are ways for the other party to enable the court to determine the existence of the arbitration agreement by an application for setting aside the arbitration award by virtue of Article 36 of the Korean Arbitration Act;
(c) the other party can challenge the existence of the arbitration agreement when one party applies for the recognition and enforcement of an arbitration award pursuant to Article 37 of the Korean Arbitration Act; and
(d) Article 6 of the Korean Arbitration Act provides that '[i]n matters governed by this Act, no court shall intervene except as provided in this Act.'[282]

In sum, interim measures staying the arbitration proceedings pending the arbitration are prohibited because, in fact, they are likely to prejudice the principle of competence-competence of an arbitration tribunal and the independence of arbitration clauses. Similarly, as the said rationales also apply to anti-arbitration orders, these too cannot be allowed.[283]

The second issue is whether an anti-suit injunction is available under Korean law. Article 300 of the Korean Civil Enforcement Act[284] states that:

---

279 Ruling issued by the Korean Supreme Court on 11.06.1996 (Case No. 96ma149). Article 10 of the Korean Arbitration Act prescribes that: 'A party to an arbitration agreement may request, before or during arbitral proceedings, from a court an interim measure of protection.'

280 Judgment rendered by the Korean Supreme Court on 25.06.2004 (Case No. 2003da5634).

281 Article 17, Korean Arbitration Act.

282 Judgment rendered by the Korean Supreme Court on 25.06.2004 (Case No. 2003da5634).

283 G. Lee, 'A Study on International Commercial Arbitration and Its Parallel International Litigation' (2010) 16 *Korea Private International Law Journal* 99.

284 K.H. Suk, 'Arbitration Agreement and Anti-suit Injunction in International Commercial Arbitration' (2010) 50 *Advanced Commercial Law Review* 32.

> '(1) Provisional dispositions with regard to the objects of dispute may be effected in cases where, if the existing situations are altered, the party will be unable to exercise his/her rights, or there exists a concern about a substantial difficulty in exercising it.
> (2) Provisional dispositions may also be effected in order to maintain the status quo against the disputed legal relations. In this case, such provisional dispositions shall be effected specially to avoid a significant damage on a continuing legal relations or to prevent an imminent danger, or where there exists other necessary reasons.'

In order for Article 300(2) of the Korean Civil Enforcement Act to be satisfied, the necessity to avoid significant damage or imminent danger needs to be proved. Based on this provision, the courts in Korea can issue an anti-suit injunction order. There is a certain limitation. The provision mentioned above is applicable only to preliminary anti-suit injunction orders. In other words, a permanent anti-suit injunction order is not permitted.[285] In order to secure the effectiveness of the preliminary anti-suit injunction order, indirect compulsory performance[286] along with the order can be ordered.[287]

The third issue is whether an applicant for an international arbitration can seek a motion for a pro-arbitration order before a court in Korea. As the court's intervention in arbitration needs to be minimised, pro-arbitration orders must not be allowed. In particular, pro-arbitration orders are not permitted because they can violate the principle of *kompetenz-kompetenz* and the party autonomy principle.[288]

The last issue is whether a party to an arbitration agreement can sue for damages against the other party to the agreement who refused to perform it. In this case, it is reasonable to say that the party refusing to perform the agreement needs to pay reasonable litigation costs to the opposing party on the basis of a substantive law approach.[289] However, when the arbitration agreement is analysed on the basis of a procedural law approach, particularly the major effect theory,[290] and the agreement is considered as a procedural act rather than a substantive act, the violation of the agreement can constitute a tort only if its breach essentially interferes with parties' procedural fundamental human

285 G. Lee, *supra* n. 1, p. 99.

286 Article 261 of the Korean Civil Enforcement Act provides that: 'In cases where the nature of debts enables one to make an indirect compulsory performance, the court of first instance shall, upon request of a creditor, render a ruling on ordering an indirect compulsory performance. Such ruling shall clarify an obligation to perform the debts and an appropriate period for performance, and when the order requires him to make an immediate compensation for damages. An immediate appeal may be raised against a judgment on the request under paragraph (1).'

287 Cf. Ruling rendered by the Korean Supreme Court on 14.06.2007 (Case No. 2006ma910).

288 *Ibid.*

289 K.H. Suk, *supra* n. 280, p. 32.

290 According to this theory, it is classified as a procedural act that an act does not satisfy its procedural requisites but its main effect is to create procedural effect.

rights.[291] Faced with this practical difficulty, I would like to propose to explicitly prescribe the liability for damages arising out of breach of an arbitration agreement.[292]

## 4.9. CANCELLATION OF ARBITRAL AWARDS

Article 36 of the Korean Arbitration Act prescribes the action for setting aside arbitral awards. Recourse against an arbitral award may be raised only by an action for cancellation of the arbitral award to a court.[293] The Korean Arbitration Act enumerates the four reasons on which a party making an application may base his/her action for setting aside an arbitral award and the two reasons which a court can find, *ex officio*, to cancel the arbitral award. An arbitration award may be set aside by the court only if a party making an application for cancellation of the arbitral award presents proof that: (a) a party to the arbitration agreement was under some incapacity under the law applicable to him/her, or the said agreement is not valid under the law to which the parties have subjected it, or failing any indication thereon, under the Korean law; (b) the party making the application was not given proper notice of the appointment of an arbitrator or of arbitral proceedings or was otherwise unable to present his/her case; (c) the award has dealt with a dispute not contemplated by or not falling within the terms of the submission to arbitration, or contains decisions on matters beyond the scope of the submission to arbitration; or (d) the composition of the arbitral tribunal or arbitral proceedings were not in accordance with agreement of the parties, unless such agreement was in conflict with any mandatory provision of the Korean Arbitration Act from which the parties cannot derogate, or failing such an agreement, were not in accordance with the Korean Arbitration Act.[294] In terms of (c), if the decisions on matters submitted to arbitration can be separated from those not submitted, only that part of the award which contains decisions on matters not submitted to arbitration may be set aside.[295] Also, an arbitration award may be set aside by the court if the court finds, ex officio, that the subject matter of the dispute is not capable of settlement by arbitration under the Korean law or that the award is in conflict with the good morals and other forms of social order of the Republic of Korea.[296]

In cases where arbitrators merely erred in fact-finding or their legal determination violates Korean law and regulation so that the contents of an

---

291 Cf. Judgment rendered by the Korean Supreme Court on 05.12.1995 (Case No. 95da21808).

292 G. Lee, *supra* n. 1, p. 100.

293 Article 36(1), Korean Arbitration Act.

294 Article 36(2), Korean Arbitration Act.

295 Article 36(2)(1)(c), proviso of the Korean Arbitration Act.

296 Article 36(2)(2), Korean Arbitration Act.

arbitral award can be regarded to be unreasonable, it is not safe to say that the award is in conflict with the good morals and other forms of social order of the Republic of Korea. Rather, the legal wording means that the outcome which the award results in violates the good morals and other forms of social order of the Republic of Korea.[297] The mere fact that an arbitral award differs from the decisions rendered by the Korean Supreme Court in the same type of cases depending on different interpretation of law and regulation or contract does not fall under the category in which the enforcement of the award is in conflict with the good morals and other forms of social order of the Republic of Korea.[298]

The substantive facts of *KOICA v. Hi-Net Trade Co. Ltd*,[299] which dealt with the cancellation of arbitration issues, were as follows:

(a) the plaintiff, KOICA, and the defendant, a Korean corporation, entered into an agreement whereby Hi-Net would export various goods for the purpose of foreign aid on behalf of KOICA and KOICA would make payments to Hi-Net for such goods;
(b) Hi-Net reported its tax-exemption status for value added tax (VAT) throughout the terms of the agreement and did not pay VAT;
(c) the VAT exemption was acknowledged by the relevant tax authorities;
(d) following the termination of the contract, the tax authorities informed Hi-Net that the exports were not exempted from VAT payments and requested its payments; and
(e) Hi-Net paid the VAT and then initiated arbitration against KOICA, arguing that KOICA was responsible for the VAT payments.

The procedural facts of *KOICA v. Hi-Net Trade Co. Ltd* were as follows:

(a) the arbitration tribunal rendered an arbitral award in favour of Hi-Net and ruled that KOICA should pay a portion of the VAT;
(b) KOICA sought to set aside the arbitration award by virtue of Articles 32(2) and 36(2)(1)(d) of the Korean Arbitration Act, alleging that the arbitral tribunal did not conduct the arbitration proceedings pursuant to the parties' agreement by failing to offer reasons for its decision properly and that the arbitration award conflicted with the public policy of Korea in accordance with Article 36(2)(2)(b) of the Korean Arbitration Act; and
(c) the Seoul High Court in Korea refused to cancel the arbitral award.[300]

---

297 Judgment rendered by the Korean Supreme Court on 24.06.2010 (Case No. 2007da73918).
298 *Ibid.*
299 *Ibid.*
300 Judgment rendered by Seoul High Court on 12.09.2007 (Case No. 2006na107687).

As KOICA filed an appeal before the Korean Supreme Court, the Court held that an arbitral award may be set aside for lack of reasoning if the parties had not agreed to waive the requirement under Article 32(2)(1)(d) and the arbitral tribunal did not provide reasoning to support its award.

According to the *KOICA* court, an arbitral award that does not state the reasoning upon which it is based refers to limited cases where: '(i) no reasoning was provided by the arbitral tribunal; (ii) the reasoning of the tribunal is so unclear that a court cannot determine on what factual finding or legal determination the arbitral award is based; and/or (iii) the reasoning of the tribunal is contradictory.'[301]

As far as this issue is concerned, the *KOICA* court found that: (a) its decision may resort to equitable principles without reference to any specific statute so long as the award includes some reasoning; (b) the arbitration award is sufficient if the award includes a general explanation of how the arbitrator or the tribunal reached its final conclusion; and (c) the mere fact that an award is, in part, unreasonable or incomplete does not comprise a failure to state reasoning for the purpose of cancellation of the award.[302]

Even though the *KOICA* case is a domestic case, the rationale of the *KOICA* court will be applied to the enforcement of international arbitration awards in Korea.[303]

An action for setting aside an arbitral award shall be raised within three months from the date on which the party making such application has received the duly authenticated copy of the award or the duly authenticated copy of a correction or interpretation or an additional award under Article 34 of the Korean Arbitration Act.[304] After a final and conclusive judgment for recognition

---

301 Judgment rendered by the Korean Supreme Court on 24.06.2010 (Case No. 2007da73918); E.Y. Park, 'Reconfirming Continued Support for the Autonomy of Arbitrations: Recent Developments in Korea' (2011) 16 (1) *IBA Arb. News* 48, 49.

302 E.Y. Park, *supra* n. 297, p. 50.

303 *Ibid.*

304 Article 36 (3) of the Korean Arbitration Act. See cf. Article 34 of the Korean Arbitration Act provides that:

'(1) Within thirty days of receipt of the authentic copy of an arbitral award, unless another period has been agreed upon by the parties, a party may request the arbitral tribunal to make a correction, interpretation or an additional award under any of the following subparagraphs:

1. To correct any errors in computation, any clerical or typographical errors or any errors of similar nature;
2. To give an interpretation of a specific point of or part of the award, if so agreed by the parties;
3. To make an additional award as to claims presented in arbitral proceedings but omitted from the award: Provided, That this shall not apply if agreement between the parties exists.

(2) In cases of making any request under paragraph (1), a party shall give notice to the other party to such effect.

or enforcement of the relevant award by a Korean court is rendered, no action for cancelling the award may be brought.[305]

An action for setting aside an arbitral award is designed to invalidate the award retroactively by cancelling the award. The action for cancellation of an arbitral award can be brought before a court only if Article 36(2) of the Korean Arbitration Act is applicable to the arbitral award which satisfied the formal requirements prescribed by law and was rendered on the merits. Hence, the arbitral award cannot be the subject of an action for setting aside the award in cases where the motion for the award is dismissed due to the fact that the arbitrator has no power to render the award in terms of the dispute on which a party applied for the award.[306]

In cases where an action for cancellation of an arbitral award is pending, the action is not legal if the enforcement judgment on the arbitral award is rendered and finalised. It does not make any difference if the action for setting aside the arbitral award was brought before the Korean court prior to the commencement of the action seeking its enforcement.[307] The reasons on which the Korean Supreme Court based its decision were the promotion of judicial efficiency and the prevention of inconsistency of judgments in the same country because the grounds for setting aside an arbitral award are identical to the ones for refusing to recognise an arbitral award rendered in Korea and are very similar to the ones for refusing to recognise an arbitral award under the New York Convention.[308]

According to Article V(1)(e) of the New York Convention, recognition and enforcement of an arbitral award may be refused if the award has not yet become binding on the parties, or has been set aside or suspended by a competent authority of the country in which, or under the law of which, that award was made. In this regard, the law under which an arbitral award was made does not mean the law which arbitrators apply to the substance of a case, but it refers to the law governing arbitration proceedings.[309]

---

(3) The arbitral tribunal shall decide within thirty days of the receipt of a request under paragraph (1) 1 or 2, and within sixty days of the receipt of the request under paragraph (1) 3 respectively. In such cases, interpretation under paragraph (1) 2 shall form part of the award.

(4) The arbitral tribunal may correct, *ex officio,* any error of the type under paragraph (1) 1 within thirty days of the date of the award.

(5) The arbitral tribunal may extend, if necessary, any period under paragraph (3).

(6) Article 32 shall apply mutatis mutandis to the form of a correction or interpretation of the award or to an additional award.'

305 Article 36(4), Korean Arbitration Act.

306 Judgment rendered by the Korean Supreme Court on 14.10.2004 (Case No. 2003da70249, 70256).

307 Judgment rendered by the Korean Supreme Court on 23.06.2000 (Case No. 98da55192).

308 Y.J. Mok, *supra* n. 154, pp. 262–263.

309 Judgment rendered by the Korean Supreme Court on 26.02.2003 (Case No. 2001da77840).

## 4.10. RECOGNITION AND ENFORCEMENT OF ARBITRAL AWARDS

Recognition or enforcement of an award shall be confirmed by the judgment of a court.[310] The party applying for recognition or enforcement of an arbitral award shall submit the duly authenticated original award or a duly certified copy thereof or the original arbitration agreement or a duly certified copy thereof.[311] If the award or arbitration agreement is made in a foreign language, it shall be accompanied by a duly certified translation into the Korean language.[312] A domestic arbitral award shall be recognised or enforced, unless any ground for setting aside the award can be found. Recognition or enforcement of a foreign award which is subject to the New York Convention shall be governed by that Convention.[313] The recognition of a foreign judgment under Article 217 of the Korean Civil Procedure[314] and enforcement of a foreign judgment under Article 26(1)[315] and 27[316] of the Korean Civil Enforcement Act shall apply *mutatis mutandis* to the recognition and enforcement of a foreign award which is not subject to the New York Convention.[317] A Korean court will review an arbitral award rendered in countries that are not a signatory to the New York Convention and tried to be enforced in Korea in order to make sure that the award meets the requirements for recognition and enforcement under Korean law. The requirements are as follows: (a) the award is final and conclusive; (b) the

---

310 Article 37(1), Korean Arbitration Act.

311 Article 37(2), Korean Arbitration Act.

312 Article 37(2), proviso of the Korean Arbitration Act.

313 Article 39(1), Korean Arbitration Act.

314 Article 217, Korean Civil Procedure Act provides that: 'A final and conclusive judgment by a foreign court shall be acknowledged to be valid, only upon the entire fulfillment of the following requirements: That an international jurisdiction of such foreign court is recognised in the principles of an international jurisdiction pursuant to the Acts and subordinate statutes of the Republic of Korea, or to the treaties; That a defeated defendant received, pursuant to a lawful method, a service of a summons or a document equivalent thereto, and a notice of date or an order, with a time leeway sufficient to defend (excluding the case pursuant to a service by public notice or similar service), or that he responded to the lawsuit even without being served; That such judgment does not violate good morals and other social order of the Republic of Korea; and That there exists a mutual guarantee.'

315 Article 26(1), Korean Civil Enforcement Act provides that: 'A compulsory enforcement based upon the judgment of a foreign court may be conducted only if a court of the Republic of Korea has made a declaration of its legality by means of an enforcement judgment.'

316 Article 27, Korean Civil Enforcement Act set forth as follows:
'(1) An enforcement judgment shall be made without making any examination as to whether the judgment is right or wrong.
(2) A lawsuit seeking an enforcement judgment shall be dismissed if it falls under any of the following subparagraphs:
  (1) When it has not been proved that the judgment of a foreign court has become final and conclusive; and
  (2) When the foreign judgment fails to fulfill the conditions under Article 217 of the Civil Procedure Act.'

317 Article 39(2), Korean Arbitration Act.

jurisdiction of the foreign tribunal is granted under international jurisdictional principles; (c) the Korean party was legally and timely served with the pleadings; (d) the award does not conflict with Korean public policy; and (e) there is a mutual guarantee by the foreign country where the award was rendered.[318]

## 5. CONCLUSION

After reviewing the arbitration law in Korea, it is safe to say that the following need to be noted or proposed.

First, the *LG Electronics Inc.* case is a landmark case in which the Korean Supreme Court unanimously held that the validity of a patent, including the non-obviousness requirement, can be heard and determined by a court in the patent infringement action for damages and injunction. In this regard, I think that the *LG Electronics Inc.* case and the following *Kyphon SARL* and the *HIWOOD Inc.* cases expanded the scope of the subject matter of arbitral disputes in intellectual property cases.

Second, the Korean Arbitration Act does not explicitly prescribe the confidentiality obligation of the various participants in the arbitral proceedings and the Korean courts have never interpreted that an arbitration agreement included confidentiality as its implied term.[319] Hence, where one or more parties to an arbitration agreement seated in Korea are concerned with the confidentiality of arbitral proceedings or evidence submitted in the arbitration, those parties need to take into account the arbitration agreement and the agreed applicable procedural rules.[320]

Article 9 of the KCAB's Arbitration Rules for a domestic case provides that '[t]he arbitration proceedings shall be kept confidential'. There is no further guidance in terms of the ambit of the confidentiality obligation, so the KCAB's Arbitration Rules are silent as to the kind of information required to be kept secret or as to the persons to whom the confidentiality obligation applies.[321] On the other hand, Article 52 of the KCAB's International Arbitration Rules, entitled 'Confidentiality,' states:

> '1. The arbitration proceedings, and records thereof, shall be closed to the public;
> 2. The members of the Arbitral Tribunal and the Secretariat, the parties and their representatives and assistants shall not disclose facts related to arbitration cases or facts learned through arbitration cases except where disclosure is consented to by the parties, required by law or required in court proceedings.'[322]

---

318 Cf. T.F. MacLaren, *supra* n. 130, §17:31.

319 *Ibid.*, p. 43.

320 *Ibid.*, p. 44.

321 B. Hughes, *supra* n. 134, p. 45.

322 B. Hughes, *supra* n. 134, p. 45 (arguing that 'as with the international ad hoc and institutional rules, there is a lack of consistency in approach to confidentiality even as between the two sets

Hence, as far as the confidentiality of the arbitral proceedings is concerned, the Korean Arbitration Act and the KCAB's Arbitration Rules for a domestic use need to be reformed so that they can be in line with the KCAB's International Arbitration Rules.

Finally, in Korea, a party to an arbitration agreement is not allowed to apply to an emergency arbitrator, or the competent court, as an interim measure before the arbitral tribunal is constituted. Taking into account the ICDR Rules and SCC Arbitration Rules regarding emergency arbitrator proceedings, the Korean legal community needs to incorporate an emergency arbitrator system into the Korean Arbitration Act.[323]

---

of KCAB arbitration rules' and thus 'IBA Rules provide a convenient, consistent, efficient and fair framework for addressing confidentiality and other discovery issues in arbitration').

323 K.-H. Ahn and S.R. Kim, 'A Study on Emergency Arbitrator System of SCC and Requirements for Granting of Interim Measures' (2011) 21(2) *Arbitration Review* 65–83.

# PHILIPPINES

Donemark J.L. Calimon

**Contents**

## 1. INTRODUCTION

The two main types of ADR devices commonly used in the Philippines are arbitration and mediation. While Philippine law recognises other modes of ADR, for example early neutral evaluation or mini-trial, there are no rules currently in place for these other types of ADR devices. The latest legislation and administrative issuances on ADR are geared towards ensuring efficient and effective enforcement of agreements to submit to arbitration and mediation, mediated settlements and arbitral awards.

A distinction needs to be made between two classes of ADR laws and administrative issuances under Philippine law. The first pertains to ADR laws/issuances governing voluntary ADR mechanisms, i.e. alternative modes of dispute resolution which parties to a commercial agreement may avail themselves of by mutual agreement. Arbitration within the context of the UNCITRAL[1] Model Law or the New York Convention[2] or arbitrations and mediations under the rules of various international arbitral or mediation institutions, including the ICC, WIPO, SIAC, HKIAC or the PDRCI,[3] fall

1 United Nations Commission on International Trade Law.

2 The New York Convention on the Recognition and Enforcement of Foreign Arbitral Awards, entered into force for the Philippines on 04.10.1967.

3 Philippine Dispute Resolution Center, Inc., the main arbitral institution in the Philippines.

within this first class of ADR laws. The second pertains to ADR laws/issuances which, while recognising the advantages of arbitration and mediation, regulate the use thereof by parties, e.g. by making them mandatory and/or allowing merits review of arbitral awards. Falling within this class are arbitrations/mediations under the Philippine Labor Code,[4] the Local Government Code,[5] the Philippine Mining Act,[6] the Construction Industry Arbitration Law,[7] or mediations pursuant to Supreme Court regulations. Solely for ease of reference, the first class of ADR laws/issuances are referred to as 'commercial' or 'voluntary' ADR laws, while the second class are referred to either as 'statutory', 'statute-based', or 'rules-based' ADR laws.

## 2. DEVELOPMENT OF ADR IN THE PHILIPPINES: AN OVERVIEW

Commercial arbitration found its place in the Philippine ADR system through the Spanish Civil Code which became effective in the Philippines beginning in the late nineteenth century. Subsequent legislation, particularly the Civil Code of the Philippines[8] and the Arbitration Law,[9] provided for more comprehensive domestic arbitration rules. In 2004, the Philippines enacted the ADR Act expanding its arbitration laws to cover international arbitrations as well.[10] The Philippines is a party to the New York Convention,[11] with the ADR Act as its implementing legislation. Throughout the development of commercial arbitration in the Philippines, various laws have also been enacted providing for arbitration, mostly mandatory, of specific types of disputes, e.g. labour disputes which fall within the exclusive and original jurisdiction of labour arbiters. These laws have the same purpose of decongesting court dockets and should naturally

[4] Presidential Decree No. 442, 'A Decree Instituting a Labor Code, thereby Revising and Consolidating Labor and Social Laws to Afford Protection to Labor, Promote Employment and Human Resources Development and Ensure Industrial Peace based on Social Justice', approved on 01.05.1974.

[5] The Local Government Code of 1991, became effective on 01.01.1992.

[6] Republic Act No. 7942, 'An Act Instituting a New System of Mineral Resources Exploration, Development, Utiliation, and Conservation', approved on 03.03.1995.

[7] Executive Order No. 1008, 'Creating an Arbitration Machinery in the Construction Industry of the Philippines', issued on 04.02.1985, became effective immediately.

[8] Republic Act No. 386, 'An Act to Ordain and Institute the Civil Code of the Philippines', approved on 18.06.1949, became effective on 30.08.1950.

[9] Republic Act No. 876, 'An Act to Authorize the Making of Arbitration and Submission Agreements, to Provide for the Appointment of Arbitrators and the Procedure for Arbitration in Civil Controversies, and for other purposes', approved on 19.06.1953, became effective on 19.12.1953.

[10] Republic Act No. 9285, 'An Act to Institutionalize the Use of an Alternative Dispute Resolution System in the Philippines and to Establish the Office for Alternative Dispute Resolution and for Other Purposes', approved on 2.04.2002, became effective on 28.04.2004.

[11] *Supra* n. 2.

supplement commercial arbitration. However, in certain instances, the effect of these laws, perhaps unintentionally, is to limit the effectiveness of commercial arbitration, e.g. some statute-based arbitrations are designed to replace commercial arbitration without offering parties the full benefits of commercial arbitration, such as exclusion of merits-review or ability to choose arbitrators.

Mediation as a mode of dispute resolution had also been adopted in various pieces of legislation, e.g. the Labor Code and the Local Government Code. Through initiatives of the Supreme Court, mediation was also institutionalised and incorporated into the Philippine judicial system. The first types of mediation adopted by the Supreme Court were mandatory mediations or court-annexed mediations, which are mediations conducted under the auspices of the courts. The success of court-annexed mediation encouraged the Supreme Court to further expand its mediation rules to include judge-presided mediations, known as judicial dispute resolution (JDR), and mediation in the appellate court level, known as appellate court mediation (ACM). These various forms of rules-based mediation have significantly helped the Supreme Court in its efforts to reduce the volume of cases pending with the courts. With the enactment of the ADR Act, the Philippines also formally recognised and provided rules governing commercial or voluntary mediation. This latter type of mediation, however, is still in its formative stages and has yet to become a preferred mode of mediation among parties to a dispute.

## 3. PHILIPPINE LAW ON ARBITRATION

Not one but several pieces of legislation govern arbitration in the Philippines. The ADR Act[12] is the Philippines' most comprehensive law to date on commercial arbitration, covering both domestic and international arbitrations. However, several other laws provide for or require arbitration for specific types of disputes. This section discusses the history of arbitration in the Philippines and comments on some of the important distinctions between commercial and statute-based arbitrations.

### 3.1. SPANISH CIVIL CODE AND EARLY JURISPRUDENCE ON ARBITRATION

#### 3.1.1. *Spanish Civil Code*

Arbitration was first formally introduced into the Philippine legal system in 1889 with the adoption of certain provisions of the Civil Code of Spain (Civil Code of

12 *Supra* n. 10.

1889),[13] including the provisions on compromise and arbitration. Pursuant to Article 1821 of the Spanish Civil Code, provisions of the said Code with respect to compromises were also applicable to arbitrations. Article 1820, on the other hand, provided that persons capable of making a compromise may also submit their contentions to a third person for decision.

In *Cordoba v. Conde*,[14] the Supreme Court described what was then (i.e. in 1901) a common and well-known practice for resolving commercial disputes – litigation by means of friendly adjusters, known as *juicio de amigables componedores*. The procedure for this method of resolving disputes were said to involve the following:

> 'As said by the counsel for the appellee in the argument, litigation by means of friendly adjusters (juicio de amigables componedores) was thoroughly well known at the time this contract was made, and it was the method which the parties intended to follow in the settlement of their differences. The procedure in this kind of litigation was minutely described in the former Ley de Enjuiciamiento Civil. Twenty-one articles, including those incorporated by reference, are devoted to it. (Arts. 810–822.) The adjusters had to be men who could read and write. The number had to be odd, and could not exceed five. A third person could not be given the power to name them. Unless the agreement of submission was executed before a notary, it was void. It was also void if it did not contain five specified particulars. An adjuster could be challenged if he had an interest in the subject-matter of the suit or was manifestly antagonistic to either party, provided the cause for challenge arose or came to the knowledge of the party after the appointment. If the adjuster challenged refused to withdraw, the matter had to be tried in the Court of First Instance where the adjuster resided. The decision of the dispute by the adjusters was void if not made before a notary. Against this decision the party aggrieved could, within sixty days, prosecute a writ of error in the Supreme Court of Spain, on the grounds that the judgment was rendered outside of the time limited therefor, or that it decided questions not submitted. (Art. 1670, par. 3; sec. 1673, par. 3; art. 1756.) If no writ of error was sued out, or if it was dismissed, the judgment of the adjusters was to be executed by the Court of First Instance of the district where the decision was made in the same manner as other judgments.'

In the *Cordoba v. Conde* case, however, the Supreme Court ruled that Articles 1820 and 1821 could no longer be enforced in view of the repeal of the Spanish Law on Civil Procedure and refused to enforce an arbitration agreement contained in a partnership agreement. The Supreme Court reasoned that the power 'given by article 1820 is expressly limited by article 1821, which declares that not only the form of procedure but also the effect of these agreements shall be controlled by the [Law of Civil Procedure]. When that was repealed, the Civil Code was left without any declaration as to what the effect of such an agreement

---

13 Ambrosio Padilla, *Civil Law – Civil Code Annotated*, vol. 1, 1961 ed.

14 GR No. 1125, 24.08.1903.

would be. These articles, 1820 and 1821, have therefore been repealed.'[15] As discussed below, however, the Supreme Court nevertheless recognised the limited enforceability of arbitration agreements in other cases.

### 3.1.2. *The concept of arbitration in early twentieth-century jurisprudence*

Shortly before the ruling in *Cordoba v. Conde*, the Supreme Court rendered the decision in *Wahl et al. v. Donaldson, Sims & Co.*[16] Dealing with the issue of whether an arbitration clause should be enforced, the Supreme Court took the view that arbitration is valid only if it is availed of as a means to ascertain the amount of damage sustained arising from a breach of contract and only as a condition precedent for the filing of a suit in court. The Supreme Court ruled that:

> 'a condition in a contract that disputes arising out of it shall be referred to arbitration is good where the amount of damages sustained by a breach of the contract is to be ascertained by specified arbitration before any right of action arises, but that it is illegal where all the matters in dispute of whatever sort may be referred to arbitrators and to them alone. In the first case a condition precedent to the accruing of a right of action is imposed, while in the second it is attempted to prevent any right of action accruing at all, and this can not be permitted.'[17]

The Court further ruled that agreements to refer matters in dispute to arbitration have been regarded generally as attempts to oust the jurisdiction of the court and that 'where there is a stipulation that all matters in dispute are to be referred to arbitrators and to them alone, such stipulation is contrary to public policy.'[18] Notably, the court in *Wahl et al. v. Donaldson, Sims & Co.* refused enforcement of the arbitration agreement involved therein, but nevertheless impliedly recognised that arbitration agreements may be valid under certain limited circumstances. Subsequent decisions of the Supreme Court followed the view expressed in this case that arbitration is a means to ascertain factual disputes between parties and is a condition precedent for the institution of actions in court – rather than as an actual alternative to traditional court litigation.[19]

In *Chang et al. v. Royal Exchange Assurance Corporation of London*,[20] the Supreme Court upheld the validity of an arbitration agreement providing for arbitration as 'a condition precedent to the institution of any suit upon this policy and to the liability and obligation of the corporation to pay or satisfy any

15 The Civil Code of 1889 was expressly repealed on 30.08.1950.
16 GR No 1085, 16.05.1903.
17 *Ibid.*, citing *Clark on Contracts*, p. 432.
18 *Ibid.*
19 Notwithstanding the subsequent ruling in *Cordoba v. Conde*, *supra* n. 14, the Supreme Court continued to follow the ruling in *Wahl, et al. v. Donaldson, Sims & Co. supra* n. 17.
20 GR No. L-3567, 20.08.1907.

claim or demand based upon this policy'. The Supreme Court ruled that 'such a condition is a valid one in law, and unless it be first complied with no action can be brought'.

In *Allen v. the Province of Tayabas*,[21] the Supreme Court ruled that a condition precedent in a construction contract requiring a certificate of acceptance by the Director of Public Works or his representative before any payment shall be made on any public work for the Government is a 'species of arbitration'. The Supreme Court clarified the earlier ruling in *Wahl et al. v. Donaldson, Sims & Co.*, explaining that 'unless the agreement is such as absolutely to close the doors of the courts against the parties, which agreement would be void, courts will look with favor upon such amicable arrangements and will only with great reluctance interfere to anticipate or nullify the action of the arbitrator.' It further ruled that 'it would be highly improper, for courts out of untoward jealousy to annul laws or agreements which seek to oust the courts of their jurisdiction.'

In *Puentebella et al. v. Negros Coal Co. Ltd et al.*,[22] the Supreme Court ruled that an arbitration clause which requires parties to 'submit each and every one of the differences that may arise between the party of the first part and the party of the second part to the decision of arbitrators, two of whom shall be selected by the party of the first part and two by the party of the second part, who, in case of a disagreement, shall select a fifth arbitrator, and they shall respect and abide by the decision of said arbitrators or any three of them, as the case may be' is contrary to public policy and is not binding upon the parties. This type of arbitration clause, according to the court, 'does not merely provide for arbitration as a condition precedent to recourse to the courts; it provides for a final determination of legal rights by arbitration.' In other words, the Court stated, 'an attempt was made to take the disputes between the parties out of the jurisdiction of the courts.'

Arbitration, as defined in these early Philippine cases, was viewed more as providing a means to determine factual questions. Moreover, as a condition precedent to court action, the award in an arbitration is not final and is merely a stage in the judicial process. Thus, in *Allen v. the Province of Tayabas*,[23] the Supreme Court confirmed that awards in arbitration proceedings may be questioned before the trial courts if there was fraud or mistake. In *Chan Linte, v. Law Union and Rock Insurance Co. Ltd*,[24] the Supreme Court ruled that 'the plaintiff, having agreed to arbitration after the action was commenced and submitted his proof to the arbitrator, in the absence of fraud or mistake, is estopped and bound by the award.'

---

21 GR No. 12283, 25.07.1918.
22 GR Nos. 26216 and 26217, 6.03.1927.
23 GR No. 12283, 25.07.1918.
24 GR No. 16398, 14.12.1921.

## 3.2. COMMERCIAL ARBITRATION

### *3.2.1. The New Civil Code*

On 30 August 1950, the New Civil Code (Civil Code) took effect, repealing the Spanish Civil Code. As earlier noted, the arbitration-related provisions of the Spanish Civil Code were deemed repealed by the repeal of the Law on Civil Procedure. Notably, Article 2042 of the Civil Code re-enacted the former Article 1820 of the Spanish Civil Code providing that 'the same persons who may enter into a compromise may submit their controversies to one or more arbitrators for decision'.

A significant provision of the Civil Code was Article 2044 which provided that 'any stipulation that the arbitrators' award or decision shall be final, is valid.' The award, however, is subject to review by the courts if there is mistake, fraud, violence, intimidation, undue influence, or falsity of documents.[25] This is consistent with the rulings in *Allen v. the Province of Tayabas*[26] and *Chan Linte v. Law Union and Rock Insurance Co. Ltd.*[27] It would have been more correct, however, to make arbitration agreements subject to challenge on these grounds, rather than the arbitral awards themselves. Arbitration agreements, being contracts, may be questioned on grounds of mistake or fraud or anything that vitiates consent. But the arbitral award is not a contract and should not be subject to the same challenges to which contracts are subject.

The Civil Code, like the Spanish Civil Code, also recognised the applicability of the provisions on compromise to arbitration. Article 2043 provided that the provisions thereof on compromises shall also be applicable to arbitrations. It is unclear, however, and Philippine jurisprudence has not been able to clarify, how the provisions on compromise would actually apply to arbitrations considering that neither arbitration agreements nor arbitral awards constitute compromise agreements. It is likewise not clear whether the rules on compromises were intended to apply either to the arbitration agreement, or the arbitral award or both. In fact, certain provisions of the Civil Code on compromise are not applicable to arbitration. The provision that 'a compromise is a contract whereby the parties, by making reciprocal concessions, avoid a litigation or put an end to one already commenced'[28] does not exactly apply to arbitral awards which may

25 Article 2038 of the Civil Code was made applicable to arbitration. Article 2038 provides: 'A compromise in which there is mistake, fraud, violence, intimidation, undue influence, or falsity of documents, is subject to the provisions of article 1330 of this Code. However, one of parties cannot set up a mistake of fact as against the other if the latter, by virtue of the compromise, has withdrawn from a litigation already commenced.' Under article 1330, 'a contract where consent is given through mistake, violence, intimidation, undue influence, or fraud is voidable.'

26 *Supra* n. 24.

27 GR No. 16398, 14.12.1921.

28 Article 2028, Civil Code.

not necessarily involve reciprocal concessions. In the same manner, the provision that the 'court shall endeavour to persuade the litigants in a civil case to agree upon some fair compromise',[29] is likewise inapplicable. The function of arbitration is not necessarily to enable the parties to reach a compromise, but to be able to resolve a dispute through an award.

The Civil Code continued to reflect the early notion of arbitration expressed in Philippine jurisprudence. Even if the Civil Code provided that arbitral awards are final, they are subject to review on broad grounds – including mistake or fraud. Moreover, the applicability of the rules on compromises to arbitration is indicative of how Philippine Law continued to consider arbitration as a condition precedent to filing actions in court and/or that they are intended to ascertain factual issues, such as the amount of damages. The court shall endeavour to persuade the litigants in a civil case to agree upon some fair compromise.[30] This provision would only apply to arbitration on the premise that it is a condition precedent to court action.

It is, therefore, not apparent how and whether the Civil Code actually improved Philippine arbitration law. If the intention was to make arbitration an effective alternative to court litigation, it is not clear how this could have been achieved through the enactment of the Civil Code provisions on arbitration.

### *3.2.2. Domestic Arbitration Law*

On 19 December 1953, Republic Act No. 876, or the Arbitration Law,[31] was passed providing for a law on domestic arbitration. The Arbitration Law was enacted not to repeal but to supplement the provisions of the Civil Code. It provided for specific rules governing the arbitration process as well as proceedings relating to enforcement of arbitration agreements and the arbitral awards. Although this law is more than 50 years old, most of its provisions continue to apply to domestic arbitration.

#### 3.2.2.1. The Arbitration Law (Republic Act No. 876)

The Arbitration Law provides that 'arbitration agreements are valid, enforceable and irrevocable, save upon such grounds as exist at law for the revocation of any contract'[32] and that the subject matter thereof may either be existing or future disputes and may include questions arising out of valuations, appraisals or other controversies which may be collateral, incidental, precedent or subsequent to any issue between the parties.[33] With respect to the form of arbitration agreements,

29 Article 2029, *ibid.*
30 *Ibid.*
31 *Supra*, n 9.
32 Section 2, Arbitration Law.
33 *Ibid.*

the Arbitration Law requires not only that arbitration agreements be in writing, the same must likewise be subscribed by the party sought to be charged or by his lawful agent.[34] The Arbitration Law was effectively a legislative correction of the rulings in earlier cases, beginning with *Wahl et al. v. Donaldson, Sims & Co.*, which considered arbitration agreements as contrary to public policy unless they are mere conditions precedent to court action.

The rules governing the appointment of arbitrators,[35] the qualifications of arbitrators and requirements for disclosure,[36] and challenges against arbitrators[37] were likewise addressed by the Arbitration Law. To ensure that arbitrators discharge their duties properly, the law required arbitrators to be placed under oath to conduct the arbitration faithfully and fairly and to make a just award according to the best of their ability and understanding.[38]

Arbitrators were given the power to administer oaths to all witnesses,[39] to issue subpoena and subpoena *duces tecum*.[40] Significantly, the Arbitration Law already recognised the tribunal's power to issue interim measures in aid of arbitration by allowing it to take measures to safeguard and/or conserve any matter which is the subject of the dispute in arbitration.[41] The Arbitration Law further recognised the power of arbitrators to be the sole judge as to the relevancy and materiality of evidence without being bound by the rules of evidence governing court proceedings.[42] A notable feature of the law is the prohibition that 'no arbitrator shall act as a mediator in any proceeding in which he is acting as arbitrator; and all negotiations towards settlement of the dispute must take place without the presence of the arbitrators.'[43] Arbitrators are expressly allowed to grant any remedy or relief which they deem just and equitable as long as it is within the scope of the agreement of the parties, including specific performance of a contract.[44] They may assess in their award the expenses of any party against another party, when such assessment shall be deemed necessary.[45]

In order to give teeth to contractual agreements to arbitrate, the Arbitration Law provided for the enforcement of arbitration agreements by the courts[46] and for the courts' powers to refer parties to arbitration in cases where court

34 Section 4, *ibid.*
35 Section 8, *ibid.*
36 Section 10, *ibid.*
37 Section 11, *ibid.*
38 Section 13, *ibid.*
39 *Ibid.*
40 Section 14, *ibid.*
41 *Ibid.*
42 Section 15, *ibid.*
43 Section 20, *ibid.*
44 *Ibid.*
45 *Ibid.*
46 Section 6, *ibid.*

litigation is commenced before arbitration and to stay any civil action commenced in violation of arbitration agreements.[47] The law also provided for the rules relating to enforcement of awards, giving awards the same effect as court decisions.[48] Thus, at any time within one month after the award is made, any party to the dispute which was arbitrated may apply to the court having jurisdiction for an order confirming the award.[49]

The grounds for modifying or correcting an award are: (a) evident miscalculation of figures or evident mistake in the description of any person, thing or property; (b) award upon matters not submitted to arbitration when they do not affect the merits of the award upon matters submitted; or (c) imperfection in the award in a matter of form not affecting the merits of the controversy.[50] Notably, under the Arbitration Law, the power to correct or modify awards rests with the courts.

On the other hand, the grounds for setting aside an award are: (a) procurement of the award through corruption, fraud, or other undue means; (b) evident partiality or corruption of the arbitrators; (c) misconduct of arbitrators in refusing to postpone the hearing upon sufficient cause shown, or in refusing to hear evidence pertinent and material to the controversy; (d) wilful non-disclosure of a disqualification of one or more of the arbitrators or any arbitrator misbehaviour which materially prejudices the rights of any party; or (e) when the arbitrators exceed their powers, or execute them imperfectly, such that a mutual, final and definite award was not made.[51] A motion to vacate (i.e. set aside), modify or correct the award must be served upon the other party or his counsel within thirty days after the award is filed or delivered.[52] Based on the foregoing provisions of the Arbitration Law, merits-review of arbitral awards appears to be precluded. However, notwithstanding the provisions of the Arbitration Law, the Supreme Court continued to take the view that arbitral awards are subject to review on the merits.

In *ABS-CBN Broadcasting Corporation v. World Interactive Network Systems (WINS) Japan Co. Ltd*,[53] the Supreme Court took the view that the judicial remedies available to a party aggrieved by an arbitral award are: (a) a petition in the proper trial court to issue an order to vacate the award, pursuant to the Arbitration Law; (b) a petition for review with the Court of Appeals under Rule 43 of the 1997 Rules of Civil Procedure on questions of fact, of law, or mixed questions of fact and law; and (c) a petition for certiorari with the Court of Appeals under Rule 65 of the Rules of Court should the arbitrator have acted

---

47 Section 7, *ibid.*
48 Section 28, *ibid.*
49 Section 23, *ibid.*
50 Section 25, *ibid.*
51 Section 24, *ibid.*
52 Section 26, *ibid.*
53 GR No. 169332, 11.02.2008.

without or in excess of his jurisdiction or with grave abuse of discretion amounting to lack or excess of jurisdiction. The Supreme Court correctly noted that the Arbitration Law did not provide for errors of fact and/or law and grave abuse of discretion (proper grounds for a Rule 43 petition for review and a Rule 65 petition for certiorari, respectively) as grounds for maintaining a petition to vacate an arbitral award in the trial court. It, however, incorrectly concluded that in cases not covered by the Arbitration Law, a Rule 43 or Rule 65 petition may be availed of in the Court of Appeals depending on the grounds available. The Supreme Court noted that Rule 43 of the 1997 Rules of Civil Procedure expressly applies to awards, judgments, final orders or resolutions of quasi-judicial agencies including voluntary arbitrators authorised by law. With respect to the availability of a Rule 65 Petition to question the arbitral award on grounds of grave abuse of discretion, the Supreme Court stressed that it will not hesitate to review a voluntary arbitrator's award where there is a showing of grave abuse of authority or discretion and there is no appeal, nor any plain, speedy remedy in the course of law.

#### 3.2.2.2. The ADR Act and domestic arbitration

In 2004, Congress enacted Republic Act No. 9285, or the ADR Act, to provide for a more comprehensive law on arbitration (i.e. covering both domestic and international arbitration), as well as ADR in general (including mediation and other modes of ADR). The ADR Act provides that the Arbitration Law shall continue to govern domestic arbitration which was defined as an arbitration that is not international as defined under the UNCITRAL Model Law.[54]

Several provisions of the Arbitration Law were amended by the ADR Act to give way to the application of certain provisions of the Model Law, such as the provisions on (a) referral of parties bound by an arbitration agreement to arbitration (Article 8), number and appointment of arbitrators, challenges against arbitrators and failure or impossibility to act by arbitrators (Articles 10, 11, 12, 13 and 14), equal treatment of parties (Article 18) and determination of rules of procedure by the tribunal (Article 19), decision making by the tribunal (Article 29), settlement (Article 30), form and contents of awards (Article 31), termination of proceedings (Article 32), as well as other provisions of the ADR Act, e.g. on interim measures of protection.[55] However, certain provisions of the Arbitration Law, including the provisions requiring that arbitration agreements must be subscribed or signed and those providing for the grounds for challenging or setting aside domestic arbitral awards, were retained.

---

54 UNCITRAL Model Law on International Commercial Arbitration, adopted by the Philippines through the ADR Act, *supra* n. 10.

55 Section 33, ADR Act.

The ADR Act was a significant development in Philippine arbitration history inasmuch as it provided the implementing legislation for international commercial arbitration in the Philippines and the recognition and enforcement of foreign arbitral awards. However, it fell short of uplifting the standards with respect to domestic arbitration. It made little sense, for example, that the provisions of the Model Law granting the tribunal powers to correct, interpret and make additional awards were not expressly made applicable to domestic arbitration. Moreover, why the grounds for challenging or setting aside awards under the Model Law were not adopted for domestic arbitration escapes any rational explanation. Domestic arbitration would have been significantly improved had the ADR Act simply adopted the Model Law for domestic arbitrations as well. Instead, to date, domestic arbitration continues to be governed by the Arbitration Law, while international commercial arbitration is governed by the Model Law – a dual commercial arbitration system.

### *3.2.3. Law on enforcement of foreign arbitral awards*

After the enactment of the Arbitration Law in 1953, the next significant development in Philippine arbitration took place in 1958 when the Philippines became a signatory to the United Nations Convention on the Recognition and Enforcement of Foreign Arbitral Awards or the New York Convention.[56] The Philippines signed the convention with the reservation that it did so on the basis of reciprocity and with a declaration that the Philippines will apply the same to the recognition and enforcement of awards made only in the territory of another convention State. Subsequently, the Philippine Senate, upon ratification of the convention, adopted a second reservation that it will apply the convention only to disputes arising out of commercial legal relationships.[57]

In giving its concurrence to the ratification of the New York Convention, the Philippine Senate recognised that the Arbitration Law did not contain any provision wherein an arbitration agreement between parties of different nationalities could be validly enforced in the Philippines.[58] Even prior to the signing of the New York Convention, however, the Supreme Court had already recognised the enforceability of foreign arbitral awards in the Philippines. In *Eastboard Navigation Ltd v. Juan Ysmael and Company, Inc.*, the Supreme Court

56 *Supra* n 2.

57 The reservations were pursuant to Article I(3) of the New York Convention which provides that '[w]hen signing, ratifying or acceding to this Convention, or notifying extension under article X hereof, any State may on the basis of reciprocity declare that it will apply the Convention to the recognition and enforcement of awards made only in the territory of another Contracting State. It may also declare that it will apply the Convention only to differences arising out of legal relationships, whether contractual or not, which are considered as commercial under the national law of the State making such declaration.'

58 Senate Resolution No. 71, 6th Whereas Clause.

directed the enforcement of an award issued in New York, ruling that 'arbitration, as an inexpensive speedy and amicable method of settling disputes, and as a means of avoiding litigation, should receive every encouragement from the courts which may be extended without contravening sound public policy or settled law.'[59] The Supreme Court noted that Congress had officially adopted this modern view when it reproduced in the Civil Code the provisions of the Spanish Civil Code on arbitration and when it approved the Arbitration Law.

The ADR Act of 2004 implements the provisions of the New York Convention. It clarified that arbitral awards are not foreign judgments and shall be enforced as foreign arbitral awards even if confirmed by a foreign court.[60] However, foreign arbitral awards issued in arbitrations seated in countries not party to the New York Convention may nevertheless be enforced on grounds of comity and reciprocity as a convention award.[61]

Under the ADR Act, the grounds to oppose or refuse recognition of foreign arbitral awards are limited to those provided in the New York Convention.[62] Thus, the rule that corporations doing business in the Philippines without licence do not have standing to sue before a Philippine court does not apply to enforcement of foreign arbitral awards. According to the court:

> 'Indeed, it is in the best interest of justice that in the enforcement of a foreign arbitral award, we deny availment by the losing party of the rule that bars foreign corporations not licensed to do business in the Philippines from maintaining a suit in our courts. When a party enters into a contract containing a foreign arbitration clause and, as in this case, in fact submits itself to arbitration, it becomes bound by the contract, by the arbitration and by the result of arbitration, conceding thereby the capacity of the other party to enter into the contract, participate in the arbitration and cause the implementation of the result.'

### 3.2.4. *Law on international commercial arbitration*

In 2004, the ADR Act was enacted and the Philippines began to pull itself alongside the rest of the modern arbitration world. Since it is procedural in nature, its provisions may be given retroactive effect.[63] The ADR Act covers both commercial arbitration and commercial mediation/conciliation, as well as other modes of ADR including early neutral evaluation, mini-trial, or any combination thereof.

The ADR Act declared it a policy of the State to actively promote party autonomy in the resolution of disputes or the freedom of the parties to make

59 GR No. L-9090, 10.09.1957, citing 3 *Am. Jur.*, p. 835.
60 Section 43, ADR Act.
61 *Ibid.*
62 *Tuna Processing, Inc. v. Philippine Kingford, Inc.*, GR No. 185582, 29.02.2012.
63 *Korea Technologies Co. Ltd v. Hon. Alberto A. Lerma, et al.*, GR No. 143581, 07.01.2008.

their own arrangements to resolve their disputes[64] and required the courts to give due regard to the policy of the law in favour of arbitration.[65] Being a special law on ADR, the Act must take precedence over laws of general application.[66]

Under the Act, the ADR system is defined as any process or procedure used to resolve a dispute or controversy, other than by adjudication of a presiding judge of a court or an officer of a government agency in which a neutral third party participates to assist in the resolution of issues.[67] In other words, the ADR Act excludes from its coverage statutory ADR. Similar to the limitations in domestic arbitration, the ADR Act further excludes from its application, resolution or settlement of disputes relating to the civil status of persons, the validity of a marriage, any ground for legal separation, the jurisdiction of courts, future legitime (or share of compulsory heirs in a person's estate), criminal liability, and those rights which by law cannot be compromised.[68]

The ADR Act adopted the 1985 version of the UNCITRAL Model Law. It provided that in interpreting the provisions of the Model Law, regard shall be had to its international origin and to the need for uniformity in its interpretation.[69] Following the Model Law, the requirement under the Arbitration Law that an arbitration agreement must be subscribed by the parties thereto does not apply to international arbitrations.[70] Moreover, the ADR Act recognised the power of an arbitral tribunal to rule on its own jurisdiction, or the principle of competence-competence.[71]

To differentiate it from domestic arbitration under the Arbitration Law, the ADR Act adopted the meaning of international arbitration under the Model Law, thus:

> '(3) An arbitration is international if:
> (a) the parties to an arbitration agreement have, at the time of the conclusion of that agreement, their places of business in different States; or
> (b) one of the following places is situated outside the State in which the parties have their places of business: (i) the place of arbitration if determined in, or pursuant to, the arbitration agreement; (ii) any place where a substantial part of the obligations of the commercial relationship is to be performed or the place with which the subject-matter of the dispute is most closely connected; or
> (c) the parties have expressly agreed that the subject-matter of the arbitration agreement relates to more than one country.'

64 Section 2, ADR Act.
65 Section 25, *ibid.*
66 *Tuna Processing, Inc. v. Philippine Kingford, Inc., supra* n. 63.
67 Section 3(a), ADR Act.
68 Section 6, *ibid.*
69 Sections 19 and 20, *ibid.*
70 Article 7(2), UNCITRAL Model Law.
71 Article 16, *ibid.*

Courts are mandated to refer parties to arbitration for as long as an action involves a matter which is the subject matter of an arbitration agreement and it does not find that the arbitration agreement is null and void, inoperative or incapable of being performed.[72] Where an action is commenced by or against multiple parties, one or more of whom are parties to an arbitration agreement, the court shall refer to arbitration those parties who are bound by the arbitration agreement although the civil action may continue as to those who are not bound by such arbitration agreement.[73] The ADR Act slightly deviated from the Model Law when it set the deadline for requesting referral to arbitration to before the pre-trial conference,[74] as opposed to the Model Law which sets the time to before the submission of a party's first statement on the substance of the dispute.[75] Like in domestic arbitration, the ADR Act recognised the power of the courts and of the tribunal in international arbitration to grant interim measures of protection.[76]

The default appointing authority for purposes of international arbitration (which was also made applicable to domestic arbitration) is the National President of the Integrated Bar of the Philippines[77] or his duly authorised representative. On the other hand, when the agreement provides for institutional arbitration, the appointing authority shall be the person or institution named in the arbitration agreement as the appointing authority; or the regular arbitration institution under whose rules the arbitration is agreed to be conducted.[78]

### 3.2.5. *Special Rules of Court on ADR*

The Supreme Court's Special Rules on Alternative Dispute Resolution (ADR Rules)[79] finally provided clear guidelines on the role of the courts in relation to commercial ADR proceedings.

The ADR Rules apply to and govern court proceedings relating to petitions: (a) to determine the existence, validity, or enforceability of the arbitration agreement; (b) to refer parties to ADR; (c) for interim measures of protection; (d) for appointment, challenge and termination of mandate of arbitrators; (e) for assistance in taking evidence; (f) for confirmation, correction or vacation of award in domestic arbitration; (g) for recognition and enforcement or setting aside of an award in international commercial arbitration; (h) for recognition

---

72 Section 24, *ibid.*
73 Section 25, *ibid.*
74 Section 24, *ibid.*
75 Article 8(1), UNCITRAL Model Law.
76 Sections 28–29, ADR Act.
77 The Integrated Bar of the Philippines is the official organisation of all Philippine lawyers, membership of which is necessary to enable one to practice law in the Philippines.
78 Section 26, ADR Act.
79 Supreme Court Administrative Matter No. 07-11-08-SC, 30.10.2009.

and enforcement of a foreign arbitral award; and (i) for confidentiality/protective orders.[80]

The ADR Rules clarified that where the parties have agreed to submit their dispute to arbitration, courts must refer the parties to arbitration. It further stated that the courts shall not refuse to refer parties to arbitration simply because the referral tends to oust a court of its jurisdiction, or that the courts are in a better position to resolve the dispute, or that the referral would result in multiplicity of suits, among others.[81] On the other hand, if court intervention is proper, courts are not to refuse to intervene on the grounds that the principal action is the subject of an arbitration agreement or that it is already pending before an arbitral tribunal.[82] All in all, the ADR Rules sent a strong message to the lower courts to give effect to arbitration agreements.

It further clarified that all proceedings relating to the foregoing are special proceedings and, therefore, do not require service of summons on the other party for the court to acquire personal jurisdiction.[83] Moreover, except with respect to confirmation, correction or vacation of award in domestic arbitration, recognition and enforcement or setting aside of an award in international commercial arbitration and recognition and enforcement of a foreign arbitral award, proceedings under the ADR Rules are summary in nature and are to be resolved in 30 days.[84]

The ADR Rules expressly recognised the principles of *kompetenz-kompetenz* and of the separability of arbitration agreements for both domestic and international arbitrations.[85] Courts are required to accord the arbitral tribunal the first opportunity to rule on the issue of whether or not it has the competence or jurisdiction to decide a dispute submitted to it for decision, including any objection with respect to the existence or validity of the arbitration agreement.[86] The courts must exercise judicial restraint and defer to the competence or jurisdiction of the arbitral tribunal by allowing the arbitral tribunal the first opportunity to rule upon such issues[87] and if it has to make a determination, it must make no more than a prima facie determination of that issue.[88] Pursuant to the principle of separability of the arbitration clause, an arbitration clause shall be treated as an agreement independent of the other terms of the contract of which it forms part.[89]

---

80 Rule 1.1, *ibid.*
81 Rule 2.2, *ibid.*
82 *Ibid.*
83 Rule 1.2, *ibid.*
84 Rule 1.3, *ibid.*
85 *Ibid.*
86 Rule 2.4, *ibid.*
87 *Ibid.*
88 *Ibid.*
89 Rule 2.2, *ibid.*

Peculiarly, the ADR Rules broadened the application of the rule in domestic arbitration that no arbitrator shall act as a mediator in any proceedings in which he is acting as arbitrator or vice-versa, to international arbitrations.[90] This, however, does not preclude parties to a settlement agreement from agreeing that the mediator shall become the sole arbitrator for purposes of issuing a consent award.[91]

With respect to review of arbitral awards, the ADR Rules provide that an agreement to refer a dispute to arbitration shall mean that the arbitral award shall be final and binding and that, consequently, a party to an arbitration is precluded from filing an appeal or a petition for certiorari questioning the merits of an arbitral award.[92]

As a general rule, the court can only vacate or set aside an award upon a clear showing that the grounds provided under the Arbitration Law, the Model Law or the New York Convention are present. If the court is asked to set aside or refuse recognition of an arbitral award in a domestic or international arbitration on any ground other than those provided in the ADR Rules, the court shall entertain such ground only if the same amounts to a violation of public policy. The courts shall not set aside or vacate the award of the arbitral tribunal merely on the ground that the arbitral tribunal committed errors of fact, or of law, or of fact and law. The court cannot substitute its judgment for that of the arbitral tribunal.[93] With respect to foreign arbitral awards, the court can deny recognition and enforcement of a foreign arbitral award only upon the grounds provided in the New York Convention and they cannot vacate or set aside a foreign arbitral award.[94]

## 3.3. STATUTE-BASED ARBITRATIONS

Along with the development of commercial arbitration in the country, various legislation also provided for arbitration as a mode of alternative dispute resolution for specific disputes. The essential characteristic of these forms of arbitration is that they are statute-based, i.e. the law prescribes their use – which begs the question as to whether they can really be considered to be 'alternative' modes of dispute resolution considering that they are most of the time 'compulsory' which goes against the voluntary nature of commercial arbitration.

90 Rule 2.6, *ibid.*
91 Rule 2.7, *ibid.*
92 Rule 19.7, *ibid.*
93 Rule 19.10, *ibid.*
94 Rule 19.11, *ibid.*

### 3.3.1. *Arbitration under the Labor Code*

#### 3.3.1.1. Labor Code

On 29 October 1936, Commonwealth Act No. 103 created the Court of Industrial Relations.[95] This Act was subsequently repealed by the Labor Code of the Philippines, a more comprehensive legislation relating to labour-related matters, but it nevertheless set the stage for what was to become an institutional use of ADR in the resolution of labour-related disputes. In *Chung Fu Industries (Philippines) Inc. et al. v. Court of Appeals et al.*,[96] the Supreme Court described arbitration as having found a 'fertile field in the resolution of labour-management disputes in the Philippines.'

The Court of Industrial Relations was empowered to 'take cognizance for purposes of prevention, arbitration, decision and settlement, of any industrial or agricultural dispute causing or likely to cause a strike or lockout, arising from differences as regards wages, shares or compensation, hours of labor or conditions of tenancy or employment, between employers and employees or laborers and between landlords and tenants or farm-laborers.'[97] Describing the procedure to be taken by the Court of Industrial Relations, the Act provides that the court 'shall, before hearing the dispute and in the course of such hearing, endeavor to reconcile the parties and induce them to settle the dispute by amicable agreement.'[98] If an agreement is reached, a written memorandum of its terms, which will be binding as a decision or award, shall be signed and acknowledged before a judge of the court and filed in the office of the clerk of the court.[99]

The Commonwealth Act No. 103 was subsequently repealed and ultimately replaced by Presidential Decree No. 442 or the Labor Code.

#### 3.3.1.2. Jurisdiction of the Secretary of Labor and the NLRC

The Secretary of Labor and Employment continued to have the power to assume jurisdiction over a dispute and decide it or refer the same to the National Labor Relations Commission for compulsory arbitration when, in his opinion, there

---

95 Commonwealth Act No. 103: 'An act to afford protection of labour by creating a Court of Industrial Relations empowered to fix minimum wages for labourers and maximum rentals to be paid by tenants, and to enforce compulsory arbitration between employees or landlords, and employees or tenants, respectively; and by prescribing penalties for the violation of its orders', 29.10.1936.

96 GR No. 96283, 25.02.1992.

97 Section 4, Commonwealth Act No. 103.

98 *Ibid.*

99 *Ibid.*

exists a labour dispute causing or likely to cause a strike or lockout in an industry indispensable to the national interest.[100]

The National Labor Relations Commission was given the powers previously vested in the Court of Industrial Relations. Disputes arising from wage distortions,[101] if not resolved through voluntary arbitration or conciliation are likewise subject to the compulsory jurisdiction of the National Labor Relations Commission.[102]

#### 3.3.1.3. Labour arbiters

The Labor Code established the office of the Labor Arbiter which was given the original and exclusive jurisdiction to hear and decide cases involving unfair labour practice cases, termination disputes, cases involving wages, rate of pay, hours of work and other terms and conditions of employment if accompanied with a claim for reinstatement, claims for actual, moral, exemplary and other forms of damages arising from the employer–employee relations, cases involving the legality of strikes, lockouts and certain prohibited activities, and all other claims arising from employer–employee relations involving an amount exceeding five thousand pesos, except claims for employees' compensation, social security, medicare and maternity benefits.[103]

The procedure before labour arbiters is akin to commercial arbitration in that the rules of evidence prevailing in courts of law are not controlling, and it is the spirit and intention of the Labor Code which shall prevail in proceedings before labour arbiters. Thus, labour arbiters are required to take every reasonable means to ascertain the facts in each case speedily and objectively, without regard to technicalities of law or procedure, in the interests of due process.[104]

However, unlike commercial arbitration, decisions of labour arbiters may be appealed to the National Labor Relations Commission which has exclusive appellate jurisdiction over all cases decided by labour arbiters.[105] The grounds for appeal are abuse of discretion, fraud or coercion or graft and corruption, pure questions of law and serious errors in the findings of facts causing grave or irreparable damage or injury to the appellant.[106]

---

100 Article 263, Labor Code, *supra* n. 4.

101 A situation where an increase in prescribed wage rates results in the elimination or severe contraction of intentional quantitative differences in wage or salary rates between and among employee groups in an establishment as to effectively obliterate the distinctions embodied in such wage structure based on skills, length of service, or other logical bases of differentiation.

102 Article 124, Labor Code.

103 Article 217-A, *ibid.*

104 Article 221, *ibid.*

105 Article 217-B, *ibid.*

106 Article 223, *ibid.*

### 3.3.1.4. Voluntary arbitrators

Parties to labour proceedings may agree to submit their dispute to voluntary arbitration.[107] While the ADR Act excludes labour disputes from its coverage, it does not follow that labour disputes may not be arbitrated. Parties to a labour dispute may submit to the jurisdiction of a voluntary arbitrator. The jurisdiction of voluntary arbitrators[108] covers the following disputes:

(a) original and exclusive jurisdiction to hear and decide all unresolved grievances arising from the interpretation or implementation of collective bargaining agreements, except violations thereof which are gross in character (i.e. flagrant and/or malicious refusal to comply with the economic provisions of such agreement) and those arising from the interpretation or enforcement of company personnel policies;[109] all grievances submitted to the grievance procedure which are not settled within 7 calendar days from the date of its submission are automatically referred to voluntary arbitration prescribed in the collective bargaining agreement;[110]
(b) upon agreement of the parties, voluntary arbitrators may also hear and decide all other labour disputes including unfair labour practices and bargaining deadlocks;[111]
(c) disputes causing or likely to cause a strike or lockout in an industry indispensable to the national interest may before or at any stage of the compulsory arbitration process, be referred to voluntary arbitration upon agreement of the parties;[112] and
(d) disputes arising from wage distortions, before they are submitted for compulsory arbitration, are to be resolved through the grievance procedure in the collective bargaining agreement between the parties, and, if they remain unresolved, by voluntary arbitration.

The procedure in voluntary arbitration is quite similar to the procedure in commercial arbitration insofar as it gives the parties and the tribunal much freedom so far as procedural matters are concerned.

---

107 Article 262, *ibid.*

108 Article 212 of the Labor Code provides that voluntary arbitrations are to be presided by voluntary arbitrators, who are persons who may be accredited by the National Conciliation and Mediation Board, or any person named or designated in the collective bargaining agreement by the parties to act as their voluntary arbitrator, or one chosen pursuant to a selection procedure agreed upon in the collective bargaining agreement, or any official that may be authorised by the Secretary of Labor and Employment to act as voluntary arbitrator.

109 Articles 217(c) and Article 261, Labor Code, *supra* n. 4.

110 Article 260, *ibid.*

111 Article 262, *ibid.*

112 Article 263, *ibid.*

(a) The parties generally name and designate in advance a voluntary arbitrator or panel of voluntary arbitrators, or include in the agreement a procedure for the selection of such voluntary arbitrator or panel of voluntary arbitrators. In case this fails, the National Conciliation and Mediation Board designates the voluntary arbitrator or panel of voluntary arbitrators.[113]
(b) Voluntary arbitrators may hold hearings, receive evidence and take whatever action is necessary to resolve the issue or issues subject of the dispute. They may include efforts to effect a voluntary settlement between parties, in effect acting as mediators.
(c) Upon the motion of any interested party, a writ of execution may be issued requiring either the sheriff of the Commission or of the regular courts or any public official whom the parties may designate in the submission agreement to execute the final decision, order or award.[114]

While voluntary arbitration under the Labor Code may be considered very similar to commercial arbitration, it presents a significant downside in that awards in voluntary arbitration are subject to merits review by the Court of Appeals. Rule 43 of the 1997 Rules of Civil Procedure provides the Court of Appeals with jurisdiction to review awards of voluntary arbitrators on questions of law or fact.[115]

#### *3.3.2. Arbitration under the Local Government Code*

In 1992, arbitration was also institutionalised under the Local Government Code[116] as a means of resolving disputes among members of a village or neighbouring villages (called *Barangay(s)* in the Filipino language). This dispute resolution mechanism is called *Katarungang Pambarangay* (literally, 'village justice').

The *Katarungang Pambarangay* system consists of the *Lupong Tagapamayapa* or *Lupon* (literally, 'Council of Peacemakers') composed of the chairman of the barangay and ten to twenty members and the *Pangkat ng Tagapagkasundo* or *Pangkat* (literally, conciliation panels) consisting of three members who shall be chosen by the parties to the dispute from the list of members of the *Lupon*.

The *Lupon* of each *barangay* has jurisdiction over disputes between parties who are residents of the same city or municipality, except: (a) where one party is the government, or any subdivision or instrumentality thereof; (b) where one party is a public officer or employee, and the dispute relates to the performance of his official functions; (c) offences punishable by imprisonment exceeding one

113 Article 260, *ibid.*
114 Article 262-A, *ibid.*
115 Rule 43, Section 3, 1997 Rules of Civil Procedure.
116 *Supra* n. 5.

year or a fine exceeding PhP 5,000; (d) where the offence does not involve any private offended party; (e) where the dispute involves real properties located in different cities or municipalities unless the parties agree; (f) where the dispute involves residents of *barangays* of different cities or municipalities, except where such *barangay* units adjoin each other and the parties agree; and (g) such other classes of disputes which the President may determine in the interests of justice or upon the recommendation of the Secretary of Justice. The court in which non-criminal cases not falling within the authority of the *Lupon* are filed, may *motu proprio* refer the case to the *Lupon* concerned for amicable settlement.[117]

Under the *Katarungang Pambarangay* system, no covered action or proceedings shall be filed directly in court or any other government office, unless there has been a confrontation between the parties before the *Lupon* chairman or the *Pangkat*, and no conciliation or settlement has been reached or unless the settlement has been repudiated by the parties thereto.[118] Parties may directly resort to court only: (a) where the accused is under detention; (b) where a person has otherwise been deprived of personal liberty; (c) where actions are coupled with provisional remedies such as preliminary injunction or attachment, among others; and (d) where the action may otherwise be barred by the statute of limitations.[119]

The *Katarungang Pambarangay* system involves the use of both mediation and arbitration. The procedure for mediation is discussed in the latter part of this chapter. The pendency of mediation/arbitration proceedings suspends the prescriptive period for the offence for a period of not more than 60 days from the filing of the complaint.[120]

The parties may, at any stage of the proceedings, agree in writing that they shall comply with the award of the *Lupon* chairman or the *Pangkat*. Such an agreement may be repudiated within five days from the date thereof. The arbitration award shall be made after the lapse of the period for repudiation and within ten days thereafter.[121] The arbitration award shall be in writing in a language or dialect known to the parties.[122] The parties must appear in person without the assistance of counsel or representative, except for minors and incompetents who may be assisted by their next-of-kin who are not lawyers.[123]

The award shall have the force and effect of a final judgment of a court upon the expiration of ten days from the date thereof, unless the same is repudiated or a petition to nullify the award is filed before the proper city or municipal

117 Section 408, *ibid.*
118 Section 412(a), *ibid.*
119 Section 412(b), *ibid.*
120 Section 410(c), *ibid.*
121 Section 413(a), *ibid.*
122 Section 413(b), *ibid.*
123 Section 415, *ibid.*

court.[124] Repudiation may be made on the basis of vitiated consent, either due to fraud, violence, or intimidation. It may be made within ten days from the date of the settlement by filing a sworn statement with the *Lupon* chairman. A repudiation provides sufficient basis for the issuance of certification for the filing of a complaint with the court.[125]

The amicable settlement or arbitration award may be enforced by execution by the *Lupon* within six months from the date of the settlement. Thereafter, the settlement may be enforced by action in the appropriate city or municipal court.[126]

### 3.3.3. *Construction arbitration*

Construction arbitration in the Philippines may be characterised as having characteristics peculiar to both commercial and statute-based arbitrations. While construction disputes are considered commercial under Philippine law,[127] the ADR Act provides that construction arbitrations are to be governed by Executive Order No. 1008[128] or the Construction Industry Arbitration Law.[129]

Construction arbitration was given a special place in Philippine arbitration in view of the importance of the construction industry to the Philippine economy. In 1985, then President Ferdinand Marcos issued Executive Order No. 1008 and declared it a policy of the State to encourage the early and expeditious settlement of disputes in the Philippine construction industry.[130] The Order also established the Construction Industry Arbitration Commission or the CIAC.[131]

#### 3.3.3.1. CIAC original and exclusive jurisdiction

The CIAC has original and exclusive jurisdiction over disputes arising from, or connected with, contracts entered into by parties involved in construction in the Philippines, whether the dispute arises before or after the completion of the contract, or after the abandonment or breach thereof and whether the dispute arises from government or private contracts.[132]

For the CIAC to acquire jurisdiction, the parties must agree to submit the same to voluntary arbitration, whether before or after the dispute arises.[133] This

124 Section 516(b), *ibid.*
125 Section 418, *ibid.*
126 Section 417, *ibid.*
127 Section 21, ADR Act.
128 *Supra* n. 7.
129 Section 34 of the ADR Act provides that the CIAC shall continue to exercise original and exclusive jurisdiction over construction disputes even though the arbitration is commercial.
130 Section 2, *ibid.*
131 Section 3, *ibid.*
132 Section 4, *ibid.*
133 *Ibid.*

agreement must be in writing but it need not be signed by the parties, as long as the intent is clear that the parties agree to submit a present or future controversy arising from a construction contract to arbitration.[134]

In the landmark case of *China Chang Jiang Energy Corporation (Philippines) v. Rosal Infrastructure Builders and the Court of Appeals*,[135] the Supreme Court ruled that 'an arbitration clause in a construction contract or a submission to arbitration of a construction dispute shall be deemed an agreement to submit an existing or future controversy to CIAC jurisdiction, notwithstanding the reference to a different arbitration institution or arbitral body in such contract or submission.' While parties are free to choose arbitration as a mode of dispute resolution, they may not divest the CIAC of its jurisdiction. A court before which a construction dispute is filed shall, upon becoming aware, not later than the pre-trial conference, that the parties had entered into an arbitration agreement, dismiss the case and refer the parties to arbitration to be conducted by the CIAC.[136]

#### 3.3.3.2. CIAC jurisdiction over construction contracts or construction disputes

In the case of *Prudential Guarantee and Assurance Inc. v. Anscor Land Inc.*,[137] the Supreme Court explained that 'EO No. 1008 expressly vests in the CIAC original and exclusive jurisdiction over disputes arising from or connected with construction contracts entered into by parties that have agreed to submit their dispute to voluntary arbitration. Under the aforementioned provision, it is apparent that a dispute must meet two (2) requirements in order to fall under the jurisdiction of the CIAC: first, the dispute must be somehow connected to a construction contract; and second, the parties must have agreed to submit the dispute to arbitration proceedings.' In *Philrock, Inc. v. CIAC*,[138] the Supreme Court ruled that the CIAC has original and exclusive jurisdiction over disputes arising from or connected with construction contracts entered into by parties that have agreed to submit their dispute to voluntary arbitration. The test would appear to be whether the contract involved is a construction contract.

The Rules of Procedure of the CIAC,[139] however, focuses not on the nature of the contract but of the dispute. Section 2.1 provides that the CIAC shall have original and exclusive jurisdiction over 'construction disputes'. CIAC's jurisdiction covers those disputes involving violation of specifications for materials and workmanship, violation of the terms of agreement, interpretation and/or application of contractual provisions, maintenance and defects,

134 *Ibid.*, see also Section 4.1.2, CIAC Rules, *infra* n. 138.
135 GR No. 125706, 30.09.1996.
136 Section 39, ADR Act.
137 GR No. 177240, 8.09.2010.
138 (2001) 412 *Phil.* 236.
139 Revised Rules of Procedure Governing Construction Arbitration, 19.11.2005.

payment, default of employer or contractor and changes in contract cost, amount of damages and penalties, commencement time and delays and maintenance and defects.[140] 'Construction' was defined as referring to 'all on-site works on buildings or altering structures, from land clearance through completion including excavation, erection and assembly and installation of components and equipment' in *Gammon Philippines, Inc. v. Metro Rail Transit Development Corporation*.[141] In another case, the Supreme Court ruled that the jurisdiction of the CIAC is not limited to those enumerated by law but may include disputes which are of the same or a closely related kind or species.[142] The ADR Act further defined 'construction dispute' as including those between or among parties to, or who are otherwise bound by, an arbitration agreement, directly or by reference, whether such parties are project owner, contractor, subcontractor, fabricator, project manager, design professional, consultant, quantity surveyor, bondsman or issuer of an insurance policy in a construction project.[143]

Philippine rules and jurisprudence have described the CIAC's jurisdiction broadly either by reference to construction contracts or to construction disputes. It is not clear, however, whether or not the CIAC would have jurisdiction if a dispute arises from a construction contract but does not technically involve a construction dispute or if the dispute may be characterised as a construction dispute but does not arise from a purely construction contract.

#### 3.3.3.3. Appointment of arbitrators in CIAC arbitrations

As a general rule, only CIAC-accredited arbitrators may be appointed as arbitrators in CIAC arbitrations.[144] CIAC may appoint an arbitrator who is not CIAC-accredited only when the nominee: (a) is the parties' common nominee; (b) possesses the technical/legal competence to handle the construction dispute involved; and (c) has signified his availability/acceptance of his possible appointments.[145]

After the enactment of the ADR Act,[146] the CIAC revised its rules to allow appointment of foreign arbitrators. A foreign arbitrator not accredited by CIAC

140 Section 2.1.1, *ibid.*

141 GR No. 144792, 31.01.2006.

142 *Fort Bonifacio Development Corporation vs. Domingo*, GR No. 180765, 27.02.2009.

143 Section 2.2, CIAC Rules; see also Section 35, ADR Act.

144 Section 14, EO 1008.

145 Section 8.2, CIAC Rules.

146 Section 37, ADR Act provides: 'Appointment of Foreign Arbitrator. – The Construction Industry Arbitration Commission (CIAC) shall promulgate rules to allow for the appointment of a foreign arbitrator or coarbitrator or chairman of a tribunal a person who has not been previously accredited by CIAC: Provided that: (a) the dispute is a construction dispute in which one party is an international party; (b) the person to be appointed agreed to abide by the arbitration rules and policies of CIAC; (c) he/she is either coarbitrator upon the

may be appointed as a co-arbitrator or chairperson of an arbitral tribunal for a construction dispute under the following conditions: (a) the dispute is a construction dispute in which one party is an international party i.e. one whose place of business is outside the Philippines; and (b) the foreign arbitrator to be appointed is not a national of the Philippines and is not of the same nationality as the international party in the dispute.

### 3.3.3.4. Tribunal's powers in a CIAC arbitration

The arbitral tribunal in a CIAC arbitration has authority to resolve a motion to dismiss based on lack of jurisdiction[147] and a party's jurisdictional challenge is not waived by participating in the nomination process including challenging the qualifications of a nominee, applying for extension of time to file appropriate pleadings/motion to dismiss, opposing an application for interim relief and the filing of a motion to dismiss/suspend proceedings.[148] The arbitral tribunal may direct any person, board, body, tribunal, or government office, agency or instrumentality, or corporation to produce real or documentary evidence necessary for the proper adjudication of the issues.[149]

While the ADR Act states that construction arbitration shall continue to be governed by Executive Order No. 1008, certain provisions thereof, e.g. granting of interim measures,[150] directly apply to construction arbitration, suggesting that construction arbitration should be considered a form of ADR within the meaning of the ADR Act.[151] The arbitral tribunal may issue interim measures of protection to ensure the enforcement of the award, to prevent irreparable loss or injury or deterioration of property, to minimise or avoid undue delays in the project or contract implementation, to provide security for the performance of any obligation, to produce or preserve any evidence, and such other measures deemed by the arbitral tribunal to be necessary to prevent a miscarriage of justice or abuse of rights of any of the parties.[152]

---

nomination of the international party; or he/she is the common choice of the two CIAC-accredited arbitrators first appointed, one of whom was nominated by the international party; and (d) the foreign arbitrator shall be of different nationality from the international party.'

147 Section 2.4, CIAC Rules.

148 Section 2.5, *ibid.*

149 Section 13.5.1, *ibid.*

150 Section 33, ADR Act.

151 Section 3(a) of the ADR Act defines ADR as 'any process or procedure used to resolve a dispute or controversy, other than by adjudication of a presiding judge of a court or an officer of a government agency, as defined in this Act, in which a neutral third party participates to assist in the resolution of issues, which includes arbitration, mediation, conciliation, early neutral evaluation, minitrial, or any combination thereof.'

152 Section 14.1, CIAC Rules.

### 3.3.3.5. Proceedings in CIAC arbitrations

CIAC tribunals must act according to justice and equity and merits of the case, without regard to technicalities or legal forms and need not be bound by any technical rule of evidence. The tribunal, however, has the power to exercise complete control over all proceedings to ensure a speedy, adequate and justifiable disposition of the disputes and cases submitted to them for resolution.[153] Instead of a formal hearing, the parties may agree to submit the issues for resolution after the filing of pleadings, evidence, memoranda or draft decisions.[154]

The prohibition on arbitrators against acting as mediators for the same dispute in commercial arbitrations does not apply to CIAC Arbitrations. Rather, a person may act as arbitrator in an arbitration even if he previously acted as conciliator/mediator for the same case when brought to arbitration if both parties consent to his appointment in writing.[155]

### 3.3.3.6. Arbitral awards

The final award shall contain the issues involved, a brief statement and discussion of the facts, and the authority relied upon for the resolution or disposition of the issues.[156] In the case of non-monetary claims or where the parties agreed that the sharing of fees shall be determined by the arbitral tribunal, the final award shall fix the costs of the arbitration, and/or decide which of the parties shall bear the cost(s) or in what proportion the cost(s) shall be borne by each of them.[157] Tribunals in CIAC arbitrations may render consent awards if the parties settle their dispute during the course of the arbitration.[158] Thus, a compromise agreement settled by mediation under CIAC mediation rules shall be treated as an arbitral award if so expressly stipulated by the parties in the settlement agreement.[159]

A motion for correction of an award may be filed before the CIAC in the case of evident miscalculation of figures, a typographical error, evident mistake in the description of any party, person, date, amount, thing or property referred to in the award, or where the arbitrators have awarded upon a matter not submitted to them, not affecting the merits of the decision upon the matter submitted, or where the arbitrators have failed or omitted to resolve certain issue(s) formulated by the parties in the Terms of Reference and submitted to them for resolution,

---

153 Section 21.2, *ibid.*

154 Section 13.17, *ibid.*

155 Section 36, ADR Act; see also Section 9.7, CIAC Rules.

156 Section 16.3, CIAC Rules.

157 Section 16.5, *ibid.*

158 Section 16.4, *ibid.*

159 Section 16.4.1, *ibid.*

and where the award is imperfect in a matter of form not affecting the merits of the controversy.

Unlike awards in commercial arbitration which may not be appealed on the merits, CIAC awards may be appealed to the Court of Appeals on questions of law or fact pursuant to Rule 43 of the 1997 Rules of Civil Procedure. Although Executive Order No. 1008 provides that appeal on questions of law may be made to the Supreme Court, the CIAC Rules provide that appeal of a CIAC award may be made to the Court of Appeals on questions of law or fact.[160] The petition, however, shall not stay the execution of the final award sought to be reviewed unless the Court of Appeals directs otherwise.[161] The jurisdiction of the tribunal over the dispute terminates upon the finality of the final award or decision, which takes place after the appeal is finally resolved.[162]

An arbitral tribunal appointed under CIAC Rules may issue writs of execution of final and executory decisions, ordered or final awards. Awards rendered by CIAC arbitrators may be executed through writs of execution issued by the arbitral tribunal or the single arbitrator with the concurrence of the CIAC[163] requiring any sheriff or proper officer to execute said decision, order or final award. If there are no remaining/surviving appointed arbitrator(s), the Commission shall issue the writ requested.[164]

#### 3.3.3.7. Small claims

For small claims cases, where the claim does not exceed PhP 1 million, the same shall be handled by a sole arbitrator. The fees shall be at a fixed rate of 3% of the claim but not less than PhP 10,000 or as may be prescribed by the CIAC.[165] All prescribed periods under normal procedure shall whenever practicable, be abbreviated to 50% of that required.[166]

### *3.3.4. Other statute-based arbitrations*

Aside from the Labor Code and the Local Government Code, several other laws provide for arbitration as a mode of settling specific disputes. In most of these

160 Section 18.1, *ibid.*; see also Rule 43 of the 1997 Rules of Civil Procedure, which provides: 'Scope. – This Rule shall apply to appeals from judgments or final orders of the Court of Tax Appeals and from awards, judgments, final orders or resolutions of or authorized by any quasi-judicial agency in the exercise of its quasi-judicial functions. Among these agencies are x x x Construction Industry Arbitration Commission.'

161 Section 18.4, CIAC Rules.

162 Section 16.6, *ibid.*

163 Section 20, *ibid.*

164 Section 18.5, *ibid.*

165 Section 20.1.1, *ibid.*

166 Section 20.1.2, *ibid.*

laws, arbitration is mandatory and constitutes a condition precedent to commencing proceedings before the courts or other government agencies.

3.3.4.1. Administrative settlement and adjudication of disputes among government agencies and corporations

Presidential Decree No. 242[167] prescribes the procedure for the administrative settlement and adjudication of disputes among the different offices and instrumentalities of the government arising from the interpretation and application of statutes, contracts or agreements.[168] Under the Decree, disputes involving only questions of law are to be adjudicated by the Secretary of Justice whose determination is conclusive and binding.[169] Disputes involving mixed legal and factual issues or only factual issues are to be settled or adjudicated either by the Solicitor General for disputes among offices and agencies of the government, the Government Corporate Counsel for disputes among government-owned or controlled corporations and the Secretary of Justice for all other disputes.[170]

The Decree allows the Secretary of Justice, the Solicitor General or the Government Corporate Counsel to refer questions of fact to an arbitration panel, and to designate the chairman of the tribunal for this purpose.[171] Referring to the Decree, the Supreme Court noted that it provides 'an alternative to, or a substitute for, traditional litigation in court with the added advantage of avoiding the delays, vexations and expense of court proceedings.'[172] However, considering that only questions of fact may be referred to arbitration, this does not actually seem to be the case. Moreover, the Decree does not fully empower the parties to appoint the tribunal, thereby excluding one of the essential characteristics of commercial arbitration.

3.3.4.2. Administrative or judicial arbitrations

Republic Act No. 7942, the Philippine Mining Act,[173] vests the Panel of Arbitrators of the Mines and Geosciences Bureau original and exclusive jurisdiction over disputes involving rights to mining areas, mineral agreements or permits, those involving surface owners, occupants and claimholders/

---

167 'Prescribing the Procedure for Administrative Settlement or Adjudication of Disputes, Claims and Controversies between or among Government Offices, Agencies and Instrumentalities, Including Government-Owned or Controlled Corporations, and for other Purposes', 09.07.1973.

168 Section 1, *ibid.*

169 Section 2, *ibid.*

170 Section 3, *ibid.*

171 Section 4, *ibid.*

172 *Philippine Veterans Investment Development Corp. v. Velez*, GR No. 84295, 18.07.1991.

173 *Supra* n. 6.

concessionaires, and those pending before the Bureau and the Department at the date of the effectivity thereof.[174] A decision or order of the panel of arbitrators may be appealed by the party not satisfied thereto to the Mines Adjudication Board.[175]

For consumer-related claims, Republic Act No. 7394, otherwise known as the Consumer Act of the Philippines, vests consumer arbitration officers with original and exclusive jurisdiction to hear and adjudicate all consumer complaints.[176] However, unlike commercial arbitration, the jurisdiction of consumer arbitration officers does not preclude parties from pursuing the proper judicial action.[177] The consumer arbitration officer may summon witnesses, administer oaths and affirmations, issue subpoena and subpoena *duces tecum*, rule upon issues of proof and receive relevant evidence, take or cause deposition to be taken whenever the ends of justice would be served thereby, regulate the course of the hearing, rule on any procedural request or similar matter and decide the complaint.[178] Decisions of consumer arbitration officers are final and executory unless appealed to the Secretary of Trade and Industry but only on grounds of grave abuse of discretion, excess of jurisdiction, lack factual bases and/or serious error in the findings of fact.[179]

The Downstream Oil Industry Deregulation Act of 1998 or Republic Act No. 8749[180] mandated the Department of Energy to monitor the relationship between oil companies (refiners and importers) and their dealers, haulers and LPG distributors to help ensure the observance of fair and equitable practices and to ensure the enforcement of existing contracts.[181] To this end, the Department of Energy is empowered to conciliate and arbitrate any dispute that may arise with respect to the contractual relationship between the oil companies and the dealers, haulers and LPG distributors involving the dealers' mark-up, the freight rate in transporting petroleum products and the margins of LPG distributors for the protection of the public and to prevent ruinous competition.[182] The arbitration award of the Department of Energy shall be subject to judicial review under existing law.[183]

Disputes arising from transactions involving government procurement are also required to be submitted to arbitration under Republic Act No. 9184, also known as the Government Procurement Reform Act.[184] Said disputes are to be

174 Section 77, *ibid.*
175 Section 78, *ibid.*
176 Section 162, *ibid.*
177 Section 162, *ibid.*
178 Section 163, *ibid.*
179 Section 165, *ibid.*
180 'An Act Deregulating the Downstream Oil Industry, and for other Purposes', 12.02.1998.
181 Section 7, *ibid.*
182 *Ibid.*
183 *Ibid.*
184 Became effective on 26.01.2003.

submitted to arbitration in the Philippines according to the provisions of the domestic Arbitration Law, except if the dispute is within the competence of the Construction Industry Arbitration Commission. The parties may agree in writing to resort to alternative modes of dispute resolution.[185] A likely problem that may arise is if the dispute does not fall under the domestic arbitration law but is international in nature. Would the Model Law be applied in this case? Regrettably, the Act further provides that any arbitral award thereunder shall be appealable to the Court of Appeals on questions of law pursuant to the Rules of Court.[186]

The Supreme Court also plans to establish a system for court-annexed arbitrations. It is currently envisioned to be a voluntary dispute resolution conducted with the assistance of the court in which one or more arbitrators appointed in accordance with an arbitration clause and as agreed upon by the parties, resolve a dispute by rendering an award.[187] There are yet no rules governing court-annexed arbitrations and it remains to be seen whether the same would follow the commercial arbitration process or whether it would take a form similar to statute-based arbitrations.

# 4. PHILIPPINE LAW ON MEDIATION

## 4.1. COMMERCIAL MEDIATION

As discussed above, the ADR Act also covers commercial mediation, whether ad hoc or institutional, other than court-annexed mediations. The term 'mediation' includes 'conciliation'.[188]

An agreement to submit a dispute to institutional mediation shall be deemed to include an agreement to have the rules of the institution govern the mediation.[189]

The ADR Act provides the rules for enforcing mediated settlement agreements – a process much faster than prosecuting an ordinary civil action for specific performance to enforce a contract. Mediated settlement agreements may be issued in the form of consent awards if the parties agree that the mediator shall become an arbitrator for the purposes of issuing the award.[190] The parties may deposit such settlement agreement with the court and where there is a need to enforce the settlement agreement, a petition may be filed for the purpose of

185 Section 59, *ibid.*
186 Section 60, *ibid.*
187 Supreme Court Administrative Order No. 33-08.
188 Section 7, ADR Act.
189 Section 16, *ibid.*
190 Section 17(d), ADR Act.

enforcing the same. Proceedings to enforce mediated settlement agreements shall be summary.[191]

## 4.2. COMPULSORY MEDIATION UNDER SUPREME COURT RULES

Even prior to the ADR Act coming into effect, the Supreme Court had already institutionalised the use of mediation in relation to court proceedings with the objective of de-clogging the dockets of the courts. ADR, in the context of the Supreme Court's mediation rules, is defined as 'the provision of an alternative system for settling disputes between two or more parties, which operates independently of, or, as an adjunct to the judicial litigation system, through the intervention of a qualified person or persons trained to intercede in, facilitate and coordinate the interaction of the disputants in a settlement process.'[192]

The Philippine Mediation Centre (PMC) has the primary responsibility for the expansion, development, implementation, monitoring and sustainability of the Supreme Court's ADR programs, namely: court-annexed mediation (CAM), appellate court mediation (ACM), judicial dispute resolution (JDR), mobile court-annexed mediation (MCAM), and eventually court-annexed arbitration.[193]

CAM is a mediation process backed by the courts. ACM, on the other hand, is a mediation program in the Court of Appeals.[194] JDR is a process whereby a judge employs conciliation, mediation or early neutral evaluation in order to settle a case at the pre-trial stage. In the event the JDR fails, then another judge performs the duties of a trial judge of hearing and deciding a case.[195] MCAM is a form of CAM except that the mediation proceedings are conducted in a mobile court (bus) deployed in an area for a certain period.[196]

Although these various ADR mechanisms are covered by separate Supreme Court issuances, it should be noted that they complement each other. CAM/MCAM, JDR and ACM are but three stages of diversion of court cases to ADR. During CAM, the first stage, the judge refers the parties to the PMC Office for mediation to be conducted by trained and accredited mediators. If CAM fails, the second stage, called the JDR, is undertaken by the JDR judge, acting as a

191 Section 17, *ibid.*; see also Rule 15, ADR Rules.
192 SC AO 33-08.
193 Section 1, *ibid.*
194 Sections 7(d) and 7(e), *ibid.*
195 Section 7(e)*, *ibid.*
196 Section 7(f), *ibid.*

mediator-conciliator-early neutral evaluator.[197] The third stage is during appeal where covered cases are referred to ACM.

Cases subject to mandatory CAM/JDR include (a) civil cases and the civil liability of criminal cases covered by the Rules on Summary Procedure; (b) special proceedings for the settlement of estates; (c) all civil and criminal cases filed with a certificate to file action; (d) the civil aspect of certain criminal cases including estafa (or fraud), theft and libel; (e) all civil cases, probate proceedings, forcible entry and unlawful detainer (i.e. detention of real property) cases and civil cases involving title to or possession of real property or an interest therein, which are brought on appeal from the exclusive and original jurisdiction of first level courts; and (f) habeas corpus cases under certain circumstances.

On the other hand, cases subject to ACM include (a) civil cases brought on ordinary appeal or petition for review; (b) appeals from final orders, awards, judgments, resolution of quasi-judicial agencies in the exercise of their quasi-judicial functions; (c) special civil actions for certiorari, except those involving pure questions of law; (d) habeas corpus cases involving custody of minors, with the consent of the parties, provided that the minor is not detained for commission of a criminal offence; and (e) criminal cases covered by the *Katarungang Pambarangay* law, i.e. offences punishable by imprisonment not exceeding one year or a fine not exceeding PhP 5,000.

The objective of CAM and JDR is 'to put an end to pending litigation through a compromise agreement of the parties and thereby help solve the ever-pressing problem of court docket congestion'.[198] This also applies to ACM. Without expressly repudiating the recognised rule that criminal cases may not be the subject of compromise, the rules on mediation clearly suggest that the ultimate objective of compulsory mediation is to end litigation including, in many instances, criminal cases. The civil aspect of less grave felonies punishable by correctional penalties not exceeding six years' imprisonment, where the offended party is a private person, may be submitted to CAM or JDR.[199]

CAM, JDR and ACM are confidential and information or communications obtained therein are inadmissible as evidence in any other proceedings. JDR judges and all court personnel or any other person present during the proceedings, are prohibited from disclosing information obtained in the course

197 The JDR judge acts as a mediator, neutral evaluator and/or conciliator. As mediator and conciliator, he facilitates the settlement discussions between the parties and tries to reconcile their differences. As a neutral evaluator, he assesses the relative strengths and weaknesses of each party's case, makes a non-binding and impartial evaluation of the chances of each party's success in the case and persuades the parties to a fair and mutually acceptable settlement of their dispute.

198 Resolution A.M. No. 11-1-6-SC-PHILJA 'Consolidated and Revised Guidelines to Implement the Expanded Coverage of Court-Annexed Mediation [CAM] and Judicial Dispute Resolution [JDR]', General Provisions and Coverage.

199 Part 1(3), *ibid.*

of the mediation to the trial judge or to any other person. Lawyers are encouraged to act more as advisers, rather than as advocates.

### *4.2.1. CAM procedure*

Under the Guidelines, CAM begins with the judge issuing an order requiring the parties to appear before the PMC Unit, usually upon the filing of the last pleading by the relevant party. The parties then select an acceptable accredited mediator. Otherwise, the mediator shall be chosen by lottery from a list of suitable candidates. The process starts with the mediator explaining the procedure and purpose of CAM. It is possible for the mediator to hold a separate meeting with each of the parties, if the parties consent. If no settlement is reached within 30 days from the date when the parties first appeared for the initial conference, the case is returned to court, unless the court extends the period. On the other hand, if full settlement is reached, the parties shall draft the compromise agreement for approval by the court and, if compliance has been made, the court shall dismiss the case upon the submission by the parties of a satisfaction of claims or a mutual withdrawal of the case. If only a partial settlement is reached, the parties shall submit the terms thereof for the appropriate action of the court. The court shall proceed to conduct JDR proceedings with respect to the unsettled parts.

### *4.2.2. JDR procedure*

JDR proceedings, on the other hand, are commenced by the judge by pre-setting the case for JDR, at the time he refers the case to CAM, not earlier than 45 days from the parties' first appearance at the PMC Unit for CAM. Cases may be referred to JDR even during the trial stage upon written motion of one or both parties. Generally, the judge to whom the case was originally assigned shall be the JDR judge and shall preside over the first stage. All incidents or motions filed during the first stage shall be dealt with by the JDR judge. If the case is not resolved during JDR, it shall be allocated to another branch for the second stage. As a general rule, the JDR judge shall not preside over the trial of the case. The parties may, however, file a joint written request that their case be tried by the JDR judge. If full settlement of the dispute is reached, the parties shall submit the compromise agreement for approval by the court. If there has been compliance, the court shall dismiss the case upon submission by the parties of a satisfaction of claims or a mutual withdrawal of the parties' respective claims and counterclaims. In case of partial settlement, the same may be submitted to the court for approval and rendition of a judgment on partial compromise, which may be immediately enforced by execution. In criminal cases, if settlement is reached on the civil aspect thereof, the parties shall submit the compromise agreement for appropriate action by the court. Action on the criminal aspect of the case will be determined by the public prosecutor, subject to the appropriate action of the court.

### *4.2.3. ACM procedure*

In ACM, division clerks of courts, with the assistance of the PMC, shall identify pending cases which may be referred to mediation, subject to approval by the appropriate judge. Parties to a case pending before the Court of Appeals may likewise submit written requests to the Court of Appeals to submit a case to mediation. For cases yet to be filed, parties commencing a proceeding before the Court of Appeals are required to indicate whether the case is one which may be mediated.

The division may then refer the case to mediation after submission of the appellant's brief or petition. The period within which to submit the response to the brief or petition is suspended until further orders of the court. The parties are to choose the mediators from among accredited mediators of the CA.

The mediator shall endeavour to complete the mediation proceedings within 30 days from the date of the initial mediation conference, but the period may be extended upon the motion of the parties and concurrence of the mediator if significant progress towards a settlement has been achieved. Parties are required to attend in person or through a duly authorised representative, who must be a corporate officer, and authorised in writing to negotiate, accept and decide to enter into settlement without need of further approval. Any agreement reached during mediation shall be put in writing by the mediator and signed by the parties and their counsels for submission to the court.

The court may render a judgment upon full or partial compromise. The parties may likewise agree to withdraw the appeal and enter into mutual satisfaction of claims and counterclaims, after receipt of which the court shall dismiss the appeal. If there is no settlement, the mediator shall return the case to the division of origin and make a confidential note to the PMC stating the reasons for the failure.

## 4.3. STATUTORY MEDIATION UNDER THE LOCAL GOVERNMENT CODE

The *Katarungang Pambarangay* system under the Local Government Code also provides for a dispute resolution mechanism that involves mediation.[200] The procedure is commenced with the filing of the complaint, orally or in writing,

[200] Section 410, Local Government Code.

with the *Lupon* chairman of the *barangay*.[201] The subsequent proceedings involve the following steps: (a) issuance of summons by the *Lupon* chairman; (b) constitution of the *Pangkat*, within 15 days from the first meeting of the parties if mediation fails;[202] (c) the *Pangkat* shall convene not later than three days from its constitution to hear both parties and their witnesses, simplify issues, and explore all possibilities for amicable settlement;[203] (d) the *Pangkat* shall mediate the dispute for a period of between 15 to 30 days, which may be extended in clearly meritorious cases.[204] If an amicable settlement is reached, the same shall have the force and effect of a final judgment of a court upon the expiration of ten days from the date thereof, unless repudiation of the settlement has been made[205] within the same period. The settlement may be enforced by execution by the *Lupon* within six months from the date of the settlement. After the lapse of such time, the settlement may be enforced by action in the appropriate city or municipal court.[206]

## 4.4. ADMINISTRATIVE MEDIATION

Mediation is also available in proceedings before administrative agencies.

### *4.4.1. Mediation under the Labor Code*

In proceedings before the labour arbiter, the Labor Code provides that the labour arbiter shall exert all efforts towards the amicable settlement of a labour dispute within his jurisdiction on or before the first hearing.[207]

With respect to disputes arising from a collective bargaining negotiation, if the employer and employee's union are unable to resolve the same, the National Conciliation and Mediation Board shall intervene upon request of either or both parties or at its own initiative and immediately call the parties to conciliation meetings.[208] The National Conciliation and Mediation Board shall exert all efforts to settle disputes amicably. But if the parties are unable to settle their disputes, the said Board shall encourage them to submit their case to a voluntary arbitrator.[209]

---

201 Section 410(a), *ibid.* Commencement and pendency of mediation and arbitration proceedings suspends the prescriptive period for offences and causes of action under existing laws and shall resume upon the termination thereof, which interruption shall not exceed 60 days from the filing of the complaint with the punong barangay (Section 410(c)).

202 Section 410(b), *ibid.*

203 Section 410(d), *ibid.*

204 Section 410(e), *ibid.*

205 Section 416, *ibid.*

206 Section 417, *ibid.*

207 Article 221, *ibid.*

208 Article 250, *ibid.*

209 Article 250, *ibid.*

### 4.4.2. *Mediation of intellectual property disputes*

The Philippine Intellectual Property Office recognises that the adjudication of cases before it will be facilitated and complemented by the adoption of alternative modes of dispute resolution, such as mediation. The mediation rules of the Intellectual Property Office require mediation for the following cases: (a) administrative complaints for violations of intellectual property rights and/or unfair competition; (b) *inter partes* cases; (c) disputes involving technology transfer payments; (d) disputes relating to the terms of a license involving the author's rights to public performance or other communications of his work; (e) cases appealed to the Office of the Director General from decisions of the Bureau of Legal Affairs and the Documentation, Information and Technology Transfer Bureau; and (f) all other cases which may be referred to mediation during the settlement period by the Director General.[210]

Mediators are either chosen by mutual consent of the parties or by raffle.[211] Mediators shall give every opportunity to the parties to present their respective positions with the objective of reaching an agreement or settlement and are not bound by technical rules of evidence.[212]

A compromise agreement submitted by the parties shall be submitted to the director of the Bureau of Legal Affairs for approval. An approved compromise agreement shall have the effect of a decision or judgment and shall be enforced accordingly.[213] A compromise agreement may be disapproved if the terms thereof are contrary to law and regulations, morals, public policy and/or public interest.[214]

## 5. OTHER FORMS OF ADR

The ADR Act also recognises other forms of ADR and the right of the parties to refer one or more or all of their issues or disputes to any form of ADR, such as, but not limited to, (a) evaluation of a third person, (b) a mini-trial, or (c) mediation-arbitration, or a combination thereof.[215]

The Supreme Court's programs on mediation, particularly JDR, encourage the use of early neutral evaluation. They require judges, who are acting as JDR judges, as opposed to trial judges, to make an early evaluation of the parties'

210 Section 1, Intellectual Property Office Order No. 134 Series of 2004, 'Rules on Mediation of Cases in the Bureau of Legal Affairs', 22.12.2004.

211 Section 4, *ibid.*

212 *Ibid.*

213 Section 5, *ibid.*

214 *Ibid.*

215 Section 18, *ibid.*

respective positions with a view to helping the parties arrive at an amicable settlement.

## 6. PRESENT PERSPECTIVES AND FUTURE PROSPECTS

Philippine ADR law has undergone a significant transformation in the last few years. The enactment of the ADR Act in 2004 was a huge step, setting the stage for making the Philippines an attractive venue for international arbitrations. The Supreme Court's ADR Rules, promulgated in 2009, was a clear and strong message that the judiciary strongly supports voluntary ADR. Recent Supreme Court decisions have also affirmed the Court's support for ADR. The 2012 decision in *Tuna Processing, Inc. v. Philippine Kingford, Inc.*,[216] for example, provides an assurance that foreign arbitral awards covered by the New York Convention will not be enforced only on the basis of the limited grounds provided under the Convention. Certain government agencies have also started to embrace voluntary ADR as a mode of resolving industry-specific disputes; for example, the Intellectual Property Office recently came up with its own arbitration rules based on the arbitration rules of, and prepared in coordination with, the World Intellectual Property Office.

Another positive development took place recently when, in July 2012, the Office of the President issued Executive Order No. 78[217] mandating that all contracts involving public-private partnership (PPP) projects shall include provisions on the use of ADR mechanisms, at the option and upon agreement of the parties to said contracts.[218] Pursuant to the Order, all parties who enter into similar contracts with Local Government Units are encouraged to stipulate the use of ADR mechanisms.[219] The Order encourages the use of either domestic or international ADR mechanisms giving the parties complete freedom to choose the venue, forum and rules of procedure to govern the resolution of their dispute.[220]

In August 2012, the Department of Justice, through the initiative of the Office for Alternative Dispute Resolution, issued Department Circular No.

---

216 See *supra* n. 63.

217 Executive Order No. 78, 'Mandating the Inclusion of Provisions on the Use of Alternative Dispute Resolution Mechanisms in all Contracts involving Public-Private Partnership Projects, Build-Operate and Transfer Projects, Joint Venture Agreements Between the Government and Private Entities and Those Entered into by Local Government Units', 04.07.2012.

218 Section 1, *ibid.*

219 *Ibid.*

220 *Ibid.*

049[221] providing accreditation guidelines for ADR provider organisations and training standards for ADR practitioners. The aim of the circular is to promote quality and accountability among ADR providers and practitioners through the establishment of professional standards relating to qualifications, competence and performance.[222] While accreditation under the Circular is generally voluntary, the Circular makes accreditation mandatory for private ADR provider organisations or practitioners offering ADR services to government agencies or in partnership with said agencies.[223]

While the ADR environment in the Philippines is generally positive, there is still much room for improvement.

Firstly, the enactment of the ADR Act has made Philippine ADR law more robust; however, the Philippines should nevertheless consider aligning its domestic and construction arbitration laws with the Model Law.

The provisions of Executive Order No. 78, allowing parties to choose the rules governing arbitrations relating to PPP projects, could likely clash with the original and exclusive jurisdiction of the Construction Industry Arbitration Commission under Executive Order No. 1008.

The requirement under the Arbitration Law that arbitration agreements need to be subscribed or signed by the parties is no longer in keeping with the advances in technology worldwide which relies more and more on electronic documents. This may prove to be a setback insofar as promoting domestic arbitration is concerned.

Moreover, there is a huge amount of court decisions around the world amplifying the various grounds for challenging arbitral awards under the Model Law. These decisions could enhance Philippine jurisprudence on domestic arbitration should the Philippines decide to adopt the Model Law grounds for challenging awards to domestic arbitration as well.

With respect to construction arbitration, the availability of merits review of awards in CIAC arbitration could be a disincentive to parties who might otherwise prefer to arbitrate. Aligning construction arbitration rules with the Model Law could further improve the efficiency of construction arbitration since appellate proceedings to question arbitral awards in construction arbitration may also take several years to resolve – effectively negating the benefits of an efficient arbitration process.

However, secondly, and in addition to this, if Philippine ADR history teaches anything, there is a need to recognise that commercial ADR is different from statute-based ADR and acknowledge the essential distinctions between the two. They both have their own advantages and, more importantly, can serve to

221 Department of Justice Circular No. 049, 'Adopting accreditation guidelines for alternative dispute resolution provider organizations and training standards for alternative dispute resolution practitioners', 17.08.2012.

222 3rd Whereas Clause, *ibid.*

223 Section 3, *ibid.*

supplement each other. If parties are not minded to engage in commercial or voluntary ADR, it makes sense for some form of statute-based ADR rules to automatically apply as it provides an opportunity for parties to engage in meaningful settlement discussions. However, the existence of statute-based ADR rules must not preclude parties from choosing other forms of voluntary ADR mechanisms.

In *Benguet Corporation v. Department of Environment and Natural Resources et al.*,[224] the Supreme Court correctly acknowledged the distinction between voluntary and compulsory arbitration. It ruled that an arbitration clause in a contract refers to voluntary arbitration which is different from the compulsory arbitration before the Panel of Arbitrators of the Department of Environment and Natural Resources. Even if the Philippine Mining Act vests the Panel of Arbitrators with original and exclusive jurisdiction over said dispute, the parties are bound to comply with the arbitration clause and submit to voluntary arbitration.

However, the Supreme Court has not been consistent on this point. In *China Chang*,[225] the Supreme Court dealt with more or less a similar issue. When faced with the issue of whether parties to a construction dispute can submit their dispute to an arbitral institution other than the CIAC, the Supreme Court ruled in the negative stating that 'when the law provides that the [CIAC] acquires jurisdiction when the parties to the contract agree to submit the same to voluntary arbitration, the law in effect, automatically gives the parties an alternative forum before whom they may submit their disputes. The alternative forum is the CIAC.' Unlike the ruling in *Benguet*, the *China Chang* ruling favoured the original and exclusive jurisdiction of the CIAC over the parties' choice of forum.

Finally, the effectiveness of the ADR Act and the ADR Rules will depend on how courts implement their provisions in enforcing arbitration agreements and arbitral awards. This is a given. Unless litigants believe that they can rely on the courts for support in connection with ADR proceedings, ADR will not become the preferred mode of dispute resolution.

224 GR No. 163101, 13.02.2008.
225 *Supra* n. 134.

# SINGAPORE

Joel Lee*

**Contents**



* The writer wishes to thank Ms Carol Liew (Supreme Court of Singapore) and Ms Teh Hwee Hwee (Supreme Court of Singapore) whose work the writer has drawn heavily upon and has acknowledged in footnotes where appropriate. The writer would also like to thank Mr Kwah Chee Hian whose contributions have been invaluable to the section on arbitration.

## 1. INTRODUCTION

Singapore is a small island state, approximately 700 square kilometres with a population of over 5 million people made up of many ethnicities, including the Malays, the Chinese and the Indians.[1] It was colonised by the British in 1824, occupied by Japan during the Second World War and, after the Japanese surrender, remained a British colony until its independence in 1965. Since then, Singapore has gone from strength to strength and is now a developed country with all the trimmings of modernity and a strong economy. The country is governed by a democratically elected unicameral parliament and the legal system is based on the English common law system. As with many common law systems, litigation in the courts is a significant way of resolving civil disputes and this of course brings with it the attendant tangible and intangible costs.

In this context, the ADR movement has made a significant impact upon the legal landscape in Singapore. It is well known that ADR refers to the dispute resolution processes of arbitration, mediation and negotiation.[2] These are considered alternative relative to what is perceived as the main form of dispute resolution, i.e. litigation.

The chapter seeks to explore in two parts the two main forms of ADR in Singapore: arbitration and mediation. While the writer has tried to mirror the headings in each part, because arbitration and mediation are very different

---

1 Singapore – Wikipedia <http://en.wikipedia.org/wiki/Singapore> accessed 27.09.2012.

2 See J. Lee, 'The ADR Movement in Singapore', in K. Tan Yl (ed.), *The Singapore Legal System*, Singapore University Press, Singapore 1999, p. 414.

creatures, there will be some asymmetry. Further, a larger portion of this chapter will focus on mediation, as that has been the area of most growth in recent years.

## 2. ARBITRATION

In recent years, international commercial arbitration has become a highly prominent form of dispute resolution around the world. The Singaporean experience has been no different. Being in close proximity to major Asian economies, Singapore's advantageous geographical position has drawn many international commercial arbitration cases. Apart from the country's geographical position, the government has also taken various steps to make Singapore more attractive as an arbitration venue. Such steps include enacting favourable arbitration laws and setting up the necessary infrastructure.

Historically, the idea of arbitration is not new to Singapore. Some writers have tracked the presence of arbitration in Singapore to as early as the 1830s, where there was case law which mentioned arbitration clauses.[3] The first piece of arbitration-related legislation in Singapore, the Arbitration Act (AA),[4] was enacted in 1953 although it only came into force in 1987.

Until 1991, as there were no local arbitral institutions, the arbitrations that took place were mostly *ad hoc* in nature. This meant that the disputing parties organised and took charge of the entire arbitration process themselves.

The early 1990s saw a series of developments that entrenched arbitration firmly in the Singaporean legal landscape. First, the Singapore International Arbitration Centre was formed in 1991. Secondly, 1992 saw the removal of restrictions against foreign lawyers representing clients in arbitral proceedings in Singapore. Thirdly, Singapore adopted the UNCITRAL Model Law for International Commercial Arbitration (the Model Law) in 1994. Finally, also in 1994, the International Arbitration Act (IAA)[5] was enacted which led to the current dual regime system. These developments set the stage for arbitration's growth in Singapore as a form of dispute resolution and shifted the nature of arbitration towards institutional arbitration.[6]

---

3 M. Hwang SC, A. Chan, and R. Selvaraj, 'Singapore', in M.J. Moser, *Arbitration in Asia*, 2nd ed., Juris Publishing Inc, Hong Kong, 2008, at [1.1] of Part M.

4 Arbitration Act, Cap 10, 2002 (Rev. Ed).

5 International Arbitration Act, Cap 143A, 2002 (Rev. Ed).

6 S. Menon SC, 'International Arbitration: The Coming of a New Age for Asia' (Opening Plenary Session at the International Council of Commercial Arbitration Congress 2012) <www.arbitration-icca.org/media/0/13398435632250/ags_opening_speech_icca_congress_2012.pdf> accessed 27.09.2012, p. 5.

## 2.1. FRAMEWORK OF ARBITRATION IN SINGAPORE

As just mentioned, arbitration in Singapore is governed by a dual regime system.[7] A distinction is drawn between international arbitrations and domestic arbitrations. The former is governed by the IAA, while the latter is governed by the AA.

The dual regime system requires one to characterise whether an arbitration is considered international in nature. If it is then the IAA will apply. An arbitration is international if one of the parties has its place of business outside Singapore, or the place of arbitration is different from the place of business, or a substantial part of the business obligations are to be performed in a place different from the place of business, or parties have expressly agreed that the subject matter of the arbitration agreement relates to more than one country.[8] Alternatively, even if an arbitration is not international in nature, the IAA can still apply if parties expressly agree in writing.[9]

Conversely, parties can choose to 'opt out' even if the arbitration is international in nature,[10] in which case it will be considered a domestic arbitration and the AA will apply in its place. The issue of 'opting out' used to be a controversial one, as the Singapore courts had held that the adoption of arbitration rules, e.g. the International Chamber of Commerce Arbitration Rules, would implicitly exclude the application of the IAA.[11] This meant that even if the arbitration rules failed to provide for a specific procedure, the parties could not rely on the IAA to fill the gap.[12] As such, the decision drew much criticism from the international arbitral community. This prompted a response from Parliament, which resulted in the amendment of the IAA.[13]

Section 15 of the IAA now states that any 'opting out' has to be express. If there was no express 'opting out', section 15(A) provides for any arbitration rules that have been agreed upon to be given effect insofar as they are not inconsistent with the IAA. In the event of inconsistency, then the IAA would apply. The arbitration rules are not considered inconsistent if they provide for a matter on which the IAA is silent, or are silent on a matter governed by the IAA, or provide for a matter which the IAA allows parties to derogate from. It can thus be said

---

7 By way of completion, it is useful to note that there is a third regime that deals with investment disputes involving States. This is governed by the Arbitration (International Investment Disputes) Act, Cap 11, 2012 (Rev. Ed).

8 Section 5(2) of the IAA.

9 Section 5(1) of the IAA.

10 Section 5(2) of the IAA.

11 *John Holland v. Toyo Engineering Corp. (Japan)* [2001] 2 SLR 262.

12 'The Effect of the International Arbitration Act on Contractually Specified Arbitral Rules' November 2004, Rajah & Tann, Knowledge & Risk Management, p. 1.

13 Section 15 was amended and Section 15(A) was inserted via Amendment Act 38/2001 and Amendment Act 28/2002.

that the law now views arbitration laws and arbitration rules as two separate things, which can co-exist and complement each other.[14]

Whether an arbitration is governed by the IAA or the AA can have practical consequences. These differences can most clearly be felt in relation to appealing the appointment of the arbitrator, ruling on its own jurisdiction, enforcing the arbitral agreements or appealing the arbitral award. Before looking at these, it is useful to briefly refer to those aspects of arbitration that are common across both regimes.

Parties are free to choose whomever they want to represent them in arbitration proceedings, and do not necessarily have to choose lawyers. Further, while foreign lawyers are not allowed to take part in court proceedings,[15] there is no such prohibition with respect to arbitration.

In arbitral procedures, the judicial rules of evidence do not apply.[16] As such, the arbitral tribunal has the power to determine the admissibility, relevance, materiality and weight of any evidence.[17]

The doctrine of separability is also common across both regimes. This doctrine is expressly recognised by the IAA and the AA.[18] Therefore, even if the contract is void, it does not automatically mean that the arbitration clause or agreement is void.[19]

We will now turn to the practical effects of the differences between the two regimes.

### 2.1.1. *Appointment of arbitrators*

Under both the AA and the IAA, parties are free to choose the number of arbitrators, and whom they want as these arbitrators. If the number is not specified, the number is assumed to be one.[20] Where parties cannot agree on the appointment of the sole arbitrator, either party may apply to the Deputy Chairman of the Singapore International Arbitration Centre for appointment.[21] If parties choose to appoint an even number of arbitrators, and the arbitrators do

---

14 See L. Chew, *Introduction to the Law and Practice of Arbitration in Singapore*, LexisNexis, Singapore 2010, pp. 23–31 for a discussion of this area.

15 The Legal Profession Act, Cap 161, 2009 (Rev. Ed).

16 Section 2(1) of the Evidence Act, Cap 97, 1997 (Rev. Ed).

17 Article 19(2) of the Model Law and section 23(3) of the AA.

18 Article 16(1) of the Model Law; section 21(2) of the AA.

19 *Government of the Republic of the Philippines v Philippine International Air Terminals Co., Inc.* [2007] 1 SLR 278.

20 Section 12(2) of the AA; section 9 of the IAA and rule 6, SIAC (Singapore International Arbitration Centre) Rules.

21 Section 13(3)(b) of the AA; Article 11(3)(b) of the Model Law, IAA read with Article 6 of the Model Law and section 8(2) of the IAA. See L. Boo, *International and Domestic Arbitration in Singapore* <www.singaporelaw.sg/content/%C2%ADarbitration1.html> accessed 27.09.2012, para 4.2.13.

not agree, then there can be no enforceable award.[22] Finally, where parties have agreed on a panel of three, but cannot agree on the appointment of the third arbitrator, the Deputy Chairman of SIAC as the statutory appointing authority, upon the request of either party, will appoint the third arbitrator.[23]

The difference between the international and domestic regimes is that the decision of the Deputy Chairman of SIAC with regard to the appointment of the arbitrator is not subject to any appeal under the IAA, but can be challenged under the AA on the grounds of justifiable doubt as to independence and impartiality or lack of qualifications agreed by the parties.[24]

### 2.1.2. *Ruling on own jurisdiction*

This is unique to the IAA in that, in giving the force of law to Article 16(3) of the Model Law,[25] it incorporates the doctrine of *kompetenz-kompetenz* which is the power of the tribunal to rule on its own jurisdiction.[26]

In the past, the IAA only allowed parties to appeal if the tribunal ruled that it had jurisdiction over the matter. After the recent amendments in 2012, parties are now able to appeal negative jurisdictional rulings as well.[27]

### 2.1.3. *Arbitral agreements*

It is well recognised that in order to give real effect to an agreement to arbitrate, any existing court proceedings need to be stayed. This is therefore a matter of great practical concern, and is also one of the more important differences between the international and domestic regimes.

Under the AA, one can apply for a stay if five conditions apply. The applicant must be a party to the arbitration agreement, the agreement must cover the matter in dispute before the court, the applicant must enter an appearance in the court proceedings, the applicant must not have delivered pleadings or taken any step in the proceedings, and the applicant must remain ready and willing to arbitrate.[28] Under the IAA, the conditions to be met are largely similar.[29]

The main difference however is that under the AA the power to grant a stay of court proceedings is discretionary. Put another way, the court can choose not to stay proceedings. Under the IAA, the court has no discretion and must stay the court proceedings.

---

22 Section 19 of the AA and Article 29 of the Model Law require that the award be made by a majority of the arbitrators.

23 Section 13(4) of the AA; section 9A of the IAA·

24 Section 14(3) of the AA.

25 Section 3 of the IAA gives the force of law to the Model Law.

26 L. Chew, *supra* n. 14, p. 45.

27 Section 10(3) of the IAA.

28 Section 6 of the AA.

29 Section 6(1) of the IAA.

### 2.1.4. *Arbitral awards*

#### 2.1.4.1. Appealing the award

Another important difference between the international and domestic regimes is the right of appeal with respect to the arbitral award. The AA allows appeals on questions of law. Section 49(5) of the AA incorporates *The Nema*[30] guidelines which have been adopted in Singapore.[31] Effectively, the award can only be appealed if the arbitral tribunal has made a mistake on a point of law. Otherwise, leave to appeal will only be granted if the question was of general public importance and the court is satisfied that the tribunal's decision is at least open to serious doubt.[32]

The right of appeal can be excluded by agreement.[33] Further, an appeal may only be brought if all the parties consent or if leave is sought from the High Court, and the appeal must be made within 28 days after the award has been made.[34]

There is no right of appeal under the IAA and the only options open to the parties are to either set aside the award or resist enforcement of the award.

#### 2.1.4.2. Setting aside the award

Although the IAA does not allow appeals on the award, both the IAA and the AA allow parties to apply to the court to set aside the award.[35] The grounds on which the award can be set aside are largely similar for both the IAA and the AA. These grounds include situations where:

(a) a party was under some form of incapacity when the arbitration agreement was made;
(b) the arbitration agreement is not valid under the applicable law;
(c) the applicant was unable to present his case;
(d) the tribunal acted outside its jurisdiction (i.e. the award was not within the scope of the arbitration agreement);
(e) the composition of the arbitral authority or the arbitral procedure was not in accordance with the agreement of the parties;

---

30 *Pioneer Shipping v. BTP Tioxide Ltd (The Nema)* [1982] AC 724.

31 *Hyundai Engineering v. Sembawang Kimtrans* [2001] 1 SLR 739.

32 L.S. Chen, 'The International Arbitration Act of Singapore', Singapore Chamber of Maritime Arbitration 2009 <www.scma.org.sg/pdf/rules_iaa.pdf> accessed 27.09.12, p. 2.

33 Section 49(2) of the AA.

34 Section 50(3) of the AA.

35 Section 19B(2) of the IAA incorporates Articles 33 and 34 of Model Law; section 24 of the IAA; section 48 of the AA.

(f) the subject matter was not arbitrable under the laws of Singapore or the award was contrary to public policy;
(g) the making of the award was induced or affected by fraud; or
(h) there was a breach of the rules of natural justice.

2.1.4.3. Enforcing the award

If the award is upheld but not complied with, the party with the award can seek to enforce the award through the courts. For the purpose of enforcement of an award locally, whether under the IAA or the AA, leave must be obtained from the High Court.

The application must be supported by an affidavit exhibiting the arbitration agreement and the original award, stating the name and the usual or last known place of residence or business of the applicant and the person against whom it is sought to enforce the award, and stating that the award has not been complied with or the extent to which it has not been complied with at the date of the application.[36]

After the order is served, the party who received the order has 14 days to apply to refuse enforcement.[37] The AA is silent with respect to the grounds on which the court can refuse to enforce an award. However, section 31 of the IAA, which reflects Article V of the New York Convention on the Recognition and Enforcement of Foreign Arbitral Awards 1958, provides largely similar grounds to those required for the setting aside an award.

So far, the discussion has centred on the arbitration framework as it operates in Singapore. There are of course intersections with the international arbitration framework. We will now look at two areas; the enforcement of a Singaporean award overseas and the enforcement of a foreign award in Singapore.

### *2.1.5. Enforcing a Singaporean award internationally*

As Singapore is a party to the New York Convention, awards made in Singapore will be recognised and can be enforced in other Convention countries. However, this is subject to certain requirements.

Under the New York Convention, a party seeking to enforce an award needs to produce before the foreign court a duly authenticated original award or a duly certified copy, and the original arbitration agreement or a duly certified copy. If parties require certification, the Singapore International Arbitration Centre Registrar may certify and authenticate any award made in

---

36 Order 69, rule 14(1) of the Rules of Court for AA awards; Order 69A, rule 6(1) of the Rules of Court for IAA awards.

37 Order 69, rule 14(4) of the Rules of Court for AA awards; Order 69A, rule 6(4) of the Rules of Court for IAA awards.

SIAC arbitrations. Ever since 1 January 2005, the SIAC has also provided certification services to *ad hoc* arbitrations, provided that certain conditions can be met.[38]

Further, although service of an order for enforcement of an award out of the jurisdiction is not subject to the same requirements as service of an originating process out of Singapore (which requires the leave of the Court), the service of an order for enforcement of an award out of the jurisdiction still needs to comply with the methods for service of originating process stipulated under the Rules of Court.[39]

Unlike the service of an enforcement order locally (which only gives parties 14 days to apply to set the order aside[40]), the period in which parties can apply to set aside an enforcement order served overseas is fixed by the Court at the time the order is made. The award cannot be enforced until this period of time has expired, or if there is an application to set aside the order, until the application is finally disposed of.[41]

### *2.1.6. Enforcing a foreign award in Singapore*

Part III of the IAA gives effect to the New York Convention. As such, an award made in a Convention country will be recognised and can be enforced in Singapore.[42] It should also be noted that following the amendments to the AA in 2003, foreign awards made in countries which are not signatories to the New York Convention may also be enforced in Singapore.[43]

Part III of the IAA lists the steps to enforce a foreign award in Singapore. This is essentially the same procedure as enforcing a Singaporean award in Singapore, with the additional step of producing a certified English translation if it is a foreign language award.[44]

As with the enforcement of a Singaporean award, parties can apply to the court to refuse enforcement and the grounds on which the court can refuse enforcement are similar to the grounds on which the court can set aside the award.[45]

Apart from the enforcement mechanism based on the New York Convention, section 33 of the IAA also allows foreign awards to be enforced under other

---

38 L. Boo, *supra* n. 21, para. 4.2.52.

39 L.S. Chen *supra* n. 32.

40 Order 69, rule 14(4) of the Rules of Court for AA awards; Order 69A, rule 6(4) of the Rules of Court for IAA awards.

41 Order 69, rule 14(4); Order 69A, rule 6(4) of the Rules of Court.

42 Section 29 of the IAA, giving effect to Article III of the New York Convention.

43 Section 46(1) read with section 46(3) of the AA.

44 Section 30 of the IAA.

45 Section 31 of the IAA.

provisions of law, such as those pieces of legislation that provide for the reciprocal enforcement of foreign judgments.[46]

## 2.2. SOURCES OF ARBITRATION

There are five main sources of arbitration services in Singapore.

### *2.2.1. Singapore International Arbitration Centre*

The Singapore International Arbitration Centre (SIAC) is one of Singapore's first sources of arbitration. Set up in 1991 with the assistance of the Trade Development Board and the Economic Development Board, the SIAC has become the main arbitral institution in Singapore.

The SIAC is a one-stop venue for parties to resolve their disputes. It provides the venue and necessary facilities to conduct the arbitration. It also maintains a panel of arbitrators from which appointments can be made at the parties' request. These arbitrators consist of former judges, senior lawyers, and other legal professionals who are top in their chosen field. There are currently over 250 arbitrators from over 28 different countries on SIAC's panel.[47]

Generally, arbitrations by the SIAC will be carried out under its own arbitration rules, although the SIAC is also able to administer arbitrations under any other rules agreed to by the parties.

### *2.2.2. Singapore Institute of Arbitrators*

Another source of arbitration is the Singapore Institute of Arbitrators (SIArb). This is the oldest arbitral institution in Singapore, and is more of a training institute rather than a source of arbitration. It works closely with the Chartered Institute of Arbitrators in London to conduct training courses for arbitrators to provide a pool of arbitrators from which the SIAC can draw on. As such, it can be said that the SIArb and the SIAC have a complementary relationship.[48]

### *2.2.3. Industry-specific providers*

The third source of arbitration can be termed industry-specific providers. These are arbitral bodies which cater to specific industries, such as the shipping or construction industry. For example, the Singapore Chamber of Maritime

---

46 See the Reciprocal Enforcement of Commonwealth Judgments Act, Cap 264, 1985 Ed., and the Reciprocal Enforcement of Foreign Judgments Act, Cap 265, 2001 Ed.

47 See SIAC Panel <www.siac.org.sg/index.php?option=com_content&view=article&id=64&Itemid=86> accessed 27.09.2012.

48 J. Lee, *supra* n 2, p. 429.

Arbitration separated from the SIAC in 2009[49] and caters specifically to maritime disputes.

These industry specific providers will conduct their own training, maintain their own panels and administer their own arbitration sessions. One clear advantage of these industry specific providers is that the arbitrators will have specialised industry knowledge as well as an understanding of the needs of the industry and their members. They will thus be more suited to resolve the dispute.

### 2.2.4. *Private service providers*

Apart from institutions, there are also private service providers. These are arbitrators who are not affiliated with any particular organisation, but who offer their services as arbitrators. Such arbitrations tend to be *ad hoc* arbitrations where parties do not specify any particular set of arbitration rules to govern the conduct of their arbitration. The procedural rules would be specially drawn up by the parties, or left to the arbitrator to decide. Although such services are generally cheaper than institutional arbitration, they are also more susceptible to possible deadlocks and delay tactics.[50]

### 2.2.5. *Statute-based arbitration*

The last source can be termed statute-based arbitration. Normally, arbitration is used as a dispute resolution mechanism when parties choose to do so. However, in some instances, statute makes it mandatory for parties to refer a matter to arbitration.

Recognised as an exception to the general rule, this form of statute-based arbitration is likely to have grown out of a need to resolve certain disputes quickly or by very specialised personnel.[51] One such statute is the Industrial Relations Act,[52] which sets up the Industrial Arbitration Court to arbitrate industrial disputes when negotiations between employers and trade unions have broken down.[53] The award made by the Industrial Arbitration Court is final and conclusive.[54]

49 See <www.scma.org.sg/aboutus.html> accessed 27.09.2012.

50 F. Xavier, B.L. Chong and C. Mohan, 'An overview of arbitration internationally and in Singapore', *Law Gazette*, 2001 <www.lawgazette.com.sg/2001-8/Aug01-focus4.htm> accessed 27.09.2012.

51 J. Lee, *supra* n. 2, p. 430.

52 Cap. 136, 1985 (Rev. Ed).

53 Section 32 of the Industrial Relations Act, Cap. 136, 2004 (Rev. Ed).

54 *Ibid.*, section 47.

## 2.3. PROMOTING ARBITRATION IN SINGAPORE

### 2.3.1. *Educational initiatives*

There are two law schools in Singapore, one at the National University of Singapore (NUS) and the other at the Singapore Management University (SMU). Both of these universities offer arbitration-related modules, which students in the upper years can choose to read. Both law schools offer a module on international commercial arbitration, which covers the basic concepts of arbitration such as, *inter alia*, the doctrine of separability, enforcement of awards, and the Model Law. NUS also has a link with New York University to teach commercial arbitration to students in the NYU-NUS LLM programme. In addition, NUS also teaches arbitration of investment disputes, which aims to familiarise students with the area of investment treaties and arbitration clauses.

NUS and the SIArb also provide the chance for continuous legal education in the area of arbitration for graduates and professionals. The most common course would be the Graduate Certificate in Commercial Arbitration, which is organised jointly by NUS and SIArb. This course is designed for both lawyers and non-lawyers who want to practise arbitration. Students will be taught the basics of the law of contract, tort and evidence, the law and practice of arbitration and will receive training in drafting directions, orders and the arbitral award. Upon completing the course successfully, students will be qualified for direct admission as Fellows of the SIArb. Students can also choose to read an additional 20 credits of maritime-related modules at NUS, and graduate with a Graduate Diploma in Maritime Law & Arbitration.

Apart from its link with NUS, the SIArb also has its own courses. First, there is the International Entry Course, which is a two and a half day course, followed by a written examination. The course covers subjects including arbitration agreements, appointment of arbitrators, preliminary meetings, pleadings, and more. Upon successful completion, and subject to other conditions, students may qualify for admission as a Member of the Singapore Institute of Arbitrators, and as an Associate Member of the Chartered Institute of Arbitrators. Secondly, there is the Fellowship Assessment Course, which is available to both lawyers and non-lawyers. The course teaches arbitration concepts, and also basic legal concepts to non-lawyers. Successful completion of the course will qualify students for direct admission as Fellows of the SIArb.

### 2.3.2. *Maxwell Chambers*

Established in 2010, the Maxwell Chambers was developed with the idea of being a premier integrated dispute resolution complex, housing both top-class hearing facilities as well as top international ADR institutions. The Maxwell Chambers, while not a source of arbitration *per se*, is home to many ADR institutions. These ADR institutions include arbitral institutions such as the SIAC, the International Chamber of Commerce, the Permanent Court of Arbitration,[55] and also non-arbitral institutions like the Singapore Mediation Centre and the International Mediation Institute.[56]

Currently, there are 14 custom-designed and fully equipped hearing rooms and 12 preparation rooms in the Maxwell building. Prices for hearing rooms range from $250/hr for the smallest room to $1,080/hr for the biggest room.[57]

In 2012, Maxwell Chambers expanded by setting up a second concurrent hearing facility in Centennial Tower to keep up with the expected increase in the number of arbitrations in Singapore over the next few years.

### *2.3.3. Institutional support for arbitration*

There has been tremendous institutional support for arbitration in Singapore. This effort has been a holistic one coming from all three branches of the government, as well as independent bodies in the market.

First, the judiciary has been very supportive of arbitration by upholding arbitral awards and keeping judicial intervention to a bare minimum.[58] This can be clearly seen from the case of *Tjong Very Sumito v. Antig Investments*,[59] where the Singapore Court of Appeal observed that 'the role of the court is now to support, and not to displace, the arbitral process'.[60] A supportive judicial attitude is crucial to promoting Singapore as an international arbitration hub, as international commercial entities are primarily concerned with interference from the local courts. This can be due to reasons such as perceived biasness of the local laws and courts, or that international commercial entities come from different legal systems and are not comfortable being subject to a different type of legal system.[61] The autonomy that the judiciary gives to the arbitral community is thus essential in keeping the business of these international commercial entities.

Second, the legislature amends and enacts laws frequently to ensure that Singapore is up to date with international business and arbitral norms. In this

---

55 See <www.maxwell-chambers.com/index.php?option=com_content&view=article&id=16&Itemid=13> accessed 27.09.2012.

56 See <www.maxwell-chambers.com/index.php?option=com_content&view=article&id=2&Itemid=14> accessed 27.09.2012.

57 For the most up-to-date prices, see <www.maxwell-chambers.com/index.php?option=com_content&view=article&id=15&Itemid=11> accessed 27.09.2012.

58 Ministry of Law, Media Release, 'Background Brief on Arbitration in Singapore' (27.07.2009) <http://app2.mlaw.gov.sg/LinkClick.aspx?fileticket=sy0sqEET3VY%3d&tabid=204> accessed 27.09.2012.

59 [2009] 4 SLR(R) 732.

60 *Ibid.*, para [29].

61 L. Chew, *supra* n. 14, p. 75.

respect, the legislature works closely with the executive to find out the necessary changes to be made to the law. This commitment to implement the necessary legal changes is most clearly seen from the Law Ministry's pledge to constantly review Singapore's 'arbitration laws to ensure that it supports the growth and development of international arbitration practice in Singapore'.[62] Recently, the Minister of Law, K. Shanmugam, reaffirmed this commitment in his press statement, where he explained that the government's approach is driven by the needs of industry, and that industry partners are consulted actively and regularly, so that laws and policies can be swiftly changed whenever necessary.[63] These laws make international arbitration possible by giving the force of law to key areas such as enforcing the arbitration agreement, compelling the attendance of witnesses, and enforcing the final arbitral award.[64]

## 2.4. THE WAY FORWARD

The future of international commercial arbitration in Singapore is bright and hopeful. However, it is appropriate to point out certain potential problem areas.[65] The most potent problem area is the increasingly complex nature of international arbitration, which can lead to exorbitant costs.[66] Another potential problem area is the convoluted nature of arbitration law. With no unifying appellate control and no doctrine of binding precedent, the results are often conflicting.[67] Unsurprisingly, this unpredictability, coupled with its high cost, has frustrated many arbitration users. Finally, there is also the threat of moral hazard, as arbitrators are ultimately businesspeople (unlike judges) who have to look for their own clients and appointments.[68]

These problems are not peculiar to Singapore, and are present in other arbitration venues as well. The important point is how Singapore tackles these problems, as this will differentiate the country from the rest and determine if it can remain a prominent player in the international arbitration scene.

There have been suggestions of formulating a code of conduct for arbitrators and arbitral institutions to follow.[69] Such a code should ideally deal with issues of conflicts of interest, and explain how rules of natural justice can be upheld. On a more ambitious note, the Chief Justice of Singapore (then Attorney-General

62 *Supra* n. 58.

63 Ministry of Law, Media Release, 'Arbitration Dialogue 2012' (10.07.2012) <www.news.gov.sg/public/sgpc/en/media_releases/agencies/minlaw/press_release/P-20120610-1/AttachmentPar/0/file/Arbitration%20Dialogue%202012.pdf> accessed 27.09.2012.

64 L. Chew, *supra* n. 14, p. 77.

65 S. Menon SC, *supra* n. 6, p. 11.

66 *Ibid.*, p. 11.

67 *Ibid.*, p. 13.

68 *Ibid.*, p. 14.

69 *Ibid.*, p. 25.

of Singapore), Sundaresh Menon SC, has suggested that the code could even provide for all arbitrators to be appointed by a single independent body, so as to guarantee the independence of the arbitrator. Further, to enhance arbitrator accountability, Menon SC pointed out the need to 'distinguish between issues pertaining to the conduct of the arbitrator such as conflicts of interest and allegations of misconduct, and substantive issues relating to the dispute'.[70] From the perspective of the end users, it is only important to keep the latter confidential. The former needs to be disclosed to ensure the fairness and integrity of the arbitral process.

## 3. MEDIATION

As mentioned in the introduction, Singapore has a dense population in a small space. As a result, informal methods of dispute resolution, including mediation have traditionally been used to resolve social and community disputes. Indigenous forms of mediation in Singapore have been *ad hoc,* unstructured and have often involved the intervention of respected community leaders. These community leaders or other persons of authority would bring disputants together to talk out their differences and counsel them along the way. Within the Chinese communities, the mediators would have been the heads of the family or the leader of a clan association and disputes would generally be settled according to Chinese rules and customs.[71] These would include considerations of 面子 (*mianzi*),[72] social harmony and 关系 (*guanxi*).[73] Within the Malay communities, the mediators would have been the head of the village or religious leaders helping parties resolve disputes non-confrontationally and informally in accordance with Islamic principles, customary standards and etiquettes of social interaction.[74] Within the Indian community, disputes were also amicably settled by *panchayat* or community councils and mediations may have also taken place in Hindu temples.[75]

70 *Ibid.*, p. 27.

71 L. Boulle and H.H. Teh, *Mediation – Principles, Process and Practice*, Butterworths Asia, Singapore 2000, p. 191; L.Y. Lim, *The Theory and Practice of Mediation*, FT Law and Tax Asia Pacific 1997, p. 366.

72 面子 (*mianzi*) can be loosely translated to 'face', which includes the permutations of saving, giving, asserting and restoring face. See J. Ng, 'The Four Faces of Face', in J. Lee and H.H. Teh (eds.), *An Asian Perspective on Mediation*, Academy Publishing, Singapore 2009.

73 关系 (*guanxi*) can be loosely translated to 'relationship' or 'connection'. See S.F. Law, 'More than Collectivism – A Guanxi-oriented Approach to Mediation', in J. Lee and H.H. Teh (eds.), *An Asian Perspective on Mediation,* Academy Publishing, Singapore 2009.

74 L. Boulle and H.H. Teh, *supra* n. 71, p. 191; L.T. Lim and C. Liew, 'Community Mediation – Cultural Roots and Legal Heritage', paper delivered at the 2nd Conference on Alternative Dispute Resolution: Mediation: Yesterday's Ideas, Today's Techniques, National University of Singapore, 27 March 1999; Conference Proceedings at p. 34; L.Y. Lim, *supra* n. 71, p. 368.

75 L. Boulle and H.H. Teh, *supra* n. 71, pp. 191–192; J. Lee, *supra* n. 2, pp. 414–447, 427.

It might be assumed that in these traditional contexts, the mediators would largely have been male. However, while the Chinese and Muslim communities are considered largely patriarchal, this is not to say that the mediators, especially in informal situations could not have been female. Further, the Peranakans (an ethnic group arising out of the inter-marriages between the indigenous Malays and immigrant Chinese)[76] can be said to have a matriarchal structure and the matriarchs in those contexts are likely to have been mediators for extended family disputes. What is important to note is that mediators in traditional Singaporean society were always people in positions of authority and these traditional community mediators would resolve disputes by bearing on his or her authority and social and community norms in a bid to persuade parties to resolve their dispute.[77]

With modernisation and Westernisation, indigenous forms of mediation in Singapore became less common[78] and Singaporeans went through a period of having their disputes resolved by the courts and other official forums.[79] There was a resurgence of interest in mediation in the 1990s at a time when Singaporean society was becoming more litigious and there was a need in modern society for strong and long-term social and business relationships that could survive disputes.[80]

It should be noted that modern mediation practice in Singapore differs from indigenous mediation practice. As mentioned, indigenous mediation practice was *ad hoc*, informal and unstructured. There were no explicit rules and mediators were untrained and credible by virtue of their positions of authority in their respective contexts.[81]

On the other hand, modern mediation practice is characterised by formal mediation rules and procedures, a mediators' code of conduct, agreements to mediate, confidentiality agreements, settlement agreements, prescribed fee schedules and mediator training and accreditation.[82] Modern mediation

76 See Peranakan <http://en.wikipedia.org/wiki/Peranakan> accessed 27.09.2012.

77 J. Lee and H.H. Teh, 'The Quest for an Asian Perspective on Mediation', in J. Lee and H.H. Teh (eds.), *An Asian Perspective on Mediation*, Academy Publishing, Singapore 2009, paras. 1.16–1.19.

78 See the speech of the former Chief Justice P.H. Yong at the launch of DisputeManager.com (31.07.2002) <http://app.subcourts.gov.sg/Data/Files/File/eJustice/Archives/CJSpeech_LaunchDisputeManagerDotCom.pdf> accessed 27.09.2012.

79 J. Lee and H.H. Teh, *supra* n. 77, para. 1.6; *supra* n. 78; see also the speech of the retired Justice J.S. Goh, the first Chairman of the Singapore Mediation Centre at the 6th Lawyers Engaged in Alternative Dispute Resolution (LEADR) International Conference in Australasia on Alternative Dispute Resolution (03.10.1998), Christchurch, New Zealand <www.mediation.com.sg/speech_5.htm> accessed 27.09.2012.

80 See the speech of the former Chief Justice P.H. Yong at the launch of the Singapore Mediation Centre (16.08.1997) <www.mediation.com.sg/speech_1.htm> accessed 27.09.2012.

81 See H.H. Teh, 'Mediation Practices in ASEAN: The Singapore Experience', paper presented at the 11th General Assembly of the ASEAN Law Association, Bali, 15–18 February 2012, pp. 3–4.

82 *Ibid.*, pp. 3–4.

practice was, of course, heavily influenced by mediation training and practice overseas, in particular 'Western' sources[83] like those in the United States, Australia and the United Kingdom. Considering that one view is that mediation has its roots in Asian culture,[84] this irony was not lost on the former Chief Justice Dr Yong Pung How who remarked that Singapore had to relearn mediation from the West.[85]

## 3.1. SOURCES OF MEDIATION IN SINGAPORE

The resurgence of interest in mediation in the 1990s saw three main initiatives to promote mediation in Singapore.[86] These three initiatives were the establishment of firstly court-based mediation in the Subordinate[87] and Family Courts;[88] secondly, Community Mediation Centres[89] for community-based disputes and thirdly, the Singapore Mediation Centre[90] for private commercial disputes. These still constitute the main forms of mediation in Singapore today. This chapter will now look at each of these in turn.

### *3.1.1. Court-based dispute resolution: subordinate courts*

In Singapore, the court system comprises of the Subordinate Courts and the Supreme Court. The former is made up of, *inter alia*, the District Courts, the Magistrates' Courts and the Family Courts. The latter is made up of the High Court and the Court of Appeal.[91]

In 1994, court-based mediation was introduced through the Court Dispute Resolution procedures in the Subordinate courts. The Court Mediation Centre

---

83 J. Lee and H.H. Teh, *supra* n. 77, para. 1.20.

84 H.H. Teh, *supra* n. 81, p. 2.

85 Speech at the launch of DisputeManager.com (31.07.2002) <http://app.subcourts.gov.sg/Data/Files/File/eJustice/Archives/CJSpeech_LaunchDisputeManagerDotCom.pdf> accessed 27.09.2012.

86 H.H. Teh, *supra* n. 81, p. 3.

87 J. Lee and H.H. Teh, *supra* n. 77, para. 1.7.

88 T.L. Liew, D. Hong, C.R. Ong and H.M. Lim, 'Mediation in the Family Court', in R. Magnus *et al.* (eds.), *Families in Conflict*, Butterworths Asia, Singapore 2000, p. 47; D. Hong, 'Mediation and Counselling in the Family Court', in N.T. Tan and J.E. Lee-Partridge (eds.), *Alternative Dispute Resolution – In Business, Family and Community: Multidisciplinary Perspectives*, Centre for Advanced Studies, Singapore 2000, p. 57; M. Bay, S.G. Nair and A. Mendis, 'The Integration of Alternative Dispute Resolution Within The Subordinate Courts' Adjudication Process' (2004) 16 *SAcLJ* 501.

89 J. Lee and H.H. Teh, *supra* n. 77, para. 1.11.

90 *Ibid.*, paras. 1.9–1.11.

91 See R.C. Beckman, B.S. Coleman and J. Lee, *Case Analysis and Statutory Interpretation*, Faculty of Law, National University of Singapore 2001, pp. 32–33; T.M. Yeo, 'Jurisdiction of the Singapore Courts', in K.Y.L. Tan (ed.), *The Singapore Legal System*, Singapore University Press, Singapore 1999.

was formed a year later. The Court Mediation Centre has since evolved into the Primary Dispute Resolution Centre (PDRC).

The PDRC provides a variety of ADR processes for civil suits filed in the courts. Neutral evaluation is provided for motor vehicle accident cases and personal injury claims, and mediation for all other civil matters. Of the matters that are referred to the PDRC for mediation, these can be categorised into two types of cases. The first category involves motor vehicle accident cases which do not involve injury. These cases are routinely referred to the PDRC for resolution. The second category comprises civil matters where parties have requested and consented to mediation.[92]

Initially, mediation was done by district judges specially designated as 'settlement judges'. The pool of mediators has now been expanded to include lawyers and other legally trained persons who have at least three years' post-qualification experience. Parties interested in being mediators with the PDRC have to undergo and pass an Associate Mediator training and accreditation programme. In late 2009, a pilot training and accreditation programme was run jointly by the Subordinate Courts and the Singapore Mediation Centre. This programme was run again in 2010 and 2011.

The Associate Mediator training and accreditation consists of two days of mediator training which seeks to provide trainees with knowledge of the process and skills of mediating through a series of informative sessions, mediation role plays and debriefs of those role plays. The model of mediation taught is the facilitative interests-based model and for the PDRC, the trainings also have a particular focus on the guidelines and code of ethics for mediating in the court-context.

In addition, there is a half day of assessment where trainees will mediate a role play in front of assessors and be provided with feedback. If the trainees pass this assessment, the mediator will undergo a period of mentoring and coaching where they will be assigned to co-mediate at least three cases with an experienced mediator before being allowed to mediate a case on their own.

Mediation sessions at the PDRC are generally set for periods of two to three hours. The parties and their counsel appear before the mediator and an attempt is made to resolve the dispute. If the dispute is not resolved in the first session, up to two more sessions may be scheduled.

For motor vehicle accident cases which generally involve questions of liability and quantum of damages, the mediator tends to act more as a neutral evaluator. The parties and their counsel, having heard the neutral evaluation can go on to see if a settlement can be negotiated.[93] In this category of case,

---

92 J. Low and D. Quek, 'The ADR Form in the Subordinate Courts: Finding the Appropriate Mode of Dispute Resolution', *Singapore Law Gazette*, April 2010 <www.lawgazette.com.sg/2010-04/feature1.htm> accessed 28.09.2012.

93 Court Dispute Resolution <http://app.subcourts.gov.sg/civil/page.aspx?pageid=54106> accessed 27.09.2012.

evidence is sometimes referred to in order for the neutral evaluation to be made.

For the other categories of cases, mediators will generally facilitate an exploration of the interests and concerns of the parties and generate options that parties can potentially agree upon. The mediator also assists the parties in understanding the implications of going ahead to trial in the event that there is no agreement. The mediation generally begins in a joint session where all parties and counsel are present with the option of, but not necessarily, moving into private sessions with one of the parties and their counsel.[94]

If the parties reach a settlement, counsel for both parties help draft either a settlement agreement or a consent judgment. The latter can be enforced directly should one party default on the agreed payment. In the former, there is a usually a clause allowing the plaintiff to extract an order of Court to enforce the settlement agreement in the event of default in payment. If the case is not settled, it will proceed to trial as scheduled and will be heard by another judge.[95]

So far, we have only considered civil cases. Mediation in the Subordinate Courts has been extended beyond civil cases to other types of cases. The Family Courts were established in 1995 with the goal, *inter alia*, of offering parties a less confrontational means for the resolution of family-related matters.[96]

The Family Court offers both mediation and counselling services for matters relating to, *inter alia*, dissolution of marriage, custody of children, matrimonial property division and maintenance.[97] Typically, questions of custody, maintenance and matrimonial property division happen in the petition for a dissolution of a marriage. In contested divorce petitions, after the documents have been filed and exchange, mediation and counselling generally occur after the Pre-Trial Conference.[98]

There is a clear distinction made between mediation and counselling, the former dealing with practical matters and the latter with emotional ones. In practice, the practical and emotional are often intertwined and the Family Court exercises its discretion whether to refer a matter to one or the other, or to one first before the other, or to a session where the panel is made up of a mediator and a counsellor.[99]

Mediations are often conducted by District Judges and Deputy Registrars of the Family Court as well as experienced volunteer mediators who are legally

---

94 See the Subordinate Courts of Singapore, Court Dispute Resolution/Mediation <http://app.subcourts.gov.sg/civil/page.aspx?pageid=54106#Public_Process4> accessed 27.09.2012.

95 See paragraph 25 of the Subordinate Courts Practice Directions <http://app.subcourts.gov.sg/Data/Files/File/PracticeDirections/MasterPD_31082011.pdf> accessed 27.09.2012.

96 T.L. Liew, D. Hong, C.R. Ong and H.M. Lim, *supra* n. 88, p. 47; D. Hong, *supra* n. 88, p. 57; M. Bay, S.G. Nair and A. Mendis, *supra* n. 88.

97 T.L. Liew, D. Hong, C.R. Ong and H.M. Lim, *supra* n. 88, pp. 47–48.

98 *Ibid.*, p. 76.

99 *Ibid.*, pp. 49–50.

qualified and experienced in handling family law matters.[100] Examples of volunteer mediators would be retired judges, senior practitioners and legal academics in the field of family law.

Counselling is conducted by professionals trained in counselling and social work. These can be drawn from the Family Conciliation and Resolution Centre and other external organisations like the Eagles Mediation and Counselling Centre.[101]

Family Court mediators must undergo training before being allowed to mediate. The trainings range from those conducted in-house to two-day workshops conducted by the Singapore Mediation Centre.[102] While in some respects, mediation training is generic, due to the nature of family matters, mediators are made sensitive to the possibility of reconciliation, indications of family violence and the needs of persons who are not immediate parties to the matter e.g. children of the union.

When a settlement agreement eventuates between parties, it will be formalised by the recording of a consent order by the mediator, if s/he is a district judge. If the mediator is not a district judge, the parties will be sent to the duty judge to record the consent order. Occasionally, where the consent order may be complex, parties and their lawyers may need some time to formalise the consent order and a future date will be set for the recording of the consent order.

A specialised unit within the Family Court, the Maintenance Mediation Chambers, was established in 2007 to address maintenance complaints for failure to provide financial support for a child or spouse, for breach of orders made by the Tribunal for the Maintenance of Parents, or for breach of Syariah Court orders pertaining to the non-payment of *iddah* and *mutaah*.[103]

There is no disputing that court-based mediation in Singapore has been successful in keeping case backlog at bay, reducing the trial waiting period and filtering out cases unsuitable for court litigation.

In recent years, court-based mediation has focussed on ethics and cultivating best practices.[104] To that end, a Code of Ethics and Basic Principles on Court Mediation has been developed to provide guidance to judicial officers, court counsellors and volunteers who mediate in the Subordinate Courts.[105] The PDRC has also drawn on community resources by managing Court Support Groups comprising lawyers, social workers, court interpreters and other lay

---

100 *Ibid.*, pp. 51–52.

101 *Ibid.*, p. 52.

102 *Ibid.*, p. 52.

103 See Annual Report of the Subordinate Courts 2009, p. 20 <www.courtexcellence.com/pdf/SubCourts_AR09.pdf> accessed 27.09.2012. See also the Family Court website <http://app.subcourts.gov.sg/family/page.aspx?pageid=3656> accessed 27.09.2012.

104 H.H. Teh, *supra* n. 81, p. 6.

105 The Code of Ethics and Basic Principles on Court Mediation is available online: <http://app.subcourts.gov.sg/Data/Files/File/cdr/Code%20of%20Ethics%20and%20Basic%20Principles%20on%20Court%20Mediation%20June%20201010.pdf> accessed 27.09.2012.

persons trained as counsellors or mediators.[106] One of the strengths of court dispute resolution is that mediation is only one of a number of ADR mechanisms in CDR.[107] This allows for selection of the most appropriate form of dispute resolution for any particular dispute which ensures that only suitable cases are mediated.

It is clear that court-based mediation is therefore a significant part of ADR in Singapore. Of course, while the theoretical lines between court-based mediation and other sources of mediation can be drawn, there are, in reality, overlaps. For instance, since 1996, Magistrates' Complaints in the Subordinate Courts concerning relationships involving relatives, friends and neighbours were referred to mediation either before a Magistrate or in the Community Mediation Centres.[108] This is in the hope that mediation would heal the broken relationships and prevent future recurrences in the future. The chapter will now turn to community mediation.

### *3.1.2. Community Mediation Centres*

Due to Singapore's small area and dense population, managing community and social disputes has always been a priority. As mentioned earlier, many such disputes were resolved through indigenous forms of mediation. With the development of a more litigation-centric society, the Ministry of Law formed the Committee on Alternative Dispute Resolution in May 1996 to look into the use of mediation as a harmonious way to resolve community disputes.[109] In its report, the committee noted the need for a framework to resolve disputes outside the court system that was fast, inexpensive and non-confrontational.[110] It went on to recommend that a network of community mediation centres be set up where community leaders and volunteers were trained to mediate disputes. The idea was to replicate the traditional and indigenous mechanisms for resolving community disputes and to foster community spirit.

---

106 C. Liew, 'Recent Developments in Mediation in East Asia', in A. Ingen-Housz (ed.), *ADR in Business: Practice and Issues across Countries and Cultures, Volume II*, Kluwer Law International, The Netherlands 2011, pp. 526–27.

107 The PDRC commenced a pilot programme to introduce neutral evaluation from October 2011. See Registrar's Circular No. 3 of 2011 <http://app.subcourts.gov.sg/Data/Files/RC3%20of%202011.pdf> accessed 27.09.2012. See also D. Quek and C.L. Seah, 'Finding the Appropriate Mode of Dispute Resolution: Introducing Neutral Evaluation in the Subordinate Courts', *Singapore Law Gazette*, November 2011 <www.lawgazette.com.sg/2011-11/247.htm> accessed 30.12.2011.

108 L. Boulle and H.H. Teh, *supra* n. 71, p. 224. Also see the Subordinate Courts – Court Dispute Resolution/Mediation website <http://app.subcourts.gov.sg/civil/page.aspx?pageid=54106#Public_About5> accessed 27.09.2012.

109 H.H. Teh, *supra* n. 81, p. 8.

110 Report of the Committee on Alternative Dispute Resolution dated 04.07.1996.

These recommendations were accepted by the government and the first Community Mediation Centre (CMC) was set up in 1998[111] under the Community Mediation Centres Act.[112] CMCs served to mediate disputes that were family, social or community based and which did not involve any seisable offences under any written law.

There are two CMCs and seven CMC satellite mediation centres.[113] Cases come to CMCs from three sources; direct intake, referrals from other public agencies and Magistrate referrals.[114] These cases generally fall into two categories. The first category involves community disputes that have not yet been escalated to the courts and having a matter referred to mediation is voluntary. The second category involves those community disputes that have escalated into court proceedings before a Magistrate. Magistrates can compulsorily refer appropriate cases to the CMCs without the parties' consent.[115]

Mediators at the CMCs are typically community leaders who volunteer their time and effort.[116] They include professionals from the fields of law, business, counselling and teaching. The demographic of the mediation panel is meant to replicate the mediators of traditional times who were typically respected members or leaders of the community.[117]

Persons interested in becoming CMC mediators have to first undergo a two-day training workshop which teaches them the basics of mediation. Participants who have distinguished themselves will then have an opportunity to undergo a period of 'apprenticeship' where they are assigned to conduct co-mediations with more experienced mediators. Ideally, each co-mediation would be with a different co-mediator so that the 'apprentice' mediator is exposed to as large a range of experiences as possible. When the 'apprentice' mediator is deemed ready, formal recommendations are made to the Minister of Law who then appoints them as CMC mediators for terms of two years.[118] These terms are renewable.

---

111 J. Lee and H.H. Teh, *supra* n. 77, para. 1.12.

112 Community Mediation Centres Act, Cap. 49A, 1998 (Rev Ed).

113 There were originally three CMCs but this was reduced in early 2012 in a move to centralise efforts and maximise available resources.

114 G. Lim, C. Lim and E. Tan, 'Promoting Mediation as an Alternative Dispute Resolution Process to Resolve Community and Social Disputes – A Singapore Perspective', paper presented at the 1st Asian Mediation Association Conference, Singapore, 4–5 June 2009, p. 5 <www.asianmediationassociation.org/conference/pdf/AMA%20Conference%202009%20-%20Promoting%20Mediation%20As%20An%20Alternative%20Dispute%20Resolution%20Process%20To%20Resolve%20Community%20&%20Social%20Disputes%20by%20Gloria%20Lim.pdf> accessed 27.09.2012.

115 *Ibid.*, pp. 6–7.

116 While CMC mediators receive a token amount to defray costs, CMC mediators are essentially engaged in *pro bono* work.

117 G. Lim, C. Lim and E. Tan, *supra* n. 114, p. 3.

118 Section 8, Community Mediation Centres Act, Cap 49A, 1998 (Rev Ed.).

CMC mediation services are free with an administration fee charged to the complainant at the point of registration. This fee is to deter frivolous case registrations. Mediation sessions are typically set for one to two hours and the CMC adopts a co-mediation model. The diversity of the mediation panel allows for a meaningful matching of mediators to the parties in terms of skills, language, gender, race, age group, profile and experience.[119]

Mediation sessions at the CMCs are conducted with as little formality and technicality as possible with a view to expeditiously resolving the dispute. Mediators take a facilitative approach and are forbidden to adjudicate or arbitrate the dispute.[120] As with most facilitative approaches, the mediation process is both flexible and dynamic with the mediation occurring largely in joint sessions with both parties and then moving to private sessions where appropriate. The main focus is to solve the problem of the parties by focusing on their interests and restoring the harmony and relationship between the parties.

When an agreement eventuates, it must be reduced to writing with a signed statement by or on behalf of the parties of its binding effect.[121] The mediators typically draft the settlement agreement which is then enforceable as a matter of contract in the civil courts in the event of a breach. While the CMCs do not have powers of enforcement, it does provide parties with the option of re-mediating their matter in the event of a dispute arising out of a previously mediated settlement. This is also facilitated with the insertion of a dispute resolution clause in the template settlement agreement used by the CMCs.[122]

The success of the CMCs can be attributed to the support and political will of the Government of Singapore. Concerted efforts have been made to increase public awareness of community mediation and its availability.[123] This has included educating the general public and since 2006, educating youths to enable students to gain insights into amicable conflict resolution through mediation.

### *3.1.3. Singapore Mediation Centre*

Many mediations in the commercial arena are done at the Singapore Mediation Centre (SMC). The SMC began its life as the Commercial Mediation Service when it was launched by the Supreme Court and the Singapore Academy of Law in 1996[124] in response to the idea mooted at the 1996 Opening of the Legal Year by the then Attorney-General Chan Sek Keong, of setting up a national

119 G. Lim, C. Lim and E. Tan, *supra* n. 114, p. 3.

120 *Ibid.*, 5. See also Section 10(4), Community Mediation Centres Act, Cap 49A, 1998 (Rev Ed.).

121 Section 13(2), Community Mediation Centres Act, Cap 49A, 1998 (Rev Ed.).

122 G. Lim, C. Lim and E. Tan, *supra* n. 114, p. 4.

123 *Ibid.*, pp. 7–9; C. Liew, *supra* n. 106, p. 527.

124 L. Boulle and H.H. Teh, *supra* n. 71, p. 207.

mediation centre. It differed from court-based mediation in that it was not part of the court process and was chargeable.[125]

Initially, the cases that were mediated at the SMC were referred from the Supreme Court. As institutionalised private mediation was new to the legal profession, a significant amount of time and effort was invested in educating lawyers about mediation, to enable them to advise their clients on the option. Much of that was done at pre-trial conferences in the Supreme Court, where the mediation process, advantages and costs of mediation, and the role of the lawyers in that process was explained.[126] Now, matters are also referred independently and directly to the SMC from the Subordinate Courts, lawyers and professional bodies.[127]

Within a year, 84 cases were mediated with a 75% success rate.[128] This prompted the establishment of the Singapore Mediation Centre in August 1997,[129] which was tasked with providing mediation services, training and accrediting mediators and promoting mediation.

The SMC offers three types of paid mediation services. The first is for matters where the quantum of the claim is more than Singapore $30,000. The amounts charged by the SMC to mediate these disputes range from Singapore $900 to Singapore $2,800 per party per day depending on the quantum claimed.[130] An administrative fee of Singapore $250 per party is also payable.

The second type is the Small Case Commercial Mediation Scheme (SCCMS) which is for commercial disputes where the quantum claimed is under Singapore $30,000. These are typically cases involving tenancy, car repairs, unpaid salaries and renovation matters. The fees payable for this service are Singapore $160.50 per party.

Relatively recently, the SMC has also introduced a third service, the Family Law Mediation Scheme (FLMS). This is in material respects similar to the first type of mediation service with three main differences. First, it is intended to assist couples who are going through divorce or separation to resolve issues of, *inter alia*, custody of children, spousal maintenance and division of family assets. Secondly, in a bid to encourage the use of mediation in family disputes, SMC offers a discounted rate of Singapore $2,140 per party per day (regardless of quantum). An administrative fee of Singapore $267.50 per party is also payable. Finally, apart from undergoing training and accreditation, the mediators are

---

125 In addition to an administrative fee of $250, the current schedule of mediation fees of the Singapore Mediation Centre starts from $900 per party per day. For the complete fee schedule, see <www.mediation.com.sg/pdf/mediation_annex_c.pdf> accessed 27.09.2012.

126 L. Boulle and H.H. Teh, *supra* n. 71, pp. 208–209.

127 J. Lee and H.H. Teh, *supra* n. 77, paras. 1.10 and 1.26.

128 L. Boulle and H.H. Teh, *supra* n. 71, p. 211.

129 J. Lee and H.H. Teh, *supra* n. 77, paras. 1.10 and 1.11.

130 For quantum amounts above Singapore $5,000,000, Singapore $2900 per party per day is charged plus a pro-rated portion of 0.05% of the quantum above Singapore $5,000,000. *Supra* n. 125.

drawn from a group of experienced family lawyers who are familiar with the intricacies of family disputes.

The SMC maintains three panels of mediators; principal mediators, associate mediators and international mediators. The mediators in the principal and associate mediator panels consist of professionals from many areas; there are lawyers, accountants, architects, engineers, doctors, IT specialists and other professionals. Associate mediators tend to deal with the SCCMS cases while principal mediators tend to deal with the higher value commercial cases. The mediators on the international panel consist of internationally recognised peacemakers and who may be called upon to mediate cross-border disputes.[131]

While there have been a number of accreditation mechanisms over the years, the most current that typically applies to associate mediators consists of attending a two-day basic workshop, a three-day advanced workshop and an accreditation test. Mediators are trained in the facilitative interests-based model of mediation and the accreditation test consists of a half-day of assessment where trainees will mediate a role play in front of assessors and be provided with feedback. They will also have to undergo a written test. Variations of these trainings have been conducted for the PDRC and the Family Law Mediation Pilot Project to take into account the unique training needs of the participants in those programmes.

When a case is referred to the SMC, mediators (or in some cases co-mediators) are selected to match the needs of the case, either in terms of language, expertise or experience. It is also open for parties to select their own mediators from the panel.[132] Depending on the mediation scheme involved, a mediation may be scheduled from half a day (SCCMS mediations) to two days (standard and FLMS mediations). Legal counsel is generally in attendance for the standard and FLMS mediations. In the SCCMS mediations, only parties are in attendance. Lawyers play an important role by assisting the mediators and advising their clients during the mediation.

Mediations at the SMC are governed by a standard Mediation Procedure.[133] This Mediation Procedure explains the roles of the mediator, the mediation centre and the parties; outlines the mediation process and makes provision for confidentiality. As mediators are trained in the facilitative interests-based model of mediation, parties are guided through the process of problem-solving and ideally, mediators will not intervene in the substantive aspects of the dispute either by evaluating the merits of the matter or suggesting solutions.

---

131 For the list of international mediators, see < www.mediation.com.sg/mediation_panel.htm> accessed 27.09.2012.

132 *Supra* n. 125.

133 See The Mediation Procedure <www.mediation.com.sg/Mediation%20Procedure_1%20 April%202007.htm> accessed 27.09.2012.

At this point, it is useful to mention that the SMC's Code of Conduct[134] and the Mediation Procedure do allow for a mediator to make an evaluation of the parties' case where the request is made by all the parties and if s/he is satisfied that s/he is able to make the evaluation.

Should an agreement be reached, the lawyers, and in the case of SCCMS mediations the mediator, drafts the settlement agreement. These can be enforced in civil proceedings as a contract should a breach occur. Settlement agreements can also be filed as consent orders in the High Court.

In the fifteen years since its inception, the SMC has since gone from strength to strength. Apart from mediation, it also provides a range of ADR services including adjudication,[135] neutral evaluation and the Singapore Domain Name Dispute Resolution Service.[136] The SMC has also expanded its services to mediation in other industries through specialist mediation schemes. These are:

- the Alternative Dispute Resolution Sports Scheme: launched in 2008 in partnership with sports organisations[137] and other ADR service providers,[138] this sought to resolve sports related disputes – these disputes to could relate to the selection of athletes, contractual disputes and matters of discipline;[139]
- the Medical Mediation Scheme: launched in 2008 in partnership with the Ministry of Health, this sought to resolve healthcare disputes – these disputes may relate to patients' or their families' claims for financial compensation against the doctor or hospital, other claims for lapses in the standards of the clinical services delivered by medical practitioners, and billing and financial matters;[140]

134 See Code of Conduct <www.mediation.com.sg/pdf/mediation_annex_b.pdf> accessed 27.09.2012.

135 Adjudication occurs under the framework of the Building and Construction Industry Security of Payment Act, Cap 30B, 2006 (Rev Ed.), Statutes of Singapore. The SMC Adjudication Procedure Rules may be found at <www.mediation.com.sg/Adjudication.htm> accessed 27.09.2012.

136 The Singapore Domain Name Dispute Resolution Service (SDRS) provides a low-cost and quick mechanism for parties to resolve their disputes concerning the use of '.sg' domain names. For more details, see <www.disputemanager.com.sg/SDRP/what.htm> accessed 27.09.2012.

137 These include the Singapore Sports Council and the Singapore National Olympic Council.

138 These include the Singapore International Arbitration Centre and the Singapore Institute of Arbitrators.

139 Press release by the Singapore Sports Council at the launch of the ADR Framework for Sports on 07.01.2008 <www.ssc.gov.sg/publish/Corporate/en/news/media_releases/2008/alternative_dispute.html> accessed 27.09.2012. This scheme utilises a blend of mediation and arbitration to allow disputants to first mediate their dispute, and in the event that mediation is unsuccessful, proceed for arbitration. C. Liew, *supra* n. 106, p. 521.

140 C. Liew, *supra* n. 106, p. 521; see also Ministry of Health, Inquiries and Complaints Guide <www.moh.gov.sg/content/moh_web/home/about-us/feedback/inquiries_and_complaintsguide.html> accessed 27.09.2012.

- the SMC-Medical Council Mediation Scheme: governed by the SMC-Medical Council Mediation Rules, the Complaints Committee of the Singapore Medical Council can refer matters for mediation where it was unanimously agreed that no investigation was necessary into the conduct of the registered medical practitioner;[141]
- the Council for Private Education Mediation-Arbitration Scheme: launched in 2010 and provided for in the Council for Private Education Act and the Private Education (Dispute Resolution Schemes) Regulations 2010,[142] this was set up to resolve a growing number of disputes arising from or in relation to the provision of services by registered private education providers;[143] and
- the Council for Estate Agents Mediation-Arbitration Scheme: launched in 2011 and provided for in the Estate Agents Act 2010 and the Estate Agents (Dispute Resolution Schemes) Regulations 2011,[144] this was established to resolve disputes between a licensed estate agent and his or her client.

### *3.1.4. Other sources of mediation*

The previous sections cover the larger providers of mediation in Singapore. It is not possible to document every mediation service provider in this chapter. There are a number of smaller service providers that are context or industry specific. Some examples are:

- the Consumer Association of Singapore (CASE) Mediation Centre: this primarily deals with consumer-to-business disputes and tourist-to-business disputes;[145]
- the Financial Industry Disputes Resolution Centre (FIDREC): this provides both mediation and adjudication services for disputes stemming from the financial industry.[146] These services were crucial in managing the recent financial crisis caused by the collapse of, *inter alia*, Lehman Brothers;

141 See Section 42(4)(b)(ii), Medical Registration Act (Cap 174, 2010 Rev. Ed.) and Rule 5.1, Singapore Mediation Centre and Singapore Medical Council Mediation Rules. See also the Second Reading Speech by Mr Khaw Boon Wan, then the Minister for Health, in Parliament on 11.01.2010.

142 The legislation provides for dispute resolution services to be provided by the SMC and the Singapore Institute of Arbitrators. See Private Education Act, Cap 247A, 2009; Private Education (Dispute Resolution Schemes) Regulations 2010 (S272/2010).

143 See Brochure for CPE Mediation-Arbitration Scheme <www.cpe.gov.sg/cpe/slot/u100/Publication/publication/Dispute%20Resolution%20Brochure.pdf> accessed 27.09.2012.

144 The SMC is one of the approved mediation centres prescribed by the Estate Agents (Dispute Resolution Schemes) Regulations 2011. See Second Schedule, Part I, Estate Agents (Dispute Resolution Schemes) Regulations 2011.

145 CASE, Mediation <www.case.org.sg/mediation.html> accessed 27.09.2012.

146 See FIDREC: Dispute Resolution Process <www.fidrec.com.sg/website/disputerp.html> accessed 27.09.2012; FIDReC, About Us <www.fidrec.com.sg/website/background.html>

- the Singapore Institute of Surveyors and Valuers (SISV) Mediation Centre: this seeks to resolve disputes amicably in the construction and real estate industry;[147]
- the Law Society's SCMediate Scheme: this provides for the mediation of disputes on legal costs[148] between law practices by Senior Counsel[149] and the Law Society's Cost Dispute Resolve scheme for the mediation of disputes on legal costs;[150] and
- the Eagles Mediation and Counselling Centre: this provides mediation services for, *inter alia*, personal and family contexts.[151]

Apart from these industry service providers, there are various agencies and tribunals that also provide mediation services some of which are mandated by legislative framework. Examples of these are:

- Ministry of Manpower: mediation services are provided for disputes between employers and employees as well as mandatory tripartite mediation under the framework of the Industrial Relations Act;[152]
- the Industrial Arbitration Court: the Registrar of the Industrial Arbitration Court conducts mediation to assist parties in resolving their disputes so as to avoid arbitration;[153]
- the Maintenance of Parents Tribunal: before hearing an application for maintenance orders by parents, it is mandated that the differences between the parties be referred by the Tribunal to a conciliation officer for mediation;[154]

accessed 27.09.2012; FIDReC Annual Report 2009/2010 <www.fidrec.com.sg/website/annualreports/FIDReC%20AR%202009-2010.pdf> accessed 27.09.2012, p 18.

147 See SISV Dispute Resolution Centre <www.sisv.org.sg/drc> accessed 27.09.2012.

148 The Law Society of Singapore: Cost Dispute Resolve <www.lawsociety.org.sg/forMembers/ResourceCentre/MembershipBenefits/Members'SupportSchemes/CostDisputeResolve.aspx> accessed 27.09.2012.

149 The Law Society of Singapore: SCMediate <www.lawsociety.org.sg/forMembers/ResourceCentre/MembershipBenefits/Members'SupportSchemes/SCMediate.aspx> accessed 27.09.2012.

150 The Law Society of Singapore: Cost Dispute Resolve <www.lawsociety.org.sg/forMembers/ResourceCentre/MembershipBenefits/Members'SupportSchemes/CostDisputeResolve.aspx> accessed 27.09.2012.

151 See < www.emcc.org.sg/typeofmediation.aspx> accessed 28.09.2012.

152 A Guide to Tripartite Mediation <www.mom.gov.sg/Documents/employment-practices/Tripartite%20mediation%20brochure.pdf> accessed 27.09.2012.

153 See IAC Proceedings, Industrial Arbitration Court website <www.iac.gov.sg/Home/Pages/proceedings.aspx> accessed 27/09.2012.

154 See section 5(6) of the Maintenance of Parents Act. See also Commissioner for the Maintenance of Parents, Ministry of Community Development Youth and Sports website, <http://app1.mcys.gov.sg/AboutMCYS/OurPeople/DivisionsatMCYS/FamilyFormationStability/FamilyServicesDivision/TribunalfortheMaintenanceofParents.aspx> accessed 27.09.2012.

- the Strata Titles Board: all applications for an order for collective sale of property must first be mediated;[155] and
- the Intellectual Property Office (IPOS): IPOS' Hearings and Mediation Division facilitates the resolution of intellectual property disputes.[156]

## 3.2. PROMOTING MEDIATION IN SINGAPORE

There is no doubt that mediation has been firmly established as part of the landscape of the Singapore legal system. While it would be fair to say that Singapore has achieved some success, it has not been content to rest on its laurels. Instead, it has continually looked for ways to promote mediation and its use. This section will look at some recent developments and initiatives.

### *3.2.1. Singapore Mediation Centre*

#### 3.2.1.1. Asian Mediation Association

Part of the strategy for promoting mediation in Singapore involves the promotion of mediation in the wider region. With this in mind, the Singapore Mediation Centre took the initiative to establish the Asian Mediation Association (AMA) in August 2007. The AMA seeks to promote mediation in Asia and to facilitate the sharing of resources, best practices and local knowledge as well as to provide an infrastructure for regional dispute resolution to support cross-border investment and trade activities in Asia. The AMA Charter was adopted in April 2008 which sets out its objectives, principles, membership, structure, and decision-making mechanism.[157]

The founding members of the AMA are the Singapore Mediation Centre, the Hong Kong Mediation Centre, the Indonesian Mediation Centre, the Malaysian Mediation Centre and the Philippines Mediation Centre. Membership has been expanded to include the Delhi Mediation Centre, the Thai Mediation Centre, the Indian Institute of Arbitration and Mediation, the Ministry of Labour, Industrial Relations and Employment of Fiji (Mediation Unit).

The AMA held its inaugural conference in June 2009 in Singapore.[158] The theme of the conference was 'Mediation Diversity – Asia and Beyond' and it

---

155 See General Information on Application for Collective Sale of Property, Strata Titles Board website <www.mnd.gov.sg/stb/generalInformation.html> accessed 27.09.2012.

156 See Hearings & Mediation, Intellectual Property Office of Singapore for more details: <www.ipos.gov.sg/Services/HearingsandMediation.aspx> accessed 27.09.2012.

157 See Charter of the Asian Mediation Association <www.asianmediationassociation.org/pdf/AMACharter.pdf> accessed 27.09.2012.

158 For the conference materials see <www.asianmediationassociation.org/Resources.html> accessed 27.09.2012.

brought together participants from around the world comprising ADR practitioners, lawyers, academics and other professionals interested and involved in ADR. A second conference was held in February 2011 in Kuala Lumpur, Malaysia centred on the theme 'Rediscovering Mediation in the 21st Century'.[159]

### 3.2.1.2. International Mediation Institute

Apart from regional initiatives, the Singapore Mediation Centre is also involved in international initiatives to promote mediation. One such initiative was the founding of the International Mediation Institute (IMI) in 2007. The IMI is a global public service initiative to drive transparency and competency standards in mediation practice worldwide.[160] The IMI was established by founding organisations, the American Arbitration Association, the Netherlands Mediation Institute, the Singapore International Arbitration Centre and the Singapore Mediation Centre.

The impact of Singapore's influence and development in the field of mediation, not just in Asia but worldwide is most notable here. Singaporeans have been appointed to the Advisory Council and Board of Directors,[161] the Independent Standards Commission[162] and the Intercultural Taskforce.[163]

### 3.2.1.3. Mediation Charter

The most recent initiative of the Singapore Mediation Centre in promoting the use of mediation was the launching of the Mediation Charter in 2011. The Mediation Charter is a pledge that organisations undertake to signal their commitment to promote mediation through five core actions, including using

---

159 See the 2nd AMA Conference Flyer <http://barcouncil.org.my/conference1/index.html> accessed 27.09.2012.

160 See <www.fidrec.com.sg/website/background.html> accessed 28.09.2012.

161 Singapore's Ambassador-at-large, Professor Tommy Koh is a member of the Advisory Council and Mr George Lim SC a member of the Board of Directors. See respectively <http://imimediation.org/imi-advisory-council> and <http://imimediation.org/imi-board-of-directors> accessed 27.09.2012.

162 Initially chaired by Singapore's Ambassador-at-large, Professor Tommy Koh, members include Associate Professor Joel Lee, Faculty of Law, National University of Singapore, this was convened to inter alia set high competency standards for mediators, review and approve programmes to qualify mediators for IMI certification, ensure continuing quality of approved programmes, monitor the IMI Code of Professional Conduct and appoint assessors to review complaints made under the Code of Professional Conduct. See <http://imimediation.org/imi-independent-standards-commission> accessed 27.09.2012.

163 Co-chaired by Professor Harold Abramson and Joanna Kowalski, members include Associate Professor Joel Lee, Faculty of Law, National University of Singapore. This was convened to develop criteria for inter-cultural mediator training and IMI Certification. The Task Force's goals were to develop criteria that are succinct, flexible, and feasible to implement by trainers and QAPs (Qualifying Assessment Programs). See <http://imimediation.org/intercultural-taskforce> accessed 27.09.2012.

mediation as a first resort to resolve the organisation's disputes with other persons or organisations.[164]

### *3.2.2. Court-based initiatives*

One of the challenges of promoting the use of mediation in Singapore is getting support from the gatekeepers of the legal system i.e. the lawyers. Singapore has adopted a number of recent court-based initiatives to encourage the use of mediation.

#### 3.2.2.1. ADR Form

On 22 April 2010, the Subordinate Courts released ePractice Direction No. 2 of 2010.[165] Taking effect on 17 May 2010, the practice direction introduced the 'ADR Form' which was required to be filed by lawyers when taking out or responding to a summons for directions pursuant to O 25 of the Rules of Court.[166]

The ADR Form requires 'Solicitors […] to indicate in the form the salient characteristics about the case. These include the nature and value of the claim and the projected length of the trial.'[167] It also provides that 'parties must […] certify on the form that their solicitors have explained to them the various ADR options and their respective benefits. The form includes basic information about mediation and arbitration for the parties' reference.'[168]

The ADR Form seeks to 'introduce the practice of considering ADR options in all cases'[169] at a point where all the issues in dispute would have crystallised after the filing of the pleadings and before the high legal costs of preparing for trial are incurred.

Upon submission of the ADR Form, the judicial officer will make recommendations for the appropriate form of dispute resolution for the dispute in question.[170] The forms of dispute resolution are to be either mediation (at the Primary Dispute Resolution Centre or the Singapore Mediation Centre),

164 See welcome address by the Honourable Justice Belinda Ang, Chairman, SMC, at SMC's annual appreciation lunch and launch of the Singapore Mediation Charter (09.09.2011) <www.sal.org.sg/Lists/Speeches/DispForm.aspx?ID=92> accessed 27.09.2012. For a list of the organisations that signed the Mediation Charter, see <www.sal.org.sg/Lists/NewsReleases/Attachments/46/Annex%201.pdf> accessed 27.09.2012.

165 Available at <www.singaporelawwatch.sg/legal/ln2/rss/noticedirect/67217.pdf?utm_source=rss%20subscription&utm_medium=rss> accessed 27.09.2012.

166 Cap 322, R 5, 2006 (Rev. Ed.).

167 ePractice Direction No. 2 of 2010, para. 6(a).

168 ePractice Direction No. 2 of 2010, para. 6(b).

169 Except cases involving non-injury motor accidents as these are already dealt with by Court Dispute Resolution sessions. See ePractice Direction No. 2 of 2010, para. 5.

170 J. Low and D. Quek, *supra* n. 92, pp. 18 and 20.

arbitration (under the Law Society Arbitration Scheme) or adjudication (in the courts).[171]

This is a significant development as the requirement to fill in this form encourages lawyers and their clients to have a meaningful discussion regarding the ADR processes available and the attendant risks and costs of litigation. While it is too early to gauge its success, it is certainly to be welcomed as a step to '[encourage] a paradigm shift and a culture change through the active encouragement of ADR and facilitating greater awareness of ADR'.[172]

#### 3.2.2.2. Presumption of ADR

Supporting the ADR Form is the Subordinate Court's most recent court-based initiative. These are various changes introduced via the Practice Directions Amendment No. 2 of 2012. One of these changes relates to the introduction of the Presumption of ADR. Put simply, this provides for automatic referral of all civil cases for ADR unless parties opt out of ADR.

Cases are sorted into two categories. The first are cases that fall into 'Recommended ADR' category. These are generally claims of lower value. The idea is that the early settlement of these lower value claims would result in more substantial savings in terms of time and costs. Therefore cases with a value of $20,000 or less, or cases between $20,000 and $60,000 that will take more than three days of trial, fall into this category.

Parties may opt out of ADR in the 'Recommended ADR' category in three situations: first, where ADR has been attempted before; secondly, where the dispute involves a question of law; and thirdly, where parties can produce some other good reason. Where parties opt out for an unsatisfactory reason, they may face cost sanctions under Order 59 r 5.[173]

Cases that do not fall into the 'Recommended ADR' category fall into the 'General Track' category. This category allows for parties to opt out for any reason.

In addition to the Presumption of ADR, the amendment also creates a new ADR section in the Subordinate Courts Practice Direction. Further, the amendment also clearly sets out the expected standards relating to the preparation for and the attendance of mediation and neutral evaluation.

#### 3.2.2.3. Costs sanctions

The final recent development was the amendment of Order 59 r 5 of the Rules of Court which provided for the court to take into account various considerations

---

171 ePractice Direction No. 2 of 2010, para. 6(c).

172 J. Low and D. Quek, *supra* n. 92, pp. 18 and 20.

173 See *infra* section 3.2.2.3.

when exercising its discretion in awarding costs. The original was amended by organising its content into subsections and by the insertion of a new consideration.[174] The amendment empowers the court to take into consideration 'the parties' conduct in relation to any attempt at resolving the cause or matter by mediation or any other means of dispute resolution'.[175]

This introduction of costs sanctions is intended to encourage lawyers and parties to consider the use of mediation to resolve their disputes as any unreasonable refusal to consider mediation[176] or a lack of good faith effort[177] to engage in mediation would clearly be caught. It is important to note that there is a gap in the rules in that it only operates where parties or their counsel bring up the possibility of mediation. Where they do not, it is arguable that this consideration will not apply, in which case, it no longer serves the purpose of encouraging lawyers and parties to consider the use of mediation to resolve their disputes.[178]

### 3.2.3. *Educational and training initiatives*

Education and training remain key ways to promote the use of mediation in Singapore. Some initiatives have been around for some time. For example, since 1996, the Faculty of Law of the National University of Singapore has been running skills-based mediation workshops as an elective subject for its law students and is the first law school in Asia to have done so. Graduates who successfully complete the mediation workshop can apply to be accredited as an Associate Mediator of the Singapore Mediation Centre upon passing the assessment module.[179]

The Singapore Mediation Centre has, since its inception, been conducting training on a regular basis. Most mediators in Singapore have been trained under the auspices of the Singapore Mediation Centre. Through this training, many have become advocates in their respective industries and have played a key role in promoting mediation. The Singapore Mediation Centre also conducts training overseas including for the Judiciary of Brunei, the Courts of the Dubai International Financial Centre, the Court of Appeal of the Philippines, the

---

174 Rules of Court (Amendment No 3) Rules 2010 (GN No S 504/2010) with effect from 15.09.2010.

175 Order 59 Rule 5(c).

176 It is not clear what would constitute a reasonable refusal to mediate. See brief discussion at J. LEE, 'Court-based initiatives for mediation in Singapore' [2011] *Asian JM* 60, 65–66.

177 There are of course tremendous difficulties in showing a lack of good faith. LEE, *ibid.*, p. 66.

178 *Ibid.*, p. 65.

179 Students from the NUS Law Faculty's Mediation workshop were exempted from both the basic and advanced mediation workshop though not the assessment for accreditation. Information on SMC workshops can be found at <www.mediation.com.sg/training.htm> accessed on 27.09.2012).

Supreme Judiciary Council of the State of Qatar and the Office of the Judiciary of Thailand.[180]

More recently, the Singapore Management University School of Law, established in 2007, has been running a 'Negotiation and Mediation for Lawyers' workshop since 2009. In the same year, it established the SMU Centre for Dispute Resolution which is tasked with fostering ADR research and teaching.

A more recent development in 2011 was the changes made to the Part B of the Singapore Bar Exams,[181] administered by the Singapore Institute of Legal Education. Part B is a compulsory five-month postgraduate practical law course and examination required of every qualified lawyer seeking admission to the Singapore bar. The new curriculum incorporated compulsory modules on negotiation skills and mediation advocacy skills as well as a separate optional module on mediation skills.

### *3.2.4. Developing an Asian perspective*

It was mentioned earlier that modern mediation practice in Singapore was influenced by mediation training and practice from the 'West' and differed from indigenous forms of mediation. Even as early as the mid-1990s, academics, commentators and practitioners questioned whether the facilitative interests-based model of conflict resolution was appropriate in the Asian context and what modifications needed to be made to take into account relevant cultural differences.[182]

A working group was set up in 2003 under the auspices of the Singapore Mediation Centre to study this question. After five years, the study bore fruit in the publication of *An Asian Perspective on Mediation*[183] launched at the first Asian Mediation Association Conference (4–5 June 2009).

Instead of accepting the dichotomous choice of 'West versus East',[184] the book proceeded from the assumption that the interests-based model of conflict resolution provided a functional paradigm that was universal to the human condition. What sometimes caused an uncomfortable fit with cultures outside

180 H.H. Teh, *supra* n. 81, p. 17.

181 See generally the Legal Profession Act (Cap. 161) and the Legal Profession (Qualified Persons) Rules. Part B is a compulsory 5 month postgraduate practical law course and examination.

182 J. Lee and H.H. Teh, *supra* n. 77, paras. 1.35–1.39.

183 J. Lee and H.H. Teh (eds.), *An Asian Perspective on Mediation*, Academy Publishing, Singapore 2009.

184 In writing this paper, the author is well aware of the dangers of using sweeping terms like the 'East', 'West' or even 'culture'. It is outside the scope of the paper to explore the problems of this definitional minefield. Suffice it to say that this issue is explored thoroughly in *An Asian Perspective on Mediation*, *ibid.*

the West were the cultural assumptions inherent within the model which had their origin in the West.[185]

By identifying these 'Western' cultural assumptions and replacing them with cultural assumptions appropriate to the context of Singapore (and other cultures which share its heritage),[186] it was possible to preserve the usefulness of the interests-based model of conflict resolution and harmonise it with the culture of Singapore. Having said that, it is important to note that there is no attempt to prescribe any 'Asian model' of mediation. Instead, it offers *one* Asian perspective, that of Singapore, and provides academics and practitioners of mediation in other Asian countries a methodology for contextualising the interests-based model in their own cultures.

The ideas in this book have been well received and have been described as a significant contribution to the thought leadership and understanding of mediation in Asia.[187] The Singapore Mediation Centre has recently conducted, in July 2012, a workshop based on *An Asian Perspective on Mediation*.

### *3.2.5. Other initiatives*

There are also a number of other initiatives that are worth mentioning. First, apart from the sources of mediation mentioned earlier, there is anecdotal evidence to suggest that an increasing number of private mediations are being conducted. These mediators can be from Singapore or from other jurisdictions. Regrettably, it is not possible track and list these. However, if we accept the anecdotal evidence to be accurate, then mediation is set to grow in Singapore.

Secondly, there has been a private initiative by a group of mediators to organise a Peacemakers' Workshop. The inaugural workshop was in June 2010 and has been replicated every year since. The goal of this workshop was to empower youths to better manage conflict situations and to promote peer mediation. Students from secondary schools (from 13 to 16 years of age) in Singapore were taught conflict management skills within a basic mediation framework. The cornerstone of Peacemakers was a competition where students mediate simulated disputes and awards were given to the best mediators and parties. This is a heartening development in two ways. The author supports the importance of inculcating a culture of peace-making in Singapore's youths and Peacemakers is certainly a step in the right direction. It is also heartening in that this private initiative involved the participation of mediators from the various

---

185 See generally the discussion in J. Lee and H.H. Teh, 'Appropriateness of the Interests-Based Model for the Asian Context', in J. Lee and H.H. Teh (eds.), *An Asian Perspective on Mediation*, Academy Publishing, Singapore 2009.

186 See generally the discussion in J. Lee and H.H. Teh, 'Asian Culture: A Definitional Challenge', in J. Lee and H.H. Teh (eds.), *An Asian Perspective on Mediation*, Academy Publishing, Singapore 2009.

187 C. Liew, *supra* n. 106, p. 530.

mediation institutions in Singapore like the CMC, EMCC, PDRC and SMC, and symbolises the importance of bringing together mediators, despite their institutional affiliations, under the banner of peace-making. The Peacemakers movement is set to grow. Apart from demand from schools for peace-making and peer mediation programmes, there have been indications of interest in Peacemakers by the International Mediation Institute as well as plans to replicate Peacemakers in some of the member countries of the Asian Mediation Association.

The final initiative is relatively recent and involves the creation of an informal network where mediators, mediation teachers, mediation trainers and mediation providers meet from time to time to discuss issues relating to mediation, developments and initiatives in mediation and ideas as to how to develop mediation in Singapore. This initiative is cross-institutional and to the author's mind, an important collaborative development in order for mediation to continue to flourish in Singapore.

## 3.3. THE WAY FORWARD

It is of course difficult to say with any certainty how ADR will develop in Singapore. The author, adopting the right of speculative licence, would like to make three predictions.

First, is the move towards collaborative legal practice. The writer started this chapter acknowledging that the traditional interpretation of the acronym 'ADR' was 'Alternative Dispute Resolution'. Over the years, there have been suggestions to replace the word 'Alternative' with 'Appropriate'.[188] This is more than a semantic difference. Words affect how we perceive the world. The author submits that labelling mediation as an 'alternative' to litigation already stacks the deck in litigation's favour. After all, one only goes to one's alternatives if the main option does not work out. Further, since a lawyer's legal education is largely based on the win-lose zero-sum paradigm, this only ensures that lawyers perceive mediation as something less desirable. The word 'appropriate' removes this stigma and also focuses the lawyer's attention on what the proper issue is, i.e. which method of dispute resolution is the appropriate one for the client's matter at hand. In a sense, this is already a reflection of the evolution of the legal system in Singapore in both case law,[189] legal processes, i.e. the ADR Form, and legal education at both the university and post-graduate levels.

---

188 J. Lee, *supra* n. 2, pp. 415–416, and J. Lee, 'ADR and Mediation: The Future of Legal Practice', in H.W. Tang, M. Hor, and S.Y. Koh (eds.), *The Practice of Law*, Lexis Nexis, Singapore 2011.

189 In *Lock Han Chng Jonathan v. Goh Jessiline* [2008] 2 SLR(R) 455, the Singapore Court of Appeal highlighted the importance of lawyers to assist their client to make an informed choice about the options available to proceed with the matter. This involves a duty on the part of the lawyer to ensure that the client is provided with relevant information about the choices

This is a significant step forward. By way of speculation, the author suggests the next step in ADR's evolution in Singapore is to move from thinking about 'Appropriate' dispute resolution to that of 'Amicable' dispute resolution. This move reflects the real distinction between dispute resolution processes like arbitration and litigation on one hand and negotiation and mediation on the other. For years, arbitration was considered part of the alternative dispute resolution processes and from one perspective this is of course accurate. It was an alternative to litigation. However, due to the similarity of its dispute resolution to litigation, it was far easier for lawyers to transit to the use of arbitration. Arbitration is now so common place that it is no longer accurate to refer to it as 'alternative'. The suggested classification accurately places arbitration and litigation as adversarial forms of dispute resolution while mediation and negotiation are considered more amicable forms of dispute resolution. Many mediators have had the experience of having to deal with lawyers or parties who come to mediation with an adversarial mindset. The suggested classification makes explicit the mindset required when using each form of dispute resolution.

In Australia and the United States, there is a strong and growing number of practitioners of collaborative law. The idea is that these practitioners primarily focus on collaborative ways of resolving their clients' disputes and where it is necessary to utilise more adversarial forms of dispute resolution, they will refer it on to other practitioners. This has the advantages of allowing for specialisation as well as defining the scope of practice for liability purposes. While collaborative law is not yet a reality in Singapore, the author can certainly see this as one possible reality. It is perhaps apt that at this point of writing, there are plans for an ADR conference organised by the Subordinate Courts where a key topic is on 'collaborative law'.[190]

A second point is the professionalisation of mediation and its related industries. To date, mediation has been a labour of love. Mediators are generally volunteers and even if they are paid, the amounts are small compared to what they might get in terms of commercial rates in their respective professions. And to be fair, this has been necessary to get mediation on its feet. After all, in Singapore, it is the poorer cousin to arbitration, which has received tremendous institutional and financial support. Just as there are now those who can claim arbitration as a profession, the next step is for mediation to move in the same direction. Leathes suggests, and the writer agrees, that this is vital to ensuring the mediation movement's well-being into the next decade.[191] Good mediators

available, the tangible and intangible risks involved with each choice and the consequences of each choice. See J. Pinsler, 'Litigation and the Client's Right to Make an Informed Choice' (2008) 20 *SAcLJ* 21 for more detailed discussion on this case.

190 See <www.lawsociety.org.sg/conference/ADR/programme.aspx> accessed 27.09.2012.

191 See M. Leathes, 'Making Mediation Mainstream' (2nd Keynote Address delivered at the 2nd AMA Conference, Kuala Lumpur, Malaysia, 25.02.2011 <http://barcouncil.org.my/conference1/pdf/9.MAKINGMEDIATIONMAINSTREAM.pdf> accessed 27.09.2012.

should be able to charge fair commercial rates for their services. The professionalisation of mediation should also see the rise of mediation advocates who are either lawyers (possibly practitioners of collaborative law) or other professionals who specialise in assisting parties in assessing whether mediation is suitable for their dispute, helping them prepare for a mediation and even representing them in a mediation.

The final prediction is the importance mediation will play in the region. As mentioned earlier, one of the regional initiatives was the establishment of the Asian Mediation Association. Another regional grouping that Singapore is a part of is the Association of South East Asian Nations (ASEAN). Established in 1967, one of ASEAN's purposes is to 'maintain and enhance peace, security and stability and further strengthen peace-oriented values in the region'[192] via 'reliance on peaceful settlement of disputes'.[193] Teh makes a case for mediation as a way of resolving disputes between member states, between members states and nationals (whether of member states or not) and between nationals of member states within the framework of ASEAN.[194] With the leadership, both formal and informal, that Singapore plays in the context of ASEAN, the author agrees with Teh that mediation can and should be key to peace-keeping and peace-making in the region.

At the end of the day, ADR, and in particular mediation, has come a long way. Only time will prove the accuracy (or not) of the author's predictions. ADR is certainly here to stay and if it stays on its present course, its prospects are bright indeed.

---

192 Article 1, ASEAN Charter, <www.aseansec.org/publications/ASEAN-Charter.pdf> accessed 30.09.2012.

193 *Ibid.*, Article 2(2)(d).

194 For more developed arguments, see H.H. Teh, *supra* n. 81, pp. 22–25.

# THAILAND

Suparb VONGKIATKACHORN*

## Contents



---

* Note that unless otherwise specified in this Thailand chapter, all referenced materials or sources are in the Thai language. The current exchange rate is approximately 30 Baht for one US Dollar. BE (Buddhist Era) is officially used for Thai calendar; BEs are maintained for the convenience of research in Thai-language materials. The years have been converted to Christian Era or AD, which in most cases are shown in parentheses. Statistics in this chapter are provided, as available or provided, from different sources and thus not shown to the same extent or in the same format. For the convenience of the reader, acronyms of titles of laws, regulations, or organisations may be given more than once.

## 1. SCOPE AND GENERAL BACKGROUND

Undoubtedly, if ADR is defined broadly as a means of settling a dispute without resorting to a State's institutionalised system of justice administration like a court of law, ADR would have been in existence in Thailand since the Sukhothai Kingdom (thirteenth to fifteenth centuries AD), the generally recognised beginning of Thailand's national history. Without going further into it, particularly the history of the codified Law of the Three Seals,[1] to ascertain if certain court officers in the Ayutthaya Kingdom (fourteenth to eighteenth centuries AD) were chosen by disputing parties to decide a dispute (thereby constituting an element of arbitration), written law that has apparently authorised or provided for various frameworks of ADR will be discussed below, with a particular focus on the field of civil and commercial matters.

1 See Justice for the People, p. 186, an excerpted document for downloading from the Ministry of Justice's website at <www.moj.go.th/upload/mini106_km/uploadfiles/8267_9439.pdf>. For a detailed description of this enactment, see Y. Isshii, *The Kotmai Tra Sam Duang or the Laws of the Three* Seals, at <http://adap.crma.ac.th/index.php?option=com_wrapper&view=wrapper&Itemid =72>. The acronym 'adap' in the foregoing link stands for Ayutthaya Digital Archive Project, which was funded by Thailand's Office of the Higher Education Commission (see <http://adap.crma.ac.th/wiki/index.php/Main_Page>).

As a general background, all bills will enter into force after they have been enacted with the advice and consent of the bicameral National Assembly of Thailand, signed or deemed to have been signed by the King, and published in the Royal Gazette.[2] The legal process is an accusatorial system. Decisions of the courts of law are not law, but only interpretations and the outcome of the application of law and facts at issue before them. Broadly speaking, international conventions, treaties or agreements will not be enforceable without, among other things, the National Assembly's approval or implementing enactment.[3]

# 2. LEGAL DEVELOPMENTS

## 2.1. OUT-OF-COURT MEDIATION

The Office of the Judiciary (OOJ) under the Courts of Justice (being the Judiciary branch) defines 'mediation' as a means of dispute resolution facilitated by a neutral third person who assists the parties in finding mutually acceptable solutions. If the parties reach an amicable solution, they may enter into a binding and enforceable compromise agreement.[4] See further *infra* subsection 3. 'Compromise agreements'. Further, the OOJ proposed a definition of out-of-court mediation, which can be summarised to mean mediation conducted without any court involvement either before or after a party's filing of a lawsuit.[5]

However, if one were to specify other details, e.g., non-judicial State officials' involvement or a post-judgment mediation process, so as to qualify the above-mentioned definition, the initial type of out-of-court mediation in Thailand would, in terms of legislative developments, be a mediation process where a State official is involved for the purposes of dispute settlement. This process first appeared in the Local Administration Act BE 2440 (1897) (LAA 1897)[6] where a subdistrict headman (*Kamnan*) had the power to make an assessment of

2 See sections 90 and 150 of the current Constitution of Thailand BE 2550 (2007) (Constitution). The Royal Gazette is the government's publication in which enactments of law, notices, appointments, and ceremonies are announced officially for the general public's knowledge.

3 See section 190 of the Constitution.

4 International Affairs Division of the OOJ: *Mediation: Thai-English*, Booklet (undated), pp. 1–2.

5 *Ibid.*, p. 3.

6 Announced on 20 May RE 116 (1897) (see Annual Collection of Laws (*Prachoom Khot Mhai Prajam Sok*), Vol. 16: Laws between RE 116–117 (1897–1898 AD or BE 2440–2441), first printing on 01.06.1935 (BE 2478), pp. 22–67). Note: RE stands for Rattanakosin Era, which was first used in 1889 (RE 108 or BE 2432) during the reign of King Rama V to mark the period of time from the establishment of Rattanakosin (Bangkok) by King Rama I in 1782 (BE 2325), which was the first year of RE. RE was replaced with BE in 1912 (RE 131 or BE 2455) during the reign of King Rama VI.

certain disputes pursuant to which disputing parties made an agreement and as a result no party was entitled to file a lawsuit afterwards.[7]

Subsequently, the mediation scheme under the LAA 1897 and its subsequent amendments was replaced with the mediation scheme under the State Administration Amendment Act No. 7 BE 2550 (2007) (SAA No. 7)[8] where a three-mediator panel (presided over by the chief district officer, a provincial public prosecutor, or the assistant chief district officer) has a duty to comply with stipulated ethics and is empowered to conduct mediation, and the resultant compromise agreement entered into by the disputing parties will have the effect of an arbitral award in accordance with the law on arbitration. If any party fails to comply with the compromise agreement, the other party may apply to a competent public prosecutor for him to apply on the party's behalf (not later than three years from the date the compromise agreement may be enforced) to a competent court (by filing a motion) to issue a legal execution order in accordance with the compromise agreement by applying the law on arbitration *mutatis mutandis*. No statistics provided. See further *infra* subsection 6.1. 'LAA 1897 and SAA No. 7 (2007)'.

Further, the Ministry of Justice (MOJ) formulated a policy in 1997 to promote alternative dispute resolution to reduce the caseloads of the courts of law. Hence, the MOJ set a community volunteer mediation program in motion. The program is now being carried out by the OOJ's Alternative Dispute Resolution Office

---

7 It is noteworthy that after the LAA 1897 a common legal basis or formality of dispute settlement and its effect did not come into existence until the Civil and Commercial Code of Thailand (CCC) took effect on 1 January 1925. Under sections 850–852 of the CCC, a dispute is settled by means of parties entering into a compromise agreement. See further *infra* subsection 3.1. 'Out-of-court compromise agreements'.

8 Prior to this amendment, in 1987 the Interior Minister issued the Bylaws of the Interior Ministry on the Implementation of Dispute Conciliation by Village Committees BE 2530, dated 24.12.1987, which is still effective (see 2011 Handbook for Networks and Volunteers for Rights and Liberties Protection, first printing, pp. 50–51 at <www.rlpd.moj.go.th/rlpd6/images/stories//kumu%20k5% 2054.pdf>). A village committee (VC) is one from each village, which consists of approximately 200 persons or not fewer than five houses, under the LAA 1914 (see *infra* subsection 6.1. 'LAA 1897 and SAA No. 7 (2007)') or one from each village, which consists of one or more than one such village, under the Administration of Voluntary Development and Self-Defence Villages Act BE 2522 (1979). In respect of civil matters, a VC is empowered to mediate when disputing parties consent to the VC's mediation and the disputes arise in such a village or a village in which either party is domiciled. After the disputing parties have given their written consent to the VC's mediation, such VC, which may be represented by at least two members and invitees, will begin its mediation without delay. The VC will apply principles of law or lawful local customs. The invitees may include the chief district officer, the assistant chief district officer, a police officer with a rank not lower than police sub-lieutenant in the district, and a public prosecutor. The mediation will terminate if the disputing parties cannot reach an agreement, and a report will be made to the chief district officer for further action. But if the disputing parties can agree, the VC will prepare and arrange for the disputing parties to execute a compromise agreement. Whether the mediation is successful, a record will be made in the written consent for safekeeping by the village headman (*Phu Yai Baan*), who will report the outcome of mediated cases to the chief district officer on a monthly basis.

(ADRO) in accordance with the Notification re Rules for Training of Community Volunteer Mediators BE 2545, dated 20 March 2002. Currently, there are approximately 1,200 community volunteer mediators (CVMs) in 57 provinces. See further *infra* subsection 6.7. 'CVMs (1997)'. Between October 2002 and September 2011, the CVMs helped settle 11,899 civil cases and 3,108 criminal cases.[9]

Also with regard to the MOJ, the Conflict Management Promotion Division (CMPD) was set up under the Rights and Liberties Protection Department (RLPD) of the MOJ by virtue of the Ministerial Regulation on the Assignments of the RLPD under the MOJ BE 2545, dated 9 October 2002. Among the CMPD's power and duties, it will develop systems and procedures to promote dispute settlement with the emphasis on participation of the general public and communities, promote such dispute settlement, and coordinate with related organisations to organise training and disseminate knowledge to communities to promote dispute settlement. The CMPD's current vision is to promote and encourage communities to manage conflicts by peaceful means and with participation of the general public.[10] In 2005, the minister of the MOJ issued the Regulation of the MOJ re Networks and Volunteers for Rights and Liberties Protection BE 2548, dated 6 September 2005. The powers and duties of networks and volunteers (basically, recognised groups of people and qualified individual persons) include conducting and coordinating management of conflicts and community dispute settlement and reporting its operations to the RLPD annually or as required by the RLPD. There are numerous organs and activities recognised by the RLPD in relation to dispute settlement; however, the foregoing regulations, organs, and activities do not affect the legal effect of an out-of-court compromise agreement, discussed under subsection 3.1. 'Out-of-court compromise agreements'.

As regards the Department of Intellectual Property (DIP) of the Ministry of Commerce (MOC), mediation services began only after the DIP's re-assignments in 2002[11] by virtue of the Ministerial Regulation on the Assignments of the DIP of the MOC BE 2545, dated 9 October 2002.[12] See further *infra* subsection 6.12. 'DIP's Ministerial Regulation (2002)'. Between December 2002 and June

---

9 Statistics provided by the courtesy of the ADRO.

10 See <www.rlpd.moj.go.th/rlpd6/index.php?option=com_content&task=blogcategory &id=20 &Itemid=38>.

11 It is noteworthy that the WIPO Arbitration and Mediation Centre, located in Geneva, Switzerland, was established in 1994 (see <http:// www.ipthailand.go.th/ ipthailand/index.php?option=com_content&task=view&id=340&Itemid=273>).

12 The DIP was established by virtue of the Royal Decree on the Assignments of the DIP of the MOC BE 2535, effective on 03.05.1992, which was superseded by the Royal Decree on the Assignments of the DIP of the MOC BE 2542, effective on 01.10.1999. However, both Royal Decrees did not include provision of mediation and arbitration services in the assignments of the DIP. Generally speaking, a royal decree is an enactment issued by the King by virtue of the constitution or an act of parliament for the purpose of state administration, with the advice of the cabinet of ministers and countersigned by the Prime Minister.

2010, the DIP's statistics showed that 187 of 349 mediated cases were successful.[13]

As for other State or governmental agencies or interested bodies, out-of-court mediation services are provided as an alternative to arbitration when an arbitration proceeding is requested. The substantive laws, for example the Securities and Exchange Act BE 2535 (1992) (SEC Act), the Agricultural Futures Trading Act BE 2542 (1999) (AFT Act), the Derivatives Act BE 2546 (2003) (Derivatives Act), and the insurance enactments in 2008, except the Metropolitan Electricity Authority Act BE 2501 (1958), the Metropolitan Waterworks Authority Act BE 2510 (1967), the Petroleum Act BE 2514 (1971), and the Provincial Waterworks Authority Act BE 2522 (1979), are discussed below.

Regarding the SEC Act, the Stock Exchange of Thailand (SET) issued, by virtue of section 201 of the SEC Act, a notification dated 6 November 1995 relating to arbitration. Under the notification, members of the SET and customers of the members may apply with the SET for dispute resolution by conciliation concerning the purchase or sale of securities traded on the SET although the conciliation is not expressly provided for by law. The conciliation process will begin prior to an arbitration hearing. No statistics of cases are available. As for the SEC Office (including the SEC Commission) (the regulator of the SET), four notifications, dated 28 November 2001, 15 November 2002, 13 October 2004, and 16 May 2008 (the latter being the most current), were issued, without specific reference to provisions of the SEC Act relating to dispute resolution, to provide for dispute resolution by arbitration and conciliation (the latter is not required by law). No statistics of cases are available.

Regarding the AFT Act, the Agricultural Futures Trading Commission (AFTC) issued, in pursuance of section 116 of the AFT Act, a notification No. Gor Thor 2/2546 re principles and procedure for the AFTC Secretary General's review and determination of disputes, dated 16 July 2003, to provide for a scheme of dispute resolution. Pursuant to the notification, the AFTC Secretary General will, when requested, make a determination of disputes arising from or in connection with futures trading between the Agricultural Futures Exchange of Thailand (AFET) members and their customers. An administrative fee will be levied at the rate of 2% of the claim amount but not less than Baht 5,000. See further *infra* subsection 6.11. 'AFT Act (1999)'. To date, no cases have been determined under this provision.

As for the AFET, the AFET Board of Directors issued, in pursuance of section 114 of the AFT Act, the Regulation re Arbitration Procedures, dated 19 August 2004 (as amended by the Regulation No. 2 BE 2552, dated 20 November 2009), to provide for dispute resolution by conciliation (which is not required by law)

---

13 See <www.ipthailand.go.th/ipthailand/index.php?option=com_docman&task=cat_view&gid=536&Itemid=81>, then select 'stat_arbi_53June.doc'.

concerning disputes arising from or in connection with agricultural futures trading between AFET members and their customers. See further *infra* subsection 6.11. 'AFT Act (1999)'. To date, there has been no case mediated.

Regarding the Derivatives Act, the SEC Office (including the SEC Commission) (the regulator of the Thailand Futures Exchange (TFEX)) issued a notification, dated 16 May 2008 (mentioned above), to provide for dispute resolution by conciliation (which is not required by law) for disputes arising under the Act. The TFEX issued its Regulations and Procedures, dated 24 February 2006 (see section 1006), to provide for a scheme of dispute resolution by conciliation between its members regarding disputes over the purchase or sale of futures traded on the TFEX, although this process is not required by law. See further *infra* subsections 2.4.1. 'Progress' and 6.14. 'Derivatives Act (2003)'. No statistics of cases are available.

Regarding insurance enactments, in 2008 the new Insurance Against Lost Act BE 2535 (1992) and the new Life Insurance Act BE 2535 (1992) were amended in sections 36/1 and 37/1, respectively to empower the Secretary General of the Office of Insurance Commission (OIC), as registrar,[14] to review complaints and conduct mediation. See *infra* subsection 6.8. 'Insurance ADR (1998)'. According to the 2010 Annual Report of the OIC, in 2010 there were 3,049 cases mediated and 2,877 cases were successful.

In a related development, King Prajadhipok's Institute (KPI) was established under the King Prajadhipok's Institute Act BE 2541 (1998), as amended, as a juridical person under the supervision of the president of the National Assembly, for 'democracy development' (defined under section 3 of the Act to include 'research and collection of information on democracy and constitutional monarchies as well as promotion, dissemination, and education of democratic ideals among the general population'). Its objectives under section 6 of the Act include to provide and promote education for personnel in the public and private sectors and the general public concerning politics, public administration, and economic and social conditions under the democratic regime and to support academic work of the National Assembly. According to the KPI's website,[15] the Office for Peace and Governance was initially set up as a program of the KPI in 2001 and since 2006 has been upgraded to function as a principal organ of the KPI. The Office's main responsibilities currently include promotion of study and research in the knowledge of peaceful prevention and resolution of conflicts, promotion of the use of peaceful means and public participation in the prevention and resolution of conflicts, promotion of capability building for personnel in various organisations, and provision of training courses on management and peaceful resolution of conflicts. Although the Office is chiefly

---

14 See section 4 of the Insurance Against Loss Act BE 2535 (1992) and section 5 of the Life Insurance Act BE 2535 (1992).

15 See <www.kpi.ac.th/ kpith/index.php?option=com_content&task=view&id=34&Itemid=9>.

responsible for providing the aforementioned education to a large number of personnel in government and private organisations, it allegedly participated in the management and resolution of certain environmental conflicts but did not administer mediation services.

Further, the Centre for Peace in Health Care was set up by the Order No. 2032/2547, dated 24 September 2004 of the Office of the Permanent Secretary of the Public Health Ministry to carry out capability building activities for personnel at all levels in the health industry for the purpose of peaceful conflict resolution by means of mediation (allegedly, with more emphasis on the prevention aspect) and to develop systems and procedures for proper and efficient management in health care.[16] To date, it has provided training courses to more than 1,000 doctors, nurses and other personnel including legal staff so they are able to have a basic understanding of peaceful conflict management by way of negotiation and has trained a number of mediators, at hospitals in all provinces of Thailand. Allegedly, it has set up mediation networks in all provinces through which it has occasionally provided mediation services based on certain guidelines; however, it has not been able to obtain a sufficient budget to strengthen the networks, or even to reasonably monitor or evaluate the performance of working groups in the networks.

Recently, the Bureau of Public Participatory Promotion (Bureau) of the Department of Environmental Quality Promotion (DEQP) under the Ministry of Natural Resources and Environment was involved in and trained mediators for environmental conflicts. Arguably, despite the Ministerial Regulation on the Assignments of the DEQP, dated 9 March 2012, assigning (a) the Bureau to assume the responsibility to develop mechanisms for management of environmental disputes and (b) the DEQP to set up a centre for prevention and resolution of environmental disputes, the training responsibility would allegedly be assigned for the fiscal year 2013 to the Institute of Environmental Training and Technology Transfer instead (this Institute is under the Environmental Research and Training Centre of the DEQP) while the assignment for the setting up of the centre would seem to be left unattended. It is noteworthy that a conciliation centre under the Bureau existed from 2004 to 2009.

As regards post-judgment mediation, which is a relatively recent development, it was adopted in 2005 by the Legal Execution Department (LED) of the MOJ on the grounds that it is a consequential part of a court judgment but before or during the execution process. See further *infra* subsection 6.15. 'Legal Execution Department ADR (2005)'. From February 2011 to April 2012, there were a total of 5,653 cases that were entered at the LED (excluding provincial execution offices) and were followed by execution. Of these 5,653 executions, 361 executions were referred to mediation and 121 were mediated successfully.[17]

---

16 See <www.peaceinhealth.com/index.php/ features/rokbox.html>.

17 Statistics provided by the courtesy of the LED.

There is a specific pre-trial mediation process (before the filing of a lawsuit) under the Regulation of the Central Intellectual Property and International Trade Court re Pre-trial Dispute Mediation BE 2554 (2011) (Pre-trial Mediation Regulation). See further *infra* subsection 6.17. 'Pre-trial mediation (2011)'. As of May 2012, seven cases have been mediated under the Pre-trial Mediation Regulation: three cases were successful, one failed, and three are still pending. Another pre-trial mediation process is administered by the ADRO in accordance with its 'unofficial' Out-of-Court Mediation Rules in its bilingual (Thai and English) publication, dated January 2004.[18] These rules were not stated to be issued by virtue of any authority. Today these rules are rarely used as the court-annexed mediation process is purportedly believed to be more efficient, but they are still offered by the ADRO for disputing parties to adopt for their pre-trial mediation process.

As regards out-of-court mediation where a State official(s) is not involved or where mediation services are not provided by governmental or State agencies, a domestic private organisation has a role. In 2001, the Board of Trade of Thailand (BTT)[19] issued its Dispute Conciliation Rules on 30 April 2001 (TC Conciliation Rules), by virtue of its Thai Commercial Arbitration Rules (TC Arbitration Rules), which were issued on 1 July 1968. The TC Conciliation Rules were superseded by a new version on 24 April 2009. By virtue of Article 6 of the TC Arbitration Rules, a registrar, as designated by the BTT's Thai Commercial Arbitration Committee, will call a meeting of disputing parties for negotiation and settlement of disputes before submission thereof to an arbitration tribunal under the TC Arbitration Rules. If the registrar deems it appropriate and the parties agree, one or more conciliators will be appointed in accordance with the TC Conciliation Rules. However, no records of cases conducted under the TC Conciliation Rules are available.

## 2.2. COURT-ANNEXED MEDIATION

The OOJ defines court-annexed mediation as the mediation of a dispute which is still pending before the court and which is arranged by the court.[20]

Almost 11 years after the Civil and Commercial Code (CCC) entered into force in 1925, court-annexed mediation first appeared in sections 19[21] and 20 of the Civil Procedure Code (CPC), which entered into force on 1 October 1935. See

18 Included in the publication are the Code of Conduct for Mediation and, in Thai only, forms: request for mediation, statement of independence and impartiality, acknowledgement of mediation process, and schedule of mediation costs.

19 See *infra* subsection 2.4.1. 'Progress'.

20 Mediation: Thai-English, p. 3.

21 Section 19 of the CPC empowers a court to require disputing parties to appear in court in person so that they might reach an agreement or make a compromise.

further *infra* subsection 6.2. 'CPC (1935 and 2008) and 2011 Stipulation'. Also under the CPC, there is a mediation scheme for petty lawsuits, which is provided for by virtue of an amendment to section 193 in 1999. See further *infra* subsection 6.9. 'Petty lawsuits (1999)'. Basically, the foregoing provisions have provided and still provide for disputing parties to make a compromise agreement before the court so that they can avoid running the full course of a court action which is, in Thailand, relatively time-consuming and prejudicial to continued working relationships between the litigating parties. The legal basis of court-annexed mediation for dispute settlement is based on section 138 of the CPC. See further *infra* subsections 3.2. 'In-court compromise agreements' and 4. 'Mediation'.

In furtherance of the court-annexed mediation process, section 20 *bis* of the CPC, added in 1999, was amended in 2008, and in pursuance of the amendment the Supreme Court President issued the Stipulation on Mediation BE 2554, dated 28 September 2011 (2011 Stipulation) to set forth detailed rules and procedure of court-annexed mediation at all levels of courts of justice (i.e., the Court of First Instance, the Court of Appeal, and the Supreme Court), appointment of mediators, and powers and duties of the mediators. See further *infra* subsection 6.2. 'CPC (1935 and 2008) and 2011 Stipulation'. Further, pursuant to the 2011 Stipulation, a mediation centre will be set up as necessary at any court of justice, which includes provincial courts throughout the country and specialised courts, e.g., the Bankruptcy Court, the Intellectual Property and International Trade (IPIT) Court, the Labour Court, and the Tax Court. Specifically, other procedural laws that contain a court-annexed mediation process include the Labour Court Establishment and Procedure Act BE 2522 (1979) (LC Act),[22] the Juvenile and Family Court Establishment and Procedure Act BE 2534 (1991),[23] the Intellectual Property and International Trade Court Establishment and Procedure Act BE 2539 (1996) (IPIT Act),[24] the Bankruptcy Court Establishment and Procedure Act BE 2542 (1999),[25] the Tax Court Establishment and Procedure Act BE 2528 (1985),[26] and the Consumer Litigation Procedure Act BE 2551 (2008) (CLP Act).[27]

At all civil courts of first instance throughout the country (excluding the labour courts, the juvenile and family courts, the IPIT court, the bankruptcy court, and the tax court mentioned below), between October 2010 and September 2011, of 442,288 cases, 184,208 cases were mediated and 136,507 cases were

22 See further *infra* subsection 6.3. 'Labour ADR (1979)'.

23 Superseded by the Juvenile and Family Court and Procedure Act BE 2553 (2010) (see *infra* subsection 6.4. 'Juvenile and family ADR (1991)').

24 See further *infra* subsection 6.6. 'IPIT Act (1996)'.

25 See further *infra* subsection 6.10. 'Bankruptcy ADR (1999)'.

26 See further *infra* subsection 6.13. 'Tax ADR (2002)', relating to the Tax Mediation Regulation in 2011, which superseded its prior regulation of 2002.

27 See further *infra* subsection 6.16. 'Consumer ADR (2008)'.

successful. It is likely that the foregoing numbers include those of petty lawsuits and consumer litigations.

At the Central Labour Court in Bangkok and regional Labour Courts (all courts of first instance), between October 2010 and September 2011, of 6,153 cases, 3,928 cases were mediated and 1,747 cases were successful.[28]

At the Central Juvenile and Family Courts in Bangkok and at Min Buri branch and provincial juvenile and family courts throughout the country, between October 2010 and September 2011, of 9,673 cases, 4,479 cases were mediated and 2,847 cases were successful.[29]

At the Central IPIT Court, between 2008 and 2011, 443 cases were mediated and 153 cases were successful.[30]

At the Central Bankruptcy Court, between October 2010 and September 2011, of three cases mediated, one case was unsuccessful, one case was disposed of (for reason of, for example, abandonment of the complaint), and one case is still pending.[31]

At the Central Tax Court, between October 2010 and September 2011, of 233 cases, 56 cases were mediated and 17 cases were successful.[32]

At courts of first instance throughout the country regarding consumer litigation under the CLP Act in 2010, 104,661 consumer litigation cases were mediated and 76,513 such cases were successful.[33]

## 2.3. COURT-ANNEXED ARBITRATION

Since its enactment in 1935, the CPC has contained provisions for court-annexed arbitration under sections 210–222, except for section 221 which deals with out-of-court arbitration. To date, there has been no court-annexed arbitration case instituted pursuant to those provisions.

## 2.4. OUT-OF-COURT ARBITRATION

### *2.4.1. Progress*

Arbitration was paid more and earlier attention than mediation, probably because of international circumstances after (a) the 24 September 1923 Geneva Protocol

28 Statistics provided by the courtesy of the ADRO.

29 *Ibid.*

30 Statistics provided by the courtesy of the Mediation and Compromise Section of the Central IPIT Court.

31 Statistics provided by the courtesy of the ADRO.

32 *Ibid.*

33 The OOJ's Annual Judicial Statistics, Thailand, BE 2553 (2010) (see <www.oppb.coj. go.th/userfiles/file/AnnualJudicialStatistics BE2553_TH.pdf, p.30>).

on Arbitration Clauses, which entered into force on 28 July 1924, (b) the 26 September 1927 Geneva Convention on the Execution of Foreign Arbitral Awards, which entered into force on 25 July 1929, and (c) the 10 June 1958 New York Convention on the Recognition and Enforcement of Foreign Arbitral Awards, which entered into force on 7 June 1959. Thailand ratified the Geneva Protocol[34] on 3 September 1930, the Geneva Convention[35] on 7 July 1931, and the New York Convention[36] on 21 December 1959. Currently, by virtue of Article VII.2 of the New York Convention, only the New York Convention is available for enforcement of foreign arbitral awards in Thailand.[37] Incidentally, Thailand signed the Convention on the Settlement of Investment Disputes between States and Nationals of Other States (ICSID) on 6 December 1985 but has not deposited an instrument of ratification.[38] So according to Article 68 of the Convention in effect at the time of Thailand's signature, so far as Thailand is concerned the Convention has not entered into force in favour of, and thus dispute settlement by arbitration under the Convention is unavailable to, a national of another contracting State. Further, on 20 October 2000[39] Thailand completed membership requirements under the Convention Establishing the Multilateral Investment Guarantee Agency (MIGA), adopted on 11 October 1985.[40] See further *infra* subsection 2.4.2.1. 'Cabinet resolutions' (first paragraph and the footnote on MIGA).

In terms of domestic legislation, section 28(1) of the Chambers of Commerce Act BE 2509 (1966) (Chambers Act) requires every chamber of commerce,[41] including the BTT to act as an arbitrator to determine commercial disputes out

---

34 Registration: 28.07.1924, No. 678. See <http://treaties.un.org/pages/LONViewDetails.aspx?src=LON&id=543&lang=en>.

35 Registration: 25.07.1929, No. 2096. See <http://treaties.un.org/pages/LONViewDetails.aspx?src=LON&id=544&lang=en>.

36 Registration: 07.06.1959, No. 4739. See <http://treaties.un.org/pages/ViewDetails.aspx?src=TREATY&mtdsg_no=XXII-1&chapter=22& lang=en>.

37 Booklet entitled '50 Questions re Arbitration', p. 28, by the Thai Arbitration Institute (TAI) of the ADRO.

38 See <http://icsid.worldbank.org/ICSID/FrontServlet?requestType=ICSIDDocRH&actionVal=ContractingStates&ReqFrom=Main>.

39 According to the Savings and Investment Policy Bureau of the Fiscal Policy Office under the Ministry of Finance.

40 <www.miga.org/whoweare/index.cfm?stid=1788> and <www.miga.org/whoweare/index.cfm?stid=1789>.

41 It is defined under section 4 of the Chambers Act (a) originally, as an institution which persons set up for promotion of trade, industry, agriculture, finance, or economy other than for profit or revenue sharing, and (b) in 2007 per Chambers of Commerce Act No. 2 BE 2550 (2007), as an institution which persons set up for promotion of trade, services, professional occupation, industry, agriculture, finance, or economy other than for profit or revenue sharing. Under section 6 of this Act, there are four types of chambers of commerce: (a) provincial chamber of commerce, (b) the Thai Chamber of Commerce, (c) foreign chamber of commerce, and (d) the Board of Trade of Thailand. Under section 14 of this Act, each province may have only one chamber of commerce and the chamber of commerce for Bangkok Metropolis will be called the Thai Chamber of Commerce. Under section 15 of this

of court. The BTT, by its Thai Commercial Arbitration Committee, issued the TC Arbitration Rules on 1 July 1968 (superseded by a new version on 20 May 2003) for its Office of the Arbitration Tribunal (OAT) to administer. Since 1968, the OAT has conducted out-of-court arbitration proceedings in Thailand.[42] See further *infra* subsection 7.1. 'Office of the Arbitration Tribunal'. According to recent unofficial records provided by the OAT of the BTT, the OAT conducted cases/issued awards as follows: 4/0 cases in 2008, 9/1 cases in 2009, 7/4 cases in 2010, 6/9 cases in 2011, and 0/1 cases in 2012, respectively.

A key milestone in the development of out-of-court arbitration is the enactment of the first Arbitration Act in 1987. The law was enacted when section 221 of the CPC was revised[43] in the same year to allow more complete legislation, namely, the first Arbitration Act BE 2530 (1987) to govern out-of-court arbitration. Subsequently, in order to improve the law for greater acceptance, the first Arbitration Act 1987 was superseded in 2002 by the Arbitration Act BE 2545 (2002),[44] which was based substantially on the 1985 UNCITRAL Model Law on International Commercial Arbitration. Currently, the Arbitration Act 2002 has become the essential legal framework for all out-of-court arbitration proceedings in Thailand and the ADRO under the OOJ, formerly the Arbitration Office (AO) of the Office of the Judicial Affairs (OJA) under the MOJ, has been actively promoting use of out-of-court arbitration as a means of dispute settlement. Between the inception of the AO in 1990 and 31 December 2011, a total of 1,251 cases were settled by out-of-court arbitration through the AO and the ADRO; in 2011 alone, a total of 120 cases were completed and 332 cases were pending.[45]

There are substantive laws that specifically provide for out-of-court arbitration as a means of dispute settlement (even before the enactment of the repealed Arbitration Act 1987), namely, the Metropolitan Electricity Authority Act BE 2501 (1958),[46] the Metropolitan Waterworks Authority Act BE 2510 (1967),[47] the Petroleum Act BE 2514 (1971),[48] the Provincial Waterworks

---

Act, the Thai Chamber of Commerce, the foreign chambers of commerce, trade associations, State enterprises, and co-operatives may join to form the Board of Trade of Thailand.

42 See <http://rss2.thaichamber.org/rss/view.asp?nid=1145 and http://rss2.thaichamber.org/rss/view.asp?nid=1169>.

43 See further *infra* subsection 5.2. 'Out-of-court arbitration'.

44 *Ibid.*

45 Statistics provided by the courtesy of the TAI of the ADRO.

46 Section 34(2).

47 Section 36(2).

48 Section 67(3). Incidentally, section 53 of this Act requires a dispute that cannot be settled in connection with: (a) a ministerial order for a concessionaire to rectify a circumstance being a ground for revocation of concession (under section 52) or (b) a question whether the concession has been complied with, to be referred to arbitration in accordance with the procedure set forth in the concession. Further, if the concessionaire refuses to comply with the arbitral award or fails to comply with the award within a specified time the Minister of Energy will have power to revoke all or parts of the rights and benefits of the concessionaire or to revoke the concession.

Authority Act BE 2522 (1979),[49] and the Agricultural Land Lease Act BE 2524 (1981).[50] These laws, except for the last Act, similarly require an owner or possessor of land who is injured by the relevant authority in the performance of their duties to submit to arbitration his dispute over any amount of compensation to be payable by the authority. As for the last Act, the court will be required to treat final decisions or orders of the provincial or district agricultural land lease committee as out-of-court arbitral awards.

There are two governmental agencies that provide arbitration services in connection with their functions, namely, the Department of Insurance (DOI) and the DIP.

In 1998, the DOI[51] of the MOC issued the Rules on Arbitration BE 2541, dated 1 September 1998, as amended by the Rules on Arbitration No. 2 BE 2546, dated 23 July 2003 (DOI's Arbitration Rules) to lay down rules of arbitration proceeding under its administration. In addition, the DOI Director General issued his order No. 95/2541, dated 19 November 1998, that all insurance policies were required to include insurer consent to arbitration pursuant to the foregoing Rules. Subsequently, functions of the DOI were transferred to the OIC in 2007[52] and the OIC Secretary General applies section 32(2) of the Insurance Business Regulation and Promotion Commission Act BE 2550, effective on 1 September 2007 (also known as the Insurance Commission Act (IC Act)), which does not expressly provide for an ADR means, to lay down regulations for arbitration and mediation processes. By virtue of the provision, the OIC Secretary General issued out-of-court arbitration regulations, i.e., the Regulation of the OIC re Arbitration BE 2551, dated 25 July 2008, as amended by the Regulation of the OIC No. 2 BE 2553, dated 7 September 2010 (OIC's Arbitration Regulation). In effect, the OIC's Arbitration Regulation replaced the DOI's Arbitration Rules.[53] See further *infra* subsection 6.8. 'Insurance ADR (1998)'. According to the OIC Annual Report 2010, in 2010 the OIC conducted 200 new arbitration cases, rendered 183 arbitral awards, and carried over 87 pending cases to 2011.

---

49 Section 29(3).

50 Section 58(1).

51 It is unclear whether the DOI had power and duties with regard to ADR before 1998, but only in 1999 the Royal Decree on the Re-assignments of the DOI of the MOC BE 2542, effective on 01.10.1999 empowered the Legal Division of the DOI to have power and duties to consider and mediate and to determine disputes over insurance claims and proceeds. Subsequently, there were further re-assignments of the DOI in 2002 by the Ministerial Regulation on State Agency Assignments of the DOI of the MOC BE 2545, dated 09.10.2002. According to Clause 1(3) of this Ministerial Regulation, the DOI had power and duties to carry out, manage, and develop a scheme, form, and procedure for resolution of civil and commercial disputes in relation to insurance by means of arbitration. In addition, according to Clause 3(2)(d) of this Ministerial Regulation, the Legal Division of the DOI had power and duties to consider and mediate and to determine disputes over insurance claims and proceeds.

52 Functions of the DOI under the MOC were transferred to the OIC under the Finance Ministry by virtue of sections 49–52 of the IC Act.

53 See Clause 42 of the OIC's Arbitration Regulation.

In 2002, the MOC's DIP was assigned to carry out mediation and arbitration services and the Rules of the MOC re Intellectual Property Arbitration, dated 11 July 2002, were issued to deal with arbitration. See further *infra* subsection 6.12. 'DIP's Ministerial Regulation (2002)'. Between December 2002 and June 2010, the DIP's statistics showed that two out of four arbitrated cases resulted in an arbitral award rendered.[54]

Similar to the above arbitration services of the governmental agencies, dispute settlement by out-of-court arbitration is provided for under the following substantive laws: the SEC Act (1992),[55] the Derivatives Act (2003),[56] and the AFT Act (1999).[57]

Sections 201–203 of the SEC Act entitle members of the Stock Exchange of Thailand (SET) and their customers to apply with the SET for dispute settlement by arbitration concerning the purchase or sale of securities traded on the SET. However, under the Notification of the SET, dated 6 November 1995, a conciliation process may begin prior to arbitration hearings. Arbitrators' fees will be levied at a minimum amount of Baht 10,000 for a claim amount not exceeding Baht 500,000 and at a maximum amount of Baht 250,000 for a claim amount exceeding Baht 50 million. The fee will be allocated equally among the arbitrators. According to the Legal Department of the SET, there has been no arbitration case since 1995.

The SEC Office (including the SEC Commission) (the regulator of the SET and the Thailand Futures Exchange (TFEX) mentioned below) issued four notifications, dated 28 November 2001, 15 November 2002, 13 October 2004, and 16 May 2008 to provide for dispute settlement by arbitration and conciliation (the latter is not required by law). Under the current notification, dated 16 May 2008, disputes arising under the SEC Act and the Derivatives Act are included. The law on arbitration was stipulated to supplement the notifications.

On 28 April 2006, the TFEX, set up in accordance with the Derivatives Act, began trading. The TFEX provides for schemes of dispute settlement by arbitration (see section 1001 of the TFEX's Regulations, dated 24 February 2006) and conciliation (see section 1006 of the TFEX's Regulations; this process is not required by law) between its members for disputes over the purchase or sale of futures traded on the TFEX (as the disputes between TFEX members and their customers will be settled by arbitration under the auspices of the SEC Office). A panel of three arbitrators will be appointed, one by each of the disputing parties and the chairman by the TFEX. The arbitrators' fees and the allocation will be the same as levied by the SET mentioned above. According to the Legal Department of the TFEX, there has been no arbitration case filed with the TFEX.

---

54 See <www.ipthailand.go.th/ipthailand/index.php?option=com_docman&task=cat_view&gid=536&Itemid=81>, then select 'stat_arbi_53June.doc'.

55 Sections 201–203.

56 Sections 47–48.

57 Sections 114–117.

Under the above-mentioned SEC Office's current notification, a dispute over the purchase or sale of securities traded on the SET under the SEC Act[58] or futures traded on the TFEX under the Derivatives Act,[59] between an injured claimant and a respondent, i.e., (a) a securities company, (b) a local share selling agent, (c) a mutual fund supervisor, (d) a private fund custodian, or (e) a derivatives business operator, that qualifies for settlement in accordance with the foregoing SEC Office's notification includes (i) a dispute with a claim value not exceeding Baht 1 million[60] and (ii) a dispute that has been filed in the complaint system in accordance with the notification of the SEC Commission or the notification of the SEC Office relating to the handling of customer complaints, as the case may be, and it appears that: (a) the claimant receives no communication from the complaint handling officer according to the relevant notification within 15 days from the date the complaint is filed, (b) the complaint is not resolved within 45 days from the date the complaint is filed, unless the claimant agrees to extend such period, or (c) the claimant is not satisfied with the resolution.

Further, arbitrators will be selected from the roster maintained by the SEC Office. An arbitrators' fee will be levied at the rate of 2% of the claim amount but not less than Baht 5,000, and in the case of aggregation of related disputes, not less than Baht 100,000 per dispute or, where there are three arbitrators, each will receive a remuneration not exceeding Baht 100,000 per dispute. The most recent statistics, from 2009–11,[61] showed that there was an arbitration case in 2009 with an award given in the same year and there were two arbitration cases in 2010 with one award rendered in the same year and another award rendered in 2011. All of those cases were related to futures trading.

In pursuance of section 114 of the AFT Act, the Board of Directors of the Agricultural Futures Exchange of Thailand (AFET) issued a regulation regarding arbitration procedures, dated 19 August 2004 (as amended by the Regulation No. 2 BE 2552, dated 20 November 2009) to provide for dispute settlement by conciliation (which is not required by law) and arbitration concerning disputes arising from or in connection with agricultural futures trading between AFET members and their customers. Arbitrators and certain conciliators are those

58 The SEC Office has created a Symbol of Arbitration for securities companies to apply for and to show to the general public that they have made a commitment in writing with the SEC Office to resolve their disputes by arbitration with their customers (see <www.sec.or. th/enforcement/Content_0000000459.jsp?categoryID=CAT0000438&lang=en>).

59 By virtue of section 47(1) of the Derivatives Act, a customer may request to enter into an arbitration process that is organised by the SEC Office for settlement of a civil dispute incidental to or resulting from a derivatives business. In making the request, the customer has to give the derivatives business operator a notice expressing his intent to settle the dispute by arbitration. Upon the derivatives business operator's receipt of the notice, it will be deemed that both parties have agreed to enter into an arbitration agreement to settle such dispute.

60 See Notification of the SEC Commission 'No. KorThor/Nor/Khor. 4/2551 re Amount of Damages Arising from Derivatives Transaction for Settlement by Arbitration', dated 02.04.2008.

61 Provided by the courtesy of the Office of the SEC Secretary General.

registered with the AFET; the third conciliator as chairman is appointed by the AFET. The conciliators' remuneration, allocated equally among them, will be levied at the rate of 1% of the claim amount but not less than Baht 5,000 and not more than Baht 125,000. The arbitrators' remuneration, 40% of which goes to the chairman and 30% to each of the two arbitrators, will be levied at the rate of 2% of the claim amount but not less than Baht 30,000 and not more than Baht 250,000. To date, there have been two arbitration cases conducted under the auspices of the AFET: the first case was initiated in 2006 with an award rendered in 2009 and the second case was initiated in 2009 with an award rendered in 2010.[62]

The next thing in terms of development that has yet to happen is another arbitration administrative body in addition to the TAI of the ADRO. (On the TAI, see *infra* subsection 7.2. 'Thai Arbitration Institute'.) On 19 December 2006, the MOJ was granted the Cabinet approval for setting up another arbitration institute in addition to the TAI, which is under the administration of the OOJ. On 17 July 2007, the Arbitration Institute Act BE 2550 (2007) entered into effect. However, as of May 2012 the Arbitration Institute under the Act has not been set up.[63]

#### *2.4.2. Setbacks*

As things do not always go the way one would wish, we will now look at certain setbacks, impact of which is unnecessarily restricted to investment, in the development of arbitration as a means of dispute settlement in Thailand.[64]

##### 2.4.2.1. Cabinet resolutions[65]

It is noteworthy that on 28 July 2009 the Cabinet of Ministers of Thailand (Cabinet) passed two resolutions which unfavourably[66] affected the development

---

62 Provided by the courtesy of the Legal Department of the AFET.

63 For the purpose of completeness, the Office of the Thai Rubber Arbitration Committee under the Ministry of Agriculture and Cooperatives which has been dormant on account of scarce activities will not be discussed.

64 The Immovable Property Expropriation Act BE 2530 (1987) repealed and replaced the Immovable Property Expropriation Act BE 2497 (1954) and no longer uses arbitration as a means of determining disputes over compensation amounts. By virtue of section 36(2) of the replacement Act, any arbitration set up under the repealed Act and pending an award was revoked and replaced with an appeal process. The remark annexed to the replacement Act seems to imply that the replacement appeal process would be a quicker resolution of disputes over compensation amounts. This aversion to arbitration has not been responded to negatively, compared to the Cabinet resolutions discussed under subsection 2.4.2.1. 'Cabinet resolutions'.

65 Generally speaking, they are not law but, as applicable, only directives of the Executive branch to all agencies under its administration.

66 Position Paper on Arbitration in Thailand, dated 10.2009, by the American Chamber of Commerce in Thailand at <www.google. co.th/url?sa=t&rct=j&q=&esrc=s&source=web&cd=6&sqi=2&ved=0CGIQFjAF&url=http%3A%2F%2Fwww.amchamthailand.com%2Fasp%2Fview

of dispute settlement by arbitration in Thailand: one concerned a proposed amendment to the Arbitration Act 2002 and the other concerned a general directive for State agencies when making concession contracts with private parties. The directive was subsequently revised to include all kinds of State contracts. The first movement (A) appeared to end well in the following year but the other (B) appeared to continue to have a negative impact on the Thai government's role to promote[67] the use of dispute settlement by arbitration in Thailand.

(A) According to a webpage of the Secretariat of the Cabinet, listing 'Cabinet resolutions approving in principle – for the purpose of reference or adoption for practice (only those used routinely)',[68] there appears item 1.20 – arbitration, which contains a concluding resolution dated 31 August 2010 on a draft amendment to the Arbitration Act 2002.[69] The originating resolution was passed on 28 July 2009,[70] as mentioned above, to instruct the Office of the Council of State[71] to consult with the MOJ, the OOJ, the Office of the Attorney General, the SEC Office, and the BTT in considering an amendment to the Arbitration Act 2002 which was proposed by the MOJ to prohibit the use of dispute settlement by arbitration in State contracts with private parties, realising that such amendment

_doc.asp%3FDocCID%3D2518&ei=DGUbUOrLK62fiAe9-oGYDQ&usg=AFQjCNGIrry_qCpWNGS2HGYf7BtEt7H1BQ &sig2=UNlq86VY2fRoOqyjixM1pA>.

67 In 1992, the Office of the Prime Minister by way of its Circular Ref. Naw Raw (GawWawPaw)/Waw 116, dated 01.04.1992 (BE 2535) notified all departments and divisions of the Thai government to use in their operation model contracts that the Procurement Committee under the Regulation of the Prime Minister's Office on Procurement BE 2535 (1992) prepared as annexes to the Regulation. These model contracts have been in use since 01.04.1992. An annexed model contract on general hire of work contains Clause 21 – Dispute and Arbitration, which provides for dispute settlement by arbitration as a prerequisite to court action. Moreover, in 2000, the Cabinet issued the Royal Decree Prescribing Professions and Occupations Prohibited to Aliens No. 3 BE 2543, effective on 16.11.2000 (see section 60 of the Working of Aliens Act BE 2551 (2008)), lifting the ban under item (39) – Legal Services and Litigation to allow (a) performance of duties as arbitrators and (b) when the governing law is not Thai law or the award will not be enforced in Thailand, representation in arbitral proceedings. Lastly, on 03.07.2001, the then Prime Minister with the approval of the Cabinet then issued the Regulation of the Prime Minister's Office on Performance of Arbitral Awards BE 2544, effective on 04.07.2001, to require State agencies to comply with arbitral awards on disputes with private parties unless the awards are against the law applicable to the disputes, made as a result of an unlawful act or means, or not within the scope of the arbitration agreement. In the exception cases, there is a detailed procedure to follow. However, if the award is on a dispute between the Multilateral Investment Guarantee Agency (MIGA) and a State agency under the 1985 Convention Establishing the Multilateral Investment Guarantee Agency, the State agency will not follow the procedure but will speedily apply for a disbursement according to the award.

68 <www.soc.soc.go.th/principle_mati.htm>.

69 See confirmed text in Circular Ref. Naw Raw [Office of the Prime Minister] 0503/Waw 162, dated 09.09.2010.

70 See confirmed text in Circular Ref. Naw Raw [Office of the Prime Minister] 0503/13544, dated 04.08.2009.

71 <www.krisdika.go.th/wps/portal/general>.

would affect investor confidence and Thailand's obligations in various conventions and international agreements.

On 31 August 2010, the Cabinet passed the concluding resolution, resolving to turn down the proposed amendment and set forth in the foregoing footnoted circular to all departments and divisions of the Thai government that State agencies suffered losses in arbitration proceedings because of problems in making and managing contracts and appointing arbitrators, not because of problems in the arbitration system, the latter which may be solved through management by the State agencies.

(B) Also, according to the above-mentioned webpage of the Secretariat of the Cabinet, there appears item 1.11 – making concession contracts, listing two resolutions, dated 27 January 2004 (Initial Resolution)[72] and dated 28 July 2009 (Finalised Resolution).[73] There was in fact also an intervening Cabinet resolution on 4 May 2004[74] passed to clarify the Initial Resolution; thereafter, both the Initial Resolution and the clarifying resolution were finalised in the Finalised Resolution. Nevertheless, the Cabinet subsequently passed a resolution dated 11 November 2011[75] making two exceptions (see items (i) and (ii) under (B.2) below) to the Finalised Resolution, in addition to an exception (see item (iii) under (B.2) below), which was previously contained in another Cabinet resolution dated 16 March 2004.[76] The exceptions result in eliminating the requirement of submission for a case-by-case approval as specified therein.

(B.1) According to the footnoted circular of the Finalised Resolution in 2009, the following directive is for all State agencies and State enterprises to follow:[77]

(a) in a contract of any kind, whether it is in the administrative nature, that a State agency makes with a Thai or foreign private party, there should be no obligation to use arbitration for dispute settlement; and if there is a problem or a necessity or a demand of the contracting party that cannot be avoided,

72 See confirmed text in Circular Ref. Naw Raw [Office of the Prime Minister] 0504/Waw 31, dated 09.02.2004.

73 See confirmed text in Circular Ref. Naw Raw [Office of the Prime Minister] 0506/Waw 155, dated 07.08.2009.

74 See confirmed text in Circular Ref. Naw Raw [Office of the Prime Minister] 0504/Waw 100, dated 06.05.2004.

75 See confirmed text in Circular Ref. Naw Raw [Office of the Prime Minister] 0506/25266, dated 18.11.2011.

76 See a brief at <www.cabinet.thaigov.go.th/cc_main21.htm> and select item '16 March BE 2547' (2004) to find a Thai text for 'Dispute Settlement Mechanisms between State and Private Parties under Agreements with Other Countries for the Promotion and Protection of Investments'.

77 There was no submission for approval after the date of the Initial Resolution, but between the date of the Finalised Resolution and 24.04.2012 there were about twelve submissions and eleven approvals granted: Thai Airways International PCL's submission was turned down when it purportedly applied for a blanket approval for making future contracts with an arbitration clause with its partners.

the matter must be submitted to the Cabinet for approval on a case-by-case basis;
(b) the principal contract that is binding between the parties must be made in the Thai language; a foreign-language version should be treated as a translation; and
(c) Thai law should be stipulated for the interpretation and enforcement of contract.

(B.2) The above-mentioned three exceptions are as follows:

(i) Krung Thai Bank PCL may use arbitration for dispute settlement for its ISDA Master Agreement and/or Credit Support Annex (CSA) with foreign financial institutions;
(ii) State-enterprise financial institutions may use arbitration for dispute settlement in their cross-border syndicated loan agreements; and
(iii) as a guideline for negotiation of promotion and protection of investments in Thailand, the Ministry of Foreign Affairs may agree to provide private investors a choice of *ad hoc* or institutional international arbitration.

2.4.2.2. Bilateral Investment Treaties[78]

Bilateral investment treaties (BITs) provide private parties with recourse to international commercial arbitration with regard to disputes with the host country. Thailand has 36 BITs in force, that with Myanmar being the next one to come into force, according to the Division of the International Economic Policy (Division) of the Department of International Economic Affairs under the Ministry of Foreign Affairs. In respect of the BITs, the Cabinet's position regarding the above-mentioned third exception (16 March 2004) was clear until its Finalised Resolution was passed in 2009. As a consequence, on 13 November 2009 the Division issued a statement on its website[79] setting forth its position. Briefly, according to the statement, the Cabinet's position in 2009 would send a negative signal to investors that the Thai government did not accept arbitration as a means of dispute settlement between Thailand and private parties and would constitute a 'back track' (*sic*) on the obligations Thailand committed in prior bilateral investment treaties and free trade agreements.

In view of the statement, the Cabinet's position does not seem to affect Thailand's position in those international agreements in that regard, particularly the agreements made in the past. This is because although the Cabinet would not grant its specific approval for a given investment contract, the investors should

78 See a list of Thailand's agreements on the promotion and protection of investments at <www.mfa.go.th/web/989.php>.

79 <www.mfa.go.th/business/2318.php?id=3836>.

still have recourse to arbitration under an applicable, effective bilateral investment treaty with Thailand, assuming that the treaty contains provisions similar to those below:[80]

> 'Article 11
> Settlement of Disputes between Investor and the Contracting Party
>
> 1. In case of *dispute with respect to investments* between a Contracting Party and an investor of the other Contracting Party, consultations shall take place between the parties concerned with a view to solving the case amicably.
> 2. If these consultations do not result in a solution within three months from the date of request for settlement, the investor may submit the dispute, at investors'choice, for settlement to:
>    a) the competent courts of the Contracting Party in the territory of which the investment has been made; or
>    b) an arbitrator or international *ad hoc* arbitral tribunal established under the Arbitration Rules of the United Nations Commission on International Trade Law (UNCITRAL); or
>    c) the International Centre for Settlement of Investment Disputes in case both Contracting Parties are Contracting States to the Convention on the Settlement of Investment Disputes between States and Nationals of other States, opened for signature at Washington D.C. on March 18, 1965.
> 3. The arbitral tribunal established under this Article shall reach its decision on the basis of national laws and regulations of the Contracting Party, which is a party to the dispute, the provisions of the present Agreement, as well as applicable rules of international law.
> 4. All arbitral awards shall be final and binding on the parties to the dispute and shall be enforced in accordance with the laws of the Contracting Party to the dispute.
> 5. All sums received or payable as a result of a settlement shall be freely transferable in a freely usable currency.'

The wording 'dispute with respect to investments' in Article 11.1 of the Thailand Model above appears to be a clarification of its earlier broad position in, e.g., Article 10.1 of its treaty with Egypt in 2000[81] where only 'any dispute' was used. An obvious interpretation resulting from the clarification would be that the investor–State dispute settlement provision could be invoked only when the dispute concerns investments under a given treaty. Thus, if such investor–State dispute settlement provision does not qualify further with wording like 'dispute

---

80 Article 11 – Settlement of Disputes between Investor and the Contracting Party of the Thailand Model (version 2002), as posted on the United Nations Conference on Trade and Development (UNCTAD) website: <www.unctad.org/sections/dite/iia/docs/Compendium//en/Thai_model_2002.PDF>. Emphasis added.

81 See Bilateral Investment Treaties 1995–2006, Trends in Investment Rulemaking <www.unctad.org/en/Docs/iteiia20065_en.pdf>, p. 101.

concerning an alleged breach of an obligation under the Agreement which causes loss or damage to the investor or its investment', disputes based purely on investment contract claims rather than on treaty claims could be argued successfully to be within the jurisdiction of the arbitral tribunals constituted under the applicable treaties.[82]

## 2.5. OMBUDSMEN

Apart from arbitration and mediation, another major development is ombudsmen, who, under the Organic Act on Ombudsmen BE 2552 (Ombudsmen Act), effective on 5 August 2009,[83] have neither power nor duties to adjudicate complaints about constitutional organisations or judicial agencies or wrongdoing by public officials or people holding political office. However, they simply have power and duties, among other things, to consider and undertake fact-finding investigations into a complaint where: (a) a government official, official, or employee of a governmental agency, State agency, State enterprise, or local government organisation fails to comply with law or acts beyond the scope of his power and duties as prescribed by law; (b) a government official, official, or employee of a governmental agency, State agency, State enterprise, or local government organisation unjustly commits an act causing injury to the complainant or the public, whether such act is consistent with his power or duties; and (c) there is an investigation into any omission to perform a duty or any unlawful performance of a duty of a constitutional organisation or judicial agency, excluding the trial and adjudication of the courts.[84] Further, the ombudsmen may consider and undertake the investigations without a complaint if the ombudsmen are of the opinion that the acts under (a), (b), or (c) above have a prejudicial impact on the public in general, or intend to protect public interests.[85] If the ombudsmen find that any rule, regulation, by-law, order, or act of any person under item (a) gives rise to a question of constitutionality or legality, they may, without delay, submit the case together with their opinion to the Administrative Court for adjudication.[86]

---

82 *Ibid.*, pp. 99–104, and see Investor–State Dispute Settlement and Impact on Investment Rulemaking, pp. 26–30 <www.unctad.org/en/Docs/iteiia 20073_en.pdf>.

83 Repealing (a) the Organic Act on Parliamentary Ombudsmen BE 2542 (1999) and (b) the Announcement of the Council for Democratic Reform under the Constitutional Monarchy No. 14 BE 2549, dated 21.09.2006. For further information on ombudsmen in Thailand, see <www. ombudsman.go.th/10/eng/index1.asp>.

84 Section 13(1) of the Ombudsmen Act.

85 Section 13(2) of the Ombudsmen Act.

86 Section 14(2) of the Ombudsmen Act.

# 3. COMPROMISE AGREEMENTS

## 3.1. OUT-OF-COURT COMPROMISE AGREEMENTS

Generally speaking, the compromise provisions of sections 850–852 of the CCC constitute the basis or formality of any form of out-of-court ADR in Thailand for a dispute settlement to be agreed upon and become valid, binding, and enforceable between concerned parties, unless otherwise specified by other laws. The foregoing provisions were enacted under Title 17 (Compromise) of Book 3 (Specific Contracts): (a) initially, pursuant to the Royal Decree Promulgating Book 3 and Re-Promulgating Book 1 and Book 2 of the CCC (all Books entering into force on 1 January 1925 (BE 2468) (announced on 1 January 1924 (BE 2467));[87] and (b) subsequently, pursuant to the superseding Royal Decree Promulgating Revised Book 3 of the CCC (entering into force on 1 April 1929 (BE 2472) (announced on 1 January 1928 (BE 2471)).[88] Claims established by a compromise agreement have a statute of limitations requiring a claim to be brought[89] within ten years, regardless of the original claim's statute of limitations.[90] As sections 850–852 are fundamentally significant, their current provisions are quoted as follows:

> Section 850: 'A compromise is an agreement whereby the parties settle a dispute, be it existing or contemplated, by mutual concessions.'
> Section 851: 'A compromise agreement is not enforceable by action unless there be some written evidence signed by the liable party or his agent.'
> Section 852: 'The effect of the compromise is to extinguish the claims conceded by each party and to secure to each party the rights which are declared therein to belong to him.'

## 3.2. IN-COURT COMPROMISE AGREEMENTS

Since 1935, section 138 of the CPC has provided as follows:

> 'If parties to a lawsuit make an agreement or a compromise on the issues of the lawsuit without withdrawing the plaint and if such agreement or compromise is not

87 See Annual Collection of Laws (*Prachoom Khot Mhai Prajam Sok*), Vol. 37 BE 2467 (1924), first printing on 09.08.1934 (BE 2477), pp. 308, 406–407.

88 See Annual Collection of Laws (*Prachoom Khot Mhai Prajam Sok*), Vol. 41 BE 2471 (1928), first printing on 05.03.1933 (BE 2476), pp. 349, 449–450. A significant change appeared in section 851 which previously provided that a compromise agreement was void unless made in writing. Currently, section 851 provides that 'A compromise agreement is not enforceable by action unless there be some written evidence signed by the liable party or his agent.'

89 Mediation: Thai-English, p. 9.

90 Section 193/32 of the CCC.

contrary to law, the court shall write down in detail the terms of the agreement or compromise and issue its judgment accordingly.

The judgment shall not be appealed, except on any of the following grounds:

(1) when it is alleged that a party commits a fraud;
(2) when the judgment is alleged to contravene a provision of law relating to public order;
(3) when the judgment is alleged not to be in accordance with the agreement or compromise.'

By virtue of the above provision, parties to a lawsuit may make a compromise[91] in court at any level of the courts (i.e., the Court of First Instance, the Court of Appeal, or the Supreme Court)[92] on issues of the case as long as it has not been withdrawn and the compromise is not found to be contrary to any provision of law so that the court may render a judgment pursuant to the compromise. Such a compromise is binding only on the contracting parties[93] and the judgment pursuant thereto will be issued only at the time the court renders a judgment for the whole lawsuit.[94] Such judgment in a court of first instance may not be revoked[95] but may only be appealed on the grounds of the exceptions specified above. Failure to comply with such a compromise will be remedied simply by submitting an application for an execution of the judgment without starting a new lawsuit.[96]

## 4. MEDIATION

Different mediation processes under various laws will be discussed under subsection 6. 'ADR processes under various laws', not necessarily in a comparative or parallel manner. However, the mediation processes will result in disputing parties making a compromise agreement in settlement of their dispute. Thus, generally speaking so long as a mediation process does not start upon or after the filing of a lawsuit, the legal effect of making a compromise agreement (as discussed under subsection 3.1. 'Out-of-court compromise agreements') will apply to all kinds of out-of-court or pre-trial mediation, except for post-judgment mediation.

---

91 i.e., under sections 850–852 of the CCC.

92 Practical Guidelines for Making A Compromise and Resultant Judgment, Chotechuang Tapwong, Former Presiding Justice of the Court of Appeal (Knowledge of Civil Law for Mediation of Disputes, 04.2007, published by the ADR Knowledge Centre of the ADRO under the OOJ), pp. 69 and 74.

93 *Ibid.*, pp. 69 and 73.

94 *Ibid.*, pp. 69 and 74.

95 *Ibid.*, pp. 69 and 75, citing Supreme Court Decision No. 768/2534 (1991 AD).

96 Mediation: Thai-English, p. 9.

As for the in-court or court-annexed mediation process, it first appeared in section 19 of the CPC (under Division 1 – General Provisions, of the CPC), by virtue of which, since its inception in 1935, the court will order any or all parties to appear in court in person although the party or parties may be represented by a lawyer if the court views that such appearance may bring about an agreement or a compromise (as set forth in sections 20 and 20 *bis* of the CPC). In 1999, section 193 of the CPC was amended so that a mediation process is provided for in respect of petty lawsuits and a compromise can be reached in settlement of the dispute. In both cases, the compromise is subject to section 138 of the CPC (which provision is also under Division 1 – General Provisions, of the CPC). See *supra* subsection 3.2. 'In-court compromise agreements'. Moreover, as other procedural laws, e.g., the JFC Act, the IPIT Act (see *infra* subsection 6. 'ADR processes under various laws') apply provisions of the CPC, including section 138 of the CPC, in the absence of any applicable provisions thereunder to the contrary, the common legal basis of all court-annexed mediation processes for dispute settlement would be based on section 138 of the CPC.

## 5. ARBITRATION ACTS

Under Thai law, each of court-annexed arbitration and out-of-court arbitration has its own legal framework. Both frameworks were originally embodied in the CPC and have been classified as a type of special procedure in the Court of First Instance under sections 210–222 of Chapter 3 (Arbitration) of Title 2 (Special Procedures in Courts of First Instance) of Division 2 (Procedure in the Court of First Instance) of the CPC. Sections 210–222 (except section 221) govern court-annexed arbitration, and section 221 governed out-of-court arbitration.

In 1987, the CPC was amended by the CPC Amendment Act No. 11 BE 2530 (1987), which removed the out-of-court arbitration framework under section 221 for it to fall under the Arbitration Act BE 2530 (1987) instead. In 2002, the Arbitration Act BE 2530 (1987) was superseded by the Arbitration Act BE 2545 (2002) in order to, among other things, better accommodate the use of foreign arbitration.[97]

### 5.1. COURT-ANNEXED ARBITRATION

Sections 210–222 (except section 221) of the CPC govern court-annexed arbitration. When a lawsuit is pending before a court of first instance, the parties may agree to submit any or all of the issues in dispute to one or more arbitrators for settlement by filing a joint application with the court stating their terms of

97 See Remarks annexed to the Arbitration Act BE 2545 (2002).

agreement. If the agreement does not specify otherwise, each of the plaintiff and the defendant may appoint one arbitrator. If there are joint plaintiffs or joint defendants, only one arbitrator may be appointed for the joint plaintiffs or the joint defendants, respectively. However, a party or a third party may be agreed to appoint the arbitrators. Any of the foregoing appointments must be made in writing. If the court does not approve any of the appointed arbitrators, it will require a new appointment. If the parties do not appoint their arbitrator, the court has power to appoint arbitrators for them as it deems fit. Once the parties have appointed their arbitrator, the arbitrator cannot be removed without the other parties' consent. The appointment of an arbitrator may be challenged and the provisions for challenge of a judge under the CPC will apply *mutatis mutandis*.

The arbitrators are required to hear all the parties and may make such inquiries as they think fit regarding the dispute before them. They may request that the court provide them with all pleadings and other documents of the lawsuit for their review. They may also request the court to summon witnesses, administer oath taking, or order production of documents, subject to court fees. Unless their terms of agreement specify otherwise, the arbitrators may conduct proceedings as they think fit.

Unless the parties' agreement specifies otherwise, an arbitral award is to be made by majority decision of the arbitrators; in the event that the votes are tied, the arbitrators or the court by their motion will appoint a chairman to give a casting vote. The arbitrators will submit their award to the court for a judgment to be made in accordance therewith. An appeal cannot be made against a court order refusing to issue a judgment in accordance with the award nor against a judgment issued in accordance therewith, unless: (a) there is an allegation that the chairman or the arbitrators are dishonest or any party has committed a fraud; (b) the court order or judgment is contrary to law relating to public order; or (c) the judgment is not in accordance with the award.

## 5.2. OUT-OF-COURT ARBITRATION

### *5.2.1. Process*

The original section 221 of the CPC, which was the only provision under the CPC dealing with out-of-court arbitration, provided briefly for the enforcement of an award with which a party has failed to comply.[98]

[98] The original section 221 of the CPC provided that: 'As regards a dispute which was determined by out-of-court arbitration, if a party refuses to comply with the arbitral award, the award will not be enforced unless the other party has applied with a competent court and the court has given a judgment in accordance with the award. In that case, the court having competent jurisdiction shall be the court designated in the agreement by the parties or, in the

In 1987, this whole section was revised by the CPC Amendment Act No. 11 BE 2530 (1987) to provide simply that 'Submission of a dispute to arbitration out of court shall be in accordance with law governing arbitration'. The Arbitration Act BE 2530 (1987) was the law that was referred to. The foregoing Arbitration Act entered into effect in the same year. The law was intended to meet the demand for resolving disputes out of court, to expand the scope of this means which was under a single section of law, and to provide for the recognition and enforcement of foreign arbitral awards that was problematic and not acknowledged by any national law despite Thailand's ratification of relevant treaties.[99] In 2002, the first Arbitration Act 1987 was superseded by the Arbitration Act BE 2545 (2002). A summary of the replacement Arbitration Act follows.

An arbitration agreement is defined as a clause in a contract or a separate agreement, made in writing and signed by the parties, by which the parties agree to settle by arbitration all or certain disputes which have arisen or may arise between them in respect of a legal relationship, whether contractual or not. However, it may be deemed to exist: (a) where the agreement appears in an exchange of letters, facsimile, telegrams, telexes, an exchange of information with electronic signature, or other means that records the agreement; (b) where the agreement is asserted in a claim or an objection and the non-asserting party does not deny it; or (c) where a contract evidenced in writing refers to any document that has an agreement to resolve a dispute by arbitration and to intend to incorporate the agreement into the principal contract. An arbitration agreement is transferred together with the related claims or liability.

A government agency is not entitled to refuse to settle its dispute by arbitration if it has entered into an arbitration agreement with a private party, regardless of whether the agreement is in an administrative contract.[100]

---

absence of the designation, the court which would have competent jurisdiction to try and adjudicate the dispute. If the court is of the opinion that the award is contrary to law in any respect, the provisions of the last paragraph of section 218 shall apply.' (The last paragraph of section 218 provides that 'However, if the court is of the opinion that the award is contrary to law in any respect, it shall have power to issue an order refusing to make a judgment in accordance with the award. If the award can be rectified, the court may require the arbitrators or concerned parties to make the rectification within a time it considers reasonable.')

99 See Remarks annexed to the Arbitration Act BE 2530 (1987).

100 'Administrative contract' is defined under section 3 of the Administrative Court Establishment and Procedure Act BE 2542 (1999) to include a contract, at least one of whose parties is an administrative agency or a person acting on behalf of the State and which has the nature of a concession contract or a contract for providing public services, procuring infrastructure, or exploiting natural resources. 'Administrative agency' is defined under the foregoing section 3 as a ministry, sub-ministry, department, governmental body called by any other name and ascribed the status of a department, provincial administration, local administration, State enterprise established by an act or a royal decree, or other State agency and includes an agency entrusted to exercise administrative powers or carry out administrative acts.

A court will dispose of a lawsuit the plaintiff has filed without first referring the dispute to arbitration as mutually agreed if, after its examination, it sees that (a) there exists no cause to render the arbitration agreement void, unenforceable, or incapable of performance and (b) the defendant has applied to the court (not later than the date for submitting an answer or within the time allowed for submitting an answer) for it to dispose of the lawsuit in order for the parties to engage in arbitration.

The competent courts[101] under the Arbitration Act 2002 are the court having jurisdiction over a party's domicile, the court having jurisdiction to adjudicate the disputes submitted to the arbitrators, the court having jurisdiction over the place of the arbitration proceedings, the Central IPIT Court, the Regional IPIT Court,[102] and the Administrative Court.[103]

Unless otherwise agreed by the disputing parties, if they cannot agree on a sole arbitrator to be appointed, a party may apply to a competent court to

---

101 Sections 9 and 45(2) of the Arbitration Act 2002.

102 Section 7(1) of the IPIT Act provides that: 'The intellectual property and international trade courts shall have jurisdiction over the following matters: (1) criminal cases relating to trademarks, copyrights, and patents; (2) criminal cases relating to offences under Sections 271–275 [on trademarks] of the Criminal Code; (3) civil cases relating to trademarks, copyrights, patents, and cases arising from technology transfer or licensing agreements; (4) civil cases in connection with offences under Sections 271–275 of the Criminal Code; (5) civil cases relating to international sale or exchange of goods or financial instruments, international services, international carriage, insurance, and other related juristic acts; (6) civil cases relating to letters of credit issued in connection with transactions under (5), inward or outward remittances of funds, trust receipts, and guarantees in connection therewith; (7) civil cases relating to ship arrests; (8) civil cases relating to dumping and subsidisation of goods or services from abroad; (9) civil or criminal cases relating to disputes over integrated circuit layout designs, scientific discoveries, trade names, geographic indications, trade secrets, and plant varieties protection; (10) civil or criminal cases that are prescribed to be under the jurisdiction of the intellectual property and international trade courts; and (11) civil cases relating to arbitration to settle disputes under (3)–(10).'

103 Section 9 of the Administrative Court Establishment and Procedure Act BE 2542 (1999) provides that: 'The Administrative Court has the competence to try and adjudicate or give orders in the following matters: (1) a disputed case relating to an unlawful act done by an administrative agency or a State official, whether in connection with the issuance of a rule or order, or any other acts done without power, beyond the scope of powers or duties, inconsistent with the law or not complying with formality, process, or procedure which is essentially required of such acts, in bad faith, having the nature of unfair discrimination, creating unnecessary process, or causing undue burden to the public, or constituting undue exercise of discretion; (2) a disputed case relating to an administrative agency or a State official neglecting duties required by law to be performed or performing such duties with undue delay; (3) a disputed case relating to a wrongful act or other liabilities of an administrative agency or a State official arising from exercise of power under the law, from a law, administrative order, or other orders, or from neglecting duties required by law to be performed or performing such duties with undue delay; (4) a disputed case relating to an administrative contract; (5) a case where the law requires an administrative agency or a State official to file a lawsuit to compel a person to do or refrain from doing an act; and (6) a disputed case relating to a matter prescribed by law to be under the jurisdiction of the Administrative Court.'

appoint an arbitrator for them. If there is more than one arbitrator to be appointed, each party is entitled to appoint one arbitrator. The appointed arbitrators will appoint a chairman, failing that within 30 days of the appointment, a party may apply to a competent court to appoint the chairman for them. If any party does not appoint its own arbitrator within 30 days from the date of receiving the notice thereof, the party or the other party may apply to a competent court to appoint the arbitrator. If the disputing parties cannot agree on the number of arbitrators, there will only be one arbitrator to be appointed. And when there is more than one arbitrator to be appointed, the arbitrators to be appointed will be odd in number. If the parties have specified an even number of arbitrators, the arbitrators are required to appoint umpire chairman.

The arbitrators are required to be impartial and independent in the performance of their duties and, at any time before or after their appointment, to disclose to disputing parties without delay facts that may cause a suspicion of their impartiality or independence unless they have already been made aware of such facts. An arbitrator may be removed by mutual agreement of the parties. Unless otherwise agreed by the parties, an arbitrator can be challenged within 15 days of a party becoming aware of the appointment or the facts giving rise to a suspicion of impartiality, independence, or disqualification. If the challenge procedure proves unsuccessful, the challenging party may submit an application of objection to a competent court within 30 days from the date of receiving the decision on the challenge, the date of becoming aware of the appointment, or the date of becoming aware of the facts giving rise to such suspicion, as the case may be.

The arbitrators will not be subject to civil liability in their conduct as arbitrators unless they commit a wilful or grossly negligent act to injure any disputing party. An arbitrator who demands, receives or agrees to unlawfully receive property or any other benefits for himself, herself, or other persons in order to do or refrain from doing an act in the performance of their duties will be liable to imprisonment for a term not exceeding ten years or a fine not exceeding Baht 100,000, or both. Any person who provides, offers to provide, or promises to provide property or any other benefits to any arbitrator to induce him or her to do, refrain from doing, or delay doing any act in contravention of his or her duties will be liable to imprisonment for a term not exceeding ten years, a fine not exceeding Baht 100,000, or both.

The arbitrators have the power to make a determination of their scope of their authority, including the existence or validity of the arbitration agreement, the validity of their appointment, and disputed issues falling under the scope of their authority. The determination of their authority may be made as a preliminary one or at the time of making the award on the issues in dispute. In the case of preliminary determination, a disputing party may apply to a competent court to decide on the determination within 30 days from the date of receiving the preliminary determination. Although the arbitrators may determine that the principal contract is void or invalid, that determination will not affect the arbitration agreement.

The statute of limitations of the issues in dispute is interrupted in accordance with section 193/14(4) of the CCC[104] on the occurrence of one of the following events and arbitration proceedings will start:

(a) when a disputing party receives a written notice from the other party requiring dispute settlement by arbitration;
(b) when a disputing party notifies the other party in writing to appoint an arbitrator or its approval for appointment of arbitrators for dispute settlement;
(c) when a disputing party notifies the arbitrators in writing of its disputes intended to be settled; or
(d) when a disputing party submits its disputes to a mutually agreed institution set up to administer arbitration proceedings.

A party may apply to a competent court for a preliminary order before or during the arbitration proceedings or for issuance of a subpoena or an order to deliver any documents or objects and the court may grant the order if it would be able to if it was conducting the proceedings. Provisions of the CPC in this regard (sections 253–270) would be applied *mutatis mutandis*.

If the parties do not agree otherwise or this law does not provide otherwise, the arbitrators have the power to conduct proceedings in ways they consider appropriate. The power includes the power to determine the admissibility and weight of any evidence. In this regard, they may apply relevant provisions of the CPC.

Unless the disputing parties agree otherwise, the arbitrators may choose the place and language of the arbitration and may hold oral hearings or hear and decide a case on the basis of documents only.

The arbitrators are required to apply the governing law of the dispute that the parties specify and the law will, if not specified, be the substantive law, excluding the law on conflict of laws. If the parties do not specify the governing law, it will be Thai law in the absence of a conflict of laws issue. The parties may require the arbitrators to determine the dispute on the basis of the principles of good faith and fairness and in accordance with the terms of the contract and, in the case of a commercial dispute, will take into account usages of the trade applicable to the transaction. Unless otherwise agreed by the parties, any award, order or decision of the arbitrators will be made by a majority of votes; failing that, the chairman will make the determination. The chairman may be authorised by the parties or other arbitrators to decide on issues of arbitration proceedings.

---

104 Section 193/14 of the CCC provides that 'Statute of limitations is interrupted in the following cases: [...] (4) the creditor submits its claims to arbitration.'

During the arbitration proceedings, if the parties make a compromise agreement, the arbitrators will terminate the proceedings. If the arbitrators consider, at the parties' request, that the terms of their agreement or the compromise agreement is not contrary to law, the arbitrators will issue an award in accordance with the agreement. Such award will fall under section 37 of this Act (see the following paragraph) and have the status of an award on the issues in dispute. Arbitration proceedings will terminate upon issuance of the award or an order of the arbitrators.

Under section 37 of the Act, an award must be made in writing and signed by at least a majority of the arbitrators. If the parties have not agreed otherwise, the award must state clearly the reasons of the award and may not exceed the scope of the arbitration agreement or the request of the parties unless the award is made in accordance with the compromise agreement in the preceding paragraph or in respect of fees and expenses for the arbitration or remuneration of the arbitrators. In addition the award must state the dates and place of the arbitration and the stated place will be regarded as the place where the award was made. The arbitrators must send every disputing party a copy of the award.

A party may have recourse against an arbitral award by submitting an application to a competent court for setting aside within 90 days of the date of receipt of a copy of the award, or, if there is an application to amend or interpret an award or make an additional award, within 90 days of the date of amending or interpreting the award or making an additional award.

A court may set aside an arbitral award when:

(a) the applicant can prove that:
   (i) a party to the arbitration agreement was under some incapacity under the law applicable to that party;
   (ii) the arbitration agreement is not valid under the law to which the parties have agreed or, failing any indication thereon, under Thai law;
   (iii) the party making the application was not given proper notice of the appointment of the arbitrators or of the arbitral hearings or was otherwise unable to present his case;
   (iv) the award deals with a dispute not falling within the scope of the arbitration agreement or the award does not fall within the scope of the terms of the submission to arbitration, provided that, if the decisions on matters falling within the scope can be separated from those that are not, only that part of the award which contains decisions on matters not falling within the scope of the arbitration agreement or the terms of the submission to arbitration may be set aside; or
   (v) the composition of the arbitral tribunal or the arbitral procedure was not in accordance with the agreement of the parties, or, failing such agreement, was not in accordance with this law; or

(b) the court finds that:
  (i) the dispute under the award is not capable of settlement by arbitration under the law; or
  (ii) the recognition or enforcement of the award is in conflict with the public order or good morals.

When asked to set aside an award, the court may, where appropriate and requested by a party, suspend the setting aside proceedings for a period of time determined by it in order to give the arbitral tribunal an opportunity to resume the arbitral proceedings or to take such other action as in the arbitral tribunal's opinion will eliminate the grounds for setting aside.

### *5.2.2. Recognition and enforcement*

An arbitral award, be it domestic or foreign, would invariably be recognised and enforced, i.e. enforcement on the basis of an application instead of a plaint, provided that in the case of a foreign arbitral award it falls under the treaties, conventions, or international agreement to which Thailand is a party and they would be enforceable only to the extent Thailand agreed to be bound thereby. After a competent court has received the application, it will speedily hold an inquiry and render a judgment without delay.

An application for recognition and enforcement of an arbitral award must be submitted within a period of three years from the date the award may be enforced. According to Clause 1(b) of Schedule 1 (Filing Fees) annexed to the CPC, (a) an application for enforcement of or setting aside a domestic arbitral award is charged with a filing fee at the rate of 0.5% (but not exceeding Baht 50,000) of the claim amount not exceeding Baht 50 million and at the rate of 0.1% of any excess amount, and (b) an application for enforcement of or setting aside a foreign arbitral award is charged with a filing fee of 1.0% (but not exceeding Baht 100,000) of the claim amount not exceeding Baht 50 million and at the rate of 0.1% of any excess amount. The foregoing rates would also apply to the filing with the Central IPIT Court[105] and the Administrative Court.[106] An arbitral award requires no stamp duty.[107]

A court may refuse enforcement of an arbitral award if the party against whom the award will be enforced can prove that:

(a) a party to the arbitration agreement was under some incapacity under the law applicable to that party;

105 Section 26 of the IPIT Act.
106 Section 45(4) of the Administrative Court Establishment and Procedure Act BE 2542 (1999).
107 Royal Decree No. 374 BE 2543, issued pursuant to the Revenue Code and effective on 16.11.2000.

(b) the arbitration agreement is not valid under the law to which the parties have agreed or, failing any indication thereon, under the law of the country where the award was made;
(c) the party against whom the award will be enforced was not given proper notice of the appointment of the arbitrators or of the arbitral hearings or was otherwise unable to present his case;
(d) the award deals with a dispute not falling within the scope of the arbitration agreement or the award does not fall within the scope of the terms of the submission to arbitration, provided that, if the decisions on matters falling under the scope can be separated from those that are not, only that part of the award which contains decisions on matters falling within the scope of the arbitration agreement or the terms of submission to arbitration may be enforced;
(e) the composition of the arbitral tribunal or the arbitral procedure was not in accordance with the agreement of the parties, or, failing such agreement, was not in accordance with the law of the country where the award was made; or
(f) the award has not yet become binding on the parties or has been set aside or suspended by a competent court or under the law of the country in which that award was made.

The court may refuse enforcement in the preceding paragraph if the court finds that:

(a) the dispute under the award is not capable of settlement by arbitration under the law; or
(b) the recognition or enforcement of the award is in conflict with the public order or good morals.

An order or judgment of the court under this Act may not be appealed to the Supreme Court or the Supreme Administrative Court unless:

(a) the recognition or enforcement of the award is contrary to public order or good morals;
(b) the order or judgment is contrary to the provisions of law relating to public order or good morals;
(c) the order or judgment is not in accordance with the arbitral award;
(d) the judge who tried the case gave a dissenting opinion in the judgment; or
(e) it is an order relating to the preliminary measures (under section 16).

Unless otherwise agreed by the parties or determined by an institution established for dispute settlement by arbitration, fees and expenses incurred in the arbitral proceedings as well as remuneration of the arbitrators except lawyers' fees and expenses are as stipulated in the arbitral award; failing that, any disputing party or the arbitral tribunal may request a competent court for an order on fees, expenses, and remuneration of the arbitrators as it thinks fit.

## 6. ADR PROCESSES UNDER VARIOUS LAWS

### 6.1. LAA 1897 AND SAA NO. 7 (2007)

This out-of-court mediation process first appeared in the LAA 1897, under which a non-judicial State official acted as a mediator. Under Clause 3 of section 27 of the LAA 1897,[108] regarding a civil case where the plaintiff complained to a sub-district headman (*Kamnan*) for a disputed amount or compensation not exceeding Baht 100, the sub-district headman had the power to demand that the defendant and witnesses appear in person for assessment and settlement without recourse to court action. If the parties were unable to reach an agreement, the sub-district headman would advise the plaintiff to take the matter to court. If the parties had made an agreement pursuant to the assessment, no party was entitled to file a lawsuit afterwards and in the event of non-compliance with the agreement, the sub-district headman would request a court to enforce the agreement. Subsequently, the LAA 1897 was superseded by the Local Administration Act BE 2457 (1914) (LAA 1914), in effect repealing the assessment power of the sub-district headman under the foregoing section 27.

Further, under Clause 3 of section 55 of the LAA 1897, regarding a civil case where the plaintiff complained to the District Committee (*Grom Gaan Amphoe*) for an amount not exceeding Baht 1,000, the District Committee had the power to demand the defendant and witnesses to appear in person for assessment. If the parties were unable to reach an agreement, the District Committee would dispose of the case for the parties to take court action. If the parties had made an agreement pursuant to the assessment, no party was entitled to file a lawsuit afterwards and in the case of non-compliance with the agreement, the District Committee had the power to take the non-compliant party to court for enforcement in accordance with the agreement. Subsequently, the assessment power of the District Committee under the foregoing section 55 was retained and revised by virtue of section 108 of the LAA 1914.

Under section 108 of the LAA 1914, regarding a civil case where the plaintiff complained to the District Committee for a value not exceeding Baht 200, the District Committee had the power to demand that the defendant appear in person for assessment. If the parties were unable to reach an agreement, the District Committee would dispose of the case for the parties to take court action. If the parties had made an agreement pursuant to the assessment, no party was

108 See the LAA 1897 in the above-mentioned Annual Collection of Laws, Vol. 16, pp. 42–43.

entitled to file a lawsuit afterwards and the settled case would be treated as though it were settled by arbitration. In the case of non-compliance with the agreement, the District Committee had the power to take the non-compliant party to court for enforcement in accordance with the agreement. A nominal fee was charged to the losing party but could be waived by the District Committee.

However, the above-mentioned section 108 was revised by the Local Administration Amendment Act No. 7 BE 2527 (1984) (LAA No. 7) to instead entrust the chief district officer (*Nai Amphoe*) with similar power. Under the revised provisions, a chief district officer had the following judicial powers in civil cases. Regarding a civil case where the disputed amount did not exceed Baht 20,000 and the cause of the dispute occurred in the district or the person complained about was domiciled in the district, if the complainant requested the chief district officer to require the other party to come for mediation and assessment for settlement without recourse to court action, the chief district officer had the power to so require. If the chief district officer had made an assessment and the parties did not agree, he would terminate the case for the parties to take court action. However, in the course of the assessment if the parties did agree to accept any person's testimony or determination, he had the power to issue a warrant to require such person to give testimony or make a determination for settlement of the case. If the parties agreed to such person's assessment, he would write down the terms of agreement for their and his signatures, each would retain one copy of the agreement. Failure to comply with the terms of the agreement would entitle the other party to bring a signed copy to court for a judgment to be issued in accordance with the agreement. A case agreed by the parties as a result of the chief district officer's assessment was regarded as a case finally settled by arbitration and the parties no longer had the right to court action. Unless the chief district officer waived fees at his discretion, a fee of Baht 5 for issuing the warrant and completing the application and a fee of Baht 10 for preparing the agreement would be charged to the losing party or shared between the parties as agreed. Eventually, the revised section 108 of the LAA 1914 was repealed by the Local Administration Amendment Act No. 11 BE 2551 (2008) (LAA No. 11).

Before the above-mentioned repeal in 2008, section 61/2 was, by virtue of the State Administration Amendment Act No. 7 BE 2550 (2007) (SAA No. 7), added to the State Administration Act BE 2534 (1991) (SAA 1991) to provide for a mediation process to be conducted by a panel of mediators which has jurisdiction in its district (*Amphoe*). This mediation scheme applies to all districts throughout Thailand, including districts (*Khet*) of Bangkok Metropolis.[109] Currently, the scheme has been supplemented by the Ministerial Regulation on Mediation of Civil Disputes BE 2553, dated 25 August 2010, which specifies rules and

109 Section 61/2, last paragraph.

procedure for the preparation of rosters, ethics, mediation procedure, making of a compromise agreement, and remuneration of mediators.

A summary of the mediation scheme under SAA No. 7 as supplemented by the above-mentioned Ministerial Regulation is as follows.

There will be a number of mediators in each district (*Amphoe* and *Khet*) throughout Thailand to be selected to operate as a panel to mediate civil disputes between parties, a party to which must be domiciled in the district. The mediated disputes must be related to land, inheritance, other civil disputes, not exceeding Baht 200,000 in value, or other civil disputes of a higher amount that will be specified in a ministerial regulation or a royal decree.

No fewer than 20 mediators will be on a roster maintained by the chief district officer of the district. The mediators on the roster are selected from their applications by the chief district officer with subsequent approval of the relevant provincial council (*Kana Grom Gaan Changwat*),[110] which consists of the provincial governor, the provincial vice governor or his designee, the provincial deputy governor (*Palad Changwat*), the provincial public prosecutor, the commander of provincial police, and chiefs of field staffs from various ministries or a representative from each ministry.

Ethical conduct requirements of the mediators include impartiality, independence, fairness, non-discriminatory performance of duties, not calling for or accepting property or interests from disputing parties or other related persons, keeping confidential information relating to the mediation, and neither determining disputes nor forcing any party to sign a compromise agreement. A disputing party may trigger a process of investigation into an allegation that a mediator has breached an ethical conduct requirement.

When a dispute arises and a disputing party intends to have it mediated, the party may notify the chief district officer of its intention by submitting its application in writing, in person, by post, or orally. The chief district officer will notify the other party/parties and inquire whether they also intend to engage in mediation. If the disputing parties agree to resolve the dispute by mediation, the chief district officer will notify all parties in writing that all parties agree to engage in mediation and specify a date, time, and place for all parties to meet to select their mediator and the presiding mediator, who may be the chief district officer, the provincial public prosecutor, or the assistant chief district officer (*Palad Amphoe*). Failing an agreement on a presiding mediator, the chief district officer has power to appoint the presiding mediator. If a party does not agree to engage in mediation, the chief district officer will dispose of the application for mediation and so notify the applicant.

Within seven days of complete selection of all mediators, the presiding mediator will convene a meeting of the panel of mediators to deliberate on the application for mediation. If they see that the applicant is exercising his right in

110 Section 53 of the SAA 1991.

bad faith or further action will cause any disputing party to gain or lose advantages in taking legal proceedings, the panel of mediators will resolve not to accept the application for mediation.

Within seven days after the panel of mediators has accepted the application for mediation, the chief district officer will send a notice of the mediation meeting, which normally takes place at the district office, to all concerned parties. Notices of subsequent meetings will be issued by the presiding mediator. All mediators are required to attend every meeting and are prohibited from determining the disputes. When the panel of mediators has reasons to doubt if the disputed claims are legally enforceable on grounds other than statute of limitations, they will cease the mediation and strike the disputes from their mediation docket.

During the mediation if a disputing party is unwilling to continue participating in the process, the party is entitled to notify the presiding mediator of its termination in writing or orally. Consequently, the panel of mediators will dispose of the application for mediation and order to cease the mediation and it will be regarded that the panel of mediators has never received the application for mediation.

The mediation must be finished within three months from the date the chief district officer enters the disputes in the mediation docket unless it is necessary and the disputing parties agree, the mediation may be extended each time not exceeding three months and altogether not exceeding one year. If the mediation is not finished within the foregoing timeframes, the panel of mediators will dispose of the disputes.

The panel of mediators has the power and duty to hear disputes directly from disputing parties and to conduct mediation to speedily bring about an agreement between the parties. If the disputing parties reach an agreement, the panel of mediators will arrange for them to enter into a binding compromise agreement. If they fail to agree, the panel of mediators will dispose of the dispute. The compromise agreement will have the effect of an arbitral award in accordance with the law on arbitration. If any party fails to comply with the compromise agreement, the other party may apply to a competent public prosecutor for him to apply (not later than three years from the date the compromise agreement may be enforced) to a competent court (without filing a plaint) to issue a legal execution order in accordance with the compromise agreement by applying the law on arbitration[111] *mutatis mutandis*.

After the panel of mediators has accepted the dispute for mediation, the statute of limitations is interrupted as from the date of submitting the dispute to mediation until the panel of mediators disposes of the dispute or until the date the disputing parties enter into a compromise agreement, as the case may be.

---

111 See sections 42, 43 and 44 of the Arbitration Act 2002.

The mediators are entitled to remuneration and travelling expenses in accordance with the schedule attached to the Ministerial Regulation on Mediation of Civil Disputes BE 2553 (2010).

## 6.2. CPC (1935 AND 2008) AND 2011 STIPULATION

Court-annexed mediation first appeared in sections 19[112] and 20 of the CPC, which entered into force on 1 October 1935.[113] In 1999 by virtue of the CPC Amendment Act No. 17 BE 2542 (1999), section 20 was revised[114] and section 20 *bis*[115] was added, thereby constituting a basis for a systemised scheme of court-annexed mediation to be formulated afterwards. Hence, subsequent to the 1999 Amendment Act to the foregoing sections 20 and 20 *bis*, after the OOJ was set up in 2000[116] to be in charge of the administration of courts of justice, independently of the Executive branch, the OOJ's Judicial Administration Commission (JAC) systemised the mediation scheme in existence then by issuing: (a) the Regulation on Mediation for Financial Dispute Resolution BE 2544 on 22 March 2001 (by virtue of section 17(1) of the Judicial Administration Act BE 2543 (2000) (JA Act)) and (b) the Regulation on Mediation BE 2544 on 23 August 2001[117] (by virtue of section 17(1) of the JA Act).

However, in 2008 the third and fourth paragraphs of section 20 *bis* of the CPC were revised and added, respectively[118] to provide for (a) rules and procedure of court-annexed mediation, (b) appointment of mediators, and (c) power and duties of mediators, to be set forth in a stipulation of the Supreme Court President which will be effective by publication in the Royal Gazette. In

---

112 Section 19 of the CPC empowers a court to require disputing parties to appear in court in person so that they might reach an agreement or make a compromise.

113 Subsequently, the Regulation of the Civil Court re Mediation for A Compromise BE 2537 (1994), dated 15.11.1994, and the Supreme Court President's Recommendations on Mediation for A Compromise BE 2539 (1996), dated 29.03.1996, were issued.

114 Section 20 of the CPC originally empowered the court to attempt to make an assessment so that the parties would reach an agreement or make a compromise on the matters in dispute at any stage of the trial. Currently, section 20 of the CPC empowers the court to *mediate* for the disputing parties to reach an agreement or make a compromise on the matters in dispute at any stage of the trial, i.e. before the Court of First Instance, the Court of Appeal, or the Supreme Court, as the case may be, renders its judgment or disposes of the lawsuit by a judgment or an order, unless the Court of Appeal or the Supreme Court may instruct otherwise (see Clauses 45 and 49 of the 2011 Stipulation).

115 Section 20 *bis* (1) empowers the court, in the interest of mediation when it sees fit or with an application of a party, to order the mediation to be conducted *in camera* with the presence of a party or all parties appearing in person with or without their lawyers. The second paragraph further empowers the court, when it sees fit or with an application of a party, to appoint a person or a group of persons to be a mediator or mediators to assist it in the mediation for the parties to make a compromise.

116 By virtue of section 37 of the JA Act, as amended by the JA Act No. 2 BE 2551 (2008).

117 As amended by its Regulations on Mediation No. 2 BE 2547, effective on 14.07.2004.

118 By virtue of the CPC Amendment Act No. 24 BE 2551 (2008).

2011, in pursuance of the foregoing section 20 *bis*, paragraph 3 of the CPC, the Supreme Court President issued the Stipulation on Mediation BE 2554, dated 28 September 2011 (2011 Stipulation) to override all conflicting provisions of previous regulations, notifications, rules, or orders on the foregoing matters. Thus, the following summary of the 2011 Stipulation would affect the JAC's two Regulations mentioned in the preceding paragraph. Moreover, it would also affect the mediation processes that have been supplemented by regulations, notifications, rules or orders, discussed under subsections 6.3. 'Labour ADR (1979)', 6.4. 'Juvenile and family ADR (1991)', 6.6. 'IPIT Act (1996)', 6.10. 'Bankruptcy ADR (1999)', 6.13. 'Tax ADR (2002)', and 6.16. 'Consumer ADR (2008)', unless stated otherwise.

A mediation centre at each court of justice nationwide will, free of charge, administer mediation of disputes pending before the court pursuant to this 2011 Stipulation when the judges in quorum of a lawsuit in question deem it appropriate or all parties to the lawsuit agree thereon by notifying their agreement to the mediation centre or the judges in quorum during the court proceeding unless the judges in quorum decide to mediate by themselves or by assigning one or more of them to mediate.

When the judges in quorum do not decide to mediate a lawsuit in question by themselves or by assigning one or more of them to mediate, a sole mediator or a panel of mediators (for convenience, shortened to 'mediator') will be appointed. Such a mediator may be: (a) the mediators designated to the court in question who are selected from judiciary officers and government servicemen or employees of the OOJ; (b) those on the court rosters, either the roster which is registered by the OOJ Secretary General or the roster which is maintained at the discretion of the Chief of the Court[119] as approved by the Mediation Administration Committee of the court in question; or (c) those not listed on the court rosters. As for either (a) or (b), the court's appointment will take into account the suitability of the mediator and the satisfaction of the parties participating in the mediation. As for (c), the court's appointment is subject to the consent of all mediating parties and their agreement on the responsibility for the remuneration and expenses of the mediator. The mediating parties may challenge the mediator's impartiality before the start of the mediation process or within seven days of their knowledge of the relevant fact but not later than the end of the mediation process.

Where the parties are natural persons, they are required to attend mediation meetings in person. In the event of force majeure or unavoidable necessity, they may appoint an agent, who has power to make decisions and a compromise, to

[119] Namely, the President of the Supreme Court, the President of the Court of Appeal, the Presidents of the Regional Courts of Appeal, and the Chief Judges of the Courts of First Instance, the Chief Judges of the Court, an acting person, or a person designated by the foregoing persons to act in accordance with this 2011 Stipulation (see Clause 4 of the 2011 Stipulation).

attend the meetings in their place. Where the parties are legal persons, they will issue a power of attorney in writing (to be delivered to an officer at the mediation centre) to authorise a person with power to make decisions and a compromise to attend the meetings on their behalf.

The mediator may specify the mediation process and directions of the proceedings as they deem fit unless the parties agree otherwise and subject, however, to the rules and directions that that court may specify in respect of the methods, time, and place of the mediation.

The mediation may be conducted in camera and no details of the mediation will be recorded unless the parties agree to record them in whole or in part at their expense. The mediator may disclose dispute-related information of a party to another party unless the former party specifies otherwise. The mediator, disputing parties, and persons relevant to the mediation are prohibited from referring to or producing as evidence or using, in any way in arbitration, court or other similar proceedings, among other things, confidential statements or admissions of disputing parties made during the mediation.

The mediator on the court rosters will receive remuneration and expenses in accordance with the rules and procedures prescribed by the OOJ Secretary General. However, mediators appointed from judiciary officers and government servicemen or employees of the OOJ are not entitled to receive such remuneration. As for mediators not on the court rosters, their remuneration and expenses will be borne equally by the parties unless agreed otherwise.

A mediation process may begin at the time the plaintiff files his lawsuit (then he will be requested to complete forms for indicating intention to engage in mediation to resolve disputes) or at the time the plaint is served (then the defendant will be requested to complete forms for such intention). As a consequence, the mediation process may be finished before the first court hearing of the lawsuit. If not, the court, on the first court hearing of the lawsuit, may introduce the plaintiff and the defendant to the mediation scheme so that the parties may decide whether they wish to engage in the mediation process.[120] Note that the mediation process may even begin at the Court of Appeal or the Supreme Court.[121]

It is noteworthy that the 2011 Stipulation does not specify the consequence of failure to comply with a judgment issued in accordance with the compromise agreement, so it is believed that section 138 of the CPC would apply. See *supra* subsection 3.2. 'In-court compromise agreements'.

---

120 See Clause 4.3 of the ADRO's 'Handbook for Organising Court-Annexed Mediation', second printing, BE 2549 (2006), which is purportedly still in use.

121 See Chapters 5 and 6 of this 2011 Stipulation.

## 6.3. LABOUR ADR (1979)

A mediation process[122] is specified in sections 37–39 and 43 of the Labour Court Establishment and Procedure Act BE 2522 (1979) (LC Act). According to section 37 of the LC Act, after a labour court has accepted a case for trial, it will set a time and date for hearing at an early date and issue a subpoena to require the defendant to appear in court on schedule. In that subpoena, there will be, for the defendant's knowledge, a list of allegations and the relief applied for. The court will also order the plaintiff to appear in court on the same schedule. When the plaintiff and the defendant are present before the court, the court will mediate so that the parties will reach an agreement or make a compromise. In so doing, by virtue of Clause 8/2 of the Stipulation of the Labour Court re Conduct of Labour Court Proceeding, dated 27 February 1980 (BE 2523) (issued by virtue of section 29 of the LC Act), as revised by its amendment act No. 3 in 2000, the court may instruct the parties to meet a labour court legal officer for negotiation. If the parties reach an agreement, the officer will help prepare a case withdrawal application or a compromise agreement, and then report to the court. But if they cannot, he will bring the parties to the court for further proceedings.

The court is required to regard that any labour court case has a special nature and should be settled with good understanding between the parties for their continuing relationships. In the course of the court's mediation, if a party makes a request or the court thinks it appropriate, it may order the mediation to be conducted in camera in the presence of the parties only. After the court has mediated but the parties are unable to reach an agreement or make a compromise, the court must continue with its proceedings.[123] Within the purview of the foregoing, the court always has the power to mediate for the parties to reach an agreement or make a compromise at any stage of the proceedings.[124] If there are issues that cannot be settled or compromised, the court must note down the issues in dispute, record the plaintiff's statement and the defendant's answer and read the same to them, and have them affix their signature thereon. The court may specify which party is to adduce evidence first or later and immediately set the date for taking evidence. If the defendant refuses to give its answer, the court must make a record accordingly and continue with the proceedings.[125] See also *supra* subsection 6.2. 'CPC (1935 and 2008) and 2011 Stipulation'.

---

122 The following matters under the Labour Relations Act BE 2518 (1975), as supplemented by the Regulation of the Labour Relations Committee re Review and Determination of Labour Disputes BE 2548 (2005) which repealed its prior regulation in 2003, will not be discussed here: (a) the mediation process conducted by a Labour Dispute Conciliation Officer before a labour dispute becomes unresolved and (b) the determination of unresolved labour disputes by the Labour Relations Committee.

123 Section 38 of the LC Act.

124 Section 43 of the LC Act.

125 Section 39 of the LC Act.

## 6.4. JUVENILE AND FAMILY ADR (1991)

Although Thailand has had a special court and procedure for cases involving minors since 1951,[126] a mediation process only appeared in the replacement Acts, namely, the Juvenile and Family Court Establishment and Procedure Act BE 2534 (1991) and its amendments. Under another subsequent replacement Act, namely, the Juvenile and Family Court and Procedure Act BE 2553 (JFC Act), effective on 22 May 2011, the mediation process remains limited to Family Court cases.

The term 'Family Court case' was expanded and is defined under section 4 of the JFC Act as a civil action where a plaint or an application is filed with a court[127] or an act involves judicial power in regard to a minor[128] or a family which requires a sanction in compliance with the CCC, a law on family registration, or other laws relating to family. Trial and adjudication of Family Court cases fall under Chapter 13, sections 146–164 of the JFC Act.

In the trial and adjudication of a Family Court case, at any stage of the proceedings, the court has a duty to attempt to make an assessment, taking into account the peacefulness and togetherness of living in the family so that the parties will reach an agreement or make a compromise on their disputes.[129] Further, where there is a dispute in a Family Court case, before the first hearing the court has a duty to appoint a conciliator[130] to mediate so that the parties will

---

126 The governing laws then were the Children's and Juvenile Court Establishment Act BE 2494 (1951) and the Children's and Juvenile Court Procedure Act BE 2494 (1951) and their amendments.

127 Under section 10(3) of the JFC Act, a juvenile and family court has power to try and adjudicate Family Court cases and issue orders in those cases. A juvenile and family court is defined under section 4 of the JFC Act as the Central Juvenile and Family Court, a Provincial Juvenile and Family Court, and a Juvenile and Family Division of a provincial court which is established under this Act.

128 According to sections 19, 20, and 1448 of the CCC, 'minor' means a person who has not attained majority, which is either at the age of 20 or by marriage at or over the age of 17 or, with court consent, under the age of 17.

129 See section 146 of the JFC Act.

130 A Family Court case conciliator will not be appointed if the defendant is in default of appearance (see Work Manual under the JFC Act, undated and revised in compliance with Chapter 13 of the JFC Act, published by the Central Juvenile and Family Court, p. 105 <www.jvnc.coj.go.th/human/Manual071054.pdf>). According to section 150(2) of the JFC Act, a Family Court case conciliator is entitled to remuneration in accordance with a regulation of the Judicial Administration Commission (JAC) subject to approval of the Finance Ministry. In addition, by virtue of sections 50(3) and 51(4) of the JFC Act, a social worker is empowered and entrusted with duties to carry out court orders in search of living conditions of a family and *mediate* and compromise disputes in Family Court cases and to call the parties or any person to meet for *mediation* and compromise of disputes in Family Court cases. See further Rules of the Supreme Court President re Basic Knowledge, Principles, and Procedure for Registration and Deregistration of Family Court Case Conciliators BE 2554, issued by virtue of sections 7 and 149 of the JFC Act on 19.08.2011 and effective on 27.09.2011. The Thai word for 'conciliator' is different from 'mediator' and in fact has a slightly different meaning from 'mediator'; however, in the context of this Act, the conciliator is appointed to *mediate*

make a compromise; the principles and methods of mediation and the reporting of outcome will be in accordance with rules prescribed by the President of the Supreme Court.[131] However, if the parties are unable to make a compromise or the nature of the case will not permit a compromise, the court will terminate the mediation and continue with its proceedings and will, in its hearings, not admit records or testimonies taken during the mediation.[132]

After the appointed family conciliator has performed his duty as mentioned above, he must report the outcome of the mediation to the court. If the mediation is successful, the family conciliator must cause a compromise agreement to be made and make a report to the court or make an appointment with or request the court to call the parties to appear and make a compromise agreement before the court.[133] If the court considers that the compromise agreement is not against the law or public order or good morals of the people, it will issue a judgment in accordance with the compromise agreement. However, if the court will not issue a judgment it may prescribe conditions or time conditions for parties to comply with the agreement on a trial basis, particularly in respect of the exercise of parental powers or the raising of minors or incompetent persons. Notwithstanding the foregoing, if a minor receives a benefit or has an interest in the Family Court case, the court must principally take into account the best interest of the minor.[134] On the other hand, if the court considers that the compromise agreement is against the law or public order or good morals of the people or it is a case where the minor receives a benefit or has an interest and the best interest of the minor has not been taken into account, the court must refuse to issue a judgment in accordance with such agreement.[135] See also subsection 6.2. 'CPC (1935 and 2008) and 2011 Stipulation'.

## 6.5. SEC ACT (1992)

See *supra* subsections 2.1. 'Out-of-court mediation' and 2.4.1. 'Progress'.

---

disputes. For the purposes of this Act and broadly speaking any other Thai laws, the words 'conciliator' and 'mediator' can be used interchangeably.

131 See section 148(1) of the JFC Act. By virtue of this paragraph and section 7 of the JFC Act, the Rules of the Supreme Court President re Rules, Procedure, and Reporting of Outcome of Mediation in Family Court Cases BE 2554, issued on 27.09.2011, took effect on 26.11.2011. According to Clause 3 of these Rules, the 2011 Stipulation will apply *mutatis mutandis* where these Rules are silent.

132 See section 151 of the JFC Act.

133 See section 148(3) of the JFC Act.

134 See section 148(4) of the JFC Act.

135 See section 148(5) of the JFC Act.

## 6.6. IPIT ACT (1996)

The IPIT Act does not contain specific provisions for dispute settlement by arbitration or mediation. Since section 26 of this Act requires that proceedings in this court be in accordance with this Act and stipulations issued pursuant to section 30 of this Act and where there is no applicable provision, provisions of the CPC would apply, the chief justice of the Central IPIT Court issued, with the approval of the President of the Supreme Court, the Stipulation for IPIT Court Cases BE 2540, dated 28 November 1997.

Under Clause 27 of the Stipulation in the preceding paragraph, before taking evidence, the court may order all parties to come before it for determining directions of the case, e.g. to adopt an arbitration method or to mediate for a compromise. In furtherance of the court's mediation, three sets of regulations were issued successively, each replacing its predecessor. They were: the Regulation of the Central IPIT Court on Dispute Mediation BE 2541 (1998), the Regulation of the Central IPIT Court on Dispute Mediation BE 2543 (2000), and the Regulation of the Central IPIT Court on Dispute Mediation BE 2545 (2002). The latter (IPIT Regulation) was dated 10 September 2002 and supplemented by the Regulation of the Central IPIT Court on Dispute Mediation No. 2 BE 2553, dated 19 April 2010. See also *supra* subsections 6.2. 'CPC (1935 and 2008) and 2011 Stipulation' and 6.17. 'Pre-trial mediation (2011)'.

## 6.7. CVMs (1997)

As mentioned earlier in respect of mediation involving State officials, in 1997 the Ministry of Justice (MOJ) formulated a policy to promote ADR to reduce caseloads of the courts of justice. Community volunteer mediation started off as a program to promote ADR nationwide. In implementing the policy, the Arbitration Office (AO) of the OJA under the MOJ was tasked with setting up regional dispute resolution centres nationwide to promote community participation in dispute resolution. Subsequently, a village arbitration training course was adopted for training local leaders to have a basic understanding of the law and the techniques to mediate their local disputes. In 1998, the AO implemented its program to establish dispute resolution centres and to promote dispute resolution in the regions which were based on the nine jurisdictional regions of the courts of justice nationwide. Further, the Regulation of the MOJ on Community Volunteer Mediators BE 2541, dated 6 November 1998, was issued.

As the local leaders were trained to become local mediators for out-of-court mediation, the title of the program was changed from 'Village Arbitration Training' to 'Community Volunteer Mediation Training'. The working and selection committee consists of provincial governors, presidents of provincial administration organisations, commanders of provincial police, chief judges of provincial courts, and executives of various State agencies or private organisations.

As a result of section 37 of the JA Act in pursuance of section 275 of the Constitution BE 2540 (1997) of Thailand, the judicial administration under the MOJ was transferred to the OOJ, effective 20 August 2000 (BE 2543). Accordingly, the community volunteer mediation program was transferred from the AO of the OJA to the ADRO of the OOJ. In 2002, the ADRO issued its Notification re Rules for Training of Community Volunteer Mediators BE 2545, dated 20 March 2002, in effect replacing the above-mentioned 6 November 1998 regulation of the MOJ. Under the Notification, the community volunteer mediators (CVMs) have power and duties, among other things, to formulate and determine mediation methods in accordance with issues in dispute and prepare a compromise agreement in accordance with an agreement of the disputing parties if they can reach a compromise and wish to make such an agreement. As local leaders, the CVMs purportedly receive and charge no fees for the performance of their duties.

## 6.8. INSURANCE ADR (1998)

Subsequent to the issuance of DOI's Arbitration Rules in 1998 and 2003 (see *supra* subsection 2.4.1. 'Progress'), in 2008 the new Insurance Against Loss Act BE 2535 (1992) and the new Life Insurance Act BE 2535 (1992) were amended in sections 36/1 and 37/1 respectively, to empower the OIC Secretary General, as registrar, to review complaints and conduct mediation. See also subsection 2.1. 'Out-of-court mediation'.

Although the IC Act does not specify a basis for issuing implementing regulations on an ADR means like other substantive laws, the OIC Secretary General applies section 32(2) of the IC Act as follows to lay down regulations for arbitration and mediation processes.

> 'Section 32 The secretary general has power and duties as follows:
> [...] (2) to lay down regulations in relation to the operation of the Office [of the Insurance Commission] which shall not be contrary to, nor inconsistent with, rules or resolutions of the Commission.'

By virtue of the provision, the OIC Secretary General issued out-of-court arbitration regulations, i.e., the Regulation of the OIC re Arbitration BE 2551, dated 25 July 2008, as amended by the Regulation of the OIC No. 2 BE 2553, dated 7 September 2010 (OIC's Arbitration Regulation), to replace the DOI's Arbitration Rules. See *supra* subsection 2.4.1. 'Progress'. Further, by virtue of

Clause 26 of the OIC's Arbitration Regulation, the OIC Secretary General issued the out-of-court mediation Regulation of the OIC re Dispute Conciliation in the Arbitration Procedure BE 2553, dated 7 September 2010 (OIC's Conciliation Regulation). The OIC Secretary General stated the reason for issuing the OIC's Conciliation Regulation in the remarks section at the end of the Regulation to the effect that the OIC wants to serve the parties who wish to mediate disputes before going to arbitration.

Both the arbitration and mediation procedures the OIC has established are for resolving disputes between a claimant, being a party who submits its disputes based on a claim under an insurance agreement, and a respondent, being an insurance company whose liability thereunder is sought by the claimant.

### *6.8.1. OIC's mediation*

Under the OIC's Conciliation Regulation, a dispute means a dispute in connection with an insurance contract subject to the OIC's operation for dispute resolution by arbitration that may be settled by an agreement or a compromise of the parties, as defined under the OIC's Arbitration Regulation. This mediation process is part of, and commences prior to, the arbitration proceedings under the OIC's Arbitration Regulation. Before the parties agree to appoint an arbitrator(s), if the OIC Secretary General sees fit or a party or both parties to the dispute wish to mediate their dispute prior to the appointment, an OIC officer will call a meeting for mediation. If the parties fail to reach a settlement and they wish to appoint a conciliator (a person or a panel who are registered with the approval of the Arbitration Committee)[136] to conduct mediation under the OIC's Conciliation Regulation, the officer will appoint a conciliator accordingly and arrange for the parties to sign their agreement to enter into mediation. The conciliator and the parties may establish their particular procedure before starting the mediation. Information exchanged in the mediation will be kept confidential and will not be used in any subsequent arbitration or court proceedings, unless the parties agree otherwise.

The conciliator must complete the mediation within 30 days from the date of his appointment. The time may be extended at the parties' request no more than twice, each time not exceeding seven days. Thereafter, the mediation will terminate. The officer may order the termination of the mediation if the conciliator finds that any party intends to delay the process or is acting in bad

136 According to Clause 1 of the OIC's Arbitration Regulation, it consists of the OIC Secretary General, his assistant Secretary General (legal), his assistant Secretary General (litigation), a representative from the OOJ, a representative from the Office of the Attorney General, the President of the General Insurance Association, the President of the Thai Life Assurance Association, the President of the Thai Insurance Brokers Association, not more than three learned persons appointed by the OIC Secretary General, and the director of the OIC Dispute Settlement and Arbitration Department.

faith. If the parties can reach a compromise, the conciliator will prepare a compromise agreement which will terminate the mediation. The mediation will terminate if the conciliator finds that the dispute may not be settled by means of mediation or the parties will not benefit from the mediation. The conciliator will, among other things, not make any comment in the nature of deciding the dispute unless the parties agree otherwise and will not be responsible to the parties for any acts done for the purpose of mediating and settling the dispute unless such acts or omissions thereof are committed intentionally or with gross negligence to the prejudice of the parties.

The conciliator will be entitled to remuneration and expenses at the rates prescribed by the Arbitration Committee which will be paid out from the Security Deposit (see OIC's Deposit Notification in the following subsection). According to the OIC's Remuneration Notification (see 6.8.2.), Baht 1,000 remuneration is charged for each dispute. If the disputes are closely related, a total of not more than Baht 3,000 remuneration will be charged. If it is a complicated case and the mediation meetings take more than eight hours, the OIC Secretary General may fix a remuneration not exceeding the foregoing and not more than Baht 3,000 remuneration for each dispute. Notwithstanding the foregoing, expenses will be charged as actually incurred but not to exceed Baht 1,000 for each dispute.

### *6.8.2. OIC's arbitration*

The OIC's Arbitration Regulation is applicable to any disputes, conflicts, or claims between the above-mentioned claimant and an insurance company that is subject to the operation of the OIC, and supplemented by an agreement of the parties, the discretion of the arbitrators, or the provisions of the Arbitration Act 2002. However, it is also supplemented by notices and regulations of the Arbitration Committee.

A claimant is required to make his submission to the OIC, a provincial OIC, or a regional OIC (a) where he is domiciled, (b) with a reasoned statement of convenience, where the insurance agreement was made, (c) where the insurance policy was issued, or (d) where the incident occurred, together with enough copies for the arbitrators and the respondent. Included in the submission must be a copy of an agreement or a clause on dispute settlement by arbitration. An officer, designated by the OIC Secretary General, will send a notice of the submission and a copy of the submission to the respondent without delay by registered mail or other means as prescribed by the OIC Secretary General. The respondent is required to file an answer within 15 days of receiving the notice and the copy of the submission or, in the case of unavoidable necessity, within a time extended by the officer but not to exceed 15 days.

A party may appoint a representative(s) or any person(s) to assist it in the proceedings. The number of arbitrators appointed will depend on the claim amount: a sole arbitrator for an amount of claims from zero to Baht 2,000,000 and, unless the parties agree to a sole arbitrator, three arbitrators for an amount of claims exceeding Baht 2,000,000. Unless the parties agree otherwise, the officer will call a meeting of parties within 15 days from the date of receiving the answer and at the meeting they will appoint the arbitrator(s) from the roster of arbitrators registered with the OIC. The arbitrators will select one of them to be the chairman. The arbitrator(s) may be challenged as to impartiality or substituted for this and other reasons in accordance with the provisions of this Regulation. The arbitrators may not be adduced as witnesses in court proceedings with regard to the dispute being the basis of the arbitration proceedings.

The arbitrator(s) will set a date for the first hearing. If the claimant fails to appear on that date without a request for postponement or a notice of excuse for non-appearance, the arbitrator(s) may dispose of the case. If the respondent fails to appear on that date or any party fails to appear on the next hearing date without a request for postponement or a notice of excuse for non-appearance, the arbitrator(s) may proceed *ex parte* as they deem appropriate and may levy a fine on an actual basis on the non-appearing party as reimbursement to the other party or as expenses for the conduct of the hearings. It is noteworthy that as part of the arbitration procedure, the arbitrator has the power to mediate the dispute at any time during the arbitration proceedings.[137]

An award with clear reasons for each decision must be made by the majority of the arbitrators within 90 days after the date of completing the appointment of arbitrator(s), unless reasonably extended on account of necessity at the discretion of the arbitrator(s). The award must be based on the rule of law and equity; in the interpretation of insurance contracts regard must be had to the likely nature and trade practices of such insurance contracts. The award may be disclosed by the OIC without the consent of the parties except for *in camera* proceedings.

The remuneration and expenses the arbitrators will receive in the proceedings will be at the rates prescribed by the Arbitration Committee. According to Clause 2 of the Notification of the Arbitration Committee re Rates for Arbitrators' Remuneration and Expenses Incurred in the Proceeding BE 2553, dated 7 September 2010 (OIC's Remuneration Notification), the rates of arbitrators' remuneration will be as follows: (a) Baht 5,000–10,000 if there is no disputed amount; (b) 1% of not over Baht 1 million disputed amount, but not less than Baht 5,000; (c) 1.5% of over Baht 1 million but not over 2 million disputed amount, but not less than Baht 22,500; (d) 1.5% of over Baht 2 million disputed amount but not over Baht 5 million, but not less than Baht 52,500; and (e) 1.5% of over Baht 5 million disputed amount, but not less than Baht 150,000 and not

[137] See Clause 27 of the OIC's Arbitration Regulation.

over Baht 200,000. The chairman will receive 40% of the total amount of remuneration and the other two arbitrators each will receive 30% of the total amount of remuneration.

According to Clause 4 of the Notification of the Arbitration Committee re Rates of Security Deposit for Payment of Arbitrators' Remuneration and Expenses Incurred in the Proceeding BE 2551, dated 11 November 2008 (OIC's Deposit Notification), the claimant and the respondent will make a deposit as security (Security Deposit) for payment of arbitrators' remuneration and expenses to be incurred in the proceedings on the date of submission of the claim and on the date of filing the answer, respectively at the following rates, failing which the OIC Secretary General will order not to accept the submission, the answer, or otherwise as applicable: (a) Baht 10,000 each if there is no disputed amount; (b) for a disputed amount not over Baht 500,000: the claimant, Baht 5,000, and the respondent, Baht 5,000; (c) for a disputed amount over Baht 500,000 but not over Baht 1,000,000: the claimant, Baht 5,000, and the respondent, Baht 10,000; (d) for a disputed amount over Baht 1 million but not over Baht 2 million: the claimant, Baht 22,500, and the respondent, Baht 45,000; (e) for a disputed amount over Baht 2 million but not over Baht 5 million: each, no less than Baht 90,000; and (f) for a disputed amount over Baht 5 million, each no less than Baht 180,000.

## 6.9. PETTY LAWSUITS (1999)

The CPC provides for a mediation scheme of petty lawsuits. Pursuant to section 189 of the CPC, a petty lawsuit means (a) a lawsuit where relief applied for can be computed in terms of money not exceeding Baht 40,000 or a sum as prescribed in a royal decree, or (b) a lawsuit for eviction of any person from an immovable property that is generating a rent or may be let, at the time of entering the plaint in an amount not exceeding Baht 4,000 per month or a sum as prescribed in a royal decree.

According to sections 193,[138] 193 *ter*,[139] 193 *quarter*,[140] 193 *quinque*,[141] and 194 of the CPC, in the case of a petty lawsuit a court will fix an early hearing date, notify the defendant to appear in court for mediation, testifying, and adducing evidence on the same date, and order the plaintiff to appear in court on the initial hearing date. On the initial hearing date when both the plaintiff and the defendant are present in court, the court will mediate for the parties to come

138 Amended by the CPC Amendment Act No. 17 BE 2542 (1999) and the CPC Amendment Act No. 24 BE 2551 (2008).

139 Added by the CPC Amendment Act No. 17 BE 2542 (1999) and revised by the CPC Amendment Act No. 24 BE 2551 (2008).

140 Added by the CPC Amendment Act No. 17 BE 2542 (1999).

141 *Ibid.*

to an agreement or a compromise on the disputes. If they fail to do so and the defendant has not submitted its answer, the court will require the defendant to give its answer in writing or orally. If the defendant fails to do so, the court may (a) consider that the defendant is in default of the answer and proceed with the case accordingly, or (b) adduce evidence and proceed with the case accordingly. As for a petty lawsuit, the court may sit for hearing without any adjournment; however, in cases of necessity the court may adjourn each time for not more than seven days. Thereafter, the court may render its judgment orally.

## 6.10. BANKRUPTCY ADR (1999)

By virtue of section 19, as amended by the Bankruptcy Court Establishment and Procedure Act No. 3 BE 2548 (2005), of the Bankruptcy Court Establishment and Procedure Act BE 2542 (1999), the chief justice of the Central Bankruptcy Court issued a stipulation in relation to the conduct of proceedings and admission of evidence in the bankruptcy courts (currently, only the Central Bankruptcy Court, located in Bangkok, has been established) for the purposes of smooth, speedy and just conduct of bankruptcy proceedings, namely the Stipulation on Bankruptcy Actions BE 2542, dated 26 May 1999, which was superseded by the Stipulation on Bankruptcy Actions BE 2549, dated 25 May 2006. Both stipulations contain similar provisions, empowering the court to order all parties to appear before it prior to taking of evidence, in order to agree, among other things, a plan for the proceedings (including a means of ADR) and a timetable thereof. But while the former stipulation (Clause 12(4)) allowed only mediation and arbitration, the latter stipulation (Clause 14(1)) allows the foregoing means as well as any other means of ADR. There has been no guideline as to how the 2011 Stipulation would be applied to bankruptcy cases. See also *supra* subsection 6.2. 'CPC (1935 and 2008) and 2011 Stipulation'.

## 6.11. AFT ACT (1999)

See *supra* subsection 2.4.1 'Progress'.

## 6.12. DIP'S MINISTERIAL REGULATION (2002)

According to the Ministerial Regulation on the Assignments of the DIP of the MOC BE 2545, dated 9 October 2002, (a) the DIP had powers and duties, among other things, to conduct mediation and resolve disputes relating to intellectual property (Clause 1(6)), and (b) the DIP's Office of Prevention and Suppression of

Intellectual Property Rights Violation[142] had powers and duties, among other things, to conduct arbitration on intellectual property, to conduct mediation for a compromise of disputes on intellectual property, and to be in charge of registering learned persons on intellectual property to act as arbitrators (Clause 4(1)).

However, the foregoing ministerial regulation was revoked by the Ministerial Regulation on the Assignments of the DIP of the MOC BE 2553, dated 16 March 2010,[143] which (a) removes the mediation and arbitration functions of the Office of Prevention and Suppression of Intellectual Property Rights Violation, and instead (b) entrusts the DIP's Legal Office with the powers and duties to mediate disputes and conduct arbitration on intellectual property and other relevant laws (Clause 7).

Notwithstanding the above changes, two sets of Rules of the MOC re Conciliation of Intellectual Property Disputes and re Intellectual Property Arbitration, both dated 11 July 2002 (BE 2545), remain in force. Both rules provide the same definition of a dispute, which is: (a) a dispute or controversy over any kinds of intellectual property including patent, trademark, copyright, integrated circuit layout design, trade secret, geographical indication, trade name, and plant species, and (b) a dispute or controversy that gives rise to an intellectual property related issue.

Under the above-mentioned Rules of the MOC re Conciliation of Intellectual Property Disputes, these rules may be varied by the mutual agreement in writing of the disputing parties. Prior to submission of the dispute to conciliators, the DIP Director General will arrange a meeting of the disputing parties for negotiation and settlement of dispute. If he considers it necessary and the disputing parties consider it suitable, one or more conciliators may be appointed by the disputing parties from those unregistered with the recommendation and approval of the Arbitration Committee, which is appointed by the Commerce Minister and chaired by the DIP Director General. The disputing parties may make the appointments with or without the DIP Director General's recommendation or may request the DIP Director General to make the appointments for them. The conciliators will apply the principle of fairness with reference to the rights and duties of the disputing parties, trade customs, and relevant circumstances including the course of past practice between them. The conciliators will prepare a conciliation agreement for the disputing parties to sign when the conciliation is successful.

The DIP and the conciliators are required to keep the conciliation proceedings and the conciliation agreement confidential, and the conciliators will not be required to testify in arbitration or court proceedings. The disputing

---

142 As amended by the Ministerial Regulation on the Assignments of the DIP of the MOC No. 2 BE 2547, dated 08.01.2004.

143 According to Clause 2(8) of this regulation, the DIP has powers and duties to mediate disputes and conduct arbitration on intellectual property.

parties will not adduce as evidence in an arbitration or court proceeding the following items, regardless of whether they are related to issues in dispute during the conciliation proceedings: (a) views or suggestions offered by the other disputing party in the conciliation proceedings; (b) admissions of the other disputing party in the conciliation proceedings; (c) proposals or views offered by the conciliators; and (d) the fact that the other disputing party is ready to accept a conciliatory proposal made by the conciliators.

The disputing parties will equally bear the expenses for the conciliation, including the conciliators' remuneration and travelling and other expenses for the conciliators and witnesses. The DIP Director General may require the disputing parties to equally make a deposit as security for payment of the foregoing expenses before or additionally during the conciliation; failing which, the DIP Director General may cease the conciliation process.

Under the above-mentioned MOC Rules re Intellectual Property Arbitration, these rules may be varied by the mutual agreement in writing of the disputing parties subject to the approval of the DIP Director General. Matters not dealt with by these rules will be dealt with in accordance with the mutual agreement of the disputing parties, at the discretion of the arbitrators, or the Arbitration Act 2002. Arbitrators may be either those registered with the recommendation and approval of the above-mentioned Arbitration Committee or those so unregistered but appointed by the disputing parties. Prior to submission of the dispute to arbitrators, the DIP Director General will arrange a meeting of the disputing parties for negotiation and settlement of the dispute. If he considers it necessary and the disputing parties consider it suitable, one or more conciliators will be appointed and will not later become arbitrators for the same dispute. Hence, the above-mentioned MOC Rules re Conciliation of Intellectual Property Disputes will apply until the conciliation proceedings terminate by, among other things, a disputing party making a written statement to that effect on the grounds that it is of no use to continue with the proceedings.

The respondent is required to submit his answer to the DIP within 15 days of receiving a copy of the notice of claim for dispute resolution by arbitration. The DIP will start the arbitrator's appointment process. As for a panel of three arbitrators, each party will appoint one arbitrator from the registered list and the two arbitrators will appoint the chairman. If a disputing party does not appoint its arbitrator within 30 days of receiving a notice for appointment of an arbitrator, or the chairman is not appointed within 30 days of the two appointments of arbitrators, the Arbitration Committee will instead appoint the arbitrator or the chairman, as the case may be. An award must be made within 90 days after the appointment of the last arbitrator and, if necessary, the arbitrator(s) can extend the deadline by not more than 90 days. The arbitrators will render an award in accordance with legal principle and the principle of fairness. The award may not be disclosed unless with the consent of the disputing parties.

In the case of a sole arbitrator, his remuneration will be (a) between Baht 5,000–10,000, calculated at the rate of 1% of the claim amount not exceeding Baht 1 million, (b) between Baht 20,000–50,000, calculated at the rate of 1% of the claim amount exceeding Baht 1 million but not exceeding Baht 5 million, and (c) between Baht 75,000–120,000, calculated at the rate of 1.5% of the claim amount exceeding Baht 5 million. In the case of a panel of three arbitrators, the remuneration will be three times the amount that a sole arbitrator would be entitled to, but five-elevenths of the total amount will be allocated to the chairman and three-elevenths to each of the two arbitrators.[144] The claimant is required to make a deposit as security for payment of expenses in the initial amount of Baht 2,000 on the date of claim submission. Within 30 days of setting up the arbitration proceedings, each disputing party will make a deposit for the payment of arbitrators' remuneration and expenses incurred in proceedings at the following rates: no less than Baht 7,500, no less than Baht 30,000, and no less than Baht 70,000 for the above-mentioned claim amounts (a) to (c), respectively. The DIP Director General may require a higher amount of deposit. If the respondent fails to make the required deposit, the claimant is required to make the payment instead. An additional deposit of not more than Baht 5,000 may be required each time to cover expenses during the proceedings.

## 6.13. TAX ADR (2002)

In 2002, the chief justice of the Central Tax Court (CTC) issued the Regulation of the CTC re Mediation to Reach A Compromise BE 2545, dated 19 September 2002, which is superseded by the Regulation of the CTC re Mediation of Disputes BE 2554, dated 20 May 2011 ('Tax Mediation Regulation), issued by virtue of the general power under section 17 of the Tax Court Establishment and Procedure Act BE 2528, effective on 6 September 1985. See *supra* subsection 6.2. 'CPC (1935 and 2008) and 2011 Stipulation'.

Under the Tax Mediation Regulation, the CTC chief justice may appoint a judge or a judiciary officer who, unless specified by the parties, is neither a judge in quorum nor a judge in charge of the case to be mediated, and a person or persons from a registered list to be a mediator or mediator(s). As opposed to a judge or a judiciary officer who acts as a mediator, mediator(s) appointed from the registered list will be remunerated and receive expenses. The mediators will not be liable for any act carried out for the purposes of mediation and dispute

144 See the Notification of the Arbitration Committee re Arbitrator's Remuneration and Expenses in the Arbitration Proceeding, dated 17.12.2002.

resolution unless their action or inaction is done with intent or gross negligence to the prejudice of the parties.

A case may be mediated if it is subject to the jurisdiction of the CTC and the judge in charge of the case or the CTC chief justice or his deputy is of the view that it should be mediated or the parties wish to mediate it. The judge in charge of the case or the CTC chief justice or his deputy may, with the mutual agreement of the parties, order the case to be mediated at any stage of the court proceedings. But if the foregoing person, as the case may be, is of the view that the mediation will unduly suspend or delay the court proceedings, he may, in the interests of the parties, order the proceedings to be conducted simultaneously with the mediation.

The mediation process is separate from the court proceedings and is not a reason to delay the court hearings. Either party may apply for mediation at the mediation centre at the CTC before the initial court hearing. If the other party agrees to participate, the mediation centre will prepare a case file and present it to the CTC chief justice for appointment of a mediator or mediators. If the mediation is successful and the parties withdraw the case or reach a compromise, the CTC staff members will present the case file for the judge in charge of the case to issue an order or a judgment; if not, the mediation will be terminated and the case file will be returned to the judge in charge of the case for further court proceedings. Notwithstanding the above, if the CTC chief justice or his deputy is of the view that the mediation is no longer appropriate, he may order the case file be returned to the judge in charge of the case to continue with the court proceedings.

Before the mediation begins, the mediator(s) may consult with the parties in order to set up steps or a plan for conducting the mediation. The mediation proceedings will be conducted in camera and without recording in writing or electronically unless the parties mutually agree on recording in whole or in part at their expense. The parties will agree that facts and transactions of the mediation may not be used as evidence in court proceedings and the mediator(s) or the CTC staff members may not be required to testify in court with respect to the subject matter or details of negotiation in the mediation. However, if the parties settle only a part of the dispute or admit certain facts and agree to use them in the court proceedings, the mediator(s) will prepare a memorandum of the agreement and notify the same to the court.

The mediation will terminate when: (a) the parties settle their disputes by withdrawing the court case or requesting the court to render a judgment in accordance with their compromise agreement; (b) a party withdraws from the mediation; (c) the mediator(s) does not succeed in the set timeframe; (d) the mediator(s) is of the view that the dispute may not be settled by mediation; or (e) the court is of the view that the dispute may not be settled by mediation or the mediation is of no further use to the case.

## 6.14. DERIVATIVES ACT (2003)

See *supra* subsection 2.4.1. 'Progress'.

## 6.15. LEGAL EXECUTION DEPARTMENT ADR (2005)

This is a post-judgment mediation conducted under the auspices of the Legal Execution Department (LED) of the MOJ. Because of, to name just a few, a huge backlog of executions resulting from difficulties in locating assets of judgment debtors, multiple steps in the execution process though streamlined, expenses involved, depreciation of assets subject to execution, etc., a mediation centre was set up in 2005, initially under the Central Deposit of Property Office of the LED.[145] Subsequent to the Order of the LED No. 220/2550, dated 21 May 2007, the mediation centre was changed to be under the Seizure of Property Division of the LED. Currently, it was set up as a unit operating directly under the LED and has been entrusted with powers and duties, among other things, to conduct dispute mediation after the pronouncement of judgment and before[146] or during execution of judgment, to train mediators, and to disseminate knowledge about mediation related to execution of judgments. The LED charges neither fees nor expenses for the conduct of the mediation.[147] As of June 2012, the LED is purportedly in the process of formulating a regulation to govern the mediation process.

A judgment debtor would file an application for mediation with the mediation centre of the LED or a provincial execution office in order to: (a) prevent an execution of judgment after a judgment has been pronounced;[148] (b) cease an execution of judgment after the court has pronounced its judgment and issued a writ of execution as a result of a judgment debtor's non-compliance within a period of time specified in the court decree;[149] or (c) to prevent a seizure or attachment of assets of the judgment debtor. Also, such an application may be filed after the assets of the judgment debtor have been seized, attached or ordered to be sold at auction so that the seizure, attachment or auction may be removed or cancelled.[150]

If the parties reach an agreement, the legal execution officer will cease the execution. According to the LED's website,[151] the LED is of the view that: (a) on the basis of the Supreme Court Decision No. 1950/2551 (2008 AD) the agreement

---

145 <http://branch.led.go.th/drc/about.asp>.
146 <http://branch.led.go.th/drc/plan.asp>.
147 <http://branch.led.go.th/drc/about.asp>.
148 *Ibid.*
149 Sections 271, 273, and 276 of the CPC.
150 <http://branch.led.go.th/drc/about.asp>.
151 *Ibid.*

is regarded as a binding consequence in compliance with the judgment, and (b) if it is breached, the legal execution officer may continue with the execution in accordance with the agreement without requiring a new lawsuit. If the parties fail to agree completely, the mediator will make a report to the legal execution officer so that the legal execution officer will carry out the execution to the extent it is disagreed. In most cases, it would take one to three months to determine the outcome of mediation.[152]

## 6.16. CONSUMER ADR (2008)

Court-annexed mediation in relation to the Consumer Protection Act BE 2522 (1979) was subject to sections 19, 20 and 20 *bis* of the CPC as mentioned above. Currently, it would specifically be subject to sections 24 and 25 of the CLP Act, as supplemented by the Stipulation, particularly Clauses 14–17, of the Supreme Court President on the Conduct of Proceeding and Litigation Officers' Performance of Duty in Consumer Litigation BE 2551 (2008) (CLP Stipulation), issued by virtue of provisions of the CLP Act and effective on the date the CLP Act became effective (i.e. 24 August 2008). Notwithstanding, the 2011 Stipulation would be applied by the Mediation and Compromise Centre of the Civil Court to override conflicting provisions of the CLP Stipulation. A summary of the CLP Stipulation (in the ensuing paragraphs) would be affected by the 2011 Stipulation although it might be arguable whether in light of section 7 of the CLP Act,[153] the 2011 Stipulation, which was issued *under the CPC* and not under section 6 of the CLP Act, could be applied to override the conflicting provisions of the CLP Stipulation.

Court-annexed mediation under the CLP Act is limited to 'consumer litigation', which is defined under section 3 of the CLP Act as: (a) a civil case between (i) a consumer or a person entitled to take court action on behalf of the consumer under section 19 of this Act[154] or under other laws and (ii) a business operator on a dispute over legal rights or duties in connection with the

152 *Ibid.*

153 Section 7 of the CLP Act provides that: 'Consumer Litigation proceeding shall be in accordance with the provisions of this Act and stipulations of the President of the Supreme Court *under Section 6*. Where there are no such provisions or stipulations, the provisions of the Civil Procedure Code shall be applied *mutatis mutandis*' (emphasis added). The above section 6 provides that: 'The President of the Supreme Court shall be in charge of this Act and have power to issue stipulations so that Consumer Litigation proceeding will be conducted smoothly, speedily, and justly; provided that the stipulations shall not lessen the right of the parties to present a defence. The stipulations of the President of the Supreme Court *under this Act* shall be enforceable after having been approved by the plenary meeting of the Supreme Court and published in the Royal Gazette' (emphasis added).

154 i.e., the Consumer Protection Board or an association recognised by the Consumer Protection Board under the Consumer Protection Act 1979.

consumption of goods or services; (b) a civil case under the law on liability for damage arising from unsafe goods (i.e., the Act on Liability for Damage Arising from Unsafe Goods BE 2551 (2008)); (c) a civil case related to a case under (a) or (b); or (d) a civil case specified by law to apply the procedure under this Act.

As regards consumer litigation above, a mediation procedure is provided for under sections 24 and 25 of the CLP Act and supplemented by Clauses 14–17 of the CLP Stipulation. Moreover, litigation officers are appointed by the OOJ Secretary General to primarily assist the court in the conduct of consumer litigation when assigned to, among other things, mediate in consumer litigation and, in rendering such assistance, perform other duties pursuant to the CLP Act or the CLP Stipulation.[155] A summary of the mediation procedure is as follows:

After the court has accepted the plaint, the court must fix an early date for the first hearing and summon the defendant to appear in court on the fixed date for engaging in mediation, giving testimony, and adducing evidence on that day. The court must supply the defendant with a copy of the plaint or a copy of the memorandum of the plaint, and order the plaintiff to appear in court on that day. On the date of the first hearing, when the plaintiff and the defendant are both present, the litigation officer will conduct mediation for the parties to reach an agreement unless the court sees fit to appoint a mediator of the court to conduct the mediation instead. However, if they intend to have another person mediate, they must inform the litigation officer and provide details of the address and telephone number of that person. The court may instruct the litigation officer to contact the person to invite him or her to be the mediator. If the person cannot be contacted or the person does not accept or the instruction would result in a delay which would damage the case, the court may instruct the litigation officer or the mediator of the court to proceed with the mediation. In the course of mediation, if any party makes a request or the mediator considers it appropriate, the mediator may order that the mediation be conducted in camera in the presence of any or all parties.

If the parties reach an agreement, which will result in withdrawal of the case or in making a compromise agreement, the person conducting the mediation must recommend and assist them to make a request or a statement or the necessary compromise agreement and speedily report to the court for issuing a judgment or an order. If the parties cannot reach an agreement and a party wishes to submit an answer or a list of evidence, the court may assign a litigation officer to assist the party to prepare the answer or the list of evidence in good order and report to the court for it to convene a hearing on that day or another hearing date as it sees fit.

---

155 See section 4(1) of the CLP Act. Under section 4(2) of the CLP Act, a litigation officer is an official under the Criminal Code and has power to issue a summons calling any person to furnish information or to deliver documents for his review in respect of any matters within his power and duties.

It is believed that a judgment would be issued in accordance with the compromise agreement which would thus be subject to section 138 of the CPC mentioned above.[156]

## 6.17. PRE-TRIAL MEDIATION (2011)

On 22 July 2011, the chief justice of the Central IPIT Court issued the Regulation of the Central IPIT Court re Pre-trial Dispute Mediation BE 2554 (2011) (Pre-trial Mediation Regulation). This Pre-trial Mediation Regulation appears to be, among all court-issued regulations, the only one that deals specifically with out-of-court mediation. Clause 4 of this Regulation specifically requires that where this Regulation is silent, the Regulation of the Central IPIT Court on Dispute Mediation BE 2545 (2002) and the Regulation of the Central IPIT Court on Dispute Mediation No. 2 BE 2553 (2010) will be applied. Since the 2011 Stipulation overrides the two foregoing Regulations with respect to conflicting provisions, the 2011 Stipulation would be applied and affect the summary below accordingly, for the purpose of the foregoing Clause 4 of the Pre-trial Mediation Regulation.

Under this Pre-trial Mediation Regulation, mediation starts when a party submits its application to the Mediation and Compromise Section of the Central IPIT Court to begin this mediation process before the filing of a lawsuit. The Section will terminate the process when the other party, after receiving the Section's notice of allegations and the process, refuses to participate in the process. But if the other party agrees, the Section will arrange a meeting of all concerned parties for appointing a conciliator. A mediation dossier will be opened and a case number assigned for the entry and disposition of the case. Information obtained during mediation will be kept confidential unless the parties agree otherwise, the disclosure is required by law, or the disclosure is beneficial to the performance or enforcement of an agreement resulting from the dispute settlement.

The mediation before going to trial will cease when (a) the parties agree to the settlement of the case, (b) a party withdraws from the process, (c) the conciliator finds that the dispute may not be settled by mediation, or (d) a party brings the case to court before the process ceases. Where the parties agree to settlement, the parties concerned may request to do either of the following: (a) prepare their memorandum of agreement as a compromise agreement for use as evidence for the purpose of compliance with the terms of the agreement; or (b) together with (a), a party files a plaint with the court together with a joint statement to the effect that the case has been agreed and attaches the prepared

156 See *supra* subsection 3.2. 'In-court compromise agreements'.

compromise agreement for the court to adjudicate the case in accordance therewith.

## 7. INSTITUTIONS AND THEIR RULES

### 7.1. OFFICE OF THE ARBITRATION TRIBUNAL

According to a booklet of the BTT entitled 'The Thai Commercial Arbitration Rules' (TC Arbitration Rules), printed on 25 February 2010, the first version of the TC Arbitration Rules was adopted on 1 July 1968 and revised for use on 15 December 2000. That version was superseded by a new version with improvements to accord with the Arbitration Act 2002, trade, and economy. The new version was adopted for use on 20 May 2003.

According to a CD publication of the BTT entitled 'The Thai Commercial Arbitration Office, Arbitration CD-ROM Version 2.0', the BTT issued its Conciliation Rules on 30 April 2001 and, by virtue of Article 6 of the TC Arbitration Rules, substituted them with a new version on 24 April 2009. There are no available records of cases conducted under these Conciliation Rules.

A summary of the TC Arbitration Rules follows. The BTT appoints the Thai Commercial Arbitration Committee, consisting of 18 members who are experts in related fields of activity and familiar with the arbitral process. This committee has duties, among other things, to lay down rules, regulations, and procedures for the conduct of arbitration, to supervise the operation of the arbitration, to promote the process of arbitration, and to act as an intermediary for disputing parties.

According to Article 41 of the TC Arbitration Rules, if disputing parties wish to settle their disputes under the TC Arbitration Rules, they should adopt the following proposed clause: 'Both parties agree to accept the Thai Commercial Arbitration Rules to govern the settlement of disputes. In the event of any disagreement or dispute concerning or arising from this contract where the parties are unable to reach an agreement, such disagreement or dispute shall be finally and exclusively settled by arbitration under the Thai Commercial Arbitration Rules then in force.'

The disputing parties may jointly appoint a sole arbitrator. They may, within 30 to 60 days of the notice of the committee's registrar, appoint one arbitrator each from the list of persons maintained by the committee or they may appoint a non-listed person. If each disputing party appoints its arbitrator, the two arbitrators will appoint a chairman, who has the casting vote. If the chairman is not appointed within 30 days of the prior arbitrators' appointment, the committee will make the appointment within 45 days from the date of being so notified by the committee's registrar.

The submission of claim must be made in the required application form and accompanied by the required documents. An answer must be given within 30 days of receiving a copy of the submission. The arbitration proceedings commence when the committee's registrar provides the arbitration tribunal with a file of the dispute and its relevant documents. The arbitration tribunal will continue with the proceedings despite either party's subsequent refusal or discontinued desire to have the arbitration tribunal decide the dispute.

The arbitration tribunal will hear the dispute of the parties and render its award on the basis of documents and any other evidence presented to it during the proceedings. It will determine the dispute in accordance with the rule of law and the agreement between the parties, taking into account the applicable commercial usage as it considers appropriate and applicable to the determination. Only at the express written request of the disputing parties, the arbitration tribunal may 'act as amiable compositeur or decide ex aequo et bono' (Article 25).

After the arbitration tribunal has rendered its award, which must be made in writing within 180 days from the date of the appointment of the last arbitrator or within such time extension as mutually agreed by the parties, the award will be sent by registered mail to all concerned parties within seven days of the date it was rendered and will be binding on the parties and enforceable under applicable law, including the New York Convention, from the day on which it reaches the parties.

The committee, its registrar, and the arbitration tribunal will not be liable to any damages arising from the performance of their work or from the arbitration of the dispute during or after the arbitration proceedings.

## 7.2. THAI ARBITRATION INSTITUTE

Consequent to the Arbitration Act 1987, on 3 January 1990 the minister of the MOJ issued (a) the Rules of the MOJ re Dispute Conciliation and (b) the Rules of the MOJ re Arbitration. On 22 May 1990 the Cabinet passed a resolution granting an approval for the setting up of the AO under the OJA of the MOJ.[157] After the judicial administration was transferred from the MOJ to the OOJ in 2000, the functions of the AO were transferred to the ADRO under which the Thai Arbitration Institute (TAI) and the Thai Mediation Centre were organised. Pursuant to the current Announcement of the Judicial Administration Commission re Internal Assignments and Prescription of Powers and Duties of Organs under the Jurisdiction of the OOJ No. 3, dated 28 December 2007, the ADRO has powers and duties, among other things: (a) to promote, coordinate

[157] See Preface to the Cases and Materials on Arbitration, Vol. 1, dated 14.02.1992, by the then MOJ Permanent Secretary, Prasert Boonsri.

and engage in dispute settlement by mediation, conciliation, arbitration and other alternative means; (b) to advise and issue legal opinions for governmental agencies and the general public in the conduct of proceedings of mediation, conciliation, arbitration and other alternative means of dispute settlement; (c) to develop law, regulations and rules and lay down systems and develop systems of mediation, conciliation, arbitration and other alternative means of dispute settlement; and (d) to develop systems, formats, measures, principles, procedures and standards of dispute settlement by mediation, conciliation, arbitration and other alternative means in or out of court.

Consequent to the replacement Arbitration Act 2002, the above-mentioned 3 January 1990 Rules of the MOJ re Arbitration were replaced with the Rules of the OOJ re Arbitration by the TAI, dated 2 May 2003, issued by the OOJ Secretary General. These rules will apply to arbitration conducted by the TAI, unless agreed otherwise by the disputing parties with the approval of the TAI Director. A summary of these rules follows.

Contracting or disputing parties may adopt the following proposed arbitration clause of the TAI: 'Any dispute, controversy or claim arising out of or relating to this contract or the breach, termination or invalidity thereof, shall be settled by arbitration in accordance with the Arbitration Rules of the Thai Arbitration Institute, the Office of the Judiciary applicable at the time of submission of the dispute to arbitration and the conduct of the arbitration thereof shall be under the auspices of the Thai Arbitration Institute.'

The disputing parties may appoint a sole arbitrator or a panel of three arbitrators. In the case of a sole arbitrator, each disputing party will propose three nominees and the TAI may propose three nominees. Each disputing party will list all nominees in order of preference for the TAI to approach the preferred nominees in that order. In the case of three arbitrators, each disputing party will appoint one arbitrator and a chairman will be appointed in accordance with the foregoing procedure for the appointment of a sole arbitrator. A party may not adduce an arbitrator as its witness in court proceedings concerning the subject matter of the arbitral proceedings. According to Rule 14(2) of the TAI, all arbitrators are subject to the Code of Ethics for Arbitrators of the TAI.[158]

The disputing parties may agree on the language(s) to be used in the proceedings. Unless otherwise stipulated in the arbitration agreement, the arbitral tribunal will conduct any proceedings in camera as it considers appropriate by taking into account the principle of justice. The arbitral tribunal will decide in accordance with 'legal principle and the rule of justice' unless the parties request the arbitral tribunal to decide the dispute '*ex aequo et bono*' (Rule 29). The award will be made within 180 days from the date the last arbitrator was appointed. The arbitrators, TAI Director and the TAI may not disclose the award to the public without the consent of the parties.

---

158 <www.coj.go.th/adro/userfiles/file/Code%20of%20Ethics_th.pdf>.

Costs and expenses in the arbitral proceedings as well as the arbitrators' fee but not including the attorneys' fee and expenses will be specified by the arbitral tribunal in its award. The TAI issued the Announcement on Rate of Costs, Expenses, and Arbitrator's Fee for Arbitral Proceedings on 4 January 2011.[159] For example, costs and expenses for refreshments, recording, overtime remuneration of officials, and delivery of documents are charged as quoted in the announcement.

In regard to the arbitrators' fee, an arbitrator's fee for a sole arbitration will be Baht 4,000 per session when there is no disputed amount and a total amount of Baht 30,000 when the disputed amount does not exceed Baht 2,000,000. When the disputed amount is, for example, between Baht 50,000,001 and 100,000,000, the arbitrator's fee will be Baht 155,000 + 0.1% of the amount in excess of Baht 50,000,000. Further, when the disputed amount is more than Baht 2,000,000,000, the arbitrator's fee will be Baht 725,000 + 0.01% of the amount in excess of Baht 2,000,000,000.

An arbitrators' fee for more than one arbitrator will be Baht 20,000 per session when there is no disputed amount and a total amount of Baht 60,000 when the disputed amount does not exceed Baht 2,000,000. When the disputed amount is, for example, between Baht 50,000,001 and 100,000,000, the arbitrators' fee will be Baht 310,000 + 0.2% of the amount in excess of Baht 50,000,000. Further, when the disputed amount is more than Baht 2,000,000,000, the arbitrators' fee will be Baht 1,450,000 + 0.02% of the amount in excess of Baht 2,000,000,000. Also, there is a table of arbitrators' fees in the case of an award rendered following the disputing parties' compromise. The foregoing rates may be varied depending on the factors stipulated in the announcement and as determined by the TAI Director.

Before commencing any arbitral proceedings, if the TAI Director deems it appropriate, he may request the disputing parties to deposit a security for payment of costs, administrative fees, and arbitrators' fee. If the parties fail to pay the required security for costs, administrative fees, or arbitrators' fee, as the case may be, within the period specified by the TAI Director, the TAI Director may report the same to the arbitral tribunal to consider suspending the arbitral proceedings.

## 8. FINAL REMARKS

It is noteworthy that it took 15 years from the first Arbitration Act BE 2530 (1987) to the current Arbitration Act BE 2545 (2002) for arbitral awards rendered in and outside of Thailand to have an equal footing in terms of their enforcement in the

159 <www.coj.go.th/adro/userfiles/file/Announcement%20of%20Rate%20of%20Costs%20and%20Expenses%202011.pdf> (English text).

Thai courts. However, it took 72 years from the entry into force of section 138 of the CPC in 1935 to the entry into force of SAA No. 7 in 2007 for court-annexed mediation and out-of-court mediation, respectively to have a similar footing[160] in terms of enforcement of a resulting compromise agreement made by the disputing parties. So, for the purposes of dispute settlement one should consider if a compromise agreement conceded by interested parties themselves (being out-of-court mediation) has been paid enough attention, compared to an arbitral award rendered by a disinterested person or persons (being out-of-court arbitration).

Given all the discussion from the beginning of this chapter and the following statistics of the courts of first instance throughout Thailand, ADR in Thailand, particularly those out-of-court/pre-trial mechanisms, should get more attention and efforts if they really are expected to play a greater role in improving the efficiency of the administration of justice in a traditionally Eastern and non-litigious society like Thailand for the betterment of Thailand's society and economy. In 2010, 253,019 civil cases (excluding consumer cases) were filed with the courts of first instance and only 202,256 cases (excluding consumer cases) were disposed of, while 90,060 civil cases (excluding consumer cases) were mediated (i.e. court-annexed), and only 49,433 cases (excluding consumer cases) were successful.[161] In 2011, 517,625 new civil cases (all kinds) were filed with the courts of first instance throughout Thailand, excluding 87,779 civil cases (all kinds) which were carried over from the preceding year; at the end of 2011, a total of 507,618 civil cases (all kinds) were disposed of and a total of 97,786 civil cases (all kinds) were carried over to 2012.[162]

Those who believe it would be beneficial to attach more importance to mediation may question whether it would be more efficient to have a specific or single piece of legislation to govern all mediation processes under various laws and regulations. The reasons would be, for example, (a) he could avoid forum-shopping, judge-shopping, or the like and (b) mediation could be on the same footing as arbitration in all respects, particularly the enforcement aspect and effect on the statute of limitations.

However, according to point 1.6 of the present policy[163] of the President of the Supreme Court in regard to development work in the administration of justice, he will encourage alternative dispute resolution in order for people to settle disputes harmoniously, attach importance to promotion of potential and ethics of mediators, and promote mediation in the Court of Appeal and the Supreme Court. Therefore, one should at least expect more developments of court-annexed ADR mechanisms in Thailand.

---

160 For example, out-of-court compromise agreement additionally requires a public prosecutor's involvement in the enforcement process.

161 The OOJ's Annual Judicial Statistics, Thailand BE 2553 (2010), see <www.oppb.coj. go.th/userfiles/file/AnnualJudicialStatistics BE2553_TH.pdf> pp. 28 and 30.

162 <www.oppb.coj.go.th/userfiles/file/SJanToDecLegal2.pdf> p. 40.

163 <www.opsc.coj.go.th/info.php?cid=1>.

# UNITED STATES: ARBITRATION

George A. BERMANN*

**Contents**



* The author is deeply grateful for the invaluable assistance provided by Catherine Bratic, JD Columbia Law School, expected May 2013.

## 1. ORIGINS

American lawyers, businesses and scholars are at the forefront of the practice of arbitration and alternative dispute resolution today. Arbitration is widely accepted in the United States, and American practitioners lead many of the advances in the field.

Yet arbitration is hardly new or unique to the US. Arbitration as a method of alternative adjudication greatly predates the founding of the United States.[1] Within North America, arbitration was prevalent before the founding of the

---

1 A. FRASER, 'A Sketch of the History of International Arbitration' (1925–26) 11 *Cornell L.Q. (Cornell Law Quarterly)* 179, 188.

United States or its federal court system.[2] Native Americans are reported to have used arbitration to resolve disputes between different tribes.[3] The first European settlers of the continent, deeply religious Puritans, developed dispute resolution tools such as 'gospel order' and 'brotherly fashion' that resembled arbitration.[4] This tradition continued in the American colonies.[5] In 1768, the New York Chamber of Commerce was founded, with one of its purposes being a forum for arbitration of member disputes.[6] Further, the 1777 Articles of Confederation, which predates the United States Constitution, provided a mechanism for resolving disputes between states before five 'commissioners or judges' chosen by the parties.[7] The United States' first president, George Washington, included an arbitration clause in his will stipulating that a panel of three arbitrators was to decide by final and binding decision any dispute over the wording of his last will and testament.[8]

Early America also sought to arbitrate disputes with foreign nations. Shortly after declaring its independence from Great Britain and establishing peace, the United States signed Jay's Treaty with its former ruler. The treaty established multiple arbitral mechanisms for resolving claims between the two nations and their citizens.[9] Those two nations in particular frequently resorted to arbitration throughout the eighteenth and nineteenth centuries to settle boundary disputes and Civil War-related claims.[10] The 1848 Treaty of Guadalupe Hidalgo provided for the resolution of disputes between the United States and Mexico by arbitral commissioners appointed either by the countries themselves or by a mutual ally.[11]

---

2 R. Massey, Jr., 'History of Arbitration and Grievance Arbitration in the United States' <www.laborstudiesandresearch.ext.wvu.edu/r/download/32003> accessed 03.09.2012.

3 M. Arbaugh, 'Making Peace the Old Fashioned Way: Infusing Traditional Tribal Practices in Modern ADR' (2002) 2 *Pepp. Disp. Resol. L.J. (Pepperdine Dispute Resolution Law Journal)* 303.

4 R. Ackerman, 'Disputing Together: Conflict Resolution and the Search for Community' (2002)18 *Ohio St. J. on Disp. Resol. (Ohio State Journal on Dispute Resolution)* 27, 46–57 n. 58; J. Daly, 'Arbitration: The Basics' (2006) 5 *J. Am. Arb. (Journal of American Arbitration)* 5.

5 J. Daly, *supra* n. 4, p. 6.

6 L. Sarpy, 'Arbitration as a Means of Reducing Court Congestion' (1965) 41 *Notre Dame L. (Notre Dame Lawyer)* 182; *Red Cross Line v. Atlantic Fruit Co.*, 264 U.S. 109, 118 (1924).

7 J. Ralston, *International Arbitration from Athens to Locarno*, Stanford University Press, Stanford 1929, p. 190; Articles of Confederation, Article IX (1781).

8 R. Bales, *Compulsory Arbitration: The Grand Experiment in Employment*, ILR Press, Ithaca 1997.

9 Jay's Treaty (1794). The 1871 Treaty of Washington with Great Britain stipulated further arbitral procedures.

10 J. Ralston, *supra* n. 7, pp. 194–195.

11 Treaty of Guadalupe Hidalgo (1848), Article XXI.

## 2. EVOLUTION

Arbitration's greatest impetus in United States law came, however, from labour unions. The first use of an arbitration clause in a labour contract dates to 1829, when the Journeymen Cabinet-Makers from Philadelphia included a clause in their union constitution creating a mechanism to resolve contractual disputes between the employer and union members.[12] As the Industrial Revolution gained steam in the United States in the mid-nineteenth century, trade groups began to adopt arbitration as a method of resolving conflicts without judicial interference.[13] At the same time, private enterprises came to believe that commercial disputes were best settled by arbitrators who would have a better sense than judges of the businesses' commercial objectives and who would not necessarily impose the formalities and inefficiencies of the national judicial system on the dispute.[14] Opting for arbitration also eliminated the risk of costly appeals that undermined judicial finality.[15] In many ways, arbitration exemplified the American ethos: valuing efficiency and individual determinism, while maintaining fidelity to the rule of law.[16]

### 2.1. LEGISLATIVE INITIATIVE

In the early twentieth century, New York's court systems became increasingly clogged and Wall Street businesses put pressure on legislators to legitimise arbitration with an official endorsement. Arbitration was not prohibited at this time, but courts would not compel arbitration based on an agreement to submit future disputes to an arbitrator. The New York State legislature enacted an arbitration law in 1920 to address this issue.[17] The New York Arbitration Law allowed parties to bind themselves to arbitrate future disputes rather than only pre-existing ones. The concept was revolutionary in the United States at the time.[18] Justice Cardozo, a highly esteemed American judge, summarised the

---

12 W. Nelles, 'The First American Labor Case' (1931) 41 *Yale L.J. (Yale Law Journal)* 165.

13 J. Ralston, *supra* n. 7, p. 186; G. Gwynne, 'The Oldest American Tribunal', (1937) 1 *Arb. J. (Arbitration Journal)* 117, 120; (1925) 50 *ABA Rep. (American Bar Association Reporter)* 357.

14 B. Benson, 'An Exploration of the Impact of Modern Arbitration Statutes on the Development of Arbitration in the United States' (1995) 11 *J.L. Econ. & Org. (Journal of Law, Economics & Organization)* 479, 482.

15 *Ibid.*

16 T. Carbonneau, *Carbonneau on Arbitration: Collected Essays*, JurisNet, New York 2010, p. 360, n. 32; T. Carbonneau, 'Judicial Approbation in Building the Civilization of Arbitration' (2009) 113 *Penn St. L. Rev. (Pennsylvania State Law Review)* 1343, 1367; J. Daly, *supra* n. 4, p. 6.

17 N.Y. Arbitration Law, L.1920, C.275, Consol. C. 72; S.4214, 67th Cong., 4th Sess., 64 Cong. Rec. 732 (1922) (bill introducing the FAA).

18 F. Emerson, 'History of Arbitration Practice and Law' (1970) 19 *Clev. St. L. Rev. (Cleveland State Law Review)* 155, 161.

attitude of New York courts shortly after the passage of the Arbitration Act as follows:

> 'The question is one of intention, to be ascertained by the same tests that are applied to contracts generally. [...] Our own favor or disfavor of the cause of arbitration is not to count as a factor in the appraisal of the thought of others. [...] Parties to a contract may agree, if they will, that any and all controversies growing out of it in any way shall be submitted to arbitration. If they do, the courts of New York will give effect to their intention.'[19]

By 1925, Congress followed with its own support for arbitration. The 1925 Federal Arbitration Act (FAA), based on the earlier New York statute, likewise targeted traditional judicial hostility to the enforcement of agreements to arbitrate.[20] According to the Congressional Record:

> 'The need for the law arises from an anachronism of our American law. Some centuries ago, because of the jealousy of the English courts for their own jurisdiction, they refused to enforce specific agreements to arbitrate upon the ground that the courts were thereby ousted from their jurisdiction. This jealousy survived for so long a period that the principle became firmly embedded in the English common law and was adopted with it by the American courts. The courts have felt that the precedent was too strongly fixed to be overturned without a legislative enactment.'[21]

The FAA passed easily in both the Senate and the House of Representatives, bolstered by the support of the American Bar Association and the business community.[22] Through this Act, 'Congress declared a national policy favoring arbitration and withdrew the power of the states to require a judicial forum for the resolution of claims which the contracting parties agreed to resolve by arbitration.'[23] Section 2 of the FAA reads:

> 'A written provision in any maritime transaction or a contract evidencing a transaction involving commerce to settle by arbitration a controversy thereafter

---

19 *Marchant v. Mead Morrison Mfg Co.*, 252 N.Y. 284, 169 N.E. 386 (1929).

20 See Federal Arbitration Act, 9 U.S.C. §§1–16 (1925); *Scherk v. Alberto-Culver Co.*, 417 U.S. 506, 511 (1974) (the FAA intended to put agreements to arbitrate on 'the same footing as other contracts').

21 65 Cong. Rec. 1931 (1924).

22 G. Born, *International Commercial Arbitration*, 3rd ed., Kluwer Law International, The Hague 2009, pp. 35–36; S. Rep. No. 536, 68th Cong., 1st Sess. 3 (1924); Committee on Commerce, Trade and Commercial Law, 'The United States Arbitration Act and its Application' (1925) 11 *ABA J.* 153, 155–56; see Federal Arbitration Act, 9 U.S.C. §§1–16 (1925). Title 9, §§1–14, enacted on 12.02.1925 (43 Stat. 883), codified 30.07.1947 (61 Stat. 669), amended 03.09.1954 (68 Stat. 1233). Chapter 2, §§201–208, was added on 31.07.1970 (84 Stat. 692); Chapter 3, §§301–307, was added on 15.08.1990 (Pub. L. No. 101–369). Chapters 2 and 3 address arbitration proceedings in an international context.

23 *Southland Corp. v. Keating*, 465 U.S. 1, 10 (1984).

> arising out of such contract or transaction [...] shall be valid, irrevocable, and enforceable, save upon such grounds as exist at law or in equity for the revocation of any contract.'[24]

This provision in particular was meant to combat state legislation disfavouring arbitration agreements and overcome the refusal by courts to enforce such contracts.[25]

## 2.2. JUDICIAL SUPPORT

Arbitration could not have achieved the success it has in the United States without substantial judicial support. In fact, until well into the twentieth century, US courts remained largely hostile to arbitration as a dispute resolution mechanism.[26] Arbitration agreements were frequently invalidated out of concerns about procedural fairness and displacement of the judiciary.[27] The FAA was intended to address this obstacle. Although the FAA is invariably described as articulating a strong federal policy favouring arbitration, this interpretation is largely due to the Supreme Court's characterisation of the statute.[28] The Court may be credited with solidifying arbitration's place in United States law through its frequent pronouncements in support of arbitration as a litigation alternative.

Shortly after passage of the FAA, the Supreme Court invalidated the power of federal courts to create federal common law rules of decision affecting state substantive rights. This decision, in *Erie Railroad Co. v. Tompkins*[29] did not prevent the courts' power to vest Congress with broad authority to create rules of decision applicable in both state and federal courts.

The Court made this clear in the case of *Prima Paint Corp. v. Flood & Conklin Manufacturing Co.* by relying on the language of the FAA rendering arbitration

24 9 U.S.C. §2 (1994).

25 *Allied-Bruce Terminix Cos. v. Dobson*, 513 U.S. 265, 273–274 (1994).

26 G. Born, *supra* n. 22, p. 35.

27 See *Kulukundis Shipping Co. v. Amtorg Trading Corp.*, 126 F.2d 978 (2d Cir. 1942) (summarising the history of the enforceability of arbitration agreements in the US); *Gilmer v. Interstate/Johnson Lane Corp.*, 500 U.S. 20, 24 (1991) (the FAA was enacted 'to reverse the longstanding judicial hostility to arbitration agreements that had existed at English common law and had been adopted by American courts'). G. Born, *supra* n. 22, p. 36.

28 *See Allied-Bruce Terminix*, 513 U.S. at 283 (O'Connor J concurring) ('over the past decade, the Court has abandoned all pretense of ascertaining congressional intent with respect to the Federal Arbitration Act, building instead, case by case, an edifice of its own creation'). See also *Prima Paint, Corp. v. Flood & Conklin Mfg Corp.*, 388 U.S. 395, 405 (1967) (in holding that the scope of pre-arbitral review is limited, 'we not only honor the plain meaning of the statute but also the unmistakably clear congressional purpose').

29 *Erie R.R. Co. v. Thompkins*, 304 U.S. 64 (1938).

agreements 'involving commerce' enforceable.[30] The Court held that Congress had enacted the FAA pursuant to its broad powers to regulate interstate and foreign commerce under the Constitution.[31] The Supreme Court has also given the phrase 'involving commerce' a broad interpretation 'consistent with the Act's basic purpose' of legitimising agreements to arbitrate.[32]

### *2.2.1. The Supreme Court trilogies*

#### 2.2.1.1. First trilogy

In what is known as the 'first arbitration trilogy', the Supreme Court addressed the role of arbitration in US labour law; however, as US courts became more broadly supportive of arbitration, they applied these decisions beyond the collective bargaining context.[33] The three cases in the first trilogy were argued by the same lawyers on behalf of the unions, and the Supreme Court handed down decisions in all three cases on the same day in 1960.

The first case, *United Steelworkers of America v. American Manufacturing*, arose out of an attempt to compel arbitration of a labour dispute.[34] Upon a company's refusal[35] to reinstate an injured employee, the United Steelworkers Union filed a grievance and attempted to force the company to arbitrate the dispute pursuant to a clause in the collective agreement. When the case reached the Sixth Circuit Court of Appeals, the panel held that the employee and his union had no right to arbitrate because the claim advanced in the grievance was 'frivolous, patently baseless'.[36] The Supreme Court ordered the company to arbitrate, although it did not deny that the underlying claim lacked merit.[37] The agreement to arbitrate all disputes meant exactly that, the Court said. 'The courts, therefore, have no business weighing the merits of the grievance' before compelling arbitration.[38]

The second case, *United Steelworkers of America v. Warrior & Gulf*, distinguished between labour arbitration and general commercial arbitration. According to the Court, commercial arbitration might be viewed as '[a]

---

30 9 U.S.C. §2 (1994).

31 *Prima Paint*, 388 U.S. at 405. The justices then characterised the power to craft rules of decision applicable to all cases as 'supplementary' to Congress' commerce power. *Ibid.* at 405 n. 13.

32 *Allied-Bruce Terminix*, 513 U.S. at 275 (quoting *Scherk v. Alberto-Culver Co.*, 417 U.S. 506, 511 (1974)).

33 The first trilogy was applied to commercial arbitration in *Moses H. Cone Mem'l Hospital v. Mercury Constr. Corp.*, 460 U.S. 1 (1983).

34 363 U.S. 564 (1960).

35 *Ibid.*

36 *United Steelworkers of Am. v. Amer. Mfg Co.*, 264 F.2d 624, 628 (6th Cir. 1959).

37 *Amer. Mfg*, 363 U.S. at 568 ('The processing of even frivolous claims may have therapeutic values of which those who are not a part of the plant environment may be quite unaware').

38 *Ibid.* at 568.

substitute for litigation', but labour arbitration was 'the substitute for industrial strife'.[39] By the 1960s, labour arbitration was not only an alternative dispute resolution process but a substantive right for workers. This understanding, the majority said, justified a broader reading of an agreement to arbitrate.[40] If there was an arbitration clause broad enough to cover the dispute, the court should compel arbitration without further inquiry. Although consent is the cornerstone of arbitration, in this context 'doubts should be resolved in favour of coverage'.[41] This principle has come to be known both in labour disputes and in arbitration law as a whole as the 'presumption of arbitrability'. However, it was not fully espoused in *Warrior & Gulf* since only four of the nine Supreme Court justices signed on to that part of the opinion, with two others concurring but refusing to endorse any such presumption.[42]

The third case in the trilogy, *United Steelworkers of America v. Enterprise Wheel & Car*, addressed the enforcement of arbitral awards.[43] The theme, again, was that the courts were required to apply the law of the FAA regardless of their assessments of the merits of the underlying dispute. The Court restated the general rule in labour arbitrations that an arbitral award 'is legitimate only so long as it draws its essence from the collective bargaining agreement'.[44] Anticipating further disputes, the Court went on to say that an award's failure to clearly indicate its basis 'is not a reason for refusing to enforce the award. Arbitrators have no free-standing obligation to the court to give their reasons'.[45] This language reflects another frequently-cited presumption in the law of arbitration: that awards draw upon the proper law in the absence of manifest evidence to the contrary.

Together, these rulings stand for the general proposition that arbitrators are better-placed than federal judges to rule on disputes over arbitrability and to evaluate the merits of the dispute appropriately. But while promptly accepted in the federal courts, the first trilogy encountered greater resistance in state courts.[46] Although state judges paid lip service to the Supreme Court's rulings on federal policy, they frequently went on to ignore this counsel and apply traditional state law defences to arbitration.[47]

---

39 363 U.S. 574 (1960).

40 *Ibid.*

41 *Ibid.* at 582–583.

42 *Ibid.*, 363 U.S. 564 (Harlan J and Brennan J concurring.).

43 363 U.S. 593 (1960).

44 *Ibid.* at 597.

45 *Ibid.* at 598.

46 B. Aaron, 'Arbitration in the Federal Courts: Aftermath of the Trilogy', in M. Kahn (ed.), *Collective Bargaining and the Arbitrator's Role*, BNA Incorporated, Washington 1962, p. 60 <www.naarb.org/proceedings/pdfs/1962–60.pdf> accessed 03.09.2012.

47 L. Hirschman, 'The Second Arbitration Trilogy: The Federalization of Arbitration Law' (2009) 71 *Va. L. Rev. (Virginia Law Review)* 1305, 1307.

### 2.2.1.2. Second trilogy

The FAA notwithstanding, federal and state courts alike still showed concern that arbitration agreements might reflect unequal bargaining power between the parties.[48] In 1974, this attitude began to soften when the Supreme Court held that 'any dispute arising out of [the parties'] international commercial transaction is to be respected and enforced by the federal courts', and affirmed that arbitration would not be a less fair forum than a courtroom trial for parties to an agreement to arbitrate under US law.[49] The Supreme Court's very public assessment that arbitration was both procedurally and substantively fair seriously limited the ability of courts to rely on their distrust of the process in order to avoid compelling arbitration.

The second trilogy consisted of *Moses H. Cone Memorial Hospital v. Mercury Construction Corp.*,[50] *Southland Corp. v. Keating*,[51] and *Dean Witter Reynolds Inc. v. Byrd*.[52] This second group of decisions is commonly said to have 'federalised' arbitration law by establishing the supremacy of federal arbitration policies over state law.[53] *Moses* recognised that federal arbitration legislation represented a body of substantive law and legislative policy that pre-empted contrary state legislation.[54] The Court declared that there was 'a liberal federal policy favouring arbitration' that governed in both state and federal courts.[55]

The Court drove home this point in *Southland Corp. v. Keating*, compelling the arbitration of state statutory claims which were non-arbitrable under California law.[56] *Southland Corp.* not only compelled states to give effect to the FAA in their own courts, it compelled them to ignore any local policies to the contrary.[57] In *Dean Witter Reynolds*, the Supreme Court ordered the parties to arbitrate state securities law claims pendent to federal securities law claims that at that time were deemed non-arbitrable under federal law.[58] The ruling ended all use of the 'intertwining doctrine' and made clear that parties could not evade

---

48 G. Born, *International Arbitration: Cases and Materials*, Aspen, 2010, p. 48; G. Born, *supra* n. 22, p.133.

49 J. Daly, *supra* n. 4, p. 8.

50 460 U.S. 1 (1983).

51 465 U.S. 1 (1984).

52 470 U.S. 213 (1985).

53 L. Hirschman, *supra* n. 47.

54 *Moses H. Cone Mem'l Hospital v. Mercury Constr. Corp.*, 460 U.S. 1, 24 (1983).

55 *Ibid.*

56 *Ibid.*

57 *Southland Corp. v. Keating*, 465 U.S. 1, 16 (1984) ('In creating a substantive rule applicable in state as well as federal courts, Congress intended to foreclose state legislative attempts to undercut the enforceability of arbitration agreements').

58 *Dean Witter Reynolds, Inc. v. Byrd*, 470 U.S. 213 (1985). The Supreme Court subsequently held federal securities claims to be arbitrable. *Shearson/American Express v. McMahon*, 482 U.S. 220 (1987); *Rodriguez de Quijas v. Shearson/American Express, Inc.*, 490 U.S. 477 (1989).

arbitration by tying in federal securities action claims.[59] Throughout the 1990s, the Supreme Court reaffirmed that federal arbitration law was pre-emptive of all contradictory state law, immunising arbitration from existing and contemplated conflicting state regulation.[60]

#### 2.2.1.3. Third trilogy

The third and very recent arbitration trilogy expands even further the Court's self-avowed pro-arbitration policy, to the point of limiting the application of the ordinarily valid state law contract defences to arbitration.

The decision in *Rent-A-Center* appears to stand for the proposition that parties may delegate to an arbitral tribunal the gateway issue of whether an agreement to arbitrate is unconscionable. In the face of such a delegation, courts appear to lose the power to police arbitration agreements for unconscionability and to deny the enforcement of arbitration agreements 'upon such grounds as exist at law or in equity for the revocation of any contract',[61] though the delegation itself could be challenged under at least some traditional contract law defences. The majority in *Rent-A-Center* took the opportunity to use the traditional concept of separability in US law to distinguish between challenges to the arbitration agreement and its delegation provision. Because the consumer failed to attack the delegation provision uniquely, the challenge could be viewed as an attack on the arbitration agreement as a whole, thus leaving its determination to the arbitral tribunal rather than a court.[62]

In *Stolt-Nielsen v. AnimalFeeds*, the Court refused to extend the benefits of class litigation to the arbitration context, finding the suggestion to be so at odds with the basic purposes of arbitration that consent to class arbitration could not be inferred but had to be stated expressly.[63] The decision does not sit well with the traditional understanding that arbitrators – chosen by the consent of the parties – have primary authority to interpret the parties' contract and, in the absence of clear direction from the parties, to determine the procedural contours of the arbitration.[64]

The final case in the trilogy further extended the broad federal policy in favour of arbitration. The Court held in *AT&T Mobility LLC v. Concepcion* that the FAA pre-empted a California law treating as unconscionable and denying

---

59 L. Hirschman, *supra* n. 47, p. 1340.

60 See *Doctor's Associates, Inc. v. Casarotto*, 517 U.S. 681 (1996); *Allied-Bruce Terminix Cos. v. Dobson*, 513 U.S. 265 (1994); *Gilmer v. Interstate/Johnson Lane.*, 500 U.S. 20, 26 (1991) (so long as the arbitration was procedurally sufficient to vindicate the plaintiff's statutory rights, an employment discrimination claim could be brought in an arbitration).

61 *Perry v. Thomas*, 482 U.S. 483, 489 (1987).

62 G. Bermann, 'The Supreme Court Trilogy and its Impact on U.S. Arbitration Law' (2011) 22 *Am. Rev. Int'l Arb. (American Review of International Arbitration)* 551, 554.

63 *Stolt-Nielsen, S.A. v. AnimalFeeds Int'l*, 130 S. Ct. 1758 (2010).

64 See, e.g., *Howsam v. Dean Witter Reynolds, Inc.*, 537 U.S. 79 (2002).

enforcement of contract provisions by which consumers waive their rights to class arbitration.[65] Lower courts have cited the case for the assertion that 'the unavailability of class arbitration [...] is not a ground for a finding of substantive unconscionability'.[66] *Concepcion* gives little attention to traditional concerns of fairness in arbitrations as well as the efficiency that class action arbitration brings.

In this most recent arbitration trilogy, the Supreme Court has moved beyond promoting arbitration and shielding it from judicial hostility. It has gone some distance in eliminating safeguards that help ensure arbitration's legitimacy.[67] The net effect of this last set of rulings in US arbitration law is not yet entirely clear, as lower courts are exhibiting an unusual amount of confusion over them and resistance to them.[68]

### *2.2.2. General attitude of the courts*

The US judiciary, led by the Supreme Court, thus has vigorously supported arbitration as an alternative means of dispute resolution, treating the FAA as the expression of a 'liberal federal policy favouring arbitration agreements'.[69] The Supreme Court has also protected the autonomy of arbitral regimes from political interference.[70]

## 2.3. PUBLIC SUPPORT

Over the years, public enthusiasm for arbitration has grown steadily in the US, to the point that arbitration clauses now regularly appear in boilerplate contract language.[71] Sophisticated parties tend to view arbitration as an equally effective

65 131 S. Ct. 1740 (2011).

66 *Sanders v. Forex Capital Markets*, 2011 U.S. Dist. LEXIS 137961, at *17 (S.D.N.Y. 29 November 2011).

67 G. Bermann, *supra* n. 62, p. 571.

68 Compare *Chen-Oster v. Goldman, Sachs & Co*, 785 F. Supp. 2d 394, 404–405 (S.D.N.Y. 2011); *Sanders v. Forex Capital Mkts, LLC*, 2011 U.S. Dist. LEXIS 137961, at *28 (S.D.N.Y. 29 November 2011); and *In re California Title Ins. Antitrust Litig.*, 2011 U.S. Dist. LEXIS 71621, at *13 (N.D. Cal. 27 June 2011) *with Opalinski v. Robert Half Int'l, Inc.*, 2011 U.S. Dist. LEXIS 115534, at *10 (D. N.J. 6 October 2011) (class arbitration not necessarily foreclosed merely because arbitration agreement is silent on the issue); *Botello v. COI Telecom, LLC*, 2010 U.S. Dist. LEXIS 138572, at *16 (W.D. Tex. 30 December 2010) (same); and *Sutter v. Oxford Health Plans LLC*, 2011 U.S. Dist. LEXIS 17123, at *12–16 (D.N.J. 22 February 2011).

69 *Moses H. Cone*, 460 U.S. at 24.

70 J. Daly, *supra* n. 4, p. 8.

71 T. Stipanowich, 'Rethinking American Arbitration' (1988) 63 *Ind. L.J. (Indiana Law Journal)* 425, 426; S. Mentschikoff, 'Commercial Arbitration' (1961) 61 *Colum. L. Rev. (Columbia Law Review)* 846, 848–856.

alternative to litigation.[72] The growth reflects both a growing confidence in the competence and integrity of arbitrators and a growing dissatisfaction with the cost, delay and formality of traditional litigation.[73] In large commercial disputes, businesses perceive juries as dangerously unpredictable. In the international context, arbitration offers the obvious advantage of neutrality.

Arbitration has also won the attention, mostly positive, of academic writers in the US. The Arbitration Society of America, organised in 1922, began the process by presenting arbitration as a legitimate field of academic inquiry and committing a full-time staff devoted to its intellectual development.[74] The Society distributed literature, held conferences, and published articles on arbitration. Although the Society was short-lived, dissolved as early as 1926, it is credited with lending important public support to passage of the FAA.[75] The Society's successor, the American Arbitration Association (AAA), continues today as the premier institution for arbitration – domestic and international alike – in the US. Both in practice and in academia, interest in arbitration continues to grow.

On the other hand, while arbitration has always had its detractors in the US, public criticism has clearly grown over the past decade. On the one hand, companies are showing frustration over the growing complexity of arbitral procedure and the introduction of traditional courtroom formalities and delays into the arbitral process, to the point that they view arbitration as no better than litigation in terms of cost and efficiency.[76] On the other hand, a growing body of opinion holds that consumers and other disadvantaged interests are being deprived, without meaningful consent, of the right of access to courts for the resolution of their claims. The legislative initiative known as the Arbitration Fairness Act (AFA) is a manifestation of this development. The AFA would add a Chapter 4 to the FAA prohibiting the enforcement of pre-dispute agreements to arbitrate in consumer, employment and civil rights disputes. The proposed legislation would not prevent the parties from arbitrating these disputes so long as assent was freely given after the dispute arose.[77] Still, the use of arbitration continues to rise in the US, as in so many other parts of the world.

72 B. Goldstein, 'Alternatives for Resolving Business Transaction Disputes' (1983) 58 *St. John's L. Rev. (St. John's Law Review)* 69.

73 T. Stipanowich, *supra* n. 71, p. 428.

74 F. Emerson, *supra* n. 18, p. 161.

75 *Ibid.*

76 The most illustrative situation might be found in the debates relating to the proposed Arbitration Fairness Act in the US Congress. (S. 1782/H.R. 3010).

77 Arbitration Fairness Act (S. 1782/H.R. 3010) (2011).

# 3. KEY TEXTS

## 3.1. FEDERAL LAW

The Federal Arbitration Act is the primary US text on arbitration, domestic and international alike. It consists of three chapters, the first addressing domestic arbitration agreements and arbitral awards affecting interstate commerce, the second implementing the New York Convention, and the third implementing the Inter-American (or Panama) Convention.[78]

The FAA is the oldest arbitration statute still enforced in a major jurisdiction.[79] In comparison to its foreign counterparts, it is terse and minimalist, and seriously outdated.[80] The FAA does not address the competence of arbitrators and courts to resolve questions of jurisdiction, provisional relief, the conduct of arbitral proceedings, separability, form of the award, or costs, among many other things.[81] Even on subjects that the FAA does address, such as grounds for challenging an award, the law is remarkably abrupt and not particularly well drafted.

As mentioned, the central purpose of the FAA was to require the enforcement of agreements to arbitrate.[82] Section 2 of the FAA's first chapter makes these agreements 'valid, irrevocable, and enforceable, save upon such grounds as exist at law or in equity for the revocation of any contract'. Other sections of the FAA provide the machinery for giving arbitration agreements such an effect. Sections 3 and 4 direct federal courts to stay proceedings pending before them if the court finds that a valid agreement to arbitrate exists and the matter is 'referable to arbitration'. The sections then require the courts to compel the parties to arbitrate those issues.[83]

The remainder of Chapter 1 bears on federal trial courts' powers to assist in arbitral proceedings. The district court may appoint arbitrators if the parties are unable to agree and may enforce an arbitral tribunal's issuance of a subpoena or otherwise assist in the taking of evidence.[84] The final three sections provide for the confirmation, vacatur, or correction of arbitral awards within the United States.[85] The role of the federal courts in arbitration is discussed in section 4 of the chapter.

---

78 9 U.S.C. §§1–16; 9 U.S.C. §§201–10; 9 U.S.C. §§301–07.

79 G. Born, *supra* n. 22, p. 48.

80 *Ibid.*, p. 49. Compare the FAA's 17 articles to the English Arbitration Act or the UNCITRAL Model Law.

81 G. Born, *supra* n. 22, p. 50.

82 9 U.S.C. §2.

83 9 U.S.C. §§3–4.

84 9 U.S.C. §§5, 7.

85 9 U.S.C. §§9–11.

## 3.2. STATE LAW

Although the FAA pre-empts inconsistent state law on arbitration, it does not pre-empt state law in the sense of occupying the field.[86] Thus, state legislation serves an important gap-filling function within the United States federal system.[87] When the FAA, the New York or Panama conventions, or federal common law has addressed a specific issue, state law may not contradict or interfere. States retain plenary legislative authority. When there is an absence of federal law, states remain free to act. Such a situation often arises when an arbitration agreement or arbitral award does not affect interstate or foreign commerce, as Congressional power to legislate commerce is limited to those situations.

Although the power of states to enact arbitration laws is limited by the FAA, general state contract law remains highly relevant. State contract law may supply the prerequisites for the formation of a valid agreement, and state procedural rules may apply to discovery, consolidation, and interim relief insofar as the FAA is silent.[88] State law may even apply to certain arbitration issues although a case is tried in federal court.[89]

Every state in the US has adopted some form of legislation addressing arbitration.[90] Thirty-eight states have taken as their point of departure the Uniform Arbitration Act (UAA), proposed in 1924 by the Conference of Commissioners on Uniform State Laws and amended in 1955.[91] The UAA is quite similar to the FAA.[92] It reflects the policies of enforcing agreements to arbitrate future disputes and the strong presumption that arbitral awards are entitled to recognition and enforcement.

In 2000, the National Conference of Commissioners on Uniform State Laws proposed the Revised Uniform Arbitration Act (RUAA),[93] incorporating many

---

86 *Volt Info. Sciences, Inc. v. Board of Trustees*, 489 U.S. 468, 477 (1989) ('The FAA contains no express pre-emptive provision, nor does it reflect a congressional intent to occupy the entire field of arbitration. But even when Congress has not displaced state regulation in an area, state law may nonetheless be preempted to the extent that it actually conflicts with federal law.').

87 See *Southland Corp. v. Keating*, 465 U.S. 1, 16 (1984).

88 G. Born, *supra* n. 22, p. 53.

89 See *Erie R.R. Co. v. Thompkins*, 304 U.S. 64, 78 (1938) ('Except in matters governed by the Federal Constitution or by acts of Congress, the law to be applied in any case is the law of the state [...] There is no federal general common law').

90 G. Born, *supra* n. 22, p. 53; an extended list of state arbitration statutes can be found in AAA, *The International Arbitration Kit*, AAA 1993, p. 103.

91 G. Born, *supra* n. 22, p. 40. The first version only covered agreements to arbitrate existing disputes, but later revisions to the UAA added enforceability agreements to arbitrate future disputes.

92 M. Pirsig, 'The New Uniform Arbitration Act' (1956) 11 *Bus. Law. (Business Lawyer)* 44.

93 National Conference of Commissioners on Uniform State Laws, Revised Uniform Arbitration Act (2000).

provisions of the UNCITRAL Model Law, including on the constitution of the tribunal, provisional rulings, arbitral procedures, and format for awards. More than half of all states remain tied to the original UAA,[94] while others, such as Texas and California, have enacted a version of the UNCITRAL Model Law.[95]

Yet not all states have adopted the UAA or its firmly pro-arbitration stance. For example, a handful of states have adopted statutes that bar the arbitrability of certain claims or do not provide for a presumption in favour of enforcement.[96] But to that extent they are contrary to the FAA, they are pre-empted in cases involving inter-state or foreign commerce.

Obviously, parties may elect to have their contract governed by state substantive law.[97] Even if they do not, state law will provide the rules of contract law applicable to questions of the formation, validity and enforceability of agreements to arbitrate.[98]

## 3.3. CONVENTIONS AND TREATIES

### 3.3.1. *New York Convention*

The United States is a signatory to the 1958 United Nations Convention on the Recognition and Enforcement of Arbitral Awards. The US Congress ratified the New York Convention in 1970 and revised the FAA to incorporate the Convention into a second chapter of that law.[99] By then, the US had come to recognise the efficiencies offered by arbitration and was ready to extend the support system for domestic arbitrations into the international context, especially in light of the expected benefits for US companies in global markets.[100] FAA Chapter 2 thus provides for the enforcement of agreements to arbitrate and the recognition and enforcement of awards subject to the New York Convention.[101] Convention awards are governed by Chapter 1 of the FAA to the

94 G. Born, *supra* n. 22, p. 54.

95 Title 9.3, Arbitration and Conciliation of International Commercial Disputes, Ca. Civ. Proc. Code §§1297.11 *et seq.* (West 1982 & Supp. 1996) (effective 7 March 1988). Tex. Civ. Prac. & Rem. Code Ann. §§171.001 *et seq.* (West 1986 & Supp. 1996) (effective 1 September 1995). J. Coe, *International Commercial Arbitration: American Principles and Practice in a Global Context*, Transnational Publishers, Irvington-on-Hudson 1997. See also J. McClendon, 'State International Arbitration Laws: Are They Needed or Desirable?' (1990) 1 *Am. Rev. Int'l Arb.* 245.

96 G. Born, *supra* n. 22, p. 40.

97 *Volt Info. Sciences, Inc. v. Board of Trustees*, 489 U.S. 468, 470 (1989).

98 *First Options of Chicago, Inc. v. Kaplan*, 514 U.S. 938, 115 S. Ct. 1920, 1924 (1995).

99 9 U.S.C. §§201–210.

100 G. Born, *supra* n. 22, p. 37.

101 9 U.S.C. §§201, 206, 207.

extent that its application creates no conflict.[102] Chapter 1 thus performs a gap-filling function.

### 3.3.2. *Inter-American Convention*

The Inter-American, or Panama, Convention, like the New York Convention, requires the enforcement of arbitration agreements and the recognition and enforcement of foreign awards.[103] The New York Convention generally supersedes the Panama Convention when both apply, unless a majority of the parties to the arbitration are citizens of States that have signed and ratified the Panama Convention and are part of the Organisation of American States. In fact, the two conventions do not diverge markedly in content.[104] However, the Panama Convention incorporates the Rules of Procedure of the Inter-American Commercial Arbitration Commission as default provisions when the parties have not specified a choice of procedural law.[105]

### 3.3.3. *NAFTA*

The North American Free Trade Agreement, entered into by Canada, Mexico and the United States in 1992, represents a powerful joint endorsement of arbitration by the three nations. Article 2022 requires the signatory states to 'encourage and facilitate the use of arbitration', and to 'provide appropriate procedures to ensure observance of agreements to arbitrate and for the recognition and enforcement of arbitral awards in such disputes'.[106] These obligations are easily fulfilled, as all three nations have ratified the New York Convention. NAFTA also establishes an Advisory Committee on Private Commercial Disputes to report on arbitration procedures within the free trade area.[107]

### 3.3.4. *ICSID Convention*

In 1965, the Washington Convention established the International Centre for the Settlement of Investment Disputes (ICSID). The World Bank promoted the idea of ICSID, an entity designed to facilitate the resolution of investment disputes through conciliation and arbitration. The Centre's jurisdiction is not

---

102 9 U.S.C. §208.

103 9 U.S.C. §§301–307.

104 See 'United States', in J. Paulsson (ed.), *ICCA International Handbook on Commercial Arbitration*, Suppl. 44, Kluwer Law International, 2005, p. 86. See, e.g., Articles 5–6 of the Panama Convention.

105 *Ibid.*

106 Article 2022, NAFTA.

107 *Ibid.*

compulsory, even for signatories to the Convention, but is independently established through contracts and investment treaties. As a signatory, the United States is categorically bound to enforce final ICSID awards.[108]

## 3.4. SOURCES OF OTHER RULES

The skeletal nature of federal arbitration legislation leaves plenty of room for other sources of law. Foremost among them is federal common law. But not all of this gap-filling material can properly be classified, since it also comprises a large amount of rules and guidelines issued by a variety of professional associations. These texts supplement incomplete domestic legislation and give further direction to participants in international arbitration.

### *3.4.1. Federal common law*

In addition to the statutory law applicable to arbitration in the United States, a large amount of judge-created common law has emerged. Much of the emergence of common law has been a necessity due to the limited reach of the FAA.[109] The common law on arbitration deals with subjects ranging from the validity of agreements to arbitrate to the powers of courts once arbitration has commenced.

### *3.4.2. AAA Rules*

The rules of the AAA, the preeminent arbitral institution in the US, have an obvious effect on the arbitrations it administers within the United States, but they also shape the general culture of arbitration in the US. The AAA permits parties to choose among several sets of rules in arbitrations that it administers. The AAA's International Center for Dispute Resolution (ICDR) Rules, based largely on the UNCITRAL Arbitration Rules, are the default rules set for parties in an international dispute.[110] Although the Rules, like the AAA Code of Ethics, can be contracted around by the parties, most parties do not take the trouble of

---

108 Convention on the Settlement of Investment Disputes Between States and Nationals of Other States, produced at Washington, DC, 18.03.1965. See also C. Schreuer *et al.*, *The ICSID Convention: A Commentary*, 2nd ed., Cambridge University Press, Cambridge 2009.

109 A. Samuel, 'Arbitration Statutes in England and the USA' (1999) 8 *Arb. & Disp. Res. J. (Arbitration and Dispute Resolution Journal)* 1, 32 ('The [FAA] falls in the category of "small but perfectly formed." It is very resilient and loosely enough drafted in the right places to enable the court to do the right thing for the arbitral process').

110 Article 1.1, AAA Int'l Rules. The rules apply when the parties have agreed 'to arbitrate disputes under these International Arbitration Rules or have provided for arbitration of an international dispute by the [AAA] without designating particular rules.'

avoiding them.[111] The AAA also maintains a set of Commercial Arbitration Rules for domestic cases. Spun off from these rules are a number of specialised rules for certain trades.[112] If the amount of a claim exceeds $500,000, the AAA will apply its 'Procedures for Large, Complex Commercial Disputes'.[113]

Arbitrations under the Commercial Arbitration and Mediation Center for the Americas (CAMCA), an institution founded jointly by the AAA and Canadian and Mexican counterparts, are administered by the AAA under special CAMCA Rules within the United States.

Arbitrators presiding over AAA-administered cases must comply with the association's requirements for arbitrator qualifications. Notably, AAA arbitrators are not required to have any legal background whatsoever; they must simply be well-respected in their fields.[114] The Supreme Court endorses this attitude, recognising that 'the specialized competence of arbitrators pertains primarily to the law of the shop, not the law of the land'.[115]

The AAA performs detailed checks on arbitrators to root out potential conflicts of interest.[116] Beyond that, there are few constraints on AAA arbitrations. This permits the process to match the needs of each dispute. Except to the extent that the parties prescribe otherwise, the conduct of hearings and discovery is largely up to the arbitrator's discretion. Arbitrators may 'grant any remedy or relief that the arbitrator deems just and equitable and within the scope of the agreement of the parties'.[117]

Still, awards issued under the aegis of the AAA must comply with certain procedural requirements. The award must be written and signed.[118] Traditionally, the AAA has discouraged its arbitrators from giving a thorough account of the reasons behind their awards, mainly out of a concern that excessive prose exposes the award to greater scrutiny at the enforcement stage.[119] This reticence has protected the secrecy of disputes but has also limited the development of rule-based decision-making within AAA arbitrations.[120] Arbitration under the ICDR is subject to a different presumption, viz that awards will be reasoned unless the parties agree otherwise.

---

111 A. Rau and E. Sherman, 'Tradition and Innovation in International Arbitration Procedure' (1995) 30 *Tex. Int'l L.J. (Texas International Law Journal)* 89, 116–118.

112 J. Paulsson, *supra* n. 104, p. 12.

113 AAA, *Procedures for Large, Complex Commercial Disputes*, amended and effective 15.09.2005.

114 AAA, 'A Guide for Commercial Arbitrators' (2004) <www.adr.org/sp.asp?id=22016> accessed 04.09.2012.

115 *Alexander v. Gardner-Denver Co.*, 415 U.S. 36, 57 (1974).

116 AAA, *Code of Ethics* at Cannon II. AAA, *AAA Rules*, at R-17, 18.

117 T. Stipanowich, *supra* n. 71.

118 AAA, *A Guide for Commercial Arbitrators* (2004).

119 D. Thompson, 'Arbitration Theory & Practice: A Survey of AAA Construction Arbitrators' (1994) 23 *Hofstra L. Rev. (Hofstra Law Review)* 137, 158.

120 F. Schauer, 'Giving Reasons' (1995) 47 *Stan. L. Rev. (Stanford Law Review)* 633, 651, 654, 658.

### 3.4.3. *Bar Association Rules*

The AAA, in a joint effort with the American Bar Association, issued the ABA/AAA Code of Ethics in 1980.[121] This code provides ethical guidelines, particularly on issues of impartiality of arbitrators and conflicts of interest. The Code of Ethics now establishes a presumption of neutrality for all arbitrators, including those appointed by the parties.[122]

The International Bar Association has made very substantial contributions to the 'soft law' that is so prevalent in arbitration today. These include ethical rules (notably the IBA Code of Ethics[123] and the IBA Guidelines on Conflicts of Interest in Arbitration),[124] but they extend further. An excellent example is the IBA Rules of Evidence in International Arbitration, which parties can choose to apply to the taking and admissibility of evidence in any arbitration.[125]

The practice of law is also governed by the bar associations of each state, although the practice of arbitration is not considered the practice of law in many states. Nevertheless, the majority of arbitration practitioners in the US are state-qualified lawyers who maintain membership in the state bars. Consequently, state rules governing ethics and conflicts of interest also bind these lawyers.

# 4. ARBITRATION TODAY

## 4.1. PREVALENCE

Arbitration is now widespread as a means of dispute resolution in commercial, employment and consumer settings.[126] The most common method by far of entering into arbitration is through a pre-dispute agreement to arbitrate,

---

121 AAA and ABA, 'AAA/ABA Code of Ethics' (1985) *YB Comm. Arb. X (Yearbook of Commercial Arbitration Vol. 10)* 131.

122 O. BYRNE, 'A New Code of Ethics for Commercial Arbitrators: The Neutrality of Party-Appointed Arbitrators on a Tripartite Panel' (2003) 30 *Fordham Urb. L.J. (Fordham Urban Law Journal)* 1815, 1825–26.

123 INT'L BAR ASS'N, *Code of Ethics for International Arbitrators* (1988) <www.ibanet.org/Document/Default.aspx?DocumentUid=B21F3C32-190E-4FB0-9750-5459AE4E8498> accessed 04.09.2012.

124 INT'L BAR ASS'N, *IBA Guidelines on Conflicts of Interest in International Arbitration* (2004) <www.ibanet.org/Document/Default.aspx?DocumentUid=E2FE5E72-EB14-4BBA-B10D-D33DAFEE8918> accessed 04.09.2012.

125 INT'L BAR ASS'N, *IBA Rules on the Taking of Evidence in International Arbitration* (May 2010) <www.ibanet.org/LPD/Dispute_Resolution_Section/Arbitration/IBA_Rules_Evidence/Overview.aspx> accessed 04.09.2012.

126 The AAA experienced its greatest jump in arbitration filings between 1990 and 1998. By 2005, the AAA had administered more than two million cases. AMERICAN ARBITRATION ASSOCIATION, *1999 American Arbitration Association Ann. Rep.* (1999); AMERICAN ARBITRATION ASSOCIATION, *Fast Facts* <www.adr.org/FastFacts> accessed 04.09.2012.

typically in the form of a clause in a main contract. It is of course possible to stipulate to arbitration after a dispute has arisen, but this is relatively rare.[127]

The heightened popularity of arbitration is a consequence of the growing expense, delay and difficulties of litigating in US courts. The caseloads of both federal and state courts have exploded. Docket pressure is traceable to an increase in drug-related criminal cases, the greater complexity of business disputes, the ability for plaintiffs to avoid financial risk by engaging attorneys on a contingency fee basis and on a class-action basis, and the near-absence of a loser-pays system in American litigation.[128] Even though arbitration is coming in for mounting criticism on these same grounds, the majority of litigation attorneys contacted by the American Bar Association in recent surveys expressed the view that arbitration was faster and more cost-effective than litigation.[129]

## 4.2. TRENDS

Although the number of arbitrations occurring in the US increases every year, the diversity of arbitral procedures is decreasing. More and more, sophisticated parties demand submission of arbitration to established arbitral institutions operating under well-defined procedural rules.[130] Some attribute this phenomenon, called the 'judicialisation' or 'legalisation' of arbitration, to the influence of American litigators who seek to impose the habits of traditional litigation on alternative dispute resolution mechanisms as well.[131] Still, many believe that institutions and the standard rules that they promulgate legitimise arbitration and contribute to its popularity.[132]

And yet, at the same time, we observe an increasing tendency to customise arbitration clauses in individually-negotiated contracts involving significant commercial transactions.[133] The Supreme Court has approved of the parties' power

127 J. Deye and L. Britton, 'Arbitration by the American Arbitration Association' (1994) 70 *N. Dak. L. Rev. (North Dakota Law Review)* 281, 282.

128 J. Coe, *supra* n. 95, p. 97.

129 See ABA, *ABA Section of Litigation Task Force on ADR Effectiveness American Bar Association* (August 2003) <www.abanet.org/litigation/taskforces/adr/surveyreport.pdf> accessed 04.09.2012.

130 G. Kaufmann-Kohler, 'Globalization of Arbitral Procedure' (2003) 36 *Vand. J. Trans. L. (Vanderbilt Journal of Transnational Law)* 1313, 1322–1330; E. Brunet, 'Replacing Folklore Arbitration with a Contract Model of Arbitration' (1999) 74 *Tul. L. Rev. (Tulane Law Review)* 39, 62 ('there is much reason to think that arbitration signatories are knowingly demanding judicialized arbitration by contracting to arbitrate under the available judicialized rules').

131 See, e.g., A. Rau, 'The Culture of American Arbitration; and the Lessons of ADR' (2005) 40 *Tex. Int'l L.J.* 449, 460; E. Brunet, *supra* n. 130, p. 62.

132 G. Kaufman-Kohler, *supra* n. 130.

133 A. Rau, *supra* n. 131, p. 8; R. Coulson, 'Tailoring Arbitration to Business Needs' (1964) 19 *Bus. Law. (Business Laywer)* 1037, 1043–1050.

to choose their own rules and procedures in arbitration.[134] The 'customisability' of arbitration continues to enhance its popularity.[135]

On average, one year passes between the commencement of arbitral proceedings and the issuance of a final award.[136] As the time increases, so too do the fees associated with arbitration.[137] Although this does not compare unfavourably to litigation delays, arbitration is beginning to lose its edge over international arbitration in terms of cost and efficiency. On the other hand, the parties' capacity to select an arbitrator of their own choice continues to distinguish arbitration from litigation and contribute to its appeal.[138] Misgivings notwithstanding, corporate litigants in particular continue to sing the praises of arbitration.[139]

## 4.3. DOMESTIC ARBITRATION

Arbitration continues to grow in popularity in the US as an alternative to traditional court litigation. The perceived benefits of alternative dispute resolution are many. The parties may feel that arbitration offers a more neutral forum or a faster and cheaper procedure; they may also believe that arbitration will save them from the extended discovery that can be inescapable in traditional American litigation. Arbitration is also increasingly favoured because of the easy access to expertise: while the average judge may be unfamiliar with the type of dispute, the parties can hand-pick arbitrators who have knowledge pertinent to the dispute.[140] Complex and technical cases have grown disproportionately in AAA filings.[141]

Although arbitration is in theory easily customisable to the needs of the parties,[142] in reality, few have the resources or the expertise to develop their own procedures, and most end up incorporating the rules of the AAA.[143] Fortunately,

---

134 See, e.g., *Mitsubishi Motors Corp v. Soler Chrysler-Plymouth, Inc.*, 473 U.S. 614, 628 (1985); *McDonald v. City of West Branch*, 466 U.S. 284, 292 (1984).

135 See generally, A. Rau, *supra* n. 131, p. 501.

136 Federal Mediation and Conciliation Service, Arbitration Statistics Fiscal Year 2007 <www.fmcs.gov/internet/displayContent.asp?itemID=21224> accessed 04.09.2012.

137 *Ibid.*

138 K. Burton Beam, 'Administering Last Rites to Employee Rights: Arbitration Enforcement and Employment Law in the Twenty-First Century' (2003) 40 *Houston L. Rev. (Houston Law Review)* 499, 530; *Mitsubishi Motors*, 473 U.S. at 633.

139 H. Mazadoorian, 'At a Crossroad: Will the Corporate ADR Movement be a Revolution, or Just Rhetoric?' (Summer 2000) *Disp. Resol. Mag. (Dispute Resolution Magazine)* 5.

140 See *Mitsubishi Motors*, 473 U.S. at 633 ('Adaptability and access to expertise are hallmarks of arbitration').

141 American Arbitration Association, 2011 President's Letter and Financial Statements (2012) <www.adr.org/aaa/ShowProperty?nodeId=%2FUCM%2FADRSTG_019403&revision=latestreleased> accessed 04.09.2012.

142 G. Born, *supra* n. 22, p. 2.

143 T. Stipanowich, *supra* n. 71, p. 434.

the AAA offers a number of different sets of rules to deal with different categories of disputes.

The expertise that party-appointed arbitrators bring comes at a cost, however, as an experienced arbitrator can charge thousands of dollars a day in fees while a federal judge is essentially free. Nor does the expertise of arbitrators necessarily reduce the volume of attorneys' fees that continue to represent the largest cost component in arbitration, particularly when judicialised arbitral procedures are in play. Critics of domestic arbitration thus challenge arbitration's claims to being cheaper and more efficient than litigation.

The domestic arbitration culture in the United States is heavily shaped by the AAA, which, as noted,[144] stands at the forefront of the arbitration movement.[145] Established largely by legal academics in 1926, just after the passage of the FAA,[146] the AAA administers a vast number of domestic commercial arbitrations.[147] It has also exerted influence over the shape of arbitration abroad.[148] The importance of the AAA procedural rules has already been underscored.[149]

### 4.3.1. *Employment arbitration*

Arbitration of employment disputes has skyrocketed in the past century. In the US, both collective bargaining disputes and individual grievances against employers are commonly resolved through arbitration under the FAA.

#### 4.3.1.1. Collective bargaining

Today, the vast majority of all labour contracts between employers and unions contain arbitration clauses.[150] Collective bargaining disputes frequently embrace what is termed 'interest' arbitration. After negotiations between a union and an employer fail, the parties may elect to rely on an arbitrator-driven mechanism for adjudicating respective rights. An 'interest' arbitrator goes further than a traditional arbitrator and will help actively to determine the contract provisions that will govern future relations.[151] Arbitration is particularly well-suited to this context as it is less bound than litigation by

144 *See supra*, Section 3.4.2.
145 T. Stipanowich, *supra* n. 71, p. 430.
146 J. Deye and L. Britton, *supra* n. 127.
147 J. Paulsson, *supra* n. 104, p. 11.
148 T. Ginsburg, 'The Culture of Arbitration' (2003) 36 *Vand. J. Transnat'l L. (Vanderbilt Journal of Transnational Law)* 1335, 1339.
149 See *supra*, section 3.4.2.
150 M. Hill and A. Sinicropi, 'Improving the Arbitration Process: A Primer for Advocates' (1991) 27 *Willamette L. Rev. (Willamette Law Review)* 463, 471.
151 D. Feller, 'A General Theory of the Collective Bargaining Agreement' (1973) 61 *Calif. L. Rev (California Law Review)* 663, 744–745.

traditional adversarial patterns and better accommodates a degree of activism on the part of the decision-maker.

4.3.1.2. Individual grievances

Arbitration clauses have become commonplace in individual employment contracts as well, due to the Supreme Court's decision in *Gilmer v. Interstate/Johnson Lane Corp.*,[152] which held that mandatory arbitration clauses are not unconscionable even in the context of age-discrimination claims. In mandatory arbitration disputes, an employee agrees in the initial contract to submit all future employment-related claims to binding arbitration.

These types of employment arbitrations tend to be among the most basic and routine. The allegations fall into predictable patterns and discovery turns out to play a lesser role than in commercial cases. It is typical for a company representative to act as an advocate in an employment arbitration in the place of a lawyer.[153] On the other hand, they are voluminous in number, easily outnumbering other categories of disputes.[154] In 2002, an AAA executive reported that over 6 million employees were subject to a binding arbitration clause under AAA Rules.[155] To respond to this pressure, the AAA tries to re-direct as many of these cases as possible to mediation so as to resolve them more quickly and more efficiently.[156] The AAA applies to these cases its Employment Dispute Resolution Rules, which are specifically tailored to employment disputes.[157]

While the level of concern about the fairness of compelling arbitration of employment disputes remains significant,[158] the Supreme Court has maintained its support for labour arbitration. Moreover, the data seems to undercut the

---

152 500 U.S. 20 (1991); see also *Circuit City Stores, Inc. v. Adams*, 532 U.S. 105 (2001) (holding that employment agreements with mandatory arbitration clauses were enforceable under the FAA); M. LeRoy, 'Jury Revival or Jury Reviled? When Employees are Compelled to Waive Jury Trials' (2005) 7 *U. Pa. J. Lab. & Emp. L. (University of Pennsylvania Journal of Labor and Employment Law)* 767, 768 (describing how 'employers flocked to this dispute resolution method' after the Supreme Court's decision). D. Lipsky and R. Seeber, 'Patterns of ADR Use in Corporate Disputes' (1999) 54 *Disp. Resol. J. (Dispute Resolution Journal)* 66, 68. See also D. Lipsky and R. Seeber, 'In Search of Control: The Corporate Embrace of ADR' (1998) 1 *U. Pa. J. Lab. & Emp. L.* 133, 137 (in 1996, a majority of large businesses surveyed reported that they used arbitration to resolve disputes with employees).

153 J. Daly, 'Problems with Arbitration in the USA' (2008), p. 5 <www.ialsnet.org/meetings/business/DalyJoseph-USA.pdf> accessed 04.09.2012.

154 See, e.g., Federal Mediation and Conciliation Services, Fiscal Year 2011 <www.fmcs.gov/internet/itemDetail.asp?categoryID=196&itemID=21837> accessed 04.09.2012.

155 Interview with Robert Meade, Senior Vice President, American Arbitration Association, in New York, NY (14.01.2002).

156 American Arbitration Association, 2011 President's Letter, *supra* n. 141.

157 AAA, Employment Dispute Resolution Rules (1993).

158 S. Bompey, M. Delikat and L. McClelland, 'The Attack on Arbitration and Mediation of Employment Disputes' (1997) 13 *Lab. Law. (Labor Lawyer)* 21, 37.

assertions of critics.[159] Studies have shown that the 'success rate' for plaintiffs in arbitration is at least as high as it is in litigation.[160] Arbitrations also appear to provide the claimant with a better chance of receiving a small sum, making the dispute less of an all-or-nothing game than traditional litigation.[161] There is some evidence, however, that employers fare better in iterative arbitrations with the same arbitrators.[162]

In sum, access to traditional court litigation remains limited for the lowest-compensated employees, who find it difficult to afford the costs of litigating a dispute and retaining a plaintiff's lawyer.[163] Meanwhile, thanks to the more streamlined nature of employment arbitration, lower income employees find arbitration to be a more accessible alternative, as it is tends to result in a quicker and less expensive resolution of disputes.[164]

This is not to suggest that the arena of employment disputes is entirely subject to private ordering in the US. The Equal Opportunity Employment Commission, an agency established in 1965 to enforce anti-discrimination laws in the workplace, retains authority to vindicate that objective. In *EEOC v. Waffle House*, the Supreme Court held that the EEOC could pursue enforcement actions against an employer on behalf of an employee, even if the employee was barred by a mandatory arbitration provision from conducting individual litigation.[165]

### *4.3.2. Construction disputes*

Arbitration is also an essential tool for the American construction industry. When disputes arise after construction has started, the contractor and subcontractor need a way to resolve disputes so that work on the project can continue. An arbitrator may rewrite the parties' agreement in order to fulfil the parties' original intentions or to fill gaps in the contract language. Arbitrators may also be asked to address strict liability and indemnification issues. Accordingly, the resolution of these disputes requires specific technical

---

159 See *Circuit City Stores, Inc. v. Adams*, 532 U.S. 105 (2001).

160 M. Delikat and M. Kleiner, 'Comparing Litigation and Arbitration of Employment Disputes: Do Plaintiffs Better Vindicate Their Rights In Litigation?' (2003) 6(3) *American Bar Association Litigation Section Conflict Management*; see L. Maltby, 'Private Justice: Employment Arbitration and Civil Rights' (1998) 30 *Colum. Hum. Rts. L. Rev. (Columbia Human Rights Law Review)* 29, 55–57.

161 See L. Maltby, *supra* n. 160.

162 See L. Bingham, 'Employment Arbitration: The Repeat Player Effect' (1997) 1 *Employee Rts. & Emp. Pol'y J. (Employee Rights and Employment Policy Journal)* 189, 213–214.

163 E. Hill, 'Due Process at Low Cost' (2002) 18 *Ohio St. J. Disp. Resol.* 782.

164 *Ibid.*; M. Delikat and M. Kleiner, 'An Empirical Study of Dispute Resolution Mechanisms for Employment Disputes: Do Plaintiffs Better Vindicate Their Rights in Litigation?' (2004) 58 *Disp. Res. J.* 56, 57–8.

165 *EEOC v. Waffle House, Inc.*, 534 U.S. 279 (2002).

knowledge.[166] A pool of arbitrators with experience in the construction industry supplies the requisite knowledge, and the AAA's construction division gives particularised attention to these cases. Here too, however, contractors and subcontractors are increasingly entrusting these disputes to mediation.[167]

### *4.3.3. Consumer disputes*

The United States both permits and encourages the arbitration of consumer disputes, largely unperturbed by the concerns about fundamental fairness and due process that have halted these proceedings in many foreign legal systems.[168]

Consumer disputes most frequently arise in the context of consumer purchase agreements, in which the requirement to submit disputes to arbitration may be found on the back of a receipt, or buried in a service contract with a bank, real estate agency, or phone company; or in an 'End User License Agreement' for computer software. Companies prefer arbitration because it eliminates many of the risks associated with traditional litigation in the United States. To begin with, companies involved in litigation can expect to sustain negative publicity from the mere filing of a suit against them,[169] whereas arbitration can be kept confidential. Companies may also fear the unpredictability of a jury verdict, as trial by jury is a basic constitutional right in civil cases.[170] In the United States, juries and judges alike are authorised to award punitive damages against a corporation; while arbitrators may also award such damages, they do so far less frequently.[171] Lastly, the aggregation of individual claims in a single arbitration still remains a relatively remote possibility, whereas class actions have achieved widespread acceptance in the US.[172]

---

166 T. Stipanowich, 'Beyond Arbitration: Innovation and Evolution in the United States Construction Industry' (1996) 31 *Wake Forest L. Rev. (Wake Forest Law Review)* 65, 68; J. Deye and L. Britton, *supra* n. 127, p. 281.

167 See generally T. Stipanowich, *supra* n. 166, p. 122.

168 The arbitration of consumer disputes is not immune from criticism in the United States, however. See, e.g., *Knepp v. Credit Acceptance Corp.*, 229 B.R. 821, 827 (Bankr. N.D. Ala. 1999) ('The reality that the average consumer frequently loses his/her constitutional rights and right of access to the court when he/she buys a car, household appliance, insurance policy, receives medical attention or gets a job rises as a putrid odor which is overwhelming to the body politic'); P. Carrington and P. Haagen, 'Contract and Jurisdiction' [1996] *Sup. Ct. Rev.* 331, 401; See generally D. Schwartz, 'Enforcing Small Print to Protect Big Business: Employee and Consumer Rights Claims in an Age of Compelled Arbitration' (1997) *Wis. L. Rev. (Wisconsin Law Review)* 33.

169 J. Sternlight, 'Creeping Mandatory Arbitration: Is It Just?' (2005) 57 *Stanford L. Rev.* 1631, 1638.

170 US Const. Amend. 7. See also C. Drahozal and R. Friel, 'Consumer Arbitration in the European Union and the United States' (2003) 28 *N.C. J. Int'l L. & Com. Reg. (North Carolina Journal of International Law and Commercial Regulation)* 357, 389.

171 C. Drahozal and R. Friel, *supra* n. 170, p. 390. See generally, T. Eisenberg *et al.*, 'The Predictability of Punitive Damages' (1997) 26 *J. Legal Stud. (Journal of Legal Studies)* 623.

172 See *infra*, section 6; Fed. R. Civ. P. 23.

In short, the perceived pro-consumer policies of US courts lead American businesses to favour arbitration and to provide for them in non-negotiable form contracts. Consumers, however, generally perceive arbitration to be a less fair alternative to traditional litigation.[173] The AAA has responded to these concerns. Consumers may avail themselves of the AAA's Consumer Due Process Protocol in disputes related to contracts for goods or services for personal or household use.[174] This protocol aims to promote fair procedures for consumers and remedy the imbalance in knowledge of and experience with arbitration. The AAA enforces these procedures by denying access to the institution to businesses that refuse to respect the protocol.[175] The AAA has also promulgated Supplementary Procedures for Consumer-Related Disputes, which resemble the procedures offered in American small-claims courts.

For its part, the Supreme Court has not wavered in its pro-arbitration attitude even in the consumer contract context.[176] In *Moses H. Cone v. Memorial Hospital v. Mercury Construction Corp.*, the Supreme Court declared that the strong pro-arbitration policy at the federal level favours the arbitration of all consumer disputes.[177] The Court seems, for now, to be satisfied by the procedural guarantees incorporated into arbitration.[178]

As noted earlier,[179] Congress has shown interest in protecting consumers from pre-dispute arbitration agreements through an 'Arbitration Fairness Act', though such legislation has not been enacted. However, other recently-passed legislation delegates to the Securities and Exchange Commission (SEC) the authority to prohibit arbitration clauses in customer agreements through administrative rule-making.[180] The SEC has not exercised this authority, but has undertaken to study the potential for rulemaking on the subject. Meanwhile, the SEC continues to oversee the activities and dispute resolution rules of the Financial Industry Regulatory Authority (FINRA), the institution under whose aegis many consumer arbitrations are conducted.[181]

173 J. Sternlight, *supra* n. 169, p. 1638.

174 AAA, 'Consumer Due Process Protocol: Scope of the Consumer Due Process Protocol (2001)' <www.adr.org> accessed 05.09.2012.

175 *Ibid.*

176 See, e.g., *Doctor's Associates, Inc. v. Casarotto*, 517 U.S. 681 (1996) (holding that Montana's notice requirements for arbitration provisions ran afoul of the FAA's pro-arbitration policies).

177 460 U.S. 1, 24–25 (1983).

178 See generally M. Delikat and M. Kleiner, *supra* n. 160.

179 See *supra*, section 2.3.

180 Dodd-Frank Wall Street Reform and Consumer Protection Act, H.R. 4173, 111th Cong. §921(a) (2nd Sess. 2010).

181 Section 19(b) of the Securities and Exchange Act of 1934 gives the SEC oversight authority over SRO securities arbitration. 15 U.S.C. §78s(b) (2006).

### 4.3.4. *Securities arbitration*

Though encompassed in the category of consumer disputes, securities disputes raise special concerns in the United States and merit separate discussion here. The Supreme Court has held Securities Act claims to be arbitrable, leading to a quick growth in arbitrations of shareholder claims.[182]

Arbitration is the primary method for the resolution of disputes between investors and brokers. Most frequently, the broker's standard contract contains an arbitration provision.[183] Even if the contract does not contain such a provision, the Code of Arbitration Procedure for Consumer Disputes from the largest dispute resolution forum in the securities industry (FINRA) requires brokers to submit to arbitration if a customer so demands.[184]

Despite the popularity of arbitration clauses in commercial disputes, publicly-held companies have displayed a reticence to adopt arbitration clauses in their own certificates of incorporation and contracts with shareholders.[185] Corporations favour litigation in these contexts out of a fear of limited review in 'bet the company' disputes and the limited expertise of arbitrators in securities law.[186] And yet, at the same time, many investors view the arbitral process as unfair and biased towards corporate interests.[187]

### 4.3.5. *Court-ordered procedures*

Many jurisdictions expressly permit courts to order the parties to participate in arbitration or mediation. The eligibility of cases for such treatment depends on the complexity of the dispute and the amount in controversy.[188] Non-binding arbitration, in which an arbitrator hears a case and issues a non-binding award, can also support traditional litigation by acting as a 'reality check' on the parties' expectations in litigation.[189]

---

182 *Shearson/American Express v. McMahon*, 482 U.S. 220 (1987); *Rodriguez de Quijas v. Shearson/American Express, Inc.*, 490 U.S. 477 (1989).

183 J. Gross, 'The End of Mandatory Securities Arbitration?' (2010) 30 *Pace L. Rev. (Pace Law Review)* 1174.

184 FINRA Rule 12200. See also FINRA, 'Code of Arbitration Procedure for Industry Disputes' <www.finra.org/web/groups/arbitrationmediation/@arbmed/@arbion/documents/arbmed/p117547.pdf> accessed 06.09.2012.

185 T. Eisenberg and G. Miller, 'The Flight from Arbitration: An Empirical Study of Ex Ante Arbitration Clauses in the Contracts of Publicly Held Companies' (2007) 56 *DePaul L. Rev. (DePaul Law Review)* 335.

186 S. Ware, 'Why Do Businesses Use (or Not Use) Arbitration Clauses?' (2010) 25 *Ohio S. J. on Disp. Resol. (Ohio State Journal on Dispute Resolution)* 433, 436.

187 J. Gross and B. Black, 'When Perception Changes Reality: An Empirical Study of Investors' Views of the Fairness of Securities Arbitration' 2008 *J. Disp. Resol. (Journal of Dispute Resolution)* 349.

188 J. Deye and L. Britton, *supra* n. 127, pp. 282–283.

189 *Ibid.*

Under some statutory schemes, arbitration is the exclusive remedy for certain claims. Local courts will dismiss such claims and require the plaintiff to commence arbitration. For example, New York State permits a consumer to demand repair or replacement of a defective vehicle recently purchased in the state. If the car dealer refuses to honour this demand, the consumer may file a demand for arbitration.[190] Congress has also created statutory rights that plaintiffs may vindicate only through arbitration.[191] The Supreme Court has upheld these schemes.[192]

#### 4.3.6. *Mediation*

Mediation has also exploded in the United States.[193] Although this alternative dispute resolution mechanism resembles arbitration in terms of consent, enforceability, and party control, mediation frequently occurs in the shadow of traditional litigation rather than as an entirely separate forum for resolving disputes. American judges have the power to order parties to attend formal mediation talks before a dispute goes to trial. Parties can also elect to attend mediation on their own in an attempt to avoid the expense of litigation. Increasingly, parties may also agree in advance to mediate a dispute rather than proceed to litigation or arbitration. Arbitral institutions may also oversee these proceedings. Mediations currently represent 9% of the cases before the ICDR.[194] Mediations, like arbitrations, are enforceable under the FAA. Still, mediation is met with some resistance in the US due to a traditional preference for adversarial over non-adversarial dispute resolution models.[195] Mediation is discussed in greater depth in the following chapter.

### 4.4. INTERNATIONAL ARBITRATION

The growth of international arbitration in the United States can be traced to a few significant legislative texts: the New York Convention, the Panama Convention, and the Washington Convention, the latter establishing the International Centre for the Settlement of Investment Disputes (ICSID) to deal with protection of investors' rights abroad. These texts enable US courts to enforce both agreements to arbitrate and foreign awards.

---

190 NY Gen. Bus. Law. §198-a(k) (2004).

191 See, e.g., 7 U.S.C. §136(a)(c)(1)(F) (2000) and 29 C.F.R. 1440.1 (1 July 2004). The Supreme Court rejected a challenge to the constitutionality of this law in *Thomas v. Union Carbide Agri. Prods. Co.*, 473 U.S. 568, 582 (1985).

192 *Thomas v. Union Carbide*, 473 U.S. at 582.

193 T. Stipanowich. 'Arbitration: The "New Litigation"' 2010 *U. Ill. L. Rev. (University of Illinois Law Review)* 1.

194 American Arbitration Association, 2011 President's Letter, *supra* n. 141.

195 A. Rau, *supra* n. 131, p. 495.

The popularity of arbitration in the international context is due to the same factors that underlie the rise in domestic arbitration: expediency, cost, expertise, flexibility, party control, and confidentiality. Yet one criterion rises above all of these in the international context: neutrality.[196] Parties involved in international disputes are concerned above all with finding a disinterested forum in which both sides can fairly air their concerns and neither will enjoy a 'home field advantage'. The neutrality offered by an arbitral tribunal is more important when the parties come from different countries, speak different languages, and have an imbalance of knowledge of local procedural laws. For this reason, US courts have been even more supportive of international arbitration than domestic arbitration.[197] The Supreme Court's concern for protection of foreign investors has only reinforced its pro-arbitration posture.[198] More generally, the Supreme Court has recognised that the predictability offered by international arbitration 'is an indispensable element in international trade, commerce, and contracting'.[199]

Although different concerns underlie the attraction to international and domestic arbitration, the two are not always treated as separate processes. Much of the US law on arbitration is judge-made, and courts have made few efforts to treat international arbitration differently.[200] For example, US choice-of-law rules and requirements for the exercise of personal jurisdiction do not treat international cases separately.[201] Yet, the FAA distinguishes domestic and international agreements and awards in its implementation of domestic law and the Panama and New York conventions. Some state statutes do as well.[202] Still, the distinctions are subtle.

---

196 J. Paulsson, *supra* n. 104, p. 2. See also G. Born, *International Commercial Arbitration: Commentary and Materials*, Kluwer Law International, The Hague 2010, p. 2 ('Most importantly, international arbitration is designed and accepted particularly to assure parties from different jurisdictions that their disputes will be resolved neutrally. Among other things, the parties usually seek an independent decision-maker, detached from the courts, governmental institutions, and cultural biases of either party. They also ordinarily contemplate the arbitrator's application of internationally-neutral procedural rules, rather than a particular national legal regime.').

197 G. Born, *supra* n. 196, pp. 39, 157–159, and 165–166.

198 See, e.g., *Shearson/Am. Express, Inc. v. McMahon*, 482 U.S. 220 (1987) and *Scherk v. Alberto-Culver Co.*, 417 U.S. 506, 511 (1974). In *Scherk*, the Supreme Court decided that claims under the Securities Exchange Act were arbitrable when they arose out of an international transaction. *McMahon* relied on this ruling to extend the arbitrability of SEA claims to the domestic context.

199 *M/S Bremen v. Zapata Off-Shore Co.*, 407 U.S. 1, 13–14 (1972).

200 J. Coe, *supra* n. 95, p. 99.

201 J. Paulsson, *supra* n. 104, p. 2.

202 See, e.g., Cal. Civ. Proc. Code §1297.13 (West 1982 and Supp. 1996) (defining an 'international' dispute).

### 4.4.1. *International commercial arbitration*

The United States was not always broadly supportive of international commercial arbitration. During the drafting of the New York Convention, the US delegation alternated between sitting out entirely and opposing US adoption of the Convention.[203] But the United States is now a cheerleader for cross-border dispute resolution in the form of arbitration, and US lawyers and litigants contribute immensely to the field.[204]

By the 1980s, arbitration had become the norm for the settlement of international commercial disputes involving US businesses.[205] The United States served as the seat for 5.6% of all ICC arbitrations filed in 2006.[206] US companies are the most heavily represented parties in ICC arbitrations, representing 10.7% of participants in 2006.[207] This support stems from arbitration's neutrality and confidentiality. Additionally, awards are easy to enforce and execute.[208]

The American Arbitration Association also influences international arbitration through its International Centre for Dispute Resolution (ICDR) in New York City and Dublin. The ICDR Centre is a popular institution for US businesses operating abroad. The popularity of ICDR continues to grow, with a record number of cases filed in 2011.[209]

In a recent survey of corporate decision-makers internationally, 16% of respondents listed AAA/ICDR arbitration as their preferred institution.[210] In any case, many have claimed – usually unfavourably – that arbitration is becoming increasingly 'Americanised' through increased discovery, oral practice, motion practice and adversarial methods.[211]

---

203 Official Report of the United States Delegation to the United Nations Conference on International Commercial Arbitration 2, 22 (15.08.1958), quoted in L. Quigley, 'Accession by the United States to the United Nations Convention on the Recognition and Enforcement of Foreign Arbitral Awards' (1961) 70 *Yale L.J.* 1049, 1074 n. 108.

204 M. Goldhaber, 'The Court that Came in from the Cold' (May 2001) *Am. Law. (American Lawyer)* 98.

205 L. Craig, 'Some Trends and Developments in the Laws and Practice of International Commercial Arbitration' (1995) 30 *Tex. Int'l L. J.* 1, 2 (citing numerous sources).

206 G. Born, *supra* n. 22, p. 132.

207 '2006 Statistical Report' (2007) *ICC Ct. Bull. (ICC Court Bulletin)* 6.

208 PriceWaterhouseCoopers, 'International Arbitration: Corporate Attitudes and Practices' 6 (2008) <www.pwc.co.uk/en_UK/uk/assets/pdf/pwc-international-arbitration-2008.pdf> accessed 06.09.2012.

209 AAA, *supra* n. 141.

210 Queen Mary University of London, 'Arbitration Institutions/Statistics' <www.arbitrationonline.org/research/ArbitrationInstitStat/index.html> accessed 06.09.2012.

211 L. Reed and J. Sutcliffe, 'The "Americanization" of International Arbitration?' (Apr. 2001) *Mealey's Int'l Arb. Rep. (Mealey's International Arbitration Reporter)* 11.

### *4.4.2. International investment arbitration*

The United States is a party to the Washington Convention (also known as the ICSID Convention). Americans receive more appointments as ICSID arbitrators than individuals of any other nationality.[212] Arbitrations frequently involve American businesses as claimants, while the United States appears less frequently as the respondent state.[213]

The United States operates under separate agreement with its two closest trade partners, Canada and Mexico, neither of which is a party to the ICSID Convention. The North American Free Trade Agreement authorises arbitration under the ICSID additional facility rules or the UNCITRAL Arbitration Rules.[214]

Additionally, the United States is a party to nearly fifty bilateral investment treaties with other nations.[215] These treaties generally support ICSID arbitration proceedings and assist in the enforcement of non-ICSID awards. The US Model Bilateral Investment Treaty promotes the transparency of investment arbitrations and encourages arbitrators to increase public access to the proceedings and to consider amicus filings from interested persons.[216] The Model BIT partially carves out domestic labour and environmental laws from the reach of foreign investor suits.[217]

# 5. THE ARBITRATION PROCESS SHAPED BY AMERICAN COURTS

## 5.1. ARBITRABILITY

Although US courts for decades blocked agreements to arbitrate certain subjects on the grounds of public policy, today '[t]here is virtually no subject-matter inarbitrability defence to the enforcement of arbitral agreements'.[218] Entire areas

---

212 ICSID, 'The ICSID Caseload – Statistics' (2012) <http://icsid.worldbank.org/ICSID/FrontServlet?requestType=ICSIDDocRH&actionVal=ShowDocument&CaseLoadStatistics=True&language=English31> accessed 06.09.2012.

213 *Ibid.*

214 Article 1120(1), NAFTA; see J. Coe, Jr., 'Taking Stock of NAFTA Chapter 11 in Its Tenth Year: An Interim Sketch of Selected Themes, Issues, and Methods' (2003) 36 *Vand. J. Trans. L. (Vanderbilt Journal of Transnational Law)* 1381, 1387.

215 J. Paulsson, *supra* n. 1054, p. 87.

216 Treaty Between the Government of the United States of America and the Government of [Country] Concerning the Encouragement and Reciprocal Protection of Investment <www.state.gov/documents/organization/117601.pdf> accessed 06.09.2012.

217 Articles 12(1) and 13(1), *ibid.*

218 T. Carbonneau, *Cases and Materials on the Law and Practice of Arbitration*, 3rd ed., JurisNet, Huntington 2003, p. 245.

of the law once thought to be the sole province of the federal courts – antitrust,[219] securities,[220] investor fraud,[221] and even civil rights[222] – may now be adjudicated through arbitration. Even issues of regulatory law have been handed over to tribunals.[223]

The expansive availability of arbitral fora to resolve claims derives from the parties' freedom to contract under US law, since agreements to arbitrate are enforceable 'save upon such grounds as exist at law or inequity for the revocation of any contract'.[224] The set of claims that can be excluded on the grounds of public policy has also diminished as courts have acknowledged that acceptable fora for disputes need not be procedurally equivalent to US courts in order to fulfil the requirements of due process.[225]

The presumption of arbitrability derives from the FAA. Courts will not conclude that a statutory right is non-arbitrable 'unless Congress itself has evinced an intention to preclude a waiver of judicial remedies for the statutory rights at issue'.[226] Meanwhile, due to the FAA's supremacy as federal law, states have no power to preclude arbitration of state law claims subject to the FAA.[227]

---

219 *Mitsubishi Motors Corp v. Soler Chrysler-Plymouth, Inc.*, 473 U.S. 614, 628–629 (1985).

220 *Rodriguez de Quijas v. Shearson/American Express, Inc.*, 490 U.S. 477, 483 (1989) (holding that claims under the Securities Act of 1933 are arbitrable).

221 *Shearson/American Express, Inc. v. McMahon*, 107 S. Ct. 2332 (1987) (reconciling the decision with earlier rulings which held securities claims to be non-arbitrable under older securities laws by recognizing the Court's shifting attitude towards arbitration and its growing acceptance of the ability of arbitrators to resolve complex statutory disputes).

222 *Gilmer v. Interstate/Johnson Lane*, 500 U.S. 20, 26 (1991) (holding that claims under the Age Discrimination in Employment Act are arbitrable); Penn Plaza, 129 S. Ct. at 1474 (a 'collective-bargaining agreement that clearly and unmistakably requires union members to arbitrate [civil rights] claims is enforceable as a matter of federal law'); *Circuit City Stores, Inc. v. Adams*, 532 U.S. 105, 123 (2001) (compelling arbitration of an employment discrimination lawsuit because 'arbitration agreements can be enforced under the FAA without contravening the policies of congressional enactments giving employees specific protection against discrimination prohibited by federal law').

223 See, e.g., *Mitsubishi Motors*, 473 U.S. at 640 ('Accordingly, we require this representative of the American business community to honor its bargain, by holding this agreement to arbitrate enforceable'); see also *JLM Industries, Inc. v. Stolt-Nielsen SA*, 387 F.3d 163, 179–181 (2d Cir. 2004) (antitrust claims between competitors can be arbitrated).

224 9 U.S.C. §2.

225 See, e.g., *Haynsworth v. The Corporation*, 121. F.3d 956 (5th Cir. 1997) ('The view that every foreign forum's remedies must duplicate those available under American law would render all forum selection clauses worthless and would severely hinder Americans' ability to participate in international commerce'); see also *Mitsubishi Motors*, 473 U.S. at 628 ('by agreeing to arbitrate a statutory claim, a party does not forgo the substantive rights afforded by the statute; it only submits to their resolution in an arbitral, rather than a judicial forum'). See generally A. Rau, '"Arbitrability" and Judicial Review: A Brief Rejoinder' (2002) 1 *J. of Am. Arb.* 159 (2002).

226 *Mitsubishi. Motors*, 473 U.S. at 628.

227 *Perry v. Thomas*, 482 U.S. 483, 489–492 (1987); *Southland Corp. v. Keating*, 465 U.S. 1, 10–17 (1984).

The Supreme Court's holding in the *Mitsubishi* case, which permitted the arbitration of US antitrust law claims in a Japanese tribunal applying Swiss law, is a broad affirmation of party autonomy to submit statutory disputes to arbitration. However, *Mitsubishi* also contains dicta referring to the New York Convention's 'public policy' exception to the enforcement of foreign arbitral awards, to the effect that after an award is rendered, national courts 'will have the opportunity at the award-enforcement stage to ensure that the legitimate interest in the enforcement of the antitrust laws has been addressed'.[228] This language raised concern in academic commentary that the Supreme Court was encouraging national courts to give a 'second look' to awards on matters governed by statutory law.[229] However, the courts do not appear to have taken up the Supreme Court's suggestion in *Mitsubishi*.[230]

Given the broad arbitrability of all manner of disputes, the term 'arbitrability' has come in US parlance to refer much more broadly to any inquiry into whether a valid and binding agreement to arbitrate exists, and whether it covers the dispute at issue.[231] These issues must be resolved separately from underlying contractual claims if the arbitration is to proceed expeditiously.

## 5.2. SEPARABILITY AND *KOMPETENZ-KOMPETENZ*

The responsibility for determining arbitrability questions is unclear in the US, as the FAA makes no mention of recourse to courts in advance of arbitration for resolution of these issues. The Supreme Court has spoken of 'gateway' issues that a court may determine at the outset before compelling arbitration.[232] These threshold issues include the existence and scope of an agreement to arbitrate, the ability of a type of dispute to be arbitrated as a matter of law, and traditional defences such as fraud or mistake.[233] A national court is naturally empowered to

228 *Mitsubishi Motors*, 473 U.S. at 638.

229 See, e.g., T. Carbonneau, 'The Exuberant Pathway to Quixotic Internationalism: Assessing the Folly of *Mitsubishi*' (1986) 19 *Vand. J. Trans. L.* 263, 297–298.

230 J. Coe, *supra* n. 95, p. 102; C. Alfaro and F. Guimarey, 'Who Should Determine Arbitrability? Arbitration in a Changing Economic and Political Environment' (1996) 12 *Arb. Int'l (Arbitration International)* 415, 424–426.

231 See, e.g., *AT&T Techs., Inc. v. Commc'ns Workers of Am.*, 475 U.S. 643 (1986); *Cox v. Ocean View Hotel Corp.*, 533 F.3d 1114 (9th Cir. 2008); *John Wiley & Sons, Inc. v. Livingston*, 376 U.S. 543, 547 (1964).

232 Although some argue that these claims can be brought after the arbitration has commenced, such an arrangement is inefficient and disfavoured. See generally G. Bermann, 'The Gateway Problem' (2012) 39 *Yale J. Int'l L.* 1.

233 See, e.g., *AT&T Mobility LLC v. Concepcion*, 131 S. Ct. 1740 (2011); *Granite Rock Co. v. Int'l Bhd. of Teamsters*, 130 S. Ct. 2847 (2010); *Rent-A-Ctr., W., Inc. v. Jackson*, 130 S. Ct. 2772 (2010); *Stolt-Nielsen, S.A. v. AnimalFeeds Int'l*, 130 S. Ct. 1758 (2010); *Buckeye Check Cashing, Inc. v. Cardegna*, 546 U.S. 440 (2006); *First Options of Chicago, Inc. v. Kaplan*, 514 U.S. 938 (1995); *AT&T Techs., Inc. v. Commc'ns Workers of Am.*, 475 U.S. 643 (1986).

decide on these questions because its own jurisdiction ends where arbitral jurisdiction begins; the court therefore determines its own jurisdiction in determining gateway questions. Compared with countries such as France, US law permits a much broader range of intervention by national courts at the threshold stage.[234]

The concept of *kompetenz-kompetenz*, the power of a tribunal to evaluate its own jurisdiction, confirms the ability of arbitrators to make threshold determinations as well.[235] In the United States, the doctrine has only a positive dimension: the conclusion that an arbitrator is suited to rule on a jurisdictional objection does not necessarily preclude a court from taking up the question as well.[236] While *kompetenz-kompetenz* does not determine who can resolve these questions, the notion of separability begins to provide a dividing line between court and tribunal powers.

The FAA presumes the separability of the arbitration agreement from the remainder of the contract.[237] Being a separate and autonomous portion of the contract in which it appears, the agreement thus survives even if the contract in which it is contained is found to be invalid. Thus, if a party argues that the main contract is invalid because it was procured by fraud or mistake, a broad arbitration clause within that contract will remain valid. The most recent version of the UAA also espouses the view that, for these purposes, the arbitration agreement is separable from the contract in which it is found.[238]

This basic role of separability is taken one step further in the US. If a claim attacks the validity of the contract as a whole (including the agreement to arbitrate that it contains), it clearly implicates the arbitrator's jurisdiction to decide contractual disputes. Thus, the dispute is appropriately resolved by the tribunal. On the other hand, attacks directed only at the arbitration clause are more properly decided by the courts under US law; they are treated as 'gateway' issues.[239] This distinction was announced by the Supreme Court in the 1967 *Prima Paint* case, drawing from the FAA. While a court may evaluate 'issues which g[o] to the "making" of the agreement to arbitrate', it may not evaluate the contract generally and must 'order arbitration to proceed once it

---

234 See generally G. Bermann, *supra* n. 232.

235 Institutional laws also supply this power. The AAA's Commercial Arbitration Rules specify that: 'The arbitrator shall have the power to rule on his or her own jurisdiction, including any objections with respect to the existence, scope or validity of the arbitration agreement.' R. 7(a). In *First Options*, the Supreme Court made clear that an arbitrator does not act unlawfully in deciding jurisdictional objections that are presumptively susceptible to judicial determination. 514 U.S. at 942.

236 G. Bermann, *supra* n. 232.

237 *Buckeye Check Cashing*, 546 U.S. 440; *Prima Paint, Corp. v. Flood & Conklin Mfg Corp.*, 388 U.S. 395, (1967).

238 2000 UAA §6(b)–(c).

239 G. Bermann, *supra* n. 232, p. 23. *See also Prima Paint, Corp. v. Flood & Conklin Mfg Corp.*, 388 U.S. 395 (1967).

is satisfied that "the making of the agreement for arbitration or the failure to comply [with the arbitration agreement] is not in issue"'.[240] In a more recent case, the Supreme Court held that 'a challenge to the validity of the contract as a whole and not specifically to the arbitration clause, must go to the arbitrator'.[241]

In *Howsam*, the Supreme Court characterised issues for the tribunal alone as those '"procedural" questions which grow out of the dispute and bear on its final disposition'.[242] These disputes are said to be properly put before an arbitrator because the parties would expect the tribunal to deal with issues relating to the merits of the claim.[243]

Policy reasons, particularly efficiency concerns, may also counsel that a court should determine the issue. Disputes over the very existence of a contract – as opposed to its validity – may also fall to the courts.[244] Issues left to the arbitrators include: fraud or mistake in formation of the contract as a whole,[245] unconscionability or invalidity of the whole contract,[246] claim preclusion,[247] fulfilment of conditions precedent to arbitration,[248] the expiration of a time period for bringing a claim,[249] and whether a claim is susceptible to class action arbitration.[250] American courts are divided on the issue of who may determine waiver. The Supreme Court has suggested in dicta that the responsibility falls to

240 *Prima Paint*, 388 U.S. at 403–404.

241 *Buckeye*, 546 U.S. at 449.

242 *Howsam v. Dean Witter Reynolds, Inc.*, 537 U.S. 79, 84 (2002).

243 G. Bermann, *supra* n. 232, p. 46.

244 G. Bermann, *supra* n. 232, p. 30–31, 49; *Buckeye* 546 U.S. at 444 n. 1 ('The issue of the contract's validity is different from the issue whether any agreement between the alleged obligor and oblige was ever concluded. Our opinion today addresses only the former, and does not speak to the issue decided in the cases cited by respondents (and by the Florida Supreme Court), which hold that it is for courts to decide whether the alleged obligor ever signed the contract, whether the signor lacked authority to commit the alleged principal, and whether the signor lacked the mental capacity to assent') (citations omitted); *Rent-a-Ctr., W., Inc. v. Jackson*, 130 S. Ct. 2772, 2778 (2010) ('The issue of the agreement's "validity" is different from the issue whether any agreement between the parties "was ever concluded," and, as in [Buckeye Check Cashing], we address only the former'); *Granite Rock Co. v. Int'l Bhd. of Teamsters*, 130 S. Ct. 2847 (2010).

245 *Prima Paint*, 388 U.S. at 402.

246 *Buckeye*, 546 U.S. 440.

247 See, e.g., *Shell Oil Co. v. CO2 Comm., Inc.*, 589 F.3d 1105, 1109–1110 (10th Cir. 2009); *Emilio v. Sprint Spectrum, L.P.*, 315 F. App'x 322, 324 (2d Cir. 2009); *Triangle Constr. & Maint. Corp. v. Our V.I. Labor Union*, 425 F.3d 938, 947 (11th Cir. 2005); *Klay v. United Healthgroup*, 376 F.3d 1092, 1109–1110 (11th Cir. 2004).

248 *John Wiley & Sons, Inc. v. Livingston*, 376 U.S. 543, 557–559 (1964). See also *Lumbermens Mut. Cas. Co. v. Broadspire Mgmt. Servs.*, 623 F.3d 476, 477 (7th Cir. 2010) (holding that the fulfillment of conditions precedent to arbitration is a question for the arbitrator to decide); *3M Co. v. Amtex Sec., Inc.*, 542 F.3d 1193, 1200 (8th Cir. 2008) (same).

249 537 U.S. 79 (2002).

250 *Green Tree Fin. Corp. v. Bazzle*, 539 U.S. 444, 452–453 (2003).

the arbitrator.[251] While some courts have accepted this guidance,[252] others have left the inquiry to judges.[253] Many have distinguished between contract-based and conduct-based waiver.[254]

Once a tribunal is in place and capable of exercising its competence, US courts may decline to exercise jurisdiction over gateway issues; however, they are not strictly required to do so.[255] No law limits the power of courts to determine these questions during the arbitration.[256] However, the parties apparently can delegate gateway issues to the tribunal alone in their original arbitration agreement.[257]

The fact that an issue has been ruled on by an arbitrator will not exempt it from later review by a US court. Although courts are eager to compel arbitration without first investigating all of a party's jurisdictional objections,[258] they will not forgo judicial review of the award once it is made if a party resisting

251 *Howsam v. Dean Whitter Reynolds*, 537 U.S. 79, 84–85 (2002) ('[T]he presumption is that the arbitrator should decide allegations of waiver, delay, or a like defense to arbitrability') (internal quotations omitted).

252 See, e.g., *Nat'l Am. Ins. Co. v. Transamerica Occidental Life Ins. Co.*, 328 F.3d 462, 466 (citing *Howsam* and giving the issue to the arbitrator); *Woodland Ltd. P'ship v. Wulff*, 868 A.2d 860 (D.D.C. 2005).

253 See, e.g., *Marie v. Allied Home Mortgage Corp.*, 402 F.3d 1, 12–14 (1st Cir 2005) (holding that the Supreme Court 'did not intend to disturb the traditional rule that wiaver by conduct, at least where due to litigation-related activity, is presumptively an issue for the court'); *Tristar Fin. Ins. Agency, Inc. v. Equicredit Corp.*, 97 Fed. Appx. 462, 464 (5th Cir. 2004) ('[T]he court, not the arbitrator, is in the best position to decide whether the conduct amounts to a waiver under applicable law').

254 See, e.g., *Republic of Ecuador v. Chevron Corp.*, 638 F.3d 384, 393–394 (2d Cir. 2011); *Pro Tech Indus., Inc. v. URS Corp.*, 377 F.3d 868, 871–872 (8th Cir. 2004); *Klay v. United Healthgroup, Inc.*, 376 F.3d 1092, 1109–1110 (11th Cir. 2004); *Banc One Acceptance Corp. v. Hill*, 367 F.3d 426, 430 (5th Cir. 2004). See *JPD, Inc. v. Chronimed Holdings, Inc.*, 539 F.3d 388, 393–394 (6th Cir. 2008) (suggesting that a deliberate attempt to interfere with arbitration sought against it would waive a party's right to arbitrate against the same party in the future). See also *Citibank, N.A. v. Stok & Assocs., P.A.*, 387 F. App'x 921 (11th Cir. 2010) (weighing the balance of harms), cert. granted, 131 S. Ct. 1556 (2011), cert. dismissed, 131 S. Ct. 2955 (2011); *Cox v. Ocean View Hotel Corp.*, 533 F.3d 1114 (9th Cir. 2008) (holding that an employer's rejection of an employee's claims as unripe for arbitration did not preclude the employer from invoking arbitration); *Khan v. Parsons Global Servs. Ltd.*, 521 F.3d 421, 428 (D.C. Cir. 2008) (holding that participating in litigation by filing a motion for summary judgment waived the right to subsequently invoke arbitration).

255 G. Bermann, *supra* n. 232, p. 15; C. Alfaro and F. Guimarey, *supra* n. 230, pp. 424–426. J. Barcelo, 'Who Decides the Arbitrators' Jurisdiction? Separability and Competence-Competence in Transnational Perspective' (2003) 36 *Vand. J. Trans. L.* 1115, 1125–1126 ('Thus, in the vast majority of cases the arbitral process will go forward, but parties with a legitimate basis for objecting to the arbitrators' jurisdiction will have an opportunity, after only moderate delay, to make their case to a judge').

256 A. Rau, *supra* n. 131, p. 515.

257 *Rent-A-Ctr., W., Inc. v. Jackson*, 130 S. Ct. 2772, 2777–2778 (2010); *First Options of Chicago, Inc. v. Kaplan*, 514 U.S. 938, 943 (1995) ('Did the parties agree to submit the arbitrability question itself to arbitration?').

258 *Contec Corp. v. Remote Solution Co.*, 398 F.3d 205, 208 (2d Cir. 2005).

enforcement argues that the arbitrator lacked the power to hear the dispute.[259] Instead, the Supreme Court instructs that the court should review the arbitrator's decision on jurisdictional questions de novo unless there is 'clear and unmistakable evidence' that the parties intended to submit the arbitral jurisdiction question to the tribunal alone.[260] In this case, the arbitral decision will be subject to only the general 'manifest disregard' standard on the jurisdictional point.[261] However, if 'the parties did not agree to submit the arbitrability question itself to arbitration, then the court should decide that question just as it would decide any other question that the parties did not submit to arbitration, namely independently.'[262] When reviewing an award under these circumstances, courts will thus submit jurisdictional decisions by an arbitrator to de novo review if the claim would have been susceptible to initial determination by a court.[263]

## 5.3. PRESUMPTION OF AGREEMENT TO ARBITRATE

When a party seeks an order compelling arbitration under the FAA, the question of whether or not an agreement to arbitrate exists is ordinarily an issue for a civil jury.[264] However, section 4 of the FAA Chapter 1 allows the parties to waive the right to a civil jury and submit the question to a judge instead.[265] The FAA also establishes a 'presumption in favour of arbitrability' well-known in US jurisprudence.[266] This presumption also mandates that any doubts concerning the scope of the agreement to arbitrate be resolved in favour of arbitrating all issues.[267]

The FAA and most state laws only cover written agreements to arbitrate. Both the Panama and New York conventions apply only to a written and signed agreement between the parties. Consequently, courts will not apply the strong

259 See, e.g., *Howsam v. Dean Whitter Reynolds, Inc.*, 537 U.S. 79, 86 (2002); *First Options*, 514 U.S. at 945; *Virginia Carolina Tools, Inc. v. Int'l Tool Supply, Inc.*, 984 F.2d 113, 117 (4th Cir. 1993).

260 *First Options*, 514 U.S. at 943.

261 G. Born, *supra* n. 22, p. 917.

262 *First Options*, 514 U.S. at 943.

263 *Ibid.* at 943.

264 J. Coe, *supra* n. 95, p. 106. 9 U.S.C. §4.

265 9 U.S.C. §4.

266 *AT&T Techs., Inc. v. Commc'ns Workers of Am.*, 475 U.S. 643, 650 (1986). There is a strong 'presumption of arbitrability' when the parties have drafted a broad arbitration clause. This presumption may only be rebutted if 'it may be said with positive assurance that the arbitration clause is not susceptible of an interpretation that covers the asserted dispute'. (internal citations omitted). See also *Republic of Nicaragua v. Standard Fruit Company*, 937 F.2d 469, 478 (9th Cir. 1991) ('the most minimal indication of the parties' intent to arbitrate must be given full effect, especially in international disputes').

267 J. Paulsson, *supra* n. 104, p. 29.

presumption of arbitrability articulated in these laws without a written arbitration agreement. However, many forms of writing will qualify as an agreement to arbitrate if the parties have acted on the document.[268]

The FAA does not restrict the capacity of government entities to enter agreements to arbitrate. Government agencies are statutorily authorised to resolve disputes related to administrative programs through arbitrations.[269] To render arbitration agreements with governmental entities effective, the Foreign Sovereign Immunities Act revokes state immunity in actions seeking the enforcement of an agreement to arbitrate or an arbitral award when the arbitration takes place in the United States or is governed by the New York or Panama conventions.

## 5.4. COMPELLING ARBITRATION

If a court finds there is a valid agreement to arbitrate, it should decline to hear the merits of the controversy and refer the parties to arbitration. A federal district court may only compel the parties to attend domestic arbitrations (those covered by Chapter 1 of the FAA) within its own judicial district.[270] If the arbitration is to occur in a country that has signed the New York Convention or the Panama Convention, any district court may compel arbitration if basic requirements of jurisdiction and venue to support such a declaration are met.[271]

## 5.5. CONSOLIDATION OF ARBITRATIONS

The consolidation of related arbitrations is a matter of party agreement.[272] Although a plurality opinion in the *Bazzle* case suggested that the susceptibility of the arbitration agreement to class arbitration was a question for the arbitrators, rather than a national court, to decide, the Supreme Court subsequently said in the case of *Stolt-Nielsen, S.A. v. AnimalFeeds International Corp.*[273] that the issue remained open. The Supreme Court's decision in *Stolt-Nielsen* does, however,

---

268 See *Stedor Enters., Ltd. v. Armtex, Inc.*, 947 F.2d 727, 733 (4th Cir. 1991); *Pervel Indus., Inc. v. TM Wallcovering, Inc.*, 871 F.2d 7, 8 (2d Cir. 1989).

269 Administrative Dispute Resolution Act, 5 U.S.C. §576.

270 9 U.S.C. §4.

271 9 U.S.C. §§206, 303. *Intergen N.V. v. Grina*, 344 F.3d 134, 142 (1st Cir. 2003).

272 *Green Tree Fin. Corp v. Bazzle*, 539 US 444 (2003) (plurality decision); *Stolt-Nielsen S.A. v. AnimalFeeds Int'l Corp.*, 548 F.3d 85, 100 (2d Cir. 2008) (the issue should be decided under the 'relevant substantive contract law').

273 *Bazzle*, 539 U.S. 444; *Stolt-Nielsen, S.A. v. AnimalFeeds Int'l*, 130 S. Ct. 1758, 1771–1772 (2010). Some circuit courts follow the plurality opinion in *Bazzle* to hold that the issue remains one for arbitrators. See, e.g., *Blue Cross Blue Shield of Mass., Inc. v. BCS Ins. Co.*, 671 F.3d 635, 640

make it much more difficult for a tribunal to reach the conclusion that claims can be brought by a class.[274] The Court found that it was improper for the arbitrators to have consolidated claims when the relevant arbitration agreements were 'silent' on the issue.[275] Under the FAA, party consent is central, and parties must be allowed to 'specify with whom they choose to arbitrate disputes'.[276] Consent to arbitrate a dispute is not enough to infer consent to class arbitration. According to the Supreme Court in the subsequent *AT&T Mobility* case, the two procedures are so different that a party could not be assumed to consent to the latter merely by acquiescing in the former.[277] Nor may courts consolidate disputes when the parties have not consented.[278] Public policy concerns may play no role in the court's decision to consolidate.[279]

American concerns about class arbitration echo worries about class action litigation more generally. In *Stolt-Nielsen*, the Court noted that class action arbitrations would bind absent parties, sacrifice confidentiality and privilege between the members of a class, and greatly increase the stakes for defendants.[280] State laws do not appear to share this hostility, however. The RUAA and other state statutes authorise consolidation between the same parties when there are multiple proceedings or agreements to arbitrate between them.[281]

## 5.6. APPOINTMENT OF ARBITRATORS

Parties are free to appoint arbitrators by mutual agreement as they see fit. US courts will only become involved in the process if the parties so provide, are unable to agree on a choice, or have made a selection that would in some way taint the final award.[282]

Due to the influence of the AAA, many US arbitrations are conducted by a single arbitrator, selected by mutual agreement or – failing that – by the AAA

(7th Cir. 2011); *Fantastic Sams Franchise Corporation, v. FSRO Association Ltd., et al.*, 683 F.3d 18 (1st Cir. 2012); *In Vilches v. Travelers Co.*, 413 Fed. Appx. 487 (3d Cir. Feb. 9, 2011);.

274 *Stolt-Nielsen*, 130 S. Ct. at 1775 ('[A] party may not be compelled under the FAA to submit to class arbitration unless there is a contractual basis for concluding that the party agreed to do so').

275 *Ibid.* at 1775.

276 *Ibid.* at 1773–1774.

277 *AT&T Mobility LLC v. Concepcion*, 131 S. Ct. 1740, 1749–1750 (2011).

278 *Gov't of United Kingdom v. Boeing Co.*, 998 F.2d 68, 71 and n. 1 (2d Cir. 1993). See also *BP Exploration Libya Ltd. v. ExxonMobil Libya Ltd.*, 11–20547, 2012 WL 3065317 (5th Cir. 30 July 2012).

279 *AT&T Mobility*, 131 S. Ct. at 1750.

280 *Ibid.* at 1776.

281 2000 UAA §10; T. Stipanowich, 'The Third Arbitration Trilogy: Stolt-Nielsen, Rent-A-Center, Concepcion and the Future of American Arbitration' (2011) 22 *Am. Rev. Int'l Arb.* 323.

282 See, e.g., 9 U.S.C. §303.

itself.[283] While domestic US law traditionally allowed parties to have a biased arbitrator or a tripartite panel with two of the three arbitrators acting as quasi-advocates for one of the parties,[284] this arrangement has fallen out of favour, with the disfavour spreading from the international to the domestic cases. The AAA and the ABA both discourage the use of non-neutral arbitrators.[285]

Under the FAA, a court may designate an arbitrator if the parties do not provide for a method of selecting them, if the parties do not succeed in appointing an arbitrator by the agreed-upon method, or if 'for any other reason there shall be a lapse in the naming of an arbitrator'.[286] The FAA calls for one arbitrator as a default rule.[287] In reality, it is unlikely that the parties will have failed to specify a procedure for appointing arbitrators, as most institutions provide a default procedure for appointments.[288] A court may also order the parties to appoint an arbitrator in accordance with the contract's stipulations.[289]

Once the arbitrators have assumed their positions, US courts will generally not hear challenges to the appointments until a final award is made.[290] A court may set aside an award if an arbitrator fails to disclose facts that would tend to suggest that the arbitrator was biased or had a conflict of interest.[291] However, the failure to disclose on its own may not be enough to vacate an award when no actual bias is shown.[292] The FAA does not describe with exactitude what constitutes impermissible bias on the part of an arbitrator, but case law and non-

283 J. Deye and L. Britton, *supra* n. 127, p. 281.

284 *Westinghouse Elec. Corp. v. NYC Transit Auth.*, 14 F.3d 818, 821 (2d Cir. 1994) (an employer of one of the parties could act as arbitrator so long as his decision was not 'arbitrary, capricious or grossly erroneous to evidence bad faith'); *Fidelity Fed. Bank, FSB v. Durga Ma Corp.*, 386 F.3d 1306, 1313 (9th Cir. 2004) (holding that although the arbitrators were expected to 'act neutrally', the respondent should have expected that the arbitrator named by the claimant would have some affinity for the party that appointed him); *Sphere Drake Ins. Ltd. v. All American Life Ins. Co.*, 307 F.3d 617, 620 (7th Cir. 2002) ('in the main party-appointed arbitrators are supposed to be advocates'). See also G. Born, *supra* n. 22, p. 47.

285 2004 Code of Ethics for Arbitrators in Commercial Disputes (establishing 'a presumption of neutrality for all arbitrators, including party-appointed arbitrators, which applies unless the parties' agreement, the arbitration rules agreed to by the parties or applicable laws provide otherwise'). See also AAA Commercial Arbitration Rules and International Rules.

286 9 U.S.C. §5.

287 *Ibid.*

288 See, e.g., AAA, International Rules, Article 6; UNCITRAL Rules, Articles 6–8; IACAC Rules, Article 5; CPR Int'l Rules 6.1.

289 J. Paulsson, *supra* n. 104, p. 33.

290 See, e.g., *Gulf Guar. Life ins. Co. v. Conn. Gen. Life Ins. Co*, 304 F.3d 476 (5th Cir. 2002); *Availl, Inc. v. Ryder Systems, Inc.*, 110 F.3d 892 (2d Cir. 1997).

291 200 UAA §§. 23, 12. 9 U.S.C. §10.

292 *Commonwealth Coatings Corp. v. Continental Cas. Co.*, 393 U.S. 145, 150 (1968) (courts should not 'authorize litigants to submit their cases and controversies to arbitration boards that might reasonably be thought biased against one litigant and favorable to another'); *ANR Coal v. Cogentrix of N. Caro., Inc.*, 172 F.3d 493, 500 (4th Cir. 1999) (setting out factors to consider when reviewing an arbitrator's failure to disclose a potential conflict of interest).

binding guidelines suggest that an arbitrator should disclose all potential conflicts of interest, erring on the side of disclosure.[293]

## 5.7. PARTY AUTONOMY AND ARBITRATOR DISCRETION

US courts are overwhelmingly supportive of party autonomy. The Supreme Court's 1985 decision in *Mitsubishi Motors v. Soler Chrysler-Plymouth* permitted the parties to arbitrate antitrust claims in front of a Japanese tribunal applying Swiss law as the governing law. The holding that the choice of Swiss law would not compromise the vindication of US antitrust policies has been interpreted to permit most party choices in arbitration.[294] In the years since then, the Supreme Court has ordered lower courts to enforce the parties' agreement to arbitrate and any conditions it imposes strictly.

The parties may choose the number of arbitrators and the method for selecting them, the location of the arbitration and the language, the governing law, and any special rules that they wish to apply. The broad freedom of contract in the US has translated into broad freedom in arbitration with the FAA's pro-arbitration policy, which equates agreements to arbitrate with any other type of contract. Parties may delegate to arbitrators the power to determine the scope of the arbitral agreement.[295]

Broad party autonomy translates into broad arbitrator autonomy. Few procedural tools available to courts have been denied to arbitrators; tribunals can act as freely as the parties permit them to. The parties may enable the tribunal to set the location of the arbitration and fill in any other procedural gaps in the parties' agreement.[296] US courts also view expansively the power of the arbitrator to craft relief: both equitable relief and punitive damages are available if the parties have not stated otherwise.[297] In *Mastrobuono v. Shearson Lehman Hutton*, the Supreme Court held that the decision to award punitive damages is squarely within the arbitrator's discretion unless the parties have clearly prohibited such

---

293 *ANR Coal v. Cogentrix of North Carolina, Inc.*, 172 F.3d 493, 500 (4th Cir. 1999); American Bar Association's Code of Ethics for Arbitrators in Commercial Disputes (arbitrators must disclose any 'financial or personal interest in the outcome of the arbitration, as well as business, professional, familiar, or social relationships with any party, counsel, or witness that might impugn their own impartiality').

294 J. Coe, *supra* n. 95, p. 101; see also J. Paulsson, *supra* n. 104, p. 31.

295 G. Bermann, *supra* n. 232, p. 39; *Stolt-Nielsen, S.A. v. AnimalFeeds Int'l*, 130 S. Ct. 1758 (2010); see, e.g., *Mercury Telco Grp., Inc. v. Empresa De Telecommunicaciones De Bogota*, 670 F. Supp. 2d 1350 (S.D. Fla. 2009); *Morsey Constructors, LLC v. Burns & Roe Enter., Inc.*, 2008 WL 3833588, at *4 (W.D. Ky. 13 August 2008).

296 *Aerojet-General Corp. v. Am. Arbitration Ass'n*, 478 F.2d 248, 251 (9th Cir. 1973).

297 *Willoughby Roofing & Supply Co., Inc. v. Kajima Intl, Inc.*, 598 F. Supp. 353, 362 (N.D. Ala. 1984) *aff'd*, 776 F.2d 269 (11th Cir. 1985) ('To deny arbitrators the full range of remedial tools generally available under the law would be to hamstring arbitrators and to lessen the value and efficiency of arbitration as an alternative method of dispute resolution.').

relief.[298] The eight justices of the majority held that such relief was permitted by the FAA and that state law precluding it would be pre-empted.[299]

At their discretion, arbitrators can award injunctive and interim relief.[300] The AAA's International Rules confirm this power, permitting the arbitrators to make any conceivable type of award.[301] These awards are presumptively enforceable in US courts.[302]

## 5.8. ARBITRAL ACTION IN AID OF ARBITRATION

Arbitrators do not have unlimited power, however. They do not have the inherent authority to sanction parties as a judge does; though they may of course draw adverse inferences and allocate costs in such a way as to reflect disapproval of attorney conduct. They also lack the power to issue binding subpoenas to third-party witnesses, and they cannot enforce their own awards.[303] Consequently, tribunals must rely on national courts to give their decisions effect. Under the FAA, arbitrators 'may summon in writing any person to attend before them or any of them as a witness and in a proper case to bring with him or them any book, record, document, or paper which may be deemed material as evidence in the case.'[304] Courts may enforce these orders in aid of arbitration.

A party, having consented to the tribunal's jurisdiction, cannot challenge the discovery orders or evidentiary rulings of the arbitrators before a US court.[305] A non-party who refuses to comply with a subpoena or production order is likely to find himself before a national judge. If the court agrees that the evidence demanded by the arbitrator is relevant, it will order the non-party to comply under the threat of contempt of court.[306]

The enforceability of arbitral discovery orders may be even greater, as indicated by the Supreme Court in its 2004 *Intel* decision.[307] The Eleventh Circuit

---

298 *Mastrobuono v. Shearson Lehman Hutton*, 115 S. Ct. 1212 (1995).

299 *Ibid.*

300 See *Gilmer v. Interstate/Johnson Lane*, 500 U.S. 20, 32 (1991).

301 AAA Int'l Rules, Article 27.7; CPR Int'l Rule 14.1.

302 See *infra* section 5.10.

303 Compare *In re Security Life Ins. Co.*, 228 F.3d 865, 870–71 (8th Cir. 2000) (allowing pre-hearing discovery) with *Hay Group, Inc. v. E.B.S. Acquisition Corp.*, 360 F.3d 404, 408–409 (3d Cir. 2004) (denying pre-hearing discovery). See *Hay Group, Inc. v. E.B.S. Acquisition Corp.*, 360 F.3d 404, 406 (3d Cir. 2004) (describing the limits of an arbitrator's subpoena authority); *Life Receivables Trust v. Syndicate 102 at Lloyd's of London*, 549 F.3d 210 (2d Cir. 2008); cf. Fed. R. Civ. Pro. 11.

304 9 U.S.C. §7.

305 *Stanton v. Paine Webber Jackson & Curtis*, 685 F. Supp 1241, 1242–1243 (S.D. Fla. 1988); *Thompson v. Zavin*, 607 F. Supp. 780, 783 (C.D. Cal. 1984).

306 *Burton v. Bush*, 614 F.2d 389, 390 (4th Cir. 1980).

307 *Intel Corp. v. Adv. Micro Devices, Inc.*, 124 S. Ct. 2466, 2479 (2004) (in dicta, including 'arbitral tribunals' in the definition of 'international tribunals' whose discovery rulings a district court could enforce).

Court of Appeals recently concluded that a foreign arbitral tribunal qualifies as an 'international tribunal' for the purposes of a statute which permits a district court to order a party to 'give his testimony or statement or to produce a document or other thing for use in a proceeding in a foreign or international tribunal.'[308]

## 5.9. INTERLOCUTORY REVIEW

Interlocutory review of arbitral proceedings is extremely limited in the US.[309] Under the FAA, 'a district court does not have the power to review an interlocutory ruling by an arbitration panel'.[310]

There are some exceptions to this oft-stated rule, however. A district court may review an interim ruling if the tribunal's award 'finally and definitely disposes of a separate independent claim'.[311] If the arbitrators have relinquished their authority on the issue or,[312] alternatively, if the award 'either disposes of a separate claim in an arbitration or has actual effects on the property or rights of the parties', the ruling is sufficiently final to merit review.[313]

Severable issues subject to interlocutory review must be 'self-contained' as well as 'non-dependent'.[314] Under this analysis, courts have reviewed awards of past damages, which were severable from the yet unresolved question of future damages;[315] and establishment of security, severable from a final award.[316] In

308 28 U.S.C. §1782; *Consorcio Ecuatoriano de Telecomunicaciones S.A. v. JAS Forwarding (USA), Inc.*, 685 F.3d 987 (11th Cir. 2012). But see *NBC v. Bear Stearns & Co., Inc.*, 165 F.3d 184, 188 (2d Cir. 1999) and *Republic of Kazakhstan v. Biedermann Int'l*, 168 F.3d 880 (5th Cir. 1999). See also A. Conley, 'A New World of Discovery: the Ramifications of Two Recent Federal Courts' Decisions Granting Judicial Assistance to Arbitral Tribunals Pursuant to 28 U.S.C. §1782' (2006) 17 *Am. Rev. Int'l. Arb.* 45, 46–47.

309 See generally A. Rau, 'Provisional Relief in Arbitration: How Things Stand in the United States' (2005) 22(1) *J. Int'l Arb.* 1.

310 *Michaels v. Mariforum Shipping, S.A.*, 624 F.2d 411, 414 (2d Cir. 1980).

311 *Metallgesellschaft A.G. v. M/V Capitan Constante*, 790 F.2d 280, 283 (2d Cir. 1986); see also *Zephyros Maritime Agencies, Inc. v. Mexicana De Cobre, S.A.*, 662 F. Supp 892, 894 (S.D.N.Y. 1987).

312 J. Gaitis, The Federal Arbitration Act: Risks and Incongruities Relating to the Issuance of Interim and Partial Awards in Domestic and International Arbitrations' (2005) 16 *Am. Rev. Int'l Arb.* 1, 43; *Trade & Transport, Inc. v. Nat. Petro. Charterers, Inc.*, 931 F.2d 191, 193 (2d. Cir. 1991).

313 J. Carter and J. Fellas, *International Commercial Arbitration in New York*, Oxford University Press, Oxford 2010, p. 256.

314 *Ibid.*; *Moyer v. Van-Dye-Way Corp.*, 126 F.2d 339, 341 (3d Cir. 1942). See also *Yasuda Fire & Marine Ins. Co. of Europe v. Cont. Cas. Co.*, 37 F.3d 345 (7th Cir. 1994) and *Pacific Reins. Mgmt. Corp. v. Ohio Reins. Corp.*, 935 F.2d 1019, 1022–23 (9th Cir. 1991).

315 *Island Territory of Curacao v. Solitron Devices, Inc.*, 356 F.Supp. 1 (S.D.N.Y.), *aff'd*, 489 F.2d 1313 (2d Cir. 1973), *cert. denied*, 416 U.S. 986 (1974).

316 See, e.g., *Atlas Assurance Co. of Am. v. American Centennial Ins. Co.*, No. 90 Civ. 5474 (SWK), 1991 WL 4741, at *2–3 (S.D.N.Y. 16 January 1991) (confirming an interim award which directed the respondent to establish an escrow account for the benefit of fulfilling a final award against it); *Konkar Maritime Enterprises v. Compagnie Belge D'Affretement*, 668

other cases, the pressing need for an immediate ruling on a part of a matter may result in an interim award that is clearly severable from the remainder of the claims.[317] On the other hand, evidentiary rulings are considered to be intertwined with the merits of the case and therefore they are not reviewable until a final award is issued.[318] Similarly, arbitral decisions that can be characterised as mere procedural orders – such as the fixing of the place of arbitration or the determination of which institutional rules to apply – are not immediately reviewable,[319] and probably not subject to serious judicial review even in a post-award challenge.

Although a court will not review most decisions before an award is made, it is not barred from taking other measures to protect a final judgment, for 'an arbitration clause does not deprive [the party] of the usual provisional remedies'.[320] A preliminary injunction might be issued to protect a party or preserve the funds to fulfil a potential judgment by a tribunal,[321] or otherwise preserve the status quo. Out of respect for arbitral jurisdiction, however, most courts will decline to rule on an application for an interim measure that could have been submitted to an arbitrator.[322]

## 5.10. ENFORCEMENT AND RECOGNITION

US courts act as the final gatekeeper in the arbitral process by exercising authority to vacate or enforce an award. Under no circumstance will a judge revisit the merits of the claims in the course of reviewing an award.[323] American law adheres closely to the contract theory of arbitration, acknowledging that the

---

F. Supp. 267, 272 (S.D.N.Y. 1987) (confirming an interim award ordering the parties to establish a joint escrow account to provide security for the final judgment); *Sperry Int'l Trade v. Government of Israel*, 532 F. Supp. 901, 909 (S.D.N.Y.1982), *aff'd*, 689 F.2d 301 (2d Cir. 1982) (confirming an interim award directing the respondent to place a letter of credit in escrow pending the final award).

317 *Publicis Commun. v. True North Communs. Inc.*, 206 F.3d 725, 729 (7th Cir. 2000) ('A ruling on a discrete, time-sensitive issue may be final and ripe for confirmation even though other claims remain to be addressed by arbitrators').

318 *Aerojet Gen. Corp. v. Amer. Arb. Ass'n*, 478 F.2d 248 (9th Cir. 1973). See *Compania Panemena Maritima v. J. E. Hurley Lumber Co.*, 244 F.2d 286 (2d Cir. 1957).

319 *Aerojet Gen. Corp.* 478 F.2d 248.

320 *Murray Oil Prods. Co. v. Mitsui & Co.*, 146 F.2d 381, 384 (2d Cir. 1944).

321 *Roso-Lino Beverage Distrib. Inc. v. Coca-Cola Bottling Co.*, 749 F.2d 124, 125 (2d Cir. 1984); *Ortho Pharma. Corp. v. Amgen, Inc.*, 882 F.2d 806, 812 (3d Cir. 1989). But see *Merrill Lynch, Pierce, Fenner & Smith, Inc. v. Hovey*, 726 F.2d 1286, 1292 (8th Cir. 1984) ('where the Arbitration Act is applicable and no qualifying contractual language has been alleged, the district court errs in granting injunctive relief').

322 J. Paulsson, *supra* n. 104, p. 44.

323 *United Steelworkers of Am. v. Enter. Wheel & Car Corp.*, 363 U.S. 593, 596 (1960) ('The federal policy of settling labor disputes by arbitration would be undermined if courts had the final say on the merits of the awards').

parties are free to make their own mistakes and actively relinquish their rights to full appellate review by opting for arbitration.[324]

Enforcement and confirmation is one of the few issues on which international and domestic awards are treated differently. This result is not dictated by policy but by statutory language and structure. Domestic awards, subject to Chapter 1 of the FAA, may be vacated only under a limited list of conditions found in section 10 of that text. Awards subject to the New York or Panama conventions fall under the standards for enforcement given in those texts. ICSID awards, under the guidelines of the Washington Convention, are completely immune from review.

### *5.10.1. Domestic awards*

A domestic award is subject to vacatur within one year of its issuance.[325] The action will usually come before a state court unless there is an independent basis for federal court jurisdiction.[326] Under the FAA, a court may vacate an award in any of the following circumstances:

(a) the award was procured by corruption, fraud, or undue means;
(b) there was evident partiality or corruption in any of the arbitrators;
(c) the arbitrators committed misconduct or misused their discretion in a way that prejudiced the rights of a party; or
(d) the arbitrators exceeded their powers, or imperfectly executed them such that a mutual, final, and definite award was not made on the matters submitted.[327]

These four grounds cover a range of procedural shortcomings but have been construed narrowly by courts.[328] The party seeking to vacate the award has the burden of proving the existence of one of the four grounds for vacatur. If the party meets this burden, the court may set aside the award entirely. The FAA also permits the court to modify or correct an award in limited circumstances, or to remand it to the arbitrator for reconsideration if the time limit for making an award has not yet passed.[329]

---

324 *See IDS Life Ins. Co. v. Royal Assocs.*, 266 F.3d 645, 646 (7th Cir. 2001) ('the grounds for challenging an arbitration award are narrowly limited, reflecting the voluntary contractual nature of commercial arbitration'); *Burton v. Bush*, 614 F.2d 389, 390 (4th Cir. 1980) (in agreeing to arbitrate, parties 'relinquish the right to certain procedural niceties which are normally associated with a formal trial').

325 9 U.S.C. §9.

326 *Moses H Cone*, 460 U.S. at 25 n. 32.

327 9 U.S.C. §10(a).

328 See *Hall Street Assocs. v. Mattel, Inc.*, 552 U.S. 576, 582, 584 (2008).

329 9 U.S.C. §§10(b), 11.

An additional ground not contained in the FAA is 'manifest disregard of the law'.[330] The standard was suggested by the Supreme Court and has been adopted by a number of circuits.[331] Awards are rarely vacated on this basis, as it requires more than a court's disagreement over the legal interpretation espoused by the arbitrator; the award must show 'that the arbitrator appreciates the existence of a clearly governing legal principle but decides to ignore or pay no attention to it', adding that the legal principle 'must be well defined, explicit, and clearly applicable'.[332] Recent Supreme Court rulings have called into question, but not decided, whether manifest disregard remains a proper vacatur ground.

If none of the preceding conditions is found to exist, the court must confirm the award and 'enter judgment' upon it. This process gives the award the same precedential force as a judgment of that court. To confirm an award, a party must file an application, including copies of the arbitration agreement, the tribunal's written award, and any court order modifying or correcting the arbitrator's judgment.[333]

A thoroughly-reasoned award is naturally more susceptible to negative review by a court than an award that states no reasons.[334] For many arbitrators, this operates as an incentive against extensive published analysis in their decisions.[335] It is not a prerequisite to a valid award that the tribunal heard and considered oral evidence.[336] Some consideration is required, though: an arbitrator may not make an award against a party solely on the basis of the party's default under the AAA Commercial Rules.[337] The UAA and the RUAA direct that the arbitrator should evaluate the claims on the basis of all available evidence even if a party fails to appear in the arbitration.[338]

---

330 See, e.g., *Duferco Int'l Steel Trading v. T. Klaveness Shipping AlS*, 333 F.3d 383, 389–390 (2d Cir. 2003); see also *George Watts & Son, Inc. v. Tiffany & Co.*, 248 F.3d 577,580 (7th Cir. 2001) ('an arbitrator may not direct the parties to violate the law').

331 *First Options of Chicago, Inc. v. Kaplan*, 514 U.S. 938, 942 (1995) (saying that an earlier Supreme Court case found the parties were 'bound by arbitrator's decision not in "manifest disregard" of the law'); *Williams v. CIGNA Fin. Advisors Inc.*, 197 F.3d 752, 759 (5th Cir. 1999), *cert. denied* 529 U.S. 1099 (2000); *M & C Corp v. Erwin Behr GmbH & Co.*, 87 F.3d 844, 850–851 (6th Cir. 1996); *Manion v. Nagin*, 392 F.3d 294, 298 (8th Cir. 2004); *Montes v. Shearson Lehman Brothers, Inc.*, 128 F.3d 1456, 1459 (11th Cir. 1997); *Cole v. Burns Int'l Security Servs.*, 105 F.3d 1465, 1486 (D.C. Cir. 1997).

332 *Merrill Lynch, Pierce, Fenner & Smith, Inc. v. Bobker*, 808 F.2d 930, 933–934 (2d Cir. 1986).

333 9 U.S.C. §13.

334 See *Reichman v. Creative Real Estate Consultants*, 476 F. Supp. 1276, 1282 (D.C.N.Y. 1979) ('the task of a reviewing court, especially one confronted by a claim of manifest disregard of the law, is made more difficult in the cases where no reasons are given by the arbitrator').

335 H. Marx, 'Who Are Labor Arbitration Opinions Written For? And Other Musings About Award Writing' (2003) 58 *Disp. Resol. J.* 22, 23 ('the less said the better').

336 *Intercarbon Bermuda, Ltd. v. Callex Trading & Transport Corp.*, 146 F.R.D. 64, 72–74 (S.D.N.Y 1993).

337 AAA Commercial Rules, Article 29.

338 1955 UAA §5; 2000 UAA §15(c).

### 5.10.2. Convention awards

A chief difference between review of domestic and foreign awards is that US courts have no authority to vacate an award made outside of the US.[339] A court may only decline to recognise or enforce a judgment it finds to be defective.

Within three years of the making of the award, a party may apply to a federal court to enforce the award. The New York and Panama conventions, as implemented through the FAA, provide federal court jurisdiction over enforcement actions.[340] The court must enforce the judgment unless one of the following conditions is met:

(a) the arbitration agreement is invalid or does not exist;[341]
(b) a party was not provided with proper notice of the proceedings or was otherwise denied an opportunity to present its case;[342]
(c) the arbitrators ruled on matters not submitted to arbitration;[343]
(d) the composition of the tribunal or the procedures applied by that body violate the parties' agreement or the law of the arbitral seat;[344]
(e) the award has been set aside by the law under which it was made, or the award is currently the subject of such proceedings;[345]
(f) the award addressed matters that are non-arbitrable under domestic law;[346] or
(g) enforcement of the award would be contrary to the public policy of the United States.[347]

These criteria are applied exceptionally narrowly.[348] They are also exclusive.

### 5.10.3. ICSID awards

The Washington Convention does not permit US courts to second-guess ICSID awards. Final rulings covered by that convention are automatically enforceable in national courts.

---

339 *Gulf Petro Trading Co. v. Nigerian Nat'l Petroleum Corp.*, 512 F.3d 742, 747 (5th Cir. 2008) ('a United States court [...] lacks subject matter jurisdiction over claims seeking to vacate, set aside, or modify a foreign arbitral award'); *M&C Corp. v. Erwin Behr GmbH & Co.*, 87 F.3d 844, 848 (6th Cir. 1996).

340 9 U.S.C. §§201, 203, 205.

341 Article V(1)(a).

342 Article V(1)(b).

343 Article V(1)(c).

344 Article V(1)(d).

345 Article V(1)(e).

346 Article V(2)(a).

347 Article V(2)(b).

348 *Yusuf Ahmed Alghanim & Sons, W.L.L v. Toys R Us*, 126 F.3d 15, 23 (2d Cir. 1997), *cert. denied*, 522 U.S. 1111 (1998) *Bergesen v. Joseph Muller Corp.*, 710 F.2d 928, 933 (2d Cir. 1983); *Parsons & Whittemore Overseas Co. v. Societe Generale de L'Industrie du Papier (RAKTA)*, 508 F.2d 969, 974 (2d Cir. 1974).

# 6. FUTURE DEVELOPMENT PERSPECTIVES

Due to a common law system of adjudication and a strong public interest in arbitration, the laws described in this chapter are subject to constant change. The following topics in particular are popular targets of political debate and academic criticism.

## 6.1. INCREASED OR DIMINISHED REVIEW OF ARBITRAL AWARDS

The limited availability of appeal from awards is a hallmark benefit of arbitration. Nonetheless, parties have displayed increasing interest in the power to increase or decrease the permissible scope of judicial review of arbitral awards, either to safeguard against errors in arbitration or to further expedite the final resolution of a dispute.[349]

The most direct approach is for the parties to stipulate in their arbitration agreement that the award will be subject to vacatur on grounds other than those described in the FAA. This approach is now almost universally disfavoured following the Supreme Court's decision in *Hall Street Associates v. Mattel* in 2008.[350] In that case, the Supreme Court held that the parties may not expand the ground for vacating an award by contract. *Hall Street* dealt only with vacatur under Chapter 1 of the FAA, but there is no reason to suspect that the precedent would not apply equally to refusal to enforce awards on Convention grounds.

To evade the holding of *Hall Street*, some parties have sought to achieve the same ends by instead circumscribing the arbitrator's powers in their agreement. For example, the agreement to arbitrate might require that the judge 'strictly apply' the correct law, effectively requiring the reviewing court to re-examine the tribunal's findings of law to ensure that it complied with the parties' agreement. Courts have shown mixed reactions to this practice.[351]

Parties have also sought to limit review of awards by the same means. As is frequently the case in arbitration, parties may only do this explicitly: it is not enough to contract for an award that will be 'final and binding'.[352] Some courts

349 T. Stipanowich, *supra* n. 193, p. 7.

350 *Hall Street Associates v. Mattel, Inc.*, 552 U.S. 576 (2008).

351 See *Edstrom Indus., Inc. v. Companion Life Ins. Co.*, 516 F.3d 546, 550–553 (7th Cir. 2008) (because the parties' contract required the arbitrator to strictly apply state law, the court vacated the tribunal's apparently incorrect interpretation of the state's law). But see *Wood v. Penntex Res. LP.*, 2008 U.S. Dist. LEXIS 50071 (S.D. Tex. June 27, 2008) (rejecting a similar argument).

352 See *M&C Corp. v. Erwin Behr GmbH*, 87 F.3d 844, 847 (6th Cir. 1996) (rejecting argument that ICC Arbitration Rules, which provided for waiver of appeal of an award, barred review of grounds for denying enforcement under the New York Convention); *Iran Aircraft Indus. v. Avco Corp.*, 980 F.2d 141, 145 (2d Cir. 1992) (the Iran-U.S. Claims Tribunal agreement

have permitted this practice when the intention to limit judicial review was clearly expressed, apparently more willing to view the FAA as a floor than as a ceiling.[353] Other courts and commentators would prohibit this practice, particularly for non-Convention awards, as it conflicts with the policy of achieving uniform review of arbitral awards.[354]

The parties might then seek to avoid the application of the FAA by selecting to arbitrate under the arbitration laws of a state or a foreign jurisdiction. This option was left open by the Court's opinion in *Hall Street*, which said, 'we do not purport to say that [Section 10 and Section 11 of the FAA] exclude more searching review based on authority outside the statute as well. The FAA is not the only way into court for parties wanting review of arbitration awards: they may contemplate enforcement under state statutory or common law, for example, where judicial review of different scope is arguable.'[355] The California Supreme Court has relied on this language to permit parties to select a different standard of review through selection of the California Arbitration Act.[356] State law is a limited source of recourse, however, since state law that provides a stricter standard of review than federal law is pre-empted by the FAA.

Finally, parties remain free to waive any objections that they might raise as a defence to the enforcement of an award. Because waiver does not change the applicable law, it does not offend the policies of the FAA. Nonetheless, party waiver does not preclude the possibility of a court raising certain objections sua sponte.

The matter remains controversial because it is unclear how far the recent *Hall Street* decision extends. If, as some assert, the FAA establishes vacatur and enforcement standards that state law may not override, party autonomy will be greatly reduced in this area. If *Hall Street* is read in a more limited manner, parties will have the opportunity to modify the traditional ground rules by resort to state law.

---

provision stating that awards are 'final and binding' does not displace the grounds for denying enforcement provided for in the New York Convention).

353 *Bowen v. Amoco Pipeline Co.*, 254 F.3d 925, 931 (10th Cir. 2001) (suggesting that 'parties to an arbitration agreement may eliminate judicial review by contract' containing clear and unequivocal language).

354 See *Lustfield v. Milne*, 5 Pa. D. & C.5th 469, 478 (Pa. Ct. Com. Pl. 2008) (interpreting *Hall Street* as abrogating earlier cases that had permitted parties to reduce the grounds for review). The current draft of Section 4 of the Restatement (Third) of International Arbitration also takes this position.

355 *Hall Street Assocs. v. Mattel, Inc.*, 552 U.S. 576, 582, 590 (2008).

356 *Cable Connection, Inc. v. DirectTV, Inc.*, 190 P.3d 586, 589 (Cal. 2008). See also *Roadway Package Sys., Inc. v. Kayser*, 257 F.3d 287 (3d Cir. 2001) (suggesting that the parties might have successfully contracted for a reduced standard of review by selecting to have their arbitration under Pennsylvania law).

## 6.2. CLASS ARBITRATION

The class action is a popular tool in American litigation. Extensive legislation, rule-making and judicial precedent have been devoted to ensuring that the process is efficient and fair.[357] Although multi-party arbitration remains rare, American litigants have pressed to make class arbitration a reasonable possibility, particularly in the consumer context.[358] The Supreme Court has resisted these efforts, but has not rejected the availability of class arbitration altogether.[359]

Although contracting parties need not agree in advance to the possibility of class action litigation, the Supreme Court held in *Stolt-Nielsen* that parties to an arbitration agreement must separately and explicitly consent to the availability of class arbitration.[360] The Court did not specify the language or conduct that would suffice to evince such an agreement.[361] Consequently, lower courts have debated whether anything less than explicit language is sufficient.[362]

The Supreme Court's decision in *Bazzle* made the existence of an agreement to submit to class arbitration a question for the arbitrator to decide.[363] The AAA's Supplementary Rules for Class Arbitrations followed up with guidance on this determination, first requiring the arbitrator to make a 'reasoned, partial final award' regarding the permissibility of class arbitration under the arbitration clause. The AAA's procedures resemble the American federal court procedures for class certification and notification.[364] The AAA has administered over 250 class arbitrations to date.[365]

The rise of class arbitrations has naturally provoked an interest in ensuring the fairness of the process. In a recent study, the AAA found that 36.5% of consumer arbitrations involved a class action waiver in the arbitration agreement.[366] The Supreme Court dealt a blow to state regulation of class

---

357 See, e.g., Fed. R. Civ. Pro. 23; *Wal-Mart v. Dukes*, 131 S. Ct. 2541 (2011); Class Action Fairness Act of 2005, 28 U.S.C. §§1332(d), 1453, and 1711–1715.

358 See generally, *AT&T Mobility LLC v. Concepcion*, 131 S. Ct. 1740 (2011).

359 See, e.g., *Bazzle v. Green Tree Fin. Corp.*, 569 S.E.2d 349 (2002) (permitting an arbitration award based on a class action).

360 *Stolt-Nielsen, S.A. v. AnimalFeeds Int'l*, 130 S. Ct. 1758, 1775 (2010).

361 *Ibid.* at 1776 n. 10.

362 *Jock v. Sterling Jewelers Inc.*, 646 F. 3d 113 (2d Cir. 2011) ('The problem is that the Supreme Court failed to give any clear guidance on what must be shown in the way of implicit consent, instead explicitly (and inexplicably) stating that it had "no occasion to decide what contractual basis may support a finding that the parties agreed to authorize class-action arbitration"', quoting *Stolt-Nielsen*, 130 S. Ct. 1758).

363 *See supra*, section 5.2.

364 AAA, Supplementary Rules, §§1–4.

365 W. Baker, Class Action Arbitration, (2009) 10 *Cardozo J. Confl. Resol. (Cardozo Journal of Conflict Resolution)* 335, 344.

366 C. Drazohal and S. Zyontz, 'Private Regulation of Consumer Arbitration' (2011) 79 *Tenn. L. Rev. (Tennessee Law Review)* 289.

arbitrations in *AT&T Mobility v. Conception*. The Court struck down a California law that invalidated waivers of class actions in agreements to arbitrate. The Supreme Court interpreted the statute to effectively require the availability of class arbitration.[367] Then holding that class arbitration was fundamentally different from two-party arbitration, the majority held that 'requiring the availability of class-wide arbitration interferes with fundamental attributes of arbitration and thus creates a scheme inconsistent with the FAA'.[368] The majority rejected the minority's view that the legislation did not offend federal policy because it treated litigation and arbitration alike.[369] But the majority appeared especially troubled by efficiency losses and the fairness interests of corporate defendants.[370]

The *AT&T* holding is on its face relatively narrow. As the Court noted, states remain 'free to define unconscionability as [they see] fit'.[371] But the majority's reaffirmation of the belief that class arbitration 'changes the nature of arbitration' is likely to impede further use of the class action mechanism.[372] For now, traditional contractual defences such as unconscionability remain avenues for preventing contractual waiver of class arbitration in contracts of adhesion.[373]

## 6.3. ARBITRATION FAIRNESS ACT

Hidden waiver provisions and other arguably unconscionable clauses have generated legislative concern. As noted,[374] Congress has proposed consumer protection legislation that would invalidate pre-dispute arbitration agreements in consumer, employment, or civil rights cases.[375]

This is not the first time that Congress has set its sights on arbitration. Versions of the AFA were introduced in 2007, and again in 2009, spurred by concerns about the increasing cost and complication of arbitration as well as concerns that it was unfair to consumers.[376] These bills raised concern both

---

367 *AT&T Mobility LLC v. Conception*, 1315 S. Ct. 1740, 1750 (2011).

368 *Ibid.* at 1748.

369 *Ibid.* at 1757 (Breyer J dissenting).

370 *Ibid.* at 1751–1752.

371 *Ibid.* at 1760.

372 *Stolt-Nielsen, S.A. v. AnimalFeeds Int'l*, 130 S. Ct. 1758, 1775 (2010).

373 See *Jock v. Sterling Jewelers, Inc.*, 646 F.3d 113, 125–127 (2d Cir. 2011); *In re American Express Merchants' Litigation*, No. 06-1871-cv, (2d Cir., Feb. 1, 2012).

374 *See supra*, section 2.3.

375 Arbitration Fairness Act (S. 1782/H.R. 3010) (2011).

376 See F. Massengale and K. Whitfield, 'Arbitration: Be Careful What You Wish For' (1996) 44 *La. B.J. (Louisiana Business Journal)* 120, 121; Federal Mediation and Conciliation Service, Arbitration Statistics Fiscal Year 2007 <www.fmcs.gov/internet/displayContent.asp?itemID=21224> accessed 04.09.2012 (just over a year to resolve the average dispute). Regarding fairness, see J, Public Citizen, 'The Arbitration Trap: How Credit Card Companies Ensnare Consumers' (2007) 43 <www.citizen.org/documents/ArbitrationTrap.pdf> accessed

domestically and abroad, with one French scholar saying that the 2007 text 'pose[d] a serious threat to the promotion of efficient international dispute resolution and of the United States as a friendly place to arbitrate'.[377]

Unlike earlier drafts of the AFA, the 2011 version would not prohibit pre-dispute agreements to arbitrate franchise disputes or any dispute between parties of unequal bargaining power, nor would it require that all gateway issues be resolved by a court, in violation of the *kompetenz-kompetenz* doctrine. Nevertheless, the draft legislation remains of concern to the international arbitration community.

Even without the AFA, arbitration reform can be and has been enacted by other means. An appropriations bill for the Department of Defence in 2010 banned pre-dispute agreements to arbitrate sexual harassment claims involving large defence contractors.[378] Securities and banking reform has included prohibitions on arbitrating the whistleblower claims it creates.[379] The Consumer Financial Protection Bureau, empowered by the Consumer Protection Act to regulate pre-dispute arbitration agreements involving consumer financial products and services, stands to take the lead in reform.[380] The Securities Exchange Commission has the same power for securities products and services.[381]

American judges, legislators, and scholars continue to debate the merits of regulating the practice of arbitration as well as the best ways to do so.[382] The outcomes that emerge in the next few years are likely to impact the future contours of arbitration in the United States.

---

07.09.2012. See generally D. Lindamood (2010) 45 *Wake Forest L. Rev.* 291. See HR 3010 (110th Congress) (2007); HR 1020 and S 931 (111th Congress) (2009). The 2007 AFA lacked specific language, instead employing vague terms such as 'any statute intended to protect civil rights'. It would also have prohibited any agreement giving arbitrators jurisdiction over gateway questions. The 2009 AFA improved by offering more specific language and eliminating the controversial gateway issue. Both earlier versions also prohibited pre-dispute agreements to arbitrate franchise claims.

377 E. Gaillard, 'International Arbitration Law' (22 April 2008) *N.Y.L.J (New York Law Journal)* 3.

378 Department of Defense Appropriations Act 2010, Pub. L. No. 111–118 §8116(a) 123 Stat. 3409, 3454 (2009).

379 Dodd-Frank Wall St. Reform Consumer Protection Act, 7 U.S.C. §26(n)(2).

380 12 U.S.C. §5518 (2011).

381 15 U.S.C. §78(o).

382 See generally B. Dillon-Coffman, 'Revising the Revision: Procedural Alternatives to the Arbitration Fairness Act' (2010) 57 *UCLA L. Rev. (University of California – Los Angeles Law Review)* 1095 (regarding the AFA in particular).

# UNITED STATES: MEDIATION

Shanin Specter and Jason L. Pearlman

'The courts of this country should not be the places where resolution of disputes begins. They should be the places where the disputes end after alternative methods of resolving disputes have been considered and tried.'
Supreme Court Justice Sandra Day O'Connor

**Contents**

## 1. INTRODUCTION TO MEDIATION IN THE UNITED STATES

Mediation is a procedure for resolving disputes. The procedure can take on many different forms and incorporate different philosophies, but in its purest sense, it is a process by which a neutral intervener assists two or more parties to a dispute in reaching a resolution. Three essential features of mediation are: first, the mediator has no stake or interest in the outcome of the dispute; second, the mediator has no authority to compel or dictate a binding resolution on the parties; and third, only the parties can reach an agreement as to the terms of a settlement.[1]

Mediation has been used as a tool for resolving many different kinds of conflicts from labour and collective bargaining disputes, disputes among neighbours and families such as divorce actions and custody claims, disputes with governmental agencies, and nearly all other types of disputes imaginable. Mediation can be used as an alternative to litigation as well as a device utilised by disputants and courts as supplementary to litigation.

As our laws and commerce have grown more complex, so too have mediation and other systems employed for resolving disputes. Through the years, mediation in the United States has matured from an amorphous and unstructured infancy to the sophisticated, skilled and rule-oriented practice that is common today.

## 2. HISTORICAL EVOLUTION OF MEDIATION IN THE UNITED STATES

### 2.1. MEDIATION AND THE RISE OF COMMERCE AND INDUSTRY IN THE UNITED STATES

Mediation in America from colonial times through the end of the nineteenth century was informal, unstructured, and primitive by today's standards. As trade and communities developed with the advent of the industrial revolution, so did an increase in disputes among citizens and the need for developing alternative systems, outside of the courts, for disposing of these disputes. These concerns figured most prominently in the area of labour relations and collective bargaining.

---

1 J. Alfini *et al.*, *Mediation Theory and Practice*, Lexis Publishing, New York NY 2001.

### 2.1.1. *President Theodore Roosevelt mediates the United Mine Workers Strike of 1902*

In May of 1902, 147,000 coal miners in the anthracite coal region of Pennsylvania went on strike in search of increased wages and recognition of the United Mine Workers as their union bargaining representative.[2] The labour demonstrations became violent during the summer months and the impact of the work stoppage was feared to be catastrophic for the country.[3] The perilous situation was described by author Edmund Morris as follows:

> 'Here was the nation's biggest union challenging its most powerful industrial combination – a cartel of anthracite railroad operators and absentee "barons" in total control of an exclusive resource. Already it amounted to the greatest labor stoppage in history. A visiting British economist predicted that if the current standoff lasted until cold weather came, there would be "such social consequences as the world has never seen."'[4]

With the economic and social consequences potentially far-reaching, the President of the United States, Theodore Roosevelt, was at first reluctant to interject the weight of his office in a private labour dispute;[5] such a move would have been unprecedented. But by October, as the public interest became more threatened by the potential of a winter fuel famine, Roosevelt arranged for a meeting among the parties wherein he would serve as mediator in an attempt to bring about an agreement to end the labour strike.[6] Although the initial meeting mediated by Roosevelt did not result in an agreement, the strike was later resolved, with the assistance of Secretary of War Elihu Root and banker J.P. Morgan, with the parties' agreement to the appointment of a Coal Strike Commission.[7]

The mediation of the coal miners' strike by President Roosevelt was a watershed event for mediation in the United States. This mediation was primitive by today's standards; the President had a powerful interest in the outcome of the dispute and had applied pressure through threats of a military takeover of the coal mines.[8] But Roosevelt's mediation of the labour dispute was notable in that it was 'a very big and entirely new thing [...] the definite entry of a powerful government upon a novel sphere of operation.'[9]

---

2 E. Morris, *Theodore Rex*, Random House, Inc., New York NY 2001.
3 *Ibid.*
4 *Ibid.*, p. 131. The quote of the 'British economist' was attributed to Stuart Uttley in Literary Digest, 8.02.1902.
5 E. Morris, *supra* n. 2.
6 J.T. Barrett, *A History of Alternative Dispute Resolution*, 1st ed., Jossey-Bass, San Francisco CA 2004.
7 E. Morris, *supra* n. 2.
8 J.T. Barrett, *supra* n. 6.
9 E. Morris, *supra* n. 2, p. 169, quoting *The Times* of London.

### 2.1.2. *Establishment of the US Department of Labor in 1913*

The Department of Labor was established as a cabinet-level department by act of Congress and signed into law by President Taft in 1913. The mediation of labour disputes by the executive branch espoused by President Roosevelt in 1902 was now codified in federal law as Congress prescribed the role of the Secretary of Labor to include 'the power to act as mediator and to appoint commissioners of conciliation in labour disputes whenever in his judgment the interests of industrial peace may require it to be done.'[10] In its first year, the Department of Labor mediated 33 labour disputes.[11]

With a spike in labour disputes brought on by the increased labour demands of World War I, the Department of Labor's budget was expanded in 1917 to create the United States Conciliation Service (USCS), dedicated specifically to the mediation and conciliation of labour disputes.[12] By 1919, the annual caseload of the USCS increased to 1,789. Since few individuals had experience with mediation, the USCS mediators spent much of their time educating and coaching parties regarding the nature of the mediation process.[13] The USCS, by the end of World War I, had played a major role in the proliferation of mediation and in the resolution of labour disputes.[14]

### 2.1.3. *Railway Labor Act of 1926 and the creation of the National Mediation Board*

The Railway Labor Act (RLA) was passed into law in 1926 to prevent railroad shut-downs and to promote peace between the railroads and it labourers.[15] The prominent features of the RLA survive today, including protections for unions and employees and use of mediation to resolve disputes relating to pay, work rules and working conditions.[16] The RLA established the National Mediation Board (NMB) for the purpose of mediating disputes between the railroad industry and labour. According to the NMB:

> 'As provided for in the RLA, the National Mediation Board (NMB) is responsible for providing mediation services to help the parties reach a settlement should the parties fail to reach an agreement during direct negotiations. If the parties are unable to

---

10 Public Law 426-62, Section 8, approved 4 March 1913.

11 J.T. Barrett, *supra* n. 6.

12 J.T. Barrett, *supra* n. 6.

13 USCS Director John Steelman said that 'The primary work of our mediator was educating the parties on how to negotiate and use mediation. The parties did not know what they were doing or how to do it.' J.T. Barrett, *supra* n. 6.

14 J.T. Barrett, *supra* n. 6. Following the War, the USCS caseload steadily declined to no more than 560 total cases through 1932. The caseload increased with the New Deal legislation and the Second World War. *Ibid.*

15 The Act was subsequently amended to expand coverage to airlines and airline employees: 45 U.S.C. 151 ff.

16 J.T. Barrett, *supra* n. 6.

> reach a voluntary agreement to establish or modify a collective bargaining agreement, either party may apply for the mediation services of the NMB. Once mediation is invoked, the NMB conducts mediation meetings until an agreement is reached or until the NMB concludes no agreement can be reached despite its best mediatory efforts. If the NMB reaches this conclusion, it urges both sides to resolve their dispute through binding arbitration. Upon rejection of the proffer of arbitration by either party, the NMB releases the parties into a 30 day cooling off period. During the cooling off period, neither side can alter the status quo. At the end of 30 days, the parties either reach an agreement or engage in self-help. In some situations, the parties may be required to participate in a Presidential Emergency Board (PEB) and defer any self-help action until 30 days after the PEB makes its recommendation.'

The NMB's use of mediation has played a critical role in maintaining an uninterrupted flow of commerce by preventing airline and railroad work stoppages. The Board has an impressive record ensuring that bargaining disputes rarely escalate into disruptions of passenger service and commerce. According to the NMB, 97% of all mediations in the history of the NMB have been successfully resolved without interruptions to public service. Since 1980, the success rate has been nearly 99%.[17]

## 2.2. MEDIATION IN THE 1930S AND THE RISE OF LABOUR

The elevation of Franklin Delano Roosevelt to the Presidency in 1933 resulted in substantial pro-labour legislative achievements that are characteristic of Roosevelt's 'New Deal'. The New Deal legislation and increase in labour demands from World War II ushered in an era of growth for labour unions, with corresponding growth in the use of mediation in the context of collective bargaining.[18]

### *2.2.1. Creation of the National Labor Relations Board*

Following the end of World War I and into the 1920s, hostilities between labour and employers ran high and labour strikes became widespread.[19] During this period, employers sought to quell labour strikes by seeking injunctive relief through the courts.[20] In August 1933, President Roosevelt created the National Labor Board (NLB) to mediate labour disputes and achieve compliance with

---

17 <www.nmb.gov/mediation/mrna.html>.

18 J.T. Barrett, *supra* n. 6.

19 A. Baumann, 'Play Ball: What Can Be Done To Prevent Strikes and Lockouts in Professional Sports and Keep the Stadium Lights On' (2012) 32 *Journal of the National Association of the Administrative Law Judiciary* 251.

20 <www.nlrb.gov/who-we-are/our-history/pre-wagner-act-labor-relations>.

existing labour laws. Although the NLB lacked power to enforce labour laws, by June 1934, the NLB mediated the settlement of 1,019 labour strikes and settled or averted over 2,000 other types of labour disputes.[21]

In July 1935, the Roosevelt Administration and Congress took a major step forward toward the advancement of mediation in labour disputes with the passage of the National Labor Relations Act.[22] The Act, also known as the Wagner Act,[23] created the National Labor Relations Board (NLRB), an independent agency endowed with the power to enforce the rights of labour employees and to force employers to engage in collective bargaining with their union.[24]

The NLRB exists to investigate claims of labour law violations and to 'resolve cases by settlement rather than litigation whenever possible'.[25] The NLRB also has the power to adjudicate disputes and to enforce its orders in the federal courts when necessary.[26] Today, the NLRB mediates disputes between employers and labour unions. From 2000 to 2010, the NLRB has mediated labour settlements of nearly $430,000,000 to the benefit of tens of thousands of American workers.[27]

### *2.2.2. Creation of the Federal Mediation and Conciliation Service*

With the enactment of the Taft-Hartley Act in 1947, Congress created the Federal Mediation and Conciliation Service (FMCS) as an independent agency of the United States government.[28] The agency assists with mediating private non-airline and non-railroad labour disputes across the United States.[29] The FMCS articulates its mission as follows:

---

21 *Ibid.*

22 <www.nlrb.gov/who-we-are/our-history/1935-passage-wagner-act>.

23 Senator Robert F. Wagner of New York was the chief sponsor and proponent of the law. Senator Wagner had previously served as Chairman of the NLB. <www.nlrb.gov/who-we-are/our-history/1935-passage-wagner-act>.

24 A. Baumann, *supra* n. 19, p. 251. The role of the NLRB was expanded with the passage of the Taft-Hartley Act which put both employers and workers under the jurisdiction of the NLRB. *Ibid.*

25 <www.nlrb.gov/what-we-do>.

26 *Ibid.*

27 <www.nlrb.gov/75th/settlements.html>.

28 <www.fmcs.gov/internet/itemDetail.asp?categoryID=21&itemID=15810>. The FMCS was a reincarnation of the U.S. Conciliation Service which previously operated as an arm of the Department of Labor. J.T. Barrett, *supra* n. 6.

29 Mediation of collective bargaining agreements in the railroad and airline industries fall exclusively within the jurisdiction of the National Mediation Board. Negotiation disputes in the non-rail and non-airline private sector are handled by the Federal Mediation and Conciliation Service in accordance with the Taft-Hartley Act. Collective bargaining representation of federal government employees is administered by the Federal Labor Relations Authority pursuant to the Civil Service Reform Act of 1978, Title VII. Collective bargaining representation of state, county and municipal government employees varies and

> 'The primary responsibility of the Federal Mediation and Conciliation Service (FMCS) is to promote sound and stable labor relations through mediation and conflict resolution services. We mediate collective bargaining negotiations, provide other forms of alternative dispute resolution services outside of the collective bargaining context, provide training courses to improve the workplace relationship, and refer arbitrators for settlement of contract application disputes. FMCS mediators are widely dispersed throughout the country.'[30]

'Dispute mediation – and other conflict resolution services – are the tools and techniques used by FMCS to promote collective bargaining, strengthen labour-management relations, and enhance organisational effectiveness.'[31] While labour dispute mediation continues to be the primary service offered by the FMCS today, the agency has broadened its services to include conflict prevention and other alternative dispute resolution systems.[32]

Throughout its long history, the FMCS has mediated a wide range of notable private and public sector conflicts. In the early 1970s, the FMCS was called upon by Congress and the Native American Hopi and Navajo tribes to mediate a land dispute between the tribes.[33] In 2002, the FMCS, at the request of President George W. Bush, successfully mediated a labour dispute that closed all West Coast shipping ports for ten days and put approximately $300 billion worth of economic activity at risk.[34] In 2004, the FMCS mediated an end to the 141-day strike by the United Food and Commercial Workers against Southern California supermarket chains. The strike was the longest in the grocery industry's history and affected approximately 70,000 workers.[35] In 2008, the FMCS facilitated an agreement between the Boeing Company and the International Association of Machinists and Aerospace Workers (IAMAW) to end a 52-day labour strike of 27,000 employees.[36] In 2011, the FMCS was involved in mediating negotiations of a new collective bargaining agreement between the National Football League and its Players' Association.[37] The FMCS has made significant contributions to the field of mediation by helping to resolve these disputes as well as many others, and it continues to make important contributions today.

---

depends on whether there is a state or local law which permits collective bargaining. <www.nmb.gov/mediation/faq-mediation.html>.

30 <www.fmcs.gov/>.

31 <www.fmcs.gov/internet/categoryList.asp?categoryID=12>.

32 A. Strimling, 'The Federal Mediation and Conciliation Service: A Partner in International Conflict Prevention' (2002) 2 *Pepperdine Dispute Resolution Law Journal* 417.

33 *Ibid.*, p. 417. The success of this mediation by the FMCS led to the agency's continued involvement in Native American communities.

34 <www.fmcs.gov/internet_text_only/printerPage.asp?categoryID=93&itemID=16811>.

35 <www.fmcs.gov/internet_text_only/printerPage.asp?categoryID=93&itemID=16811>.

36 <www.fmcs.gov/internet_text_only/printerPage.asp?categoryID=21&itemID=15810>.

37 <www.washingtonpost.com/wp-dyn/content/article/2011/02/17/AR2011021707365.html>.

## 2.3. THE COMMUNITY JUSTICE MOVEMENT

The judiciary in the United States has a long history of struggles in effectively handling minor civil and criminal cases among families, acquaintances and neighbours.[38] These cases typically involve small financial disputes and minor instances of assault, harassment and theft.[39] The courts are especially ill-equipped to deal with these types of cases because traditional criminal penalties such as fines and incarceration provide little hope of resolving these matters – and often cause them to escalate – and it is often difficult to distinguish the truth of the matter, leading to frustration of law enforcement, lawyers and judges.[40] The concerns among the parties to a dispute are refashioned as 'legal issues' by the traditional justice system, leaving those with fundamentally personal and emotional conflicts alienated from addressing the issues directly and resolving them constructively.[41] The cases would add to an already backlogged and overloaded court docket and the cases were of little to no significance to the community. Though the courts were widely viewed as ineffective in dispensing justice in these types of cases, there were not assessable alternatives until the advent to community mediation programs in the late 1960s.[42]

There were a number of public and private experimental community mediation programs that were birthed in urban centers in the late 1960s and early 1970s, often making use of volunteer citizens as mediators.[43] There were wide differences among these programs, but the general nature of the approach and philosophy has been described as follows:

> 'Bring all the neighbors into a room. Have them meet with one another in the presence of a community resident trained in conducting problem-solving dialogues. Try, through that discussion, to have the parties discuss their concerns, communicate their aspirations to one another, and work out arrangements acceptable to each […] The process – mediation – requires people to listen to one another, accord respect to and concern for each other's viewpoint, place fault-finding in perspective, and engage in problem solving discussions that enable participants to resolve their immediate concerns and stabilize future interactions. Doing all those things is neither easy nor straightforward; it takes time, commitment and skill from the parties, their representatives, and the mediator. The benefits though are obvious and tangible: it empowers persons and families to interact constructively as neighbors; it enables

38 D. McGillis, *Community Mediation Programs: Developments and Challenges*, National Institute of Justice, July 1997.

39 *Ibid.*

40 *Ibid.*

41 J. Alfini, *supra* n. 1.

42 D. McGillis, *supra* n. 38.

43 *Ibid.* Notable programs that became models for the development of future programs included those in San Francisco, Philadelphia, Rochester (NY), New York City, and Columbus, Ohio.

> persons to regain command of discussing the things that matter most to them; and it requires each individual to be accountable for her conduct.'[44]

Many of the private community-based programs would be 'referred' cases by judges as a means of reducing backlogged court dockets and in hopes of achieving more durable and meaningful resolutions.[45] Numerous studies on these community-based programs revealed that these mediations yielded a high rate of settlement and a high degree of party satisfaction with the process and the outcome.[46]

Increased public funding from the federal, state and local governments in addition to private financial support from non-profit organisations,[47] bar associations and industry groups,[48] led to further proliferation of community-based mediation programs in the 1970s and 1980s.[49] In 1977, the US Department of Justice initiated three experimental 'Neighborhood Justice Centers' in Atlanta, Los Angeles and Kansas City. Though each program was designed differently, each achieved a great deal of success and has become permanent fixtures in their communities. Not only have these programs flourished and survive to today, but they have spawned hundreds of similar court-sponsored and private, community-based mediation programs across the United States.[50]

## 2.4. MODERN MEDIATION IN THE UNITED STATES

### *2.4.1. Pound Conference of 1976*

The National Conference on the Causes of Popular Dissatisfaction with the Administration of Justice, known as the Pound Conference,[51] was a defining event in the mediation movement in the United States in that it birthed a re-imagination of mediation's role in the judicial process. The Pound Conference

---

44 J. Alfini, *supra* n. 1, pp. 9–10.

45 D. Hensler, 'Our Courts, Ourselves: How the Alternative Dispute Resolution Movement is Reshaping Our Legal System' (2003) 108 *Pennsylvania State Law Review*, 165.

46 J. Alfini, *supra* n. 1.

47 The Ford Foundation and William and Flora Hewlett Foundation were prominent private organisations that played a significant financial and leadership role in the development of community mediation. J. Alfini, *supra* n. 1.

48 The American Arbitration Association and Institute for Mediation and Conflict Resolution provided leadership in encouraging community mediation programs. D. McGillis, *supra* n. 38.

49 D. McGillis, *supra* n. 38.

50 J. Alfini, *supra* n. 1.

51 The namesake of the Pound Conference was Harvard Law School Professor Roscoe Pound, a celebrated advocate of 'court reform and improvements in the administration of justice in the first half of the twentieth century'. J.T. Barrett, *supra* n. 6.

was organised by Chief Justice Warren Burger to address the inefficiencies and sources of disenfranchisement with the American court system.[52]

Professor Frank E.A. Sander spoke at the conference, advocating for the concept of the 'multi-door courthouse' which offered multiple avenues toward conflict resolution.[53] Sander argued that improved case management efficiency and more impactful social outcomes could be achieved by diverting certain cases, particularly divorce cases and disputes among relatives and neighbours,[54] from the judicial caseload to mediation programs.[55] Sander argued that these types of cases were well-suited for mediation because of its 'capacity to reorient the parties toward each other, not by imposing rules on them, but by helping them to achieve a new and shared perception of their relationship [...] that will redirect their attitudes and dispositions toward one another',[56] its emphasis on the parties' responsibilities and decision making, and its potential to reinforce a sense of community.[57]

The Pound Conference generated momentum for and stimulated court-connected mediation programs in the United States. Legislation and the adoption of local rules promoting mediation and ADR were spawned from the ideas advanced by Professor Sander at the Pound Conference.[58]

### *2.4.2. Civil Justice Reform Act of 1990*

Propelled by the success of the community justice movement and in the wake of Pound Conference, Congress took a major step toward the institutionalisation of alternative dispute resolution, including mediation, in the United States federal courts with the passage of the Civil Justice Reform Act (CJRA) in 1990.[59] The CJRA required each United States district court to implement a 'civil justice expense and delay reduction plan' the purpose of which is to 'facilitate deliberate adjudication of civil cases on the merits, monitor discovery, improve litigation management, and ensure just, speedy and inexpensive resolutions of civil disputes.'[60] By 1996, mediation had become the most prominent form of ADR in the federal courts; only six years after the institution of the CJRA's pilot

---

52 J.T. Barrett, *supra* n. 6.

53 J.T. Barrett, *supra* n. 6. See 70 F.R.D. 79 for the addresses delivered at this three-day conference in 1976.

54 F. Sander at 70 F.R.D. 79.

55 D. Della Noce, 'Mediation Theory and Policy: The Legacy of the Pound Conference' (2002) 17 *Ohio State Journal of Dispute Resolution* 545.

56 F. Sander at 70 F.R.D. 79, 115, quoting L.L. Fuller, 'Mediation – Its Forms and Functions' (1971) 44 *South California Law Review* 305, 325.

57 D. Della Noce, *supra* n. 55, p. 545.

58 *Ibid.*

59 28 U.S.C. §471 (1990).

60 *Ibid.*

programs, over half of the federal district courts had developed mediation programs.[61]

The Dispute Resolution Act of 1998 expanded on the CJRA by requiring that each federal district court specifically consider mediation as a form of court-mandated dispute resolution.[62] The expansion of mediation in the federal courts attributable to the CJRA played a pivotal role in the settlement of many federal court cases, including the antitrust lawsuit brought by the Justice Department against software giant Microsoft.[63]

### *2.4.3. Administrative Dispute Resolution Act of 1990*

The Administrative Dispute Resolution Act (ADRA) was enacted by Congress in response to the growth of alternative dispute resolution procedures and the need for greater efficiency in dispute resolution with federal agencies. The law mandated each federal agency to adopt policies to address the use of alternative means of dispute resolution and case management and required a senior official to be designated within each agency to be responsible for implementation of the agency's ADR policies. The ADRA was enacted originally with a five-year sunset provision, but the law was reenacted in 2006 without a sunset.[64]

In response to the ADRA, mediation has become a widely used method for dispute resolution by federal agencies. Mediation figures prominently in the dispute resolution procedures by many federal agencies including the military, the Department of Energy, Equal Employment Opportunity Commission, and the Internal Revenue Service (IRS).[65]

61 R. Birke and L.E. Teitz, 'U.S. Mediation in 2001: The Path that Brought America to Uniform Laws and Mediation in Cyberspace' (2002) 50 *American Journal of Comparative Law* 181.

62 28 U.S.C. §651 (1998). The Findings and Declaration of Policy included strong promotion for use of mediation in the court by providing as follows: 'Congress finds that – (1) Alternative dispute resolution, when supported by the bench and bar, and utilizing properly trained neutrals in a program adequately administered by the Court, has the potential to provide a variety of benefits, including greater satisfaction of the parties, innovative methods of resolving disputes, and greater efficiency in achieving settlements; (2) Certain forms of alternative dispute resolution, including mediation, early neutral evaluation, minitrials and voluntary arbitration, may have the potential to reduce the large backlog of cases now pending in some Federal courts throughout the United States, thereby allowing the courts to process their remaining cases more efficiently; and (3) The continued growth of Federal appellate court-annexed mediation programs suggests that this form of alternative dispute resolution can be equally effective in resolving disputes in the Federal trial courts; therefore, the district courts should consider including mediation in their local dispute resolution programs.' *Ibid.* See Findings and Declaration of Policy.

63 J.T. Barrett, *supra* n. 6.

64 5 U.S.C. §571 (1990).

65 R. Birke and L.E. Teitz, *supra* n. 61, p. 181.

# 3. GOVERNING LAW AND RULES RELATING TO MEDIATION IN THE UNITED STATES

There is broad diversity among jurisdictions – state to state, district to district, county to county – in legal cultures, law and rules which are responsible for a wide range of mediation practices. With the proliferation of mediation, these inconsistencies among the various jurisdictions have led to complexities, particularly with regard to the parties' expectations relating to the issues of privilege and confidentiality of communications during mediation.[66] Efforts to address these concerns have been undertaken in recent years by state legislatures and through the promulgation of the Uniform Mediation Act.

## 3.1. MEDIATION IN THE FEDERAL COURTS

Endorsement of the use of alternative dispute resolution methods, including mediation, is codified in the Federal Rules of Civil Procedure. Federal Rule 16 governs the procedure for Pretrial Conferences and sets forth a framework for judicial management of cases in advance of trial. Federal Rule 16 authorises the court to order conferences for the purpose of 'facilitating settlement' and to 'consider and take appropriate action' on matters such as 'settling the case and using special procedures to assist in resolving the dispute' and 'facilitating in other ways the just, speedy, and inexpensive disposition of the action'.[67] The Notes of the Advisory Committee on Rules pertaining to the 1993 Amendments to Federal Rule 16 states that:

> '[Federal Rule of Civil Procedure 16] is revised to describe more accurately the various procedures that, in addition to traditional settlement conferences, may be helpful in settling litigation. Even if a case cannot immediately be settled, the judge and attorneys can explore possible use of alternative procedures such as mini-trials, summary jury trials, *mediation*, neutral evaluation, and nonbinding arbitration that can lead to consensual resolution of the dispute without a full trial on the merits.'[68]

While district courts employ many different types of ADR procedures,[69] mediation has emerged as the most consistently preferred way to resolve cases.

---

66 <www.uniformlaws.org/ActSummary.aspx?title=Mediation Act>.

67 Federal Rule of Civil Procedure 16.

68 Notes of the Advisory Committee on Rules – 1993 Amendments, Federal Rule of Civil Procedure 16. Emphasis added.

69 Most of the federal district courts have promulgated local rules governing the use of mediation. The Southern District of Florida requires, with few narrowly defined exceptions, that every civil case undergo mediation no less than 60 days before the scheduled trial date (S.D. Fla. Local Rule 16.2D). The local rules require that within seven days following the mediation, the mediator is required to file a Mediation Report with the Court, advising of the status of settlement negotiations (S.D. Fla. Local Rule 16.2F(1)). Most district courts, however,

According to a study conducted by the Federal Judicial Center in 49 district courts in a twelve month period from 2010 to 2011, of the 28,267 cases that went through an ADR process, 17,833 of those cases employed mediation.[70] 'If you have a civil case in the District of South Carolina, you will encounter mediation, and before the litigation is concluded, you likely will have discussed mediation, with your client, with opposing counsel and with the court,' explained Danny Mullis, the ADR Program Director for the District of South Carolina.[71]

## 3.2. MEDIATION IN THE STATE COURTS

Though the governing laws, rules and practices regarding court-annexed mediation, and ADR generally, vary widely from state to state, every state has enacted some form of court-sanctioned mediation or ADR procedure.[72] The proliferation of these court-sanctioned programs began in the 1970s in the wake of the community justice movement and the Pound Conference and the growth has accelerated to the present.

Court-annexed mediation practices broadly differ among states, and among the local courts within each state. Some mediation programs are mandatory for litigants while some are not; some courts will cover the cost of mediation services while others require the litigants to pay for the services of a mediator.[73]

## 3.3. CONFIDENTIALITY OF COMMUNICATIONS AND THE UNIFORM MEDIATION ACT

Confidentiality of communications in mediation is essential to creating an atmosphere of trust and candour, and thus is essential to the very nature of the

do not have mandatory mediation programs, placing the Southern District of Florida squarely in the minority. In the Eastern District of Pennsylvania, a judge may order mediation on a case by case basis, or will refer the parties to mediation with the consent of all parties to the litigation. D. Stienstra, 'Federal Judicial Center, ADR in the Federal District Courts: An Initial Report', 16 November 2011 (Appendix 5).

70 D. Stienstra, 'Federal Judicial Center, ADR in the Federal District Courts: An Initial Report', 16 November 2011.

71 <www.uscourts.gov/news/TheThirdBranch/06-07-01/In_Resolving_Disputes_Mediation_Most_Favored_ADR_Option_in_District_Courts.aspx> The Third Branch, July 2006. The District of South Carolina has codified a unique practice by Local Rule 16.03, which requires that counsel for each party file an Alternative Dispute Resolution Statement and Certification, whereby counsel certifies that he/she has discussed the availability of ADR mechanisms with the client and has discussed the advisability and timing of ADR with opposing counsel (District of S.C. Local Rule 16.03).

72 To see an extensive and evolving database of ADR programs from State to State, see the website of the National Centre for State Courts at <www.ncsconline.org/WC/Publications/ADR/default.htm>.

73 E. Ward, 'Mandatory Court-Annexed Alternative Dispute Resolution in the United States Federal Courts: A Panacea or a Pandemic?' (2007) 81 *Saint John's Law Review* 77.

process. Each state has different statutes and rules regarding the treatment of confidentiality issues in mediations. Currently, legal rules on mediation can be found in more than 2,500 state and federal statutes; more than 250 of these deal with issues of confidentiality and privileges alone.[74] The lack of uniformity leads to unpredictability as to whether communications made during mediation will be confidential. This is especially true in mediations across multiple jurisdictions because it may be unclear which state's law applies.

Most states have a common law evidentiary exclusion for offers of settlement. Such statements are excludable from evidence on the basis that they are not probative of the issues to be determined by the finder of fact. However, the practical value of this common law rule in the settling of mediation is eroded in that it does not exclude admissions of fact and all other statements made during mediation.[75]

Federal Rule of Evidence 408 is another possible source of protection to parties for communications made during mediation. The Rule states as follows:

> 'Rule 408. Compromise Offers and Negotiations
> (a) Prohibited Uses. Evidence of the following is not admissible – on behalf of any party – either to prove or disprove the validity or amount of a disputed claim or to impeach by a prior inconsistent statement or a contradiction:
> (1) furnishing, promising, or offering – or accepting, promising to accept, or offering to accept – a valuable consideration in compromising or attempting to compromise the claim; and
> (2) conduct or a statement made during compromise negotiations about the claim – except when offered in a criminal case and when the negotiations related to a claim by a public office in the exercise of its regulatory, investigative, or enforcement authority.
> (b) Exceptions. The court may admit this evidence for another purpose, such as proving a witness's bias or prejudice, negating a contention of undue delay, or proving an effort to obstruct a criminal investigation or prosecution.'

Federal Rule of Evidence 408 confers broader protection on communications than the common-law rule by expanding protection to include evidence of 'conduct' and 'statements made during compromise negotiations'. The Rule makes no mention of mediation specifically but presumably, would be encompassed by the Rule. However, the confidentiality protections afforded by the Rule are limited in scope. Section (b) enumerates various purposes for which such statements would be admissible as evidence. Further, and perhaps most significantly, the Rule speaks only to evidentiary concerns and makes no limitations on the discoverability of any statements or conduct during mediation.

---

74 <www.uniformlaws.org/Narrative.aspx?title=Why States Should Adopt UMA>.

75 'Protecting Confidentiality in Mediation' (1984) 98 *Harvard Law Review* 441, citing FRE 408 advisory committee note.

Confidentiality concerns can often be addressed by contract, wherein the parties and mediator agree to maintain the confidentiality of all communications. This has become a widespread and common practice. However, the confidentiality protections afforded by contracts are only binding on the contracting parties; these contracts cannot preclude an outsider from seeking to discover or admit as evidence a statement or conduct in a mediation.[76]

In an effort to promote greater uniformity in the practice of mediation across the United States, the Uniform Mediation Act (UMA) was drafted cooperatively by the National Conference of Commissioners on Uniform State Laws (NCCUSL) and the American Bar Association's Section of Dispute Resolution.[77] According to the NCCUSL, '[t]he Uniform Mediation Act will further the goals of alternative dispute resolution by promoting candor of the parties by fostering prompt, economical, and amicable resolution of disputes, by retaining decision-making authority with the parties, and by promoting predictability with regard to the process and the level of confidentiality that can be expected by participants.'[78] The NCCUSL summarises the UMA as follows:

> 'The UMA's prime concern is keeping mediation communications confidential. Parties engaged in mediation, as well as non-party participants, must be able to speak with full candor for a mediation to be successful and for a settlement to be voluntary. For this reason, the central rule of the UMA is that a mediation communication is confidential, and if privileged, is not subject to discovery or admission into evidence in a formal proceeding [see Sec. 5(a)]. In proceedings following a mediation, a party may refuse to disclose, and prevent any other person from disclosing, a mediation communication. Mediators and non-party participants may refuse to disclose their own statements made during mediation, and may prevent others from disclosing them, as well. Thus, for a person's own mediation communication to be disclosed in a subsequent hearing, that person must agree and so must the parties to the mediation. Waiver of these privileges must be in a record or made orally during a proceeding to be effective. There is no waiver by conduct.
>
> As is the case with all general rules, there are exceptions. First, it should be noted that the privilege extends only to mediation communications, and not the underlying facts of the dispute. Evidence that is otherwise admissible or subject to discovery does not become inadmissible or protected from discovery by reason of its use in a mediation. A party that discloses a mediation communication and thereby prejudices another person in a proceeding is precluded from asserting the privilege to the extent necessary for the prejudiced person to respond. A person who intentionally uses a mediation to plan or attempt to commit a crime, or to conceal an ongoing crime, cannot assert the privilege.

---

76 'Protecting Confidentiality in Mediation' (1984) 98 *Harvard Law Review* 441.

77 The Act was promulgated by the National Conference of Commissioners on Uniform State Laws in 2001 and amended in 2003. <www.uniformlaws.org/ActSummary.aspx?title= Mediation Act>.

78 <www.uniformlaws.org/ActSummary.aspx?title=Mediation Act>.

> Also, there is no assertable privilege against disclosure of a communication made during a mediation session that is open to the public, that contains a threat to inflict bodily injury, that is sought or offered to prove or disprove abuse, neglect, abandonment, or exploitation in a proceeding where a child or adult protective agency is a party, that would prove or disprove a claim of professional misconduct filed against a mediator, or against a party, party representative, or non-party participant based on conduct during a mediation. If a court, administrative agency, or arbitration panel finds that the need for the information outweighs the interest in confidentiality in a felony proceeding, or a proceeding to prove a claim of defense to reform or avoid liability on a contract arising out of the mediation, there is no privilege.
>
> The Uniform Mediation Act is meant to have broad application, while at the same time preserving party autonomy. While a mediation proceeding subject to the Act can result from an agreement of the parties, or be required by statute, a government entity, or as part of an arbitration, the Act allows parties to opt out of the confidentiality and privilege rules described above. Also, the Act does not prescribe qualifications or other professional standards for mediators, allowing parties (and potentially states) to make that determination. The Act generally prohibits a mediator, other than a judicial officer, from submitting a report, assessment, evaluation, finding, or other communication to a court agency, or other authority that may make a ruling on the dispute that is the subject of the mediation. The mediator may report the bare facts that a mediation is ongoing or has concluded, who participated, and, mediation communications evidencing abuse, neglect, or abandonment, or, other non-privileged mediation matters. The Act also contains model provisions calling for a mediator to disclose conflicts of interest before accepting a mediation (or as soon as practicable after discovery). His or her qualifications as a mediator must be disclosed to any requesting party to the dispute.'

The UMA has been approved by the American Bar Association and endorsed by industry stakeholders such as the American Arbitration Association, the Judicial Arbitration and Mediation Service, CPR Institute for Dispute Resolution and the National Arbitration Forum.[79] As of 2012, the UMA has been enacted into law in ten states, namely Idaho, Illinois, Iowa, Nebraska, New Jersey, Ohio, South Dakota, Utah, Vermont and Washington, in addition to the District of Columbia.[80] Other states have adopted similar mediation laws in the spirit of the UMA, including Virginia, Delaware, Florida, Montana, Nevada, Oregon and Wyoming.[81]

---

79 <www.uniformlaws.org/ActSummary.aspx?title=Mediation Act>.

80 <www.uniformlaws.org/LegislativeFactSheet.aspx?title=Mediation Act>.

81 <http://cpradr.org/Resources/ALLCPRArticles/tabid/265/ID/239/Legislation-Where-the-Uniform-Mediation-Act-Stands-in-the-States-Web.aspx>.

## 4. PRACTICAL CONSIDERATIONS REGARDING MEDIATION

The decision whether to undertake mediation is deceptively complex. No one should agree to mediation unless they are truly ready to settle. In a civil case, that means the defendant has to be willing to pay and the plaintiff has to be willing to accept payment.

Sometimes, a defendant will seek mediation in order to get a preview of the plaintiff's case. The plaintiff can ferret out an insincere request for mediation by conditioning mediation on the making of a substantial settlement offer.

Choosing a mediator is also a subtle issue. There is little point in engaging in long debate over who should be the mediator, as the mediator is not an adjudicator. Rather, someone who is a good communicator and well regarded by both sides is adequate. It may be preferable from the plaintiff's perspective to let the defendant choose the mediator, as then the mediation cannot be seen to have 'failed' because of the plaintiff's fault in choosing the mediator. As a safeguard against the possibility of the defendant choosing someone close to the defence side, the plaintiff might ask the defence to produce a list of three to five potential mediators from which the plaintiff would choose one.

As discussed above, mediations begin with the execution of a confidentiality agreement. This bars introduction of what occurs in the mediation in court. A mediator will also often add that he will not disclose to the other side anything discussed *ex parte* unless specifically instructed that he may do so. As a practical matter, this is rarely followed. A party is wise to confine their remarks to a mediator to those which they do not mind having their opponent hear.

From the defence perspective, mediation is an opportunity to put pressure on the plaintiff to settle. The defence may request the plaintiff's presence at the mediation, and may use the mediation as an opportunity to speak directly to the plaintiff. The defendant may ask the mediator to speak directly to the plaintiff if settlement discussions are not successful. Plaintiff's counsel must be cognisant of these possibilities and might decline to bring the client to the mediation. The plaintiff may also set a time limit on the mediation so as not to permit the process to wear down the plaintiff or the plaintiff's counsel.

In all mediations, the goal is to get both sides to say 'yes'. How to do so can be highly complicated. Competent counsel should be adroit in the art of settlement negotiation. Everyone has their own style and the parties must be diplomatic and understanding of differences among counsel in this regard. Often, one side or the other wishes to enter into bracketed negotiations where each side progressively gives a little and there are many offers back and forth. On other occasions, counsel may 'lay down a marker' of a specific sum that they will not pay more or will not accept less, depending upon their side in the proceeding. Such ultimata can make negotiations more difficult. The best approach is for each side to seek to sublimate their ego and desire to be seen as 'victor' and, instead, try to help the other get to 'yes'.

As a last resort, the mediator may suggest a settlement figure and request that both sides confidentially advise whether they will say yes to that number. Unless both sides say yes, the mediator will send both sides home without a resolution. This process has the advantage of permitting one side to say yes without the other side knowing they said yes, unless the other side says yes as well. That preserves the agreeing side's bargaining position in the event that the other side says no as the declining side will not be told of the agreeing side's agreement.

Other details of settlement agreements must not be overlooked in the process. The parties must discuss how long it will take for payment to be made, whether confidentiality is to be a condition of settlement, and whether non-economic considerations, such as remedial measures, are part of the bargain for resolution. We have found that it is best to discuss these matters early, rather than leaving them to the last part of settlement negotiations, after a fixed sum has been agreed.

## 5. FUTURE OF MEDIATION IN THE UNITED STATES

Mediation and alternative dispute resolution has become a big business in the United States. Private firms specialising in mediation services have become a prominent fixture in the legal landscape. These firms employ former judges and skilled practitioners to service the diverse dispute resolution needs of parties in litigation and those seeking to avoid the litigation process altogether. As long as alternatives to traditional court processes are sought, the marketplace for mediation businesses will be strong and continue to grow.

Mediation is not merely an alternative to litigation, but has become a prominent tool for resolving disputes within the context of litigation. With the proliferation of mediation in American courts, the success and future of mediation is intrinsically tied to litigation – the more complex and diverse litigation becomes, the more useful mediation can be in assisting the parties to narrow their issues and reach resolution to their disputes.

As a form of 'private justice', mediation and other ADR systems will continue to be utilised, but will never be a replacement for the indispensible American jury trial. Constitutional underpinnings ensuring the right to a trial by jury combined with American legal and cultural traditions ensure that mediation and other forms of ADR will always be just an alternative. Although disputes will often conclude without the assistance of a jury, it is through the prism of the prospect of trial by a jury that will always define the way by which legal disputes are analysed and resolved.

www.ingramcontent.com/pod-product-compliance
Ingram Content Group UK Ltd.
Pitfield, Milton Keynes, MK11 3LW, UK
UKHW051918100926
8556IPUK00021B/1236

9 781780 681399